De Gruyter Handbook of Sustainable Development and Finance

De Gruyter Handbook of Sustainable Development and Finance

Edited by
Timothy Cadman and Tapan Sarker

DE GRUYTER

ISBN 978-3-11-152365-1
e-ISBN (PDF) 978-3-11-073348-8
e-ISBN (EPUB) 978-3-11-073358-7
ISSN 2748-016X
e-ISSN 2748-0178

Library of Congress Control Number: 2022939104

Bibliographic information published by the Deutsche Nationalbibliothek
The Deutsche Nationalbibliothek lists this publication in the Deutsche Nationalbibliografie;
detailed bibliographic data are available on the internet at http://dnb.dnb.de.

Contents

Part 1: Origins and evolution

Conclusion

List of contributors

Hanna Ahlström (Sweden) Hanna Ahlström is a Postdoctoral Researcher in the Global Economic Dynamics and the Biosphere programme at the Royal Swedish Academy of Sciences. She specialises in sustainable business and finance and EU law and policy. Hanna holds a PhD from the Faculty of Law, University of Oslo. She is a Research Fellow with the Earth System Governance Network and the Task Force on Earth System Law and an external member of the research Group Companies, Markets and Sustainability at the University of Oslo. She is also a member of the International Sustainable Development Research Society Executive Board.

OrcID: 0000-0003-1177-7897

Dr Arnab Bose (India) Dr Arnab Bose is a Senior Fellow at the Centre for Study of the United Nations and faculty at OP Jindal Global University. He was Assistant Vice President (Responsible Banking) at YES Bank and Associate Fellow in The Energy and Resources Institute (TERI) in New Delhi, working in various consultancy projects on resilience, climate finance, renewable energy and local governance. Arnab has a Master's in Economics from JNU and an MBA in Finance from the University of Amsterdam, the Netherlands. His doctoral research was on smart governance of urban locations in Delhi, India and Berlin, Germany.

OrcID: 0000-0002-8423-4255

Bishwajit Basak (Bangladesh) Bishwajit Basak is currently working as a Joint Director at the Financial Stability Department of the Central Bank of Bangladesh. He has completed his graduate and postgraduate studies in Economics from University of Dhaka and also did a Master's in Public Economics at the National Graduate Institute for Policy Studies (GRIPS). His research interests are the macroeconomic issues of Bangladesh.

Tony Bradley (United Kingdom) Tony Bradley is Centre Director of SEARCH (Social and Economic Action Research Centre at Hope) and Senior Lecturer in Business Sustainability, Innovation and Social Economy at Liverpool Hope University Business School, where he co-leads the Greening Markets Research Group. He is a sociologist and political economist, specialising in interpreting the impact of the green movement on localities, business and the wider economy. He is the author of 11 books, several journal articles, reviews and reports and is, currently, completing three books on business sustainability. He lives in the English Lake District with his wife and two dogs.

OrcID: 0000-0002-0726-2674

Dr Hugh Breakey (Australia) Dr Hugh Breakey is the Deputy Director and a Senior Research Fellow in moral philosophy at Griffith University's Institute for Ethics, Governance and Law, Law Futures Centre. Hugh's work spans the philosophical sub-disciplines of political theory, normative ethics, applied philosophy and legal theory. He has extensive experience in the application of ethical, legal and political philosophy to challenging practical fields, including institutional governance, integrity systems and corruption, climate change, sustainable tourism, peacekeeping, safety industries, resource and common property, professional ethics and international law.

OrcID 0000-0002-5170-2091

https://doi.org/10.1515/9783110733488-203

Andrew Buckwell (Australia) Andrew Buckwell is an Applied Environmental and Resource Economist and Social Scientist at Griffith University. He specialises in revealing community preferences for resources use and conservation, non-market economic valuation and social benefit cost analysis. Andrew's work has been focussed on nature-based climate change adaptation in the South Pacific and on primary forest conservation through compensation schemes. Andrew has also contributed extensively to the research on how coastal councils might resource and fund adaptation strategies, such as managed retreat, and in understanding sugarcane farmer preferences for payment for ecosystem services schemes.

OrcID: 0000-0002-6441-9674

Timothy Cadman (Australia) Timothy Cadman BA Hons MA (Cantab.), PhD (UTas), Grad. Cert. Theol. (CSU) is a Research Fellow in the Law Futures Centre and the Institute for Ethics, Governance and Law at Griffith University, a Senior Research Fellow with the Earth System Governance Project and an Adjunct Research Fellow at the University of Southern Queensland. He specialises in governance of sustainable development, environmental politics and policy, climate change and natural resource management, including forestry, responsible investment and institutional performance. He works with communities and governments across the Asia-Pacific to develop governance standards for international projects and programmes.

OrcID: 0000-0002-9531-5018

Bailey Chappel (Australia) Bailey Chappel is a Dean's Rural Engineering Scholar at University of New South Wales (UNSW). He studies renewable energy engineering, business strategy and economics and is passionate about the intersection of these areas. He spent a year undertaking strategy consulting at the Climate Foundation through his role as a Consulting Director with 180 Degrees Consulting. He currently works as an Energy Markets Analyst at ITK Services Australia in addition to joining the Risk Consulting team at KPMG.

OrcID: 0000-0002-1446-3394

Diogo R. Coutinho (Brazil) Diogo R. Coutinho is a Law Professor at the University of São Paulo. He holds a Master's degree in Regulation (LSE) and a PhD in Law (USP). He has been a Visiting Professor at CTLS (Centre for Transnational Legal Studies) and a researcher at IGLP (Institute of Global Law and Policy) and at the Brazilian Centre for Analysis and Planning. His main research interests are regulation, competition and innovation policies, as well as the relationships between law, political economy and institutional change.

OrcID: 0000-0001-7810-1459

Krzysztof Dembek (Australia) Krzysztof is an experienced researcher, manager, adviser and teacher with expertise in creating, managing impact and using business models to advance sustainability and address complex social problems. He is driven by the need to ensure wicked problems are solved in ways that do not create new or aggravate existing issues. Krzysztof is a senior lecturer in social impact at the Centre for Social Impact Swinburne University, a visiting research professor at WSB University (Poland) and a Founding Member of Values 20, a global group of experts supporting the G20 leaders in developing human-centric approach to public policy and addressing global challenges.

OrcID: 0000-0003-3710-5861

Gabriela de Oliveira Junqueira (Brazil) Gabriela de Oliveira Junqueira is a PhD candidate at the University of São Paulo, Faculty of Law, Commercial Law Department. She holds a researcher position at the Green Finance and the Transformation of Property in Brazil Project. Her main research interests focus on capitalism's institutional transformations to respond to the ecological crises, especially the transformations of the corporate form.

OrcID: 0000-0002-3853-2817

Sima Rani Dey (Bangladesh) Sima Rani Dey is currently working as an Assistant Professor in Bangladesh Institute of Governance and Management (BIGM), located in Dhaka. She has completed her graduate and postgraduate studies in Statistics from Jahangirnagar University and did a Master's in Public Policy from the National Graduate Institute for Policy Studies (GRIPS). Her research interests are in issues of macroeconomics and development economics. Some of her research articles have been either accepted or published in reputed international journals including *OPEC Energy Review, International Social Science Journal, Environmental Science and Pollution Research, Economic Systems, International Journal of Emerging Markets* and *International Journal of Energy Sector Management.*

OrcID: 0000-0001-9507-0594

Tomaso Ferrando (Belgium) Tomaso Ferrando (he/his) is a research Professor at the Faculty of Law (Law and Development Research Group) and Institute of Development Policy, University of Antwerp. He researches the legal construction of the global food systems, the role of law in global production networks and the co-optation of the green transition. Currently, he is a member of the Legal Action Committee of the Global Legal Action Network (GLAN), where he is in charge of the land rights' thematic area and the President of FIAN Belgium, a non-governmental organisation engaged in the promotion of the right to food and food sovereignty.

OrcID: 0000-0001-7034-3592

Andrea Ferraz Young (Brazil) Andrea is an architect with a specialisation in Demography and Environmental Planning. She was a Young Researcher (FAPESP) at the Brazilian National Center of Monitoring and Early Warning of Environmental Disasters (CEMADEN) from the Ministry of Science, Technology, Innovation and Communication (MCTIC) between 2017–2020. She works with urban resilience, prevention of environmental disasters and support decisions through Geographic Information Systems. For the last ten years, she has been involved in scientific programmes at both national and international levels working in institutions such as Glasgow Caledonian University (2019–2020), Kings College London (2012–2013) and the Earth System Science Centre (CCST-INPE – 2009-2012).

OrcID: 0000-0002-5200-4009

Dr Robert Hales (Australia) Dr Robert Hales is the Director of the Griffith Centre for Sustainable Enterprise in the Griffith Business School at Griffith University. The Centre oversees the sustainability strategy and initiatives of the Griffith Business School. His research interests focus on the governance issues around the grand challenges of the time. His research focusses on SDGs in business and government, a business case for climate change, climate change policy, carbon management, sustainable tourism and working with First peoples on consent processes and climate change. He teaches in the Department of Business Strategy and Innovation convening masters level courses in the MBA and Master of Business.

OrcID: 0000-0002-4758-853X

Md Wasiul Islam (Bangladesh) Professor Md Wasiul Islam holds a PhD in Tourism from the University of Queensland, Australia. He did his Honours and Master's in Forestry from Khulna University, Bangladesh and a second MSc in Forest and Nature Conservation from the Wageningen University, the Netherlands. Prof Islam is a forester working at Forestry and Wood Technology Discipline of Khulna University. He started his career in the Bangladesh Forest Department where he was engaged in research on tourism and wildlife of the Sundarbans mangrove forest. His research interests are focussed on nature-based tourism, shared governance, participatory management of protected areas, co-management approach and sustainability.

OrcID: 0000-0001-9270-7748

Sikha Karki (Australia) Sikha Karki is a Postdoctoral Research Fellow working on a collaborative project (Nepal Red Panda Case Study) at Griffith University. This project focusses on forest governance, ecosystem services and natural capital valuation, improving forest information base and stakeholder engagement and capacity building, developing payments for ecosystems services, benefit sharing and incentives mechanisms for primary forest and habitat conservation. She has PhD from Griffith University. Her PhD research focussed on the impacts of climate change and food security on farm households in Nepal. Her research interests are climate change, adaptation, food security, agriculture, forests, governance, water and soil quality.

OrcID 0000-0002-9739-5584

Upama Koju (Nepal) Upama Koju is a Postdoctoral Research Fellow working in the Boreal and Temperate Primary Forest Research Project: Nepal Red Panda Case Study at Kathmandu Forestry College. Her PhD was on Cartography and Geographic Information Systems, her thesis focussed on climate change, remote sensing, GIS and modelling approaches for forest cover mapping, biomass, carbon and net productivity estimation and change analysis. She has more than ten years of experience working in multiple fields of application of GIS and remote sensing including agriculture, forestry, wildlife and the health sector. She has published 14 articles and three conference papers in international journals.

OrcID: 0000-0003-2030-8021

Zoltán Kun (Hungary) Zoltán Kun holds a Master's degree in landscape planning and a Professional degree in soil Science. He specialises on wilderness issues and forest protection and sustainable management and he works for various organisations as research consultant. He has worked for several years in managerial positions in international conservation organisations including WWF. He is member of the IUCN's World Commission on Protected Areas and the Commission on

Ecosystem Management. He is a Research Fellow of the Wildland Research Institute and works with Griffith University, Australia and Woods Hole Research Centre on investigation the role of temperate and boreal forests in climate change mitigation.

OrcID: 0000-0002-4688-8936

Dewi Ratna Kurniasari (Indonesia) Dewi Ratna Kurniasari has been a researcher at the Centre for Research and Development of Socio-Economic Policy and Climate Change, Indonesia Ministry of Environment and Forestry since 2010. She finished her Bachelor of Forestry in 2006 from the University of Lampung and continued her postgraduate education at the Bogor Agricultural Institute in the Tropical Biodiversity Conservation Study Program in 2007. The fields of study she is involved in are related to community empowerment in conservation forests, social forestry, conflict mediation, oil palm tenure and ecological-based fiscal transfers. She is actively involved in writing books, journals and policy briefs.

OrcID: 0000-0001-6175-0006

Tek Maraseni (Australia) Prof Tek Maraseni earned a double BSc (Science and Forestry) in Nepal, an MSc (NRM) in Thailand, where he was awarded a gold medal and a PhD (Environmental Science and Management) in Australia. He has over 26 years of research experience in identifying and adopting management practices that improve productivity, profitability and the sustainability of agriculture and forestry systems while reducing greenhouse gas emissions. He has successfully completed multiple research projects in 16 different countries. He has co-authored with researchers from 31 different countries and published 4 books, 32 book chapters and 175 journal papers.

OrcID: 0000-0001-9361-1983

Rebecca Marshallsay (Australia) Rebecca Marshallsay BA, MA (Writing and Literature), JD, is a Research Assistant at the Institute for Ethics, Governance and Law, a Griffith Strategic Research Centre. Her research focusses on ethics, values and governance in the blue economy, supporting Griffith University's contribution to the Blue Economy Cooperative Research Centre. Rebecca's academic interests include jurisprudence and its role in social, cultural and political applications of law, particularly as they relate to gender and the law. She completed her Master's thesis on filmic representations of new media and completed her advanced legal research project on the internet of things and Australian evidence law.

OrcID: 0000-0002-1894-6641

Iagê Miola (Brazil) Iagê Miola is a law Professor at the Federal University of São Paulo and a Researcher of the Brazilian Centre for Analysis and Planning. He holds a PhD from the University of Milan, a MA from the Oñati International Institute for the Sociology of Law (IISL), and a LLB from the Catholic University of Rio Grande do Sul. He has held visiting positions at the New York University and the IISL. His main research interests focus on the roles of lawyers and legal institutions in the economy, in topics such as green finance and the regulation of corporate power.

OrcID: 0000-0002-8840-6288

Dr Edward A. Morgan (Australia) Dr Edward Morgan is a Research Fellow at the Cities Research Institute and the Griffith Climate Change Response Program at Griffith University. His research focusses on landscape planning and governance to address environmental issues, including forest protection, sustainable development and natural resource management. He is currently undertaking interdisciplinary, participatory action research that is developing, implementing and evaluating landscape planning and governance for forest protection to support sustainable community development and climate change mitigation and adaptation in case studies in the Amazon, Melanesia and the Democratic Republic of the Congo.

OrcID: 0000-0002-9239-4320

Dr Fitri Nurfatriani (Indonesia) Fitri Nurfatriani is a Researcher at the Ministry of Environment and Forestry of Indonesia. She started her career as a researcher in 2000. She has published work in national and international journals and publications. Her expertise is in environmental policy and economics. She obtained a doctoral degree from IPB University. She has conducted several studies related to Forest Economic Valuation, Climate Change Funding, REDD+, Green Fiscal Policy, Sustainable Palm Oil Management, Social Forestry, Fire Control Policy and Ecological Fiscal Transfer. She is active in collaborative research with national and international research institutions and partners such as ACIAR, UNDP and CIFOR.

OrcID: 0000-0002-8422-7477

Bart Oor (the Netherlands) Bart Oor is the Strategic Business Developer for the Climate Foundation, where he helps establish long-term collaboration with the for-profit agricultural sector to mitigate climate change induced stress to European crops. Working in Europe, China, Taiwan and Vietnam, Bart has gained experience in product development in the consumer goods industry, IoT-services and the bicycle industry. He holds a BA of mechanical engineering from Hogeschool Arnhem Nijmegen University of Applied Science and an MBA from Maastricht University, with a specialty in Sustainability and Responsible leadership.

Susan Park (Australia) Susan Park is a Professor of Global Governance in the Department of Government and International Relations at the University of Sydney. She focusses on how international organisations and global governance can become greener and more accountable. Her most recent books include: *The Good Hegemon* (2022, OUP) *Environmental Recourse at the Multilateral Development Banks* (2020, CUP) and *Global Environmental Governance and the Accountability Trap* (2019, MIT, with Teresa Kramarz). She is incoming Editor of the journal *Global Environmental Politics*. She is Senior Hans Fischer Fellow at the Technical University of Munich (2019-2022) and Research Lead of the Earth Systems Governance project.

OrcID: 0000-0001-7932-1525

Connor Pilger (Australia) Connor Pilger is a third year Commerce (Finance and Accounting) student at the University of New South Wales (UNSW), passionate about driving social and environmental change. Through 180 Degrees Consulting, he spent nine months working with the Climate Foundation, across areas such as financing and operations. Connor is a Co-op Scholar and UNSW Business School Dean's List awardee. He also placed first in The UNSW Business School UN SDG Competition (2020), pitching an innovative clean energy strategy. Professionally, he has held investment banking internships at Citibank Australia and JP Morgan.

Flávio Marques Prol (Brazil) Flávio Prol is a Researcher of the Brazilian Centre for Analysis and Planning. He holds a PhD, a Master's degree and a LLB from the University of São Paulo Law School. He was a Fox Fellow at the MacMillan Centre for International and Area Studies at Yale University and a Visiting Researcher at the Institute of Global Law and Policy (IGLP) at Harvard Law School. His main research interests focus on the roles of legal institutions in the economy in topics such as green finance and macroeconomics.

OrcID: 0000-0002-4726-5570

Klaus Radunsky (Austria) Klaus Radunsky is a retired climate change expert with Phil degree in Chemistry. He started work in 1975 at the Austrian Ministry for Health and Environmental Protection. From 1985 he worked at the Umweltbundesamt until his retirement in July 2019, first as expert in the Department for Air Quality and from 1995 as Head of Unit. His main activities and responsibilities were representative of Austria in international forums, coordination of National Monitoring of Air Pollutant Emissions in Austria and member of respective EU and national bodies. He is still active in three working groups of the International Organization for Standardization.

OrcID: 0000-0002-8650-1046

A Amarender Reddy (India) Dr A Amarender Reddy is working as Principal Scientist (Agricultural Economics) with ICAR-Central Research Institute for Dryland Agriculture, Hyderabad. Earlier he worked as Director, National Institute of Agricultural Extension Management (MANAGE), Hyderabad. Prior to this he worked at the International Crops Research Institute for Semi-Arid Tropics (ICRISAT), the Bankers Institute of Rural Development(BIRD), the Indian Institute of Public Administration (IIPA) and at the Administrative Staff College of India (ASCI). His main interest areas are monitoring and evaluation of development programmes in Asia as well as rural and agricultural development. He is a columnist for Financial Express, Businessline and The Tribune in India. He has published more than 100 peer reviewed journal articles.

OrcID: 0000-0003-0615-0520

Hitomi Roppongi (UK) Hitomi Roppongi has researched environmental policies and laws focussing on implementation. She has led studies on low-carbon policies in Japan including Tokyo's cap-and-trade scheme and multilevel implementation. She has also taken part in research projects on global climate law and circular cities at the London School of Economics and University College London. Her recent projects focus on financial instruments and regulations associated with climate finance. She is interested in the role finance plays in delivering environmental goals. She hopes to combine her background managing risk at an investment bank and policy research in making contribution to the debate on sustainability.

OrcID: 0000-0002-9432-1918

Mimi Salminah (Indonesia) Mimi Salminah is a Researcher at the Research and Development Centre for Socioeconomics, Policy and Climate Change. Her research interests are forest landscape management, forest policy and economics, particularly with respect to climate change, ecosystem services valuation, carbon market development, green finance and subsistence market development. Mimi holds an undergraduate degree in Forestry from IPB University, and a Master's in Forest Science and Management from Southern Cross University Australia. Some of her research includes peatland restoration, inter-government fiscal transfer for green economy, market development of peatland commodities and the role of private sector in REDD+.

OrcID: 0000-0001-5094-6433

Tapan Sarker (Australia) Tapan Sarker (PhD, ANU) is a Full Professor and Finance Discipline Lead at the School of Business of the University of Southern Queensland. Tapan is an internationally renowned expert in sustainability, climate finance and public financial management. His research focusses on personal and behavioural finances as well as the factors affecting the financial participation of banks in renewable energy investment and ESG investment. He is widely published, including in top tier journals, for example, the *Global Finance Journal, Finance Research Letters, Australian Tax Forum, International Review of Economics & Finance*, and *Economic Modelling.* He is a former World Bank Scholar.

OrcID: 0000-0002-0682-2940

Seema Sharma (India) Dr Seema Sharma is Director of Resilience Relations, a certified startup in community resilience. She is working on achieving Sustainable Development Goals (SDGs) at the local level. She is a certified Artificial Intelligence professional from IIT Roorkee, India. Currently, she is a faculty member in Environment Department at the University of Delhi. She also is a developer, administrator and editor of an online journal *advait.world.*

OrcID: 0000-0002-4520-5195

Anita Shrestha (Nepal) Dr Anita Shrestha is a Postdoctoral Research Fellow at Kathmandu Forestry College. Her PhD focussed on climate change and local adaptation. She has more than 20 years of experience in research related to forests. Her areas of expertise include community forest management, natural resource management, climate change, biodiversity conservation, women's empowerment, micro enterprise development, livelihood improvement, ecotourism, gender and social inclusion (GESI), red panda conservation, governance, advocacy and lobbying. She has published more than 25 academic articles on forest, wildlife and gender-related issues in different national and international academic journals.

OrcID: 0000-0001-9581-8750

Beate Sjåfjell (Norway) Beate Sjåfjell is Professor of Law at the University of Oslo, Faculty of Law, and a Visiting Professor at College of Europe, European Legal Studies Department. Professor Sjåfjell is founder and head of the Oslo Faculty's Research Group Companies, Markets and Sustainability, as well as of several international networks and projects. Her research has become increasingly interdisciplinary, integrating a research-based concept of sustainability into corporate governance and company law. She publishes extensively in the field of company law and sustainability, including *The Cambridge Handbook of Corporate Law, Corporate Governance and Sustainability* (co-edited with Christopher M. Bruner; Cambridge University Press 2019).

OrcID: 0000-0002-5645-0225

Chris Taylor Dr Chris Taylor is a Research Fellow at the Fenner School of Environment and Society, Australian National University. Chris specialises in spatial analysis of forest ecosystems and disturbance regimes, remote sensing, environmental modelling, land use and forest certification. He has been involved with a number of research projects, ranging from the analysis of fire severity patterns across Australian forests through to climate change adaptation in Australian agriculture. Chris is also a passionate landscape photographer and has held a number of exhibitions of his photography.

OrcID: 0000-0002-7908-204X

Theresa Theuretzbacher (Norway) Theresa Theuretzbacher is the Engineering Manager at the Climate Foundation. Prior to the Climate Foundation, she gained experience in solving local water, waste and sanitation challenges in projects in rural Ghana, Alaska and DR Congo, providing numerous environmental and health benefits as well as contributing to climate change adaptation. She is engaged in the development and technology demonstrations of marine permaculture. Theresa's expertise lies in developing practical solutions by following nature's example to provide strong benefits to the economy and local ecosystems, in consideration of architectural, infrastructural, economic, environmental and social contexts into which specific technologies and their supporting infrastructures are placed.

Rebecca Truman (Australia) Rebecca Truman is the co-founder and Director of the Climate Foundation. Prior to the Climate Foundation, she helped start and run several startup companies in Silicon Valley, served as a Technical Director at Digital Productions, one of the first computer graphics companies in the US. She held responsibilities leading organisational transformation for companies such as Security First, Loyds Supply, CalTech Submillimeter Observatory, Rapid Prototypes, Inc and has convened large events. She holds a BA from the University of California, Santa Barbara.

Dr Brian von Herzen (Australia) Dr Brian von Herzen is the co-founder and Executive Director of the Climate Foundation. He is the chief architect of marine permaculture offshore seaweed mariculture. Prior to establishing the Climate Foundation in 2007, Dr von Herzen worked with Silicon Valley firms over three decades developing product solutions for tech companies large and small. He graduated magna cum laude in three years from Princeton University with a degree in Physics. He holds a PhD in planetary science from California Institute of Technology, where he was awarded the prestigious Hertz Fellowship, Hughes Doctoral Fellowship and has been awarded numerous patents. More recently, he has been selected as an Edmund Hillary Fellow in New Zealand.

Graham Wood (Australia) Graham Wood is a philosopher working in the School of Humanities at the University of Tasmania (UTAS) and is a member of the Centre for Marine Socioecology (UTAS/CSIRO). Graham's research concerns the relationship between human values and a scientific understanding of the human condition. He examines this relationship within three realms: environmental philosophy, cognitive science of religion and moral psychology. In his research environmental, religious and moral values are examined using insights from philosophy of mind, cognitive science and evolutionary psychology.

OrcID: 0000-0002-0307-9012

Jodi York (Australia) Jodi is a social impact strategist, researcher and adviser. She offers tailored support for asset owners, asset managers, businesses, non-profits and philanthropists committed to tackling entrenched social problems and delivering lasting impact. She provides evidence-led strategy to shift complex problems funding approaches, intervention design, impact management and the networks to leverage and multiply it. Jodi has a PhD in sociology from the University of

California, Berkeley and has published qualitative and quantitative research in sociology, economics, accounting and management. She has worked in business, academic, government and civil society settings in the US and across Australasia.

OrcID: 0000-0003-3986-7608

Sam Zak (Switzerland) Sam Zak is the European Lead at the Climate Foundation. He has worked at the Climate Foundation since 2019. Prior to the Climate Foundation, he completed a number of internships in different environmental organisations and sustainability think tanks. He holds an MSc in Environment and Development from the London School of Economics and Political Science and a BA in History from the University of York.

Kazi Arif Uz Zaman (Bangladesh) Kazi Arif Uz Zaman holds a PhD from the Australian National University in the field of Regional Cooperation and Sustainable Green Growth. As a Research Fellow, he has contributed to several projects conducted by the governments of Australia and Indonesia, the Association of Southeast Asian Nations (ASEAN) secretariat and the ADBI in the field of energy, sustainability, natural resources management and SDG. Dr Zaman has also engaged in a few ADBIs call-for-paper projects. He has published articles and book chapters in reputed publications including *Energy Policy*, *Springer Nature* and *International Journal of Environmental Research*. Currently, Dr Zaman works at the Financial Stability Department of Central Bank of Bangladesh.

OrcID: 0000-0001-8611-7899

Acknowledgements

The editors would like to extend their gratitude to De Gruyter for the provision of funds to enable production of this Handbook and to David Repetto, Stefan Giesen and Maximilian Gessl in particular for their help and support throughout the creative process. Thanks also go to the Law Futures Centre of Griffith University for an additional small grant to cover additional costs associated with editing, undertaken so professionally by Rebecca Marshallsay and Kirrallee Grace.

Preface

When the proposal for a Handbook on sustainable development and finance in this series was submitted to De Gruyter in October 2020, COVID-19 was a relatively new phenomenon, and its connection to sustainable development and finance appeared tenuous. Yet to comment on those relations seemed necessary, albeit foolhardy. SARSCoV-2 and its variants are hardly the domain of a political scientist or a professor of finance.

As the infection continued to spread, everyone who accepted the virus as a fact quickly became experts, at least in terms of personal hygiene, mask-wearing, maintaining social distance and the full gamut of precautionary measures. For those countries and individuals fortunate enough to have sufficient economic resources, domestic isolation and welfare became the norm, along with telecommuting and shopping online. Strange side-effects began to manifest themselves. Wild animals were seen in empty central business districts. Cafés set up tables in erstwhile parking spaces to attract COVID-safe business. Cars disappeared and bicycles became popular. Smog-laden skies turned blue and carbon emissions plummeted. Other, poorer, localities were less fortunate. Working at home was out of the question and food deliveries were not an option, forcing people outdoors. The trade in illegal wildlife escalated as impoverished householders looked for sources of income. Medical waste and throw-away masks became the new pollution problem, everywhere.

As the pandemic entered its second year, hopes for a vaccine were realised. Financial support was not provided with the same alacrity in the face of new strains of the virus and lockdowns were not reinstated – or were resisted by citizens. Gradually, as immunisation numbers increased restrictions were eased and those who died were either not vaccinated, old or socially marginalised and therefore deemed to be of less political importance than restless voters and struggling companies. Slowly, societies began to return to their old attitudes and cooperation in the face of a common enemy gave way to business-as-usual. Although not entirely. Bicycles remained popular, some cities exchanged clogged city streets for permanent outdoor venues and many people chose to keep working from home.

It is hard not to draw parallels with the history of sustainable development. The existential threat posed by human-caused environmental degradation, and climate change in particular, resulted in a short period of unprecedented collaboration in the immediate aftermath of the collapse of the Soviet Union and the global community came together to take action. Once the ministers who signed the accords returned to their respective countries however, reality took hold. Too many businesses would be affected, with impacts on employment; modernising national economies to take account of the environment would cost too much. Despite the risks, it was easier to revert to the status quo. The similarity to the pandemic may have a common cause. At the heart of the sustainability problem lies the fact that the use and transformation of natural resources into material goods causes damage but generates profit. The ongoing

https://doi.org/10.1515/9783110733488-205

destruction of the environment will remain an unavoidable trade-off – unless there is a clear separation (or de-coupling) of economic growth from environmental degradation.

The fact that fiscally conservative national governments were able to put their ideology aside, and the sky did not fall, demonstrates that where there is a will, there is a way, even if there are reversals. The transition of the global economy towards sustainability and the financing of initiatives to make it happen is underway. This may be slow and incremental, but it is happening, even if there are those opposing this progress. The climate change negotiations are a case in point. Those who attend such events for the first time often go with the expectation that this will be the moment that the world takes decisive action, when in truth it is like watching paint dry and quite mundane. It is not always easy to determine incremental, positive, developments by the absence of something far worse. An ancient forest that remains upright due to the efforts of a local community is almost rendered invisible by its ongoing presence.

Sustainable development has proven to be remarkably persistent as both a direction and a destination. Green growth emerged as an alternative discourse in the 2000s as a means of recovering from the global financial crisis through renewable energy development and has been advocated as a response mechanism for the recovery that should ensue from the pandemic. However, despite its ongoing popularity in South Korea, the EU, UK and US, the absence of the term from intergovernmental environmental conventions gives it less policy traction than sustainable development. The explicit linkage to growth, rather than development, which has greater flexibility of interpretation, may be another reason.

While the capacity for sustainable development to mean all things to all people is part of its appeal, it is also part of its rejection by some sectors of the policy community, largely due to the potential for greenwash. There is some justification for this, as the legitimacy of a number of policy instruments arising out of the global environmental agreements that have co-opted the term, such as emissions trading and eco-labelling, have been called into question. The repeated connection to finance for sustainable development from developed to developing countries in international environmental agreements, reinforces the attractiveness of the concept. Finance, or lack thereof, also explains some of the tensions and frustrations that regularly occur in intergovernmental negotiations around the implementation of those agreements. The nature of such finance is detailed and yet simultaneously vague. There are references to finance for technology transfer, the role of the private sector in delivering access to that technology, as well as funds, grants and loans, even payments. Yet there never seems to be enough. Finance might be equated to the eternally unreachable carrot, dangled in front of developing countries, with no commensurate stick for developed countries for non-delivery.

These are some of the tensions that surround the current state of play of sustainable development and finance. COVID-19 resulted in a stagnating global economy, while simultaneously reducing carbon emissions and encouraging deviation from the orthodoxies of the time. Growth, which seemed to be such an important aspect of development, proved to be less important than mechanisms for social support and public sector spending more critical to wellbeing than private finance. Despite this, as the world began the slow process of recovery, pre-pandemic economic values returned, although not entirely. Significant numbers of workers stayed at home, stimulating local business and leaving governments with inner cities in need of rejuvenation. The longer-term impacts of the virus on the trajectory of sustainable development and finance are unclear, although it is worth noting that while the climate negotiations were postponed for a year, when global leaders did convene, coal was explicitly referred to in the final text for the first time in the context of a phase down (even if a phase out was what some countries were hoping for). Furthermore, there was no drastic revision of climate policy, nor were there calls for a suspension of emissions reduction targets or other similar measures. Sustainable development, for all its contradictions, is here to stay, part of the global policy furniture, as it were.

In a volume of over 40 contributors it is not surprising that there is no one single view on the current state of, and way forward for, sustainable development and finance, with a few notable exceptions. Conventional approaches to economic development are not working, are having significant environmental and social consequences and there is an urgent need for change. There is also a certain ambiguity towards current policy instruments and market mechanisms. This second observation is directly related to the first. If the current neoliberal economic model is failing to deliver sustainability in the single bottom line world of most national economies, it is unlikely to deliver it at the international level. Market mechanisms require greater integrity if they are to function effectively and enjoy widespread support. The divisions between public and private funds for sustainable development also need to be broken down and greater collaboration between government, business and civil society is essential.

This Handbook is in five parts. In Part 1, 'Origins and evolution of sustainable development and finance,' the authors investigate some of the foundational institutions and organisations arising from of the 1992 Rio de Janeiro Earth Summit and its successors, as well as some of those aspects of (environmental) economics and (natural) resource management that should have been given closer attention. Part 2, 'Public finance' examines the current and future role of public fiscal management for sustainable development, with an emphasis on emerging technologies and their relevance to developing countries but also examining what can go wrong in developed polities when competing policy objectives collide. Part 3, 'Private Finance' mirrors the previous section, inquiring into the risks and opportunities for developing countries posed by private investment and digital infrastructure but also discussing how conventional economics in the developed world fail to value social capital and community cooperation. Part 4, 'Climate finance,' returns to the intergovernmental arena and looks at a range of institutions and approaches to financing climate change adaptation and mitigation, noting that fundamental social challenges, such as poverty and inequality, must be addressed if communities are to remain resilient in the face of future shocks. Part 5, 'The blue economy' ventures onto the high seas to explore the new frontier for development, interrogating the sustainability of existing and new activities in this space. In all sections, the impacts of the pandemic are discussed and, where relevant, recommendations provided. A concluding chapter incorporates the perspectives of all authors and reflects on the future of sustainable development and finance in a post-pandemic, post-carbon world.

Timothy Cadman
Bellingen,
New South Wales,
AMDG

Part 1: **Origins and evolution**

Timothy Cadman and Tapan Sarker

Chapter 1
Origins and evolution of sustainable development and finance

Abstract: This introductory chapter provides a broad-brush presentation of the intergovernmental regime for sustainable development that has arisen since the 1992 UN Conference on Environment and Development (UNCED), also known as the Rio Earth Summit, and beyond. The chapter begins with an outline of the origins of sustainable development as an intergovernmental and international policy agenda and delineates some of the main outcomes arising from UNCED. These include the various conventions guiding global environmental policy today, as well as the Global Environment Facility, one of the most significant channels of finance for sustainable development. Also explored are the Millennium Development Goals (MDGs), 2000–2015 and their successors, the Sustainable Development Goals (SDGs). This is followed by a discussion of the role of the private sector in financing sustainable development and the challenges inherent in unlocking private finance. The chapter continues with an exploration of the future for sustainable development and finance in the light of the alternative approaches to understanding and valuing capital and in the context of COVID-19. A final section summarises the contributions of the various authors in this section, who explore a range of issues confronting the current practice of, and potential for, sustainable development and finance.

Keywords: ecosystem services, forest certification, global environment facility, landscape planning, millennium development goals, natural capital, neoliberalism, sustainable development goals, unced, taxonomy, world bank, COVID-19

Sustainable development as an intergovernmental and international policy agenda

The current agenda for sustainable development and finance, however it has developed, is a child of global cooperation around environmental problem-solving in an era when the collapse of the Soviet Union reinforced the belief in progress towards a world of democratic, liberal internationalism. Communism was largely confined to China and capitalism was the dominant economic system. Recent environmental initiatives of the time, such as tackling the hole in the ozone caused by industrial chemicals, demonstrated how world governments could come together to develop policies and agreements in favour of the common good. Environmental problems

https://doi.org/10.1515/9783110733488-001

caused by human activity, and threats to the global commons, (i.e., the atmosphere and terrestrial ecosystems) required policies capable of responding to the impacts of global-level environmental change. The scale of the problems confronted appeared to necessitate a degree of engagement between state and non-state actors not previously seen, and a new set of institutions arose in which governance, that is, the steering or coordination of multiple interests, rather than government, was the main system for responding to the global environmental problems of the time. Understanding the impacts of the industrial-scale use of the world's resources also preoccupied the international community and it is possible to trace the trajectory of thinking around sustainable development from 1972, with the *Limits to Growth* (Meadows et al. 1972) report of the Club of Rome and the foundational and influential UN Conference on the Human Environment (UNCHE), to the 1987 Brundtland Report, which promoted the notion of sustainable development, that is, development that could meet the needs of the present without compromising the ability of future generations to meet their own needs (World Commission on Environment and Development 1987: 1). Even if the nation-state was still seen as being largely responsible for the management of domestic natural resources, this was an essentially pluralist model of international environmental cooperation (Vogler 1996) and both business and society played a role in the lead up to the 1992 UNCED (Clapp 1998). Also reflecting the involvement of business, and optimism in the evolving global economic system, was the belief that the market could solve many of the environmental challenges of the time. However, the objectives of achieving economic development and growth and protecting the environment resulted in inherent contradictions and compromises inherent in the concept of neoliberal environmentalism (Bernstein 2001).

At the heart of UNCED lies *Agenda 21* (United Nations 1993), and the various conventions that dominate global environmental policy today, notably the Framework Convention on Climate Change (UNFCCC), the Convention on Biological Diversity (UNCBD), and the Convention to Combat Desertification (UNCCD). However, the asymmetries in power brought about by the emerging regime of neoliberal global environmental governance were well-established by the UNCED and preliminary negotiations focussed on Global North concerns about climate change, biodiversity and forestry, rather than the needs of the Global South around technology transfer and trade reform and finance (controlled by the North) to bring about change. The South was obliged to accept the agenda in the main and had to satisfy itself with the Global Environment Facility, founded on the eve of Rio in 1992, as the main financial institution for sustainable development (Imber 1996). The Global Environment Facility (GEF) remains a source of funding and finance for the UNFCCC, UNCBD and UNCCD and continues to fund climate change adaptation and mitigation activities, although some space is now taken up by the Green Climate Fund. Within this regime sit the aspirations of developing and developed countries in the Sustainable Development Goals and their predecessors. Since 1992 the GEF has provided over USD 21.7 billion in grants and has mobilised USD 119 billion in cofinancing for over 5,000 projects and programmes (Global Environment Facility 2021).

One of the fundamental orientations of *Agenda 21* was (and is) its emphasis on the use of market mechanisms to deliver sustainable development (United Nations 1993). These encompass market-based initiatives from carbon trading to timber certification and more, the quality and legitimacy of which vary greatly (Cadman 2011; Cadman et al. 2015). Timber certification is investigated in more detail by Chris Taylor in Chapter Six below. The use of such mechanisms under the UNFCCC has been controversial since the days of the CDM, and now its successor under the Paris Agreement, the so-called 'mechanism to contribute to the mitigation of greenhouse gas emissions and support sustainable development' or sustainable development mechanism (SDM) (UNFCCC 2015: 7; Radunsky and Cadman 2017; Cadman et al. 2018).

As the 1990s receded and gave way to the new century, the expectations for truly sustainable development began to fade. In that sense, the Millennium Summit of 2000, its Declaration and the MDGs 2000–2015 represent an effort to revisit the ongoing and unmet needs for human development and poverty eradication, despite three decades of development (Anstee 2013). Finance from the Summit went to the World Bank, International Monetary Fund and African Development Bank to cancel developing country debt but there was no direct link to finance for sustainable development until 2015, with the reformulation of the MDGs to the SDGs and the creation of the Interagency Task Force on Finance for Development and the Addis Ababa Action Agenda of 2016. From that point, development and sustainability became more closely aligned with the various conventions, programmes and projects of UNCED. The role of the World Bank is explored in more detail below by Susan Park, in Chapter Four. The regime complex for sustainable development and finance is depicted in Figure 1.1.

The role of the private sector in financing sustainable development

In reality however, there is still little incentive for private sector transformation from business-as-usual practices. If these initiatives are to be scaled-up globally to achieve climate targets and development goals, alternative options must be explored that could unlock further funding. Rather than relying on public investments in these initiatives, which often involve private partners utilising instruments such as deferred loans government guarantees, or other mechanisms offering favourable terms can provide solutions that will be repaid and thus carry greater impact or exist as part of larger programmes where profits are reinvested. Establishing government stability and support for sustainable natural resource management are likely to increase private sector investment and foreign direct investment. Undervalued natural assets

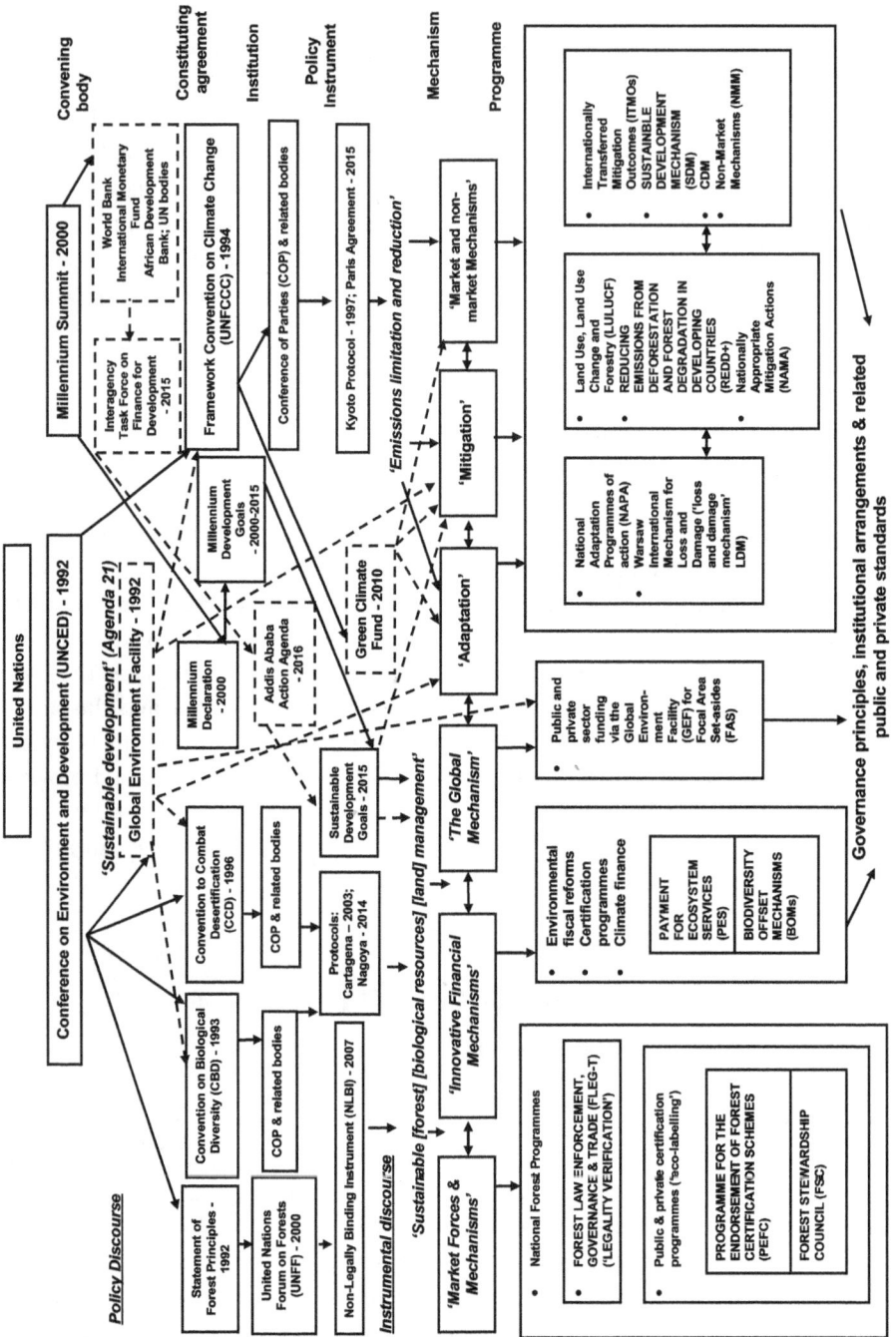

Figure 1.1: The regime complex of sustainable development and finance.
Source: Cadman et al. (2015), adapted with permission.
Note: Stippled lines indicate finance flows.

have benefitted the private sector for years largely due to weak or non-existent policies accompanied by subsidies that have essentially reduced the price of a natural
resource below the marginal cost to society (Clark, Reed, and Sunderland 2018). This
has led to unsustainable management at the landscape level and new approaches are
required to build landscape planning and sustainable finance into business practice.
This is explored by Edward A. Morgan and Andrew Buckwell in Chapter Five.

The past decade has seen a burgeoning interest in scaling-up private investment
to address persistent socioeconomic and environmental challenges globally (Clark,
Reed, and Sunderland 2018). Regulation of emission of greenhouse gases is an urgent
requirement for countries by unprecedented climate change, increasing global consensus on sustainable development. This also threatens the economic interest of developing countries at the early-stage of their industrialisation. For developed countries,
however, it is an opportunity to transfer clean technologies and to acquire soft power,
especially through advocating international agreements on global climate change.
More radically, some social scientists offer critiques of the relationship between sustainability and continuing economic growth essentially based on political economy.
Some authors have cast doubt on the value of the circular economy within corporate
capitalism, seeing it as a justification for continuing economic growth. The circular
economy has been one of the main references for rebuilding and reforming a political
economy of sustainable growth, given the social and environmental crises associated
with out-of-bounds growth capitalism (Valenzuela and Böhm 2017). The transition to a
circular economy may bring socioeconomic benefits in many ways. For example, in
terms of the creation of new employment opportunities associated with the establishment of recycling facilities, as well as the redesign of manufacturing and service systems. The circular economy is a part of social and intergenerational equity and is
fundamental to the SDGs. Economic growth and environmental costs are problematic
in establishing and developing large new business ventures (Wynn and Jones 2020).
To transform the global energy complex to be carbon neutral within a time frame designed to prevent irreparable damage to the environment presents unprecedented
challenges. The private sector must deploy financial, material and engineering resources on a scale never before undertaken with the government providing leadership, removing barriers and supporting industry efforts through policies that mobilise markets
to achieve environmental objectives.

The Sustainable Development Goals and targets are interdependent one with
another (United Nations 2018). Therefore, the goals and targets must be pursued together since progress in one area often depends on progress in other areas. However, the balanced contribution of civil society, governments, the private sector,
non-governmental organisations and the public is essential to accomplish the target
of sustainability. The key barriers faced by the private sector are policy and political
risks that cause investors to withdraw and cancel planned investments. These instruments need to be diversified to overcome these risks through leveraging available resources such as the Green Climate Fund, or the Multilateral Investment

Guarantee Agency of the World Bank (United Nations 2015). Developing countries have received funding to reduce emissions and have been encouraging the private sector and smallholder stakeholders to reduce emissions. In the case of Indonesia, fiscal instruments are encouraging the private sector to reduce forest-based emissions. The timber export ban, subsidies to palm oil (encouraging community encroachment into forests for conversion to palm oil), high fees and informal charges have acted as constraints on the viability of the forest sector (Cadman et al. 2019; Cadman et al. 2015).

There are examples of emerging economies which show the significant contribution private financing can make to achieving sustainability (Taghizadeh-Hesary and Yoshino 2019), such as corporate social and environmental responsibility contributions, notably in Indonesia and India (Yunari 2020). Powerful countries such as China have also made a series of steps to reduce emissions and finance the ecological modernisation of their industries (Yee, Lo, and Tang 2013). Making the best use of private finance will be critical if nation-states are to achieve their mitigation and adaptation objectives (Baietti et al. 2012). Although it is not without its faults, it is encouraging to see that hybrid governance systems of public and private finance such as the CDM have encouraged emissions reductions (Lund 2013); such systems now need to emerge within domestic economies to amplify sustainable business.

Private sector participation in green finance and investment can provide an opportunity for development in numerous sectors of the economy (Taghizadeh-Hesary and Yoshino 2019). Global actors including countries, regions, cities, companies, investors and other organisations are also willing to report their commitments to act on climate change, with private governance reporting mechanisms such as the Carbon Disclosure Project (NAZCA: Global Climate Action Portal Undated). This is a positive sign for economic transparency in the emerging global green economy. To unlock private finance, variations in the current systems are essential to incentivise private investment in sustainable behaviour. Free market logic and capitalism should result in an orderly allocation of capital with the proportionate blending of the private and public sectors. But this seldom happens in reality. Expecting transformational change from increasing these types of investments when they coexist with business models, financial systems and government policies that incentivise the very actions and activities responsible for the environmental damage humanity is trying to rectify is radically unrealistic.

The future for sustainable development and finance

Capitalism has speciated as a consequence of Rio and the sustainable development agenda (Cadman et al. 2015). Alongside conventional neoliberal market ideology are a range of alternative models, the most well-known of which is the notion of the triple bottom line, which acknowledges the need to account not just for economic activity, but for the social and environmental costs and benefits of doing business (Elkington and Rowlands 1999). Conservation biologists and environmental economists have explored various approaches to valuing nature, with the aim of placing biodiversity conservation and on a level playing field with government and the private sector. This aspiration has only been partially achieved. International activities undertaken by international actors (e.g., non-governmental organisations, intergovernmental organisations and other international organisations) is dominated by capacity building. In other words, aid and development, rather than systemic economic transformation, have been the focus of activities to date. The international community is not effectively using the concept to value nature in order to inform sustainability and finance-related decisions. A greater reflection on the concept of ecosystem services and related programmes of action is needed if the unfulfilled promise of natural capital accounting is to be realised (Allan et al. 2021).

The global pandemic poses its own challenges to sustainable development and finance. Health, social inequality and other aspects of sustainable development targeted by the SDGs have all been affected by the pandemic. While the impact of the pandemic has been negative on many aspects of society, the potential of the virus to transform society has also been noted. Business-as-usual may reassert itself post-pandemic, leading to an increase in emissions, as industry and consumers seek to make up for lost opportunities (Hannam and O'Malley 2020). With the global economic downturn, the prospects for urban renewal, service delivery, sustainable production and consumption, emissions reduction and energy transition have also been highlighted (Wang and Huang 2021). As several authors in this Handbook note, the disruption brought about by COVID-19 also provides a unique opportunity to galvanise the global economy through public and private finance for sustainable development. Whether this happens remains to be seen.

Overview of chapters

In summary, the international policy community and state and non-state actors continue to struggle to resolve the challenges posed by the current economic system and the environmental and social impacts for which it is responsible. Finance for sustainable development continues to remain elusive, although some progress has been made. In this first section of the Handbook, the authors investigate some of those measures and evaluate their effectiveness.

In Chapter Two, 'Complexity and uncertainty in sustainable finance: An analysis of the EU taxonomy,' Hanna Ahlström and Beate Sjåfjell see the financial sector has a role to play in bringing about societal change, but the sector needs to significantly transform. It is often overlooked that the finance field is deeply rooted in its discipline, overlooking sustainability conceptions that are discussed in other fields, and has its own epistemological, ontological and methodological biases. Some sustainability impacts still cannot be identified and measured today. Policymakers need accurate predictions for their decision-making, but reality and models seldom coincide, leading to underestimations or blindness to tipping points. Investment and policy require information about system behaviour, which may never be available and where mathematical methods will not work. Consequently, the usefulness of quantitative and probability-based methodologies for sustainable finance when applied to Environment, Social and Governance (ESG) criteria raises questions about sustainable investment in its current form. The usefulness of establishing a taxonomy for sustainable economic activities, which has been done in the European Union (EU) through its initiative on sustainable finance, raises similar questions. Now part of the European Green Deal, this is one of six priorities 2019–2024 of the European Commission and concerns the goal in which Europe aims to be the first climate-neutral, resource-efficient economy. Establishing a taxonomy of sustainability-related activities and associated regulation is the initiative's most well-known legislative proposal and is investigated by the authors. The Taxonomy Regulation sets the criteria for determining if economic activity is sustainable, sufficient to the degree needed to establish the sustainability of an investment and is a minor improvement to EU financial regulation. Regrettably, the regulation is an outcome of limited debate about to what extent it is possible to identify and measure aspects of corporate sustainability.

In Chapter Three, 'Ecosystem services and natural capital: Application to sustainable finance,' Andrew Buckwell and Edward A. Morgan provide an overview of the current state of knowledge on the concepts of ecosystem services and natural capital. The authors focus on their application in sustainable finance and discuss the challenges and concerns arising from these ideas. These two ideas have been growing since the 1970s and now present a robust framework for thinking about environmental, social and economic costs associated with sustainable natural resource management and the distribution of benefits. Originating in the developed economies, and latterly and increasingly being taken up in the developing countries, ecosystem services and natural capital as a means of evaluating the integrity of sustainable development globally are now accepted concepts. Being able to quantify ecosystem services and natural capital, especially in terms of money via economic valuations, has meant policymakers can assess the social costs and benefits of investments in environmental conservation and provision of services by nature. These costs and benefits are useful for measuring land use change, climate change, sustainable development, disaster resilience and public health at varying temporal and spatial levels. Economic valuation techniques can now meet the challenge of measuring ecosystem services and natural capital, including public goods and common pool resources.

Such valuations have begun to guide private and public funding and finance in the direction of environmental and social investment, sustainability policies and development plans. The Economics of Ecosystems and Biodiversity (TEEB) programme was designed to develop, test and demonstrate tools and mechanisms to value ecosystem services. TEEB stimulated international policymaking, influencing fiscal, regulatory and investment policies and in international biodiversity and climate change negotiations. The private sector is now expected to account for the impacts and dependencies on natural capital and ecosystem services. The UN has taken up these valuation techniques and there are now consistent, comprehensive, standardised accounting frameworks to add to traditional measures of human wellbeing, such as GDP. The integration of changes in stocks of natural capital and flows into national accounts will make the contributions of nature to the economy more transparent – especially in implementing a post-COVID-19 inclusive and green recovery.

In Chapter Four, 'The World Bank (Group) and sustainable development, Susan Park explains the role of the World Bank as the world's preeminent multilateral development bank in financing sustainable development. Through loans, investments, guarantees and technical assistance to states for development projects and programmes, the Bank has learnt over the years since the 1980s to develop environmental and social safeguards for its development lending and moved into climate financing in the 1990s. In the last 20 years, the Bank has moved towards public private partnerships, while continuing to provide public goods. This chapter examines how the World Bank has contributed to financing for sustainable development, from an initial refusal to accept its actions had environmental consequences, and its transition from do no harm to doing good. The chapter outlines how the World Bank's internal changes helped it focus on stand-alone green projects in its portfolio and gain expertise in sustainable development. This was matched by efforts to be the major global vehicle for green funding. Here the role of the Global Environment Facility in financing and moving into the carbon markets established as part of the Parties' commitments under the UNFCCC are to be noted. The chapter also scrutinises carbon market pilot funds created in the 1990s and how the World Bank is embedded in both climate financing and carbon markets. It will be interesting to see how the Group, as a whole, responds to financing the post-COVID recovery.

In Chapter Five, on a theme which echoes much of the thinking in their previous joint chapter Edward A. Morgan and Andrew Buckwell elaborate on 'Landscape Planning and Economics for Sustainable Finance.' They examine and synthesise the main challenges confronting planning and economics at a landscape level and investigate how the two approaches can support each other and result in more sustainable and more just outcomes. Finance drives land use and resource extraction in landscapes globally. Carbon finance too is grounded in land use: carbon is found in soils, trees, forests. Sustainable finance relies on the sustainable management of the landscape (natural capital), on which it is founded. Conventional finance approaches manage landscapes with a focus on unsustainable levels of resource extraction. Other values and benefits landscapes can provide including ecosystem services are overlooked, resulting in deforestation, land degradation, biodiversity loss and pollution.

Sustainable finance needs models that better value ecosystem services at a landscape level and recognise the interconnectedness and multi-stakeholder landscapes and ecosystem services. However, the benefits of ecosystem services play out over time and space and are indirect and long-term in their provision of services. Here there are parallels with COVID-19, society as a whole needs healthy, intact landscapes for human wellbeing. Well-functioning, integrated and participatory planning and decision-making processes are a way to help stakeholders identify benefits, values and actions that will improve wellbeing in the future. Helping multiple stakeholders collaborate and learn how to maintain ecosystem integrity while managing change and how to identify ways to share sharing benefits and avoid inequalities, will deliver more just outcomes.

In Chapter Six, 'Certification and sustainable development,' Chris Taylor discusses the implications for society inherent in the neoliberal preference for non-state, market-driven governance and certification in particular. In the forestry sector around 40% of global trade in industrial wood products is sourced from forests certified under two global forest certification schemes, the Forest Stewardship Council (FSC) and the Programme for the Endorsement of Forest Certification (PEFC). The rationale behind forest certification was in response to global concerns over unprecedented rates of deforestation and forest degradation occurring throughout the world during the 1970s and 1980s, as well as the limitations in the effectiveness of nation-states. State and intergovernmental efforts were failing to arrest unprecedented rates of deforestation and forest degradation. The emergence of forest certification across global trade in forest and wood products was novel in that it marked a transition away from a reliance on the nation-state towards a soft law approach that was based on self-government. Forests became governed at a distance through indirect strategies of power, operating within the norms of neoliberalism and liberal environmentalism, whereby certification internalised environmental costs by including them in the price paid for certified products and externalised authority away from the state and to the market. This was an attempt to reconcile the competing sets of environmental and economic norms of development, whereby economic development was addressed within the context of environmental protection and therefore became sustainable development. The term has been subsequently used by nation-states and industry alike to justify further development, with the potential to inflict more damage on the environment and overlook the dangers of limitless growth.

References

Allan, Jen Iris, Graeme Auld, Timothy Cadman, and Hayley Stevenson. 2021. 'Comparative Fortunes of Ecosystem Services as an International Governance Concept', *Global Policy*, 13 (1), 62–75.
Anstee, Margaret Joan. 2013. 'Millennium Development Goals: Milestones on a Long Road.' in Rorden Wilkinson and David Hulme (eds.), *The Millennium Development Goals and Beyond* (London: Routledge), pp. 43–58.

Baietti, Aldo, Andrey Shlyakhtenko, Roberto La Rocca, and Urvaksh D. Patel. 2012. *Green Infrastructure Finance: Leading Initiatives and Research* (World Bank Publications).

Bernstein, Steven. 2001. *The Compromise of Liberal Environmentalism* (New York: Columbia University Press).

Cadman, Timothy. 2011. *Quality and Legitimacy of Global Governance: Case Lessons from Forestry* (New York; Basingstoke: Palgrave Macmillan).

Cadman, Timothy, Lauren Eastwood, Federico Lopez-Casero Michaelis, Tek Narayan Maraseni, Jamie Pittock, and Tapan Sarker. 2015. *The Political Economy of Sustainable Development: Policy Instruments and Market Mechanisms* (Edward Elgar Publishing).

Cadman, Timothy, Klaus Radunsky, Andrea Simonelli, and Tek Maraseni. 2018. 'From Paris to Poland: A Postmortem of the Climate Change Negotiations', *The International Journal of Social Quality*, 8 (2), 27–46.

Cadman, Timothy, Tapan Sarker, Zahrul Muttaqin, Fitri Nurfatriani, Mimi Salminah, and Tek Maraseni. 2019. 'The Role of Fiscal Instruments in Encouraging the Private Sector and Smallholders to Reduce Emissions from Deforestation and Forest Degradation: Evidence from Indonesia', *Forest Policy and Economics*, 108, 101913.

Clapp, Jennifer. 1998. 'The Privatization of Global Environmental Governance: ISO 14000 and the Developing World', *Global Governance*, 4 (3), 295–316.

Clark, Robyn, James Reed, and Terry Sunderland. 2018. 'Bridging Funding Gaps for Climate and Sustainable Development: Pitfalls, Progress and Potential of Private Finance', *Land Use Policy*, 71, 335–346.

Elkington, John, and Ian H Rowlands. 1999. 'Cannibals with Forks: The Triple Bottom Line of 21st Century Business', *Alternatives Journal*, 25 (4), 42.

Global Environment Facility. 2021. *Who We Are*, <https://www.thegef.org/who-we-are> [Accessed 15 February 2022].

Hannam, Peter, and Nick O'Malley. 2020. 'Carbon Emissions Will Drop, but Experts Fear 'Revenge Pollution'', *Sydney Morning Herald*, 29/03/2020. <https://www.smh.com.au/environment/climate-change/carbon-emissions-will-drop-but-experts-fear-revenge-pollution-20200327-p54eft.html> [Accessed 24 February 2022].

Imber, Mark F. 1996. 'The Environment and the United Nations.' in John Vogler and Mark F. Imber (eds.), *The Environment and International Relations* (London and New York: Routledge), pp. 138–54

Lund, Emma. 2013. *Hybrid Governance in Practice: Public and Private Actors in the Kyoto Protocol's Clean Development Mechanism* (Lund University).

Meadows, Donella H., Dennis L. Meadows, Jørgen Randers, and William W. Behrens. 1972. *The Limits to Growth* (Club of Rome).

NAZCA: Global Climate Action Portal. Undated. *About*, <https://climateaction.unfccc.int/about> [Accessed 14 February 2022].

Radunsky, Klaus, and Timothy Cadman. 2017. 'Afterword: The Long Road to Paris: Insider and Outsider Perspectives.' in Timothy Cadman, Rowena Maguigre and Charles Sampford (eds.), *Governing the Climate Change Regime: Instituional Integrity and Integrity Systems* (Abingdon, UK: Routledge), pp. 250–65 Afterword.

Taghizadeh-Hesary, Farhad, and Naoyuki Yoshino. 2019. 'The Way to Induce Private Participation in Green Finance and Investment', *Finance Research Letters*, 31, 98–103.

United Nations. 1993. *Agenda 21: Programme of Action for Sustainable Development, Rio Declaration on Environment and Development, Statement of Forest Principles* (New York: United Nations Publications Department of Public Information).

——.·2015. *Trends in Private Sector Climate Finance*, (UN Secretary General Office), <https://reliefweb.int/sites/reliefweb.int/files/resources/SG-TRENDS-PRIVATE-SECTOR-CLIMATE-FINANCE-AW-HI-RES-WEB1.pdf> [Accessed 24 February 2022].

——.·2018. *Helping Governments and Stakeholders Make the SDGs a Reality*, (United Nations Division for SDGs), <https://www.sdg.gov.bd/page/goalDescription/4#1> [Accessed 24 February 2022].

United Nations Framework Convention on Climate Change. 2015. *Paris Agreement as Contained in the Report of the Conference of the Parties on Its Twenty-First Session*, <https://unfccc.int/sites/default/files/english_paris_agreement.pdf> [Accessed 5 February 2022].

Valenzuela, Francisco, and Steffen Böhm. 2017. 'Against Wasted Politics: A Critique of the Circular Economy', *Ephemera: Theory and Politics in Organization*, 17 (1), 23–60.

Vogler, John. 1996. 'Introduction. The Environment in International Relations: Legacies and Contentions.' in Mark Imber and John Vogler (eds.), *The Environment and International Relations* (London and New York: Routledge), pp. 11–33

Wang, Qiang, and Rui Huang. 2021. 'The Impact of Covid-19 Pandemic on Sustainable Development Goals–a Survey', *Environmental Research*, 202, 111637.

World Commission on Environment and Development.·1987. *Our Common Future: Report of the World Commission on Environment and Development*, World Commission on Environment and Development, <https://sustainabledevelopment.un.org/content/documents/5987our-common-future.pdf> [Accessed 10 February 2022].

Wynn, Martin, and Peter Jones. 2020. 'The Sustainable Development Goals, the ICT Industry and ICT4D Research.' in Tay Keong Tan, Milenko Gúdić and Patricia M. Flynn (eds.), *Struggles and Successes in the Pursuit of Sustainable Development* (London: Routledge), pp. 84–95

Yee, Wai-Hang, Carlos Wing-Hung Lo, and Shui-Yan Tang. 2013. 'Assessing Ecological Modernization in China: Stakeholder Demands and Corporate Environmental Management Practices in Guangdong Province', *The China Quarterly*, 213, 101–29.

Yunari, Sri Bakti 2020 *Corporate Social Responsibility Settings in Indonesia and India as a Comparison* (Proceedings on the International Conference of Science Management Art Research Technology)

Hanna Ahlström and Beate Sjåfjell

Chapter 2
Complexity and uncertainty in sustainable finance: An analysis of the EU taxonomy

Abstract: The financial sector has the potential to facilitate societal change, but there is still a need for the sector to significantly transform. What is currently missed in the academic debate is that the finance field is deeply rooted in its discipline, which creates blindfolds to crucial aspects for enabling sustainability. Many investment strategies require ample information about issues of relevance, but complete information of all sustainability aspects may never become available. In these instances, it will not be possible to use prediction models and standard mathematical methods. This sheds light on the problem with using ESG (environmental, social, governance) rating metrics in their current form. It also gives rise to questions about the usefulness of establishing a taxonomy for sustainable economic activities. The European Union's (EU's) Sustainable Finance Initiative and its affiliated Taxonomy Regulation are therefore used as a case in this chapter. The Taxonomy Regulation is symptomatic of the lack of debate about to what extent it is possible to (a) identify and (b) measure all important aspects relevant for corporate sustainability. The chapter integrates and proposes the further use of multiple policy principles, including propositions on how to translate complexity and uncertainty into methodological and legal concerns. Emerging policy tensions from the EU's post-COVID-19 recovery plan are also discussed, including implications for future research.

Keywords: eu sustainable finance initiative, EU taxonomy regulation, ESG, complexity, uncertainty, COVID-19

Acknowledgements: The authors thank the editors of this volume, in particular Timothy Cadman and the anonymous reviewers for valuable insights and guidance. Hanna Ahlström's contribution was funded in part by the Erling-Persson Family Foundation through the program Global Economic Dynamics and the Biosphere at the Royal Swedish Academy of Sciences. The chapter is based on previous work in the project Sustainable Market Actors for Responsible Trade (SMART), funded by the European Union's Horizon 2020 Research and Innovation Programme [Grant Agreement No. 693642] and both authors are grateful to the whole SMART team for the many insightful and thought-provoking discussions, which also has inspired our further work

https://doi.org/10.1515/9783110733488-002

Introduction

The role of finance in achieving global sustainability goals is increasingly recognised. This is reflected in a spectrum of interest ranging from mainstream policymakers' and investors' commitment to financing the attainment of the Sustainable Development Goals (Esposito, Gatti, and Mastromatteo 2019; United Nations 2018) to an increasing awareness of industry's effects on the Earth system and subsequent sustainability impacts (Galaz et al. 2018). Financial technical product innovations have contributed to creating systemic risk with implications including the global financial crisis of 2007–2008 (e.g., Tooze 2018). The financial crisis in turn played a part in instigating and triggering policy change towards sustainable finance (e.g., Ahlström 2019).

While the financial sector has an increasingly important role in the sustainability discourse, the discussion on this role has become ambivalent and even paradoxical (Ahlström and Monciardini 2021). On the one hand, the contribution of business to the current unsustainability of the global economic system has often been attributed to the excessive financialization of the economy (Durand 2017; Lapavitsas 2011). On the other hand, particularly in recent years, policymakers, civil society and business have increasingly turned to the financial sector as part of the solution rather than the problem, because of its potential positive knock-on effects on the entire economy. The financial sector has a potential to facilitate societal change but there is still a need for the sector itself to significantly transform. What has not received enough attention in the academic debate is that the finance field is deeply rooted in its discipline and suffers from epistemological, ontological and methodological biases (Lagoarde-Segot 2019). For instance, Fatemi and Fooladi (2013) call for a radical paradigm shift in the context of the urgent sustainability challenges. Similarly, Paranque and Pérez (2016) call for a reconsideration of and fundamental reformulation of finance. The disciplinary bias seems to create blind spots in aspects that are crucial for enabling sustainability, and which are in focus in other distinct fields, notably in sustainability research. For example, there are many sustainability impacts that are not possible to identify and measure today due to extreme levels of complexity and uncertainty. Optimal investment strategies, just like many policy strategies, benefit from complete information about all relevant systems, but such information may never be available. This situation creates challenges for using quantitative and probability-based methodologies for sustainable finance generally. It also sheds light on challenges with establishing a taxonomy for sustainable economic activities. This gives rise to the fundamental question of to what extent it is possible to make use of a taxonomy that is based on the prerequisite that all important aspects of sustainability are a) identifiable and b) measurable. This chapter accordingly uses the European Union (EU) taxonomy for sustainable activities (European Commission 2020a) as a case, as this is such a significant regulatory instrument for contemporary investment strategies for sustainability internationally.

The chapter also discusses the directly related issue of the very basis for measuring sustainability in finance, namely the use of Environment, Social and Governance (ESG) rating metrics, which is one of the key assumptions and rationales informing the 2018 report by the European Commission appointed High Level Expert Group (HLEG) on sustainable finance. In the report it is argued that incorporating ESG factors into investment decision-making would strengthen financial stability (European Commission 2018b: 5). Addressing financial stability is indeed key. However, addressing the question of identifiability and measurability of all important aspects of sustainability also means questioning to what extent ESG rating metrics as basis for sustainable investing is useful in its current form (see Crona, Folke, and Galaz 2021).

The chapter is structured as follows: the following section presents key regulatory challenges for sustainable finance, including the limited understanding of sustainability within the financial industry, with the main emphasis being on complexity and uncertainty as regulatory concerns.

Next, the case study of the EU sustainable finance regulation is analysed. This starts out by introducing the EU Sustainable Finance Initiative, including the initial *Commission Action Plan on Financing Sustainable Growth* (European Commission 2018a) and the new *Strategy for Financing the Transition to a Sustainable Economy* (European Commission 2021i).The analysis concentrates on the EU Taxonomy Regulation (European Commission 2020a), specifically the possibilities and limitations of such a taxonomy in contributing to more sustainable investments. In light of the ongoing pandemic, the possibility of financing sustainability in the aftermath of COVID-19 through the EU's COVID-19 recovery plan is also discussed.

Drawing on the preceding analysis, which identifies a set of regulatory challenges, the final section discusses how these may be overcome. This section introduces a set of policy principles that should be integrated into the field of finance, which have the potential to create more effective responses.

Regulatory challenges for sustainable finance

In spite of all references to sustainability by thought leaders in business and finance, the discourse in sustainable finance is still dominated by hegemonic traits, characterised by simplistic, compartmentalist and economics-centred reasoning, as opposed to a research-based and systemic informed approach that recognises complexity and uncertainty. Practice still very much represents sustainability talk rather than sufficient sustainability action.

To move from rhetoric to action with regard to sustainability in society, sustainability needs to become a guiding strategy for a desired future (Hugé et al. 2013). In this chapter, sustainability is conceptualised as securing social foundations (Raworth

2012, 2017) for people all over the world, now and for the future, while staying within planetary boundaries (Rockström, Steffen, Noone, Persson, Chapin, et al. 2009; Rockström, Steffen, Noone, Persson, Chapin III, et al. 2009; Steffen et al. 2015). The concept of corporate sustainability is employed as a term for when business contributes to society's overarching sustainability goals, with a suggested operationalised definition of 'creating sustainable value within planetary boundaries' (Sjåfjell et al. 2019: 12).

A distinction is sometimes drawn between weak or strong sustainability (Neumayer 2003; Roome 2012). Weak sustainability approaches builds on a business-as-usual action agenda with a strong belief in technological solutions (Ekins et al. 2003) and is focussed on trade-offs, reporting and transparency (Cullen and Mähönen 2019). Weak sustainability action agenda informs most traditional corporate related policy approaches (Sjåfjell and Taylor 2019). Strong sustainability approaches, on the contrary, integrate corporate action – including financial market activities – with their patterns of production and consumption to be limited to levels that are within the capacity of the planet (Roome 2012). Accordingly, only strong sustainability is actual sustainability and should be referred to as such (Sjåfjell and Bruner 2019).

A common denominator in these hegemonic ideas informing business and finance is the social norm of shareholder primacy. It is a systemically entrenched barrier for corporate sustainability. Here shareholder primacy is used as a short form for a complex mix of market signals and economic incentives and informed by path-dependent corporate governance assumptions (Sjåfjell et al. 2015). The shareholder primacy drive has given rise to legal myths inspired by postulates from law and economics theories, dictating that the Board and senior managers are the agents of the shareholders and have a duty to maximise returns to shareholders as measured by the current share price (Ireland 1999; Sjåfjell et al. 2015; Stout 2012, 2013).

The capital markets function to funnel and exacerbate the shareholder primacy drive, supported by securities regulation and stock exchange rules that have as their primary aim to protect investors, not the various other interests affected by corporate activity (Bruner 2011; Cullen and Mähönen 2019). The shareholder primacy drive is exacerbated by the chasm between corporate law's approach to corporate groups and the dominance and practice of such groups, and the extensive use of global value chains, and other non-equity modes of control, allowing for an intensified externalisation of environmental, social and economic costs (Sjåfjell et al. 2015; Sjåfjell et al. 2018).

The legislative response to corporate unsustainability has until recently mainly taken the shape of reporting requirements (Villiers and Mähönen 2015), leading at best to incremental improvements and weak sustainability, combined with the persistent belief that markets will self-correct through pressure from investors and corrections to share price where there is misconduct or failure to disclose material information.

With this somewhat gloomy backdrop for the analysis, this chapter builds on the notion that the financial sector has significant power and leverage, meaning potential to facilitate societal change, but there is still a need for the sector to significantly transform. There are other scholars who make use of more optimistic entry points where the financial industry is viewed as a driver for change that can enable more sustainable markets (Eccles and Klimenko 2019; Zadek 2019). The analysis in this chapter suggests that sustainable finance and its regulation is neither an oxymoron, nor the ultimate solution for sustainability (see Ahlström and Monciardini 2021). However, what is currently missing in the discussion is that even when focussing on finance as a positive force in society, biases of the finance field still persist (Lagoarde-Segot 2019).

Complexity and uncertainty as regulatory concerns

Key amongst the regulatory concerns is the inherent complexity and uncertainty that the sustainability challenge entails. Complex systems cannot be reduced to a composition of different parts without being significantly changed or transformed and their functioning is not possible to anticipate from the study of their parts (Morin 1990; Orsini et al. 2020). In the global financial context, banks, firms, investors and a range of financial intermediaries seek to engage in profitable deals based on available market information, with the potential for unexpected alterations that can result in market crashes as reinforcing feedback kick in (Sornette 2004). In the aftermath of the financial crisis, there has been an increased focus on sustainable finance as an antidote to the failures of the financial system (Ahlström and Monciardini 2021), which has enhanced the financialization of the global economy (Aalbers 2016; Krippner 2011). Moreover, business practice is today characterised by a deep complexity and opacity, through organisation, control and governance decoupling, financial engineering and increasing digitalisation (Anker-Sørensen 2019). A further complexity driver in financial markets is novel technologies (Galaz 2014), a tendency that is generally insufficiently recognised. The progression of algorithmic trade, which relies on high-speed computer linkages as well as uses of sophisticated statistical, econometric, machine learning, and other quantitative techniques where traders hold positions for very short periods of time (microseconds). This result in a financial system that is 'superconnected, hyperfunctional, and ultrafast' (Galaz and Pierre 2017: 12). The role of algorithmic trade in financial and commodity derivative markets is defined by atomistic behaviour, resulting in extremely high speed of transactions and a global reach (Galaz and Pierre 2017).

Across various disciplines, it is essential that predictive models have high-quality and are accurate. This is specifically addressed in the environmental sciences, considering the critical role of accurate models in scientific evidence for decision-making and policy (Li 2017). This has implications for sustainability. There is often a mismatch between accuracy and quality, which, in the case of environmental problems, can lead to an underestimation or ignorance of the occurrence of tipping points (Carpenter, Ludwig, and Brock 1999; Crépin 2007; Keys et al. 2019; Mäler, Xepapadeas, and De Zeeuw 2003). This means that even if the estimation of a geophysical hazard is largely correct, the level of adaptation may need to be aligned. Considering a scenario with a largely incorrect estimation, this requires unprecedented rates of adaptation. Moreover, if the understanding of a complex system is only superficial, decision-makers may tend to overestimate the carrying capacity and resilience of their system. If decisions are taken based on these simplified assumptions, financial market actors may contribute to pushing systems beyond critical thresholds, ultimately inducing abrupt undesirable environmental impacts (Galaz 2014). Optimal investment strategies, just as many policy strategies, require complete information about system behaviour. Ironically, this often entails that only when actors push a system beyond a threshold (e.g., through excessively polluting) does that information become available (Crépin 2007: 208). This problem can be translated to a situation characterised by deep uncertainty, a concept increasingly used in sustainability science and notably climate change research and referred to as the dismal theorem (Weitzman 2009: 10; 2011). This theorem explains situations that may result in indefinitely large expected losses from a high-consequence, low-probability event. Deep uncertainty cannot be modelled through standard mathematical methods (Aglietta and Espagne 2016), which means that other approaches need to be introduced into the discussion on the future role of finance for sustainability. Hence, this problem challenges the use of quantitative and probability-based methodologies for sustainable finance significantly (Kedward, Ryan-Collins, and Chenet 2020).

ESG analyses and metrics

In the contemporary stage of market developments, financial actors generally distinguish between (i) financial products that are specifically dedicated to projects with some kind of ESG signature and (ii) financial products that have been developed to support either issuers or borrowers with their development of products and their degree of ESG (Driessen 2021). A common way to describe the former (i), is when a bond or a loan has the purpose to finance a certain green or social project. These products are commonly referred to as green bonds/loans or social bonds/loans (Driessen 2021). In cases when the funding is related with issuer or borrower behaviour more generally, the products can be referred to as sustainability-linked or ESG-linked (ii). In the case of debt products, this often means that the interest payable by the issuer/borrower will be lower if certain ESG scores or behaviours are achieved (Driessen 2021).

Internationally, the development of ESG is mainly based on voluntary action, guided by different principles, guidelines and initiatives (Driessen 2021). However, in the EU there are provisions in existing legislative instruments that do promote or even mandate ESG considerations, for example, the EU Disclosure Regulation (European Commission 2020b).

As ESG-related products are being further developed, consistency in terminology and standards will (hopefully) increase (Driessen 2021). Yet, significant deficiencies have recently been revealed where ESG approaches have been standardised into ratings with high precision but with low accuracy. The problem has been described as 'refining ESG metrics without incorporating measures of impact will increase precision but fail to address accuracy' [. . .]. Therefore, it may well be better to be 'generally right than precisely wrong' (Crona, Folke, and Galaz 2021: 624). Moreover, the current state of ESG does not capture investments' impact on sustainability and is characterised by low agreement across ESG raters (Crona, Folke, and Galaz 2021). This knowledge trap needs to be made very clear to investors interested in ESG investments, but also to the regulators that are seeking to regulate those activities. When overstating or failing to accurately label investments, there is a risk for the investors themselves as well as for society. Firstly, a risk of increase of sustainability problems and secondly, gradual erosion of confidence and trust in the financial system (Crona, Folke, and Galaz 2021).

The ESG rating industry has its own distinguished problems such as its reliance on perspectives of weak sustainability (Muñoz-Torres et al. 2019). The industry has grown in response to rising demand for quality ESG data (Avetisyan and Hockerts 2017) and has had a clear influence on the behaviour of investors and companies (Slager, Gond, and Moon 2012). Credit rating agencies issue ratings focussed on ESG factors where each actor applies its own criteria (e.g., Moody's 2021; Standard and Poor's 2021). Since 2005, the ESG rating industry has witnessed a number of national and cross-border consolidations (Avetisyan and Hockerts 2017). This development was motivated firstly by concerns regarding economies of scale where ESG rating agencies aimed to become more stable, delivering more sophisticated products and services internationally (Avetisyan and Hockerts 2017). The second motive was market power where synergies with acquiring firms have been evident, including integration and collaboration, standardisation and reputational benefits. Avetisyan and Hockerts (2017) show that the dynamics of mergers and acquisitions by the big ESG rating firms have paradoxically produced a partial institutional retrogression. This means that despite ambitious aims and norms of the credit rating industry, it seems to have failed in terms of acting as change agent to the financial industry and has resulted in greater focus on traditional financial norms and values. This seems to have resulted in the ESG ratings losing some of their potential to produce real institutional changes (Avetisyan and Hockerts 2017).

Perhaps even more interesting, as well as concerning, is that the increased use of ESG metrics stands in stark contrast to the latest developments in sustainability research. The field of sustainability research has moved away from the three pillars of environmental, social and economic sustainability (Dawe and Ryan 2003; Dhahri and Omri 2018; Hansmann, Mieg, and Frischknecht 2012; Lachman 1997; United Nations 2005: 12) to emphasising systems thinking. This thinking is what informs the understanding of sustainability also employed in this chapter: securing social foundations (Raworth 2012, 2017) within staying within planetary boundaries (Rockström, Steffen, Noone, Persson, Chapin, et al. 2009; Rockström, Steffen, Noone, Persson, Chapin III, et al. 2009; Steffen et al. 2015).

Sustainable finance regulation in the EU

The EU introduced the topic of sustainable finance in two green papers in 2010 and 2011 (European Commission 2010, 2011). These papers discussed the regulatory failures that led to the financial crisis and concluded that there was a need for a reform of financial market regulation and address 'short-termism, poor risk management and a lack of responsibility of certain actors in the financial sector' (European Commission 2010: 2).

The Sustainable Finance Initiative was introduced as a strategic direction in 2016 with the establishment of the HLEG on sustainable finance (European Commission 2016b), which had the objective to provide recommendations for a comprehensive EU strategy on sustainable finance by the end of 2017, as part of the Capital Markets Union (European Commission 2015). The establishment of the HLEG was announced in the *Communication on Accelerating Implementation of the Capital Markets Union* (European Commission 2016a). On 8 March 2018, the EU launched its initiative on sustainable finance through adopting the *Action Plan on Financing Sustainable Growth* (European Commission 2018a). This policy field is now a strategic priority of the EU and is part of the European Green Deal; that is, one out of six priorities of the European Commission for 20192024, notably concerning the goal of Europe aiming to be the first climate–neutral continent by becoming a modern, resource-efficient economy (European Commission 2021e). The process has been exceptionally fast with legislative instruments adopted already in 2019 and 2020; Disclosure Regulation and Taxonomy Regulation, respectively (European Commission 2020a, 2020b).

To date, the regulation of financial markets and their relationship to business has drawn on two ideas: the hypothesis of the efficient market, and the corporate purpose being to maximise returns to shareholders. The latter is based on the ideas of shareholders as residual claimants in corporations and all other interests being satisfied before stakeholders receive anything (forgetting the original caveat of externalities) (Sjåfjell et al. 2015; Sjåfjell et al. 2018).

While in the initial Sustainable Finance Action Plan it is acknowledged that short-termism is a problem, the shareholder focus is not deemed one. Notably, the action plan does not discuss whether it is possible to continue with infinite economic growth or the implications of the shareholder primacy drive for achieving sustainability. Rather than the limits of the planet being the boundaries, the boundaries seem to be those of the business case, reflecting a narrow recognition of the financial risks of unsustainability (Sjåfjell, Häyhä, and Cornell 2020).

In the concretisation, the action points and the proposals initially focussed mainly on the environment and specifically on climate change (European Commission 2018a). This approach has now been somewhat expanded and a social taxonomy is under development (European Commission 2021a). However, the approach of first focussing on climate change and planning later to expand the policy approaches to other aspects of sustainability is contrary to sustainability research where an integrated approach and urgent action on all fronts is called for.

Many of the suggestions made by the HLEG that focussed on systemic changes such as short-termism, clarity concerning investor fiduciary duties and the need for financial markets to reflect the values of society was left behind (European Commission 2018b). It is clear that the Commission places its main emphasis on the need to develop markets and new financial products (Ahlström and Monciardini 2021).

New sustainable finance strategy

The EU's renewed strategy for sustainable finance, the *Strategy for Financing the Transition to a Sustainable Economy* was published on 6 July 2021 (European Commission 2021i). The strategy sets out additional initiatives to tackle climate change and other environmental challenges. The increased need for inclusion of and investment in small and medium-sized enterprises (SMEs) is targeted, all of which are part of the aim of the EU to transitioning towards a sustainable economy (European Commission 2021b). The strategy includes six sets of actions: (1) extending the existing sustainable finance toolbox to facilitate access to transition finance; (2) improving the inclusiveness of SMEs and consumers by giving them the right tools and incentives to access transition finance; (3) enhancing the resilience of the economic and financial system to sustainability risks; (4) increasing the contribution of the financial sector to sustainability; (5) ensuring the integrity of the EU financial system and monitor its orderly transition to sustainability; and (6) developing international sustainable finance initiatives and standards, and supporting EU partner countries (European Commission 2021b).

At the same time as the strategy was launched, the EU also adopted its proposal for a Green Bond Standard, which aims to create a high-quality voluntary standard for bonds financing sustainable investment (European Commission 2021b). A third measure that was also adopted was the Delegated Act that lays out information that should be disclosed by companies on their activities and to what extent they are sustainable, supplementing Article 8 of the Taxonomy Regulation.

It is clear that the renewed strategy for sustainable finance has come with broadening of scope and seems to tackle some of the many concerns that have been addressed by stakeholders in consultations and in other forums. For example, in comparison to previous critique, greater emphasis has been put on both financing SMEs (e.g., Hainz, Wackerbauer, and Stitteneder 2021: 32) and better acknowledging the European financial market's role and interdependence on the global financial system (e.g., Ahlström and Sjåfjell 2020). Thus, the Commission also emphasises how it intends to work with international partners, notably under the collaboration scheme of the International Platform on Sustainable Finance, with an aim of cooperating internationally to build a robust and sustainable financial system (European Commission 2021b).

EU sustainable finance initiative: EU taxonomy

Part of the EU Sustainable Finance Initiative, and perhaps the most well-known among its legislative instruments, is the establishment of a taxonomy for sustainable activities and its affiliated regulation. The Technical Expert Group on Sustainable Finance (TEG), was set up by the Commission with a mandate to help developing legislative proposals in which the taxonomy was one of the most important ones (see European Commission 2018c).

The EU taxonomy for sustainable activities is established through *Regulation (EU) 2020/852 of the European Parliament and of the Council of 18 June 2020 on the establishment of a framework to facilitate sustainable investment, and amending Regulation (EU) 2019/2088* [Taxonomy Regulation] (European Commission 2020a). The Taxonomy Regulation establishes the criteria for determining whether an economic activity is environmentally sustainable and the degrees of environmental sustainability of an investment, or a classification system for sustainable economic activities (European Commission 2021c).

This initiative is welcomed, as it represents a significant shift regarding the integration of sustainability in financial market and business law, which has for far too long been disregarded in important areas (e.g., Ahlström 2020; Sjåfjell 2021; Sjåfjell and Wiesbrock 2014). However, criticism has emerged from notably civil society organisations and academia (e.g., Ahlström and Monciardini 2021) creating doubt about what effect the EU Sustainable Finance Initiative and its taxonomy will have in practice. This includes the criticism that the Taxonomy Regulation does not cover all aspects of the sustainability challenge (Cullen, Mähönen, and Nilsen 2020). Moreover, the Taxonomy Regulation reflects the lack of debate about to what extent all the important aspects relevant for corporate sustainability can be (a) identified and (b) measured.

The Taxonomy Regulation establishes the basis for the EU taxonomy by setting out conditions that an economic activity has to meet in order to qualify as environmentally sustainable. Based on these conditions, taxonomies for each objective are formulated in the form of delegated acts under the regulation. The Commission has adopted the first Delegated Act on sustainable activities for climate change adaptation and mitigation objectives, with the plan to move further with additional environmental objectives (European Commission 2021a). Recently, the Commission published a complementary Delegated Act that sets out technical screening criteria for additional economic activities in the energy sectors including the natural gas and nuclear energy sectors, with much controversy (Bloss 2021). The additional objectives under the Taxonomy Regulation are the sustainable use and protection of water and marine resources; the transition to a circular economy; pollution prevention and control; and the protection and restoration of biodiversity and ecosystems. Taxonomies on these focus areas are currently being developed by the Commission (European Commission 2021c).

The choice of starting with a narrowed down focus on climate change creates risk for a general interpretation that climate change is the only important sustainability issue at hand relevant for the corporate sector. Different regulatory initiatives in the EU deal with other sustainability issues, which may be seen to reflect the siloed approach, still, of the EU (Sjåfjell and Taylor 2019). An example is the Commission's work on sustainable corporate governance that aims to help companies to better manage sustainability-related matters in their own operations and value chains as regards social and human rights, climate change and the environment (European Commission 2021j). This initiative has basis in the Action Plan on Financing Sustainable Growth (see Action 10: Fostering sustainable corporate governance and attenuating short-termism in capital markets European Commission 2018b) and has later also been emphasised in the *European Green Deal* (European Commission 2021e) and the *Communication on the COVID-19 Recovery Plan* (European Commission 2021h). Further, in 2021, the Commission presented its proposal for a new Corporate Sustainability Reporting Directive European Commission (2021g). Yet there does not seem to be any coordination on the issues dealt with or a research-based approach to sustainability as a common starting point. This siloed approach tends to further aggravate the fragmentation and lack of coherence in the EU's sustainability policies (see also Ahlström and Sjåfjell 2020). A comprehensive and coherent set of legislative reforms would be easier for market actors to engage with and implement, rather than to be subject to a continued piecemeal approach to legislating for sustainability (Cullen, Mähönen, and Nilsen 2020; Sjåfjell, Häyhä, and Cornell 2020).

The possibilities and limitations of the taxonomy

Considering the short time that has elapsed since the EU taxonomy of sustainable activities was adopted, there has only very recently emerged relevant literature on the topic. Amongst the especially relevant publications in this context, the analysis by Migliorelli (2021) is a starting point for the further discussion.

Migliorelli (2021) focusses on the role of finance to support the transition to sustainability and the recognition that this is possible. On that basis, sustainable finance would be better referred to as 'finance for sustainability' (Migliorelli 2021: 10). This would better reflect the complexity of the market and also steer theory and practice in a desired direction (Migliorelli 2021).

Migliorelli (2021) argues that a definition of sustainable finance should facilitate and refer to contemporary debates on the identification of relevant sustainability dimensions, sectors and activities. 'Labels and taxonomies should be created along this pattern with the aim to ensure clarity to market investors' (Migliorelli 2021: 15). The rationale is also that defining sustainable finance coherently is not a mere exercise of style. Rather, this choice is based on the understanding that if being able to define and identify sustainable activities that are easily comprehended by the industry, it will be a key enabler in developing the market (Migliorelli 2021).

The added value of defining sustainable finance differs depending on whether the perspective of the industry or policymaker is used. This difference spans the issue with defining of what this field or activity means, to the inclusion of the articulation of ESG metrics and a taxonomy. Migliorelli (2021: 11–15) lists several risks with defining sustainable finance through establishing labels and taxonomies and their possible policy and financial implications, including rebranding without additionality, greenwashing, disordered adjustment in cost of capital spreads, and differences between jurisdictions in labels and operational standards. There are clear values to refocussing and avoiding greenwashing as well as taking the issue of additionality seriously. The question of level of additionality is notably important from the perspective of the regulator. This concept refers to whether an intervention has an effect or not, compared to the status quo (e.g., Gillenwater 2012). Such analyses are thus necessary to establish whether the regulatory interventions have had the desired effect, including measuring the wider socioeconomic effects as well as for increasing accountability for sustainable finance policies. It is important to establish possibilities for knowledge production and diffusion of sustainable finance practices within the European region and beyond. It is not the benefits for those directly involved in the financial industry that should be measured (Ahlström and Monciardini 2021). This is even more important from an international perspective, which is the focus of this volume.

Importantly, the definition of sustainable finance that Migliorelli (2021) advocates for, does not aim at redefining finance. In this chapter, the significant calls for reshaping the whole financial industry are acknowledged, as it in its current form does not serve society. This means to draw on the notion of finance for sustainability, but at the same time recognising the complexity of financial markets and the extreme level of uncertainty that surrounds the prospects of achieving sustainability. Clearly, the field of finance is yet to fully acknowledge that sustainable finance should be part of transforming whole societies, including the global economy (Ahlström and Sjåfjell 2020). Until such a recognition informs legislative initiatives and regulatory follow-up, the potential of sustainable finance will remain limited.

The world has entered a new geological epoch, the Anthropocene, in which humans are the dominant driver of Earth system changes (Crutzen and Stoermer 2000). In this current era, complexity and uncertainty is increasing (Chester et al. 2021), which means that it makes more sense to focus on what is known, than what is not. This is the reason for this chapter's focus on what in many cases are denoted as brown or black economic activities or financial assets, as opposed to the environmentally friendly green. This terminology is however problematic (Cullen, Mähönen, and Nilsen 2020). Black or brown are unspecific as terms describing (un)sustainability impacts and they have understandably been reacted against by communities whose skin colour can be described with those references (Kraft 2020). The terms unsustainable or harmful are therefore used here when describing activities that are harmful to the environment and the humanity. This is furthermore in line with the 'do no significant harm' principle in the taxonomy to start with (European Commission 2020b).

The term green is also problematic, emphasising only the environment and ignoring social, economic and governance aspects of sustainability (Cullen, Mähönen, and Nilsen 2020). The reason for the unprecedented interest in the EU taxonomy is that a vast number of businesses now understand that if their activities are not classified as sustainable, this may indicate that their business model not belonging to the future (sustainable) economy. However, obviously, not all businesses are sustainable, and some will never be. To create results as fast as possible, to create clarity in markets and to allow for certain businesses to steer away from their middle range unsustainable activities (and thus eventually become sustainable), it makes more sense to first focus on harmful activities. The need to broaden the taxonomy is in line with what the TEG emphasises in its final report: 'By establishing "brown" criteria, the taxonomy would effectively create three performance levels within the taxonomy structure: substantial contribution (green), significant harm (brown, or perhaps red) and a middle category of neither substantial contribution nor significant harm' (European Commission 2020c: 51).

The do no significant harm principle is defined in Article 2(17) of the Disclosure Regulation (European Commission 2020b). A legal basis for considering a broad taxonomy (beyond current ambitions) regarding the principle can be found in Article 3(b) and 17 in the Taxonomy Regulation (European Commission 2020a) and in the requirements for the delegated screening criteria according to Articles 1012 and 1315. In this context, Cullen, Mähönen, and Rapp Nilsen (2020: 18) note that for every set sustainability objective, 'a uniform criteria for considering economic activities to be substantially contributing to that objective should be laid down.' This means that one component of the criteria needs to include considerations to avoid significant harm for all set objectives. This may mitigate the risks of investments being considered sustainable even though related economic activities do cause harm to people or the environment, while benefitting from the green branding. This interpretation is already facilitated in the Taxonomy Regulation since the criteria should take into account the life cycle of products and services provided by that economic activity (Articles 28, 40 and 44). This requires a research-based approach, and where possible based on life cycle assessments, and more broadly systems thinking, taking into account the whole life cycle of a product (Maitre-Ekern 2021).

The discussed risks outline some of the reasons why this chapter suggests shifting focus to the unsustainable, or harmful activities of corporations. It is high time that these considerations are brought to the forefront of the current debate on sustainable finance, in line with the recommendations of the TEG. The do no significant harm taxonomy would add more value considering the need for very swift shift in pollution rates, notably from extractive and highly harmful industries.

Financing sustainability in the aftermath of the COVID-19 pandemic

The COVID-19 pandemic demonstrates the interconnectedness, complexity and vulnerabilities of society to large-scale environmental shocks (Sjåfjell, Häyhä, and Cornell 2020). It is evident that societies depend on a resilient environmental support system (European Environment Agency 2020). While it has been long recognised in health and sustainability research that biodiversity loss and intensive food systems make zoonotic diseases more likely (European Environment Agency 2020; World Health Organization and Convention on Biological Diversity Secretariat 2020), it has now been brought to the forefront in many policy discussions (Van Langevelde et al. 2020). Environmental factors, such as air quality that are often related to social inequalities, also appear to influence societal responses and outcomes in the wake of the pandemic (European Environment Agency 2020).

Especially relevant for this chapter is that during the pandemic, the level of global interconnectivity and interdependence of the economic system revealed deep vulnerabilities of the global economic system. A focus on reshaping the unsustainable production and consumption systems is therefore vital. Thus, this has created a unique opportunity for the EU to transform its economy (Sjåfjell, Häyhä, and Cornell 2020).

The EU's post-COVID-19 recovery plan is called the Next Generation EU stimulus and its temporary key instrument, the Recovery and Resilience Facility allows the Commission to raise funds to help repair the immediate economic and social damage brought about by the pandemic. To benefit from the support of the facility, Member States have to submit their National Resilience and Recovery Plans to the Commission and each plan sets out the reforms and investments to be implemented by end of 2026 (European Commission 2021h). The EU stimulus comprise EUR 750 billion (USD 830 billion) developed into EUR 390 billion (USD 430 billion) in grants and EUR 360 billion (USD 400 billion) in loans for Member States (European Commission 2021h). The package will support the European Green Deal (European Commission

2021i) through different environmental measures. In shaping the guidelines for land use policies and for enhancing nature conservation efforts, the biodiversity and farm–to–fork strategies appear to have been particularly relevant (Vivid Economics 2021b). Relatable, and relevant for additional sustainability aspects are the EU's stimulus of nearly EUR 1 billion in grants for new energy infrastructure investments (European Commission 2021f) and the issuance of a EUR 17 billion (USD 18.75 billion) inaugural social bond under the EU SURE instrument to help protect jobs and keep people in work (European Commission 2021d).

It is critical that all Member States drive through the aims of the EU stimulus by using the grants and loans to achieve the dual purpose of economic recovery and environmental sustainability (Vivid Economics 2021b). Some countries in the EU did orient their stimulus so that their trajectory shifted. It is indeed positive that the Commission sets out to assess the national plans against sustainability targets. Unfortunately, these only target 37% of expenditure for climate investments (European Commission 2021h). The EU recovery packages have been criticised for being unambitious and missing opportunities for moving towards a sustainable future (Sjåfjell, Häyhä, and Cornell 2020). Generally, it has been suggested that the recovery plans have done more harm than good for nature (Vivid Economics 2021a). As is increasingly being argued, it is important to distinguish between climate and nature impacts and that policies can come with unintended negative impacts (e.g., Locatelli et al. 2015). Vivid Economics (2021a) found that 98% of climate-relevant spending would reduce emissions, however, they could show that more than half of nature-relevant spending was harmful to nature. There seems to also be an imbalance between the size of spending that contributes to different nature-related investments and climate change-related investments. The spending seems to significantly disadvantage nature. This means that the Commission's goals to holistically address the environmental ambitions of the recovery package seem to fail (Vivid Economics 2021b).

More economic rescue packages and incentives may be introduced in the future. It is vital that these support the transition to sustainability, which means that the need for recovery cannot justify relaxing requirements for sustainable banking and finance (Sjåfjell, Häyhä, and Cornell 2020). It is in this context the next section introduces a discussion on how to better address complexity and uncertainty that surrounds sustainable finance. This includes propositions on how these concepts may be translated into methodological and legal concerns relevant for sustainable finance. It is also an attempt to integrate established policy principles to create more effective responses to complexity and uncertainty.

Policy responses to complexity and uncertainty

The Sustainable Finance Initiative does not position itself within a framework grounded on sustainability research with its inherent complexity and uncertainty, nor does it encompass and engage with the complexity of the global financial system, which it aims to shift towards sustainability. This is symptomatic of the initiative's broader failure in not challenging the problematic aspects of mainstream approaches to business and finance. Although it is laudable that the Sustainable Finance Initiative attempts to bring sustainability into finance, it does not address the fundamental problems of the current system. Its proposals create forward momentum, but there is danger that these will be incremental steps rather than contributions to the necessary transition. It lacks the systemic, sustainability-based approach, which dares question the fundamental aspects of a given system and tries rather to tweak limited aspects of the existing system.

Sustainable finance needs to recognise the complexity of markets, with emerging phenomena such as hyperfunctionality, surprise and propagating shocks (Galaz and Pierre 2017), and place this in the context of the complexity and uncertainty of the sustainability challenge (Brondizio et al. 2016). An analysis on this basis would inform a more systemic approach and a fundamental reassessment of the current system.

Moreover, the Sustainable Finance Initiative is informed by and reflects a narrow and limited approach to financial risk. Although it is positive that an emerging recognition of the financial risks of unsustainability is starting to break down the silos between business and finance and sustainability goals, this has its clear limitations: The only relevant sustainability impacts are those for which action is justified through a business case. Combined with a lack of understanding of the extent of the financial risks of unsustainability and a lack of integration of sustainability research, this means that the approach to which issues are relevant and that the initiative aims to deal with will be quite random (Cullen and Mähönen 2019).

The Sustainable Finance Initiative seems to be attempting to reform a system that it does not fully grasp; to shift it towards a goal that is not properly articulated or understood; with measures that do not engage with the fundamental barriers towards sustainability in that system. The initiative ignores the inherent complexity and uncertainty of the sustainability challenge, and indeed of the financial system itself, opting instead for simple answers based on mechanistic and simplistic approaches to environmental protection.

Considering the increased need for addressing complexity and uncertainty in sustainable finance, there is a need for new legal thinking. Polasky et al. (2020: 1139) suggest four policy principles that can be applied in order to create more effective responses in order to peer through the mist of uncertainty, which prevents decisions to be made that are timely and appropriate. These principles are to a) follow the strongest and most direct path between policy decisions on outcomes, b) focus on finding sufficient evidence for policy purpose, c) prioritise no-regrets policies by avoiding options with controversial, uncertain, or immeasurable benefits and d) aim for getting the big picture roughly right rather than focussing on details (Polasky et al. 2020). They specifically denote their approach as 'identifying corridors of clarity,' as this means to help create an understanding of critical phenomena or causal pathways sufficiently well to justify taking policy action. This is a critical and important difference in comparison to much other evidence-based decision-making, which may not be possible to use due to increased complexity and uncertainty. This approach can be compared to the propositions made by Crona, Folke, and Galaz (2021: 624) where it is argued that it may be better to be 'generally right than precisely wrong.' This continuum of policy choices is specifically useful for the discussion on level of measurability regarding ESG metrics and the EU Taxonomy. It is notably policy principle (d) that aims for getting the big picture roughly right rather than focussing on details (Polasky et al. 2020) that speaks the same language in this case. This means to focus on unsustainable, or harmful activities of corporations and emphasising the do no significant harm principle. There are clear-cut cases, where one example is the scientifically well documented fact that greenhouse gas (GHG) emissions result in climate change, which can without doubt be put in the category of harmful economic activities. In light of the need for very swift shift in pollution rates, the Taxonomy needs to be as powerful as possible on everything that needs to be shifted away from, while allowing sufficient flexibility in terms of what needs to be shifted towards. Exercising the policy principle (d) by Polasky et al. (2020) in the context of sustainable finance thus means to shift focus from a green or sustainable taxonomy to one that signifies and create market signals on what is unsustainable and harmful.

Decision-making in the face of risk and considerable uncertainty requires integrating the precautionary principle at the fundamental level. This legal principle emphasises thorough review before taking actions. The reason is that benefits and consequences of potential interventions to the system need to be assessed and typically results in prevention or at least temporary non-action (De Sadeleer 2012; Garnett and Parsons 2017; Harremoës et al. 2001). While this principle is well–established in environmental policy, this approach is highly relevant for financial supervision and the management of nature-related risks as well (Kedward, Ryan-Collins, and Chenet 2020).

Another principle of EU law that can inform a policy response to complexity and uncertainty is that of policy coherence. In a complex and uncertain world with global interconnectedness and deep unsustainability of markets, policy coherence can form a basis for a smart mix of regulatory initiatives. While a taxonomy probably cannot successfully define a sustainable economy, other regulatory initiatives can help create a coherent framework for stimulating innovation for sustainability. The concept of policy coherence is here defined as 'the process where policymakers design a set of policies in a way that, if properly implemented, they can potentially achieve a larger goal' (Cejudo and Michel 2017: 755). This notion helps to emphasise the role of finance, not only in the EU but internationally. Thus, the interconnections between sustainable finance and other different aspects of the EU's external relations are key (Ahlström and Sjåfjell 2020). A good example here is the EU's initiative on sustainable corporate governance, which goes to the heart of the regulatory infrastructure for corporate decision–making (Sjåfjell 2021). The proposal for the directive is expected in the first quarter of 2022 (European Commission 2021j). If the proposal for a directive does as originally announced and engages properly with company law and corporate governance, it would be the hitherto missing link in the EU's aim at shifting business and finance towards sustainability. Integrating sustainability properly into company law and corporate governance is a prerequisite for realising the full potential of the Sustainable Finance Initiative (as reflected in Action 10 of the first Action Plan (European Commission 2018a)), as well as the corporate sustainability reporting requirements (see directive proposal by the European Commission (2021g)) and the work with the broader context of achieving a sustainable circular economy (Ahlström and Sjåfjell 2020; Sjåfjell, Häyhä, and Cornell 2020). It also connects with sustainability public procurement (Sjåfjell et al. 2019). Channelling public capital to promote sustainability is indeed crucial, as the private sector will not be able to fill the investment gaps alone, which is why the role of the EU's and the Member States' central banks also are fundamental (Cullen, Mähönen, and Nilsen 2020).

The new *Strategy for Financing the Transition to a Sustainable Economy* may seem to a greater extent to reflect the principle of policy coherence at least in some respects, with greater attention being paid to improving the link between European financial market policy and international economic policy. This is formulated in section IV on *Fostering Global Ambition* (European Commission 2021i: 18–19) and under Action 6 where the Commission set a high level of ambition in developing international sustainable finance initiatives and standards and to support EU partner countries (European Commission 2021i: 20).

As regards improvement of ESG metrics, the example of metrics of biodiversity emphasises a long overlooked and important factor for sustainable investments (Lambooy et al. 2018; Smith et al. 2020). A greater awareness amongst investors concerning the role of biodiversity is emerging, mainly targeting the palm oil industry (United Nations Principles for Responsible Investment 2021) and tobacco industry (e.g., Blitz and Swinkels 2021). New methodologies for analysing biodiversity impact have started to emerge related to the food sector also, where land use change, freshwater eco-toxicity, fertilisation (with impacts such as eutrophication) and emissions of GHGs are used (Natixis 2021). Valid and well-performing indicators for biodiversity are still in the future, however, there is hope for improvement especially considering the recent awakening in regard to biodiversity issues in the private sector generally. Finance sector-led initiatives have recently established the Natural Capital Finance Alliance, which has developed a number of tools to integrate nature-related financial risks in pricing (Natural Capital Finance Alliance and Price-waterhouseCoopers 2018). Individual financial institutions are also developing their own in-house pricing approaches, where the ASN Bank's Biodiversity Footprint for Financial Institutions is an example (Biodiversity Working Group of the Sustainable Finance Platform 2020). More recently a Task Force on Nature-related Financial Disclosures has been established (Global Canopy et al. 2020).

However, the question of measurability remains. Again, deep uncertainty cannot be modelled through standard mathematical methods (Aglietta and Espagne 2016) and it may not be possible to use quantitative and probability-based methodologies at all (Kedward, Ryan-Collins, and Chenet 2020). In the context of deep uncertainty, many sustainability impacts cannot and will never be able to be captured in ESG metrics. Therefore, this chapter proposes re-evaluating how to think about measuring sustainability impact in finance through ESG metrics generally and the EU taxonomy specifically. It is suggested to establish a continuum of measurability, spanning non-negotiable and thus not measurable considerations, such as human rights at the one end and other well-established quantifiable aspects such as climate change indicators and metrics in the other.

Conclusion

The EU taxonomy has been well received by the private sector, and notably the financial sector, since it is deemed to create clarity in markets, influencing the cost of capital and contributing to avoiding risks of greenwashing. From a regulatory perspective, the notion of additionality is key and yet to be evaluated. However, it is unlikely that it will contribute to push the financial sector onto a path towards supporting real sustainability, where approaches that recognise and embrace complexity and uncertainty are used. If these phenomena are to be addressed, fundamental assumptions on which laws and policies regulating business and finance are based on today need to be reassessed. Indeed, complexity and uncertainty will most likely only increase in the future, which is why these aspects should receive increased attention in financial regulation generally, and in regard to sustainability specifically. This is not something that can be fully addressed and measured through ESG metrics or in a taxonomy. Therefore, this chapter proposes to enhance focus on risks analyses, rather than focussing on measuring aspects of sustainability (e.g., certain ESG metrics) that may not be accurate, possible to assess or in the worst cases, even possible to identify. It is better to get the big picture roughly right, rather than focussing on details and risking being precisely wrong on them. Finally, sustainable finance can only realise its potential if it is complemented by other regulatory initiatives in the EU, notably the EUs initiative on corporate governance. A question, to which the answer can ultimately only be found in the future, is the feasibility of these and other proposals. This chapter has aimed to bring attention to the need to better address uncertainty and complexity as regulatory concerns for sustainable finance. As such, this is a contribution to a necessary debate and one in which all sustainability and finance-oriented scholars, policymakers and practitioners should engage.

References

Aalbers, Manuel B. 2016. 'Corporate Financialization.' in Douglas Richardson (ed.), *International Encyclopedia of Geography: People, the Earth, Environment and Technology* (New York: John Wiley and Sons), pp. 960–69.

Aglietta, Michel, and Étienne Espagne. 2016. 'Climate and Finance Systemic Risks, More Than an Analogy?: The Climate Fragility Hypothesis', *CEPII, Centre d'Etudes Prospectives Et d'Informations Internationales*, 10, 1–30.

Ahlström, Hanna. 2019. 'Policy Hotspots for Sustainability: Changes in the EU Regulation of Sustainable Business and Finance', *Sustainability*, 11 (2), 499.

——. 2020. *Achieving Sustainability in EU Business and Financial Market Law – A Systems Thinking Approach*, Doctoral Dissertation, University of Oslo.

Ahlström, Hanna, and David Monciardini. 2021. 'The Regulatory Dynamics of Sustainable Finance: Paradoxical Success and Limitations of EU Reforms', *Journal of Business Ethics*, 177 (1), 193–212.

Ahlström, Hanna, and Beate Sjåfjell. 2020. 'Reversing the Hierarchy of Business, Finance and Circular Economy: Enabling Policy Coherence for the Transition to Sustainability', *University of Oslo Faculty of Law Research Paper* (2020-06).

Anker-Sørensen, Linn. 2019. The Multifaceted Corporate Group. Testing EU's Response to Hidden Control Structures, Doctoral Dissertation, University of Oslo.

Avetisyan, Emma, and Kai Hockerts. 2017. 'The Consolidation of the ESG Rating Industry as an Enactment of Institutional Retrogression', *Business Strategy and the Environment*, 26 (3), 316–30.

Biodiversity Working Group of the Sustainable Finance Platform.·2020. *Biodiversity Opportunities and Risks for the Financial Sector*, (De Nederlandsche Bank), <https://www.dnb.nl/media/cy2p51gx/biodiversity-opportunities-risks-for-the-financial-sector.pdf> [Accessed 24 October 2021].

Blitz, David, and Laurens Swinkels. 2021. 'Who Owns Tobacco Stocks?', Journal of Asset Management, 1–15.

Bloss, Michael. 2021. *Kommissionschefin Zerstört Glaubwürdigkeit Der Grünen EU-Taxonomie Mit Atom & Gas*, <https://michaelbloss.eu/de/presse/themenhintergrund/kommissionschefin-zerstoert-glaubwuerdigkeit-der-gruenen-eu-taxonomie-mit-atom-gas> [Accessed 1 January 2022].

Brondizio, Eduardo S., Karen O'Brien, Xuemei Bai, Frank Biermann, Will Steffen, Frans Berkhout, Christophe Cudennec, Maria Carmen Lemos, Alexander Wolfe, and Jose Palma-Oliveira. 2016. 'Re-Conceptualizing the Anthropocene: A Call for Collaboration', *Global Environmental Change*, 39, 318–27.

Bruner, Christopher M. 2011. 'Corporate Governance Reform in a Time of Crisis", *Journal of Corporation Law*, 36, 309–41.

Carpenter, Stephen R., Donald Ludwig, and William A. Brock. 1999. 'Management of Eutrophication for Lakes Subject to Potentially Irreversible Change', *Ecological Applications*, 9 (3), 751–71.

Cejudo, Guillermo M., and Cynthia L. Michel. 2017. 'Addressing Fragmented Government Action: Coordination, Coherence, and Integration', *Policy Sciences*, 50 (4), 745–67.

Chester, Mikhail, B. Shane Underwood, Braden Allenby, Margaret Garcia, Constantine Samaras, Samuel Markolf, Kelly Sanders, Benjamin Preston, and Thaddeus R. Miller. 2021. 'Infrastructure Resilience to Navigate Increasingly Uncertain and Complex Conditions in the Anthropocene', *NPJ Urban Sustainability*, 1 (1), 1–6.

Crépin, Anne-Sophie. 2007. 'Using Fast and Slow Processes to Manage Resources with Thresholds', *Environmental and Resource Economics*, 36 (2), 191–213.

Crona, Beatrice, Carl Folke, and Victor Galaz. 2021. 'The Anthropocene Reality of Financial Risk', *One Earth*, 4 (5), 618–28.

Crutzen, Paul J., and Eugene F. Stoermer. 2000. 'The "Anthropocene"', *Global Change Newsletter* (41), 17–18.

Cullen, J., and J. Mähönen. 2019. 'Taming Unsustainable Finance: The Perils of Modern Risk Management.' in Beate Sjåfjell and C. M. Bruner (eds.), *Cambridge Handbook of Corporate Law, Corporate Governance and Sustainability* (Cambridge, UK: Cambridge University Press), pp. 100–13

Cullen, Jay, Jukka Mähönen, and Heidi Rapp Nilsen. 2020. 'Financing the Transition to Sustainability: Smart Reform Proposals', *University of Oslo Faculty of Law Research Paper/ Nordic and European Company Law Working Paper*, 2020-10/20-09.

Dawe, Neil K., and Kenneth L. Ryan. 2003. 'The Faulty Three-Legged-Stool Model of Sustainable Development', *Conservation Biology*, 17 (5), 1458–60.

De Sadeleer, Nicolas. 2012. *Implementing the Precautionary Principle: Approaches from the Nordic Countries, EU and USA* (London: Earthscan).

Dhahri, Sabrine, and Anis Omri. 2018. 'Entrepreneurship Contribution to the Three Pillars of Sustainable Development: What Does the Evidence Really Say?', *World Development*, 106, 64–77.

Driessen, M. 2021. 'Sustainable Finance: An Overview of ESG in the Financial Markets.' in Danny Busch, G. Ferrarini and S. Grünewald (eds.), *Sustainable Finance in Europe: Corporate Governance, Financial Stability and Financial Markets* (Cham, Switzerland: Palgrave Macmillan), pp. 329–50

Durand, Cédric. 2017. *Fictitious Capital: How Finance Is Appropriating Our Future* (London: Verso Books).

Eccles, Robert G., and Svetlana Klimenko. 2019. 'The Investor Revolution', *Harvard Business Review*, 97 (3), 106–16.

Ekins, Paul, Sandrine Simon, Lisa Deutsch, Carl Folke, and Rudolf De Groot. 2003. 'A Framework for the Practical Application of the Concepts of Critical Natural Capital and Strong Sustainability', *Ecological Economics*, 44 (2-3), 165–85.

Esposito, L., E.G. Gatti, and G. Mastromatteo. 2019. *Sustainable Finance, the Good, the Bad and the Ugly: A Critical Assessment of the EU Institutional Framework for the Green Transition* (Milan: Dipartimento di Politica Economica, Università Cattolica del Sacro Cuore).

European Commission. 2010. *Regulating Financial Services for Sustainable Growth*, (Brussels: EC), <https://eur-lex.europa.eu/legal-content/EN/TXT/?uri=celex%3A52010DC0301> [Accessed 20 October 2021].

———. 2011. *Green Paper – the EU Corporate Governance Framework*, (Brussels: EC), <https://eur-lex.europa.eu/legal-content/EN/ALL/?uri=CELEX%3A52011DC0164> [Accessed 20 October 2021].

———. 2015. *Action Plan on Building a Capital Markets Union*, (Brussels: EC), <https://eur-lex.europa.eu/legal-content/EN/TXT/?uri=CELEX%3A52015DC0468> [Accessed 20 October 2021].

——.·2016a. *Capital Markets Union – Accelerating Reform Com/2016/0601 Final*, (Brussels: EC), <https://eur-lex.europa.eu/legal-content/EN/TXT/?uri=CELEX%3A52016DC0601> [Accessed 20 October 2021].

——. 2016b. *European Commission Appoints Members of the High-Level Expert Group on Sustainable Finance*, <https://ec.europa.eu/commission/presscorner/detail/en/IP_16_4502> [Accessed 20 October 2021].

——.·2018a. *Commission Action Plan on Financing Sustainable Growth*, <https://ec.europa.eu/info/publications/sustainable-finance-renewed-strategy_en> [Accessed 26 May 2021].

——.·2018b. *Final Report of the High-Level Expert Group on Sustainable Finance*, <https://ec.europa.eu/info/files/180131-sustainable-finance-final-report_en> [Accessed 20 October 2021].

——. 2018c. *Technical Expert Group on Sustainable Finance (TEG)*, <https://ec.europa.eu/info/publications/sustainable-finance-technical-expert-group_en> [Accessed 24 October 2021].

——. 2020a. *Information About the Regulation (EU) 2020/852 (Taxonomy) on the Establishment of a Framework to Facilitate Sustainable Investment Including Date of Entry into Force*, < https://ec.europa.eu/info/law/sustainable-finance-taxonomy-regulation-eu-2020-852/law-details_en> [Accessed 20 October 2021].

——. 2020b. *Regulation (EU) 2019/2088 of the European Parliament and of the Council of 27 November 2019 on Sustainability-Related Disclosures in the Financial Services Sector*, (European Parliament) <https://eur-lex.europa.eu/legal-content/EN/TXT/?uri=CELEX:32020R0852> [Accessed 26 October 2021].

——.·2020c. *Taxonomy: Final Report of the Technical Expert Group on Sustainable Finance*, < https://ec.europa.eu/info/sites/default/files/business_economy_euro/banking_and_finance/documents/200309-sustainable-finance-teg-final-report-taxonomy_en.pdf> [Accessed 24 October 2021].

——.·2021a. *Call for Feedback on the Draft Reports by the Platform on Sustainable Finance on a Social Taxonomy and on an Extended Taxonomy to Support Economic Transition*, <https://ec.europa.eu/info/publications/210712-sustainable-finance-platform-draft-reports_en> [Accessed 24 January 2022].

——. 2021b. *Commission Puts Forward New Strategy to Make the EU's Financial System More Sustainable and Proposes New European Green Bond Standard*, <https://ec.europa.eu/commission/presscorner/detail/en/ip_21_3405> [Accessed 13 October 2021].

——. 2021c. *EU Taxonomy for Sustainable Activities – What the EU Is Doing to Create an EU-Wide Classification System for Sustainable Activities*, <https://ec.europa.eu/info/business-economy-euro/banking-and-finance/sustainable-finance/eu-taxonomy-sustainable-activities_en> [Accessed 26 May 2021].

——. 2021d. *European Commission Issues First Emission of EU SURE Social Bonds*, <https://ec.europa.eu/commission/presscorner/detail/en/IP_20_1954> [Accessed 18 October 2021].

——. 2021e. *A European Green Deal*, <https://ec.europa.eu/info/strategy/priorities-2019-2024/european-green-deal_en> [Accessed 21 September 2021].

——. 2021f. *Investing in New Energy Infrastructure: Green Light for EU Grants Worth Nearly €1 Billion*, <https://ec.europa.eu/commission/presscorner/detail/en/IP_20_1803> [Accessed 18 October 2021].

——.·2021g. *Proposal for a DIRECTIVE OF THE EUROPEAN PARLIAMENT AND OF THE COUNCIL Amending Directive 2013/34/EU, Directive 2004/109/EC, Directive 2006/43/EC and Regulation (EU) No 537/2014, as Regards Corporate Sustainability Reporting*, <https://eur-lex.europa.eu/legal-content/EN/TXT/?uri=CELEX:52021PC0189> [Accessed 18 October 2021].

——. 2021h. *Recovery and Resilience Facility*, <https://ec.europa.eu/info/business-economy-euro/recovery-coronavirus/recovery-and-resilience-facility_en> [Accessed 21 September 2021].

——. 2021i. *Strategy for Financing the Transition to a Sustainable Economy*, ‹https://ec.europa.
   eu/info/publications/210706-sustainable-finance-strategy_en› [Accessed 13 October 2021].
——. 2021j. *Sustainable Corporate Governance*, ‹https://ec.europa.eu/info/law/better-regulation/
   have-your-say/initiatives/12548-Sustainable-corporate-governance_en› [Accessed
   27 October 2021].
European Environment Agency.·2020. *EEA Briefing. Covid-19 and Europe's Environment: Impacts of
   a Global Pandemic*, ‹https://www.eea.europa.eu/publications/covid-19-and-europe-s/covid-
   19-and-europes-environment› [Accessed 18 October 2021].
Fatemi, Ali M., and Iraj J. Fooladi. 2013. 'Sustainable Finance: A New Paradigm', *Global Finance
   Journal*, 24 (2), 101–13.
Galaz, Victor. 2014. *Global Environmental Governance, Technology and Politics: The Anthropocene
   Gap* (Cheltenham, UK: Edward Elgar Publishing).
Galaz, Victor, Beatrice Crona, Alice Dauriach, Bert Scholtens, and Will Steffen. 2018. 'Finance and
   the Earth System–Exploring the Links between Financial Actors and Non-Linear Changes in the
   Climate System', *Global Environmental Change*, 53, 296–302.
Galaz, Victor, and Jon Pierre. 2017. 'Superconnected, Complex and Ultrafast: Governance of
   Hyperfunctionality in Financial Markets', *Complexity, Governance and Networks*, 3 (2), 12–28.
Garnett, Kenisha, and David J. Parsons. 2017. 'Multi-Case Review of the Application of the
   Precautionary Principle in European Union Law and Case Law', *Risk Analysis*, 37 (3), 502–16.
Gillenwater, M. 2012. 'What Is Additionality? Part 3: Implications for Stacking and Unbundling',
   GHG Management Institute, Discussion Paper (003), 1–14.
Global Canopy, United Nations Development Programme, United Nations Environment Programme
   Finance Initiative, and World Wildlife Fund. 2020. *Taskforce on Nature-Related Financial
   Disclosures*, ‹https://tnfd.global/› [Accessed 24 October 2021].
Hainz, Christa, Johann Wackerbauer, and Tanja Stitteneder. 2021. 'Economic Policy Goals of the
   Sustainable Finance Approach: Challenges for SMEs', *CESifo Forum* 3(22),30–33.
Hansmann, Ralph, Harald A. Mieg, and Peter Frischknecht. 2012. 'Principal Sustainability
   Components: Empirical Analysis of Synergies between the Three Pillars of Sustainability',
   International Journal of Sustainable Development and World Ecology, 19 (5), 451–59.
Harremoës, Poul, David Gee, Malcolm MacGarvin, Andy Stirling, Jane Keys, Brian Wynne, and
   S. Guedes Vaz. 2001. *Late Lessons from Early Warnings: The Precautionary Principle 1896-
   2000* (Copenhagen: European Environment Agency).
Hugé, Jean, Tom Waas, Farid Dahdouh-Guebas, Nico Koedam, and Thomas Block. 2013. 'A
   Discourse-Analytical Perspective on Sustainability Assessment: Interpreting Sustainable
   Development in Practice', *Sustainability Science*, 8 (2), 187–98.
Ireland, Paddy. 1999. 'Company Law and the Myth of Shareholder Ownership', *The Modern Law
   Review,* 62 (1), 32–57.
Kedward, Katie, Josh Ryan-Collins, and Hugues Chenet.·2020. *Managing Nature-Related Financial
   Risks: A Precautionary Policy Approach for Central Banks and Financial Supervisors*, UCL
   Institute for Innovation and Public Purpose Working Paper Series, ‹https://www.ucl.ac.uk/
   bartlett/public-purpose/publications/2020/aug/managing-nature-related-financial-risks›
   [Accessed 26 May 2021].
Keys, Patrick W., Victor Galaz, Michelle Dyer, Nathanial Matthews, Carl Folke, Magnus Nyström,
   and Sarah E. Cornell. 2019. 'Anthropocene Risk', *Nature Sustainability*, 2 (8), 667–73.
Kraft, Andrew 2020 'No More Inflammatory Jargon: Change Blacklist to Blocklist' *AdExchanger*
   ‹https://www.adexchanger.com/data-driven-thinking/no-more-inflammatory-jargon-change-
   blacklist-to-blocklist/› [Accessed 26 October 2021]
Krippner, Greta R. 2011. *Capitalizing on Crisis: The Political Origins of the Rise of Finance*
   (Cambridge, MA: Harvard University Press).

Lachman, Beth E. 1997. *Linking Sustainable Community Activities to Pollution Prevention: A Sourcebook* (Santa Monica, CA: Rand).

Lagoarde-Segot, Thomas. 2019. 'Sustainable Finance. A Critical Realist Perspective', *Research in International Business and Finance*, 47, 1–9.

Lambooy, Tineke E., K.E.H. Maas, S. van 't Foort, and R. van Tilburg. 2018. 'Biodiversity and Natural Capital: Investor Influence on Company Reporting and Performance', *Journal of Sustainable Finance and Investment*, 8 (2), 158–84.

Lapavitsas, Costas. 2011. 'Theorizing Financialization', *Work, Employment and Society*, 25 (4), 611–26.

Li, Jin. 2017. 'Assessing the Accuracy of Predictive Models for Numerical Data: Not R nor R^2, Why Not? Then What?', *PloS One*, 12 (8), e0183250.

Locatelli, Bruno, Charlotte Pavageau, Emilia Pramova, and Monica Di Gregorio. 2015. 'Integrating Climate Change Mitigation and Adaptation in Agriculture and Forestry: Opportunities and Trade-Offs', *Wiley Interdisciplinary Reviews: Climate Change*, 6 (6), 585–98.

Maitre-Ekern, Eléonore. 2021. 'Re-Thinking Producer Responsibility for a Sustainable Circular Economy from Extended Producer Responsibility to Pre-Market Producer Responsibility', *Journal of Cleaner Production*, 286, 1–25.

Mäler, Karl-Göran, Anastasios Xepapadeas, and Aart De Zeeuw. 2003. 'The Economics of Shallow Lakes', *Environmental and Resource Economics*, 26 (4), 603–24.

Migliorelli, Marco. 2021. 'What Do We Mean by Sustainable Finance? Assessing Existing Frameworks and Policy Risks', *Sustainability*, 13 (2), 975.

Moody's. 2021. *ESG*, <https://esg.moodys.io/insights-analysis#insights-MIS> [Accessed 19 October 2021].

Morin, E. 1990. *Introduction À La Complexité* (Paris: Le Seuil).

Muñoz-Torres, María Jesús, María Ángeles Fernández-Izquierdo, Juana M. Rivera-Lirio, and Elena Escrig-Olmedo. 2019. 'Can Environmental, Social, and Governance Rating Agencies Favor Business Models That Promote a More Sustainable Development?', *Corporate Social Responsibility and Environmental Management*, 26 (2), 439–52.

Natixis. 2021. *Biodiversity: The Missing Piece in the ESG Puzzle*, <https://www.im.natixis.com/en-institutional/insights/biodiversity-the-missing-piece-in-the-esg-puzzle> [Accessed 21 October 2021].

Natural Capital Finance Alliance, and PricewaterhouseCoopers. 2018. *Integrating Natural Capital in Risk Assessments: A Step-by-Step Guide for Banks*, (Geneva, Oxford and London: NCFA and PWC), <https://www.greengrowthknowledge.org/sites/default/files/downloads/resource/NCFA-Phase-2-Report.pdf> [Accessed 20/11/2021].

Neumayer, Eric. 2003. *Weak Versus Strong Sustainability: Exploring the Limits of Two Opposing Paradigms* (Cheltenham, UK: Edward Elgar Publishing).

Orsini, Amandine, Philippe Le Prestre, Peter M. Haas, Malte Brosig, Philipp Pattberg, Oscar Widerberg, Laura Gomez-Mera, Jean-Frédéric Morin, Neil E. Harrison, and Robert Geyer. 2020. 'Complex Systems and International Governance', *International Studies Review*, 22 (4), 1008–38.

Paranque, Bernard, and Roland Pérez. 2016. *Finance Reconsidered: New Perspectives for a Responsible and Sustainable Finance* (Bingley, UK: Emerald Group Publishing Limited).

Polasky, Stephen, Anne-Sophie Crépin, Reinette Biggs, Stephen R. Carpenter, Carl Folke, Garry Peterson, Marten Scheffer, Scott Barrett, Gretchen Daily, and Paul Ehrlich. 2020. 'Corridors of Clarity: Four Principles to Overcome Uncertainty Paralysis in the Anthropocene', *BioScience*, 70 (12), 1139–44.

Raworth, Kate. 2012. 'A Safe and Just Space for Humanity: Can We Live within the Doughnut', *Oxfam Policy and Practice: Climate Change and Resilience*, 8 (1), 1–26.

Raworth, Kate. 2017. 'A Doughnut for the Anthropocene: Humanity's Compass in the 21st Century', *The Lancet Planetary Health*, 1 (2), e48-e49.

Rockström, Johan, Will Steffen, Kevin Noone, Åsa Persson, F. Stuart Chapin, Eric F. Lambin, Timothy M. Lenton, Marten Scheffer, Carl Folke, and Hans Joachim Schellnhuber. 2009. 'A Safe Operating Space for Humanity', *Nature*, 461 (7263), 472–75.

Rockström, Johan, Will Steffen, Kevin Noone, Åsa Persson, F. Stuart Chapin III, Eric Lambin, Timothy M. Lenton, Marten Scheffer, Carl Folke, and Hans Joachim Schellnhuber. 2009. 'Planetary Boundaries: Exploring the Safe Operating Space for Humanity', *Ecology and Society*, 14 (2), 32.

Roome, Nigel. 2012. 'Looking Back, Thinking Forward: Distinguishing between Weak and Strong Sustainability.' in Pratina Bansal and A. J. Hoffman (eds.), *The Oxford Handbook of Business and the Natural Environment* (Oxford: Oxford University Press), pp. 620–29

Sjåfjell, Beate. 2021. 'Reforming EU Company Law to Secure the Future of European Business', *European Company and Financial Law Review*, 18 (2), 190–217.

Sjåfjell, Beate, Tiina Häyhä, and Sarah Cornell. 2020. 'A Research-Based Approach to the UN Sustainable Development Goals. A Prerequisite to Sustainable Business', *A Prerequisite to Sustainable Business (January 28, 2020). University of Oslo Faculty of Law Research Paper* (2020-02).

Sjåfjell, Beate, Andrew Johnston, Linn Anker-Sørensen, and David Millon. 2015. 'Shareholder Primacy: The Main Barrier to Sustainable Companies.' in Beate Sjåfjell and J. B. Richardson (eds.), *Company Law and Sustainability: Legal Barriers and Opportunities* (Cambridge, UK: Cambridge University Press), pp. 79–147

Sjåfjell, Beate, Jukka Mähönen, Andrew Johnston, and Jay Cullen. 2018. 'Obstacles to Sustainable Global Business: Towards EU Policy Coherence for Sustainable Development', *University of Oslo Faculty of Law Research Paper/Nordic and European Company Law Working Paper*, 2019-02/19-10.

Sjåfjell, Beate, Jukka Mähönen, Mark B. Taylor, Eléonore Maitre-Ekern, Maja van der Velden, Tonia Novitz, Clair Gammage, Jay Cullen, Marta Andhov, and Roberto Caranta. 2019. 'Supporting the Transition to Sustainability: Smart Reform Proposals', *University of Oslo Faculty of Law Research Paper/Nordic and European Company Law Working Paper*, 2019-63/20-05.

Sjåfjell, Beate, and Mark B. Taylor. 2019. 'Clash of Norms: Shareholder Primacy Vs. Sustainable Corporate Purpose', *International and Comparative Corporate Law Journal*, 13 (3), 40–66.

Sjåfjell, Beate, and Anja Wiesbrock. 2014. *The Greening of European Business under EU Law: Taking Article 11 TFEU Seriously* (Oxford: Routledge).

Sjåfjell, Beate., and C. M. Bruner. 2019. 'Corporations and Sustainability.' in B. Sjåfjell and C. M. Bruner (eds.), *Cambridge Handbook of Corporate Law, Corporate Governance and Sustainability* (Cambridge, UK: Cambridge University Press), pp. 3–12

Slager, Rieneke, Jean-Pascal Gond, and Jeremy Moon. 2012. 'Standardization as Institutional Work: The Regulatory Power of a Responsible Investment Standard', *Organization Studies*, 33 (5-6), 763–90.

Smith, Thomas, Lucy Beagley, Joseph Bull, E.J. Milner-Gulland, Matt Smith, Francis Vorhies, and Prue F.E. Addison. 2020. 'Biodiversity Means Business: Reframing Global Biodiversity Goals for the Private Sector', *Conservation Letters*, 13 (1), e12690.

Sornette, Didier. 2004. 'Why Stock Markets Crash: Critical Events in Complex Financial Systems', *Physics Today*, 57 (3), 78–79.

Standard and Poor's. 2021. *ESG in Credit Ratings*, <https://www.spglobal.com/ratings/en/prod ucts-benefits/products/esg-in-credit-ratings> [Accessed 19 October 2021].

Steffen, Will, Katherine Richardson, Johan Rockström, Sarah E. Cornell, Ingo Fetzer,
    Elena M. Bennett, Reinette Biggs, Stephen R. Carpenter, Wim De Vries, and Cynthia A. De Wit.
    2015. 'Planetary Boundaries: Guiding Human Development on a Changing Planet', *Science*,
    347 (6223).
Stout, Lynn A. 2012. *The Shareholder Value Myth: How Putting Shareholders First Harms Investors,*
    Corporations, and the Public (San Francisco: Berrett-Koehler Publishers).
——. 2013. 'The Toxic Side Effects of Shareholder Primacy', *University of Pennsylvania Law Review*,
    161 (7), 2003–23.
Tooze, Adam. 2018. *Crashed: How a Decade of Financial Crises Changed the World* (New York:
    Penguin Random House).
United Nations 2005 *2005 World Summit Outcome: Draft Resolution Referred to the High-Level*
    Plenary Meeting of the General Assembly by the General Assembly at Its 59th Session <
    https://digitallibrary.un.org/record/556532> [Accessed 13 October 2021].
——. 2018. *UN Secretary-General's Strategy for Financing the 2030 Agenda*, <https://www.un.org/
    sustainabledevelopment/sg-finance-%20strategy/> [Accessed 13 October 2021].
United Nations Principles for Responsible Investment. 2021. *Investor Working Group on*
    Sustainable Palm Oil, <https://www.unpri.org/collaborative-engagements/investor-working-
    group-on-sustainable-palm-oil/6271.article> [Accessed 24 October 2021].
Van Langevelde, Frank, Hugo René Rivera Mendoza, Kevin D. Matson, Helen J. Esser, Willem F.
    De Boer, and Stefan Schindler. 2020. *The Link between Biodiversity Loss and the Increasing*
    Spread of Zoonotic Diseases, (Brussels: European Parliament), <https://www.europarl.europa.
    eu/RegData/etudes/IDAN/2020/658217/IPOL_IDA(2020)658217_EN.pdf> [Accessed
    27 October 2021].
Villiers, Charlotte, and Jukka Mähönen. 2015. 'Accounting, Auditing and Reporting: Supporting or
    Obstructing the Sustainable Companies Objective?' in Beate Sjåfjell and Richardson J. B
    (eds.), *Company Law and Sustainability: Legal Barriers and Opportunities* (Cambridge, UK:
    Cambridge University Press), pp. 175–225
Vivid Economics. 2021a. *Fund Nature, Fund the Future*, https://www.vivideconomics.com/wp-
    content/uploads/2021/06/Fund-Nature-Fund-the-Future.pdf> [Accessed 18 October 2021].
——. 2021b. *Greenness of Stimulus Index. An Assessment of Covid-19 Stimulus by G20 Countries*
    and Other Major Economies in Relation to Climate Action and Biodiversity Goals,
    <https://www.vivideconomics.com/casestudy/greenness-for-stimulus-index/> [Accessed
    18 October 2021].
Weitzman, Martin L. 2009. 'On Modeling and Interpreting the Economics of Catastrophic Climate
    Change', The Review of Economics and Statistics, 91 (1), 1–19.
——. 2011. 'Fat-Tailed Uncertainty in the Economics of Catastrophic Climate Change', *Review of*
    Environmental Economics and Policy, 5 (2), 275–92.
World Health Organization, and Convention on Biological Diversity Secretariat. 2020. *Biodiversity*
    and Infectious Diseases: Questions and Answers, <https://www.cbd.int/health/infectiousdi
    seases> [Accessed 27 October 2021].
Zadek, Simon. 2019. 'Financing a Just Transition', *Organization and Environment*, 32 (1), 18–25.

Andrew Buckwell and Edward A. Morgan

Chapter 3
Ecosystem services and natural capital: Application to sustainable finance

Abstract: This chapter introduces the concepts of natural capital and ecosystem services, highlights their application in sustainable finance and discusses the challenges their use raises. The terms present a framework for thinking through environmental, social and economic problems associated with sustainable natural resource management and the distribution of benefits. Their quantification in monetary terms enables policymakers to assess the social costs and benefits of investments in environmental conservation, sustainable development and resource use at differing spatial and temporal scales. The approach by The Economics of Ecosystems and Biodiversity (TEEB) study, to reveal, demonstrate and capture ecosystem service values helps bring the concepts out of academia and into policymaking and, recently, into business so it can measure its impacts and dependencies on nature. The concepts have also been integral to developing consistent, comprehensive, standardised accounting frameworks to augment traditional measures of human wellbeing, such as gross domestic product (GDP), thus making the contributions of nature to the human economy more transparent. The concepts have their critics. Non-linearity and complexity in ecosystem service provision, as well as economic values, notably monetary value can confound valuation techniques. These obscure the reality that nature has intrinsic value, regardless of human systems of valuation.

Keywords: valuing nature, total economic value, accounting for nature, natural resource management, metrics for wellbeing, COVID-19

Introduction

The planet's living systems and the climatic stability of the Holocene, on which complex human society has depended and thrived, is now widely recognised to be under considerable pressure and is likely to have already exceeded crucial ecological and geochemical planetary boundaries, which represent the upper limits of a safe operating space for humanity (Rockström et al. 2009). The Great Acceleration of the post-World War II era saw global consumption expand and capital investments into intensification of activities that increase this pressure (Steffen et al. 2015). The demands on the planet's natural resources and its waste assimilation capacities – its natural capital and the services provided by its ecosystems – are unsustainable (Costanza and Daly 1992). Established measures of human socioeconomic

https://doi.org/10.1515/9783110733488-003

development have erroneously interpreted extraction and depletion of natural capital as income because its negative impacts on ecosystems are not easily integrated into the dominant paradigm of private property rights, the role markets play in the allocation of resources or traditional measures of wellbeing.

Social and economic pathways and their impacts and dependencies on natural capital are guided by the global, national and local financial systems and their evolving design – its regulation, standards and institutions. Without information on how and the extent to which economies and societies are interdependent on natural capital, financial capital will not flow towards investments that support sustainable development and ecological regeneration. An understanding of the twin concepts of natural capital and ecosystem services (ES) can inform the application of sustainable finance through: (i) informing where investments can produce positive spillovers, such as environmental and social benefits, for which compensation may be secured by the providers; (ii) informing policy on internalising externalities, such as pollution and environmental risks like climate change; (ii) generating more holistic measures of social and economic progress; (iii) project evaluation; and (iv) informing private capital on its impacts and dependencies on nature. To do this, it is necessary first to understand how the concepts of natural capital and ES are understood in the literature in terms that are readily comparable to conventional goods and services produced by the economy, that is, using economic valuation.

Developments in valuation methods to quantify natural capital and ES, particularly in monetary terms, and innovation in the design of policy instruments is allowing policymakers, investors and, to an extent, consumers to consider these values in their decision-making. Economic valuation techniques have rapidly evolved to meet the challenge of measuring the full gamut of natural capital and ES. This, in turn, has begun to provide signals to private and public funding and finance towards environmentally and socially sustainable investments. This chapter provides an overview of the current state of knowledge on natural capital and ES, highlights their application in sustainable finance and discusses the challenges and concerns these concepts raise.

Natural capital and ecosystem services: Conceptual evolution

Natural capital

Natural capital is the stock of nature, material and the sum of the complex relationships between them, which contribute to society as inputs into the production of goods and services. It is the foundational determinant of human wellbeing (Millenium Ecosystem Assessment 2003). Natural capital can be considered non-renewable (fossil fuels, minerals, biodiversity), or renewable (primary production, ongoing physical processes) in relation to the nature of its exploitation. For example, minerals, fossil fuels and genetic diversity, once exploited, will not regenerate, at least on a temporal scale relevant to human decision-making. Other forms of natural capital, such as forests or soil, can regenerate so long as the rate of its exploitation does not exceed its rate of regeneration.

Early economic theorists did not explicitly consider nature in their theories of production of goods and services. (Hereon goods and services are referred to as simply services – economics need not distinguish between the two.) Instead, it was loosely wrapped up in the concept of land, see Ricardo (1817), which was considered immutable – it could not be degraded, renewed nor exhausted. The stocks of wood and coal driving the industrial revolution were simply free inputs as physical scarcity was not considered. JS Mill (1884) argued for the consideration of the environment, and its provision of services and contribution to human quality of life, and he importantly drew a connection between unlimited industrial growth with damage to nature. Later, Hotelling began to better model resource scarcity over time and devised models of the interaction of physical resource depletion and maximisation of economic efficiency (Gaudet 2007). The first use of the term natural capital is popularly ascribed to Schumacher from his 1973 book *Small is Beautiful*. Schumacher critiqued non–renewable resources being construed as income; instead arguing it should be treated as a form of capital, as should nature's assimilating capacity. Natural capital was further expanded in two seminal papers: the first by Pearce, *Economics, equity and Sustainable development* (1988) which posited that '[s]ustainability requires at least a constant stock of natural capital, construed as the set of all environmental assets' (1988: 599); the second, by Costanza and Daly, *Natural Capital and Sustainable Development* (1992), which explored the degree of substitutability of manufactured capital for natural capital, quantification of ES and natural capital, and the role of discount rates in valuing natural capital.

Since, mentions of natural capital in the literature has increased significantly and it is now firmly embedded in environmental economics literature and in policy circles. Natural capital is considered as one of many capitals, which when combined with other forms of capital, generates the services that provide benefit to people. Classifications consider natural capital as the foundational capital, upon which the other capitals are contingent. This popular framing aligns with the concept of strong sustainability and implies that investment in natural capital is a necessary component in the production of services for human wellbeing.

Figure 3.1 depicts the six capitals model. This conceptualisation presents natural capital as being the container for all capitals and that manufactured capital and financial capital are, in turn, dependent on the socially-centred capitals (Gleeson-White 2015).

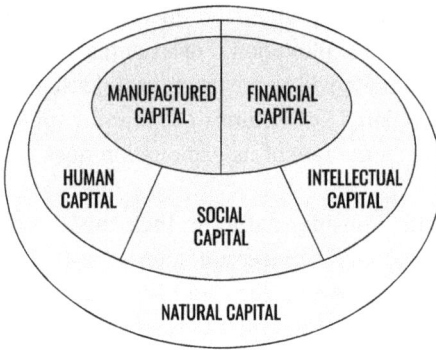

Figure 3.1: The six capitals model.

Substitutability: Strong vs. weak sustainability

There is an enduring canonical contest between concepts of weak and strong sustainability, which hinges on the substitutability of natural capital – that is, the extent to which other forms of capital can be substituted in upon natural capital's loss. Weak sustainability contends that natural capital is substitutable for both human-centred capitals (notably, human and manufactured capital) and many abiotic forms of natural capital (e.g., minerals and fossil fuels), which have historically been automatically substituted out in short run fluctuations in competitive markets. Thus, natural capital can be depleted and traded off to a socially optimal level to maximise the flow of benefits from all forms of capital, which changes over time, so long as future generations are left no worse off across all potential flow of benefits from all forms of capital (Pearce and Atkinson 1993). From a sustainability financing perspective, the investment of Norway's royalties from its exploitation of its oil and gas reserves into its transition economy is an example of weak sustainability in action, which fulfils the principle of investing all rents from exhaustible resources in reproducible capital goods (Hartwick 1977). Conversely, the strong sustainability perspective challenges this assumption and maintains that natural capital is not fully substitutable. Certain ecological functions cannot feasibly be replicated, at all, technologically or at necessary scale. Natural capital is fundamentally different as it is: (a) subject to irreversible loss (e.g., species extinction); (b) subject to the threshold phenomenon and sudden, positive feedback loops; and (c) cannot be scaled-up beyond natural sustainable yields, in the same way factory output can be scaled, such as the protection from UV radiation provided by the ozone layer. Such natural capital can be described as critical natural capital (Neumayer 2003). Determining the criticality of natural capital is a function of both ecological criteria, such as scale, yield, condition etc. (the realm of natural sciences), but also of societal values, ethics and risk (the realm of social sciences) (Pelenc and Ballet 2015).

Ecosystem services

If natural capital represents the stocks of nature, ES are flows of services that provide benefits into human society, directly, or indirectly, from the functions and processes of natural capital stock, usually only biotic services, but different conceptualisations include abiotic services (Haines-Young and Potschin-Young 2018). This anthropocentric perspective signifies that ES are defined by the people and communities in which they are utilised. Though ecological processes will continue whether or not humans utilise their services, ES arise only when humans benefit. The transformation of ES into benefits (wellbeing) may require effort, such as time, work, resources and money. Other ES are readily available to people without effort, but require humans to experience them (Sarkki 2017). Therefore, ES are considered to coproduced 'using societal institutions and nature's components and processes' (Spangenberg, Görg, and Settele 2015: 202) – in other words they are a product of a combination of different capitals (see above). The Millennium Ecosystem Assessment's (MEA) *Ecosystems and Human Well-being* (2003) was the seminal attempt to define a conceptual framework for ES (see Table 3.1). Its proposal classified ES along functional lines, using the categories: provisioning, regulating, cultural, and supporting services, on which the three former are dependent (see Figure 3.2). The rhetorical significance of this should not be underestimated, as this framing has become the default for university teaching and journal publications and influences how people conceive of ES, which services are accounted for and, importantly, which are economically valued.

PROVISIONING SERVICES	REGULATING SERVICES	CULTURAL SERVICES
Products obtained from ecosystems	*Benefits obtained from regulation of ecosystem processes*	*Non-material benefits obtained from ecosystems*
• Food • Fresh water • Fuelwood • Fiber • Biochemicals • Genetic resources • Mineral resources (only in CICES framework)	• Climate regulating • Disease regulation • Water flow regulation • Water purification • Erosion control • Pollination	• Spiritual and religious • Recreation and eco-tourism • Aesthetic • Inspirational • Educational • Sense of place • Cultural heritage

SUPPORTING SERVICES
Services necessary for the production of all other ecosystem services
• Nutrient cycling   • Soil formation   • Primary production

Figure 3.2: The Millennium Ecosystem Assessment's conception of categories of ecosystem services.
Source: Millenium Ecosystem Assessment (2003).

Reinforcing operationalisation of ES was The Economics of Ecosystems and Biodiversity (TEEB) initiative (2010), was originally inspired by the Stern review into the economic case for taking early action to combat climate change. TEEB used MEA's functional classification of ES and set out to (i) recognise the benefits provided by nature; (ii) demonstrate the extent of that contribution through biophysical and economic evaluation and (iii) shed light on how that value of nature may be captured through design of new institutions of property rights and governance structures.

Over time, the growing institutional and academic operationalisation of ES and natural capital has demanded tighter codification. If policymakers were to start considering biodiversity and ecosystems, particularly in terms of their economic value for comparing to investments in capital that degrade biodiversity, then greater precision would be needed to satisfy the policymakers undertaking project assessment, applying diligence to investment decisions, and accountants formulating national accounts. Boyd & Banzhaf (2007) argued that to fully compare ES with conventional services a standardised method is required for it to be taken seriously (2007: 617). In particular, they noted the problem of double-counting intermediate, or indirect, ES. Since the MEA supporting and most regulating services had been considered not to be delivering final ES and economically valuing both would be erroneous.

Standardisation was furthered refined through the UN's System of Environmental Economic Accounting (SEEA) process (United Nations et al. 2014). The SEEA is an internationally agreed framework for organising and presenting statistics on the flow of natural capital assets (water, timber etc) into the economy. It enabled national statistics offices to report in ways compatible with the long-established System of National Accounts, which reports on GDP and national asset balance sheets. In 2021, the UN Statistical Office adopted an extension of the SEEA with the Ecosystem Accounting (SEEA–EA) framework, which takes a landscape view of ecosystem and natural capital accounting. To support the standardisation work, the Common International Classification of Ecosystem Services (CICES) was developed by the European Environment Agency to codify the emerging consensus from MEA, TEEB and the US Environmental Protection Agency's Final Ecosystem Goods and Services Classification System (2013). CICES also classifies along the same functional lines, leaving aside underlying supporting services. Later versions of CICES have included both biotic and abiotic services to enable it to fully align with sectoral natural capital accounting.

The nature of goods and services

Before describing the varying economic valuation methods for ES, it is germane for conceptual understanding to quickly digress into the nature of the services in an economy. Table 3.1 shows a classification scheme of services defined along two axes: excludability and rivalry.

Table 3.1: Classification of goods and services.

		Defined, to a great extent, by institutions (e.g., private property rights regimes), but also, to an extent, the attributes of the good or service		
		Difficult to exclude beneficiaries	Some potential to exclude beneficiaries	Easy to exclude beneficiaries
Defined by the innate properties of the good or service	**Non-rival**	**Pure public goods (resources and sinks)** – Aesthetic beauty – Public forests, wildlife refuges – Genetic diversity		**Inefficient market good** (Costs to exclude, but no cost and no benefit in excluding)
	Congestible	**Public goods (resources and sinks)** – Waste and toxic emissions – Non-timber forest products		**Toll good** – Public services – Private beach – Ecotourism
	Rival	**Open access resources** – Open ocean fishery – Climate stability	**Common pool resource** – Customary fishery – Mineral resources	**Private good** – Private parks – Timber extraction

Source: adapted from Randall (1983).

Excludability is based on how easily beneficiaries can be prevented from benefitting. It is not an inherent property but is institutionally defined, that is, with boundaries enforceable by property law, agreed community understandings or technology, thus it is subject to change and evolution. ES are considered non-excludable where it is either impossible to exclude beneficiaries or it is not cost-effective to create property rights regimes to do so. For example, until technologies existed to monitor and attribute non-point source (or diffuse) pollution back source, regulating businesses from using the environment as a sink for industrial waste was not feasible. While the excludability of a good is largely defined by institutions, the attributes of the resource also influence the institutions. For example, enforcing customary rights of a common pool resource fishery is only really feasible on a small-scale basis and could not extend into the open ocean. ES tend to be public goods or common pool resources (see Table 3.1) where the lack of capacity to exclude beneficiaries leads to externalities, such as overexploitation by free-riders, or the tragedy of the commons (Hardin 1968).

Rivalry is an innate property (they are commonly tangible goods of direct use), regardless of the institutional setting. A purely non-rival service is one that is not diminished no matter how many beneficiaries use that service. If carbon emissions are regulated and a stable atmosphere is secured, it is the attributes of a stable climate that make it a non-rival good. A purely rival ecosystem service is one where one person's utility is diminished by the same unit as another's benefit, such as a fishery. However, rival services are congestible. For example, non-timber forest product extraction sustainably sourced can become a rival good if poor community governance results in it being harvested beyond the forest's regenerative capacity.

Valuation of ecosystem services and natural capital

To set the conditions for capital to flow towards investments in sustainable capital, the right signals to investors need to be presented. The signals will depend on how natural capital and ES are valued. Effective valuation can be useful for informing policy and behaviour by: (i) informing where investments can produce positive spillovers, such as environmental and social benefits, for which compensation may be secured by the providers; (ii) informing policy on internalising externalities, for example, through taxes, such as pollution and environmental risks like climate change; (iii) generating more holistic measures of social and economic progress; (iii) project evaluation; and (iv) informing private capital on its impacts and dependencies on nature.

Valuation of ES and natural capital is an assessment of people's preferences over how, when, and to what extent they obtain benefits from the environment, or conversely, the value of how much worse off they are as a result of environmental degradation (Costanza et al. 2017). Economic valuation is a way of demonstrating these preferences in monetary terms. Through economic valuation, the utilitarian value of nature is ascertained, which incorporates both ethical and social dimensions, that is, the total economic value of the full gamut of both use and non-use values (Daily 1997). Thus, economic valuation is anthropocentric, based on or derived from, the preferences held by individuals and not by any objective, ecological measure.

Economic valuation of ES allows for ready comparison with services commonly exchanged in markets, or economic valuation of natural capital can enable comparison with other forms of capital stocks. Expressing value in monetary terms, therefore, has proven useful in helping to consistently frame trade-offs between options that have to address multiple assessment criteria. Within this context, economic valuation has three broad purposes (Laurans et al. 2013). It can be:
- Informative, such as raising awareness of the value of biodiversity (Kumar 2010) and providing data for ecosystem accounting for integration into green GDP (Andrade and Garcia 2015; Secretariat of the Convention on Biological Diversity 2010) and for full cost corporate accounting (Capitals Coalition 2016; Epstein et al. 2011);

- Technical, such as setting compensation rates for loss of environmental amenity, or pollution (Aultman et al. 1993); and
- Decisive, such as informing policymaking in land use, using benefit cost analysis (Barbier 2007; Gashaw et al. 2018).

Economic valuations can be used to reveal a range of formulations of prices and values. A common, and useful, measure is that of reporting the value of the annual flow of an ecosystem service, for example, on a per hectare per year basis (and potential per capita), or a flow of all ES from a landscape to provide a total ecosystem service value (TESV) (Gashaw et al. 2018; Buckwell et al. 2020). Annual valuations can also be used to determine an ecosystem's net present value (NPV), or asset value. The NPV of an asset is the value of the flow of its benefits into the future, discounted back to today's prices.

As alluded to above, estimating TESV requires making judgements as to what constitutes intermediate and final ES to avoid double-counting (Boyd and Banzhaf 2007). In general, regulating services are intermediate to the final benefits enjoyed and therefore should not be totalised in a TESV (though nevertheless present useful information for decision-making). The exceptions to this are (i) air quality regulation (an end in itself), (ii) climate regulation, which, although this provides a measure of an intermediate service (a stable climate) that contributes to local food production, for example, it also provides a final service to global society either as a public good, or a private good, if emissions reductions are converted into a carbon permit; and (iii) the moderation of disturbance functions of coral reefs and mangroves, providing coastal protection (an end in itself) (Buckwell et al. 2020).

Importantly, ES are not provided in the abstract but within a real spatial and temporal distribution specific to the context and the location of the natural capital generating that service and to identifying beneficiaries. Thus, a forested catchment provides certain ES, such as water filtration or water flow regulation only to beneficiaries downstream. Other ES, climate regulation, for example, deliver benefits omni-directionally, at a global scale (Kemkes, Farley, and Koliba 2010). This spatial specificity can create mismatches between the managers of an ecosystem – the agent who must bear the costs, or opportunity costs, of protecting that ecosystem – and the beneficiary of an ecosystem service. In economic terms, this is known as a principal-agent problem. For example, a forest dwelling community may suffer costs (perhaps in terms of opportunity costs, see below) from not cutting the forest and benefitting from a timber harvest, while the beneficiary of the water regulation and erosion control ES downstream (e.g., a coastal hotel) reaps the benefits. The temporal scale is also important, particularly in how this relates to the concept of discounting future benefits. Keeping with the forest example, when land managers apply high discount rates to decision-making, perhaps to earn a business rate of return to be captured privately, the present value (PV) of future ecosystem service benefits is annually discounted and, as a result, there is an incentive for the managers to extract timber in the near-term by liquidating natural capital. Alternatively, where the decision maker applies a low, or even zero, discount rate, the PV of benefits from ES remains constant. Two famous counterexamples here are: (1) The virtually zero-discount rate applied to future damage caused by climate change in the Garnaut Climate–Change–Review (Garnaut 2008) – as a result, in benefit cost analysis, the case for acting now to reduce emissions was strong. (2) In contrast, Lomborg (2010) applied a higher discount rate to future damage and was able to conclude that mitigation actions to reduce carbon emissions ranked the lowest on a list of international development initiatives.

Finally, while it is evident people have an observable preference for the sustainability of services from natural capital, this does not mean that all values are economic. Many people would profess to believing some things hold intrinsic value – the value that resides in something, regardless of whether or not they have expressed a preference for utilising it. This is particularly so when considering the natural world. However, '[c]osting nature does not tell us that it is devoid of intrinsic value. It actually presupposes that nature has both intrinsic and instrumental value. Instrumental value derives from its contribution to intrinsic value' (Daly 2020: 101051). As will be explored, environmental economists have developed methodologies to compare these often seemingly incommensurable environmental values into a common metric.

Universalistic valuation: Total economic value

The environment, like many traded services, can be differentiated based on features of its characteristics. For example, typically, the benefits of many provisioning services (e.g., timber) can be readily calculated using market values, as the benefits have attendant cash flows: sale of timber. In contrast, conservation benefits are often more associated with non-market benefits, with no cash flows. As cash flows are captured as private goods and governments are incentivised by the potential for taxation and royalty capture of such activities, decisions are biased towards these uses: there is a misplaced concreteness to these cash flow values (Georgiou et al. 1997: 7). Therefore, conservation benefits need to be internalised into decision-making to ensure non-market values are made visible to policymakers and sustainable investors. Conservation benefits are thus measured by their total economic value (TEV) (see Figure 3.3), which includes both use and non-use values.

Direct use values are conceptually straightforward and relatively easy to estimate. For example, the value of timber can be ascertained through analysis of market prices of timber and subtracting the costs of labour and other capitals to ascertain the residual value provided by ES. Tourism (a cultural ES) is also directly utilised and the value provided by nature can be calculated through related market-based methods. Indirect use values are also utilised personally, however are more

TOTAL ECONOMIC VALUE

USE VALUES

Direct use values

Output consumed directly

- Water sales
- Contribution to food & fibre production
- Recreation & tourism

Indirect use values

Functional benefits

- Carbon sequestration
- Water purification
- Flood mitigation
- Pollination
- Erosion control

Option values

Future direct and indirect use values

- Biodiversity & forest conservation
- Stable climate protection

NON-USE VALUES

Bequest values

Preservation of habitat and natural resources for future generations

- Habitats
- Cultural reproduction
- Resistance to irreversible changes

Vicarious values

Value obtained from others having use value (in the present)

- Distant habitats
- Another's benefits

Existence values

Value resides in something regardless of instrumental value

- Altruism

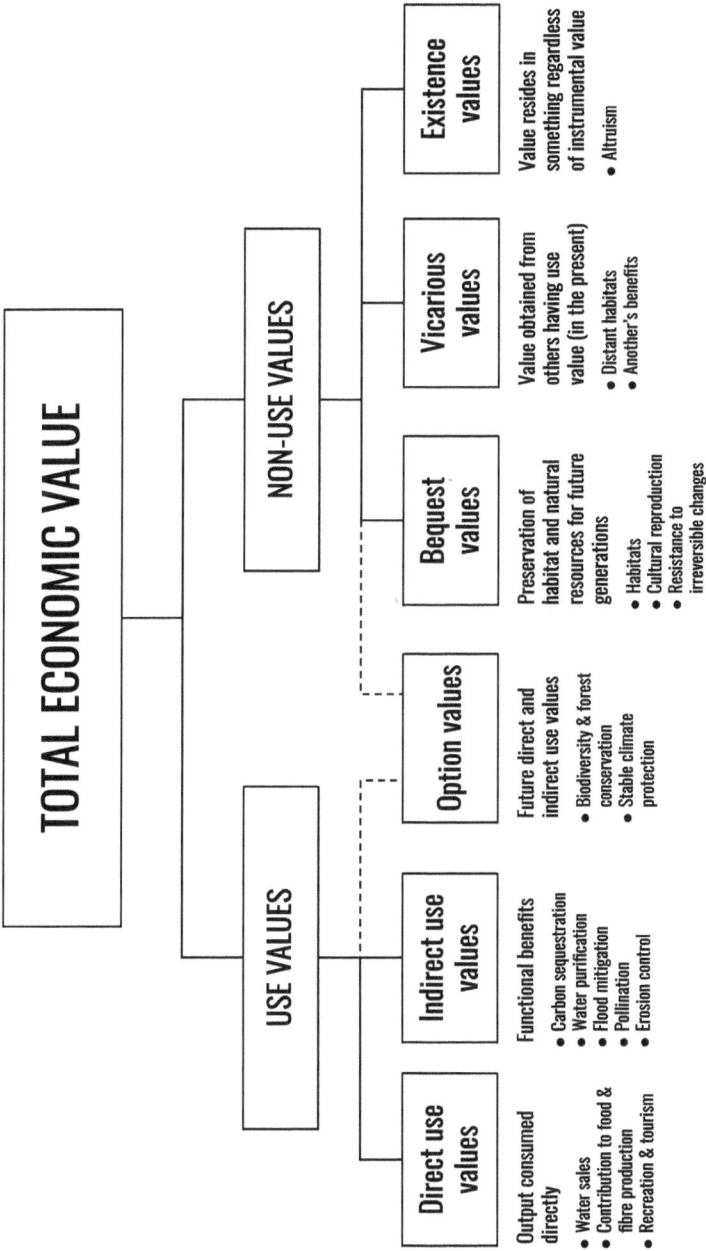

Figure 3.3: The total economic valuation framework.

associated with regulating services (ecological functions). Carbon sequestration or water filtration services provided by forests or coastal protection provided by mangroves are examples. Commonly, indirect use values are enjoyed as public goods or common pool resources (see Table 3.1).

Non-use values are more nebulous and subtly differentiated (but empirically less important to distinguish). Bequest values and vicarious values are dependent on an individual's preferences for future generations, or other contemporaries to benefit. Existence values relate to an individual's benefit from the mere existence of a natural asset. (Note this is different to intrinsic values, where the value resides within something.) It is recognised in the literature that despite the bias in policy towards extractive direct use values because of their attendant cash flows and tax revenues, non-market values are a substantial component of TEV (Taye et al. 2021).

Economic valuation of ecosystem services and natural capital

In neoclassical economics, the value of a service in well-functioning markets, containing only private goods, is calculated by observing an individual's monetary preference for it, or their willingness-to-pay (WTP), which is continually revealed in their behaviours in market transactions. An individual's marginal WTP (synonymous with the term demand) generally fits a model of diminishing utility in every additional unit consumed. Thus, the demand for each additional unit of, for example, bottled water falls until no more is demanded (demand is choked off). A market equilibrium, in terms of the quantity traded and the price paid, is reached where the marginal cost (MC) of producing an additional bottle of water is equal to the marginal WTP of the consumer. The next unit of water will not sell, as the cost of production is greater than the WTP of the consumer. The value of the market is equilibrium price multiplied by quantity consumed.

Investments in sustainable finance to secure ES are commonly made in poorly functioning markets and no property rights, or in markets where producers can externalise social costs or gain free inputs, thus making their products cheaper than they otherwise should be. As many ESs are non-excludable, testing WTP relies on more complex methods. In response, environmental economists have developed numerous methods to estimate that value. The optimal method of valuation is determined by what aspect of economic value is being assessed and the type of ecosystem service being estimated. Figure 3.4a shows a classification of these valuation methods. They fall into two broad categories:

1. Market-based methods estimate the contribution of ES by way of using exchange values – that this is the product of the quantity of benefit from an ES being produced multiplied by the determine shadow price per unit. This generates values compatible with the SEEA and national accounting; and

ECONOMIC VALUATION METHODS

MARKET BASED METHODS

Residual method
Gross margin net of natural capital inputs
- Direct use values

Replacement cost
Total costs of replacement due to loss
- Indirect use values

Opportunity cost
Differential with best alternative option
- Indirect use value of regulating ecosystem services

Damage cost avoided
Potential costs of avoided losses
- Indirect use value of regulating ecosystem services

NON-MARKET BASED METHODS

Revealed preferences

Travel cost analysis
Consumer travel preferences as proxy for natural area value
- Direct use recreation values

Hedonic pricing
Value attributed to specific attribute of environmental benefit
- Direct use benefits (e.g. proximity to natural areas)

Stated preferences

Contingent valuation
Value placed on hypothetical loss or gain of environmental benefit
- All use and non-use values

Choice experiment
Value placed on hypothetical loss or gain of basket of environmental benefits
- All use and non-use values

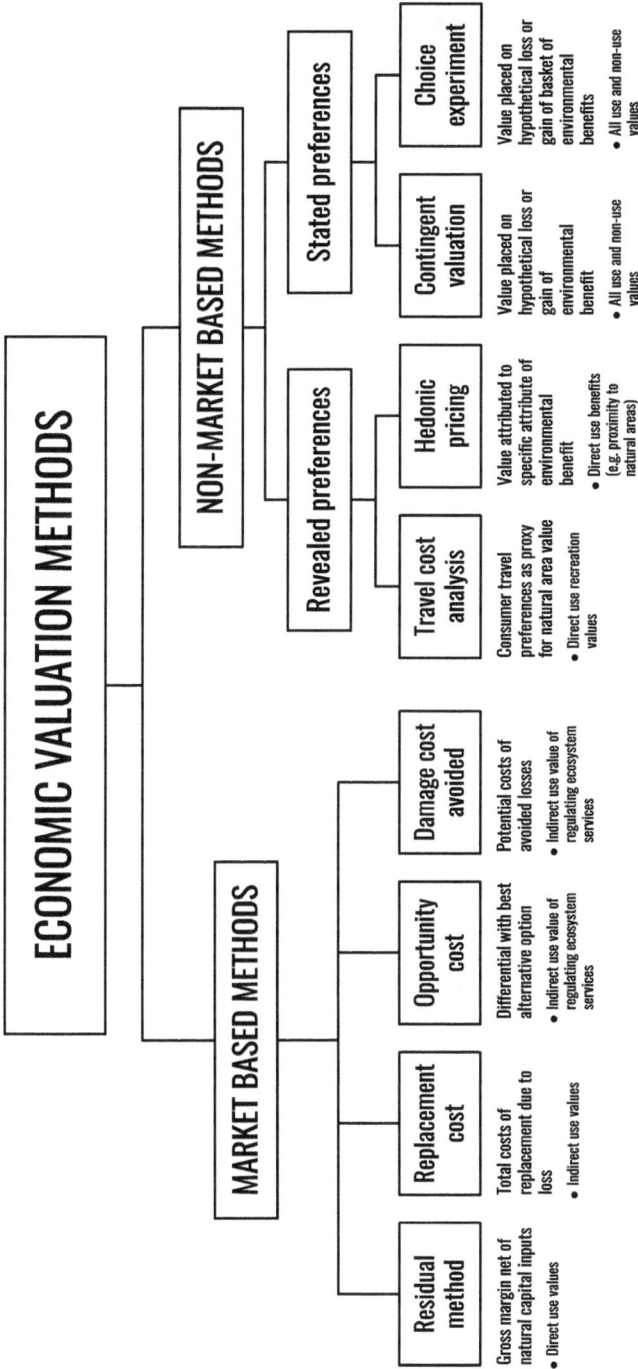

Figure 3.4a: Standard environmental economic valuation methods classification.

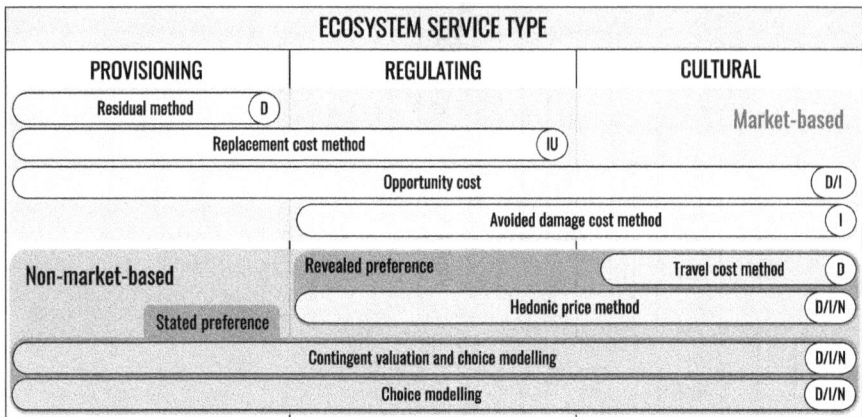

Figure 3.4b: How environmental valuation methods map to ecosystem service type and the total economic valuation framework.
Note: D = Direct use, I = Indirect use, N = Non-use.

2. non-market methods determine total welfare, or welfare changes as a result of utility gained from an ES.

Figure 3.4b references how these methods relate to ES classification and the source of the value from the TEV framework (see Figure 3.3).

Market-based valuation methods use exchange value proxies to estimate the economic contribution of ES. This group of methods rely on the behavioural trail left by individuals as they make decisions that affect their lives' (Georgiou et al. 1997: 27). Hence, like traditional market analysis, they observe how people have actually behaved. The residual method can be used to value the contributions of ES to the production of innately rival, provisioning services, which may be subsequently traded in markets, such as food or fresh water. The residual method involves subtracting production costs of non-natural capital inputs (generally, transparently priced) from the gross margin earned – the remainder being implicitly attributed to intermediate ES, for example, pollination or soil formation. For provisioning services not traded in markets, such as subsistence production, functioning markets can provide a replacement proxy, or shadow price, to measure ES contribution using the replacement cost method. Opportunity cost is the value of the forgone benefits of an option when compared to the next best alternative option. For example, in 2007, President Rafael Correa, announced Ecuador would relinquish its right to exploit oil beneath the Yasuni National Park in return for financial compensation from the global community for forgone resource rent, estimated to be ~$3.6 billion, or around half the likely royalties. By 2013, only $300 million was pledged (only $13 million actually deposited) and the idea was abandoned (Fierro 2017). Avoided damage is a measure of the value of damage that would otherwise have been caused were it not for the intervention of an ES. An example is the social cost of carbon (Ackerman and Stanton 2012), which represents the cost of future damage to infrastructure and health associated with the emission of each extra tonne of carbon into the atmosphere. Another well studied example is the value of coastal protection services provided by mangrove forests to coastal communities (Barbier 2016).

Since many ESs, particularly regulating and cultural services, are non–excludable (public goods or common pool resources) and thus free at point of use, people can enjoy an increase in welfare without any notional exchange or the giving up of something else they value. Non-market valuation methods estimate this change in welfare. Some non-market aspects can be revealed through observation of *ex post* behaviours. Two example methods are the hedonic price and the travel cost. Hedonic price can be deployed to determine the contribution of environmental quality to the overall market price of a differentiated good and is commonly used to determine the impact of environmental quality to the price of real property. However, this method is also used to isolate ES contributions of forest certification premiums, ecotourism products or wages. Travel cost (Hotelling 1947) uses surveys to elicit the value of public goods recreation areas – nominally free at the point of entry as a (congestible) public good – by using the survey respondents' reported costs of travel as proxy for the monetary value they place on that recreational area.

Where preferences cannot be revealed through past behaviours, for example, in the case of valuing spiritual and cultural services, or TEV, analysts must resort to stated preferences in contrived experiments. Two key methods are in the armoury: contingent valuation (CV) and choice experiments (CE). Both methods ask a statistically representative set of respondents (to enable scaling-up of the results to make conclusions about the whole population) about their WTP to secure a specified change in environmental condition (as proxies for ES). Stated preferences therefore demand hypothetical case studies (experiments) to generate institutional scenarios (i.e., a payment method) under which the respondent can express their preferences. Therefore, CV and CE can be used to quantify public WTP for potential future changes in environmental condition. In one sense, stated preference methods enable each respondent to have a democratic, equal voice as they are forced to express preferences from a list of choices made available to everyone, rather than express a preference in accordance with their own experience of their wealth. Another is that new, novel institutions can be tested. Extensive literature exists showing that individual choices to act in environmentally sustainable ways are constrained by the lack of appropriate institutions and property rights regimes that govern society (Georgiou et al. 1997). Conversely, stated preference method by definition are hypothetical and are thus subject to biases if experimental design is poor (Andreoni 1990).

Economic valuation and sustainable finance

With this broad understanding of methods, it is possible to now turn to their application to sustainable finance. This section describes, in broad terms, how valuation can inform decisions that can encourage the flow of capital towards environmentally sustainable activities and its corollary, discouraging the continuation of investments towards unsustainable activities.

Compensation for the provision of ecosystem services

Inclusion of the benefits from ES, commonly ignored in markets and policy, into economic thinking can challenge the dominant narrative of what constitutes production in an economy. Investments in schemes that compensate stakeholders for conserving natural capital and the ES it generates are becoming increasingly important in sustainable finance. Instead of conservation investments being framed in terms of forgone production, decisions to conserve habitat from agricultural production, for example, are being seen in terms of production of ecosystem, for which compensation is due. While agricultural goods produce private benefit (financial income), ES tend to generate non-excludable, public goods or important free inputs into traditional market-based activities.

Such compensation arrangements: can be voluntary – broadly dubbed payment for ecosystem service, or PES, schemes (Bishop and Hill 2014) and pursued for internal organisational reasons, such as corporate social responsibility; they can be externally driven by regulation – governments can demand pollution emissions permits, biodiversity offsets for developments, can institute ecological compensation schemes; or they can be driven normatively by international policy action in solving global pollution problems through grant schemes to combat climate change, such as the Global Climate Fund or Reducing Emissions from Deforestation and Forest Degradation (REDD+) schemes (Wallbott, Siciliano, and Lederer 2019). In addition, as trust in biophysical data and ecosystem service valuation grows and estimates stabilise, compensation schemes can become relevant at a landscape level, where value can be exchanged between stakeholders at scales commensurate with the ecosystem service under consideration. For example, two stakeholder communities in the same catchment, with at least *de jure* property rights, may use economic valuation to determine fair value from resisting commercial deforestation in exchange from stakeholders further down the catchment who value clean drinking water, flood retention or a silt-free coral reef for their ecotourism visitors. A commonly cited example of such Coasian bargaining (Coase 1960) is the scheme set up by the City of New York to secure a clean but unfiltered water supply to avoid the costs of implementing federal requirements on drinking water quality, by purchasing avoided deforestation in the upper catchments of the Catskill Mountains (Pires 2004). Similar principles have been deployed implementing China's ecological compensation schemes (Deng et al. 2011). These schemes attempt to reduce the conflict between development and conservation by having ecosystem service beneficiaries (e.g., urban provinces downstream) financially compensate ecosystem service suppliers (e.g., forested habitats and agricultural areas in provinces upstream) to protect ecosystems for specific services, for example, maintaining clean drinking water. Compensation funds ecological restoration and environmental protection and discourages land conversion and, as a result, has created opportunity costs for social and economic development.

This landscape approach (see Chapter Five in this volume), combining economic valuation of ES with the development of institutions that can enable the trading of value in nominal public goods, can also promote investments that best harness ecosystem co-benefits. For example, while securing carbon in a forest project may be the primary goal of a REDD+ project, conserving this forest also secures a broader basket of benefits that forest provides, such as water flow and sediment regulation, pollination services and cultural and spiritual values (Morgan et al. 2021). As compensation schemes, regulatory or voluntary, trade in contrived markets (there is rarely an innate demand for a carbon sequestration) they demand strict additionality – a stakeholder cannot double-dip and claim credits for more than one ecosystem service when that ecosystem service will be already by secured with the original payment. (Note this is not always the case, as habitats can be managed in ways that maximise certain ES.) If additionality is not achieved, it is economically inefficient – the funds would have been better deployed securing further conservation. However, this demand for strict additionality impedes conservation and the practice of credit stacking, assessing the TESV of a landscape, has potential for broad application (Deal, Cochran, and LaRocco 2012).

Internalising the costs of environmental damage

That capital flows towards where it will achieve the best rate of return is a leitmotif of economics. High returns are achieved where costs of production can be externalised, or socialised, to the greatest extent or where market power or information asymmetries can be exploited in the market or the policymaking process. Despite capital maximising its returns, societal welfare will not be maximised where the social costs of pollution exceed the private costs. As such, environmental costs can be a drag on a national economy; consider the forgone benefits from poor human health, loss of biodiversity and soil, or damage emanating from climate change. From a firm's perspective, if the economic costs of managing emissions from their production process can be avoided, returns will be higher than for a competitor. This might occur where two competing plants are: (a) in different jurisdictions with different pollution regulations but share the same waste sink (e.g., the atmosphere); (b) in the same jurisdiction, but one firm has negotiated more favourable regulation; (c) where the two plants produce the same service (e.g., electricity) but use different inputs (brown coal vs. fossil gas); or (d) where two plants produce different but substitutable goods through different processes with different pollution levels. Exploiting this capacity to emit without financial penalty continues favours unsustainable financing for pollution-generating activities to the detriment of investments in sustainable activities. Economic valuation methods can be used to value this external cost and hence inform pollution policy through the levying of taxes or charges on pollution.

Some of the most significant pollutants are greenhouses gases (GHGs), which are predominantly emitted from the burning of fossil fuels, deforestation and agriculture. While the quantity of emissions from human activities is the function of science and engineering, assigning an economic value to this carbon is the function of environmental economics. When reflecting on GHG pollution, the ES considered in CICES is regulation of chemical composition of atmosphere and ocean. Carbon emissions can be economically valued in a number of ways, depending on the context or the arguments to be made. For example, if a project proponent was seeking to access a scheme to purchase emissions permits in jurisdictions with emissions trading, the appropriate valuation of carbon would be determined by the price at which permits can be traded. Policymakers seeking to drive finance towards sustainable investments would demand sufficient permits from polluters, who would either install technologies to reduce their emissions (at a cost), or purchase emissions permits for surrender. If a jurisdiction deploys pollution taxes, such as a Pigouvian tax – a tax levied in proportion to the amount of pollution generated, which is equal to the margin social cost borne by the victim of that pollution – firms face a similar decision: pay the tax or reduce emissions (Nye 2008). Either way, increasing the relative burden on polluting industries by internalising the social costs of GHG pollution will benefit investments in sustainable enterprises and increase social welfare.

Augmenting national accounts

National accounts record monetary flows of transacted services through an economy. Accounts, such as GDP, have come to be considered important proxies for measures of wellbeing and development but are not without criticism, particularly for what is counted and what is not counted and what is, at best, merely estimated (Giannetti et al. 2015; Mitchell 2017). Widely implemented national accounts are deficient in their treatment of ES and natural and the social capitals that bring nature's services into the economy (see Figure 3.1), ignoring the value of the first and then latter and erroneously considering liquidation of natural capital as income. Reporting starts at the point of extraction and ends at the point of discharge into the environment. Consequently, activities that increase the exchange of services in markets that align with the current paradigm of property rights are favoured, or property rights are extended into services traditionally considered commons, systematically undervaluing contributions provided by nature, women and communally-based activities (Raveendran 2010). For example, national development plans, policies or fiscal settings tend to support the privatisation of community lands (enclosure) for transformation to commercial agriculture and its attendant environmental costs, such as overexploitation of provisioning ES, such as timber getting and wild fisheries. As a result, the invisible aspects of nature's contributions remain unaccounted for in national accounts and measures of wellbeing.

Natural capital and ecosystem accounting, as now codified in the SEEA's Central Framework and the Ecosystem Accounting framework begin to address this blind spot. Economic valuation plays an important role in converting SEEA's biophysical accounts of flows of environmental services into monetary measures that are compatible with and integrated into national monetary accounts to provide a more holistic view of national income, which can now include both marketed and non-marketed contributions. Economic valuation can also be used in determining the value of changes in stocks of natural capital; again, compatible with other national accounts, such as balance sheets. This can provide a clearer assessment of the non-marketed contributions to wellbeing. For example, several studies into the TESV provided by landscapes have demonstrated the significant importance of ES to wellbeing (Gashaw et al. 2018; Tolessa et al. 2018). In Vanuatu, this was assessed to be more than three times greater than GDP (Buckwell et al. 2020).

Project evaluation

Economic valuation of ES plays an important role in project assessment using tools, such as cost benefit analysis (CBA). CBA can guide sustainable finance by broadening the scope of material project considerations to include the commonly invisible aspects of environmental costs and benefits. A CBA is used to estimate and compare the net benefits of a project (benefits minus costs) with a business-as-usual case. To be comparable, these benefits and costs are homogenised into monetary values. CBA also considers the timing of each of the benefits and costs and converts these into today's prices using a discount rate so that all impacts can be meaningfully compared, regardless of their timing or realisation. A social CBA considers these costs and benefits from a whole of society perspective and therefore takes into account flows of social and environmental costs and benefits beyond the direct costs and benefits. Social and environmental benefits and costs can include changes to environmental quality, quantity and amenity, changes to recreational values and impacts on ES.

Thus, practitioners assessing benefits and costs using the TEV framework (see Figure 3.2) and economic valuation of ES (Venn and Quiggin 2007). Access to data, particularly locally relevant data that can be monetised, is often a limitation in analysis, however, advances in economic valuation techniques, which can include the more esoteric non-use values, have enabled broader application of TEV. Analysts also need to be cognisant of not totalising incompatible aspects of TEV (such as timber values and carbon sequestration values at the same time – carbon would be released if the forest was harvested) and of not double-counting compounding ecosystem service values. Cultural and spiritual values, or loss of these values due to development, especially those of Indigenous peoples, may be effectively economically valued, using non-market valuation techniques, such as CV and CE. However, inclusion of these values as monetary inputs might be considered insensitive or inappropriate and these decisions may be better mediated through the political decision-making processes.

Natural capital and business

As non-excludable services, policymakers face difficulties in motivating private producers of ES in market economies. If a firm cannot exclude beneficiaries from free riding, there can be no compensation for providing that service! Nonetheless, businesses depend on natural capital and the continuation of a flow of ES from integrous habitats, whether it is an obvious, tangible direct use input, such as timber or fresh water, or indirect use benefits, such as the free coastal protection provided by mangroves. Thus, business faces a conundrum. It benefits, directly and indirectly from natural capital and ES, but unless it has exclusive control (property rights) over the exploitation of that service for benefit, it will not be encouraged to invest in its sustainable continuation. It therefore faces risks on three fronts.

Business face supply-side and demand-side risks. On the supply-side, business faces input shocks. For example, flows of filtered water are essential for the operation of everything from a drink bottling plant to a hydroelectric dam. If damage to natural capital interrupts that flow, the business faces increased costs. (Note that this is based on the concept of weak sustainability, where inputs can be substituted by a manufactured capital sourced input – water shipped in from another source.) Secondly, business faces regulatory risk. For example, many businesses currently emitting GHGs without penalty (e.g., the airline industry) likely face future regulation, such as a price on carbon emissions, which drives an increase in supply-side in terms of building intellectual and human capital to expertly manage that risk and investments in lowering emissions. Thirdly, on the demand–side, businesses can face reputational risk. For example, a business can be exposed to consumer pressure if it was discovered that an input into its supply chain is the cause of deforestation. Conversely, this reputational risk can be exploited as a supply-side opportunity, where the businesses can compete on sustainability performance, fetching consumer premiums or investment through brand association with environmental performance.

Economic valuation of ES plays a crucial function in managing those risks. Frameworks, such as the Natural Capital Protocol (NCP) (Capitals Coalition 2016) can help business frame their dependencies and impacts on natural capital in terms compatible with internal accounting, in support of achieving the UN Sustainable Development Goal 12.6 (encouraging companies to integrate sustainability reporting). The NCP was created by the Capitals Coalition – a collaboration of for-profit, not-for-profit and international organisations seeking to provide advice, frameworks and model methodologies to businesses and also informing international accounting standards. It offers a comprehensive framework for businesses to identify, measure and value their impacts and dependencies on ES and natural capital in biophysical and monetary terms, which can assist in their sustainability reporting and carbon disclosures.

Conceptual critiques

As an explanatory metaphor, economic analyses of the human relationship with nature through the lens of ES and natural capital has been the subject of lively debate (Monbiot 2018; Pascual et al. 2017). These are based on the fundamental grounding of ecosystem services as embodying:

(i)   Conceptual vagueness: As the metaphorical device has matured, the definitions and classifications have evolved, suggesting the concepts lack scientific validity (the different ways that natural capital is conceived as one of four, five or six capitals is a case in point).

(ii) A separation of human society and nature: ES are depicted to flow into human society across a metaphorical divide (dualism) that is common and persistent in Western-centric philosophical traditions (Descartes 1996) and in neoclassical economic models. Waste subsequently flows outwards into the environment, where it is seen, literally, as an externality.

(iii) Anthropocentrism: Although regulating ES often serves the function of others, particularly provisioning and cultural services, ultimately it is all in service of human utility and to allocate according to dominant property rights regimes, particularly in the industrialised North, rather than being seen for its intrinsic value in and of itself, or as being sensitive to Indigenous cultures' conceptions of communality (Luke 2002; Næss 1973).

(iv) Utilitarian in focus: Nature's value is determined only in its utility to human society. Although valuation techniques are now established to determine non-use values, these are determined only by values stated by people, thus the relationship remains one of exploitation.

(v)   Naive to ecological processes: Application of economic valuation struggles with the complexity of ecological systems, which are dynamic in nature and suffer phase change and hysteresis, rather than tending towards an equilibrium.

Conceptual vagueness

Intangible, cultural ES are commonly critiqued as being vaguely defined. For example, Pröpper and Haupts (2014) argue that, as cultural benefits are more conceptual, rather than material, this has tended to lead the category of cultural ES being used as a miscellaneous basket into which newly conceived, unallocated, non-material ES get placed when no better basket can be determined. Instead, the authors suggest the term 'intangible/immaterial ecosystem services' be used to clarify boundaries around the term (Small, Munday, and Durance 2017: 65). However, it is arguably still possible to consider shared and social values, such as cultural services (more broadly) within individualistic survey methods, such as CV or CE. In a (self-described) polemic, Ravenscroft (2016) argues incorporation of monetised, non-tangible values is not necessarily problematic and merely a technical problem to resolve through elicitation methods used in the field. What is being valued is not intangible, external, shared values, but the personal satisfaction (utility) that an individual experiences from being altruistic within and between generations, which is eminently quantifiable through eliciting an individual's WTP to become completely self-serving! (Wilson and Howarth 2002). Furthermore, not only is this non-problematic, it is actually a necessary condition of valuation in informing policy, as it fulfils the Bergson-Samuelson social welfare functions – ranking in terms of maximising desirability of alternate social states – required by in CBA.

Co-production

Others have argued that cultural values pervade all other ES, often amplifying the value to a community; thus, all ES, to some extent, are coproduced. Wild fish, for example, are an important provisioning service but the harvesting of fish as a pursuit may be central to the culture of a community. Ergo, ES benefits may be captured privately (e.g., individually, or by a household) or socially, and in simple, monist ways or in complex, multifaceted and even synergistic ways – both temporally and spatially (Stoeckl et al. 2018). For example, many of the ES benefits captured from soil fertility of subsistence gardens or the collection of wild fish from healthy stocks (provisioning service) will be captured privately and immediately and therefore likely to be highly valued through some elicitation methods. The benefits of pollination of those subsistence gardens, by the insects, birds and bats of the forest (a regulating service), is more likely to be captured socially, at the community-level, over the course of the planting cycles, and while the community may intrinsically understand the importance of pollination, as the benefits (and costs of loss) are more widely shared over space and time, the services will tend to attract lower valuations. The benefits of a stable climate, as a result of sequestering carbon in the tropical forests, accrue over many years and to the benefit the entire global community. The complexity of the benefits are not only a function of the temporal and spatial scale of which the benefits are experienced, but also the invocation of group cultural identification, whereby personal relations are conducted through deep-seated and long-established sociocultural networks rather than through the market or bureaucracy (Thompson et al. 1991).

Anthropocentrism and utilitarian critiques

Further critique is made that in framing nature in anthropocentric, utilitarian terms, placing it only as a contribution in the production function for goods and services for the human economy or its retention contributes only to human welfare (Næss 1973) and outside the moral community for which legal protections are assigned (Stone 1972). The end point argument is that by speaking the language of your opponents (Monbiot 2014) it means that the argument for respecting nature cannot be won, as you are merely reinforcing the frame that nature lacks any value unless it has a value placed on it by humans.

This anthropocentrism and utilitarian perspective also present challenges to valuation methods. Monetary valuation methods (CE, CV, travel cost, hedonic, etc.) all start with the potentially flawed assumption that 'outcomes generated by free and competitive markets set the appropriate standard for welfare improvements through efficient resources allocation' (Wilson and Howarth 2002: 434). Monetary values of ES assume that WTP is derived from comparisons to substitutes with or actions in an efficiently functioning market and not one where the price is opaque or the market is distorted, which is often the *prima facie* case for undertaking the economic study in the first place. For example, basing the marginal ES value of additional subsistence production on the cost of additional goods purchased at a nearby market assumes prices at those markets have already accounted externalities in their production. This is never likely to be the case.

Purchasing decisions are based on a range of factors, of which price is only one, yet with ecosystem service valuations, this is the only factor of choice that economists attempt to reveal. Even in developed societies, it is argued the degree to which stated preference valuation techniques, which rely on hypothetical futures, can define TEV is limited – lived experiences (context) are a necessary condition of determining value (Bowers 1997). Conversely, while travel cost analysis or hedonic pricing reflect people's actual (past) behaviour, they are inappropriate in low-income contexts. Even in high-income societies people have been shown to be poor judges of value in novel, or emerging markets, such as those often presented in CV and CE surveys. Individuals need time and context to develop the 'suitable heuristic devices [. . .] which allow them to act rationally' (Bowers 1997: 133). Even accepting that people may act rationally in well-established, simple markets (e.g., food shopping), it does not follow they will also do so in highly complex (spatially and temporally) contrived markets, such as those developed for valuation (Söderqvist et al. 2005). As a result, individual WTP for improvements in ES are based on a much wider range of factors than commonly traded private services. 'This poses a major methodological challenge, as trade-offs between services are required to generate estimates of monetary value' (Kenter et al. 2011: 518). Economic valuations of ES in low-income contexts will typically yield very low WTP values. In predominantly cashless, subsistence communities, where land is majority customarily owned, there is often a poor understanding of the utility of money (Kenter et al. 2016). Indigenous communities also have a tendency accumulate and share common wealth among larger groupings of individuals or households – the standard unit of neoclassical economic analysis(Adamowicz et al. 1998; Venn and Quiggin 2007).

Non-linearity and valuation

The elegance of environmental economics defies scientific/ecological complexities, such as ecological thresholds and interrelated nature of ES, particularly for public goods or common pool resources (Koch et al. 2009; Rau, von Wehrden, and Abson 2018). This assumption is that ecosystems respond linearly with impacts and forcings on natural capital, when the reality this relationship is dynamic and non-linear, spatially and temporally (Koch et al. 2009: 29). Therefore, assuming ES can be freely traded off, with a constant linear response of supply of ES is erroneous – and, at worse, eminently risky to sustainability. Ecologists use the term hysteresis. For example, a coral reef can be subject to a perturbation, or an acute stressor, such as a coral bleaching event, or destruction from a cyclone, or be subject to parameter change, or chronic stressor, such as continual overfishing or poor water quality. Either a perturbation or a parameter change may be responsible for tipping the coral dominated ecosystem into a macro-algal dominated ecosystem. However, in both instances, neither a cessation of the chronic stressors, or an end of the perturbation precipitates a phase change back to the coral dominated ecosystem. The state change is permanent, without intervention (Harrison 2011). Three different temporal dynamics are recognised: linear, seasonal dynamics and irregular events (Rau, von Wehrden, and Abson 2018). Thus, marginal analysis and monetary valuation may be inappropriate tools, especially in the vicinity of thresholds and tipping points – is it meaningful to place a value on the Amazon rainforest, for example, when its loss would fundamentally change the regional and global climate? Similarly, an environmental justice perspective focuses on who is entitled to ES and the impacts of environmental change caused by others, not their WTP. Therefore, economic valuation should be considered only one tool of many to support decision-making in directing sustainable finance, not as an objective way to generate a definite answer.

Conclusions

Concern about the privatisation and commodification of nature is well-placed. Economic valuation methods – notwithstanding their capacity to estimate non-market values – are commonly still based in estimations of individual willingness-to-pay or scaled-up to community WTP when determining the value of public goods. Policy responses, particularly in advanced economies have indeed tended towards the extension of individual property rights into hitherto unownable aspects of the biosphere. For example, to arrest rapid climate change individual (including individual firms) property rights have been allocated through market-based mechanisms that involve permits to pollute or emissions reduction certificates. While proponents might argue this has been successful (the European Union has reduced its emissions, in part due to the presence of an emissions trading scheme), it undeniably has been as a result of the commodification of nature and the extension of property rights into what were previously common pool resources. However, the valuation of natural capital and ES in a common metric (money) does not need to assume nature is being privatised. New institutions are emerging that generate compensation through PES schemes, but the benefits (compensation) are held in trust or are collectively allocated into common property assets. Increasingly, economic valuation of social and environmental costs is now playing a significant role in the formulation of land use and industrial policy and decision-making.

The currently continuing (at time of writing) global COVID-19 pandemic has provided a forced watershed from the economic disruption generated by widespread restrictions on economic activity and local and global migration and the direct costs of human mortality. The United Nations has carried the agenda built on the central idea of building back better (O'Callaghan and Murdock 2020) recognising that the causes of the pandemic likely lies in a dysfunctional relationship between the current and accelerating trajectory of human development driving the twin crises in climate change and biodiversity loss. The agenda seeks to direct recovery towards a clean, green transition; ensuring that where taxpayers' money is used to rescue businesses, it must be tied to sustainable objectives; governments must rediscover the power of its spending power, using fiscal policy to shift from the grey to green economy; and an ending of subsidies to the fossil fuel sector and pursuing policies for the sector to internalise its environmental costs on society. While there is evidence that an agenda of carbon emissions reduction is being pursued in some countries, notably in Canada and parts of Europe and the UK, the consensus (as of 2021) is that momentum is not necessarily consolidated unequivocally. The world's largest economies, including the US, India and China have not fundamentally reoriented their material trajectory, while many emerging economies, including Indonesia, Mexico and the Philippines have merely reinforced carbon intensive economic activities. Natural capital and biodiversity have been almost entirely ignored (Vivid Economics 2021).

References

Ackerman, Frank, and Elizabeth Stanton. 2012. 'Climate Risks and Carbon Prices: Revising the Social Cost of Carbon', *Economics: The Open-Access, Open-Assessment E-Journal*, 6, 10–10.

Adamowicz, Wiktor, Peter Boxall, Michael Williams, and Jordan Louviere. 1998. 'Stated Preference Approaches for Measuring Passive Use Values: Choice Experiments and Contingent Valuation', *American Journal of Agricultural Economics*, 80 (1), 64–75.

Andrade, Daniel, and Junior Garcia. 2015. 'Estimating the Genuine Progress Indicator (GPI) for Brazil from 1970 to 2010', *Ecological Economics*, 118 (1), 49–56.

Andreoni, James. 1990. 'Impure Altruism and Donations to Public Goods: A Theory of Warm-Glow Giving', *The Economic Journal*, 100 (401), 464–77.

Aultman, S., R. Solow, P. Portney, E. Leamer, R. Radner, and H. Schuman. 1993. 'Report of the Noaa Panel on Contingent Valuation', *Federal Register*, 58 (10), 4602–14.

Barbier, Edward. 2007. 'Valuing Ecosystem Services as Productive Inputs', *Economic Policy*, 22 (49), 178–229.

——. 2016. 'The Protective Service of Mangrove Ecosystems: A Review of Valuation Methods', *Marine Pollution Bulletin*, 109 (2), 676–81.

Bishop, Joshua, and Chloe Hill. 2014. *Global Biodiversity Finance: The Case for International Payments for Ecosystem Services* (Cheltenham, UK: Edward Elgar Publishing).

Bowers, John. 1997. *Sustainability and Environmental Economics: An Alternative Text* (London: Addison Wesley Longman Ltd).

Boyd, James, and Spencer Banzhaf. 2007. 'What Are Ecosystem Services? The Need for Standardized Environmental Accounting Units', *Ecological Economics*, 63 (2), 616–26.

Buckwell, Andrew, Christopher Fleming, James Smart, Dan Ware, and Brendan Mackey. 2020. 'Challenges and Sensitivities in Assessing Total Ecosystem Service Values: Lessons from Vanuatu for the Pacific', *Journal of Environment and Development*, 29 (3), 329–65.

Natural Capitals Coalition. 2016. *Natural Capital Protocol*, (Gravenhage, The Netherlands: Natural Capital Coalition), <https://naturalcapitalcoalition.org/protocol> [Accessed 9 October 2021].

Coase, Ronald. 1960. 'The Problem of Social Cost.' in C Gopalakrishnan (ed.), *Classic Papers in Natural Resource Economics* (London: Palgrave Macmillan), pp. 87–137

Costanza, Robert, and Herman Daly. 1992. 'Natural Capital and Sustainable Development', *Conservation Biology*, 6 (1), 37–46.

Costanza, Robert, Rudolf de Groot, Leon Braat, Ida Kubiszewski, Lorenzo Fioramonti, Paul Sutton, Steve Farber, and Monica Grasso. 2017. 'Twenty Years of Ecosystem Services: How Far Have We Come and How Far Do We Still Need to Go?', *Ecosystem Services*, 28 (Part A), 1–16.

Daily, Gretchen. 1997. *Nature's Services: Societal Dependence on Natural Ecosystems* (Washington DC: Island Press).

Daly, Herman. 2020. 'A Note in Defense of the Concept of Natural Capital', *Ecosystem Services*, 41, 101051–51.

Deal, Robert, Bobby Cochran, and Gina LaRocco. 2012. 'Bundling of Ecosystem Services to Increase Forestland Value and Enhance Sustainable Forest Management', *Forest Policy and Economics*, 17, 69–76.

Deng, Hongbing, Peng Zheng, Tianxing Liu, and Xin Liu. 2011. 'Forest Ecosystem Services and Eco-Compensation Mechanisms in China', *Environmental Management*, 48 (6), 1079–85.

Descartes, Rene. 1996. *Meditations on First Philosophy* (Cambridge, UK: Cambridge University Press).

Epstein, Paul, Jonathan Buonocore, Kevin Eckerle, Michael Hendryx, Benjamin Stout III, Richard Heinberg, Richard Clapp, Beverly May, Nancy Reinhart, Melissa Ahern, Samir Doshi, and Leslie

Glustrom. 2011. 'Full Cost Accounting for the Life Cycle of Coal', *Annals of the New York Academy of Sciences*, 1219 (1), 73–73.

Fierro, Lucía. 2017. 'Rethinking Oil: Compensation for Non-Production in Yasuní National Park Challenging Sumak Kawsay and Degrowth', *Sustainability Science*, 12 (2), 263–74.

Garnaut, Ross. 2008. *Garnaut Climate Change Review*, (Canberra: Commonwealth of Australia), <https://webarchive.nla.gov.au/awa/20190509071611/http://www.garnautreview.org.au/synopsis.htm> [Accessed 24 January 2022].

Gashaw, Temesgen, Taffa Tulu, Mekuria Argaw, Abeyou W. Worqlul, Terefe Tolessa, and Mengistie Kindu. 2018. 'Estimating the Impacts of Land Use/Land Cover Changes on Ecosystem Service Values: The Case of the Andassa Watershed in the Upper Blue Nile Basin of Ethiopia', *Ecosystem Services*, 31, 219–28.

Gaudet, Gérard. 2007. 'Natural Resource Economics under the Rule of Hotelling', *Canadian Journal of Economics/Revue Canadienne D'économique*, 40 (4), 1033–59.

Georgiou, Stavros, Dale Whittington, David Pearce, and Dominic Moran. 1997. *Economic Values and the Environment in the Developing World* (Cheltenham, UK: Edward Elgar Publishing Ltd).

Giannetti, B.F., Feni Agostinho, C.M.V.B. Almeida, and Donald Huisingh. 2015. 'A Review of Limitations of GDP and Alternative Indices to Monitor Human Wellbeing and to Manage Eco-System Functionality', *Journal of Cleaner Production*, 87, 11–25.

Gleeson-White, Jane. 2015. *Six Capitals, or Can Accountants Save the Planet? Rethinking Capitalism for the Twenty-First Century* (New York: W. W. Norton and Company).

Haines-Young, Roy, and Marion Potschin-Young. 2018. 'Revision of the Common International Classification for Ecosystem Services (Cices V5. 1): A Policy Brief', *One Ecosystem*, 3 (1), e27108-e08.

Hardin, Garrett. 1968. 'The Tragedy of the Commons', *Journal of Natural Resources Policy Research*, 1 (3), 243–53.

Harrison, P. 2011. 'Sexual Reproduction of Scleractinian Corals.' in Z. Dubinsky and N. Stambler (eds.), *Coral Reefs: An Ecosystem in Transition* (Springer), pp. 59–85.

Hartwick, John. 1977. 'Intergenerational Equity and the Investing of Rents from Exhaustible Resources', *The American Economic Review*, 67 (5), 972–74.

Hotelling, Harold. 1947. *Letter to the National Park Service: An Economic Study of the Monetary Evaluation of Recreation in the National Parks* National Park Service and Recreational Planning Division US Department of the Interior.

Kemkes, Robin, Joshua Farley, and Christopher Koliba. 2010. 'Determining When Payments Are an Effective Policy Approach to Ecosystem Service Provision', *Ecological Economics*, 69 (11), 2069–74.

Kenter, J., R. Bryce, M. Christie, N. Cooper, N. Hockley, K. Irvine, I. Fazey, L. O'Brien, J. Orchard-Webb, N. Ravenscroft, C. Raymond, M. Reed, P. Tett, and V. Watson. 2016. 'Shared Values and Deliberative Valuation: Future Directions', *Ecosystem Services*, 21 (Part B), 358–71.

Kenter, J., T. Hyde, M. Christie, and I. Fazey. 2011. 'The Importance of Deliberation in Valuing Ecosystem Services in Developing Countries – Evidence from the Solomon Islands', *Global Environmental Change*, 21 (2), 505–21.

Koch, Evamaria, Edward Barbier, Brian Silliman, Denise Reed, Gerardo Perillo, Sally Hacker, Elise Granek, Jurgenne Primavera, Nyawira Muthiga, and Stephen Polasky. 2009. 'Non-Linearity in Ecosystem Services: Temporal and Spatial Variability in Coastal Protection', Frontiers in Ecology and the Environment, 7 (1), 29–37.

Kumar, P. 2010. *The Economics of Ecosystems and Biodiversity: Ecological Foundations* (London: UNEP/Earthprint).

Laurans, Yann, Aleksandar Rankovic, Raphaël Billé, Romain Pirard, and Laurent Mermet. 2013. 'Use of Ecosystem Services Economic Valuation for Decision Making: Questioning a Literature Blindspot', *Journal of Environmental Management*, 119, 208–19.

Lomborg, Bjørn. 2010. *Smart Solutions to Climate Change: Comparing Costs and Benefits* (Cambridge, UK: Cambridge University Press).

Luke, Timothy. 2002. 'Deep Ecology: Living as If Nature Mattered: Devall and Sessions on Defending the Earth', *Organization and Environment*, 15 (2), 178–86.

Mill, John Stuart. 1884. *Principles of Political Economy* (London: West Strand).

Millenium Ecosystem Assessment.·2003. *Ecosystems and Human Well-Being: A Framework for Assessment*, (Washington DC: Island Press), <https://www.millenniumassessment.org/docu ments/document.48.aspx.pdf> [Accessed 9 October 2021].

Mitchell, Alex. 2017. 'The Little Big Number: How GDP Came to Rule the World and What to Do About It', *Consumption Markets and Culture*, 20 (1), 92–94.

Monbiot, George. 2014. 'Can You Put a Price on the Beauty of the Natural World?', *The Guardian*. <https://www.theguardian.com/commentisfree/2014/apr/22/price-natural-world-agenda- ignores-destroys> [Accessed 10 November 2021].

——. 2018. 'The Pricing of Everything', *Ecological Citizen*, 2 (1), 89–96.

Morgan, Edward, Andrew Buckwell, Caterina Guidi, Beatriz Garcia, Lawrence Rimmer, Tim Cadman, and Brendan Mackey. 2021. 'The Basket of Benefits Approach: Capturing Multiple Forest Ecosystem Services for Just Benefit Sharing', *Ecosystem Services*, In press.

Næss, Arne. 1973. 'The Shallow and the Deep, Long-Range Ecology Movement: A Summary', *Inquiry*, 16 (1-4), 95–100.

Neumayer, Eric. 2003. *Weak Versus Strong Sustainability: Exploring the Limits of Two Opposing Paradigms* (Cheltenham, UK: Edward Elgar Publishing).

Nye, John. 2008. 'The Pigou Problem', *Regulation*, 31, 32–32.

O'Callaghan, Brian, and Em Murdock.·2020. *Are We Building Back Better: Evidence from 2020 and Pathways to Inclusive Green Recovery Spending*, (Oxford: United Nations Environment Programme and Smith School of Enterprise and the Environment), <https://wedocs.unep.org/ bitstream/handle/20.500.11822/35281/AWBBB.pdf> [Accessed 29 October 2021].

Pascual, Unai, Patricia Balvanera, Sandra Díaz, György Pataki, Eva Roth, Marie Stenseke, Robert Watson, Esra Başak Dessane, Mine Islar, and Eszter Kelemen. 2017. 'Valuing Nature's Contributions to People: The IPBES Approach', *Current Opinion in Environmental Sustainability*, 26, 7–16.

Pearce, David, and Giles Atkinson. 1993. 'Capital Theory and the Measurement of Sustainable Development: An Indicator of "Weak" Sustainability', *Ecological Economics*, 8 (2), 103–08.

Pelenc, Jérôme, and Jérôme Ballet. 2015. 'Strong Sustainability, Critical Natural Capital and the Capability Approach', *Ecological Economics*, 112, 36–44.

Pires, Mark. 2004. 'Watershed Protection for a World City: The Case of New York', *Land Use Policy*, 21 (2), 161–75.

Pröpper, Michael, and Felix Haupts. 2014. 'The Culturality of Ecosystem Services. Emphasizing Process and Transformation', *Ecological Economics*, 108, 28–35.

Randall, Alan. 1983. 'The Problem of Market Failure', *Natural Resources Journal*, 23 (1), 131–48.

Rau, Anna-Lena, Henrik von Wehrden, and David J. Abson. 2018. 'Temporal Dynamics of Ecosystem Services', *Ecological Economics*, 151, 122–30.

Raveendran, G. 2010. *Contribution of Women to the National Economy* (New Delhi: International Labour Organisation).

Ricardo, David. 1817. *On the Principles of Political Economy and Taxation* (London: Dent).

Rockström, Johan, Will Steffen, Kevin Noone, Åsa Persson, F. Stuart Chapin Iii, Eric F. Lambin, Timothy Lenton, Marten Scheffer, Carl Folke, Hans Joachim Schellnhuber, Björn Nykvist,

Cynthia A. de Wit, Terry Hughes, Sander van der Leeuw, Henning Rodhe, Sverker Sörlin, Peter K. Snyder, Robert Costanza, Uno Svedin, Malin Falkenmark, Louise Karlberg, Robert W. Corell, Victoria J. Fabry, James Hansen, Brian Walker, Diana Liverman, Katherine Richardson, Paul Crutzen, and Jonathan A. Foley. 2009. 'A Safe Operating Space for Humanity', *Nature*, 461 (7263), 472–72.

Sarkki, S. 2017. 'Governance Services: Co-Producing Human Well-Being with Ecosystem Services', *Ecosystem Services*, 27, 82–91.

Secretariat of the Convention on Biological Diversity.·2010. Global Biodiversity Outlook 3, (Montreal: Secretariat of the Convention on Biological Diversity), <https://www.cbd.int/doc/publications/gbo/gbo3-final-en.pdf> [Accessed 1 November 2021].

Small, N., M. Munday, and I. Durance. 2017. 'The Challenge of Valuing Ecosystem Services That Have No Material Benefits', *Global Environmental Change*, 44, 57–67.

Söderqvist, Tore, Håkan Eggert, Björn Olsson, and Åsa Soutukorva. 2005. 'Economic Valuation for Sustainable Development in the Swedish Coastal Zone', *AMBIO: A Journal of the Human Environment*, 34 (2), 169–75.

Spangenberg, Joachim, Christoph Görg, and Josef Settele. 2015. 'Stakeholder Involvement in Ess Research and Governance: Between Conceptual Ambition and Practical Experiences–Risks, Challenges and Tested Tools', *Ecosystem Services*, 16, 201–11.

Steffen, Will, Wendy Broadgate, Lisa Deutsch, Owen Gaffney, and Cornelia Ludwig. 2015. 'The Trajectory of the Anthropocene: The Great Acceleration', *The Anthropocene Review*, 2 (1), 81–98.

Stoeckl, N., C. Hicks, M. Farr, D. Grainger, M. Esparon, J. Thomas, and S. Larson. 2018. 'The Crowding out of Complex Social Goods', *Ecological Economics*, 144, 65–72.

Stone, Christopher. 1972. 'Should Trees Have Standing–toward Legal Rights for Natural Objects', *Southern California Law Review*, 45, 450–50.

Taye, Fitalew, Maja Vinde Folkersen, Christopher Fleming, Andrew Buckwell, Brendan Mackey, K.C. Diwakar, Dung Le, Syezlin Hasan, and Chantal Saint Ange. 2021. 'The Drivers of Change in the Economic Value of Global Forest Ecosystem Services: A Meta-Analysis', *Ecological Economics*, 189, 107145.

The Economics of Ecosystems and Biodiversity.·2010. *The Economics of Ecosystems and Biodiversity: Mainstreaming the Economics of Nature: A Synthesis of the Approach, Conclusions and Recommendations of TEEB*, (Malta: Progress Press), <https://www.unep.org/resources/report/economics-ecosystems-and-biodiversity-mainstreaming-economics-nature-synthesis> [Accessed 9 October 2021].

Thompson, G., J. Frances, R. Levacic, and J. Mitchell. 1991. *Markets, Hierarchies and Networks: The Coordination of Social Life* (Thousand Oaks, CA: Sage).

Tolessa, Terefe, Hailu Gessese, Motuma Tolera, and Moges Kidane. 2018. 'Changes in Ecosystem Service Values in Response to Changes in Landscape Composition in the Central Highlands of Ethiopia', *Environmental Processes*, 5 (3), 483–501.

United Nations, European Union, Food and Agriculture Organization of the United Nations, Organisation for Economic Co-operation and Development, and World Bank Group.·2014. *System of Environmental Economic Accounting 2012–Experimental Ecosystem Accounting*, (New York: United Nations), <https://unstats.un.org/unsd/envaccounting/seeaRev/eea_final_en.pd>f [Accessed 23 January 2022].

Venn, Tyron, and John Quiggin. 2007. 'Accommodating Indigenous Cultural Heritage Values in Resource Assessment: Cape York Peninsula and the Murray–Darling Basin, Australia', *Ecological Economics*, 61 (2), 334–44.

Vivid Economics.·2021. *The Greenness of Stimulus*, (London and New York: Vivid Economics), <https://www.f4b-initiative.net/publications-1/greenness-of-stimulus-index—6th-edition> [Accessed 29 October 2021].

Wallbott, Linda, Giuseppina Siciliano, and Markus Lederer. 2019. 'Beyond PES and REDD+: Costa Rica on the Way to Climate-Smart Landscape Management?', *Ecology and Society*, 24 (1).

Wilson, Matthew A., and Richard B. Howarth. 2002. 'Discourse-Based Valuation of Ecosystem Services: Establishing Fair Outcomes through Group Deliberation', *Ecological Economics*, 41 (3), 431–43.

Susan Park

Chapter 4
The World Bank (Group) and sustainable development

Abstract: The World Bank Group is an influential player in financing sustainable development. It provides loans, investments, guarantees and technical assistance to developing states. Since the turn to sustainable development in the 1980s, the Bank has established rigorous environmental and social safeguards for its development lending. In response to climate politics, the World Bank has also engaged in climate financing since the mid-1990s. Over the last two decades, the Bank has restructured to focus on public private partnerships while highlighting its provision of global public goods. This chapter has three aims: first to examine how the World Bank has contributed to sustainable development financing, moving from inaction towards a doing good approach. Second, it outlines how the World Bank's internal changes have been accompanied by its efforts to be the vehicle for green funding. Third, the chapter outlines how its consolidation as the World Bank Group over the past decade has facilitated the private sector orientation of this public institution, in addition to public private partnerships to realise global public goods such as biodiversity, climate and public health. The axes of contention remain how to offer sustainable development solutions while addressing different actors needs in ways that provide environmental payoffs.

Keywords: sustainable development, financing, development, climate finance, world bank, world bank group, COVID-19

Introduction

The World Bank is an influential player in financing for sustainable development as the world's premier multilateral development bank (MDB). The MDBs are one of the primary means for states to channel international development assistance to developing states (Organisation for Economic Co-operation and Development 2018). The World Bank provides loans, investments, guarantees, and technical assistance to states for development projects and programmes, and its private sector arm, the International Finance Corporation (IFC) both lends and invests in companies in developing countries to achieve this, and with three other institutions they comprise the World Bank Group. These other institutions are Disputes, which is not a lending body, the Multilateral Investment Guarantee Agency (MIGA) that provides political risk insurance for its borrower Member States and the International Development

https://doi.org/10.1515/9783110733488-004

Association which lends and provides grants to the lowest-income developing states. MIGA has followed the pattern identified here of being challenged for its environmental impact and having to establish environmental and social policies as the World Bank and IFC (see Park 2010). Since the turn to sustainable development in the 1980s, the World Bank has established rigorous environmental and social safeguards for its development lending, which were seen as the gold standard for international development project lending. In the 1990s, the World Bank began to move into climate financing, while IFC became a larger and more prominent player in rule-making and international project lending to the private sector in developing states.

This chapter has three aims: first to examine how the World Bank has contributed to financing for sustainable development, moving from its initial refusal to accede that its actions had environmental consequences towards a doing good focus. Second, it aims to outline how the World Bank's internal changes, such as its broader shift towards identifying stand-alone green projects in its portfolio and expanding expertise in sustainable development, was accompanied by its efforts to be the vehicle for green funding. It became an implementer of Global Environment Facility projects, and as a project developer, broker and consultant in carbon markets established as part of Conference of the Parties' commitments under the UNFCCC. Third, the chapter outlines how its consolidation as the World Bank Group over the past decade has facilitated the private sector orientation of this public institution, in addition to public private partnerships to realise global public goods such as biodiversity, climate and public health.

This gets to the internal weaknesses of the World Bank Group, from pledging to reduce upstream lending for oil and gas projects for borrowers to prevent catastrophic climate change while also preserving the need for economically viable energy solutions for developing countries. The axes of contention therefore remain how to offer sustainable development solutions while preserving borrower ownership, how to offset private sector processes while maintaining its focus on public goods, and how to provide post-COVID-19 financing for reducing carbon intensive development in ways that provide the payoffs intended for the environment.

The World Bank and the beginning of sustainable development finance

The World Bank was initially regarded as a leader for introducing environmentally aware criteria into its policies, and for establishing an Office of the Environment in 1970 (Park and Vetterlein 2010). These changes were established for three reasons: economic, political and intellectual. First, there was an increasing realisation that environmental pollution was financially costly to mitigate. Second, states began galvanising in preparation for the United Nations Conference on the Human Environment in Stockholm in 1972. The Bank felt threatened and thus sought to expand its own influence by pre-empting the emergence of an environmental organisation that might impinge on its development mandate (Le Prestre 1989: 19). Finally, the US and epistemic communities endorsed the Bank's environmental activities (Kay and Jacobson 1983). At the time, the World Bank used the United States Environment Protection Agency's (US EPA) understanding of the environment to encompass the intersection of environmental degradation and human welfare (Wade 1997: 621, 31). This included three main areas: public health, the natural and urban environment, and a social dimension (including Indigenous peoples), although early work focussed on health and 'brown' issues such as pollution, industrial activity, and energy utilisation (Le Prestre 1989: 31).

Before the 1980s the Bank did not have a consistent strategy for environmental issues in its lending activities (Reed 1997: 229), leading environmental non-government organisations (NGOs) to increasingly question the Bank's claim to be environmentally aware. The World Bank initially dismissed this challenge, but the prominence of non-state actors continued to grow (Rich 1994). Increasingly NGOs would work with the media, trade unions, the academy, churches, and parts of the state to mobilise into transnational advocacy networks to campaign against the World Bank financed problem projects that contributed to mass environmental and social devastation (Keck and Sikkink 1998). In the early 1990s decisive Bank activities, detailed below, such as substantial project, policy, and institutional changes alongside the establishment of the Global Environment Facility (GEF) in 1991, and becoming a key player in carbon markets demonstrate how the World Bank shifted from the environment as exception to the environment as routine. While the debate in the early 2000s focussed on whether the Bank could mainstream the environment, the World Bank focussed on three main concerns: economic development, poverty alleviation and the environment.

Transnational advocacy network campaigns make the World Bank the gold standard

Opposition to the World Bank emerged in the early 1980s from environmental NGOs for 'its neglect of . . . green or natural resource issues, which had been driving the growth of environmental consciousness in the West for the previous two decades' (Brenton 1994: 125). It gained momentum in 1983 with the influential 'MDB' reform campaign (Wade 1997: 637), that included the Natural Resources Defense Council, the Environment Defense Fund (now Environment Defense), Environment Policy Institute (now Friends of the Earth – US), National Wildlife Federation, and the Sierra Club (Gutner 2002: 55), and later the Bank Information Centre. Northern NGOs formed a transnational advocacy network with activists and Southern NGOs as the campaign intensified, coalescing around projects as the best way to demonstrate the ill-effects of Bank policies and practices. The campaign focussed on publicising case studies of World Bank – financed ecological disasters in Brazil, India and Indonesia, [as well as bringing Bank practices to the attention of] congressional and parliamentary hearings in the US and a number of European nations, and the mobilisation of media attention in both the developed and the developing world (Rich 1995: 189).

Previous statements by the World Bank assured members and critics that the destruction would have been worse without the Bank's involvement (Caufield 1996: 177). In 1986, then Bank President Clausen attempted to reconcile the World Bank and NGOs by asking for dialogue, which was then taken up by President Conable. This was seen as tactical, yet it had a profound influence on the way in which the Bank would approach environmental issues in the future (Wade 1997: 670–73). By 1987, the World Bank began to take an alternative approach to the perceived indifference towards NGOs (Le Prestre 1989: 193, 98). The Bank moved from explicitly ignoring, then rejecting, NGO claims, to engaging and responding to issues with more comprehensive measures.

An internal Bank restructure in 1987 integrated environmental issues into the Bank through 'integrating environmental considerations into the mainstream of the Bank's country programs' (Piddington 1992: 216) A central Environment Department was established in mid-1987 to replace the Office of the Environment (Nielson and Tierney 2003: 259). The Environment Department was to act as a 'monitor and mentor' to the vice presidents of the (then four) regional offices. Within each of the regional offices a small environmental unit was established in the Technical Department with five to ten staff (Piddington 1992: 216). These changes attempted to move the Bank from the 'environment as exception' to 'environment as routine' (Wade 1997: 675).

The Environment Department did not initially function as planned. With no direction, no leadership, a small staff, the Environment Department struggled to make an impact. The Environment Department focussed on ecological issues in response to NGO criticism, and the lack of brown (pollution) issue specialists and environmental economists meant that there was little integration between the Environment Department and the rest of the Bank (Nielson and Tierney 2003: 260). Operations staff opposed the Environment Department because it lacked 'monitorable objectives' and the means to integrate the environment into decision-making processes.

However, this was offset by the Environment Department's attempt to integrate environmental criteria into the rest of the Bank's work by recruiting environmental specialists, launching training courses on environmental analysis, preparing environmental projects and later National Environmental Action Plans (NEAPs) (Wade 1997: 680). The changes undertaken by the World Bank were incremental but demonstrate that the Bank was incorporating environmental concerns.

All through the 1970s and into the 1980s the Bank was considered a leading advocate of environmental protection among those concerned with such issues. Yet having acquired the mantle of leadership, the Bank downplayed environmental issues in the years that followed, both to the outside world and still more to itself (Wade 1997: 623).

In the aftermath of the 1972 UN Conference on the Human Environment, President McNamara made no mention of the environment in his annual report to the Board of Directors indicating his next five-year plan, and environmental considerations then lapsed without being integrated into actual Bank practice. After the 1987 Bank restructure, NGOs and the US continued to pressure the Bank for change. This led the Bank to include environmental assessment procedures in the project preparation phase, while the Bank became the largest centre for research on the environment and development. By the mid-1990s, the Bank had assisted almost all its borrowers to prepare NEAPs linking environmental criteria into macroeconomic country policies, whole incorporating the environment into its overall mandate via its mission statement.

Wade (1997: 709–10) argues that from 'around 1992 and 1993 the more comprehensive ideas of the "environmental management" paradigm began to take hold at senior management and operational levels' because of mass campaigns by transnational advocacy networks. The Bank was also aiming to reposition itself as an environmental protector via the new pilot programme, the GEF, in conjunction with United Nations Environment Program and United Nations Development Programme. The World Development Report for 1992, titled *Development and the Environment* signalled a decisive shift by the World Bank towards full incorporation of sustainable development (World Bank 1992).

Another Bank restructure at the same time further mainstreamed the environment from 1993. This established a new vice presidency for the environment with a larger and more centralised Environmentally and Socially Sustainable Department (ESSD) (Wade 1997: 710–12). By 1996, environmental issues had become central to the Bank's overall strategy for its borrowers (Haas and Haas 1995), which scholars argue demonstrated a willingness to incorporate environmental ideas into its neo-liberal approach (Goldman 2005). Moreover, expenditure on environmental work, including research and project preparation, increased at a rate of 90% per year (Wade 1997: 611; Goldman 2005). The number of environmental specialists within the Bank was five in the mid-1980s, but by 2000 had risen to 300 (Nielson and Tierney 2003: 264). From 1989, the number of environmental projects and the amount lent for stand-alone environmental projects increased cumulatively. Overall, between 1980 and 1999 the World Bank provided one–third of all environmental aid, increasing its environmental aid by 89% in this period (Hicks et al. 2008: 188). Over three decades, the World Bank would engage with external stakeholders to create a suite of ten environmental and social safeguard policies designed to protect people and their environment, which became the gold standard for international project finance (Hunter 2008).

In the 1990s Bank watchers argued that institutional difficulties stymied environmental mainstreaming (Wade 1997), leading to greenwashing (Caufield 1996;

Rich 1994). Since then, scholars have identified difficulties in the Bank's ability to implement donor demands for greater sustainability pointing to both antinomic delegation from Member States and organisational hypocrisy on behalf of the Bank (Gutner 2005; Weaver 2008). Antinomic delegation is when Member States provide international organisations like the World Bank with issues to address which perhaps may be unsolvable such as poverty alleviation, which sets up difficulties in being able to measure the effectiveness of the organisation in meeting an unattainable goal within the framework of a single organisation. This is compounded by Weaver's identification of organisational hypocrisy where the World Bank seeks to try to offset the interests and competing demands of various Member States and stakeholders. This contributes to hypocrisy because the various units within the organisation may be unable to reconcile competing and often opposing objectives.

Buntaine (2016) outlines four control mechanisms available to Member States to improve the Bank's performance, while acknowledging that sustainable development must go beyond donor driven demands: administrative procedures, accountability mechanisms, evaluation and strategic plans. Administrative procedures can be used to ensure that World Bank staff assess environmental impacts and establish environmental management plans before a project is approved. The World Bank Inspection Panel is an accountability mechanism whereby people within the project area can complain if they are or may suffer environmental and social harm because of the project. This is a last resort process if their issues have not been addressed by Bank management. The accountability process then can feedback into what types of projects and borrowers are unable to meet the Bank's environmental and social standards. Evaluation is a means of determining the outcome of past lending although the Bank's lending approval imperative means that learning remains a challenge. Donors focus on environmental improving projects linked to global public goods (discussed below) go beyond the Bank's evaluations of projects within the Bank's country assistance framework for lending. Finally, strategic planning can be used by the World Bank's Member States to help direct the organisation but without challenging the Bank's lending imperative culture makes it difficult to ensure the World Bank can successfully provide environmentally improving outcomes through its project and programme lending.

GEF

As with its initial turn to sustainable development, the World Bank feared the creation of a new organisation to finance transboundary environmental problems in the prelude to the 1992 United Nations Conference on Environment and Development (UNCED). The GEF was nonetheless created as a pilot facility in 1991 initially to facilitate financing for international environmental agreements to be agreed upon at UNCED. It became a permanent organisation in 1994, and now covers biodiversity, climate change, international waters, land degradation, the ozone layer and persistent organic pollutants. The creation and governance of the GEF reflects a careful balance of developed and donor interests (Young 2002). The World Bank was able to retain its turf however, because it became a project implementer of GEF projects. This means that GEF funds are administered by the Bank but are not part of the Bank's daily operations. Hicks et al (2008: 188) document how the GEF was the fifth largest environmental aid provider in the 1990s but has the greenest portfolio, which is unsurprising given its mandate. In comparison, the World Bank, which is the largest lender, ranks fourteenth in terms of green aid. This is backed by research highlighting that the Bank's core environmental projects are small (approximately seven million on average) and are largely financed through grants from the GEF, the Montreal Protocol Multilateral Fund, or carbon funds (Marschinski and Behrle 2009: 107). This underscores the fact that a significant portion of the Bank's portfolio does not contribute directly to improving environmental outcomes. Nevertheless, by 2009 the World Bank claimed that 74% of its lending through the World Bank (not International Development Association (IDA)) significantly addressed climate change (Michaelowa and Michaelowa 2011: 260).

Partnerships

In addition to the World Bank's country directed project and programme lending for sustainable development, the organisation has recognised the importance of global public goods, such as health, climate and biodiversity from which all states benefit. The World Bank has been described as a 'governance entrepreneur' in its work on creating partnerships with the private sector and NGOs (Andonova 2017) in these areas. Bank Presidents Zoellick and Kim extolled the virtues of working in partnerships to provide global governance beyond the limitations of international organisations and standard Bank lending to meet developing states needs and the Millennium and Sustainable Development Goals. Andonova argues that the Bank used partnerships as a strategy to manage juxtaposing pressures from globalisation and rising public expectations. Andonova suggests that this exemplifies quasi-endogenous institutional change because Bank Presidents Wolfensohn and Zoellick sought to strategically promote these new governance arrangements as a means of advancing the legitimacy, resources and mission of the organisation during turbulent times.

As a result, the Bank increasingly directed its energy to environmental partnerships from 1999, with a focus clean energy, climate, biodiversity and reducing chemical and industrial risks. By 2011, the World Bank had invested more than double the amount in environmental partnerships compared with public health, despite the well-known partnerships such as the Global Fund to Fight AIDS, Tuberculosis and Malaria and the Global Alliance for Immunizations and Vaccines. Not only was this a strategic move to manage expectations by becoming a lead partnership entrepreneur, but the World Bank is also part of a broader pattern of international organisations. As a whole, international organisations have generated more than 80% of partnerships compared with other actors (Andonova 2017: 124–28).

However, despite being the largest financier of global biodiversity initiatives, World Bank public private partnerships have been found not to deliver in terms of the supposed benefits partnerships bring increasing democracy, innovation, and funding (Kramarz 2020). Kramarz examined two biodiversity partnerships between the World Bank and environmental NGOs. The first, the Critical Ecosystems Partnership Fund was established with Conservation International, one of the largest environmental NGOs in biodiversity. The World Bank heralded this as a means of enabling the voice of civil society but its operation of the partnership was to cement a hierarchical and command and control style of management at odds with the partnerships small structure and innovative aspirations. This, they argue, stems from the organisational bureaucratic focus of the Bank to ensure the timely release of funds, and follow its internal operational processes and reporting requirements (Kramarz 2020: 91).

The second case, the Global Invasive Species Program (GISP) also established in the mid-1990s was a multi-stakeholder partnership with the International Union for the Conservation for Nature, the Commonwealth Agricultural Bureau International, and the Scientific Committee on Problems of the Environment. It would later expand to include The Nature Conservancy and the South African National Biodiversity Institute. Again, Kramarz (2020) highlights how the World Bank's attempt to highlight a global issue, invasive species, through an innovative process of networking, was undermined by its bureaucratic style. The GISP was the worst ranked global partnership as evaluated by the Bank itself. This was caused by the Bank's attempts to fit the network of scientists working on invasive species into the bureaucratic mould needed by the World Bank. Against the wishes of the network, it pressured the network to relocate to South African from the US to receive funding. Further, it was unable to ensure widespread internal Bank support for the network that would have given a boost to the issue of invasive species, owing to its environmental technical specialists being siloed in the institution (Kramarz 2020: 112–3). The partnerships for biodiversity reveal the limits of the World Bank's ability to provide global public goods.

Privatising sustainable development finance

The shift towards embracing private sector financing for sustainable development took place from the 1990s. While the private sector finance arm of the World Bank Group, the IFC, had existed since 1956, it was not until financial liberalisation in developing countries gained pace that its role became more prominent. The IFC has grown substantially from the 1990s as a means of investing in and lending to the private sector in developing states. As detailed below, it has also become a major driver within the World Bank Group, which has turned towards prioritising private sector funding for development, while the World Bank has also strived to increase its capital through private sector strategies (da Conceição-Heldt and Dörfler 2021). This has been in response to a decline in favouring public funding for international development and a broader crisis in multilateralism. However, the IFC was unable to secure a role in climate finance on a par with the World Bank (Michaelowa and Michaelowa 2011: 263).

Beginning in the 1990s, the IFC mimicked the World Bank in its sustainable development journey (Park 2005). Pre-1998 it had used some of the Bank's environmental and social policies informally. As with the World Bank, it would come under scrutiny for its impacts on people and the environment after a mass transnational campaign, this time against a large-scale dam project partly financed and invested in by the IFC on the Bio-Bio River in Chile in 1992. The financing and execution of the Pangue Dam not only contributed to accelerating deforestation of the region and led to unchecked migration, but it also revealed a highly secretive arrangement between IFC and the company undertaking the project Endesa, which contributed to the human rights abuses of the local Indigenous Pehuenche (Downing 1996; Hair 1997). The campaign against the dam contributed to the creation of an accountability mechanism for the World Bank Group called the Compliance Advisor/Ombudsman (CAO) in 1999 and the upgrading of its environmental and social policies.

The World Bank group's performance standards

After reeling from the campaign against the Pangue Dam, the IFC sought to better integrate its environmental and social safeguard policies into its work, which it did by formally adopting and adapting the World Bank's Environmental and Social Safeguard Policies in 1998. Soon after, an internal review by the Compliance Advisor Ombudsman revealed 'the weak system supporting the SPs [safeguard policies], including lack of specific objectives, weak project monitoring and supervision, and poor integration of SPs into IFC's core business' (CAO 2003: 7). In response, the IFC launched its Sustainability Initiative in 2001 to better integrate environmental ideas within the World Bank Group, dramatically increasing its environment staff, and creating new environmental units. The initiative embodied a triple bottom line approach which equals a commitment to 'people, the planet and profits' (International Finance Corporation 2002; IFC 2012b).

From 2003 the IFC's standards would be translated into the Equator Principles for private sector financiers to manage their environmental and social risk (Hunter 2008: 450). These principles were initiated by IFC and demonstrate how IFC has begun to diffuse sustainable development throughout the project finance industry. In 2006, it radically altered its approach to environmental and social policies, reframing its environmental and social safeguards into a sustainability framework with performance standards. This translated the SPs to hold the companies it lends and invests in to account, into an internal risk management framework for companies to use themselves (Wright 2006). This led IFC to include labour protections for the first time. IFC's most recent performance standards recognise that business must respect human rights, and it explicitly adopted free, prior and informed consent for Indigenous peoples (IFC 2012a: 5, 22; IFC 2012b: 1; Mares 2019: 523; Razzaque 2019: 204). The import of IFC cannot be understated. Not only has it shaped how the private international development project finance industry should understand environmental and social aspects of its lending, it has, in turn, reshaped the World Bank's approach to sustainability. This is evidenced by the Bank's 2018 Environmental and Social Framework, which also now incorporates Free Prior and Informed Consent and labour standards (Mares 2019).

Vehicles for financing sustainable development

In 2019, President Jim Kim suddenly resigned from the World Bank, stating that he could better meet the Bank's mission to end extreme poverty from the private sector. Symbolically, this undermines the very need for a multilateral development institution. Kim had steered the Bank throughout the 2000s to take advantage of the massive flows of private sector investment to developing states. Branding itself the One World Bank Group, the World Bank works more closely with the IFC, and IFC now contributes substantial sums to the IDA. The IDA, created in 1960, is a separate financing facility administered by the World Bank that provides grants and loans to low-income borrowers. Together the World Bank Group lent nearly $64 billion in 2018. Until recently, IDA was solely financed by donor Member States through three-year negotiated replenishment rounds, of which the US used to be the largest donor. It was US control over IDA replenishments that enabled the US to advance environmental NGOs agenda to green the Bank (Park 2010). In 2007 IFC began providing funding for IDA replenishments (Lowery 2013). IFC has now provided over $2.2 billion in funding for IDA, which arguably removes donor leverage to enact further change within the World Bank. IFC has also created a range of private sector financing instruments for IDA including concessional partner loans and IDA bonds (IFC n.d.), although it is unclear how much they contribute to sustainable development.

Curbing lending for fossil fuels

The World Bank remains driven by its official mandate to facilitate economic growth for development and its mission to alleviate poverty and foster sustainable development. Tensions arise between the need for energy and infrastructure, and the urgent need to eliminate the use of fossil fuels given the likelihood of catastrophic climate change. A World Resources Institute (WRI) review discovered that over 50% of the World Bank's energy sector portfolio in 2007 did not address climate change (Newell 2009: 429; WRI 2008). Demands to reduce lending for dirty projects such as coal-fired power plants, oil and natural gas again came from NGOs and powerful states like the US and European states. In 2013 the Bank recognised the need to respond and agreed to reduce investing in new coal powered projects, stating that it would continue to do so in extremely rare circumstances (Volcovici, Shalal, and Abnett 2021). In 2019 the Bank then agreed to stop funding upstream oil and gas projects. Currently, the Bank is planning a new climate strategy to align its financing to the objectives of the Paris Agreement in response to states nationally determined commitments to meet the Paris Agreement (Volcovici, Shalal, and Abnett 2021). While still in the draft phase, and absent specific commitments, the Bank needs to decide whether it will champion the transition to a decarbonised world through its development lending for projects and programmes.

Stimulating climate finance

Beyond its traditional lending focus and partnership work, the World Bank eagerly moved to meet the needs of its Member States commitments to the UNFCCC. The Conference of the Parties agreed to establish a range of financing mechanisms for mitigating and adapting to climate change. Carbon markets were agreed upon under the 1997 Kyoto Protocol as well as Joint Implementation and the Clean Development Mechanism (CDM). The CDM is part of 'a broader trajectory of voluntary market-based instruments consistent with the trend towards the "marketization of environmental governance"' (Newell 2009: 431). The CDM awards certified GHG emissions reduction credits from projects in developing states (Michaelowa and Michaelowa 2011: 262). Again, the Bank seized the opportunity to take advantage of its technical environmental and economic expertise within the Environment Department and address core borrower constituencies (Andonova 2017: 129–30). Two roles, within the CDM and in managing Climate Investment Funds, are worth exploring in more detail.

The World Bank in the CDM

As the CDM matured, the Bank created multiple roles for itself in the emerging carbon markets. It created a Carbon Finance Unit within the ESSD Vice Presidency to undertake its climate finance work. Critics have accused the Bank of being a climate profiteer and its operations have been interrogated to identify how it contributes to carbon markets while meeting its sustainable development objectives through its ordinary lending. It now has a competitive (and sometimes unfair) advantage as it 'directly acts as a project developer, broker and consultant for both the supply and the demand-side of the [CDM] market' (Michaelowa and Michaelowa 2011: 260) This means that some consider the World Bank to have an unfair advantage within the CDM market because it manages trust funds in carbon markets while also competing with private investors and private trust funds (Michaelowa and Michaelowa 2011: 260). This returns to the question of the value add of international organisations. The World Bank was created to provide loans to developing countries that were unable to obtain private financing at reasonable rates.

In the creation of new innovative governance arrangements, the World Bank was able to help catalyse new carbon finance markets (detailed further below), although concerns have been raised as to whether the World Bank is crowding in or crowding out competition with private market actors. Crowding in activities include providing development assistance to states through its ordinary programme and project lending to establish borrower capacity for CDM project development. Crowding out, or displacing market actors, does also seem to have occurred. For example, when the World Bank has taken advantage of its position with borrowers to obtain contracts for CDM projects and where the Bank has bene able to use its relations with developing countries to gain CERs [certified emissions reductions] at less than market value (Michaelowa and Michaelowa 2011: 264). This means that the World Bank does have an advantage over its private sector competitors and its peculiar role as a public investor in a now mature private market should be clarified. The basis for the World Bank's position in the CDM has been that it can generate positive sustainable development externalities. Yet its efforts in the CDM do not demonstrate evidence that it can advance its Sustainable Development Goals such as for example by using CDM projects for promoting poverty alleviation. Indeed, its efforts do not necessarily meet the external gold standard sustainable development for CDM projects, or projects that not only meet CDM criteria but also demonstrate positive development components such as having positive social and employment effects (Michaelowa and Michaelowa 2011: 264). To date, there is no evidence that the World Bank would exit the CDM market as a competitor despite evidence that it is crowding out market actors and not providing more positive development outcomes.

Climate investment funds

As the CDM was slowly emerging, the World Bank also presented an alternative by launching its Global Carbon Initiative to the UN in 1997. The Carbon Financing Unit created new financing instruments called Climate Investment Funds (CIFs), beginning with the world's first global carbon fund, the Prototype Carbon Fund, in 1999. The World Bank established the Prototype Carbon Fund (PCF) as an experimental learning institution to 'support the implementation of project-based reductions of greenhouse gas emissions envisaged by the Kyoto Protocol' (Andonova 2017: 130) Given the limited knowledge and experience of both transition and developing states, the Bank was able to provide 'considerable capacity and institution building in the areas of project preparation, assessment of baseline scenarios, carbon accounting, granting of emission reduction credits, and transaction transparency' (Andonova 2017: 130). As Andonova (2017) notes, the Bank moved quickly to take advantage of the direction of negotiations, establishing the PCF in its first phase from 2000 to 2012 with industrial states and private sector support before the Kyoto Protocol agreements on flexible mechanisms had been concluded in 2001 and before it had come into effect in 2005 (Andonova 2017: 130).

The PCF helped catalyse the market, mobilising capital for development projects from the public and private sector to reduce carbon emissions in developing countries. The PCF therefore helped to generate both 'sufficient capacity and knowledge to enable the take-off of carbon markets' (Andonova 2017: 130). The Bank was able to insulate itself from criticism of potential failure on the basis that the PCF was easily reversible (Andonova 2017: 130–31). The Bank also wanted to co-finance emissions reduction projects with the GEF, which the US rejected (Michaelowa and Michaelowa 2011: 262). By 2010, it was managing 11 of 96 funds managing carbon finance or one-sixth of the market (Alberola and Stephen 2010). This included ten new carbon funds within the PCF's first seven years of operation including the Community Development Carbon Fund (2003), the Bio Carbon Fund (2004; tranche 2, 2007), the Netherlands CDM and Facility (2002), the Netherlands European Carbon Facility (2004), the Italian Carbon Fund (2004), the Danish Carbon Fund (2005), the Spanish Carbon Fund (2006), the Umbrella Carbon Facility (2006), the Carbon Fund for Europe (2007), and the Forest Carbon Partnership Facility (Andonova 2017: 131).

As Newell states, the World Bank helps create markets and then creates their governance mechanisms (2009: 426). Indeed, the Bank itself identified its positive impact in terms of both a greater focus of its financing going towards African states, and that its approach to defining eligibility, calculating emissions, and monitoring projects were adopted up by the CDM (World Bank 2009). Critics of the CIFs argued that they focussed on mitigating GHG emissions on middle-income countries with polluting industries supporting the interests of financiers with little attention to the needs of low-income states, and its sustainable development mission. In response the World Bank would establish a broader range of CIFs to include least developed states, such as the Climate Partnership Facility and the Forest Carbon Partnership Facility. The CIFs were considered successes within and outside the Bank generating 16 billion dollars in climate finance up to 2011. By then all of the World Bank's major donors had contributed to the CIFs, demonstrating their commitment to reducing GHG emissions in international development lending. As a result of sustained pressure from developing states and activists, the CIF Board was equalised to have representatives from developed and developing states, as well as input from the private sector and civil society (Andonova 2017: 131).

In broader climate negotiations in 2009, developed states agreed to provide $30 billion in additional financing by 2012, and an annual total of $100 billion of mobilised funds by 2020, to meet developing states climate mitigation and adaptation needs (Weikmans and Roberts 2019). While states have not met their commitments, they did create the Green Climate Fund (GCF) in 2015 of which the World Bank was made its trustee. While the GCF experienced both organisational and political difficulties (Bowman and Minas 2019), the role of the Bank in climate finance should not be underestimated. Not only has the World Bank in the past pre-empted and helped shape carbon markets, currently states provide approximately the same amount (approximately $30 billion) of climate finance through both bilateral and multilateral vehicles and primarily for mitigation (OECD 2020: 7).

Conclusion

The chapter has identified the role the World Bank has played in sustainable development financing. From being touted as an environment leader in the 1970s to then rejecting NGO claims that its projects cause environmental and social harm in the 1980s and 1990s. The Bank then recognised that it did contribute to harm and created new policies, units and environmental staff to address these issues in the 1990s and 2000s. Yet it still financed 'dirty projects' despite attempts to limit financing for coal-fired power plants, oil and natural gas. In the 1990s the Bank also began to shift into partnerships for global public goods like biodiversity with mixed results, while its private sector arm, the IFC went through the same process of rejecting NGO claims to accepting them and improving its efforts. By the 2000s the Bank was working to garner more private sector investment in development by enabling the IFC to contribute to IDA and devise new financing vehicles. Meanwhile, the IFC created and exported its Sustainability Initiative to industry through the Equator Principles and the World Bank's Environmental and Social Framework. The World Bank has played multiple roles in facilitating, acting in and helping to govern climate financing through the CDM and CIFs. The axes of contention remain for the Bank: how to offer sustainable development solutions while preserving borrower ownership, how to offset private sector processes while maintaining its focus on public goods including health, and how to provide post-COVID-19 financing for reducing carbon intensive development in ways that provide the payoffs intended for the environment.

References

Alberola, E., and N. Stephen, 2010, *Carbon Funds in 2010: Investment in Kyoto Credits and Emissions Reductions*, Climate Report 23. Paris: CDC Climate Research.

Andonova, L. 2017. *Governance Entrepreneurs. International Organizations and the Rise of Global Public-Private Partnerships* (Cambridge, UK: Cambridge University Press).

Bowman, M., & Minas, S. (2019). Resilience through interlinkage: the green climate fund and climate finance governance. *Climate policy*, 19 (3), 342–353.

Brenton, T. 1994. *The Greening of Machiavelli: The Evolution of International Environmental Politics* (London: Earthscan Publications).

Buntaine, M. 2016. *Giving Aid Effectively* (Oxford: Oxford University Press).

Caufield, C. 1996. *Masters of Illusion: The World Bank and the Poverty of Nations* (London: Macmillan).

da Conceição-Heldt, Eugénia, and Thomas Dörfler. 2021. 'Orchestrating Private Investors for Development: How the World Bank Revitalizes', *Regulation and Governance*.

Downing, T., 1996, 'A Participatory Interim Evaluation of the Pehuen Foundation,' International Finance Corporation 2067, AGRA Earth and Environment, Downing and Associates.

Goldman, M. 2005. *Imperial Nature: The World Bank and Struggles for Social Justice in the Age of Globalization* (New Haven, US: Yale University Press).

Gutner, Tamar. 2002. *Banking on the Environment: Multilateral Development Banks and Their Environmental Performance in Central and Eastern Europe* (Cambridge, MA: MIT Press).

——. 2005. 'Explaining the Gaps between Mandate and Performance: Agency Theory and World Bank Environmental Reform', *Global Environmental Politics*, 5 (2), 10–37.

Haas, Peter M., and Ernst B. Haas. 1995. 'Learning to Learn: Improving International Governance', *Global Governance*, 1, 255–84.

Hair, J., 1997, 'Pangue Hydroelectric Project (Chile): An Independent Review of the International Finance Corporation's Compliance with Applicable World Bank Group Environment and Social Requirements,' IFC Internal Review, Washington D.C., IFC.

Hicks, Robert L., Bradley C. Parks, J. Timmons Roberts, and Michael J. Tierney. 2008. *Greening Aid?: Understanding the Environmental Impact of Development Assistance* (Oxford: Oxford University Press).

Hunter, David B. 2008. 'Civil Society Networks and the Development of Environmental Standards at International Financial Institutions', *Chicago Journal of International Law*, 8 (2).

International Finance Corporation, 2012, IFC Sustainability Framework: Policy and Performance Standards on Environmental and Social Sustainability, Access to Information Policy, Washington DC, World Bank Group. Accessed: https://www.ifc.org/wps/wcm/connect/topics_ext_content/ifc_external_corporate_site/sustainability-at-ifc/policies-standards/ifc sustainabilityframework_2012 Cited: 18 October 2019.

International Finance Corporation, 2012b, *The International Bill of Human Rights and IFC Sustainability Framework*, Washington DC, World Bank Group. Accessed: https://www.ifc.org/wps/wcm/connect/topics_ext_content/ifc_external_corporate_site/sustainability-at-ifc/publi cations/ibhr_ifc_sustainability_framework Cited: 18 October 2019.

Kay, David A., and Harold Karan Jacobson. 1983. *Environmental Protection: The International Dimension* (Montclair, NJ: Allanheld, Osmun and Company).

Keck, Margaret E., and Kathryn Sikkink. 1998. *Activists Beyond Borders* (Ithaca, NY and London: Cornell University Press).

Kramarz, Teresa. 2020. *Forgotten Values: The World Bank and Environmental Partnerships* (Cambridge, MA: MIT Press).

Le Prestre, P. 1989. *The World Bank and the Environmental Challenge* (Selinsgrove, US: Susquehanna University Press).

Lowery, C., 2013, "A Proposal for IDA-17: Instead of an Income Transfer, Direct the IFC to Invest Its Time, Resources, and Expertise in IDA Countries," Centre for Global Development Brief March, Centre for Global Development, Washington DC. Cited: A Proposal for IDA-17: Instead of an Income Transfer, Direct the IFC to Invest Its Time, Resources, and Expertise in IDA Countries | Center For Global Development (cgdev.org) Accessed: 7 May 2021.

Mares, R., 2019, "Securing Human Rights through Risk-Management Methods: Breakthrough or Misalignment?" *Leiden Journal of International Law* 32: 517–535.

Marschinski, R., and S. Behrle. 2009. 'The World Bank: Making the Business Case for the Environment.' in Frank Biermann and Bernd Siebenhüner (ed.), *Managers of Global Change: The Influence of International Environmental Bureaucracies* (Cambridge, MA: MIT Press), pp. 101–42

Michaelowa, Axel, and Katharina Michaelowa. 2011. 'Climate Business for Poverty Reduction? The Role of the World Bank', *The Review of International Organizations*, 6 (3-4), 259–86.

Newell, P. 2009, "Varieties of CDM Governance: Some Reflections," *The Journal of Environment & Development*, 18, 425–435.

Nielson, Daniel L., and Michael J. Tierney. 2003. 'Delegation to International Organizations: Agency Theory and World Bank Environmental Reform', *International Organization*, 57 (2), 241–76.

Organisation for Economic Co-operation and Development.·2018. *Multilateral Development Finance: Towards a New Pact on Multilateralism to Achieve the 2030 Agenda Together*, (Geneva: OECD), <http://www.oecd.org/dac/financing-sustainable-development/develop ment-finance-topics/Multilateral-Development-Finance-Highlights-2018.pdf > [Accessed 20 September 2019].

Park, S., 2005, 'How Transnational Environmental Advocacy Networks Socialise IFIs: A Case Study of the International Finance Corporation' *Global Environmental Politics*, 5(4), 95–119.

Park, Susan. 2010. *World Bank Group Interactions with Environmentalists: Changing International Organisation Identities* (Manchester: Manchester University Press).

Park, Susan, and Antje Vetterlein. 2010. *Owning Development: Creating Policy Norms in the IMF and the World Bank* (Cambridge, UK: Cambridge University Press).

Piddington, K. 1992. 'The Role of the World Bank.' in A. Hurrell and B. Kingsbury (eds.), *The International Politics of the Environment: Actors, Interests, and Institutions* (Oxford: Clarendon Press), pp. 212–27

Razzaque, J., 2019, 'A Stock-Taking of FPIC Standards in International Environmental Law,' in Turner, S., D. Shelton, J. Razzaque, O. McIntyre, J. May (eds), 2019, *Environmental Rights: The Development of Standards*, Cambridge, Cambridge University Press: 195–221.

Reed, D. 1997. 'The Environmental Legacy of Bretton Woods: The World Bank.' in O. Young (ed.), *Global Governance: Drawing Insights from the Environmental Experience* (Cambridge, MA: MIT Press), pp. 227–45

Rich, Bruce. 1994. *Mortgaging the Earth: World Bank, Environmental Impoverishment and the Crisis of Development* (Boston: Beacon Press).

——. 1995. *Statement of Bruce Rich on Behalf of Environmental Defense Fund, National Wildlife Federation, Sierra Club, Greenpeace, before the United States Congress House Committee on*

Banking and Financial Services Subcommittee on Domestic and International Monetary Policy Concerning the World Bank. (Washington DC: Environmental Defense Fund)

Volcovici, V., A. Shalal, and K. Abnett, 2021, 'Exclusive: World Bank revises climate policy but stops short of halting fossil fuel funding,' April 1, 2021, Reuters, Accessed: 2 June 2021. Cited: https://www.reuters.com/article/climate-change-worldbank-exclusive-int-idUSKBN2BN3HE

Wade, R. 1997. 'Greening the Bank: The Struggle over the Environment 1970-1995.' in J. Lewis and R.C Webb D. Kapur (ed.), *The World Bank: Its First Half Century* (Washington DC: Brookings Institute), pp. 611–734

Weaver, C. 2008. *The Hypocrisy Trap: The World Bank and the Poverty of Reform* (Princeton: Princeton University Press).

Weikmans, R., and J. Timmons Roberts, 2019, "The International Climate Finance Accounting Muddle: Is there Hope on the Horizon?" *Climate and Development*, 11 (2): 97–111.

World Bank. 1992. *Development and the Environment.* (Washington DC: World Bank)

Wright, C., 2006, 'From 'Safeguards' to 'Sustainability': The Evolution of Environmental Discourse within the International Finance Corporation,' in D. Stone and C. Wright (eds.), *World Bank and Governance: A Decade of Reform and Reaction*, London and New York, Routledge: 67–87.

Young, Zoe. 2002. *A New Green Order? The World Bank and the Politics of the Global Environment Facility* (London: Pluto Press).

Edward A. Morgan and Andrew Buckwell

Chapter 5
Landscape planning and economics for sustainable finance

Abstract: This chapter examines and synthesises the key issues in planning and economics at a landscape level and demonstrates how they can support each other to produce sustainable and more just outcomes. Currently, many landscapes are managed with a focus on unsustainable extractive resource use, driven by conventional finance approaches that ignore or undervalue other benefits the landscapes can provide. This results in unsustainable deforestation, land degradation, biodiversity loss and pollution. Truly sustainable finance requires economic processes that better value the landscape ecosystem services, at a landscape level and that acknowledge the interconnectedness and multi-stakeholder nature of landscapes and their ecosystem services. At the same time, participatory landscape planning processes are a way to combine knowledge and values to help stakeholders identify the benefits they value, decide upon acceptable trade-offs and choose activities to improve wellbeing in dynamic, multifunctional and multi-stakeholder landscapes. This chapter will show how an integrated approach to landscape economics and planning can identify the basis of institutional arrangements that, combined with strong governance, can share benefits more justly while supporting the long-term sustainability of landscapes and their ecosystems.

Keywords: landscape planning, total ecosystem valuation, landscape economics, ecosystem services, integrated landscape management, community wellbeing, stakeholder participation, COVID-19

Introduction

Sustainable finance opportunities are dependent upon and seek to encourage the sustainable use of ecosystems, which requires the sustainable management of land use and resource management. This chapter discusses the importance of thinking about and acting at the landscape level to land uses for sustainable finance.

Land use choices are often led by market demand for raw materials and lead to unsustainable extraction and exploitation of the landscape and accompanying land use change. For example, forest loss and degradation in many areas is driven by industrial exploitation by logging, mining and clearing for agriculture (Bebbington et al. 2018). In other cases, these land use choices are driven by more immediate local welfare issues, such as growing demand for land for subsistence shifting

https://doi.org/10.1515/9783110733488-005

agriculture due to population growth or loss of productivity (Curtis et al. 2018). Sustainable finance provides payments for benefits that do not demand unsustainable use (extraction or use within the capacity of the ecosystems to regenerate). Instead, sustainable finance acknowledges and pays for benefits of ecosystems other than their extractive capacity – such as carbon storage to combat climate change (Leblois, Damette, and Wolfersberger 2017; Samndong et al. 2018) or their benefits for water supply (Angelsen and McNeill 2012; Duchelle, Simonet, et al. 2018), or for conservation benefits generally (Pires 2004; Smith and Porter 2010) – incentivising sustainable land management that seeks to maintain these ecosystems and their benefits.

However, contemporary/conventional efforts at sustainable finance tend to rely on conventional land use approaches that take a narrow, sector-specific approach. Approaches under the general heading of REDD plus ['+'] conservation, sustainable management of forests, enhancement of forest stocks), for example, tend to be linked to sustainable forest management approaches that focus on forestry and industrial timber production and often fail to protect forests or improve socioeconomic outcomes for communities (Pagiola 2008; Porras et al. 2013; Zimmerman and Kormos 2012: 105–41; Sheppard et al. 2020). Payment for ecosystem services (PES) schemes tend to focus on conservation (Duchelle, Simonet, et al. 2018; Duchelle, Sassi, et al. 2018) and may not address food security or other socioeconomic challenges (Porras et al. 2013; Schomers and Matzdorf 2013; CalvetMir et al. 2015). This, in turn, encourages continuation of conventional unsustainable land management, that focuses on productive capacity in a single sector, such as agriculture in sustainable land management (Porras and Asquith 2018).

From an ecosystem services perspective (see Chapter Three), landscapes create multiple ecosystem services (Schomers and Matzdorf 2013; Branca et al. 2013) but many sustainable finance schemes focus on one or a few and fail to recognise the others (de Groot, Wilson, and Boumans 2002). Forests, for example, provide a range of benefits to people across multiple time and geographic scales, including non-use spiritual and cultural services (Vallés-Planells, Galiana, and Van Eetvelde 2014), water flow regulation and water quality benefits for those further down the catchment (Morgan et al. 2021), global and long-run biodiversity (Watson et al. 2018; Reed et al. 2017) and carbon sequestration and storage benefits (Watson et al. 2018; Mackey et al. 2020; Ngoma et al. 2018), and the benefits of avoiding potential pandemics (Dellasala et al. 2020). However, sustainable finance rarely recognises, let alone captures these benefits, while the costs (including effort, direct financial and opportunity costs) of maintaining forest largely falls on the land stewards: local owners, managers or custodians of the forest, who are often Indigenous, customary or traditional custodians.

Swapping out unsustainable finance, driven by industrial extraction, for sustainable finance mechanisms that focus on one sector or one ecosystem service risks imposing land uses on land stewards that fail to address their needs or the

drivers of unsustainable land use change. Thus, more recently, in response to these concerns, researchers and practitioners have discussed how the next step for sustainable finance is a shift to a landscape level and working across landscapes to create green or climate smart landscapes (Mackey et al. 2020: 175–213; Dobson et al. 2020; Duchelle, Sassi, et al. 2018; Nielsen 2016). These approaches recognise that land management is dependent on multiple land uses by multiple stakeholders across a landscape (Reed et al. 2017; Morgan, Cadman, and Mackey 2020; Arts et al. 2017). However, achieving this requires improved tools to support a more holistic landscape approach. This chapter discusses the benefits and challenges of a landscape approach, and how landscape planning and economics can help address these challenges to create (more) sustainable management of land for sustainable finance.

Landscape approaches and sustainable finance

Landscapes are socioecological systems that are influenced by the interaction of their biophysical features with social and cultural influences, generally resulting in a recognisable and relatively stable combinations of land uses and forms (Reed et al. 2016; Sayer et al. 2013: 17–22; Dernier et al. 2015). Landscapes are broadly defined by their biophysical attributes and their ecosystem structure and function but are also affected by social, and especially cultural, attributes, which makes landscapes recognisable on a human level (Selman 2005: 33–42; Tress and Tress 2001).

Integrated landscape approaches (commonly shortened to landscape approaches) apply a holistic focus that considers multiple sectors and stakeholders, reflecting the multifunctional nature of landscapes and they are presented as more sustainable alternatives to more conventional siloed land management approaches (Brown 2015; Taylor and Lennon 2011; Arts et al. 2017; Morgan, Cadman, and Mackey 2020; Reed et al. 2016).

Landscape approaches are usually explicitly aimed at challenging the false dichotomy of trading-off conservation and development (Sayer et al. 2013; Freeman, Duguma, and Minang 2015; Arts et al. 2017) and consequently they align with the goals of sustainable finance. These more holistic and integrated landscapes approaches are increasingly seen the next step for sustainable finance schemes such as PES and REDD+ (Milder et al. 2014; Sayer et al. 2017; Nielsen 2016).

Although there has been limited agreement on what elements constitute a landscape approach and how to implement them (Reed et al. 2017; Reed et al. 2016), there is substantial overlap and growing agreement between the multiple definitions and principles that will help guide landscape approaches (Arts et al. 2017). Landscape approaches derive from an ecological focus and aim to place ecosystems at the centre of land management into land use management, especially the ecosystem approach developed and championed by the Convention on Biological Diversity (Reed et al. 2016; Morgan, Cadman, and Mackey 2020; Convention on Biological Diversity 2007) and often used interchangeably with the landscape approach.

Importantly, landscape approaches aim to integrate the multiple ecological, economic and development, sociocultural and political aspects of the multiple land uses and sectors of a landscape (Shepherd 2008; Smith and Maltby 2003). This includes a range of activities, including landscape planning, landscape governance, landscape design and landscape restoration and conservation (Arts et al. 2017), and focus on multifunctionality, trans disciplinarity, participation, complexity, and sustainability (Freeman, Duguma, and Minang 2015).

The benefits of taking a landscape approach stem from the nature of landscapes, but this brings with it challenges to implementation due to the complexity, multifunctionality and dynamic nature of landscapes.

Landscapes as systems: Dealing with complexity and uncertainty

Defining and delineating a landscape for management purposes is challenging. Dernier et al.'s (2015: 11) definition is typical: ' … a socioecological system that consists of natural and/or human-modified ecosystems, and which is influenced by distinct ecological, historical, economic and sociocultural processes and activities' but could apply to almost any geographical area and provides little guidance on how to separate a landscape or draw a boundary to a landscape. However, Dernier et al.'s definition does share an emphasis on the biophysical, the sociocultural and the interactions between these three with other common definitions and descriptions (see, e.g., Freeman, Duguma, and Minang (2015: 17–22); Dernier et al. (2015)). Hence, landscapes are best understood as (complex adaptive) socio-ecological systems in which multiple feedbacks operate to maintain the landscape in a stable state. Consideration of a landscape as a socioecological system allows management to identify the resources, stakeholders and governance systems that make up the system (Selman 2005; Tress and Tress 2001) and that maintain the ecosystem services(s) that is/are the basis of the finance mechanism. This includes the recognition that landscapes both shape and are shaped by cultural considerations and these should be a part of land management (McGinnis and Ostrom 2014; Ostrom 2009: 33–42; Amo-Rodríguez et al. 2010).

However, treating landscapes as systems brings with it the challenge of complexity and the accompanying uncertainty. Knowledge plays a key role in managing socioecological systems. This will include scientific knowledge about ecosystems and their functions, but it requires the bringing together of multiple knowledges, including local and Indigenous knowledge (Brown 2015; Selman 2004; Mackey and Claudie 2015), and integrating this with social values and cultural considerations (McCarter and Gavin 2014). Crucially, knowledge of complex systems is always uncertain and landscape approaches have to deal with uncertainty, including irreducible uncertainty (Shackeroff and Campbell 2021). Notably, this uncertainty extends to drawing the boundaries of landscapes, which can be contested and unclear. Drawing boundaries for resource management is important (Selman 2004; Burgman, Lindenmayer, and Elith 2005) but in landscapes can be challenging and politically controversial (Martín-López et al. 2017; Ostrom 1990; Duraiappah et al. 2014), requiring participatory approaches to mapping and boundary drawing (Filer 2012; Martín-López et al. 2017; Bryan 2011).

Landscape multifunctionality: Collaboration and avoiding silos

Consideration of landscapes as socioecological systems also recognises that landscapes are multifunctional. Thus, landscape approaches avoid only focussing on one sector or one ecosystem service, with the resulting risks of failing to address the multiple drivers of unsustainable land use change, including social change. Conventional approaches to conservation management have ignored social impacts to displaced local communities and the locking up of forests, preventing any form of resource extraction (Martín-López et al. 2017), while a focus on agriculture and forestry within land management have resulted in loss of forest and a focus on plantations (Tulloch 2007; Phillips 2003; Leblois, Damette, and Wolfersberger 2017).

However, the multifunctionality of landscapes requires the collaboration and coordination of different stakeholders and groups, including across different sectors, who will have different and often conflicting values, wants and needs. Addressing this challenge requires participatory approaches to management and especially the inclusion of communities (Milder et al. 2014; Zimmerman and Kormos 2012; Sayer et al. 2013). This is reflected in calls for more community-based approaches (Selman 2004; Valencia-Sandoval, Flanders, and Kozak 2010), including in sustainable finance schemes (Lane and McDonald 2005); but these often remain governed from the top-down, where investor or donor demands impose requirements on communities (Liu and Opdam 2014: 1; Newton et al. 2015: 2).

Dynamic landscapes: Sustainability and managing change fairly/equitably

Brownson et al. (2020: 148) note that landscape systems are a temporal entity, and their inclusion of time highlights that landscapes are usually considered recognisable as something stable over time, but that change is also a part of landscapes. For example, the UN recognises cultural landscapes, which have been maintained by landscape practices for centuries (Cadman et al. 2016) – the owners, users and managers of the natural resources have sought to harness particular benefits from the ecosystems through ongoing and often changing management practices to maintain them, and the need for protection under the UN highlights the need to respond to change beyond the landscape. This understanding of change in a landscape is especially important when considering landscapes for sustainable finance. The stability or resilience (in the sense of the ability of the landscape to recover from disturbances (Tress and Tress 2001)), of the landscape is important because sustainable finance requires the same flow of ecosystem services over time. For example, if a land steward is paid to store carbon in a forest landscape under a carbon finance scheme, then there needs to be some confidence that the carbon will remain secure in the trees and not be released by significant landscape changes, perhaps due to development or climate change itself.

However, because landscapes face ongoing change interrelated drivers within the landscape (e.g., population growth, development or improved wellbeing) and beyond the immediate landscape, such as changing demands for goods or services, including the creation of new demands (sustainable finance), an important element of landscape approaches is that they recognise the need to manage change. Importantly, however, the management of this change must be done in a way that is equitable and must not only include, but ideally be led, by those within the landscape who can implement landscape management over the long-term, as highlighted by Ostrom's (2009) detailed study of long-term common pool resources. Hence, the management of change across the landscape is important for financing land uses over the long-term.

Landscape planning to support sustainable finance

Confronting the challenges of landscape level management is essential for sustainable finance. Landscape planning can help address some of the key issues of taking a landscape approach (Folke et al. 2010; Ostrom 1990; Machar 2020; Lane 2006: 21). Planning provides a way to bring knowledge together, a way to integrate actions and a way to include considerations of justice in decision-making about land uses and resources (Selman 2009: 21–22).

Land use planning: Turning knowledge into action

Land use planning is commonly described as a way to turn knowledge into action (Morgan, Cadman, and Mackey 2020) to help stakeholders make decisions about land uses in order to create desirable outcomes and balance the multiple trade-offs from different land uses. Whereas conventional land use planning has often been highly technocratic, communicative and deliberative planning approaches focus on identifying and including a broad range of stakeholders in plan making and decision-making (Campbell 2012; Friedmann 1987; Beza 2016). Landscape planning approaches draw on these participatory planning traditions to emphasise the importance of community participation in planning (Forester 1999; Innes 1995; Amo-Rodríguez et al. 2010).

These participatory planning processes bring multiple types of knowledge together to address uncertainty, complexity and conflict (Selman 2004, 2005; Angelstam et al. 2013; Campbell 2012; Jones et al. 2013), as well as build legitimacy (Selman 2004). They encourage shared (or social) learning so that stakeholders have a shared understanding of the drivers of change and issues that need to be addressed (Valencia-Sandoval, Flanders, and Kozak 2010; Legacy 2012; Albert et al. 2012; Berkes 2009; Friedmann 1981; Reed et al. 2010; Albrechts and Balducci 2013). Hence, landscape planning is a way to bring knowledge and values together to address complexity and uncertainty in a landscape approach (Friedmann 2004; Healey 2009: 21–22; Matthews and Selman 2006).

Regional and strategic planning: Scale and integration

Although land use planning is commonly associated with urban land use at a precinct scale, it is increasingly applied at a regional scale across non-urban or mixed contexts. Regional planning is in part driven by an ecological understanding of environmental impacts that recognises the links between land uses at wider scales than conventional urban land use planning (Morgan, Cadman, and Mackey 2020), but is also driven by the recognition that urban areas affect and are affected by their surrounding regions economically and socially (Selman 2004; Brunckhorst 2013).

Regional planning is commonly a more strategic planning process that seeks to provide broader goals and ways to achieve them. Strategic planning helps integrate the multiple sectors and stakeholders that affect land use and land use change across a region as a way to guide and evaluate activities (Davidson and Arman 2014; Morgan, Torabi, and Dedekorkut-Howes 2020; Albrechts and Balducci 2013) and encourages effective collaboration and coordination among stakeholders (commonly policymakers, industry and community in formal planning) (Friedmann 2004; Healey 2009).

Landscape planning operates at a landscape level and takes the more integrated and holistic view of strategic planning to include ecological and cultural considerations more equally compared to the conventional social and economic focus of traditional land use planning (Angelstam et al. 2013; Morgan, Cadman, and Mackey 2020; Dramstad and Fjellstad 2011). Again participation in the planning process is key to integrating social and environmental issues and values (Matthews and Selman 2006: 201; Selman 2009: 110–16), reflecting the importance of participation in landscape approaches (Matthews and Selman 2006: 2544; Selman 2005: 8352) and a general focus on participatory governance in land use and natural resource management (Reed et al. 2016; Sayer et al. 2013; Adger et al. 2003; Arts et al. 2014).

Radical planning: Co-production and fairness

Conventionally, planning involves highly formalised and technocratic processes, commonly resulting in a formal planning document, such as city plan that controls the day-to-day development decisions. However, planning can take place in a much more informal way, and some have argued anywhere people get together to make decisions about the future and their activities should be considered planning (Cadman 2012: 194; Ostrom 1990: 567). Similarly, radical and insurgent planning emphasises the importance of involving people not only in the planning process but also in carrying out the planned activities (Healey 2009; Thorpe 2017). These approaches highlight co-production of both planning and implementation as a way to ultimately empower communities to decide on and implement activities to manage change into the future to achieve the desired outcomes.

Fundamental to these more radical planning are ideas of justice and fairness. These types of planning focus on the role power plays in planning and the need to address power imbalances in land use and land use change decisions (Albrechts 2015: 197–205; Miraftab 2009). They argue for the need for the planning process to empower communities, and especially typically disenfranchised groups to achieve more just and equitable outcomes land and resource uses (Cameron and Grant-Smith 2014; Forester 2007; Basta 2015; Lane 2006). Again, participation is at the core of this, but goes beyond consultation, instead requiring community management and empowerment (Miraftab 2009; Osborne 2015: 197–205).

Hence, planning can help landscape approaches address issues of power, fairness and justice in managing change, which must be addressed if outcomes to be socially and culturally sustainable. Many of the unsustainable drivers of change in a landscape derive from power imbalances, as evidenced by concerns of land rights, corruption and communities' resources being exploited through the false dichotomy of choosing between conservation and development. This is essential to ensure that sustainable finance fairly rewards communities and landscape stewards and does not just become a way for the wealthy to offset their environmental damage instead of addressing its endogenous causes.

Summary: Landscape planning and sustainable finance

Sustainable finance opportunities, such as PES and ecotourism, are built on the idea of maintaining consistent use and the benefits over the long-term. However, landscapes will face a variety of drivers of change, whether biophysical (e.g., climate change) or socioeconomic (e.g., globalisation). Planning supports a participatory approach to bring multiple stakeholders together share their different knowledges, find shared goals to coordinate and collaborate on, and address inequitable distribution of benefits, and ultimately to manage change to help maintain the benefits of the landscape. It provides a way to address complexity, conflict, and uncertainty by creating a shared understanding of the key drivers of change in a landscape through social learning. It supports a more integrated approach that encourages collaboration and coordination to choose and implement land use and natural resource management activities. It can also help to address power imbalances and address injustice by encouraging a more equitable distribution of benefits (recognising, rather than dismissing, the utopian ideal of perfect equitable distribution while accepting the pragmatic limitations of planning). Landscape planning. Crucially, however, the multiple stakeholders will have differing and often competing values, wants and needs and will value the benefits of the landscape differently. As a result, understanding if the economics of the landscape and its multiple functions and benefits is needed to help stakeholders negotiate trade-offs in a way that is equitable. A landscape economics needs to recognise and demonstrate the multiple benefits of landscapes and allow stakeholder to map them and undertake bargaining to capture the benefits of the landscape in an equitable fashion.

Landscape economics

Ecosystem services in landscapes

The concept of ecosystem services provides a useful way of understanding the benefits of landscapes (see Chapter Three), and is widely used to guide planning and management at a landscape level (Arnstein 1969; Cameron and Grant-Smith 2014; Albert et al. 2014; Frank et al. 2014; Fürst et al. 2014; Jones et al. 2013; Liu and Opdam 2014). Although using the concept of ecosystem services is potentially challenging and controversial because of its human-centredness (Sitas et al. 2014; Vallés-Planells, Galiana, and Van Eetvelde 2014), which can rationalise exploitation within a utility maximising paradigm (de Groot et al. 2010; Schroter et al. 2014), it provides a useful conceptual tool for thinking about benefits of ecosystem as discussed in Chapter Three.

Using ecosystem services in landscape approaches

Ecosystem services, because they are defined by their contribution to human activity, are a function of ecological and social systems (Matulis 2015; Sullivan 2009; Duraiappah et al. 2014). The ecosystem services stem from the ecological system, that

is, ecosystem functions that are determined by ecosystem integrity, while the services, their benefits and how these are valued are determined by the sociocultural
system (including the economic system). A landscape approach requires a landscape economics, which maps ecosystem service beneficiaries to land stewards
managing the natural capital assets that provide those services and allows stakeholders to compare the values of different ecosystem services across the landscape,
which can in turn inform choices about landscape activities and uses within landscape planning. A neoclassical economic analysis would identify ecosystems service benefits that are perceived to generate the greatest net present value (NPV) to
those making decisions about the forest – that is, those who wield contemporary
power, the property rights and are included within governance system.

However, such an analysis fails to consider the value of full range of ecosystem
services in their entirety and complexity, commonly ignoring regulating and cultural services where property rights are poorly defined (they are non-excludable
goods; see Chapter Three). The Economics of Ecosystems and Biodiversity initiative
argues that the social, cultural, or economic value of ecosystem services depend
upon: (a) those services being recognised – making the link between resources and
services they provide and the benefits to people; (b) how the benefits are demonstrated – given an economic, but not necessarily monetary, value to allow for different types of benefits to be readily compared; and (c) whether those benefits are
captured – included and respected in decision-making within forest management,
which can include generating incomes from the forest and its ecosystem services
(Millennium Ecosystem Assessment Board 2005). This conceptualisation helps link
the ecological systems (landscape ecosystem structure and function) to the sociocultural systems (including the social, economic, governance and political contexts) that influence land management choices– and hence what a landscape
economics approach must consider. The recognition, demonstration and capturing
of ecosystem service values links ecosystem function, derived from landscape ecosystems and their integrity to services and benefits and ultimately forest management. The functions, services, benefits and values will be determined both the
ecological system and sociocultural system (see Figure 5.1).

Ecosystem services are increasingly used as a concept in landscape planning as
a way to help stakeholders understand the links between the social and environmental (Morgan et al. 2021; Potschin and Haines-Young 2011; Albert et al. 2014;
Frank et al. 2014; Fürst et al. 2014; Liu and Opdam 2014). Studies show that ecosystem services can play a useful role in the planning and design of landscapes (Sitas
et al. 2014; Jones et al. 2013), by providing a way to support the co-production of
knowledge and the collaboration of diverse actors (Jones et al. 2013) and to link ecosystems and ecosystem integrity to land uses, planning and community wellbeing
(Sitas et al. 2014; Albert et al. 2014). Hence, ecosystem services provide a way for
stakeholders to map and understand benefits from ecosystems within a landscape

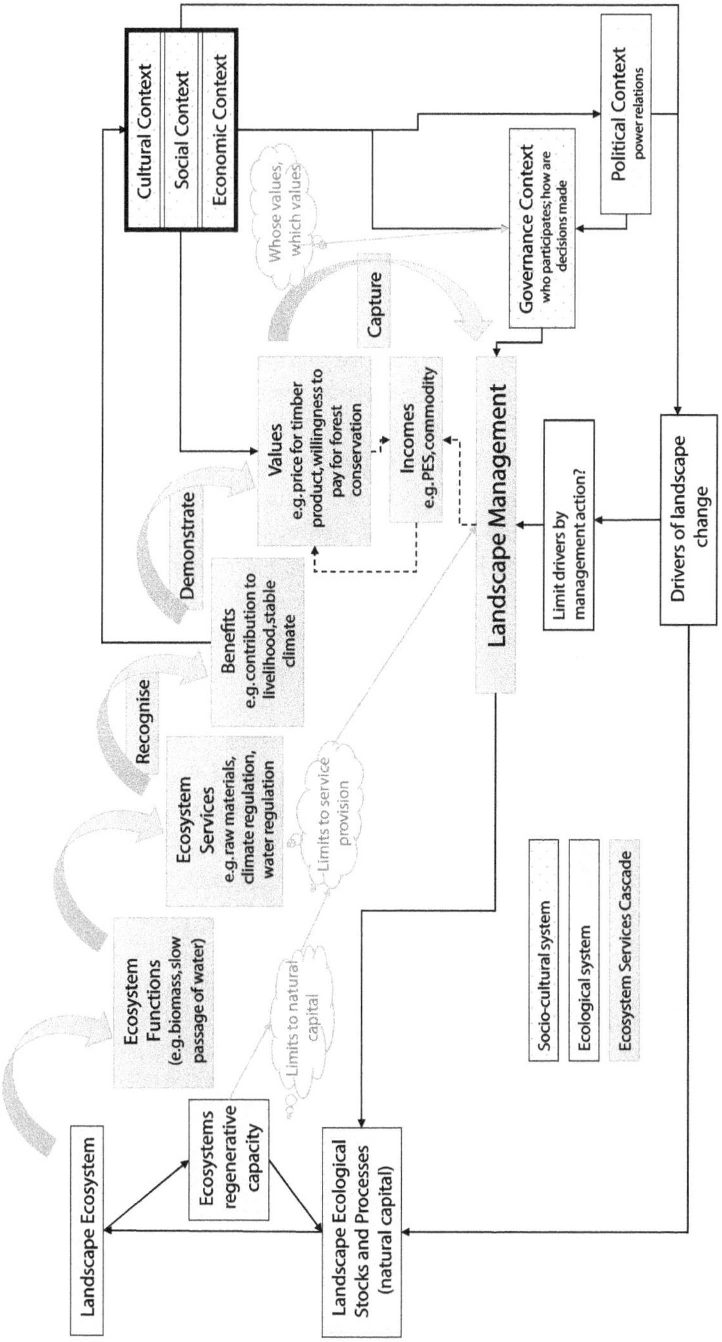

Figure 5.1: The recognition, demonstration and capturing of ecosystem service values. Adapted from. Source: Potschin and Haines-Young (2011); Kumar (2010).

planning process. However, comparing and negotiating the values of ecosystem service benefits among multiple stakeholders across a landscape requires application of economic tools (within the planning process).

Recognising ecosystem service benefits and their interactions in a landscape

The harnessing of some ecosystem services within a landscape will impact upon other ecosystem services (Liu and Opdam 2014; Morgan, Cadman, and Mackey 2020: 433–48). Logging of forests, for example, harnesses the biomass production services of forest ecosystems, but will degrade the quantity and quality of water from a catchment and climate regulation services and impact biodiversity. The loss of these services may impact the forest directly (e.g., changes to biodiversity) or elsewhere in the landscape (e.g., changes to water regulation); some losses may even impact global ecosystem services (e.g., climate regulation). This may in turn impact on the ecosystem structure and function of the forest.

From a landscape perspective, the benefits of ecosystem services accrue at different spatial and temporal scales and therefore, accrue differently to distinct stakeholders. Benefits of ecosystems services may be local, spread across a landscape or region, or even have global impacts. For example, people in the landscape will harvest food and raw materials directly from their immediate environs contemporaneously. They may change land uses to improve the harvesting of raw materials – for example, creating shifting or sedentary agriculture within a forest landscape (Felipe-Lucia, Comín, and Bennett 2014). At the same time, people may also value many timeless non-use spiritual and cultural services (Rodriguez et al. 2005) that encourage the protection and preservation of areas of the landscape, perhaps as the creation of taboo areas in some cultures rather than more formally protected areas. Other ecosystem service benefits, such as water flow regulation and water quality benefits of maintaining forest cover, may accrue to others in the landscape or beyond. Also, some benefits of landscapes are global and long-run, as highlighted by the role of primary forests in climate regulation as carbon stock (Samndong et al. 2018; Mackey et al. 2020) or as areas of biodiversity (Dellasala et al. 2020).

At the same time, the costs (including effort, direct financial and opportunity costs) fall on the land stewards, who are responsible for land management. Hence, the overall benefits of ecosystem services are often inequitably distributed, which affects how these ecosystem services are captured in forest management. Crucially, due to the interconnected nature of these ecosystem services, as people change the landscape to capture particular benefits, they change the benefits seen elsewhere.

Sustainable finance needs to take into account these socioecological interactions between ecosystem services, as well as recognise the distribution of benefits. For example, a carbon finance (REDD+) scheme that allows a forest to be replaced with a plantation, on the basis that both store carbon fails to be sustainable because it ignores the loss of other ecosystem services. The recent coronavirus pandemic has highlighted the importance of thinking broadly about ecosystem service benefits. Research has long drawn the link between land use change, and especially forest loss, and the risk of novel diseases and the resulting pandemic (Mackey et al. 2020; Watson et al. 2018; Dobson et al. 2020). Protecting certain ecosystems will reduce the risk of future pandemics, while increasing development of these areas will increase the risk.

TEV: Demonstrating ecosystem services in a landscape

A Total Economic Value (TEV) framework seeks to better demonstrate the contribution of all ecosystem services and natural capital stocks (Terraube and Fernández-Llamazares 2020; Tollefson 2020; Bush et al. 2004: 17–36); also described as Total Ecosystem Service Valuation (TESV) when inclusive only of ecosystem service flows over a defined spatial area (Ninan et al. 2007; Merlo and Croitoru 2005; Tolessa et al. 2018). The spatial aspect of TEV and TESV makes them especially relevant for a landscape approach to sustainable finance. Further, these approaches recognise both use and non-use values and also that not all ecosystem services can be given an exchange monetary value, which reflects the importance of values and meanings the recognition of the cultural in defining landscapes (Gashaw et al. 2018: 33–42; Tolessa et al. 2018). TEV and TESV frameworks can help landscape stakeholders demonstrate the value of multiple ecosystem services by seeking to place a common, comparable value on the complete bundle of ecosystem services of an ecosystem asset, even where they cannot be commodified or substituted (Brown 2015; Selman 2004; Tolessa et al. 2018).

A TEV approach classifies ecosystem services into direct and indirect use values and non-use values (see Figure 5.4). Provisioning ecosystem services are largely direct extractive uses of the landscape. Some direct uses will subtract from and degrade the ecosystem integrity of the landscape (e.g., extractive logging in a forest ecosystem), but others may be considered sustainable if they operate within the natural regenerative capacity of the landscape (e.g., non-timber forest products). Recreation services (ecotourism) are also considered a direct use value (experienced directly by the beneficiary). Although formally non-extractive in nature, provision of recreational services requires careful management for it to remain so. Therefore, sustainable uses are likely to need to be endogenous supply driven (rather than externally demand driven) to remain sustainable, that is, their use must recognise ecological limits, as defined by localised land stewards and service providers, in some way.

Indirect use values those where humans benefit from indirect use of a flow of services, and include many regulating ecosystem services, such as carbon sequestration and storage and maintenance of water quality. These benefits tend to flow as non-excludable, non-rival public goods or non-excludable, but congestible goods (see Chapter Three) and careful use is unlikely to degrade the ecosystems in the landscape. Cultural services provide non-use and existence values, which, by definition, do not subtract from a landscape's ecosystem integrity. See the schematic representation in Figure 5.2.

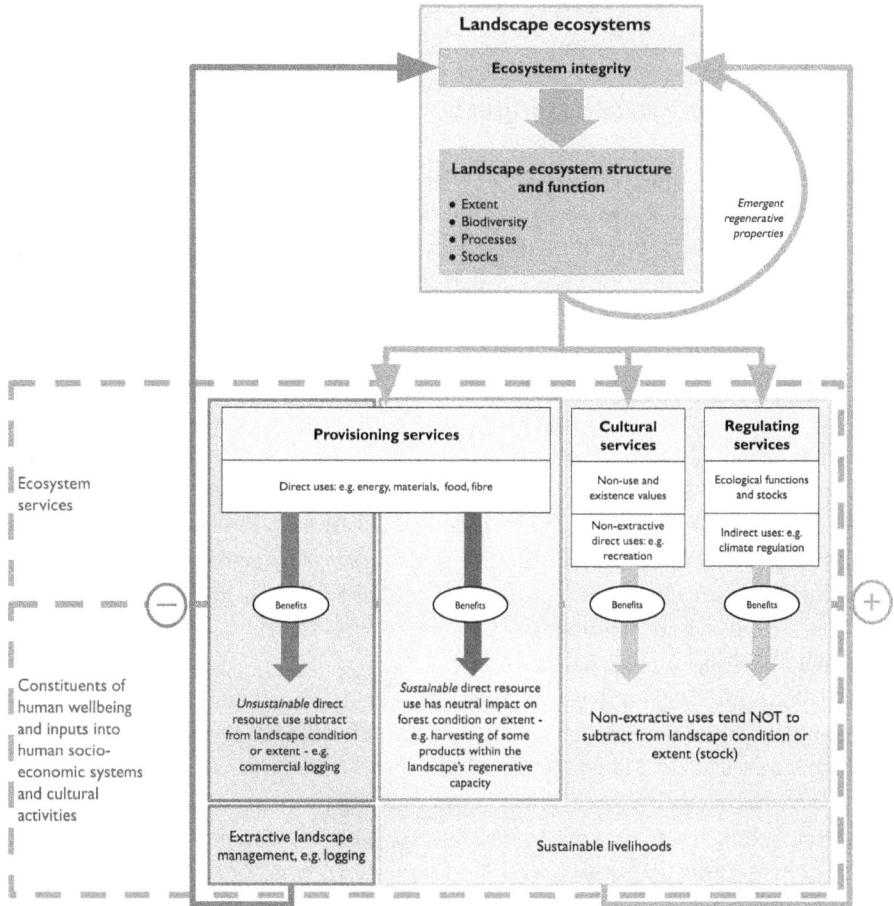

Figure 5.2: Relationships between landscape ecosystem integrity, ecosystem services and their contributions to total ecosystem service value.

As Figure 5.2 shows, some ecosystem services can be used sustainably, having a positive or limited impact on a landscape's ecosystem integrity. Other uses, including extractive processes, have a negative impact on a forest's ecosystem integrity resulting in degraded ecosystem services. Schemes that harness the sustainable use of ecosystem services are therefore more able to support sustainable livelihoods.

The demonstration of these different values, through different uses, will affect if and how they are represented within land management decisions (e.g., within landscape planning) and whether and how they are harnessed to generate incomes. These decisions will involve trade-offs and negotiation about the ecosystem services, the management ecosystems that provide them and the benefits that accrue from them, including recognition of how some direct uses of ecosystem services are often incompatible with other direct and indirect uses and non-uses. These can then support the co-production of goals and management actions to maximise and share these benefits justly.

Capturing ecosystem service benefits for sustainable finance

Humans have always collectively planned how to harness the ecosystem services of landscapes and in doing so have shaped and created the landscapes. People within the landscape harvest food, fuel and fibre from landscapes though hunting and gathering, and have also made use of the soil and water regulating services of landscapes, for example, through small-scale subsistence gardening (Gashaw et al. 2018; Tolessa et al. 2018). Recently, the capturing of the ecosystem services benefits of landscapes has increasingly focussed on creating a monetary income during the period of widespread and accelerating industrialisation, capitalism, globalisation and colonialism. This focus on maximising the NPV of production by externalising social costs and increasing economic productivity has prioritised extractive, direct uses, where benefits are commodities that have financial value in current markets and under dominant property rights regimes (e.g., timber).

Hence, those within the landscape, in seeking incomes and royalties for increased consumption and investment are presented few alternatives to activities that encourage commodity production through significant landscape change – with conservation and development presented as incompatible pathways. Importantly, however, it is not always those who live in and have attachment to the landscape that are making decisions about management. Governments and/or industry may seek to capture a particular provisioning service and encourage or require particular extractive industries (timber harvesting, mining, intensive agriculture), regardless of the impact on other ecosystem services. These activities may even be illegal, but still occur on a large-scale in landscapes (Levis et al. 2018; Ribeiro et al. 2014).

Sustainable finance mechanisms try to create income generation from either sustainable direct use or indirect use, non-market and non-use values (e.g., climate regulation, culture, biodiversity), where future, often indefinite, benefit flows are prioritised as they are either non-rival in nature (they are not diminished by others' utility) or decision-makers have applied a zero-discount rate – recognising that the value of the service benefits is maintained or increases over time. To do so, most existing approaches to sustainable finance recognise multiple ecosystem services and the interactions between them but they tend to demonstrate and capture the value of on only one (or a few) ecosystem services (Lawson 2014) – leading to these being prioritised in land management.

Schemes based on sustainable use of provisioning services, for example, non-timber forest products, implicitly recognise other provisioning, regulating and cultural ecosystem services are valuable to a broader range of stakeholders, who may not have a stake in the system of property rights (Pandey, Tripathi, and Kumar 2016). However, the demonstration of their value relies on market mechanisms and premium pricing, which are dependent on consumer perceptions and attitudes. Although certification schemes can boost consumer perceptions by providing more consistency and transparency for these market products and services, they are still reliant on demand. As the recent COVID-19 pandemic has shown for tourism, reliance on markets comes with risks.

PES approaches recognise and provide incomes for various land management actions and tend to bundle multiple ecosystem services in the value exchange but the payments are limited by what buyers of ecosystem service credits are willing to pay (Mousseau 2018: 843), most often for only indirect benefit. Payment is often based on the level of compensation needed to avoid negative impacts (Morgan et al. 2021; Wunder, Engel, and Pagiola 2008), rather than a value based on demonstration of the benefits agreed among the stakeholders. Furthermore, the schemes tend to determine the land uses that are rewarded, determining land use decisions with minimal participation (Arriagada et al. 2015).

REDD+ schemes are a type of PES that capture climate regulation services through forest-based carbon mitigation and secondarily capture other ecosystem services in management through imposed requirements. REDD+ has developed in response to the UNFCCC and international agreement on the need to reduce carbon in the atmosphere, as highlighted by the Paris Agreement. This has created a global demand for carbon credits for the public good of climate regulation. These schemes also only value the carbon through a cost influenced by a willingness to accept to avoid change, as highlighted in differences between market carbon prices around EUR 30–50, USD 35–60 per tonne of CO_2 on the European carbon trading system (Brownson et al. 2020), while a recent review of the social cost of carbon gave a range of USD 177–805 with a median cost of USD 417 per tonne of CO_2 (Wunder, Engel, and Pagiola 2008: 895).

Importantly, schemes to capture the benefits of ecosystem services for financial income also tend to be mutually exclusive, despite the common requirements to maintain or enhance ecosystem services. There are examples of REDD+ and timber certification being combined but land stewards still need to meet the separate requirements of both schemes. There are, however, alternative approaches. The concept of credit stacking is currently limited to subnational regulatory pollution abatement (EMBER 2021), but has potential for broad approaches to landscapes. Existing sustainable finance schemes, as they commonly driven by regulatory demands, tend to require robust demonstration of additionality from projects – requiring that projects should not double-dip, that is, receive compensation for ecosystem services that would have been secured anyway as co-benefits.

This practice is designed to prevent economic inefficiencies in the protection of ecosystem services: money spent on ecosystem services that would have been received anyway fails to maximise the total amount of ecosystem service delivery obtained from the total budget, which could be allocated to achieve objectives elsewhere (Ricke et al. 2018). Note that credit stacking requires an unbundling of ecosystem services – that is, each service is separated out and individually assigned a value (Deal, Cochran, and LaRocco 2012). Bundling occurs where the adoption of a land management practice receives a single payment for the provision of multiple environmental outputs. Unbundling means that the multiple environmental outputs of a land management decision are divisible and each of them could earn specific credit, potentially aimed at the ecosystem service beneficiaries at different scales. Therefore, a land management practice can generate single payment for the provision of multiple environmental outputs, regardless of to whom and what scale those benefits occur. While stacking risks economic inefficiency (and therefore overpayments to ecosystem service providers).

Although stacking risks economic inefficiency, it can provide a way to better demonstrate and capture the value of the multiple benefits of forests to reverse the trend of forest loss. Also, given the inherent uncertainties of landscapes systems (see above) and in the recognition and valuation of ecosystem services, the inefficiency of credit stacking is highly uncertain and potentially minimal, and concerns about inefficiencies maybe less important than achieving the overall goal of supporting more sustainable land management.

Synthesis: Using landscape planning and economics to support sustainable finance

This discussion of landscape planning and economics urges a more holistic and wider interpretation of ecosystem services, their link to land management and their valuation in sustainable finance to better reflect the both the reality of ecosystems and the sociocultural nature of landscapes. Current sustainable finance schemes often fail to recognise or demonstrate multiple ecosystem services across a landscape, and in doing so can lead to loss of important ecosystems or fail to equitable transfer the benefits. A landscape approach to sustainable finance needs to recognise and demonstrate the value of the multiple ecosystem services across the landscape, and then identify ways for stakeholders to capture them to ensure equitable and sustainable benefits for those in the landscape.

Recognising and mapping ecosystem service benefits across the landscape for sustainable finance

Sustainable finance is based on harnessing the ecosystem service benefits of a landscape. Recognising and mapping ecosystem service benefits requires stakeholders to understand the ecosystem structures and functions that give rise to these benefits, and to identify the trade-offs between ecosystem services related to different land use changes. Landscape planning provides processes to bring together knowledge about the landscape to help stakeholders choose land uses and activities to achieve outcomes defined by their values that support their wellbeing, and ecosystem services are increasingly used in these planning processes to support the co-production of knowledge and the collaboration of diverse actors. Introducing TEV type valuations into a planning process provides a way for stakeholders to demonstrate, map and compare the multiple ecosystem service benefits they receive, as well as identifying the benefits that flow to others beyond the landscape. Crucially, by recognising use and non-use values, and by acknowledging that not all values can directly be given a monetary value, it relies on methods that get stakeholders to identify the values of ecosystem services. Note that TEV tends to express value in monetary terms, which is useful for framing trade-offs consistently between options that have to address multiple assessment criteria (Woodward 2011: 2). In reality, this may not mean defining dollar values for each ecosystem service, but merely serve as a way to compare values of the many different benefits, and map those benefits and values to the stakeholders.

Comparing and bargaining for sustainable finance

Having recognised, mapped and demonstrated the value of these different ecosystem service benefits, stakeholders are then able to apply a bargaining process (Lankoski et al. 2015: 87–137) to transfer the benefits and costs more fairly through PES-type schemes, or to choose market-based opportunities to capture the non-use and sustainable use benefits.

Importantly, this supports sustainable finance opportunities within a landscape, or at a regional scale, alongside the more common national and international scale. For example, a TEV might help stakeholders identify and value the ecosystem service (water regulation) benefits of an area of forest upstream for an important urban catchment, reef ecosystem or ecotourism (see Figure 5.3). A landscape plan will identify the need to protect the forest, and the activities and stakeholders required to do so. If the costs (including opportunity costs) of protecting the forest fall on the community that lives in or near the forest, then they can bargain for benefit transfer from those benefitting from the water regulation services of the forest. This can lead to an agreement within a planning process that the communities who own and manage the forest will continue to protect and maintain the forest, in return for payment (in a type of PES

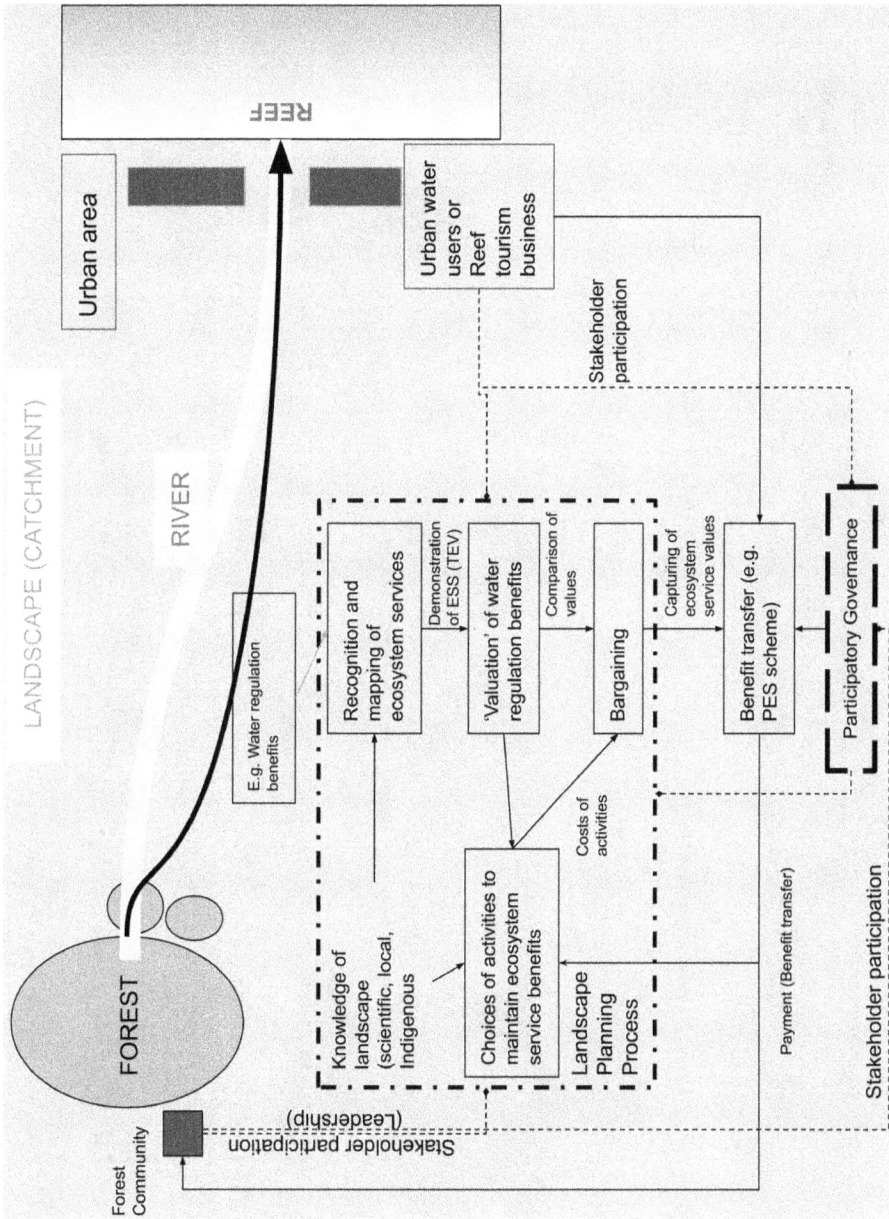

Figure 5.3: A conceptual example of the role of landscape planning processes and the valuation of ecosystem services in bargaining and creating benefit transfer across a ridge-to-reef landscape.

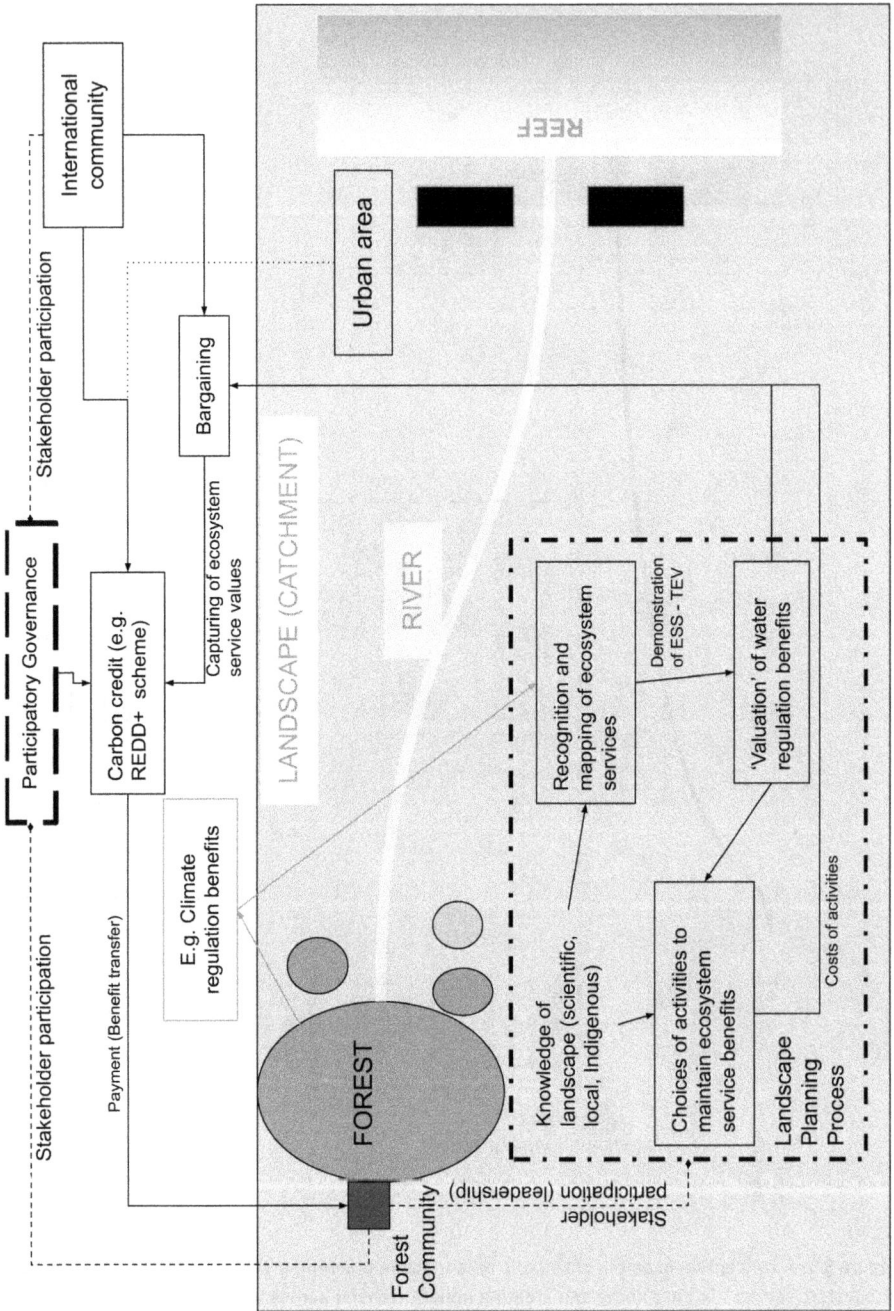

Figure 5.4: A conceptual example of the role of landscape planning processes and the valuation of ecosystem services in bargaining and creating benefit transfer using international credit schemes in a ridge-to-reef landscape.

scheme). The landscape plan provides agreement of the protection of the forest, and therefore confidence of those downstream that they will continue to receive the benefits into the future, despite likely drivers of future change.

Although this is a simple example, the mapping of the multiple ecosystem services in the landscape and identification of the activities related to maintaining them also supports sustainable finance schemes that operate at a larger scale. This provides a way to support credit stacking – by showing the multiple ecosystem service benefits of planned actions. It also provides a transparent process for the long-term maintenance of these benefits. Those paying for the ecosystem service (transferring benefit) can have greater reassurance that they are paying for multiple ecosystem services, that these ecosystem services are providing benefits, and that there is a plan that will address and mitigate risks to those benefits.

Where these benefits accrue to those beyond the landscape (e.g., global climate regulation benefits of forests), the bargaining process may be less direct. Global or national schemes are likely to need mediated credit-bases schemes, such as the European Carbon Trading System. However, the landscape planning and economics approach clearly shows both the multiple benefits and the actions that maintain them, both giving the stakeholders in the landscape (e.g., the forest community) choices over which to seek bargains for and also placing both responsibility and power in their hands – as opposed to simply placing a responsibility to carry out the requirements of a scheme imposed from above.

Governing sustainable finance in the landscape: participation and deliberation

Creating and implementing a landscape plan requires strong participatory governance. Similarly, good governance is essential for sustainable finance schemes, and governance challenges are highlighted as common problem within REDD+ and other PES (see Cadman et al. 2015). A full discussion on governance challenges is beyond the scope of this chapter but the substantial literature of governance of natural resources and governance of sustainable finance and climate change provide guidance and tools for improving governance and addressing governance challenges (Adger et al. 2003; Berkes 2010). Good governance will rely on meaningful participation and productive deliberation (Berkes 2010), and the importance of participation and involvement of stakeholders has been noted throughout this chapter. A landscape planning process must aim to include and empower stakeholders in deliberations, especially land stewards responsible for land management. A TEV approach will also support participation in the planning process, as it supports the valuation of ecosystem services by all the stakeholders. Creating the necessary institutional and governance arrangements will be a challenge but will be essential for the successful development and implementation of landscape approaches, including the planning and economics aspects discussed here.

Conclusion

This chapter has discussed the importance of a landscape approach for sustainable development, and the role of landscape planning and economics in supporting such an approach. Landscape planning provides a way for stakeholders to make decisions about landscape uses to achieve shared goals. It provides a way to manage change, integrate the differing and competing interests of stakeholders and seek fair and equitable distribution of benefits. A landscape economics approach, based on TEV methods, provides a way for stakeholders to recognise and demonstrate ecosystem services. Combined, these allow stakeholders to map and compare the multiple landscape ecosystem service benefits and instigate bargaining for benefit transfer or ways to capture sustainable use and non-use ecosystem service benefits.

Sustainable finance can be seen as high-risk, due to its long-term nature and often loosely defined systems of property rights. However, the recent COVID-19 pandemic has highlighted the need to also consider the global risk of landscape change – future pandemics are more likely the more forests and forest landscapes are disrupted, particularly in a highly interconnected, globalised world. It also highlights the need for sustainable finance to seek diversity: although ecotourism might be a useful source of sustainable finance, the pandemic has highlighted the risk of loss of tourists that must be mitigated. A landscape approach that considers the multiple ecosystem services of the landscape combines an economic approach that stacks these many benefits and a planning process that identifies drivers and risks and chooses multiple options accordingly, avoiding reliance on any one income stream.

Creating landscape approaches to long-term sustainable finance is not straightforward. Landscapes are complex socioeconomic systems; stakeholders will often be in conflict, and power disparity is common. Landscape planning and TEV economic approaches and building the necessary governance arrangements will support these approaches, but will themselves need resources and capacity building, especially for those land stewards and communities who stand to gain the most from sustainable finance – but are also most at risk of exploitation.

Crucially, decision-making needs to include those who will bear the costs of landscape management and those who receive the ecosystem service benefits of them. Participatory approaches to planning and governance are necessary to ensure that landscape stewards are involved in decision-making and can make informed choices about the ecosystem services they choose to capture and the land management options they take to do so. Too often current sustainable finance schemes determine the actions and the benefits from the top-down, and consequently risk becoming simply another way for wealthy stakeholders to offset their unsustainable practices. A landscape approach provides a way to build sustainable finance from the bottom-up, with the express goal of empowering communities and land stewards and seeking equitable and just benefit sharing.

References

Adger, Neil, Katrina Brown, Jenny Fairbrass, Andrew Jordan, Jouni Paavola, Sergio Rosendo, and Gill Seyfang. 2003. 'Governance for Sustainability: Towards a 'Thick' Analysis of Environmental Decisionmaking', *Environment and Planning A*, 35 (6), 1095–110.

Albert, Christian, James Aronson, Christine Fürst, and Paul Opdam. 2014. 'Integrating Ecosystem Services in Landscape Planning: Requirements, Approaches, and Impacts', *Landscape Ecology*, 29 (8), 1277–85.

Albert, Christian, Thomas Zimmermann, Jörg Knieling, and Christina von Haaren. 2012. 'Social Learning Can Benefit Decision-Making in Landscape Planning: Gartow Case Study on Climate Change Adaptation, Elbe Valley Biosphere Reserve', *Landscape and Urban Planning*, 105 (4), 347–60.

Albrechts, Louis. 2015. 'Ingredients for a More Radical Strategic Spatial Planning', *Environment and Planning B: Planning and Design*, 42 (3), 510–25.

Albrechts, Louis, and Alessandro Balducci. 2013. 'Practicing Strategic Planning: In Search of Critical Features to Explain the Strategic Character of Plans', *disP – the Planning Review*, 49 (3), 16–27.

Amo-Rodríguez, Silvia Del, María Del Carmen Vergara-Tenorio, José María Ramos-Prado, and Luciana Porter-Bolland. 2010. 'Community Landscape Planning for Rural Areas: A Model for Biocultural Resource Management', *Society and Natural Resources*, 23 (5), 436–50.

Angelsen, Arild, and Desmond McNeill. 2012. 'The Evolution of REDD+ ' in Arild Angelsen, Maria Brockhaus, William D. Sunderlin and Louis V. Verchot (eds.), *Analysing REDD+: Challenges and Choices* (Bogor, Indonesia: Center for International Forestry Research), pp. 31–59

Angelstam, Per, Michael Grodzynskyi, Kjell Andersson, Robert Axelsson, Marine Elbakidze, Alexander Khoroshev, Ivan Kruhlov, and Vladimir Naumov. 2013. 'Measurement, Collaborative Learning and Research for Sustainable Use of Ecosystem Services: Landscape Concepts and Europe as Laboratory', *AMBIO*, 42 (2), 129–45.

Arnstein, Sherry. 1969. 'A Ladder of Citizen Participation', *Journal of the American Planning Association*, 35 (4), 216–24.

Arriagada, R., E. Sills, P. Ferraro, and S. Pattanayak. 2015. 'Do Payments Pay Off? Evidence from Participation in Costa Rica's PES Program', *PLoS ONE*, 10 (7), e0131544.

Arts, Bas, Jelle Behagel, Esther Turnhout, Jessica de Koning, and Séverine van Bommel. 2014. 'A Practice Based Approach to Forest Governance', *Forest Policy and Economics*, 49, 4–11.

Arts, Bas, Marleen Buizer, Lumina Horlings, Verina Ingram, Cora van Oosten, and Paul Opdam. 2017. 'Landscape Approaches: A State-of-the-Art Review', *Annual Review of Environment and Resources*, 42 (1), 439–63.

Basta, Claudia. 2015. 'From Justice in Planning toward Planning for Justice: A Capability Approach', *Planning Theory*, 15 (2), 190–212.

Bebbington, Anthony, Denise Bebbington, Laura Sauls, John Rogan, Sumali Agrawal, César Gamboa, Aviva Imhof, Kimberly Johnson, Herman Rosa, Antoinette Royo, Tessa Toumbourou, and Ricardo Verdum. 2018. 'Resource Extraction and Infrastructure Threaten Forest Cover and Community Rights', *Proceedings of the National Academy of Sciences*, 115 (52), 13164–73.

Berkes, Fikret. 2009. 'Evolution of Co-Management: Role of Knowledge Generation, Bridging Organizations and Social Learning', *Journal of Environmental Management*, 90 (5), 1692–702.

——. 2010. 'Devolution of Environment and Resources Governance: Trends and Future', *Environmental Conservation*, 37 (4), 489–500.

Beza, Beau. 2016. 'The Role of Deliberative Planning in Translating Best Practice into Good Practice: From Placeless-Ness to Placemaking', *Planning Theory and Practice*, 17 (2), 244–63.

Branca, Giacomo, Leslie Lipper, Nancy McCarthy, and Maria Jolejole. 2013. 'Food Security, Climate Change, and Sustainable Land Management. A Review', *Agronomy for Sustainable Development*, 33 (4), 635–50.

Brown, Jessica. 2015. 'Bringing Together Nature and Culture: Integrating a Landscape Approach in Protected Areas Policy and Practice.' in Roberto Gambino and Attilia Peano (eds.), *Nature Policies and Landscape Policies* (Heidelberg: Springer, Cham), pp. 33–42

Brownson, Katherine, Elizabeth Anderson, Susan Ferreira, Seth Wenger, Laurie Fowler, and Laura German. 2020. 'Governance of Payments for Ecosystem Ecosystem Services Influences Social and Environmental Outcomes in Costa Rica', *Ecological Economics*, 174, 106659.

Brunckhorst, David. 2013. *Bioregional Planning: Resource Management Beyond the New Millennium* (London and New York: Routledge).

Bryan, Joe. 2011. 'Walking the Line: Participatory Mapping, Indigenous Rights, and Neoliberalism', *Geoforum*, 42 (1), 40–50.

Burgman, M., D. Lindenmayer, and J. Elith. 2005. 'Managing Landscapes for Conservation under Uncertainty', *Ecology*, 86 (8), 2007–17.

Bush, Glenn, Simon Nampindo, Caroline Aguti, and Andrew Plumptre. 2004. *The Value of Uganda's Forests: A Livelihoods and Ecosystems Approach*, (New York: Wildlife Conservation Society), <https://programs.wcs.org/portals/49/media/file/sForests.pdf> [Accessed 24 January 2022].

Cadman, Tim. 2012. 'Evaluating the Quality and Legitimacy of Global Governance: A Theoretical and Analytical Approach', The International Journal of Social Quality, 2 (1), 4–23.

Cadman, Timothy, Lauren Eastwood, Federico Lopez-Casero Michaelis, Tek Narayan Maraseni, Jamie Pittock, and Tapan Sarker. 2015. *The Political Economy of Sustainable Development: Policy Instruments and Market Mechanisms* (Cheltenham: Edward Elgar Publishing).

Cadman, Tim, Tek Maraseni, Hugh Breakey, Federico López-Casero, and Hwan Ok Ma. 2016. 'Governance Values in the Climate Change Regime: Stakeholder Perceptions of REDD+ Legitimacy at the National Level', *Forests*, 7 (10), 212.

Calvet-Mir, L., E. Corbera, A. Martin, J. Fisher, and N. Gross-Camp. 2015. 'Payments for Ecosystem Services in the Tropics: A Closer Look at Effectiveness and Equity', *Current Opinion in Environmental Sustainability*, 14, 150–62.

Cameron, Jenny, and Deanna Grant-Smith. 2014. 'Putting People in Planning: Participatory Planning, Inclusion and Power.' in Jason Byrne, Jago Dodson and Neil Sipe (eds.), *Australian Environmental Planning: Challenges and Future Prospects* (London: Routledge), pp. 197–205.

Campbell, Heather. 2012. 'Planning to Change the World: Between Knowledge and Action Lies Synthesis', *Journal of Planning Education and Research*, 32 (2), 135–46.

Convention on Biological Diversity. 2007. *Ecosystem Approach – Principles*, <https://www.cbd.int/ecosystem/principles.shtml> [Accessed 14 January 2020].

Curtis, Philip, Christy Slay, Nancy Harris, Alexandra Tyukavina, and Matthew Hansen. 2018. 'Classifying Drivers of Global Forest Loss', *Science*, 361 (6407), 1108–11.

Davidson, Kathryn, and Michael Arman. 2014. 'Planning for Sustainability: An Assessment of Recent Metropolitan Planning Strategies and Urban Policy in Australia', *Australian Planner*, 51 (4), 296–306.

de Groot, Rudolf, Matthew Wilson, and Roelof Boumans. 2002. 'A Typology for the Classification, Description and Valuation of Ecosystem Functions, Goods and Services', *Ecological Economics*, 41 (3), 393–408.

de Groot, Rudolf, R. Alkemade, L. Braat, L. Hein, and L. Willemen. 2010. 'Challenges in Integrating the Concept of Ecosystem Services and Values in Landscape Planning, Management and Decision Making', *Ecological Complexity*, 7 (3), 260–72.

Deal, Robert, Bobby Cochran, and Gina LaRocco. 2012. 'Bundling of Ecosystem Services to Increase Forestland Value and Enhance Sustainable Forest Management', *Forest Policy and Economics*, 17, 69–76.

Dellasala, Dominick, Cyril Kormos, Heather Keith, Brendan Mackey, Virginia Young, Brendan Rogers, and Russell Mittermeier. 2020. 'Primary Forests Are Undervalued in the Climate Emergency', *BioScience*, 70 (6), 445–45.

Dernier, Louisa, Sarah Scherr, Seth Shames, Paul Chatterton, Lee Hovani, and Nienke Stam. 2015. *The Little Sustainable Landscapes Book* (Bogor, Indonesia: Center for International Forestry Research).

Dobson, Andrew, Stuart Pimm, Lee Hannah, Les Kaufman, Jorge Ahumada, Amy Ando, Aaron Bernstein, Jonah Busch, Peter Daszak, Jens Engelmann, Margaret Kinnaird, Binbin Li, Ted Loch-Temzelides, Thomas Lovejoy, Katarzyna Nowak, Patrick Roehrdanz, and Mariana Vale. 2020. 'Ecology and Economics for Pandemic Prevention', *Science*, 369 (6502), 379–81.

Dramstad, Wenche, and Wendy Fjellstad. 2011. 'Landscapes: Bridging the Gaps between Science, Policy and People', *Landscape and Urban Planning*, 100 (4), 330–32.

Duchelle, Amy E., Claudio de Sassi, Erin O. Sills, and Sven Wunder. 2018. 'People and Communities: Well-Being Impacts of REDD+ on the Ground ' in Arild Angelsen (ed.), *Transforming REDD+: Lessons and New Directions* (Bogor, Indonesia: Center for International Forestry Research), pp. 131–41

Duchelle, Amy, Gabriela Simonet, William Sunderlin, and Sven Wunder. 2018. 'What Is REDD+ Achieving on the Ground?', *Current Opinion in Environmental Sustainability*, 32, 134–40.

Duraiappah, Anantha, Stanley Asah, Eduardo Brondizio, Nicolas Kosoy, Patrick O'Farrell, Anne-Helene Prieur-Richard, Suneetha Subramanian, and Kazuhiko Takeuchi. 2014. 'Managing the Mismatches to Provide Ecosystem Services for Human Well-Being: A Conceptual Framework for Understanding the New Commons', *Current Opinion in Environmental Sustainability*, 7, 94–100.

EMBER. 2021. *Carbon Price Viewer*, <https://ember-climate.org/data/carbon-price-viewer/> [Accessed 10 February 2020].

Felipe-Lucia, María, Francisco Comín, and Elena Bennett. 2014. 'Interactions among Ecosystem Services across Land Uses in a Floodplain Agroecosystem', *Ecology and Society*, 19 (1), 20.

Filer, Colin. 2012. 'Why Green Grabs Don't Work in Papua New Guinea', *The Journal of Peasant Studies*, 39 (2), 599–617.

Folke, Carl, Stephen Carpenter, Brian Walker, Marten Scheffer, and Terry Chapin. 2010. 'Resilience Thinking: Integrating Resilience, Adaptability and Transformability', *Ecology and Society*, 15 (4), 20.

Forester, John. 1999. *The Deliberative Practitioner: Encouraging Participatory Planning Processes* (Cambridge, MA: MIT Press).

——. 2007. 'Planning in the Face of Power.' in Michael Wegener, Kenneth Button and Peter Nijkamp (eds.), *Planning History and Methodology* (Cheltenham, UK: Edward Elgar Publishing), pp. 67–80

Frank, Susanne, Christine Fürst, Anke Witt, Lars Koschke, and Franz Makeschin. 2014. 'Making Use of the Ecosystem Services Concept in Regional Planning – Trade-Offs from Reducing Water Erosion', *Landscape Ecology*, 29 (8), 1377–91.

Freeman, Olivia, Lalisa Duguma, and Peter Minang. 2015. 'Operationalizing the Integrated Landscape Approach in Practice', *Ecology and Society*, 20 (1), 24.

Friedmann, John. 1981. *Planning as Social Learning.* (Berkeley, CA: Institute of Urban and Regional Development, University of California)

——. 1987. *Planning in the Public Domain: From Knowledge to Action* (Princeton, NJ: Princeton University Press).

——. 2004. 'Strategic Spatial Planning and the Longer Range', *Planning Theory and Practice*, 5 (1), 49–67.

Fürst, Christine, Paul Opdam, Luis Inostroza, and Sandra Luque. 2014. 'Evaluating the Role of Ecosystem Services in Participatory Land Use Planning: Proposing a Balanced Score Card', *Landscape Ecology*, 29 (8), 1435–46.

Gashaw, Temesgen, Taffa Tulu, Mekuria Argaw, Abeyou W. Worqlul, Terefe Tolessa, and Mengistie Kindu. 2018. 'Estimating the Impacts of Land Use/Land Cover Changes on Ecosystem Service Values: The Case of the Andassa Watershed in the Upper Blue Nile Basin of Ethiopia', *Ecosystem Services*, 31, 219–28.

Healey, Patsy. 2009. 'In Search of the "Strategic" in Spatial Strategy Making', *Planning Theory and Practice*, 10 (4), 439–457.

Innes, Judith. 1995. 'Planning Theory's Emerging Paradigm: Communicative Action and Interactive Practice', *Journal of Planning Education and Research*, 14 (3), 183–89.

Jones, K. Bruce, Giovanni Zurlini, Felix Kienast, Irene Petrosillo, Thomas Edwards, Timothy Wade, Bai-lian Li, and Nicola Zaccarelli. 2013. 'Informing Landscape Planning and Design for Sustaining Ecosystem Services from Existing Spatial Patterns and Knowledge', *Landscape Ecology*, 28 (6), 1175–92.

Kumar, Pushpam. 2010. 'Introduction.' in Pushpam Kumar (ed.), *The Economics of Ecosystems and Biodiversity: Ecological and Economic Foundations* (London: Earthscan), pp. 9–39

Lane, Marcus. 2006. 'The Role of Planning in Achieving Indigenous Land Justice and Community Goals', *Land Use Policy*, 23 (4), 385–94.

Lane, Marcus, and Geoff McDonald. 2005. 'Community-Based Environmental Planning: Operational Dilemmas, Planning Principles and Possible Remedies', *Journal of Environmental Planning and Management*, 48 (5), 709–31.

Lankoski, Jussi, Markku Ollikainen, Elizabeth Marshall, and Marcel Aillery. 2015. 'Environmental Co-Benefits and Stacking in Environmental Markets', *OECD Food, Agriculture and Fisheries Papers*, 72.

Lawson, Sam. 2014. *Illegal Logging in the Democratic Republic of the Congo*, Energy, Environment and Resources, (London: Chatham House), <https://www.chathamhouse.org/sites/default/files/home/chatham/public_html/sites/default/files/20140400LoggingDRCLawson.pdf> [Accessed 31 May 2021].

Leblois, Antoine, Olivier Damette, and Julien Wolfersberger. 2017. 'What Has Driven Deforestation in Developing Countries since the 2000s? Evidence from New Remote-Sensing Data', *World Development*, 92, 82–102.

Legacy, Crystal. 2012. 'Achieving Legitimacy through Deliberative Plan-Making Processes – Lessons for Metropolitan Strategic Planning', *Planning Theory and Practice*, 13 (1), 71–87.

Levis, Carolina, Bernardo Flores, Priscila Moreira, Bruno Luize, Rubana Alves, Juliano Franco-Moraes, Juliana Lins, Evelien Konings, Marielos Peña-Claros, Frans Bongers, Flavia Costa, and Charles Clement. 2018. 'How People Domesticated Amazonian Forests', *Frontiers in Ecology and Evolution*, 5, 171.

Liu, Juichieh, and Paul Opdam. 2014. 'Valuing Ecosystem Services in Community-Based Landscape Planning: Introducing a Wellbeing-Based Approach', *Landscape Ecology*, 29 (8), 1347–60.

Machar, Ivo. 2020. 'Sustainable Landscape Management and Planning', *Sustainability*, 12 (6), 2354.

Mackey, Brendan, and David Claudie. 2015. 'Points of Contact: Integrating Traditional and Scientific Knowledge for Biocultural Conservation', *Environmental Ethics*, 37 (3), 341–57.

Mackey, Brendan, Cyril Kormos, Heather Keith, William Moomaw, Richard Houghton, Russell Mittermeier, David Hole, and Sonia Hugh. 2020. 'Understanding the Importance of Primary Tropical Forest Protection as a Mitigation Strategy', *Mitigation and Adaptation Strategies for Global Change*, 25 (5), 763–87.

Martín-López, Berta, Ignacio Palomo, Marina García-Llorente, Irene Iniesta-Arandia, Antonio Castro, David García Del Amo, Erik Gómez-Baggethun, and Carlos Montes. 2017. 'Delineating Boundaries of Social-Ecological Systems for Landscape Planning: A Comprehensive Spatial Approach', *Land Use Policy*, 66, 90–104.

Matthews, Robin, and Paul Selman. 2006. 'Landscape as a Focus for Integrating Human and Environmental Processes', *Journal of Agricultural Economics*, 57 (2), 199–212.

Matulis, Brett. 2015. 'Valuing Nature: A Reply to Esteve Corbera', *Ecological Economics*, 110, 158–60.

McCarter, Joe, and Michael Gavin. 2014. 'Local Perceptions of Changes in Traditional Ecological Knowledge: A Case Study from Malekula Island, Vanuatu', *AMBIO*, 43 (3), 288–96.

McGinnis, Michael, and Elinor Ostrom. 2014. 'Social-Ecological System Framework: Initial Changes and Continuing Challenges', *Ecology and Society*, 19 (2).

Merlo, M., and L. Croitoru. 2005. 'Valuing Mediterranean Forests: Towards Total Economic Value.' in M. Merlo and L. Croitoru (eds.), *Valuing Mediterranean Forests: Towards Total Economic Value* (Wallingford, UK: CABI Publishing), pp. 17–36 3.

Milder, Jeffrey, Abigail Hart, Philip Dobie, Joshua Minai, and Christi Zaleski. 2014. 'Integrated Landscape Initiatives for African Agriculture, Development, and Conservation: A Region-Wide Assessment', *World Development*, 54, 68–80.

Millennium Ecosystem Assessment Board. 2005. *Ecosystems and Human Wellbeing* (Washington, D.C.).

Miraftab, Faranak. 2009. 'Insurgent Planning: Situating Radical Planning in the Global South', *Planning Theory*, 8 (1), 32–50.

Morgan, Edward A., Andrew Buckwell, Caterina Guidi, Beatriz Garcia, Lawrence Rimmer, Tim Cadman, and Brendan Mackey. 2021. 'The Basket of Benefits Approach: Capturing Multiple Forest Ecosystem Services for Just Benefit Sharing', *Ecosystem Services*, In press.

Morgan, Edward A., Tim Cadman, and Brendan Mackey. 2020. 'Integrating Forest Management across the Landscape: A Three Pillar Framework', *Journal of Environmental Planning and Management*, 64 (10), 1735–69.

Morgan, Edward A., Elnaz Torabi, and Ayşın Dedekorkut-Howes. 2020. 'Responding to Change: Lessons from Water Management for Metropolitan Governance', *Australian Planner*, 56 (2), 125–33.

Mousseau, Frederic. 2018. *The Great Timber Heist Continued: Tax Evasion and Illegal Logging in Papua New Guinea*, (Oakland, CA: Oakland Institute), <https://www.oaklandinstitute.org/sites/oaklandinstitute.org/files/great_timber_heist_cont.pdf> [Accessed 2 June 2021].

Newton, Peter, Brian Schaap, Michelle Fournier, Meghan Cornwall, Derrick Rosenbach, Joel DeBoer, Jessica Whittemore, Ryan Stock, Mark Yoders, Gernot Brodnig, and Arun Agrawal. 2015. 'Community Forest Management and REDD+', *Forest Policy and Economics*, 56, 27–37.

Ngoma, Hambulo, Arild Angelsen, Sarah Carter, and Rosa Maria Roman-Cuesta. 2018. 'Climate-Smart Agriculture: Will Higher Yields Lead to Lower Deforestation?' in Arild Angelsen (ed.),

Transforming REDD+: Lessons and New Directions (Bogor, Indonesia: Center for International Forestry Research), pp. 175–87.

Nielsen, Tobias. 2016. 'From REDD+ Forests to Green Landscapes? Analyzing the Emerging Integrated Landscape Approach Discourse in the UNFCCC', *Forest Policy and Economics*, 73, 177–84.

Ninan, K., S. Jyothis, P. Babu, and V. Ramakrishnappa. 2007. *The Economics of Biodiversity Conservation: Valuation in Tropical Forest Ecosystems* (London: Routledge).

Osborne, Natalie. 2015. 'Intersectionality and Kyriarchy: A Framework for Approaching Power and Social Justice in Planning and Climate Change Adaptation', *Planning Theory*, 14 (2), 130–51.

Ostrom, Elinor. 1990. *Governing the Commons: The Evolution of Institutions for Collective Action* (Cambridge, UK: Cambridge University Press).

——. 2009. 'A General Framework for Analyzing Sustainability of Social-Ecological Systems', *Science*, 325 (5939), 419–22.

Pagiola, Stefano. 2008. 'Payments for Environmental Services in Costa Rica', *Ecological Economics*, 65 (4), 712–24.

Pandey, Ashok K., Y.C. Tripathi, and Ashwani Kumar. 2016. 'Non Timber Forest Products (NTFPs) for Sustained Livelihood: Challenges and Strategies', *Research Journal of Forestry*, 10, 1–7.

Phillips, Adrian. 2003. 'Turning Ideas on Their Head: The New Paradigm for Protected Areas', *The George Wright Forum*, 20 (2), 8–32.

Pires, Mark. 2004. 'Watershed Protection for a World City: The Case of New York', *Land Use Policy*, 21 (2), 161–75.

Porras, Ina, and Nigel Asquith.·2018. *Ecosystems, Poverty Alleviation and Conditional Transfers*, (London: International Institute for Environment and Development), <https://pubs.iied.org/16639iied> [Accessed 24 January 2022].

Porras, Ina, D. Barton, M. Miranda, and A. Chacón-Cascante.·2013. *Learning from 20 Years of Payments for Ecosystem Services in Costa Rica*, (London: International Institute for Environment and Development), <https://pubs.iied.org/16514IIED/> [Accessed 9 February 2020].

Potschin, Marion B., and Roy H. Haines-Young. 2011. 'Ecosystem Services: Exploring a Geographical Perspective', *Progress in Physical Geography: Earth and Environment*, 35 (5), 575–94.

Reed, James, Josh Van Vianen, Elizabeth Deakin, Jos Barlow, and Terry Sunderland. 2016. 'Integrated Landscape Approaches to Managing Social and Environmental Issues in the Tropics: Learning from the Past to Guide the Future', *Global Change Biology*, 22 (7), 2540–54.

Reed, M., K. Allen, A. Attlee, A Dougill, K. Evans, J. Kenter, J. Hoy, D. McNab, S. Stead, C. Twyman, A. Scott, M. Smyth, L. Stringer, and M. Whittingham. 2017. 'A Place-Based Approach to Payments for Ecosystem Services', *Global Environmental Change*, 43, 92–106.

Reed, M., A. Evely, G. Cundill, I. Fazey, J. Glass, A. Laing, J. Newig, B. Parrish, C. Prell, C. Raymond, and L. Stringer. 2010. 'What Is Social Learning?', *Ecology and Society*, 15 (4), r1.

Ribeiro, Maria Beatriz, Adriano Jerozolimski, Pascale de Robert, Nilson Salles, Biribiri Kayapó, Tania Pimentel, and William Magnusson. 2014. 'Anthropogenic Landscape in Southeastern Amazonia: Contemporary Impacts of Low-Intensity Harvesting and Dispersal of Brazil Nuts by the Kayapó Indigenous People', *PLoS ONE*, 9 (7), e102187.

Ricke, Katharine, Laurent Drouet, Ken Caldeira, and Massimo Tavoni. 2018. 'Country-Level Social Cost of Carbon', *Nature Climate Change*, 8 (10), 895–900.

Rodriguez, Jon Paul, T. Douglas Beard, John Agard, Elena Bennett, Steve Cork, Graeme Cumming, Danielle Deane, Andrew Dobson, David Lodge, Michael Mutale, Gerald Nelson, Garry Peterson, and Teresa Ribeiro. 2005. 'Interactions among Ecosystem Services.' in SR Carpenter, PL

Pingali, EM Bennett and MB Zurek (eds.), *Ecosystems and Human Wellbeing* (New York: Island Press), pp. 433–48

Samndong, Raymond, Glenn Bush, Arild Vatn, and Melissa Chapman. 2018. 'Institutional Analysis of Causes of Deforestation in REDD+ Pilot Sites in the Equateur Province: Implication for REDD+ in the Democratic Republic of Congo', *Land Use Policy*, 76, 664–74.

Sayer, Jeffrey, Chris Margules, Agni Boedhihartono, Terry Sunderland, James Langston, James Reed, Rebecca Riggs, Louise Buck, Bruce Campbell, Koen Kusters, Chris Elliott, Peter Minang, Allan Dale, Herry Purnomo, James Stevenson, Petrus Gunarso, and Agus Purnomo. 2017. 'Measuring the Effectiveness of Landscape Approaches to Conservation and Development', *Sustainability Science*, 12 (3), 465–76.

Sayer, Jeffrey, Terry Sunderland, Jaboury Ghazoul, Jean-Laurent Pfund, Douglas Sheil, Erik Meijaard, Michelle Venter, Agni Klintuni Boedhihartono, Michael Day, Claude Garcia, van Cora Oosten, and Louise Buck. 2013. 'Ten Principles for a Landscape Approach to Reconciling Agriculture, Conservation, and Other Competing Land Uses', *Proceedings of the National Academy of Sciences*, 110 (21), 8349–56.

Schomers, Sarah, and Bettina Matzdorf. 2013. 'Payments for Ecosystem Services: A Review and Comparison of Developing and Industrialized Countries', *Ecosystem Services*, 6, 16–30.

Schroter, Matthias, Emma van der Zanden, Alexander van Oudenhoven, Roy Remme, Hector Serna-Chavez, Rudolf de Groot, and Paul Opdam. 2014. 'Ecosystem Services as a Contested Concept: A Synthesis of Critique and Counter-Arguments', *Conservation Letters*, 7 (6), 514–23.

Selman, Paul. 2004. 'Community Participation in the Planning and Management of Cultural Landscapes', *Journal of Environmental Planning and Management*, 47 (3), 365–92.

——. 2005. *Planning and the Landscape Scale* (London, UK: Routledge).

——. 2009. 'Planning for Landscape Multifunctionality', *Sustainability: Science, Practice and Policy*, 5 (2), 45–52.

Shackeroff, Janna, and Lisa Campbell. 2021. 'Traditional Ecological Knowledge in Conservation Research', *Conservation and Society*, 5 (3), 343–60.

Shepherd, Gill (eds.) 2008. *The Ecosystem Approach: Learning from Experience*, (Gland, Switzerland: International Union for Conservation of Nature).

Sheppard, Jonathan, James Chamberlain, Dolores Agúndez, Prodyut Bhattacharya, Paxie Wanangwa Chirwa, Andrey Gontcharov, Willie Cliffie John Sagona, Hai-long Shen, Wubalem Tadesse, and Sven Mutke. 2020. 'Sustainable Forest Management Beyond the Timber-Oriented Status Quo: Transitioning to Co-Production of Timber and Non-Wood Forest Products – a Global Perspective', *Current Forestry Reports*, 6 (1), 26–40.

Sitas, Nadia, Heidi Prozesky, Karen Esler, and Belinda Reyers. 2014. 'Opportunities and Challenges for Mainstreaming Ecosystem Services in Development Planning: Perspectives from a Landscape Level', *Landscape Ecology*, 29 (8), 1315–31.

Smith, Laurence, and Keith Porter. 2010. 'Management of Catchments for the Protection of Water Resources: Drawing on the New York City Watershed Experience', *Regional Environmental Change*, 10 (4), 311–26.

Smith, Richard, and Edward Maltby. 2003. *Using the Ecosystem Approach to Implement the Convention on Biological Diversity: Key Issues and Case Studies* (Gland, Switzerland: International Union for Conservation of Nature).

Sullivan, Sian. 2009. 'Green Capitalism, and the Cultural Poverty of Constructing Nature as Service Provider', *Radical Anthropology*, 3, 18–27.

Taylor, Ken, and Jane Lennon. 2011. 'Cultural Landscapes: A Bridge between Culture and Nature?', *International Journal of Heritage Studies*, 17 (6), 537–54.

Terraube, Julien, and Álvaro Fernández-Llamazares. 2020. 'Strengthening Protected Areas to Halt Biodiversity Loss and Mitigate Pandemic Risks', *Current Opinion in Environmental Sustainability*, 46, 35–38.

Thorpe, Amelia. 2017. 'Rethinking Participation, Rethinking Planning', *Planning Theory and Practice*, 18 (4), 566–82.

Tolessa, Terefe, Hailu Gessese, Motuma Tolera, and Moges Kidane. 2018. 'Changes in Ecosystem Service Values in Response to Changes in Landscape Composition in the Central Highlands of Ethiopia', *Environmental Processes*, 5 (3), 483–501.

Tollefson, Jeff. 2020. 'Why Deforestation and Extinctions Make Pandemics More Likely', *Nature*, 584 (7820), 175–76.

Tress, Bärbel, and Gunther Tress. 2001. 'Capitalising on Multiplicity: A Transdisciplinary Systems Approach to Landscape Research', *Landscape and Urban Planning*, 57 (3), 143–57.

Tulloch, David. 2007. 'Many, Many Maps: Empowerment and Online Participatory Mapping', *First Monday*, 12 (2). https://doi.org/10.5210/fm.v12i2.1620

Valencia-Sandoval, Cecilia, David Flanders, and Robert Kozak. 2010. 'Participatory Landscape Planning and Sustainable Community Development: Methodological Observations from a Case Study in Rural Mexico', *Landscape and Urban Planning*, 94 (1), 63–70.

Vallés-Planells, María, Francisco Galiana, and Veerle Van Eetvelde. 2014. 'A Classification of Landscape Services to Support Local Landscape Planning', *Ecology and Society*, 19 (1): 44. http://dx.doi.org/10.5751/ES-06251-190144

Watson, James, Tom Evans, Oscar Venter, Brooke Williams, Ayesha Tulloch, Claire Stewart, Ian Thompson, Justina Ray, Kris Murray, Alvaro Salazar, Clive McAlpine, Peter Potapov, Joe Walston, John Robinson, Michael Painter, David Wilkie, Christopher Filardi, William Laurance, Richard Houghton, Sean Maxwell, Hedley Grantham, Cristián Samper, Stephanie Wang, Lars Laestadius, Rebecca Runting, Gustavo Silva-Chávez, Jamison Ervin, and David Lindenmayer. 2018. 'The Exceptional Value of Intact Forest Ecosystems', *Nature Ecology and Evolution*, 2 (4), 599–610.

Woodward, Richard. 2011. 'Double-Dipping in Environmental Markets', *Journal of Environmental Economics and Management*, 61 (2), 153–69.

Wunder, Sven, Stefanie Engel, and Stefano Pagiola. 2008. 'Taking Stock: A Comparative Analysis of Payments for Environmental Services Programs in Developed and Developing Countries', *Ecological Economics*, 65 (4), 834–52.

Zimmerman, Barbara, and Cyril Kormos. 2012. 'Prospects for Sustainable Logging in Tropical Forests', *BioScience*, 62 (5), 479–87.

Chris Taylor
Chapter 6
Certification and sustainable development

Abstract: Non-state market-driven certification has become a critical component of global trade in natural resource commodities. This consists of companies and producers being assessed against standards that are developed by certification schemes founded and managed by non-state actors. These certification schemes are organised around a privatised form governance largely operating within norms and rationalities of neoliberalism and liberal environmentalism. They make use of identities, visibilities and concepts such as sustainable development. In this chapter, the practices of forest certification are discussed as an example of non-state market-driven certification in reference to governmentality and the mentality and rationalities of governing are considered. These schemes form a rationality of self-government that is largely independent of the state. In this sense, forests are governed at a distance through indirect impositions of power, which are exercised in the form of performance being demonstrated to an audience, consisting of consumers and interested actors, that the values of public concern are being conserved, protected or compensated. The self-government rationality of these schemes avoids the problems associated direct impositions of power as afforded by the state.

Keywords: forest stewardship council, governmentality, liberal environmentalism, neoliberalism, programme for the endorsement of forest certification, self-government, sustainable forest management, COVID-19

Introduction

Non-state market-driven certification has become a critical component of global trade in natural resource commodities (Auld 2014). This consists of companies and producers being assessed against standards that are developed by certification schemes founded and managed by non-state actors (Cashore, Auld, and Newsom 2004). These schemes typically establish environmental and social performance standards that go beyond voluntary codes of conduct and self-regulatory modes of governing by requiring independent verification of compliance with standards (Gulbrandsen 2014). There are a range of certification schemes covering a range of market sectors (Dingwerth and Pattberg 2009). The development of these certification schemes was intended to address failures in government and intergovernmental efforts to address market concerns around environmental degradation and poor working conditions (Gulbrandsen 2004). However, certification is largely a privatised form governance operating within the

https://doi.org/10.1515/9783110733488-006

norms of neoliberalism through discourses of sustainable development (Bernstein 2001; Humphreys 2009).These norms recognise economic development as the dominant paradigm through which environmental and social justice will be delivered at a global scale.

One of the most prominent examples of non-state market-driven certification is in the forestry sector, where over 440 million hectares has been certified under two major global forest certification schemes: the Forest Stewardship Council (FSC) and the Programme for the Endorsement of Forest Certification (PEFC) (FSC 2021b; FSC/PEFC 2021; PEFC 2020). Forest certification has evolved into a complex integrated mechanism of standards and procedures that has become an important component of global trade in forest products (Food and Agriculture Organization of the United Nations 2018: FAO). The share of wood products that FSC and PEFC certify as coming from certified forests under their respective standards represents 40% of global industrial roundwood production (FAO 2018). This significant share of global trade in forest and wood products demonstrates the increasing and important role that non-state market-driven governance now plays in seeking to address concerns around global environmental and social justice issues. It is therefore critical that these non-state market-driven certification initiatives be subject to increased scrutiny because they are offering the market a guarantee that a specified level of performance has been met in the sourcing and extraction of resources from forests and other natural ecosystems (Nussbaum and Simula 2005a).

The emergence of forest certification across global trade in forest and wood products is novel and addresses in part some of the failings of state and intergovernmental efforts to address deforestation and forest degradation, which reached unprecedented levels around the world during the 1970s and 1980s (Cashore, Auld, and and Newsom 2004; Williams 2006). It marks a transition away from a reliance on the nation-state and its hard law mechanisms towards a soft law approach that is based around private governance (Auld 2014). Its authority is based on market transactions and its legitimacy is based on valuations by external audiences, including those it seeks to regulate (Cashore, Auld, and Newsom 2004; Williams 2006). This is effectively where governance operates independently of state intervention and conforms with the norms of neoliberalism (Humphreys 2009) and what Bernstein (2001) has referred to as liberal environmentalism. In essence, forest certification seeks to internalise environmental costs by including them in the cost of products certified. The specific norms around liberal environmentalism are an attempt to reconcile competing sets of environment and economic development norms previously introduced at the 1972 United Nations Conference on the Environment in Stockholm (Bernstein 2002). The belief is that environmental protection can be addressed within the norms of economic development, broadly defined under the term sustainable development (World Commission on Environment and Development 1987).

The dominance of norms under neoliberalism and liberal environmentalism over other norms raises important questions of power and knowledge. Here, Michel Foucault's notion of governmentality (2007) provides important insights as to why certain strategies to address global deforestation and forest degradation gained prominence while others were rescinded. This chapter discusses as a case study the practices of forest certification within the norms of neoliberalism and liberal environmentalism and how these norms have given rise to the rationality of forest certification as a form of governing forests throughout the world. It discusses how forests and specific actors with affected interests in forests rendered objects visible and therefore governable within this privatised governance regime (Dean 2010).

Governmentality, power and liberal environmentalism

Michel Foucault (2007) introduced the notion of government as a necessary critique of the conceptions of power (Lemke 2012). This notion of government is different to the commonly held views of government as a state (Dean 2010). In his essay *The Subject and Power*, Foucault described the historical evolution of the term government as a concept that refers not simply to state management and political structures, but also to the way in which groups or individuals are directed and political and economic measures subjugate or control the range of actions available to those who are governed (Foucault 1982: 790). Therefore, government is a means to lead, direct or to guide and it presumes a set of standards or norms of conduct by which behaviour can be judged (Dean 2010). Such norms form specific rationalities of government, which are collectively termed governmentalities (Gordon 1991: 1). Foucault (2007: 108) provided three descriptions of governmentality. First as an ensemble formed by institutions, procedures, calculations and tactics allowing a specific and complex form of power. Second to have led to the development of a series of specific governmental apparatuses (*appareilis*) and knowledge (*savoirs*). Lastly as the process by which the state has increasingly taken the form of government attending to the conduct of its subjects (Hindess 1996). Combined, governmentality refers to all endeavours to shape, guide and direct the conduct of others (Rose 1999) and a way of arranging entities to suitable ends (Foucault 2007). Unlike coercive forms of power (Foucault 1995), governmentality provided for an explanation of power that was in essence productive (Lemke 2012: 11).

Mitchell Dean (2010: 33) provides dimensions upon which to analyse regimes of government which consist of 1) forms of visibility, ways of seeing and perceiving; 2) distinctive ways of thinking and questioning; 3) specific ways of acting, intervening and directing, made up of particular rationalities and expertise; and 4) characteristic ways of forming subjects, selves, persons or agents. These dimensions include the identification of problematisations, which consist of identifying specific situations in which the activity of governing becomes a problem (Dean 2010: 38). An analysis of government also includes a critique on methods of governing and the priority of these methods over others, practices of government as regimes, examining fields of visibility, technical aspects of government, its rationalities and how government forms identities.

In the context of problematisation, the political doctrine of liberalism can be approached as a related set of problematisations, interrogations and critiques of past, present and potential forms of government (Dean 2010: 63). It is based on the rule of law and the protection of individual rights and freedom against unnecessary encroachments of the state (Dean 2010: 61–62). Liberal government is effectively bound to the interests and actions of individuals who exchange in goods and services across the market. It has formed around rationality of those individuals that has allowed for an optimal functioning of the market while guaranteeing the welfare of the state and its population (Lemke 2012: 16). As a successor of liberalism, the political ideology of neoliberalism limits the influence of the state and conceives human wellbeing as advanced by liberating individual entrepreneurial freedoms and skills within an institutional framework characterised by strong private property rights, free markets and free trade (Harvey 2005: 2). In terms of governmentality, Dardot and Laval (2013) describe neoliberalism as the rationality of contemporary capitalism. Its principal characteristic is the generalisation of competition as a behavioural norm and it has permeated many aspects of social life. They consider that neoliberalism does not simply do away with rights and rules and the institutions that administer them. It also determines social relations and ways of life and constitutes a type of existence that stipulates the norms of Western behaviour and the expectations for those societies which seek to embrace modernity. Everyone exists in a state of permanent competition and economic struggle one with another, especially in the workplace, and social relations are determined by the market; inequality is justified by transforming the individual into an enterprise, resulting a mode of government that accords with the principle of competition (Dardot and Laval 2013). In this view, the role of the state is to create and preserve an institutional framework appropriate to such practices (Harvey 2005). Health, security, and welfare have been restructured and framed according to the image of the market (Rose 1999: 146).

Many concerns regarding the environment and corresponding responses have been framed around norms of neoliberalism. In this context, negative impacts on the environment are perceived as externalities, which are evaluated and costed in accordance with rules and norms of the market. For example, if forests are to be conserved, they need to be valued under market mechanisms (Humphreys 2009). Where environmental values conflict with economic imperatives agreements often fail, particularly in intergovernmental forums and when the environmental concern impacts state sovereignty. An example of this was at the United Nations Conference on the Human Environment in Stockholm in 1972, where underlying tensions arose between Northern and Southern nation-states regarding state sovereignty over resources use and policy (Bernstein 2002). Southern nation-states succeeded in placing concerns about economic growth on the agenda. This provided for institutional ways to reconcile competing sets of norms around the environment and economic development. As a breakthrough concept, sustainable development emerged during the 1980s and became the dominant conceptual framework for responses to international environmental problems (Bernstein 2002: 3).

Sustainable development was a cornerstone of the influential World Commission on Environment and Development report, *Our Common Future*, often referred to as the Brundtland Report after the then Prime Minister of Norway at the time of the report, Gro Harlem Brundtland, who was also the chair of the World Commission on Environment and Development. The report authors from the World Commission on Environment and Development defined the concept of sustainable development in the following widely cited statement:

> Sustainable development is development that meets the needs of the present without compromising the ability of future generations to meet their own needs.
>
> (World Commission on Environment and Development 1987: 43)

According to Bernstein (2000), the sustainable development concept encouraged a managed liberalism in the international economic order and integrated environmental protection goals into domestic development policies and international institutions. Bernstein (2001) argues that the thinking inherent in the concept created an entry point for liberal environmentalism to become institutionalised and resulted in an international system of governance that required environmental protection be based on maintaining, promoting and protecting the liberal economic order, including the privatisation of the global commons. The market was not only deemed to be compatible with the protection of the environment, but an essential mechanism for incorporating the concerns of state and non-state actors about the environment (Bernstein 2001).

The term sustainable development is now widely used. A targeted Google search of the term result yielded over 90 million results. It is widely used in forest management discourse, with the term sustainable forest management extensively used (Higman et al. 2005). It is also used extensively in agriculture, construction, transport and fishing. It has become a catch phrase to alleviate public concerns over environmental degradation.

Using an analytical governmentality framework, environmental concerns under the concept of sustainable development have been made visible through the rationalities of neoliberalism and liberal environmentalism. These rationalities provide for distinctive ways of thinking and questioning environmental problems, along with specific ways of acting upon them. Such problems are framed within the overall problematisation of government, that being the critique provided by liberalism, neoliberalism and liberal environmentalism. Forest certification is one such practice operating within the norms of neoliberalism as well as liberal environmentalism (Bernstein 2001).

Forest certification and neoliberal governmentality

A critique of forest certification as a type of governmentality or a rationality of government is important here. Forest certification is not only a response to widespread concerns around deforestation and forest degradation, but also part of a larger problematisation of government. Under the norms of neoliberalism, deforestation and forest degradation are viewed as the consequence of negative externalities and where forests are not valued under specific market mechanisms. Deforestation arises as a consequence of failing to effectively internalise the positive externalities associated with environmental goods and services. Forest conservation needs to be given an economic value and functions through market mechanisms. The logical assumption of this view is that if forests have no economic value, they will be threatened by deforestation and degradation (Humphreys 2009). One of the primary drivers behind forest certification is therefore to provide market incentives to manage and value forests in accordance with socially and environmentally acceptable standards (Nussbaum and Simula 2005a). Unprecedented rates of deforestation and forest degradation were occurring in the latter half of the twentieth century throughout the world (Williams 2006). The drivers behind the deforestation and forest degradation were multilayered, but land clearing for agriculture was identified as one of the most important drivers of deforestation and logging an important driver behind forest degradation (Hosonuma et al. 2012). During the 1980s, environmental NGOs and civil society actors sought to raise awareness on global deforestation and forest degradation, instigating public campaigns and consumer boycotts of wood products originating from some of the worst affected areas, such as the Brazil and surrounding areas (Cashore, Auld, and Newsom 2004).

With increasing public awareness of global deforestation and forest degradation, particularly across Europe and North America, market demands increased for verifying the source of wood products (Cashore, Auld, and Newsom 2004). An environmental NGO in the United Kingdom, Friends of the Earth UK, published their first edition of their *Good Wood Guide* and launched a seal of approval for approved wood products. It listed hundreds of UK retailers, mainly according to their involvement with tropical timbers (Counsell and Terje Loraas 2002). However, some of the guidance in the first edition could not be fully verified, because it only focussed on retailers not trading wood sourced from tropical forests (Synnott 2005). Wood sourced from other forest types, such as temperate or boreal forest, was never assessed. It resulted in Friends of the Earth UK publishing a completely revised version of the *Good Wood Guide* and the seal of approval was discontinued (Counsell 1990).

International efforts to verify forest management in the sourcing of wood products came in the form a proposal to the International Tropical Timber Organisation (ITTO). In 1988, Friends of the Earth UK sought to encourage the ITTO to consider certification and labelling as a mechanism for improving tropical forest management (Synnott 2005). The ITTO was established in 1985 based on the International Tropical Timber Agreement, which was in turn established under the auspices of the United Nations Conference on Trade and Development (UNCTAD) (Elliot 2000). The ITTO commissioned a study investigating the status of natural forest management in the tropics. It concluded that the extent of moist tropical forest being managed for the sustainable production of timber was negligible at a global scale (Elliot 2000). Following the report, a feasibility study was proposed for the identification of sustainable forest management and products sourced from those forests being recognised in export markets. It was hoped that the ITTO would facilitate this initiative (Synnott 1988). Although this initiative was endorsed by the UK government's Overseas Development Administration (Tollefson, Gale, and Haley 2008), it encountered strong opposition at the seventh International Tropical Timber Council (ITTC) session in Yokohama in November 1989, because many timber-producing countries feared that a scheme identifying wood products based on sustainable forest management would present a barrier to trade (Counsell and Terje Loraas 2002; Tollefson, Gale, and Haley 2008).

State invention in the trade of wood products from regions where deforestation and forest degradation were occurring also encountered difficulties. In Austria, state-based attempts were made to regulate the import of unsustainably produced timber (Vogt et al. 1999). The Austrian parliament proposed legislation that required mandatory labelling on wood products and imposed an import tax on products sourced from tropical forests (Chase 1993). Under this proposed legislation, the Austrian Economic Affairs Ministry was to increase the import tax on all products made from or containing tropical wood, from 8% to 70%. The labelling component was part of a selective import certification system, with tropical wood imports labelled with made from tropical wood or contains tropical wood (Chase 1993: 761). However, countries producing tropical timber contested that these proposed measures were non-compliant with the legal requirements of General Agreement on Tariffs and Trade (GATT) (now World Trade Organisation (WTO)) (Vogt et al. 1999). Critics alleged unfair discrimination and that Austria was attempting to decide unilaterally what constituted sustainably managed forests when there was no international consensus (Chase 1993). As a result, other importing nation-states moved away from using mandatory, legislative means to address timber trade issues (Vogt et al. 1999). Voluntary market-based approaches became preferable because they did not involve the enforcement of state law favouring some wood products and restricting others, which was non-compliant with GATT and later WTO Trade laws.

Intergovernmental efforts to address deforestation and forest degradation also encountered difficulties. The proposal for a legally binding Global Forest Convention at the United Nations Conference on Environment and Development (UNCED) at Rio de Janeiro in 1992 proved unsuccessful (Humphreys 1996). The notion of a legally binding convention pitted Northern states such as the US and Canada, which argued that forests were a global common, against Southern states such as Malaysia and India, which argued that forests were a sovereign responsibility (Bernstein and Cashore 2004). These Southern states argued that forests should be utilised in line with their respective development objectives (Humphreys 2005). Bernstein and Cashore (2004) explained that the failure to create a binding treaty at UNCED was in large part owing to the inability to work out how this compatibility of free trade, development and protection of forests could work in practice. Proposals to deal with the problems associated with forestry had difficulty gaining legitimacy as they had a potential to impact state resource sovereignty and the rules of free trade. Legally binding provisions for sustainable forest management, even if not directly related to trade, could nevertheless unduly impact the exports of developing countries (Bernstein and Cashore 2004). Neoliberalism, with its light-touch approach to soft law, rather than hard conventions, encouraged non-legally binding approaches, which reflect political rather than legal commitments and to this day there is no international forest convention on a par with biodiversity, desertification, or climate change (Humphreys 2009). As a result, proceeding efforts to address deforestation and forest degradation around the world considered the norms of liberal environmentalism (Bernstein 2001) and neoliberalism (Humphreys 2009). State-based and intergovernmental efforts that contravened such norms were doomed to failure, owing to the dominance and hegemony of such norms governing economic conduct. Actors worked outside of the state and conceived non-state market-based incentives to address deforestation and forest degradation. Forest certification is now one of the most important of these incentives.

The first forest certification incentive to emerge was the Forest Stewardship Council (FSC) (Cashore, Auld, and Newsom 2004). It was founded in an assembly of 130 representatives in Toronto, Canada, in September 1993 (Nussbaum and Simula 2005a). Representatives included environmental organisations, labour unions, Indigenous groups, retailers and the consultancy sector (Dingwerth 2008). The concept behind the FSC was to bring to together actors from different, and sometimes conflicting, sectors and create an interdiscursive space upon where standards constituting acceptable forms of forest management could be agreed to. Actors were organised by their sector interests into three chambers, environmental, social and economic, with its purpose to maintain the balance of equal voting power between these different chambers (FSC 2017). The governance of the organisation reflected this three-chamber system, with directors of the FSC elected by the membership and assigned to each chamber representing their respective chamber constituencies. Each chamber was further divided into two sub-chambers, each representing Northern and Southern states (Nussbaum and Simula 2005a).

Forests and plantations certified under the FSC are required to comply with approved standards for forest management based around Principles and Criteria on what the FSC agreed to constitute well-managed forests (2015a). The approved standards consist of locally adapted indicators based on the FSC Principles and Criteria, which are developed by standard development groups approved by the FSC (2009b). Wood products labelled as being sourced from FSC certified forests require that their processing streams be certified under Chain of Custody Standards approved by the FSC (2021a). Wood processors can include non-FSC certified wood into FSC labelled products on condition it complies with FSC standards on Controlled Wood (2007, 2016).

Standards, norms and technologies of government

Central to the practice of forest certification is the auditing of forest and plantation management against the approved standards of a forest certification scheme (Nussbaum and Simula 2005a). The use of the standards and the process of auditing forests and plantations against those standards in the FSC, and the practice of forest certification more broadly, forms a technology of government (Miller and Rose 1990). This is where standards and the practice of auditing is used to shape the conduct of forest and plantation management with the intent of achieving a set of outcomes. In this context standards and standardisation form a critical technology of government (Higgins and Hallström 2007). They provide ways of knowing forests and the management of these forests through procedures of notation, ways of collecting and presenting statistics, the transportation of these to centres where calculations and judgements can be made and so forth (Miller and Rose 1990: 5). The rationality behind standards is that they form knowledge of what is normal and what is abnormal in accordance with specific structures of power (Foucault 2007). This production of truth and knowledge provided for a forest, plantation or group of actors working in and around these areas to become known and measured across a specific territory. This aligns with Foucault's (2007) concept of a population and territory, which can be used to provide the basis for norms and standards. Certain actions and behaviours can thus be differentiated from others across populations and territories. Such differentiations have evolved under specific disciplines which contain expertise, knowledge, and relations of power (Foucault 1982). Disciplines classify 'individuals, places, time, actions and operations . . . into components such that they can be seen, on the one hand, and modified on the other' (Foucault 2007: 56). Foucault referred to these visibilities and modifications as 'disciplinary normalisation' (2007: 57)

In the practice of forest certification, certified forests become a type of normal forest, a forest that is known, calculable and governable. The normal forest concept is not new and has its origins in the scientific forestry of the Enlightenment (Puett-mann, Coates, and Messier 2009). However, as opposed to the normal forest under early forms of scientific forestry being a simplistic and homogenous environment (Scott 1998), the normal forest that is certified is one that reflects the perception of an acceptable forest and/or plantation to those who not only govern the standard, but to those who also accept its authority. The process of certification enables the market to differentiate a normal forest compliant with approved standards from ab-normal forests that are not certified or which do not meet the thresholds of an ap-proved forest certification standard.

The normalisation of conduct across populations and territories is a critical ele-ment of neoliberal means of industrial production and consumption. The homogeni-sation of production methods provides for efficient means of production across large scales. Such normalisation is in effect a result of standardisation. This practice dates to the ancient Babylonians producing bricks of standard dimensions and the Romans standardising axle lengths for their chariots to economise on road building. In the wake of global industrial production, standardisation provides for more efficient pro-duction of goods where homogenous production has gained prominence (Higgins and Hallström 2007). One of the driving forces behind the practice of standardisation was the rise of engineering and its formation as a professionalised body (Higgins and Hallström 2007). During the 1920s, several national associations representing engi-neering professions formed new organisations of standardisation, known as National Standards Bodies. States promoted these National Standards Bodies as facilitators of progress and trade and relied on the standards set by these bodies for their regulatory purposes. The proliferation of National Standards Bodies over multiple jurisdictions triggered the emergence of an international standardisation movement. This led to the formation of the International Organisation for Standardisation (ISO) (Higgins and Hallström 2007). The ISO's central mission was to facilitate international trade and commerce by developing common international standards for products, materi-als, and processes (Prakash and Potoski 2006). Under this rationality, the normal is an efficient means of production and consumption, the abnormal is not.

The rationality of standardisation as a form of differentiating the normal from the abnormal has its basis in liberal and neoliberal governmentalities. Liberalism seeks to establish norms of government that are derived from its economic relations with the processes that will lead to the production of the resources necessary for its subsistence and prosperity (Dean 2010: 144). Under neoliberalism, norms of productivity are less inclined to reside with the state but private enterprise and citizens. The population is encouraged to be industrious. It is normalised to perform and achieve performance targets, such as in education, employment and material wealth acquisition. Technolo-gies of government are in essence technologies of performance (Dean 2010). The push to corporatise, privatise and outsource the public service and replace previous ar-rangements for determining compliance with benchmarks, performance indicators and the like, became technical methods for improving performance and re-orienting moral and political conduct towards that goal (Dean 2010). These technologies are a means of transforming professionals within a population into 'calculating individuals' within calculable spaces, subject to particular calculable regimes (Dean 2010: 197). This encapsulates a form of self-government, where the individual is compelled to know themselves and take responsibility for themselves (Foucault 1994). The practice of forest certification is a form of self-government, where, in place of the citizen, a forest management actor or actors voluntarily elect to have their performance assessed and audited against approved standards of a forest certification scheme residing within a privatised governance regime.

Under the FSC scheme, along with other forest certification schemes, accredited certification bodies are contracted by the applicant forest management enterprise and downstream processors to assess and audit the management operations of the enterprise against the relevant approved standard of the forest certification scheme (FSC 2009a; Nussbaum and Simula 2005b). The accredited certification bodies are private enterprises, whose income is generated from the applicant forest management actors and downstream manufacturers. Once certification is achieved under the FSC, accredited certification bodies are then required to undertake at least four surveillance evaluations over a period of five years (2009a). Under the FSC, accredited certification bodies are required to conduct themselves in accordance with the norms and standards for certification approved by the FSC (2015b).

The norms and standards used under forest certification evolved with the intent of capturing the complexities surrounding forest ecosystems and the societies that value and depend on them. The practice of standardisation was not intended for this purpose, because it was initially developed to make industrial manufacturing efficient, consistent and meeting thresholds of performance (Higgins and Hallström 2007). Standards used across society cover many aspects of industrial production and social life. This is evident in safety standards, such as the fire rating of building elements or minimum safety requirements for motor vehicle components. For example, some standards specify the performance thresholds of building elements to contain the spread of fire for a set time-period allowing for the occupants of a building to escape. These standards are the product of expert working groups, convened by respective standards bodies. The expert knowledge informing the standard may be based upon documented observations of specific past events, of what succeeded and what failed. However, this information does not form the content of the standards. In the process of standardisation, expert knowledge is abstracted into a generalised measure of performance (Jacobsson 2002).The generality and abstractness of knowledge in standards became more evident as it is transferred into more complex areas of social life. For example, the ISO Quality Assurance Standards specify requirements for a quality management system that can be used for internal application by organisations, or for certification or for contractual purposes. It focusses on the effectiveness of the quality management system in meeting customer requirements (Standards Australia 2016). These standards do not specify minimum thresholds of performance for products or provide a guarantee that a minimum threshold of performance has been met. Instead, the rationality of these standards is to provide a platform to enable that is less concerned about environmental protection and more about ensuring a form of neoliberal 'rule at a distance' (Higgins and Hallström 2007: 697). Environmental management standards are similar to those standards covering quality assurance. They are based on the use of a documented management system to implement an environmental policy for the entity seeking certification under that standard (Higman et al. 2005). Environmental management standards specify no minimum threshold of environmental performance. Therefore, no guarantee of achieving a performance threshold is allowed to be labelled on products manufactured from a process certified under these environmental management standards (Higman et al. 2005). Given the ambiguity surrounding the notion of quality assurance and environmental management systems, a new market for assurance has emerged, which demands a tight coupling between quality performance and processes to ensure that this performance is visible to a wider audience (Power 1999).

This was particularly the case for forest certification, which contains elements of both performance and process-based standards (Nussbaum and Simula 2005a). Forest management standards also had to evolve with the aim of capturing greater complexities concerning the social and environmental impacts of forest management (Lindenmayer and Franklin 2002). In response to the complexities around forest management, the FSC devised a hierarchical framework of Principles, Criteria, Indicators and Verifiers to form a structure in its forest management standards (2015a). The Principles and Criteria are global in scope, with Indicators and Verifiers locally adapted to regions or nation-states (2009b). This is intended to provide consistency in the locally adapted standards used by accredited certification bodies across the world (2009b). The Principles identify essential rules or elements for the FSC of forest stewardship and the criteria provide a means of judging whether or not the Principles (of forest management) have been fulfilled. The indicators provide quantitative or qualitative variables which can be measured or described and which provides a means of judging whether a forest management unit complies with the requirements of the FSC Criteria. The indicators form the normative component of an FSC standard. The verifiers provide guidance to the accredited certification bodies and the applicants seeking certification regarding interpreting compliance with the indicators. The hierarchical structure of the FSC forest management standards marks a point of departure from the previous form and structure of standards devised under the ISO and national standard bodies (Taylor 2011). From a governmentality perspective, the intent of this structure was to increase visibility of elements in the forests, actions of forest management enterprises working in forests and actors with an interest or who are impacted by forest management operations.

This rationality of forest certification renders visible the certified forest as well as elements that comprise the certified forest, associated actions and identities. For example, an important component of the FSC forest management standards is the

High Conservation Value Forest concept (2015a). The FSC classifies a forest as being High Conservation Value based on six attributes:
1) Forests with concentrations of biological diversity and rare, threatened or endangered species, that are significant at global, regional or national levels;
2) Landscape level ecosystems and mosaics, such as intact forest landscapes and large landscape level ecosystems and ecosystem mosaics that are significant at global, regional or national levels, and that contain viable populations of the great majority of the naturally occurring species in natural patterns of distribution and abundance;
3) Rare, threatened or endangered ecosystems, habitats or refugia;
4) Forests providing critical ecosystem services, including protection of water catchments and control of erosion of vulnerable soils and slopes;
5) Forests satisfying the basic necessities of local communities or Indigenous peoples, identified through engagement with these communities or Indigenous peoples; and,
6) Forests containing cultural values of global or national cultural, archaeological or historical significance and/or of critical cultural, ecological, economic or religious/sacred importance for the traditional cultures of local communities or Indigenous peoples, identified through engagement with these local communities or Indigenous peoples.

According Tollefson et al (2008), the High Conservation Value Forest concept approach was intended make visible a wider set of values for forests. Many previous classifications of forest values focussed on values consisting of age or whether the forest was part of a large and intact area (Laestadius, Nogueron, and Lee 2003). However, these classifications did not include other forest values that were of importance to many other actors, such as Indigenous peoples whose culture and well-being are critically dependent of a suite of values not rendered visible by other forms of classification. Furthermore, the FSC found that other terms to describe forests of value, such as primary or virgin lacked, definitional clarity and risked ambiguous usage by certification bodies, as well as the inability to translate these terms into Spanish, the FSC's second official language (Tollefson, Gale, and Haley 2008: 192–93).

Various identities are made visible through its rationalities of forest certification. For example, the applicant seeking certification under the FSC is identified as the client (2015b: 10). Accredited certification bodies are required to have expertise within relevant disciplines, including those consisting of ecology, forestry, sociology, economics or anthropology (2015b: 40). Here, identities such as ecologist, forester, sociologist, economist and anthropologist are rendered visible. The rationality of the certification process affords authority to these identities. People who are affected or have an interest in the performance of the client as a forest manager are identified as stakeholders (FSC 2009a). The identity of a stakeholder is assigned to such groups as local communities, state departments, local government entities, environment groups, social organisations, workers and employees (Nussbaum and Simula 2005a). The FSC identifies two stakeholder types: the affected stakeholder and the interested stakeholder (2015a). The former makes visible any person, group of persons or entity that is or is likely to be subject to the effects of the forest under certification; the latter identifies any person, group of persons or entity that has shown an interest, or is known to have an interest, in the forest under certification. However, the authority of knowledge held by stakeholders in a certification audit can be at the discretion of the accredited certification body conducting the audit (Taylor and Lindenmayer 2021).

Forest certification enables governing at a distance. It performs an indirect mechanism of rule, which also is an important rationality in liberal democratic societies (Miller and Rose 1990: 9). This involves the mobilisation of distant places, where knowledge resides in centres of calculation in the form of maps, reports, statistics and datasets. Complex mechanisms enable the linking of calculations at one place with actions at another. This is not through the direct imposition of a form of conduct by force, but through what Miller and Rose describe as a delicate affiliation of a loose assemblage of agents and agencies into a functioning network (1990: 14–15). In the context of the FSC, knowledge of actions, identities and places resides in places distant from where they occur. Through its rationalities, it has been able to inform the conduct of actors and management of forests distant from its centres of calculation. More importantly, the FSC has been able to inform the conduct of forest management across nation-states. Where proposals of legally binding global forest conventions failed to influence the conduct of individual nation-states regarding deforestation and forest degradation (Humphreys 1996), the practices of forest certification, embedded within the rationalities of liberal environmentalism and neoliberalism, avoided the obstacles regarding state-based sovereignty and laws concerning international trade. Its success is based on its form as a non-state driven market-based mechanism (Cashore, Auld, and and Newsom 2004).

Sustainable development and certification

The concept of sustainable development has widely influenced the forest management sector. The concept of sustainability is not new, with it originally used in scientific forestry as sustained yield (Puettmann, Coates, and Messier 2009). However, the term was broadened to sustainable forest management, which attempted to sustain the flows of different sets of goods and services from forests (Sayer and Maginnis 2005). Intergovernmental organisations use the term widely, such as the Food and Agriculture Organisation of the United Nations (FAO), which states that:

> Sustainable forest management (SFM) is defined as a "dynamic and evolving concept, which aims to maintain and enhance the economic, social and environmental values of all types of

forests, for the benefit of present and future generations." Forests and trees, when sustainably managed, make vital contributions both to people and to the planet, bolstering livelihoods, providing clean air and water, conserving biodiversity and responding to climate change.

(FAO 2022)

While the term sustainable development or sustainable forest management does not feature in the FSC's Principles and Criteria, the definition of sustainable development developed by the World Commission of Environment and Development (1987) has influenced the vision of the FSC:

> FSC's vision is that the world's forests meet the social, ecological, and economic rights and needs of the present generation without compromising those of future generations.   (2015a)

In the FSC's vision, the term sustainable development as provided by the World Commission of Environment and Development (1987) is replaced with the term the world's forests. These and other examples not mentioned here demonstrate the reach and influence of the concept of sustainable development and its overarching norms of liberal environmentalism on the conduct of forest management disciplines and practices, including forest certification.

The concept of development implies economic growth. Indeed, the World Commission of Environment and Development (1987) made reviving growth the top strategic priority in a sharp departure from earlier statements of global environmental policy (Bernstein 2001). In a global context, development is widely perceived as an improvement of the quality of life for millions of people, especially where poverty has been systemic and abject. Improvements for forest management under the concept of sustainable development is viewed as providing equality and equity to millions of people around the world who are dependent on the viability of forests but who have been historically marginalised and displaced by industrial-scale logging operations (Dudley, Jeanrenaud, and Sullivan 1995). However, the term sustainable development has been widely used by wealthy nation-states and industries to promote further expansion of their respective enterprises. Often, further degrading forest ecosystems to the point of irretrievable collapse (Taylor and Lindenmayer 2020; Lindenmayer et al. 2011).

Economic development, whether it be termed under the auspices of sustainable development or something else, forms an important norm in the rationality of neoliberalism (Harvey 2005; Foucault 2008). Forest certification as a form of private governance works on the idea that if people and enterprises are free to pursue their own interests in the marketplace, the collective good will be maximised. Environmental and social standards should therefore be voluntary. Privatisation is appealing to governments because it relieves the state of its economic obligations (Humphreys 2006). However, the intent of forest certification was to complement regulation, not replace it (Cashore, Auld, and and Newsom 2004). This has inherent problems where non-compliance under a forest certification standard only results in an enterprise losing the market access afforded by that certification scheme, as opposed to being prosecuted under state-based regulation. While in some instances, forest certification standards can impose a higher level of compliance compared with state-based regulation, forest certification schemes operate in a competitive marketplace and adopt strategies of growth and expansion. This is evidenced by the strategy of the FSC (2020), which has announced that it seeks to grow its global certified area to 300 million hectares by 2030. The scheme also advocated for the forestry industry as an essential service during the COVID-19 pandemic (Carstensen 2020). Advocating for forestry as an essential service ensured that the practice of forest certification continued in a restricted economy when other market sectors were forced by governments to close.

Conclusion

The context of non-state market-driven certification schemes, whether they be concerned with forestry, fisheries or even energy efficiency, all reside within the norms of neoliberalism and liberal environmentalism. This means that these schemes have their authority in the market. However, the legitimacy of these schemes is dependent on evaluations by external audiences, including civil society actors such as Indigenous peoples' groups, environmental organisations, unions and consumer advocate groups. These schemes form a rationality of self-government that is largely independent of the state. Power is exercised in the form of performance being demonstrated to an audience, consisting of consumers and interested actors, that the values of public concern are being conserved, protected or compensated. These schemes make use of identities, visibilities and concepts, such as sustainable development. However, these non-state market-driven certification schemes do not impose themselves directly on the sovereignty of nation-states nor directly interfere with trade. The self-government rationality of these schemes provides for an indirect imposition, realised through governing at a distance. As a result, power is exercised in a productive way where certified actors can enjoy the benefits of being identified with specific schemes that have been afforded authority in the market.

References

Auld, G. 2014. *Constructing Private Governance* (New Haven, CT: Yale University Press).
Bernstein, S. 2000. 'Ideas, Social Structure and the Compromise of Liberal Environmentalism', *European Journal of International Relations*, 6 (4), 464–512.
——. 2001. *The Compromise of Liberal Environmentalism* (New York: Columbia University Press).
——. 2002. 'Liberal Environmentalism and Global Environmental Governance', *Global Environmental Politics*, 2 (3), 1–16.
Bernstein, S, and B Cashore. 2004. 'Nonstate Global Governance: Is Forest Certification a Legitimate Alternative to a Global Forest Convention?' In J.J. Kirton and M.J. Trebilcock (eds.),

Hard Choices, Soft Law Voluntary Standards in Global Trade, Environment and Social Governance (Routledge), pp. 33–63

Carstensen, Kim. 2020. *Pulling Together in a Time of Isolation*. (Bonn: Forest Stewardship Council) <https://fsc.org/en/newsfeed/pulling-together-in-a-time-of-isolation> [Accessed 24 February 2022]

Cashore, B.W, G Auld, and D And Newsom. 2004. *Governing through Markets: Forest Certification and the Emergence of Non-State Authority* (New Haven, CT: Yale University Press).

Cashore, B.W., G. Auld, and D. Newsom. 2004. *Governing through Markets: Forest Certification and the Emergence of Non-State Authority* (New Haven, CT: Yale University Press).

Chase, B.F. 1993. 'Tropical Forests and Trade Policy: The Legality of Unilateral Attempts to Promote Sustainable Development under the GATT', *Third World Quarterly*, 14 (4), 749–74.

Counsell, S. 1990. *The Good Wood Guide: A Friends of the Earth Handbook* (London: Friends of the Earth UK).

Counsell, S, and K Terje Loraas.·2002. *Trading in Credibility: The Myth and Reality of the Forest Stewardship Council*, (London: Rainforest Foundation UK).

Dardot, P, and C Laval. 2013. *The New Way of the World: On Neoliberal Society* (London: Verso).

Dean, M. 2010. *Governmentality: Power and Rule in Modern Society* (London: Sage Publications).

Dingwerth, K. 2008. 'North-South Parity in Global Governance: The Affirmative Procedures of the Forest Stewardship Council', *Global Governance*, 14, 53–71.

Dingwerth, K., and P. Pattberg. 2009. 'World Politics and Organizational Fields: The Case of Transnational Sustainability Governance', *European Journal of International Relations*, 15 (4), 707–43.

Dudley, N, JP Jeanrenaud, and F Sullivan. 1995. *Bad Harvest: The Timber Trade and the Degradation of the World's Forests* (London: WWF and Earthscan).

Elliot, C. 2000. *Forest Certification: A Policy Perspective*, (Bogor: Center for International Forestry Research).

Food and Agriculture Organization of the United Nations.·2018. *State of the World's Forests: Forest Pathways to Sustainable Development*, (Rome: FAO), <https://www.fao.org/policy-support/tools-and-publications/resources-details/en/c/1144279/> [Accessed 23 February 2022].

——. 2022. *Natural Forest Management – Sustainable Forest Management*, <https://www.fao.org/forestry/sfm/en/> [Accessed 20 February 2022].

Forest Stewardship Council. 2007. *FSC Controlled Wood Standard for Forest Management Enterprises Standard – FSC-STD-30-010 V2.0* (Bonn: FSC) <https://members.fsc.org/en/document-centre/documents/resource/374> [Accessed 23 February 2022]

——. 2009a. *Forest Management Evaluations FSC-STD-20-007 (V3-0)*. (Bonn: FSC) <https://fsc.org/en/document-centre/documents/resource/279> [Accessed 23 February 2022]

——. 2009b. *Structure and Content of National Forest Stewardship Standards FSC-STD-60-002 (V1-0)*. (Bonn: FSC) <https://fsc.org/en/document-centre/documents/resource/261> [Accessed 23 February 2022]

——. 2015a. *FSC Principles and Criteria for Forest Stewardship FSC-STD-01-001 V5-2 En*. (Bonn: FSC) <https://fsc.org/en/document-centre/documents/resource/392> [Accessed 23 February 2022]

——. 2015b. *General Requirements for FSC Accredited Certification Bodies FSC-STD-20-001 V4-0*. (Bonn: FSC) <https://fsc.org/en/document-centre/documents/resource/280> [Accessed 23 February 2022]

——. 2016. *Requirements for Sourcing FSC Controlled Wood Standard – FSC-STD-40-005 V3.1*. (Bonn: FSC) <https://au.fsc.org/preview.requirements-for-sourcing-fsc-controlled-wood-fsc-std-40-005-v3-0.a-1168.pdf> [Accessed 23 February 2022]

——. 2017. *Statutes*. (Bonn: FSC) <https://fsc.org/sites/default/files/2021-06/FSC-AC-Statutes-Sep-2017.pdf> [Accessed 23 February 2022]

——. 2020. *FSC Annual Report 2020*, (Bonn: FSC), <https://annual-reports.fsc.org/> [Accessed 24 February 2022].

——. 2021a. *Chain of Custody Certification FSC-STD-40-004 V3-1 En*. (Bonn: FSC) <https://members.fsc.org/en/document-centre/documents/resource/302> [Accessed 23 February 2022]

——. 2021b. *Facts and Figures*, <https://fsc.org/en/facts-figures> [Accessed 15 August 2021].

Forest Stewardship Council, and Programme for the Endorsement of Forest Certification. 2021. *Estimated Forest Area under Both FSC and PEFC/PEFC-Endorsed Certification in 2020*, <https://fsc.org/en/newsfeed/estimated-forest-area-under-both-fsc-and-pefcpefc-endorsed-certification-in-2020> [Accessed 23 February 2022].

Foucault, M. 1982. 'The Subject and Power', *Critical Inquiry*, 8 (4), 777–95.

——. 1994. 'Technologies of the Self.' in P Rabinow and N Rose (eds.), *The Essential Foucault* (New York: The New Press),

——. 1995. *Discipline and Punish: The Birth of the Prison*. (New York: Vintage Books).

——. 2007. *Security, Territory and Population: Lectures at the College De France 1977-1978* (New York: Palgrave MacMillan).

——. 2008. *The Birth of Biopolitics* (New York: Palgrave Macmillan).

Gordon, C. 1991. 'Governmental Rationality: An Introduction.' in G Burchell, C Gordon and P Miller (eds.), *The Foucault Effect: Studies in Governmentality* (Chicago: The University of Chicago Press), pp. 1–51

Gulbrandsen, L.H. 2004. 'Overlapping Public and Private Governance: Can Forest Certification Fill the Gaps in the Global Forest Regime?', *Global Environmental Politics*, 4 (2), 75–99.

——. 2014. 'Dynamic Governance Interactions: Evolutionary Effects of State Responses to Non-State Certification Programs', *Regulation and Governance*, 8, 74–92.

Harvey, D. 2005. A Brief History of Neoliberalism (Oxford: Oxford University Press).

Higgins, W, and KT Hallström. 2007. 'Standardization, Globalization and Rationalities of Government', *The Interdisciplinary Journal of Organization, Theory and Society*, 14 (5), 685–704.

Higman, S, J Mayers, S Bass, N Judd, and R Nussbaum. 2005. *The Sustainable Forestry Handbook* (London: Earthscan).

Hindess, B. 1996. *Discourses of Power: From Hobbes to Foucault* (Cambridge: Blackwell Publishers).

Hosonuma, N, M Herold, V De Sy, R.S De Fries, M Brockhaus, L Verchot, A Angelsen, and E Romijn. 2012. 'An Assessment of Deforestation and Forest Degradation Drivers in Developing Countries',. *Environmental Research Letters*, 7 (4), 044009.

Humphreys, D. 2006. *Logjam: Deforestation and the Crisis of Global Governance* (London: Earthscan).

——. 1996. *Forest Politics: The Evolution of International Cooperation* (London: Earthscan).

——. 2005. 'The Elusive Quest for a Global Forests Convention', *RECIEL*, 14 (1), 1–10.

——. 2009. 'Discourse as Ideology: Neoliberalism and the Limits of International Forest Policy', *Forest Policy and Economics*, 11, 319–25.

Jacobsson, B. 2002. 'Standardization and Expert Knowledge.' in N Brunsson and B Jacobsson (eds.), *A World of Standards* (Oxford: Oxford University Press), pp. 40–49

Laestadius, Lars, Ruth Nogueron, and Peter Lee.·2003. *Canada's Large Intact Forest Landscapes*, (Edmonton, Canada: Global Forest Watch Canada), <https://files.wri.org/d8/s3fs-public/pdf/gfw_canada_lifl_text_section.pdf> [Accessed 23 February 2022].

Lemke, T. 2012. *Foucault, Governmentality and Critique* (Boulder, CO: Paradigm Publishers).

Lindenmayer, D.B, and J.F Franklin. 2002. *Conserving Forest Biodiversity: A Comprehensive Multiscaled Approach* (Island Press).

Lindenmayer, D.B, R.J Hobbs, G.E Likens, C.J Krebs, and S.C Banks. 2011. 'Newly Discovered Landscape Traps Produce Regime Shifts in Wet Forests', *Proceedings of the National Academy of Sciences*, 108 (38), 15887–91.

Miller, P, and N Rose. 1990. 'Governing Economic Life', *Economy and Society*, 19 (1), 1–31.

Nussbaum, R, and M Simula.·2005a. *The Forest Certification Handbook – 2nd Edition*, (London: Earthscan).

Nussbaum, R., and M. Simula. 2005b. *The Forest Certification Handbook – 2nd Edition*. (London: Earthscan)

Power, M. 1999. *The Audit Society: Rituals of Verification* (Oxford: Oxford University Press).

Prakash, A, and M Potoski. 2006. *The Voluntary Environmentalists: Green Clubs, ISO 14001, and Voluntary Environmental Regulations* (Cambridge, UK: Cambridge University Press).

Programme for the Endorsement of Forest Certification.·2020. *PEFC Annual Review* 2020, (Geneva: PEFC), <https://cdn.pefc.org/pefc.org/media/2021-05/dac60b99-ccb7-46dd-bb87-e08a07ae0810/9c502e23-b9b4-52c6-8d80-bf71209244a5.pdf> [Accessed 23 February 2022].

Puettmann, K.J., D.K. Coates, and C. Messier. 2009. *A Critique of Silviculture: Managing for Complexity* (Washington, D.C: Island Press).

Rose, N. 1999. *Powers of Freedom: Reframing Political Thought* (Cambridge, UK: Cambridge University Press).

Sayer, J, and S Maginnis. 2005. 'New Challenges for Forest Management,.' in J Sayer, S Maginnis and M Laurie (eds.), *Forests in Landscapes: Ecosystem Approaches to Sustainability* (London: Earthscan),

Scott, JC. 1998. *Seeing Like a State: How Certain Schemes to Improve the Human Condition Have Failed* (New Haven and London: Yale University Press).

Standards Australia. 2016. *AS/NZS ISO 9001: 2016Quality Management Systems – Requirements*. <https://www.standards.org.au/standards-catalogue/sa-snz/other/qr-008/as-slash-nzs–iso–9001-colon-2016> [Accessed 23 February 2022]

Synnott, T. 1988. *Letter Addressed to Mr Koy Thompson, Draft Outline Study Proposal for the Promotion of Sustainably Produced Tropical Timber, FoE-UK*.

——. 2005. *Some Notes on the Early Years of FSC* <http://www.fsc.org/fileadmin/webdata/public/document_center/publications/Notes_on_the_early_years_of_FSC_by_Tim_Synnott.pdf> [Accessed August/5/2009]

Taylor, C. 2011. *Discourses of the Standard: Critical Discourse Analysis of the Forest Stewardship Council and the Australian Forestry Standard – Doctoral Dissertation* (Melbourne: RMIT University).

Taylor, C, and D.B Lindenmayer. 2021. 'Stakeholder Engagement in a Forest Stewardship Council Controlled Wood Assessment', *Environmental Science and Policy*, 120, 204–12.

Taylor, C, and D.B. Lindenmayer. 2020. 'Temporal Fragmentation of a Critically Endangered Forest Ecosystem', *Austral Ecology*, 45 (3), 340–54.

Tollefson, C, F Gale, and D Haley. 2008. *Setting the Standard – Certification, Governance, and the Forest Stewardship Council* (Vancouver, Toronto: UBC Press).

Vogt, D.J, B.C Larson, J.C Gordon, and A Fanzeres. 1999. *Forest Certification: Roots, Issues, Challenges, and Benefits* (Boca Raton: CRC Press).

Williams, M. 2006. *Deforesting the Earth: From Prehistory to Global Crisis, an Abridgement* (Chicago and London: The University of Chicago Press).

World Commission on Environment and Development. 1987. *Our Common Future* (Oxford: Oxford University Press).

Part 2: **Public finance**

Tapan Sarker and Timothy Cadman

Chapter 7
Public finance for sustainable development

Abstract: Part 2 of this Handbook provides an introduction to some of the key concepts, approaches and challenges to public finance necessary for sustainable economic development, using examples from both developing and developed economies. There are two primary ways to finance sustainable development designed to support the transition to a low-carbon, smart and efficient economy. The first is to integrate the agenda of sustainable development into a country's public finance and tax system. Since governments play a key role in mobilising internal revenue by formulating budgets, it is important to emphasise the role of public finance in transitioning to a low-carbon economy. The second is to incentivise private investment in line with the Sustainable Development Goals (SDGs). While the public sector is crucial in freeing up the flow of private finance, governments in developing economies often fail to provide incentives for private investors to facilitate pathways for the implementation of low-carbon investment. Some guidelines for policymakers to design and reform internal revenue mobilisation initiatives considering the context and disruptions caused by the COVID-19 pandemic are also offered. The implications of effective collaboration between government, civil society and the private sector, which in turn can configure and endure sustainable development, are highlighted.

Keywords: fiscal policy, public finance, sustainable economic development, sustainable finance, COVID-19

Background: The role of public finance in achieving sustainable development

The Synthesis Report of the UN Secretary-General at the post-2015 sustainable development agenda stated that the governments should be able to mobilise the funding sources and instruments with appropriate strategies if the ambitious sustainable development objectives are to be accomplished (United Nations Department of Economic and Social Affairs 2015: 26). The report urged that nations undertake countrywide financing techniques and strategies, regulatory frameworks, fiscal and macroeconomic rules to align private funding and public financing with the SDGs. The legal context, foreseeable socioeconomic and environmental impacts and any other hindrance that might confine or impede the viability of the financing mechanisms must be carefully considered (United Nations Development Programme 2018). Fiscal policy instruments are important tools in bridging the investment gap and assuring the sustainable use

https://doi.org/10.1515/9783110733488-007

of resources (Sarker et al. 2020). Financing flows may be classified into three categories: concessional public financing (multilateral organisations), public borrowing through the markets and private financing (Kharas and McArthur 2019). Understanding the suitable type of financing for solving different types of SDG needs is crucial. Such incentives include a country's tax system, tax subsidies, rebates and tax holidays (Sarker et al. 2020).

Domestic public finance has many roles to play, especially in a developing country. It can assist growth and provide resources to serve priorities like national defence and scientific research. It also has the potential to provide much needed resources to support economic growth along with the financial instruments in meeting the SDGs (Kharas and McArthur 2019). While public spending levels need to be focussed on as many SDG outcomes as possible, this is restrained by the paucity of public resources. In this regard, public sector objectives and expenses are cautiously considered at the country-level. A study shows that SDG-associated global public expenditure in 2015 is already large, at USD 21.3 trillion. The study further explains that even though nations with higher incomes account expend a large amount on SDG, which may surprise people who implicitly presume that the issue of SDGs are only for poorer countries (Kharas and McArthur 2019).

According to the World Bank (1988), public sector deficits rose to unsustainable levels almost without regard to economic structure and income level until 1982 when external economic shocks in the early 1980s made it impractical to finance these deficits. Consequently, a period of severe fiscal restraint became inescapable. Prudent control of fiscal deficits is just one aspect of sound public finance in the widest sense. During the late 1970s and 1980s concern about the expansion of the public sector arose in industrial and developing countries. Steady growth, high inflation, the deficit in the balance of payments, debt burdens, slow private savings and investment was observed as a result of the excessive growth of the public sector. Driving public expenditure to those areas in which the public sector can act efficiently also means increasing the necessary revenues in ways that distort prices very little. For sustainability, government plays a significant role in allocating resources, directly or indirectly, via the production and allocation of privately produced goods through subsidies, taxes and a wide range of regulatory tools such as price controls and quantitative restrictions. Both modes of intervention involve public spending and revenue and are thus equally subject to the structures of sound public finance. Public finance policies affect all sectors of the economy, either in developing countries or in industrial countries. The public sector structure has both vertical and horizontal dimensions. The vertical dimension includes the central, state/provincial and local government levels. The horizontal dimension reflects the division between government, and other autonomous or semiautonomous entities, often grouped under the heading of off-budget accounts. The public sector tends to play a more substantial role in developing countries as an investor than in industrial countries. In the developing economies the unmet backlog of physical and social infrastructure, the low levels of savings and investment, the need to foster economic growth through modernisation and the availability of concessional foreign funding for public projects explain the rapid expansion of public finance that is consistent with the public interest view (World Bank 2013).

Pragmatic approaches to public policy

A pragmatic approach to public policy analysis starts by ranking areas of economic activity according to the extent to which government intervention is desirable. Plausible criteria for ranking would be the scope for the government to promote efficiency, growth, poverty alleviation and stabilisation. Governments have certain core areas of responsibility. The public sector can effectively provide include defence, diplomacy, macroeconomic management and a legal system. Secondly, governments need to help provide social, physical and information infrastructure: education, health, transport networks, public utilities, technology development and dissemination and environmental protection. Governments, especially in developing countries, are generally not well equipped to play a major role to tackle market failure.

Fiscal reforms and environmental factors in achieving sustainable economic development

Resources alone are insufficient to achieve the SDGs. It should be accompanied by appropriate policies, incentives and institutional frameworks. A major shift in China's economy was observed in the 1990s by the introduction of the Tax Sharing System. This revenue-sharing reform led to the formation of China's substantial fiscal decentralisation and divided the financial power between central and local governments (Ahmad 2018). China has achieved tremendous economic growth with the rapid growth of fiscal revenue; however, its taxes are lacking in legal changing public finance system structures. Despite the structural problems in China, changes like fiscal reform, rationalising tax structure and revenue spending structure are the elementary ways that assist with sustainable development.

Environmental pollution has produced adverse impacts on sustainable development and the inappropriate tax legal regime is undoubtedly a grave weakness. Many countries, including China, neither have specific tax laws concerning environmental protection however, polluters have been charged for pollution activities, an approach which has had significant shortcomings. In order to address climate change and to curb and mitigate environmental pollution while working for sustainable development, a comprehensive green legal tax regime is crucial. Environmental protection can be enhanced by establishing environmental protection tax law and strictly improving the existing laws and regulations. The rationalisation of tax structures would stimulate industrial upgrading and the rational allocation of resources would be effectively supporting the growth and sustainable development. Some companies are already planting trees and forests to increase carbon sequestration. Application of greenhouse gas (GHG) tax rates would be far more effective than merely measuring pollutant gas emissions. To have a well-developed green bond market, it is crucial to define exactly what green is (Sarker, Taghizadeh-Hesary, and Yoshino 2021). With the growing environmental, social and governance (ESG) regulations in European countries, G20 countries are increasingly vulnerable in the face of similarly stringent ESG requirements into the future (Gjergji et al. 2021).

Rebalancing the Chinese economy to create new sustainable hubs is a case in point. For instance, the One Belt One Road Initiative, an interface between local, national and cross-border connectivity, along with other options for locally managed taxes, transfers, service delivery and strengthened governance mechanisms are being implemented to monitor and handle the liabilities. Creating new urban hubs will certainly improve the infrastructure facilities across China and improve the mobility of labour, capital, resources and information. This will improve fiscal transparency and benefits to China's local liability management and sustainable development. In accordance with the above, public expenditure for environmental protection, and the ecological policy of the state are designed to maintain ecological parameters in case of disruptions by the adverse effects that economic development could have on the natural environment (Calanter 2011).

An increase in the share of research and development and innovation expenditures influence the evolution of sustainable development in European Union (EU) countries (Gavriluță 2016). Studies have shown a significant relationship between the governments and sustainable development where the European Commission has competence in all areas related to services. This is to maintain a sustainable and stable economic growth through a predictable tax system, such that it can ensure the appropriate conditions for a development that responds to all current needs, without harming the resources belonging to future generations (Uryszek 2014).

Fiscal deficits resulting in financing requirements of the public sector is the major cause of macroeconomic imbalances. The goal for a prudent fiscal policy is to elevate revenue most cost-effectively and to reduce spending in the least damaging way. Public sector SDG spending can be financed through several mechanisms, including sales and income taxes, market-based government borrowing (e.g., public bond issuances), concessional international finance (e.g., grants and assistance) and non-concessional international finance (e.g., loans from multilateral development banks). Taxation can be a tool for environmental protection (Leibfritz, Thornton, and Bibbee 1997). However, there should not be a difference in the rate or amount of tax implications of CO_2 and other pollutants between countries. Otherwise, this might be used as a loophole by companies by simply relocating the factories to countries with lower tax rates (Sarker et al. 2020). Rather, it is necessary to reduce the financial pressure on taxation and strengthen fiscal institutions and the role of fiscal and budgetary policy for sustainable development (Arnăut 2014). In this case, a similar approach can be adopted for responding to the impacts of COVID-19, particularly for small to medium enterprises, which have proved resilient in some contexts, but highly vulnerable in others. Policies addressing systemic shocks like COVID-19 (or climate change and other environmental perturbations, for that matter), require not only taxation and other fiscal measures, but broader and more holistic integration of policy inputs and perspectives from a broad range of actors, from governmental agencies to primary and secondary stakeholders (Barbaglia et al. 2021).

Linking sustainable development with public financing

Sustainable development is an ethical principle that incorporates both current and future commitment to the long-term, assimilating social, economic and environmental factors and recognises the interdependence of domestic and global activities. It can engender global partnerships and also augment cooperation among governments on the federal, regional or local level, with domestic partners in industry and the non-governmental organisations (NGO) community (Ballhorn 2005). Sustainable development is an intricate multidimensional issue, which combines efficiency and equity as well as intergenerational equity based on social, economic and environmental objectives (Ciegis, Ramanauskiene, and Martinkus 2009).

Sustainable development is in its infancy as regard to its application and is still much more invoked in the abstract than operationalised in practice, in policy or the law. When operationalised, it has the potential to be transformative. Sustainable development remains an attractive but elusive concept (Ballhorn 2005).

If there is clarity on each of the underlying problems and the mechanisms by which appropriate resource to address and resolve these issues, the SDGs can be properly financed and achieved (Kharas and McArthur 2019). Every nation has its unique fiscal path to develop its respective SDG economy. According to the World Public Sector Report (United Nations Department of Economic and Social Affairs 2019), SDG economies require building public services and societal systems that make the essential public services available to every person, building flourishing social and environmentally friendly cities and industries and rectifying the advanced cities and industries which are not aligned with the SDG outcomes. Also, it further explains that the role of the private sector is inevitable in various areas of development, however, the public sector will still be the driving force to regulate the market and those management failures that can lead to the persistence of SDG challenges. The general finding of SDG-related analyses is a need for greater public spending, especially in the lowest-income economies (Kharas and McArthur 2019). Amidst plenty of important contributions to date, little attention is observed to understanding the pattern of governments expenditure on the SDGs and how it can assist in estimating incremental financing needs. Government Spending Watch (2015) is one of the only systematic databases that tries to track what is being spent in several SDG-related sectors, however, it only covers 78 developing countries and there are no proper government budget classifications and SDGs. For instance, if the infrastructure is built starting in a manner consistent with environmental sustainability and social inclusion, then there is a possibility of achieving the SDGs. If, on the other hand, infrastructure is built solely to boost aggregate economic output without concern for environmental or social impacts until the late 2020s, then it will not be possible to achieve the SDGs. These issues are particularly crucial in light of the dramatic growth in the global capital stock, which is on-trend to grow by roughly USD 100 trillion or more between 2015 and 2030, with a large share of this growth driven by developing countries (World Bank 2013).

The SDGs focus on tackling specific problems in specific places, often being faced by specific people, and thus needs a specific spending and financing strategy. Another challenge when considering spending needs is that the balance of public and private responsibilities also differs by issue area, so there are natural differences in the degree to which some issues require multi-year government budgeting and others which are best left to the competitive forces of private enterprise. Targeted, needs-based and outcome-based approaches are required to reach underserved populations and stimulate more sustainable economic activity.

The tight linkage between SDG spending and per capita income is not altogether surprising because countries can afford to spend more as they get richer (Kharas and McArthur 2019). The composition of spending also changes across income groups. For example, the share of health and social spending in total SDG public spending tends to rise as countries get richer – wealthier economies tend to provide more comprehensive old-age, disability health and other forms of support to their populations. Meanwhile, the share of spending on agriculture tends to decline at higher incomes, consistent with higher rates of urbanisation in advanced economies.

According to Global Revenue Statistics 2020, OECD countries collected an average of 33.8% of their gross domestic product (GDP) as tax, while developing countries can achieve only half this rate (OECD 2020). Taxation is a catalyst for governments that are more responsive and accountable to their citizens, and for expanding state capacity (OECD 2008). The United Nations considers that achieving the Millennium Development Goals (MDGs) will require developing countries to raise at least 20% of their GDP in taxes (Kharas and McArthur 2019). Yet presently only half of all sub-Saharan African countries still mobilise less than 17% of their GDP in tax revenues (De Paepe and Dickinson 2014a). Strengthening domestic resource mobilisation is not only essential for raising revenue but also for designing a tax system that promotes inclusiveness, encourages good governance, responds to society's concerns over income and wealth inequalities and promotes social justice (De Paepe and Dickinson 2014b). In examining the challenges faced by developing countries, it is important to stress that

increased revenue, assessing tax systems and their performance is not in itself sufficient to foster sustainable development, but it is also necessary to consider how the
revenue is distributed to ensure equity, promote inclusiveness and effectively address
social pressures. Sustainable development also requires analysis of the potential role of
taxation in reducing environmental damage or unsustainable resource use (De Paepe
and Dickinson 2014b).

Overview of chapters

Despite the greater impact on developing countries from COVID-19 and the increased challenges to achieving the SDGs arising from the pandemic, most research
to date has focussed on the advanced economies (Wang and Huang 2021). Questions have been raised as to whether developing countries can afford to implement
the SDGs for quite some time (Hoy 2016). The chapters in this section consequently
examine in some detail the public finance needs for developing countries in the
sustainability space.

In their chapter 'Public finance and fiscal instruments for sustainable development' Arif Zaman and Tapan Sarker explore how countries have pledged to meeting
the SDGs in 2030 by adopting green development strategies. They look in particular
at the Addis Ababa Action Agenda (AAAA), which provides a global framework for
comprehensive financial policies required to address national economic, social and
environmental priorities needed to reach the goals in time. Despite these commitments, the necessary finance is still not being directed at the required level and pace
to achieve the SDGs and there is still a financing gap of USD 2.53 trillion per year for
developing countries. They argue that a concerted effort from public, private and development finance partners are pivotal if the goals are to be met, but such a transition requires much stronger internal revenue mobilisation and a scaling-up of public
finance and the implementation of effective fiscal instruments to do so.

Different public finance frameworks and multiple fiscal instruments for sustainable development are used in different countries. In order to be effective, public finance and fiscal instruments for sustainable development need to take into account
both an individual government's involvement in such measures, as well the private
sector and other actors. In addition, reforms are need to such instruments, such as
recognising the environmental imperative of combatting climate change, internalising environmental costs using such avenues as Pigouvian tax, as well as distributing
benefits to less advantaged communities and thereby reducing the loss of revenue to
state coffers from the informal economy. Despite the knowledge that such instruments exist, few fiscal instruments for green development take such measures into
account, especially in developing economies.

Broader adoption of such measures, which they explore in the chapter, would, the authors suggest, provide a way forward for attaining both the targets of SDGs and Nationally Determined Contributions (NDCs)for the developing countries. However, governments have had to provide various fiscal support and stimulus packages to keep vulnerable sectors of the economy and low-income households afloat due to COVID-19. Attaining the SDGs by 2030 now will be a greater challenge than ever, and new measures will have to be implemented in the light of the pandemic to keep hopes of sustainable development alive.

The 'Financing Sustainable Development Goals (SDGs) and the role of digital finance' chapter picks up on the implementation challenges confronting sustainable development and finance in the emerging economies of South Asia. The authors, Sima Dey and Biswajit Basak, look towards digitalisation of financial services as a potential solution for critical developmental challenges in emerging economies, such as hunger, health and education. The UN has played an important role in catalysing and recommending ways to harness digital finance to accelerate the required finance necessary for achieving the SDGs. With restricted access to face-to-face financial services, digital finance has become a lifeline for billions of people struggling to survive and ensure financial sustainability during the COVID-19 pandemic. Through digital payment platforms, social safety nets involving cash transfers become easier and cheaper to manage, as the enable governments to mobilise funds for medical supplies and emergency relief to fund people in need. In this context, they explore the actions taken in Bangladesh to manage the uncertainties of crises such as COVID-19 using digital finance.

Financial inclusion has consequently become a key public policy to bring the majority of citizens into the digital economy. This strategy includes the uptake of mobile money and other digital payment platforms to provide different financial services to marginalised people. Many banks, both private and public, as well as financial service agents, are now providing digital financial services. But there is still a long way to go. The authors discuss the prominent role of digital finance in financial inclusion, how such modalities of finance operate and how digital finance can function as an efficient mechanism for achieving the SDGs. They provide some pointers as to how policymakers can take action to ensure the effective implementation of digital finance to ensure the financial sustainability of the economy and how to accelerate the financing of the SDGs for Bangladesh.

In their chapter 'Fiscal governance to support post-COVID low-carbon development in Indonesia' Fitri Nurfatriani, Mimi Salminah and Dewi Ratna Kurniasari focus on Indonesia, the world's fourth most populous nation, second-most forested country and significant developing financial power. Interestingly, it has shown a high level of interest in green taxonomy (Sustainable Finance Indonesia 2022) and is an ideal locus for study in this Handbook (see Chapter Two for an in-depth investigation of this topic).

The coronavirus pandemic has hit the global economy and plunged the world into severe recession. In Indonesia, it has caused a slowdown in growth and increased poverty, jeopardising the country's commitment to mainstreaming and implementing sustainable development, with a focus on better social, economic and environmental management. While environmental indicators have improved, poverty rates have risen sharply and fiscal capacity for environmental improvement has contracted of late. This is having an impact: climate change mitigation actions are sluggish, which is likely to lead to increased deforestation and forest degradation; and pressure on wildlife and forests is increasing due to increased human interventions arising from the need to survive during the pandemic. Ironically, encroachment into forests and associated conversion to other uses increases the interaction between wildlife and humans, and further risks transmission of animal-human viruses.

To achieve sustainable development and reduce the economic drivers behind deforestation, future growth pathways need to address post-COVID economic recovery as well as low-carbon development policies, which reconcile both environmental and economic objectives. Using fiscal policy theories and empirical investigations, the authors outline and analyse on how fiscal instruments should be governed to support post-COVID, low-carbon development. Shortly before the pandemic, the government of Indonesia estimated that approximately USD 22 billion was needed to implement a low-carbon development policy until 2024 but had at that time allocated only a fraction of what was needed. The pandemic further impacted fiscal policies to achieve this, as governmental revenue declined.

Recovery programmes aimed to protect, maintain and improve the economic capabilities of business actors affected by the pandemic but have continued to apply conventional economic approaches and have not unequivocally promoted green initiatives to create low-carbon pathways. It is therefore vital to optimise fiscal instruments, they argue, which focus on public spending targeting low-carbon development. The authors investigate and several existing fiscal instruments can be repurposed to promote green initiatives and encourage deforestation-free investments post-pandemic.

Not every green solution can be taken purely on its merits, however, and advanced liberal economies also confront their own challenges when it comes to the implementation of measures aimed to encourage sustainable development (Roulet and Touboul 2015). In the concluding chapter to this section, 'The EU renewable energy policy and its impact on forests' Zoltán Kun demonstrates how the drive for clean power in the European Union has resulted in increased deforestation and biodiversity loss, as wood is imported into the EU and burned in power stations to generate electricity.

Providing renewable energy is key to sustainable development and is acknowledged as such in the SDGs, notably through SDG7, which aims to provide affordable and clean energy to all. As part of its commitment to combat climate change under the 1997 Kyoto Protocol, the EU committed to decreasing Green House Gases, including carbon, emissions. This in turn led to the creation of the Renewable Energy Directive (RED), which promotes the increasing use renewable energy for power generation and defines the various sources from which it may be derived. One of the results of RED has been the growing use of wood-based biomass, which currently accounts for well over one-half of all EU domestic biomass supply for energy purposes. While its main use is in the heating and cooling sectors, the burning of forests for power is also growing in electricity generation overall.

The sustainability of woody biomass and whether or not bioenergy from forests should be considered as zero carbon sources of energy have recently has widely questioned. Although the RED itself includes sustainability criteria, the argument has been made these criteria a provide cover and rationale for continued logging of forests and undermine climate mitigation activities, just when the EU needs to be getting serious about preserving forests and the climate. In a potentially unfortunate combination of measures to recover from the economic impacts of COVID-19, the EU has allocated further funding to combatting both climate change and stimulating growth and with forests still counted as part of the renewable energy mix, negative impacts on biodiversity and conservation may be an outcome.

This chapter, and the others which precede it, provide timely reminders that in the rush to rebuild society and stimulate economies after the pandemic, costs may once again be externalised and unless the protection of the environment is built into public policy and fiscal measures at a systemic level, the opportunity for a genuinely sustainable recovery will be lost.

References

Ahmad, E. 2018. 'Rebalancing in China: Fiscal Policies for Sustainable Growth,' *The Singapore Economic Review*, 63 (04), 861–84.

Arnăut, Adriana 2014. *Role of Government and Civil Society in Sustainable Development, Institutional Repository of Moldova State University* (Moldova Moldova State University)

Ballhorn, Richard. 2005. 'The Role of Government and Policy in Sustainable Development', *McGill International Journal of Sustainable Development Law and Policy*, 1, 19.

Barbaglia, Martina, Vincenzo Butticè, Giancarlo Giudici, John Mendy, Tapan Sarker, Gagan D Sharma, Asha Thomas, and Ambika Zutshi. 2021. *Supporting SMEs in Sustainable Strategy Development Post-Covid-19: Challenges and Policy Agenda for the G20*, (TF5–2030 Agenda and Development Cooperation), <https://www.g20-insights.org/wp-content/uploads/2021/09/TF5_SUPPORTING_SMES_IN_SUSTAINABLE_STRATEGY_DEVELOPMENT_POST-COVID-19-_CHALLENGES_AND_POLICY_AGENDA_FOR_THE_G20.pdf> [Accessed 3 February 2022].

Calanter, Paul. 2011. 'Sustainable Urban Development Policies', *Quality-Access to Success*, 2011 Supplement, 969–75.

Ciegis, Remigijus, Jolita Ramanauskiene, and Bronislovas Martinkus. 2009. 'The Concept of Sustainable Development and Its Use for Sustainability Scenarios', *Engineering Economics*, 62 (2), 28–37.

De Paepe, Gregory, and Ben Dickinson. 2014a. 'Tax Revenues as a Motor for Sustainable Development', *Organisation of Economic Co-operation and Development (ed) Development Co-operation report*, 91–97.

――. 2014b. 'Tax Revenues as a Motor for Sustainable Development.' in, *Development Co-Operation Report 2014: Mobilising Resources for Sustainable Development* (Paris: Organisation for Economic Cooperation and Development), pp. 91–97

Gavriluță, Anca Florentina. 2016. 'Implications of Government on Sustainable Development', *Journal of Public Administration, Finance and Law* (10), 31–41.

Gjergji, Rafaela, Luigi Vena, Salvatore Sciascia, and Alessandro Cortesi. 2021. 'The Effects of Environmental, Social and Governance Disclosure on the Cost of Capital in Small and Medium Enterprises: The Role of Family Business Status', *Business Strategy and the Environment*, 30 (1), 683–93.

Government Spending Watch.·2015. *Government Spending Watch Dataset*<https://www.govern mentspendingwatch.org/spending-data> [Accessed 3 February 2022].

Hoy, Chris 2016 'Can Developing Countries Afford the SDGs' *Devpolicy Blog from the Development Policy Centre* <https://devpolicy.org/wp-content/uploads/wp-post-to-pdf-enhanced-cache/1/ can-developing-countries-afford-the-sdgs-20160209.pdf> [Accessed 3 February 2022]

Kharas, Homi, and John McArthur.·2019. *Building the SDG Economy: Needs, Spending, and Financing for Universal Achievement of the Sustainable Development Goals*, Global Economy and Development Working Paper 131, (Brookings Institute), <https://www.brookings.edu/wp-content/uploads/2019/10/Building-the-SDG-economy.pdf> [Accessed 3 February 2022].

Leibfritz, Willi, John Thornton, and Alexandra Bibbee.·1997. *Taxation and Economic Performance*, OECD Economics Department Working Papers No. 176, (Organisation for Economic Cooperation and Development), <https://www.oecd-ilibrary.org/docserver/668811115745.pdf? expires=1643839250&id=id&accname=guest&checksum=224985713CEC348703E11 DA4BBF85018> [Accessed 3 February 2022].

Organisation for Economic Co-operation and Development.·2020. *Global Revenue Statistics Database*<https://www.oecd.org/tax/tax-policy/global-revenue-statistics-database.htm> [Accessed 3 February 2022].

Organisation for Economic Cooperation and Development. 2008. *Taxation and Accountability: Issues and Practices*, DAC Guidelines and Reference Series. (Paris: OECD)

Roulet, Thomas J., and Samuel Touboul. 2015. 'The Intentions with Which the Road Is Paved: Attitudes to Liberalism as Determinants of Greenwashing', *Journal of Business Ethics*, 128 (2), 305–20.

Sarker, T., F. Taghizadeh-Hesary, A. Mortha, and A. Saha.·2020. *The Role of Incentives in Promoting Energy Efficiency in the Industrial Sector: Case Studies from Asia*, (Tokyo: Asian Development Bank Institute), <https://www.adb.org/sites/default/files/publication/634696/adbi-wp1172. pdf> [Accessed 3 February 2022].

Sarker, Tapan, Farhad Taghizadeh-Hesary, and Naoyuki Yoshino 2021. *Promoting Energy Efficiency Financing within the G20: The Role of Fiscal Instruments*, Task Force 2: Climate Change, Sustainable Energy and Environment, (G20), <https://www.g20-insights.org/wp-content/up loads/2021/09/TF2-PROMOTING-ENERGY-EFFICIENCY-FINANCING-WITHIN-THE-G20-THE-ROLE-OF-FISCAL-INSTRUMENTS.pdf> [Accessed 3 February 2022].

Sustainable Finance Indonesia.·2022. *Indonesia Green Taxonomy* Edition 1.0-2022, <https://www. ojk.go.id/keuanganberkelanjutan/en/publication/detailsflibrary/2352/taksonomi-hijau-indone%20sia-edisi-1-0-2022> [Accessed 01/02/2022].

United Nations Department of Economic and Social Affairs.·2015. *Synthesis Report of the Secretary-General on the Post-2015 Agenda*, (New York: United Nations), <https://www.un.org/en/devel

opment/desa/publications/files/2015/01/SynthesisReportENG.pdf> [Accessed
14 February 2022].

——.·2019. *Sustainable Development Goal 16: Focus on Public Institutions*, World Public Sector
Report 2019, (New York: UNDESA), <https://publicadministration.un.org/publications/con
tent/PDFs/World%20Public%20Sector%20Report2019.pdf> [Accessed 3 February 2022].

United Nations Development Programme.·2018. *Financing the 2030 Agenda – an Introductory
Guidebook for UNDP Country Offices*, (New York: UNDP), <https://www.uncclearn.org/wp-
content/uploads/library/financing_the_2030_agenda_co_guidebook.pdf> [Accessed
3 February 2022].

Uryszek, Tomasz. 2014. 'Public Finance Crisis and Sustainable Development Financing–Evidence
from EU Economies', *Copernican Journal of Finance and Accounting*, 3 (1), 161–73.

Wang, Qiang, and Rui Huang. 2021. 'The Impact of Covid-19 Pandemic on Sustainable Development
Goals–a Survey', *Environmental Research*, 202, 111637.

World Bank.·1988. *The Role of Public Finance in Development*, https://openknowledge.worldbank.
org/bitstream/handle/10986/5971/9780195206500_ch02.pdf> [Accessed 14 February 2022].

——. 2013. *Capital for the Future: Saving and Investment in an Interdependent World, Global
Development Horizons*. (Washington DC: World Bank)

Kazi Arif Uz Zaman and Tapan Sarker

Chapter 8
Public finance and fiscal instruments for sustainable development

Abstract: Public finance and fiscal policy instruments play an important role in promoting sustainable development. As countries pledge to support the United Nations 2030 Agenda, there is a need to explore the role of fiscal policy instruments that can provide the financing to achieve green development strategies in respective economies. The United Nations Secretary-General's Office (2019) reveals that the available finance is not being directed at the required level and pace towards achieving the SDGs and there is still a financing gap of USD 2.53 trillion per year for developing countries. Thus, concerted efforts from public, private and development partners are pivotal. Such a transition requires stronger internal revenue mobilisation effort and scaling-up of the public finance and effective fiscal instruments. Different public finance frameworks and multiple fiscal instruments for sustainable development are used in different countries. In this chapter an overview of the theoretical aspect and conceptual literature on green fiscal policies is provided. On the ground applications of such policies are discussed in the form of several case studies. The general framework for assessing public finance and fiscal reforms towards SDGs is also analysed.

Keywords: public finance, sustainable development goals, resource mobilisation, fiscal instruments, green fiscal reforms, carbon taxation, COVID-19

Introduction

Countries have pledged to support the United Nations 2030 Agenda through adopting multifaceted green and sustainable development strategies in respective economies for attaining the targets of the 17 Sustainable Development Goals (SDGs) by 2030. The ambitious universal goals demand some accelerated spending, investment and financing for countries. The United Nations Conference on Trade and Development (UNCTAD) (2014: 140) has estimated that the world's total annual SDG investment needs to be at roughly USD 5 to 7 trillion per year, of which more than half, amounting to 3.3 to 4.5 trillion per year, would be required in developing countries. Gaspar et al (2019: 5) estimate that an additional USD 0.5 trillion of annual spending will be needed by 2030 for low-income developing countries (LIDCs) to achieve the SDGs. While for emerging market economies (EMEs), an annual additional amount of 2.1 trillion would be required up to 2030. In aggregate, the additional spending for

https://doi.org/10.1515/9783110733488-008

LIDCs and EMEs would be equivalent to 2.5% of global GDP. However, with less than ten years left and with the devastating impact of COVID-19, which is expected to linger, the prospective attainment of SDGs has become a demanding challenge to surmount. The least developed, developing and emerging economies are especially facing mounting challenges in mobilising their financial and non-financial resources towards the successful transformation and implementation of respective sustainable and green development policies. Financial resources, particularly, are challenging as well as difficult to accumulate at this point of time when setting up the priorities and allocation of resources may substantially vary among countries amid the COVID-19 pandemic. In particular, the allocation for the environment and green growth projects is likely to be subdued following the widespread health and socioeconomic crisis that has resulted from the pandemic. Nevertheless, sustainable as well as green development is the agenda that neither should be ignored nor be delayed. The Asian Development Bank Institute (2014: xiv) highlights the importance of the quicker transition from high-carbon to low-carbon infrastructure. Their report suggests that such measures must be considered at the earliest possible opportunity as a delayed initiation would cause two to five-fold increases in mitigation expenses for each decade.

The United Nations Secretary-General's Office (2019a: 1) indicates that the available finance is not being directed at the required level and pace towards achieving the SDGs and there is still a financing gap of over USD 2.53 trillion per year for developing countries. Thus, to meet the shortfall, concerted efforts from public, private and development partners are essential. Official Development Assistance (ODA) often has notable contributions in complementing domestic efforts to mobilise resources, mainly in the least developed and low-income economies. Yet, the effectiveness of ODA or foreign grants is a contested topic that countries should meticulously consider, especially in their transitional phases of development. Elayah (2016) states that aid effectiveness in a developing country is fundamentally stalled by the country's institutional incapability, improper policies and divergent donor interests. Williamson (2010) argues that a lack of balance in terms of incentives both to the donor as well as the recipient might affect the optimal effectiveness of any foreign grant or ODA. Therefore, too much dependence on ODA or such grants may not be a better option in most cases.

Evidently, such a transition would require significant financial resources, which may not be sustainable without a stronger internal revenue mobilisation system. The Addis Ababa Action Agenda (AAAA) provides a global framework for comprehensive financing flows and policies required to accomplish the economic, social and environmental priorities of countries and reaching the goals by 2030. The agenda accentuates domestic resource mobilisation as the principal driver in SDG financing. Connected to this, the agenda further urges for accelerated economic growth in the countries with conducive environments to facilitate appropriate social, environmental and economic policies, good governance and efficient institutions at all levels (United Nations 2015). The role of the private sector's investment for SDGs is becoming increasingly important, especially, for developing countries as recent studies estimate that even scaled-up public resources alone may not be adequate to fully finance the 2030 Agenda in these countries (Rashed and Shah 2021). The private sector can facilitate a greater extent of innovation, openness, efficiency and explicit skills and resources that may be critical for widespread attainments of SDGs (Scheyvens, Banks, and Hughes 2016). The United Nations (2014: 3) advocates the central role and untapped potential of the private sector as a new paradigm in development thinking in this process. Nevertheless, it is also argued in much of literature that the alignment of the basic motive of profit maximisation of the private sector with those of equitable and pro-environmental objectives of the SDGs might be challenging (Luke 2013: 29; Pingeot 2014: 89). Some studies have also exposed a few real-world challenges the private sector is facing towards achieving SDGs. For instance, deficiency in influential leadership and harmonious partnerships, exhaustiveness and intricacy of interlinkages among the SDGs and their targets and inadequate monitoring in evaluating the progress of SDGs' implementation (Rashed and Shah 2021).

Therefore, considering the current context, the implication of public finance (i.e., fiscal policy measures), plays the most pivotal role in attaining sustainable development objectives and hence, need scaling-up along with the application of effective fiscal instruments (Sachs et al. 2019: 1).

Mobilising additional public resources demands enhanced efforts in raising government revenues and cutting down unproductive financial flows so that revenue is used most efficiently to finance planned spending towards attaining the SDGs. Though the basic essence of such deployment of fiscal instruments in sustainable development is to target environmental objectives like clean air, water and to address climatic changes, the policy measures may be adopted also to ensure efficient usage of energy, better waste and greenhouse gases management, reduction of road congestion and accidents and fostering renewable energies. Sachs et al (2019: 1) highlight the need to scale up new financial instruments and policies to support fiscal policy and carbon market instruments. Their study, however, did not assess the key barriers in implementing the policies in a developing country context. For a comprehensive policy framework, along with evaluating the varied effects of different fiscal policy instruments, the implementation barriers also need to be eased for the wide-scale adoption and diffusion of green fiscal instruments within a country context.

This chapter will provide an overview of the theoretical aspect, conceptual literature on public finance policies targeting the SDGs, and the recent on the ground applications of such policies in the form of several case studies. In addition, the general framework for assessing green public finance and fiscal reforms is also analysed including the implementation challenges and the likely ways to overcome these challenges.

Role of public financing in achieving SDGs

Government intervention and involvement are fundamental for a specific set of SDGs, such as eradicating poverty (SDG 1), zero hunger (SDG 2), good health and wellbeing (SDG 3), quality education (SDG 4), gender equality (SDG 5), clean water and sanitation (SDG 6), clean energy (SDG 7), innovation and infrastructure (SDG 9), reducing inequality (SDG 10), sustainable cities and communities (SDG 11). In general, the private sector has little involvement with these areas mainly due to higher uncertainty on the investment returns and typically a long time to receive returns (Gaspar et al. 2019: 8). According to Wagner's law, a rise in per capita income would also prompt public investment and tax revenue to rise (Wagner 1958). Hence, the impacts of public financing in advanced or high-income countries tend to be higher in fostering the SDGs attainment, particularly in the mentioned areas of education, health, and infrastructure as compared to the EMEs and LIDCs (United Nations 2019b). However, the tax to GDP ratio of LIDCs has increased from 12% in the early 2000s to around 15% in 2019, revealing that most of the EMEs and lower-income developing countries have the potential to expand their revenue collection in the near future (Gaspar et al. 2019: 15). To materialise this prospective opportunity, the Addis Ababa Action Agenda suggests four independent components for framing the strategies (United Nations 2015): (1) establishing a broad-based agreement for medium-term revenue objectives to finance the desired level of public expenditures; (2) adopting a broad tax reform comprising policy, administration, and the legal framework; (3) sustained political support over a longer period; and (4) secure sufficient resources to support the harmonised implementation of the medium-term revenue strategy.

The theoretical framework presented here explores public finance and fiscal instruments for sustainable development: economic theory, advantages and challenges of implementation. Notably, one standpoint advocates that the green development policy framework should not only consider the environmental dimensions such as discouraging the usage of fossil fuels and espousing renewables but also should assess the non-environmental dimensions to reinforce the process. For instance, policies should be explicit in specifying the potential for generating revenues, improvements of efficiencies in resource usage and appropriate distribution. Studies find that time, costs, institutional capacities and technological adaptation are a few other key factors that need to be considered in this transition process (Adenle, Manning, and Arbiol 2017; Kemp and Never 2017; Lamperti et al. 2019; Paroussos, Fragkiadakis, and Fragkos 2020).

The fundamental goal of adopting fiscal instruments such as taxes and subsidies is to reduce the gap between social and private benefits and costs (Zhang et al. 2016: 297–98). As most environmental services, including clean air and surface water, are treated as public goods, there is a likelihood of exploitation and overuse of these common resources, especially in resource constrained countries.

Consequently, environmental degradation and excessive pollution have resulted in several negative externalities such as health hazards of the population. Owing to the adverse externalities, the ideal equilibrium referring to social cost is not fully realised (Qs, Ps as shown in Figure 8.1). Rather, the actual equilibrium points towards higher usage of resources at a lower price (at Qp, Pp shown in Figure 8.1). The actual consumption thereby exceeds the socially optimal level in an uninterrupted market as the marginal social cost surpasses the marginal private cost in this context. To restore the optimal equilibrium (or close to that point), government intervention may help. For example, a plant emits toxic gases in the air and noxious chemicals into the water, which have a serious impact on the health of the locality around the plant. If there is no intervention, the plant owner has no reason to pay anything for the additional health costs borne by the locals resulting from the pollution from that plant. Therefore, some intervention by the government in form of taxation (or any other fiscal instruments such as penalty or removal of subsidy, etc.) over the amount of pollution could cover the social cost and push the equivalent point towards the ideal one.

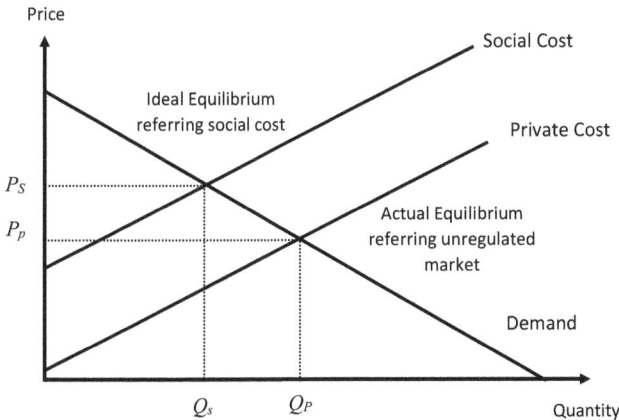

Figure 8.1: Schematic concept of taxation on public goods.

One effective technique to optimise the usage of public goods and achieve sustainable development is to embark upon the externalities through adopting the polluter-pays principle in the course of government interference into the market in the form of environmental taxation, referred to as the Pigouvian tax or other fiscal instruments (Schmidtchen, Helstroffer, and Koboldt 2015: 24). The tax may either be imposed on the final goods or services produced by the firm or on the inputs it uses in the production process that result in environmental degradation or emission. In practice, the rate of tax is set in a way that balances the negative externalities, the socially optimal outcome and price of the public good are attained. The ultimate two-fold objective of an effective environmental tax or regulation is to restrain the irresponsible actions of the economic polluting agents while accumulating public revenues expected to be invested towards a more sustainable and green develop-ment system (Crespi, Ghisetti, and Quatraro 2015; Mi and Coffman 2019).

These policies may facilitate in reinstating the balance in the form of more equi-table rights to use public goods for all. In addition, the process may eventually help to optimise the price of the natural resources and public goods which may also guarantee a more efficient usage of resources. The important result of environmen-tal taxation is to allow the government to deploy the additional funds collected in tax revenues into other development sectors focussing on different green develop-ment projects in facilitating the transition towards a green economy (Crespi, Ghi-setti, and Quatraro 2015).

Green fiscal reforms: Review of literature

Green Fiscal Reform (GFR) or Environmental Fiscal Reform is strategic adoption and integration of fiscal policies in a country's green development context. Such re-forms consist of a set of taxation and pricing instruments to attain a two-fold objec-tive: to increase domestic revenues while promoting environmental goals (Hewett and Ekins 2014). Metcalf (2016) refers to a more comprehensive outline of a GFR en-compassing all the activities having direct or partial linkages with green invest-ments. Metcalf illustrates the role of adopting green technology and infrastructure as the prospective fiscal measures under a GFR. Emphasis has also been given to other fiscal instruments focussing on generating government revenues, such as en-vironmental taxes and fees, cap-and-trade, clean energy tax credits, energy-related tax preferences, etc. The European Commission defines the environmental tax as 'a tax whose base is a physical unit (or a proxy of it) of something that has a proven, specific negative impact on the environment' (Georgescu, Pendolovska, and Cabeça 2010: 1). By designing a theoretical framework, Yoshino and Taghizadeh-Hesary (2018) state that GFR may instigate more incentives for green investors to take up more green projects with the funds accumulated through emission taxation.

To evaluate the efficacy of fiscal instruments for GFR, Dafermos and Nikolaidi (2019) apply a post-Keynesian ecological macroeconomic model to assess three sets of green fiscal policies: carbon tax, green subsidies and green investments. The out-come of this study reveals that a green fiscal policy mix, rather than any single set of policies would result in better outcomes. Chang et al (2020) use Data Envelop-ment Analysis on Chinese renewable energy firm-level panel data and discover that government subsidies and tax rebate policies have significant positive impacts on technical efficiency as well as investment efficiency of those firms. Jones (2011) also finds the green fiscal policies have noteworthy potential to uphold the objectives of both economic growth and environmental sustainability. Jones recommends that in making the green transformation effective, countries should emphasise more on imposing taxes or similar measures on environmentally harmful activities while also gradually removing the existing subsidies (if any) on them.

Gramkow and Anger-Kraavi (2018) investigate the case of Brazil to examine if GFR could influence green innovation in developing countries. The study reveals that there are some obvious impacts of fiscal policies on green innovation; however, the policies should be better coordinated and coherent for optimal outcomes. Carraro, Pandey, and Stone (2015) advocate for market-driven fiscal policies to stimulate a green economy. This study states a two-fold impact of green fiscal policies as these can generate enough revenues for environmental as well as social purposes while also shaping the market behaviours more towards low-carbon activities and green investments.

Assessing the impacts of fiscal reforms on sustainable development trajectory remains a major discussion area in contemporary literature. Metcalf (2016) proposes a simple framework based on four criteria to appraise the green fiscal policy impact: environmental improvement, fiscal solvency, efficiency and fairness and ease of administration and compliance. Elshamy and Ahmed (2017) empirically tested the efficacy of a carbon tax, solid waste tax and congestion tax adopted by European countries. Results reveal that carbon tax and congestion tax policies have positive outcomes in attaining the green and Sustainable Development Goals' objectives in the respective countries. Elshamy and Ahmed recommend that these fiscal instruments may be beneficial also to the developing countries.

Applications in public finance and fiscal instruments for sustainable development

Before discussing the characteristics of various modes of fiscal instruments for sustainable development, this section discusses the key determinants of any public finance or fiscal instrument.

Determinants of choosing policy instruments for sustainable development

The adaptation and deployment of public finance and fiscal instruments for sustainable development largely depend on two sets of determinants: policy preference and the form of reforms.

Policy preference in sustainable development

Preference in sustainable development policies remains a thought-provoking area for policymakers. Countries must find an appropriate balance between environmental and fiscal objectives to optimise the benefit of the policies (Malik 2019). Manifestly, countries' preferences are influenced by the relative development contexts and macro sociopolitical implications of the policies. Since environmental fiscal reforms directly target environmental objectives, countries with such strategic preference usually adopt policies to contain environmental degradation and emissions early on. In the case of the negative externalities, narrowing the gap between the social and private marginal costs remains the prime consideration of the policy formulation. Connected to this, policies such as gradual removal of subsidies on the consumption of fossil fuels, Pigouvian taxation on the firms emitting and polluting the environment, congestion pricing or taxes on motorists to enter the busiest parts of a city during rush hours, fuel tax for vehicles, etc. may have been deployed.

A greater preference for fiscal goals over environmental goals, conversely, emphasises more on the strengthening of fiscal management and resourceful spending towards achieving sustainable development objectives. The course of actions under this type of policy framework may constitute streamlining the tax system and its infrastructure, reducing administrative or compliance expenses and increasing public investments in sustainable and green projects. To ensure more equitable growth and income distribution, the revenues earned from environmental taxation can be balanced by allowing the exemptions and removals of many lower-income households' income or consumption taxes. Such progressivity of the taxation would also facilitate abating the administrative and compliance costs of tax collection.

Forms of fiscal reforms

In practice, countries usually adopt two forms of fiscal reform strategies: revenue-neutral and balanced budget.

The revenue-neutral strategy advocates that the burden of imposition of a particular sector's tax on an economic agent should be completely offset either by reducing other taxes or fees for that economic agent or just redistributing the revenues among vulnerable populations (Andrle et al. 2021). Therefore, this strategy results in no change in the government's overall revenue but helps to obligate the users of extended public goods to pay for the exploitation or degradation of those public goods. For instance, from a green development approach, the revenue-neutral strategy would prompt the imposition of environmental tax while offsetting this burden by decreasing other levies or fees. A balanced budget strategy, alternatively, warrants that any changes in fiscal revenues are equally harmonised by the equivalent changes in fiscal spending (Amick, Chapman, and Elkins 2020).

The preference of the fiscal reform strategy largely depends on the respective country's political will and structural settings (Hinkley 2017; Meghir et al. 2017). So often, countries implement a mixed approach in their long-term policy actions. Nevertheless, in most cases, the likelihood of future tax increase or decrease influences the behaviours of economic entities and accordingly, further modification is designed into the reform process.

Mode of fiscal instrument

The UN has proposed an array of instruments to finance SDGs (Gambetta et al. 2019). Discussion of this section will mostly follow this broad range of public instruments. Public finance and fiscal instrument measures for sustainable development are targeted to attain the environmental social, and equity objectives. Owing to differentiated objectives and applications, the environment-based instruments are discussed separately from the other social and equity-based instruments.

Instruments targeting environmental objectives

There are five main series of public finance and fiscal instruments that countries apply for attaining pro-environmental green development objectives of the SDGs, as discussed below:

Pigouvian taxations and pricing on different pollutants

Pigou presented the concept of taxation on environmental pollution and advocated for internalising the external cost, that is, to compel the private users of the public goods to pay the private cost which would set equal to the social marginal damages of the pollution (Banzhaf 2020: 2–3). The cost may be payable in terms of taxation (i.e., at a prescribed rate based on consumption or pollution amount) or in form of a lump-sum penalty. The essence of such imposition is to uphold the polluters-pay principle and to regulate the reckless behaviours of polluting firms or economic agents. For example, a congestion tax or energy tax provides important signals to the market that the government is moving its stance towards pro-environmental and sustainable fiscal strategy and going to reduce its support from pollutant behaviours. On the other hand, such a policy incentivises the pollutant firms and economic agents to become more energy-efficient over time and encourage them to transform their conventional technologies with green and sustainable technologies (Heindl and Löschel 2015: 1).

Carbon pricing initiatives

Carbon pricing initiatives are playing a central role in adopting cost-effective emission reduction strategies for countries. The initiatives are gaining increased attention around the world. In 2019, a total of 61 carbon pricing initiatives were in place or planned for implementation. Out of these, 31 are Emission Trading Systems (ETSs) and 30 are carbon taxes. Altogether, these initiatives resulted in the reduction of 12 gigatons of carbon dioxide equivalent (CO_2e) equivalent to about 22% of global GHG emissions (World Bank 2020: 9). Governments through these measures of carbon pricing raised more than USD45 billion in 2019.

Carbon pricing instruments, based on objectives and operational techniques, can be classified into two categories: carbon or emission taxes, and ETSs. ETSs are market-based instruments targets to reduce the level of emission. A central body, usually the government, sets emission caps (i.e., limit) in one or more economic sectors and allots or sells a limited number of permits. Hence, it is also known as the cap-and-trade system. The permits allow a specific pollutant to the to produce a maximum level of emission over a given time frame. Polluters are compelled to hold the number of permits based on their amount of emission. Therefore, any polluter who wants to increase their emission beyond the set level has to buy permits from other pollutants who are willing to sell their permits. Of course, the sellers in this case, have to save their permits either by improving emission reduction technologies or by reducing their production levels. Thus, the system becomes cost-effective while restricting the emission level to the set target. Because of the certainty on the emission trajectory, ETSs are enticing countries to adopt this policy instrument to attain climate change mitigation objectives.

Emission trading not only comprises of the cap-and-trade system, but also baseline-and-credit systems as adopted in British Columbia and baseline-and-offset systems as evident in Australia (World Bank 2020: 24). In a baseline-and-credit system, the emission limit is not restricted but allows the economic agent to earn credits if they can reduce their emission more than the specified baseline (i.e., permitted) level. The credits are then allowed to be sold to others in the market who require them to comply with the regulatory obligations. The baseline-and-offset system, on the other hand, incentivises agents to undertake projects which reduce emissions below the baseline, and the offsets are allocated accordingly. Reduction of subsidy on the over-usage of public goods resulting in negative externalities

Governments of most countries generally regulate the prices of public goods, such as energy. In most cases, the prices of these public goods are set at a rate below their respective marginal costs of production. More subsidised pricing on the usage of public goods and services may lead to overconsumption and, subsequently, towards negative externalities in form of unproductive environmental management and a higher extent of emission (Lahkar and Mukherjee 2019). On top of that, a substantial amount of subsidy on these public goods wields enormous pressure on the government's budget and results in substantial market distortion. As part of fiscal reforms for sustainable development, governments should implement strategies to gradually reduce the subsidy amounts by raising the prices of such public goods and services as close as to offset the social cost of their usage.

Support for subsidies on green products and technologies

To promote sustainable and green development, governments should facilitate the objectives by adopting meticulous subsidy policies on sustainable products and technologies (Yang, Tang, and Zhang 2021). Reducing import tariffs on environmental goods and technologies (i.e., capital and machinery) may also play a pivotal role in this connection. In many countries, governments subsidise households to replace their conventional appliances such as electric lights, refrigerators or air conditioners which consume more electricity and produce higher emissions with those of pro-environmental and energy-efficient appliances. Of course, such mass-scaled subsidies would exert pressure on the public budget in the short run, but its influence on common behaviours and adaptability towards sustainable development, in the long-run, is significant.

Public financing of green bonds

Government or public entities (such as municipal, state, or federal) may issue green bonds – a new fiscal instrument to support environment-friendly or climate-resilient projects and investments. In developed economies, green bonds issued by municipalities and local governments are attaining a growing market share. Even in emerging economies like China, Brazil, India, Mexico and South Africa, the green bond domestic market has been expanding in recent times (Ngwenya and Simatele 2020). Some of the most common projects under this financing belong to the field of renewable energy, smart building and green transportation.

Instruments targeting social and equitable objectives

Alongside the fiscal instruments described in the previous subsection for pro-environmentally sustainable objectives, governments may also adopt policies in the forms of public spending and regulatory measures to support the social and equity targets for sustainable development.

Social and development impact bonds

A social and development impact bond is a fiscal instrument where the government makes a contract with an intermediary (i.e., project sponsor) which agrees to implement a social and development project by raising its capital from commercial and private investors (Fraser et al. 2018). The intermediary then contracts a service provider to distribute the project's outcomes. If the project fails to deliver verifiable social and development outcomes as promised, the government does not have to pay and investors in such a case partly or entirely lose their capital. In contrast, if the project succeeds, the government has to pay the sponsors as well the investors at specified rates and terms. The key goal of this instrument is to align investments with quantifiable social and development outcomes. On one hand, it supplies adequate affordable capital to public projects targeting social and development goals; while on the other hand, the investors are insured (by the government) with regular flows of revenues as their projects become successful.

Public guarantees

Public guarantees are instruments for domestic resource mobilisation from private investors, banks, NGOs, investment funds, etc. in which the government insures the investors from the risks of non-repayment or defaults against their social and development investments (Lee, Betru, and Horrocks 2018). Guarantees provide coverage up to a stated amount in case of any non-performing assets or default of investment. Under these facilities, projects targeting the promotion of economic welfare and social development are treated as guarantees for development.

Disaster risk insurance

Under disaster risk insurance schemes, the government provides insurance to cover the insured economic agents from adverse weather and natural disasters like floods or earthquakes in exchange for premiums paid for the insurance. The schemes are targeted to enhance the resilience of individuals, companies, and public entities against unwanted natural disasters (Ray, Jain, and Thakur 2021: 17).

Enterprise challenge fund

Governments adopt the enterprise challenge funds to support the financing of the innovative enterprises to outgrowth solutions towards sustainable development (Gambetta et al. 2019). Such funds also grant concessional loans to feasible business or projects focussing on any particular development area such as agriculture, health, education and financial inclusion.

Lotteries

Lotteries are used to raise funds from the people for the development of education, health, social protection or natural conservation (Serpeninova et al. 2020).

Case studies on fiscal reforms

The financing framework for sustainable development in emerging economies: the case of Uruguay (Gambetta et al. 2019)

Uruguay, an emerging South American country, has framed its SDG financing with a major concentration on impact investment instruments. It is expected that such instruments will have a notable impact on the country's social welfare and economic advancement. Rather than adopting numerous public instruments as advised by the UN, Uruguay started with very simple forms of impact investment instruments. The reason behind not initiating complicated instruments for SDG financing is the shallow and underdeveloped financial markets which are not yet conducive to create enough demand for certain types of intricate fiscal instruments. Especially, the pro-environmental fiscal instruments were found to be more difficult to implement in this emerging state of the economy.

Uruguay imposes significant taxes on tobacco. The study reveals that more diversification in fiscal instruments is essential for emerging economies and several instruments proposed by the UN also need to be modified for emerging economies based on the respective country context. As a prerequisite, a monitoring and assessment system should be developed to reveal the expected and actual social and environmental benefits from the fiscal instruments. The study also advocates facilitating the coordination and cooperation among various economic segments of Uruguay, especially between the public and private agents. Furthermore, the international and multilateral cooperation for capacity building, training and sharing of experiences on adopting fiscal instruments for SDGs would be pivotal.

According to the observation, the key challenges for emerging economies such as Uruguay are to identify and implement appropriate instruments that blend both environmental as well as economic objectives while providing flexibility and limited usage of resources. In addition, resource mobilisation through changing the consumers' behaviour towards the financing of environmental infrastructure would be another key driver for adopting fiscal instruments for SDGs.

SDG financing options in Rwanda: A post-pandemic assessment (Lledo and Perrelli 2021)

Using a comprehensive macroeconomic framework, this study attempts to identify appropriate policy and instruments for financing the SDGs in an African economy, Rwanda. According to this study, given the current context of financing SDGs, Rwanda would not have attained its SDGs before 2050. Under an optimistic scenario where new policies and fiscal reforms could be adopted and involvement of the private sector increased, then one-third of the SDGs financing gap would have been met at the post-COVID period. Even that would enable Rwanda to achieve the SDGs by 2040. To foster this process and attaining the objectives by 2030, Rwanda has to facilitate and engage lots of resources, specifically, 13.75% of its GDP should be deployed for SDG financing per year until 2030. For countries like Rwanda, substantial public resource mobilisation may be beneficial yet difficult on the ground; hence, supportive measures such as ODA will be critical to fill the gaps.

Fiscal policy integration for green development in Bangladesh (Sarker and Zaman 2021)

The evolution towards sustainable development needs momentous reforms in fiscal policy and internal resources mobilisation for developing countries. Especially the influence of fiscal policy remains the key as it offers increased financing for social and environmental initiatives that can advance green and sustainable development.

Bangladesh was one of the forerunners in framing its Nationally Determined Contributions (NDCs) in September 2015, reflecting its intent to tackle negative environmental and climate impacts. The government has approved an array of short- and medium-term plans, roadmaps and legislation to support the cause. Despite the government's desire and pledge, the fiscal instruments for SDGs are not optimally applied in Bangladesh. Extensive financial and institutional constrictions have also hampered the efficacy of the government's development policies and programmes.

Analysing the case of Bangladesh, the study empirically evaluates the prevailing green fiscal instruments in Bangladesh and consequently, it delivers a wide-ranging prospect of each credible fiscal instrument. The study finds that with a gradual imposition of carbon taxes starting from 10 to 25% between 2021 and 2040, CO_2 emissions may reduce by 50 million mega-tonnes while earnings from the taxation revenues may stand at Bangladeshi Taka 266.3 billion by 2040. The study also reveals that subsidisation instruments would be rather futile both from fiscal as well as environmental viewpoints. The indicators suggest that a steady reduction in import tariff would be an important driver toward the evolution of consumption of environmental goods, services and technologies. In Bangladesh, the sector-wise allocations in NDCs implementation are still experiencing some trial and error to set the appropriate parameters. The study suggests that policymakers must examine more effective options for investment in the areas such as biodiversity preservation, emission control, sustainable infrastructure and stakeholders' participation towards achieving green and Sustainable Development Goals.

Assessment of the effectiveness of fiscal policies and instruments

Assessment of the effectiveness of fiscal policies and instruments is pivotal to understand whether an instrument should continue, be redesigned or aborted. The effectiveness of such policies and instruments for sustainable development may be assessed under the economic theoretical frameworks as well as from evidence-based measures. Economic theory infers that fiscal policies and instruments must ensure optimal use of public goods and resources and should send appropriate signals to the market.

Alongside the policy framework to support sustainable development objectives, instruments must also be evaluated based on other factors such as the use of revenues, costs of administration, monitoring and other applied issues. On a macro-scale, the far-reaching impacts of the fiscal instruments should also be assessed on their efficiency and distributional consequences, wider economic implications such as economic growth, labour market factors and political risks and viability.

Metcalf (2016), based on a set of questionnaires, suggests a common framework for evaluating environmental policies and fiscal reforms. The key factors remain environmental upgrading, fiscal soundness, efficiency, equality and ease of governance and compliance. Following are the set of questions:

- Are there subsidies offered to the production or consumption of energy and/or natural resources?
- Whether the market prices represent the social costs of production or consumption considering the impacts of pollution activities?
- What are the changes the environmental fiscal reforms may bring in terms of efficiency and welfare distribution?
- Whether the fiscal reforms will be revenue-neutral? If so, whether the revenue neutrality is assessed on an *ex ante* or an *ex post* basis?
- What are the related administrative, compliance and implementation challenges that the proposed reform should address?

Impact of COVID-19 on public finance for sustainable development

Regardless of countries' pledges and need to foster fiscal reforms towards SDGs, COVID-19 has appeared as the most startling and unprecedented global phenomenon that has obligated all governments to reshuffle their fiscal settings, priorities and capabilities by a substantial extent. On one hand, governments have had to install additional fiscal spending in form of various fiscal stimuli to support different vulnerable sectors of the economy as well as low-income people to sustain themselves during this critical period (Islam and Divadkar 2020). The supports come through refinancing schemes, subsidising interest rates for export-oriented businesses, SMEs, agriculture and tax breaks. COVID-19 has exposed the fact that public goods provisioning in the health and social security sectors of the developing and least developed countries is insufficient not only due to underinvestment but also owing to a lack of efficient management (Titumir 2020). In this situation, governments in all countries now have to spend more on these two particular sectors. On top of that, economic lockdown for several months, social distancing and interruption of global supply chains has led to declining income to businesses, and hence, resulted in substantial job cuts in many sectors of the economy. The cumulative impact of these put tremendous pressure on fiscal revenue generation which further hinders the government efforts and capabilities to run the fiscal reforms towards all of the SDGs.

The Organisation for Economic Cooperation and Development (2020) identifies several factors that affect the revenue collection of government. These include restraint in economic activities and employment that distresses personal as well as business incomes which affects personal income tax, corporate income taxes, social security contributions and payroll tax receipts. Due to procyclicality, consumption of high-levied products has reduced during COVID. Consumption has shifted towards essential goods in either zero tax or very low tax brackets, resulting in a decline in VAT tax receipts. Property is assumed not to be tied directly with economic cycles; hence taxes from property have been less affected due to COVID. There are some service sectors such as travel and tourism which have been severely affected owing to the COVID pandemic. A substantial decline in taxes from these sectors is thus expected. In oil-producing countries, the revenues from excises and royalty payments have declined amid the COVID as the global demand and price of oil have also dropped. The respective corporate taxes from oil companies have also been reduced.

As stated by (Belinga et al. 2014: 5), in the growing phase, economic growth and tax growth move together. However, tax revenue is assumed to fall faster than the slow or negative move of GDP, especially during crisis periods.

The impacts on public revenues vary across countries due to COVID-19. As an immediate short-term effect, reduction in tax revenues is attributable to restrictions and precautionary measures taken by governments. Countries relying more heavily on international trade and services are eventually be affected more than the others. In the long-run, the impact on tax revenues is largely determined by the implementation of effective fiscal policies and subsequent responses by the economy. Alongside this, the role of international trade channels is also pivotal.

Under these circumstances, to restore the fiscal reforms for SDGs, a post-COVID strategy needs to be framed. Experts opine that any public spending at post-COVID must target the creation of multiplier effects in the economy while addressing the public goods and respective externalities to adopt green industrialisation funds (Titumir 2020). Botzen, Duijndam, and van Beukering (2021) have also proposed that amid the crisis, countries should increase their investment in climatic adaptation to become more resilient against natural disasters. The study also suggests that attracting foreign investment may be a key solution to promote the green recovery and climate change mitigation of the developing and least developed countries.

Contemporary issues on fiscal reforms towards SDGs: Implementation challenges and ways forward

The landscape of public finance and fiscal instruments is dynamic and ever changing. While higher financing is needed for new endeavours like the SDGs to exert some pressure on countries, it also opens up remarkable opportunities for them to explore new sources to mobilise additional financial and non-financial resources and mix them up with innovative financing approaches (Florini and Pauli 2018). New partnerships, collaborations, expertise and networks have emerged throughout this evolutionary process. These are accompanied by an increased range and sophistication in financing products and instruments to meet development policy objectives. Remaining at the forefront, governments are expected to take better control and guide this course of transformation.

While such fiscal reforms may bring positive changes in the implementation of SDGs, they may present substantial challenges for the countries, the most vital challenge is to adopt appropriate sequencing of reforms and gradualism (Jakob et al. 2019). Countries cannot introduce it instantly; it requires a preparatory phase to lower the cost, to identify market limitations and policy discrepancies, and more critically, to address any negative social costs of withdrawing the subsidies (Meckling et al. 2015)

Like any innovation, these transformations are also be embedded with inherent risks and uncertainties associated with the fiscal instruments, their application and proper implementation. Increased diversity may lead towards a series of complexities, for example, in proper understanding and regulation of the new and innovative inter-connected financing approaches, in designing and blending those financing flows to attain the transformational objectives, in optimising the potentials from all financing sources, etc. Assessing country context is also crucial to ensure the appropriate adaptability of the instruments with the country's institutional settings, capacity and political motives (Drews and Van den Bergh 2016; Klenert et al. 2018). Reaching a good balance among the multi-objective nature of energy and climate-related policies is also crucial in green fiscal reforms. For instance, energy is not exclusively an environmental issue, it also impacts transport, industry, agriculture, finance and even social inclusion (Nerini et al. 2018).

To cope with the challenges, several innovative measures are recommended. Withana (2016) examines cases of both developing and developed countries and found that challenges of green fiscal reforms may be overcome mainly through three measures: targeted mitigation approach adopted for the vulnerable section of the society, use of revenues to reduce social cost and other complementary tools to fiscal measures. To overcome the political challenges, advanced countries, such as the European Union, adopt a distinct policy sequence through constructing economically motivated vested interest groups in support of decarbonisation and cost reductions in technologies used for emission mitigation (Meckling, Sterner, and Wagner 2017).

Some studies have focussed on espousing sophisticated and creative financing mechanisms to meet public policy objectives. The United Nations Development Programme (2018: 9) suggests a blended finance mode where concessional public finance could be blended with non-concessional public or private finance to support a diversified financing toolbox for fiscal reform. It also advocates the introduction of green and blue bonds in the domestic or international market to facilitate large-scaled environmental or green infrastructure. Following the increased popularity of Islamic financing instruments such as asset backed securitised sukuk bonds, this study also recommends it as a potential instrument for green public financing. Adoption of Fintech and technology-based advanced financial services could also facilitate the desired financing services at a much faster rate and at lower cost.

Conclusion

The key essence of SDG financing should ensure the plausible and efficient mix of financial and non-financial resources are deployed at the proper place at the exact time to support the pro-environmental and equitable sustainable development of a country. Understanding specific real-world problems is pivotal to develop the appropriate strategies for SDG financing. The clarity of the objectives (i.e., the underlying problems to resolve), specifications of responsibility and respective mechanisms should be defined concretely.

However, while formulating strategies on financing the SDGs encompassing a bigger range of instruments and shuffling with too many issues may result in policy muddiness rather than attaining real-world breakthroughs. While diversity and innovation should be adopted in public spending and financial approaches towards SDGs, more attention is needed to track the emerging pattern of new resources. The respective potential, as well as the challenges of such resources, should be properly analysed considering the country context. In addition, the non-financial instruments and policy support should also be aligned with the financial instruments to enhance the effectiveness of the entire process. A thorough mapping of the financial flows from a particular fiscal instrument is critical, leading to efficient decision-making.

Governments have an enormous role to support the low-carbon transition of their countries. Meticulous adoption of carbon taxation or a carbon pricing mechanism is critical. Proactive engagement and communication with the stakeholders are the key to the successful implementation of this challenging instrument. A thorough analysis, especially on the benefits of this instrument on locality and environment, should be disseminated. Carbon revenues may have a multifaceted impact on long-term solutions, not only to reduce emissions but also to fund other development plans to facilitate social infrastructure and education.

For devising a comprehensible financing strategy for SDGs, public and private investment conglomerations could make a considerable impact. A more inclusive adoption of SDG financing tools may facilitate the proper implementation of the instruments. Climate public expenditure must be synchronised and well-coordinated among various government agencies. Institutional review and capacity building on public financial management should be improved. To ease the stress on a government's part alone, SDG financing of a country would need the right balance between the internal as well as external financial resource mobilisation. Effective global, regional, bilateral and multilateral cooperation must be well-integrated with the government's effort to finance SDGs.

This chapter has significant implications in designing policy options based on the applicability and impact of various fiscal instruments for green sustainable development supported by economic theories and analysis. It provides an adequate economic breakdown as input for governments and policymakers, especially for the developing and least developed countries which are expected to diverge more as compared to advanced high-income countries in adopting appropriate strategies to support pro-environmental and equitable sustainable development public instruments. This outcome would also provide a roadmap to attain the targets of SDGs and NDCs for developing and least developed countries.

References

Adenle, Ademola A., Dale T. Manning, and Joseph Arbiol. 2017. 'Mitigating Climate Change in Africa: Barriers to Financing Low-Carbon Development', *World Development*, 100, 123–32.

Amick, Joe, Terrence Chapman, and Zachary Elkins. 2020. 'On Constitutionalizing a Balanced Budget', *The Journal of Politics*, 82 (3), 1078–96.

Andrle, Michal, Shafik Hebous, Alvar Kangur, and Mehdi Raissi. 2021. 'Italy: Toward a Growth-Friendly Fiscal Reform', *Economia Politica*, 38 (1), 385–420.

Asian Development Bank Institute.·2014. *Low-Carbon Green Growth in Asia: Policies and Practices*, (Asian Development Bank), <http://www.adb.org/sites/default/files/publication/159319/adbi-low-carbon-green-growth-asia.pdf> [Accessed 20 August 2021].

Banzhaf, H. Spencer.·2020. *A History of Pricing Pollution (or, Why Pigouvian Taxes Are Not Necessarily Pigouvian)*, (National Bureau of Economic Research), <https://www.nber.org/papers/w27683> [Accessed 24 January 2022].

Belinga, Vincent, Ms Dora Benedek, Ruud A. De Mooij, and Mr John Norregaard.·2014. *Tax Buoyancy in OECD Countries*, (Washington DC: International Monetary Fund), <https://www.imf.org/en/Publications/WP/Issues/2016/12/31/Tax-Buoyancy-in-OECD-Countries-41661> [Accessed 25 October 2021].

Botzen, Wouter, Sem Duijndam, and Pieter van Beukering. 2021. 'Lessons for Climate Policy from Behavioral Biases Towards Covid-19 and Climate Change Risks', *World Development*, 137, 105214.

Chang, Kai, Qiong Wan, Qichun Lou, Yili Chen, and Weihong Wang. 2020. 'Green Fiscal Policy and Firms' Investment Efficiency: New Insights into Firm-Level Panel Data from the Renewable Energy Industry in China', *Renewable Energy*, 151, 589–97.

Crespi, Francesco, Claudia Ghisetti, and Francesco Quatraro.·2015. *Taxonomy of Implemented Policy Instruments to Foster the Production of Green Technologies and Improve Environmental and Economic Performance*, (Vienna: WWWforEurope), <https://www.econstor.eu/handle/10419/125745> [Accessed 24 January 2022].

Dafermos, Yannis, and Maria Nikolaidi. 2019. 'Fiscal Policy and Ecological Sustainability: A Post-Keynesian Perspective.' in P. Arestis and M. Sawyer (eds.), *Frontiers of Heterodox Macroeconomics* (Springer) (pp. 277–322). New York: Palgrave Macmillan.

Drews, Stefan, and Jeroen C.J.M. Van den Bergh. 2016. 'What Explains Public Support for Climate Policies? A Review of Empirical and Experimental Studies', *Climate Policy*, 16 (7), 855–76.

Elayah, Moosa. 2016. 'Lack of Foreign Aid Effectiveness in Developing Countries between a Hammer and an Anvil', *Contemporary Arab Affairs*, 9 (1), 82–99.

Elshamy, Hany M., and Khaled I. Sayed Ahmed. 2017. 'Green Fiscal Reforms, Environment and Sustainable Development', *International Journal of Applied Economics, Finance and Accounting*, 1 (1), 48–52.

Florini, Ann, and Markus Pauli. 2018. 'Collaborative Governance for the Sustainable Development Goals', *Asia and the Pacific Policy Studies*, 5 (3), 583–98.

Fraser, Alec, Stefanie Tan, Mylene Lagarde, and Nicholas Mays. 2018. 'Narratives of Promise, Narratives of Caution: A Review of the Literature on Social Impact Bonds', *Social Policy and Administration*, 52 (1), 4–28.

Gambetta, Nicolás, Paula Azadian, Victoria Hourcade, and María Elisa Reyes. 2019. 'The Financing Framework for Sustainable Development in Emerging Economies: The Case of Uruguay', *Sustainability*, 11 (4), 1059.

Gaspar, Vitor, Mr David Amaglobeli, Ms Mercedes Garcia-Escribano, Delphine Prady, and Mauricio Soto. 2019. *Fiscal Policy and Development: Human, Social, and Physical Investments for the SDGs* (International Monetary Fund).

Georgescu, Marina Anda, Velina Pendolovska, and Julio Cesar Cabeça.·2010. *Distribution of Environmental Taxes in Europe by Tax Payers in 2007* (Eurostat), <https://ec.europa.eu/euro stat/documents/3433488/5578296/KS-SF-10-067-EN.PDF/a5bb7ce3-d8f4-484a-aeaa -85a37aeaac71> [Accessed 10 January 2022].

Gramkow, Camila, and Annela Anger-Kraavi. 2018. 'Could Fiscal Policies Induce Green Innovation in Developing Countries? The Case of Brazilian Manufacturing Sectors', *Climate Policy*, 18 (2), 246–57.

Heindl, Peter, and Andreas Löschel.·2015. *Social Implications of Green Growth Policies from the Perspective of Energy Sector Reform and Its Impact on Households*, Discussion Paper 81, (Munster, Germany: CAWM), <https://www.econstor.eu/bitstream/10419/107588/1/ 81877455X.pdf> [Accessed 28 January 2022].

Hewett, Chris, and Paul Ekins.·2014. *Environmental Fiscal Reform in Europe.*, (Green Budget Europe), <https://green-budget.eu/wp-content/uploads/UCL-no-edits-Feb-2016-1.pdf> [Accessed 12 November 2021].

Hinkley, Sara. 2017. 'Structurally Adjusting: Narratives of Fiscal Crisis in Four US Cities', *Urban Studies*, 54 (9), 2123–38.

Islam, S., and Y. Divadkar 2020 'How Bangladesh's Leaders Should Respond to the Economic Threats of Covid-19', (World Economic Forum)>https://www.weforum.org/agenda/2020/04/ covid-19-coronavirus-bangladesh/> [Accessed 22 October 2021].

Jakob, Michael, Rafael Soria, Carlos Trinidad, Ottmar Edenhofer, Céline Bak, Daniel Bouille, Daniel Buira, Hernan Carlino, Veronica Gutman, and Christian Hübner. 2019. 'Green Fiscal Reform for a Just Energy Transition in Latin America', *Economics*, 13 (1), pp. 20190017. https://doi.org/10. 5018/economics-ejournal.ja.2019-17

Jones, Benjamin. 2011. 'Driving a Green Economy through Public Finance and Fiscal Policy Reform', *Journal of International Commerce, Economics and Policy*, 2 (02), 325–49.

Kemp, René, and Babette Never. 2017. 'Green Transition, Industrial Policy, and Economic Development', *Oxford Review of Economic Policy*, 33 (1), 66–84.

Klenert, David, Linus Mattauch, Emmanuel Combet, Ottmar Edenhofer, Cameron Hepburn, Ryan Rafaty, and Nicholas Stern. 2018. 'Making Carbon Pricing Work for Citizens', *Nature Climate Change*, 8 (8), 669–77.

Lahkar, Ratul, and Saptarshi Mukherjee. 2019. 'Evolutionary Implementation in a Public Goods Game', *Journal of Economic Theory*, 181, 423–60.

Lamperti, Francesco, Mariana Mazzucato, Andrea Roventini, and Gregor Semieniuk. 2019. 'The Green Transition: Public Policy, Finance, and the Role of the State', *Vierteljahrshefte Zur Wirtschaftsforschung*, 88 (2), 73–88.

Lee, Chris, Aron Betru, and Paul Horrocks.·2018. *Guaranteeing the Goals: Adapting Public Sector Guarantees to Unlock Blended Financing for the UN Sustainable Development Goals*, (Washington DC: Milken Institute), <https://milkeninstitute.org/sites/default/files/reports- pdf/Guaranteeing-the-Goals-FINAL-4_2.pdf> [Accessed 28 January 2022].

Lledo, Victor Duarte, and Roberto A. Perrelli.·2021. *SDG Financing Options in Rwanda: A Post- Pandemic Assessment*, (International Monetary Fund), <https://www.imf.org/en/Publications/ WP/Issues/2021/04/29/SDG-Financing-Options-in-Rwanda-A-Post-Pandemic-Assessment -50252> [Accessed 28 January 2022].

Luke, Timothy W. 2013. 'Corporate Social Responsibility: An Uneasy Merger of Sustainability and Development', *Sustainable Development*, 21 (2), 83–91.

Malik, Hamza Ali 2019 *Fiscal Rules and Fiscal Space* (Bangkok: ADBI-ESCAP Seminar on Fiscal Governance for Sustainable Growth and Development) <https://www.unescap.org/sites/de fault/files/01_%5BHamza%5D%20Fiscal%20rules%20and%20fiscal%20space.pdf> [Accessed 28 January 2022].

Mattei, Fondazione Eni Enrico, Carlo Carraro, Suneel Pandey, and Steven Stone. 2015. 'Why Fiscal Policy Matters for a Green Economy Transition', *Review of Environment, Energy and Economics (Re3)*.

Meckling, Jonas, Nina Kelsey, Eric Biber, and John Zysman. 2015. 'Winning Coalitions for Climate Policy', *Science*, 349 (6253), 1170–71.

Meckling, Jonas, Thomas Sterner, and Gernot Wagner. 2017. 'Policy Sequencing toward Decarbonization', *Nature Energy*, 2 (12), 918–22.

Meghir, Costas, Christopher A. Pissarides, Dimitri Vayanos, and Nikolaos Vettas. 2017. *Beyond Austerity: Reforming the Greek Economy* (Cambridge, MA: MIT Press).

Metcalf, Gilbert E. 2016. 'A Conceptual Framework for Measuring the Effectiveness of Green Fiscal Reforms', *International Journal on Green Growth and Development* 2(2),87–126.

Mi, Zhifu, and D'Maris Coffman. 2019. 'The Sharing Economy Promotes Sustainable Societies', *Nature Communications*, 10 (1), 1–3.

Nerini, Francesco Fuso, Julia Tomei, Long Seng To, Iwona Bisaga, Priti Parikh, Mairi Black, Aiduan Borrion, Catalina Spataru, Vanesa Castán Broto, and Gabrial Anandarajah. 2018. 'Mapping Synergies and Trade-Offs between Energy and the Sustainable Development Goals', *Nature Energy*, 3 (1), 10–15.

Ngwenya, Nomhle, and Mulala Danny Simatele. 2020. 'Unbundling of the Green Bond Market in the Economic Hubs of Africa: Case Study of Kenya, Nigeria and South Africa', *Development Southern Africa*, 37 (6), 888–903.

Organisation for Economic Cooperation and Development, and Selected Partner Economies. 2020. *Tax Policy Reforms 2020*. (Paris: OECD).

Paroussos, Leonidas, Kostas Fragkiadakis, and Panagiotis Fragkos. 2020. 'Macro-Economic Analysis of Green Growth Policies: The Role of Finance and Technical Progress in Italian Green Growth', *Climatic Change*, 160 (4), 591–608.

Pingeot, Lou. 2014. *Corporate Influence in the Post-2015 Process* (Aachen, Germany: Bischöfliches Hilfswerk Misereor).

Rashed, Abdulkarim Hasan, and Afzal Shah. 2021. 'The Role of Private Sector in the Implementation of Sustainable Development Goals', *Environment, Development and Sustainability*, 23 (3), 2931–48.

Ray, Saon, Samridhi Jain, and Vasundhara Thakur.·2021. *Financing India's Disaster Risk Resilience Strategy*, (New Delhi: ICRIER), <https://www.think-asia.org/bitstream/handle/11540/13297/Working_Paper_404.pdf?sequence=1> [Accessed 25 November 2021].

Sachs, Jeffrey D., Wing Thye Woo, Naoyuki Yoshino, and Farhad Taghizadeh-Hesary.·2019. *Why Is Green Finance Important?*, (Tokyo: Asian Development Bank Institute), <https://www.think-asia.org/bitstream/handle/11540/9621/adbi-wp917.pdf?sequence=1> [Accessed 24 January 2022].

Sarker, Tapan, and Kazi Arif Uz Zaman 2021 *Fiscal Policy Integration for Green Development in Bangladesh* (Asian Development Bank Institute's Virtual Policy Dialogue on Fiscal Policy Instruments and Green Development) <https://drive.google.com/file/d/1lsw1XVEf_LmZNzHWWjLQc8k7_xTqp9zh/view> [Accessed 28 January 2022].

Scheyvens, Regina, Glenn Banks, and Emma Hughes. 2016. 'The Private Sector and the SDGs: The Need to Move Beyond 'Business as Usual", *Sustainable Development*, 24 (6), 371-82.

Schmidtchen, Dieter, Jenny Helstroffer, and Christian Koboldt. 2015. 'Replacing the Polluter Pays Principle by the Cheapest Cost Avoider Principle: On the Efficient Treatment of External Costs', *Bureau d'économie théorique et appliquée (BETA)*, Working Paper 2015 – 08.

Serpeninova, Yuliia Serhiivna, Inna Oleksandrivna Makarenko, Oleksii Leonidovych Plastun, A. Babkов, and Gunnay Gasimova. 2020. 'Mapping of the Responsible Investments Instruments in SDG 3 'Good Health and Well-Being' Financing: EU and US Experience', *Health Economics and Management Review*, 1 (1), 106-15.

Titumir, R.A.M. 2020. 'A New Fiscal, Monetary Policy Framework in Covid-19 Era', *New Age*, 25 April 2020. <https://www.newagebd.net/article/105059/a-new-fiscal-monetary-policy-framework-in-covid-19-era.> [Accessed 25 April 2021].

United Nations.·2014. *The Role of Business and Finance in Supporting the Post-2015 Agenda* (United Nations Global Compact), <https://d306pr3pise04h.cloudfront.net/docs/news_events %2F9.6%2FPost2015_WhitePaper_2July14.pdf> [Accessed 10 November 2021].

—— 2015 *General Assembly Resolution 69/313: Addis Ababa Action Agenda* United Nations (Addis Ababa, Ethiopia: Third International Conference on Financing for Development) <https://sustainabledevelopment.un.org/content/documents/2051AAAA_Outcome.pdf> [Accessed 24 January 2022].

——.·2019a. *Roadmap for Financing the 2030 Agenda for Sustainable Development 2019-2021*, (New York: United Nations Secretary General's Office), <https://www.un.org/sustainabledevel opment/wp-content/uploads/2019/07/EXEC.SUM_SG-Roadmap-Financing-SDGs-July-2019. pdf> [Accessed 10 July 2021].

——.·2019b. *The Sustainable Development Goals Report 2019*, (New York United Nations), <https://unstats.un.org/sdgs/report/2019/The-Sustainable-Development-Goals-Report-2019. pdf> [Accessed 24 January 2022].

United Nations Conference on Trade and Development.·2014. *World Investment Report – Investing in the SDGs: An Action Plan* (Geneva, Switzerland: United Nations), <https://unctad.org/sys tem/files/official-document/wir2014_en.pdf> [Accessed 28 January 2022].

United Nations Development Programme.·2018. *Financing the 2030 Agenda – an Introductory Guidebook for UNDP Country Offices* (New York: United Nations), <https://www.uncclearn.org/ resources/library/financing–the–2030–agenda–an–introductory-guidebook-for-undp-country -offices/> [Accessed 24 January 2022].

Wagner, Adolph. 1958. 'Three Extracts on Public Finance.' in Richard A. Musgrave and Alan T. Peacock (eds.), *Classics in the Theory of Public Finance* (New York: Palgrave Macmillan), pp. 1–15.

Williamson, Claudia R. 2010. 'Exploring the Failure of Foreign Aid: The Role of Incentives and Information', *The Review of Austrian Economics*, 23 (1), 17-33.

Withana, Sirini. 2016. 'Overcoming Obstacles to Green Fiscal Reform', *The International Journal on Green Growth and Development*, 2 (2), 161.

World Bank.·2020. *States and Trends of Carbon Pricing 2020*, (Washington DC World Bank Group), <https://openknowledge.worldbank.org/bitstream/handle/10986/33809/9781464815867. pdf> [Accessed 10 September 2021].

Yang, Rui, Wansheng Tang, and Jianxiong Zhang. 2021. 'Technology Improvement Strategy for Green Products under Competition: The Role of Government Subsidy', *European Journal of Operational Research*, 289 (2), 553-68.

Yoshino, Naoyuki, and Farhad Taghizadeh-Hesary. 2018. 'Alternatives to Private Finance: Role of Fiscal Policy Reforms and Energy Taxation in Development of Renewable Energy Projects.' in Venkatachalam Anbumozhi, Kaliappa Kalirajan and Fukunari Kimura (eds.), *Financing for Low-Carbon Energy Transition* (Singapore: Springer), pp. 335–57.

Zhang, Kun, Qian Wang, Qiao-Mei Liang, and Hao Chen. 2016. 'A Bibliometric Analysis of Research on Carbon Tax from 1989 to 2014', *Renewable and Sustainable Energy Reviews*, 58, 297-310.

Sima Rani Dey and Bishwajit Basak

Chapter 9
Financing sustainable development goals (SDGs) and the role of digital finance

Abstract: Digitalisation has changed the delivery patterns of financial services all over the world. On August 26, 2020, the United Nations launched a task force with a mandate of catalysing and recommending ways to harness digital finance to accelerate the required finance for Sustainable Development Goals (SDGs). Digital finance has become a lifeline for billions of people to survive and to ensure financial sustainability during the COVID-19 pandemic. Social safety nets involving cash transfers through digital payments have become convenient and they enable governments to mobilise funds for emergency relief. A number of developing countries, like Bangladesh, have done tremendously well in managing the pandemic, thanks to the use of digital financing that has delivered financial services through digital platforms, including the uptake of mobile money and other payment platforms. It is also helping to channel more resources to support all SDGs through different paths. This chapter will discuss the prominent role of digital finance and its operational mechanism to finance SDGs. The outcome of the research will be to provide an assessment of digitalisation in accelerating SDGs finance so that policymakers can take some necessary actions to ensure the effective implementation of digital finance for financial sustainability.

Keywords: digital finance, sdgs, COVID-19, sustainability, bangladesh

Introduction

Broad issues on digital finance and its role

Digital finance can be defined as financial services delivered using digital platforms in a cashless manner that requires digital infrastructure – including mobile phones and the internet. It enables seamless transactions between customers and financial service providers without paying a visit to bank branches (Manyika et al. 2016). Digital finance includes the whole range of products, services, innovation and/or infrastructure that allows individual customers and companies to access money deposits, savings, receive and send payments and credit facilities online using the internet without face-to-face interaction or bank visits (Ozili 2018: 329–40). The role of digital finance is crucial for eradicating poverty and enhancing financial inclusion in developing economies (International Telecommunication Union 2016).

https://doi.org/10.1515/9783110733488-009

The essential components for the smooth operation of digital finance include a digital transaction platform, a retail agent, customers and retail agents with a digital device – specifically a mobile phone – for performing financial transactions (Lyman and Lauer 2015). Digital finance can refer to technological innovations for executing a variety of financial services, including electronic money (e-money), mobile money, payments via debit and credit card and electronic funds transfers (Wyman 2016) from service providers to customers. In developing countries, the major role of digital finance is to facilitate and ensure financial inclusion. Moreover, it has the potential to expand basic financial services to numerous people and informal sectors since at least 50% of the global population have mobile phones (World Bank 2014).

Digital finance can deliver reachable, reasonable, convenient and safe financial services to needy individuals in the developing world (Lyman and Lauer 2015), which can also play an influential role in ensuring the accessibility and affordability of banking services. It provides easy access to various financial products and services for individuals and small, medium, and large businesses, indirectly boosting gross domestic product (GDP).

Digital innovations in the finance sector can also substantially impact banks' performances in the long-run. According to Scott, Van Reenen and Zachariadis (2017: 984–1004), innovation in digital financial services like SWIFT positively impacts banking performance and bank profitability. It also builds a significant network effect in the long-run. Digital finance may support generating higher tax revenue as the digital platform facilitates customers to increase their aggregate expenditure, subsequently increasing the size of financial transactions (Manyika et al. 2016). Fully-fledged digitalisation in delivering financial services is beneficial for financial and monetary system regulators and can considerably decrease the circulation of money on the black market. Moreover, digital finance provides customers greater freedom and control to maintain their finances, take immediate financial decisions and make money transactions within seconds (Ozili 2018: 329–40). Therefore, digital finance is capable of improving the welfare of people and small and medium-sized enterprises (SMEs) that require formal bank accounts and funds in to complete multiple financial transactions. However, all the above-mentioned expected benefits regarding digital finance can only be fully realised if the service charge of digital financial services can be made negligible or zero (Ozili 2018: 329–40).

Digital technologies for sustainable development

The digital revolution and the existing digitalisation in global financial systems will minimise potential threats in the financial sector and help achieve sustainability in the financial sector and advance SDGs simultaneously. Digitalisation in the financial sector has transformed conventional modes of financial service delivery worldwide.

This revolution occurs at every level of the financial system, starting from millions of customers' experiences managing their financial matters to operational mechanisms of the financial institutions, risk analysis and decision-making of investors, movement of capital markets and policymakers' approaches to problem-solving.

The SDG targets towards 2030 also emphasise the role of digitalisation to ensure future sustainable development because the global action plan for development necessitates a global approach to financing. To achieve the SDGs as per the roadmap, trillions of dollars are required therefore, the public sector cannot be solely liable to provide this huge amount of money. Here comes the possibility of digital finance with its new operational and financial mechanism. Now, mobile money alone contributes directly to 13 of the 17 SDGs through various means. Moreover, the green finance movement is also becoming popular because of its innovative practice of digital-enabled technologies for investment purposes and for delivering financial services achieving positive environmental impacts. Digital technologies and digital finance will be more effective in the future for financial management because capital can advance the achievement of SDGs to include everyone. However, various fields like capital markets, biodiversity and ocean health still require the reach of the digital revolution in financing.

Digital finance and financial inclusion

Financial inclusion is to bring the unbanked poor into the formal financial channels of the economy, which can be thought of as one of the sustainable provisions of digital finance (International Telecommunication Union 2016). It can also be said that financial inclusion may refer to the use of formal financial services by low-income and poor people (Beck, Demirgüç-Kunt, and Levine 2007: 27–49; Bruhn and Love 2014: 1347–76). Due to financial inclusion, the poor, particularly, are included in formal financial channels, initially owning a bank account. Because of greater financial inclusion, financially excluded individuals will be able to save their money, invest in education, start businesses and eventually get out of poverty (Beck, Demirgüç-Kunt, and Levine 2007: 27–49; Bruhn and Love 2014: 1347–76). Therefore, an ideal financial system should not be discriminating and selective, rather, it should be inclusive and equal for everyone in all respects, such as credit access and funds movement, capital expansion and risk reduction, especially for marginalised people.

Financial inclusion motivates and gives the opportunity for low-income people to save for future uncertainties that fosters stability of their financial base. Savings as bank deposits contribute to stabilising the liquidity base for banks in recession (Han and Melecky 2013), thus improving banking system stability. Higher financial inclusion creates more opportunities for poor people and encourages them to save more, invest and access credit (Ellis, Lemma, and Rud 2010). Financial inclusion comes as a great boon for people to handle income shocks such as major accidents or illnesses or loss of employment (Collins et al. 2009). Moreover, small entrepreneurs and SMEs can access more credit, which positively impacts employment growth (Prasad 2010). Financial inclusion encourages the participation of people from different sectors in affordable and formal channels of financial services as well. The role of interest rates as a key tool of macroeconomic policy and stability will be strengthened with the increase of the formal financial sector, since it exerts a positive impact on economic growth (Cecchetti and Kharroubi 2012).

When a large share of the unbanked population owns a personal cell phone, then the provision of securing financial services via their mobile phones and related devices can easily improve their access to finance (World Bank 2014). Hence, it can be presumed that the relationship between digital finance and financial inclusion is positive and greater financial inclusion can improve access to basic financial services in the lives of marginalised and low-income people in rural areas. The services of digital finance to rural and poor communities improves credit access and reduces the requirement of maintaining more branches, which can positively affect bank profitability. Digital finance can offer a convenient and reliable platform for people to conduct essential financial transactions, from money transfers to utility payments. In addition, it is necessary to mention that having a positive relationship between digital finance and financial inclusion is not uniform for people of all income groups. The strength of the positive relationship is higher for high and middle income people, but it can be different for low-income and poor people. The service providers of digital finance are corporate people and they can be responsive in terms of marketing tactics as well as the educational base of their customers. Thus, discrimination can arise between high and middle income clients and low-income and poor clients. Therefore, less focus is provided to poor and uneducated communities by digital finance service providers due to the fact they generate low net profit and their lack of financial literacy to use and realise digital finance.

Digital finance and SDGs

Billions of individuals and SMEs in developing economies lack access to credit and savings at present. They often have to pay high interest rates and have access to a limited range of products (Manyika et al. 2016). As a result, the economic growth of private investments suffers. Here, digital finance provides a package of solutions only requiring a mobile phone. It has the potential to transform the lives and economic prospects of governments, businesses and individuals across the developing world and boost GDP and materialise the goal of financial inclusion.

According to research, emerging countries will be capable of increasing their GDPs by 6%, which is equivalent to the GDP of Germany or larger than all the economies of

Africa, by 2025 with the pervasive adoption and use of digital finance (Manyika et al. 2016). This increased amount of GDP could create employment opportunities for millions of people across all sectors. Modern economies require smooth access to digital payments and financial services, enabling governments, businesses and individuals to transact reasonably and competently.

For a variety of companies, including banks, payment providers, retailers, telecommunications companies, financial technology startups and others, the possible business prospects are massive (Manyika et al. 2016). Henceforth, leaders from both the private and public sectors should make efforts to take the opportunity of digital finance in a concentrated and synchronised way. This requires mobile phones as digital infrastructure, a dynamic environment and a few essential as well as sophisticated digital financial products that can address the demands of its consumers. And most importantly, just owning a mobile phone with no additional major infrastructural investment is essential in capturing the opportunity of digital finance that can also accelerate inclusive growth in the long-run (Manyika et al. 2016).

How digital finance is enabling financial ease for both developed and least developed countries

The use of digital technologies and mobile phones worldwide is spreading at an amazing speed. A mobile phone allows customers access to digital services to perform all types of financial transactions, including government transfers, commodity purchases, utility payments, remittances transfer, salaries and payment of school fees. Mobile money is more convenient than cash for customers in terms of time, cost savings of a bank visit and risk reduction of robbery. Apart from that, it also allows access to other necessary digital financial services like managing savings or loans.

Mobile phones are omnipresent and are in almost every hand because of network coverage and quality expansion. Presently, above 90% of the populations of developing economies have mobile network coverage. Nearly 80% of people had mobile phone subscriptions and 55% of adults had a bank account in 2014. And it is expected that mobile phone subscriptions will reach nearly 90% of adults by 2020 (GMSA Intelligence 2016).

Digital financial services have cut the cost of having a digital account by around 80 to 90% in comparison to physical branches, enabling service providers to serve more customers at lower prices with a wide range of products profitably. Into the future it is likely that many people will use their digital accounts to save money. In addition, digital service providers are able to assess credit risk through their digital payment receipts and expenditure details which will lead them to design effective policies to underwrite loans and insurance with greater confidence for their borrowers. The mechanism of collecting digital repayments is quite user-friendly for service providers as it is automated. Therefore, the full package of digital credit, savings and insurance products have become cost-effective for providers to serve low-income people and very small businesses.

In 2007, the concept of mobile money was first launched in South Africa and the Philippines. In Kenya, M-PESA (M represents mobile, PESA represents money) has become a ubiquitous mobile financial service. Hence, M-PESA has been considered an innovation in the financial sector that has brought many unbanked populations into formal financial channels, ensuring their economic wellbeing and welfare. Around 96% of Kenyan households use M-PESA with their mobile phone for deposit and withdrawal purposes. A substantial number of ATMs and the 223,184 agent network has made M-PESA successful (Communications Commission of Kenya 2020; Mas and Ng'Weno 2010: 352–70). At present, a few additional financial services have also been deployed over the M-PESA network, including M-Shwari, which is a bank account of Commercial Bank of Africa, offering savings and credit services accessed entirely through the M-PESA platform, and Lipa na M-PESA which is a retail payment facility.

Digital finance has numerous benefits apart from the low costs of existing transactions and increased customer convenience. The digital finance network has become a vital part of infrastructure like amenities like roads and electricity. So, it can underpin some broader innovations in the economy and create new emerging business models.

Digital technologies to achieve the goals of sustainable development

Sustainable digital finance towards the financial system and financial institutions may contribute to achieving sustainable development. To succeed in achieving sustainable development, policymakers and international cooperation should address cross-border issues, common risks and potential market failures because digital technologies have upgraded the levels of sustainable finance. The new technologies have already underpinned digital finance with the greatest potentiality with big data, artificial intelligence, cloud computing, online and mobile platforms, blockchain and the Internet of Things (IoT) (United Nations Secretary-General's Task Force on Digital Financing of the Sustainable Development Goals 2020).

The impact of digital technologies in the financial sector and the real economy is quite remarkable and has brought several benefits to sustainable finance. First, digital finance allows greater investment in sustainable assets and projects. Its automated features and availability can process and analyse huge amounts of data cheaply, quickly and more accurately to overcome information asymmetries and identify risks.

Lastly, it enables government organisations to effectively track the regulatory aspects of sustainable development. Digital finance increases inclusion and encourages innovation, creating more financial opportunities aligning with national SDGs. When new innovations in the real economy and digital finance interact, this interaction encourages business investment reducing risks and also facilitating sustainable investments. Altogether, the interactions between sustainable development and efficient capital usage may be multifaceted and lead to unwanted consequences.

How digital finance has facilitated the financial sector during the pandemic and new learnings

Digitalisation has significantly changed the financial sector and has become a rising player in terms of new product offerings and service delivery. It motivates many existing financial institutions to digitalise their services through in-house development, acquisition, partnerships and outsourcing. Banks have allocated and invested the lion's share of their money in developing, integrating and acquiring those emerging technologies (Anton-Diaz and Khairy 2019). Even typical financial institutions are also evolving to digital-first services for their new clients through open source initiatives where mobile network operators and new innovators are key players (Fintech 2021).

Fintech investment represented about a third of global venture capital funding and hit a record high of USD 120 billion in 2018 (KPMG Fintech 2019). Meanwhile, telecom and fintech companies are also acquiring banks, for example, Lending Club's recent purchase of Radius Bank (Duberstein 2020) and Telenor's acquisition of Tameer (Telenor Group 2016). Up to now, the relationship between existing financial institutions and innovative startup firms appears to be largely complementary. This sort of partnership allows fintech firms to operate smoothly with a relatively small setup, and at the same time, the existing institutions' clients get to benefit from access to innovative technologies at a lower cost (Financial Stability Board 2019).

At present, the public finance departments of governments are investing in digitalising their financial systems as well. The use of digitalisation in financial management has improved the accountability, transparency, efficiency of budgets, efficiency gains and cost-effectiveness in payments and procurement (Lund, White, and Lamb 2017). As per the estimate of CGAP (Consultative Group to Assist the Poor), digital transfers of government benefits generated approximately 40% in savings per transaction (Cozzo 2013).

Perspective of COVID-19

During the COVID-19 pandemic, governments have established and enhanced their digital capacity to disburse social protection funds directly to citizens for protecting small businesses, saving jobs, collecting taxes and bringing relief to countless people. Fortunately, the smartphone has been turned into a wallet for many unbanked people. Digital finance has empowered citizens to open bank accounts and become savers, lenders, borrowers and investors. Digital money transfers have allowed governments and individuals during the COVID-19 pandemic to provide instantaneous financial support to needy people. Cash handling has shifted to digital payments due to the concern about the physical transmission of the COVID-19 virus through banknotes (Auer, Cornelli, and Frost 2020). Such financing has also supported SMEs to recover from the financial loss of COVID-19; those supports include emergency collateral-free digital loans, digital processing of trade financing (DBS Bank 2020; Fintech News Malaysia 2020) and government incentives with minimum interest rates, etc. China uses blockchain-powered supply chain finance, which allows SMEs to apply for loans from banks based on their receivables from large enterprises. Crowdfunding platforms also have the potential collect funds for medical supplies and emergency relief (Kulish 2020). For example, Intuit QuickBooks (BusinessWire 2020), in cooperation with GoFundMe, allowed businesses to accept donations and launch fundraisers for those affected by COVID-19. Several e-commerce platforms have been developed that sell essential goods locally for immediate or future consumption. This digital platform of e-commerce has also improved the direct connection between buyer and seller by removing the middlemen who usually consume the lion's share of businesses' profit. As a result, marginal producers are now making a better profit than before. A number of digital insurance products are also being introduced for COVID-19 patients to offer necessary health coverage. WeSure provides free insurance for Chinese COVID-19 patients with severe disease. A Mumbai-based startup offers hospitalisation and lost wages coverage (PRNewswire 2020; Wood 2020; Bhakta 2020). In all these cases, transparency of finance will play a crucial role in ensuring government accountability for crisis response and recovery spending.

Context of digital finance from developed and developing economies

Practices of digital finance through digital technologies across the globe

This section of the chapter will highlight how digital finance is overcoming the challenges of finance mobilisation, particularly because of its relevance to capital markets, private equity and venture capital. This part will also focus on how different digital technologies are being used to achieve the goals of sustainable finance.

Digital technologies built with mobile and big data are relatively prevalent, whereas applications involving blockchain and IoT are still quite nascent. Big data, MLAI and to a lesser extent, blockchain is helping to increase the institutional efficiencies, reduce information asymmetries and associated costs for designing new green financial instruments in the long-run, ensure transparency and improve the investor's capacity for identifying, assessing and pricing potential risk. Modern digital technologies such as IoT, in combination with mobile technology, are exploring the latest business models, making the expansion of sustainable capital mostly by private equity and venture capital more attractive.

Digital finance and financial development in Bangladesh

The way Bangladesh has progressed and expanded its services in the financial sector across the country is quite impressive. It is also quite satisfactory in the rural, remote and hard-to-reach areas. In this respect, the role of Bangladesh Bank, the Central Bank of Bangladesh, can be considered revolutionary and it has enhanced financial inclusion by making bank services accessible to the general people through special accounts and mobile financial services. More than 60 million Bangladeshi people are now regular users of mobile financial services. For instance, unbanked individuals like farmers, freedom fighters, the hard-core poor and people under social safety net programmes can easily open bank accounts by depositing just Bangladesh Taka (BDT) 10. Around a million people are making use of mobile banking across the country, and presently, around 50% of the population of Bangladesh has been financially included in formal financial services, an increase from 31% in 2014 (World Bank 2017). Presently, the entire stipend program of school children and all sorts of social safety net cash benefits are being transferred to beneficiaries' accounts through mobile money transfer.

Context of digital finance in Bangladesh

Previously, the financial landscape of Bangladesh was mainly dominated by the banking industry to provide diversified financial services to its customers. Unfortunately, those formal financial services were limited to only bank account holders, while many people out there remained unbanked, particularly the poor. It was really hard for the internal migrant workers (villages to towns) to send their money home. Hence, most of the time, either they needed to look for any relative or acquaintance to carry their cash home or to take support of a middleman with high charge. Against this backdrop, the necessity of an easier and accessible financial service gave rise to the digital financial service via mobile for the masses in Bangladesh, and it evolved multi-fold in 2019. Undoubtedly, the 100% coverage in owning mobile phones per 100 inhabitants has facilitated this prompt spread of mobile banking in Bangladesh (International Telecommunication Union 2021) as well as mobile financial services (MFS) (Bangladesh Bank 2021). As of December 2020, Bangladesh had 99.3 million registered MFSs accounts and performed on average 299.5 million daily transactions, which is worth BDT 56,556.88. MFS services are regulated by the Central Bank of Bangladesh, and the available service providers are bKash, Rocket, Nagad, MyCash, SureCash, among which the bKash holds the majority of the market share with the highest customer base.

The MFS industry has appeared as a one-stop solution for all kinds of financial transactions, from sending and receiving money to making payments for utility, education, medical, retail bills and transportation and even social safety net money transfers. Moreover, digital financial services have experienced a sharp increase in daily transactions during the COVID-19 pandemic. Mobile money transfers have become the major means of distributing the government's incentives and allowances, for example. the Bangladesh government provided direct financial support amounting to BDT 50 billion through mobile finance during the lockdown period.

Various government and non-government institutions also pay the regular salaries of their employees via mobile transfers. Digital financial services have already increased notably in Bangladesh and presently various providers deliver MFSs. Mainly, bKash and Rocket have stepped ahead because they have a strong and healthy customer base. Among the available service providers, the government owned Nagad has also achieved satisfactory positive growth in users. The MFS is operated through its application with various features for its customers. The customers must use the Unstructured Supplementary Service Data codes to obtain their desired services.

Undoubtedly, over time MFSs have started to influence growth largely as they offer banking facilities to customers at their doorstep. The Bangladesh Bank, the regulatory body, oversees their financial activities proactively and promotes the strategy of inclusive finance. Hence, the banking sector of Bangladesh has made substantial headway utilising digital technologies. Easy access and low-cost mobile banking services have provided advantages to become prevalent among people from all income groups. So, effective and appropriate policy is essential to maximise the benefits of digital finance and ensure fund security in the remote areas of Bangladesh.

Operational mechanism of digital finance

The tools of digital finance such as mobile phones, the internet and others that collect, store, analyse and share information in digital platforms have been widely used in recent times. Digital finance ensures easier and more prompt access to financial services, particularly for unbanked people. DFSs can reduce the cost of transactions and provide convenient, affordable and safe banking services to low-income people of developing countries (Demirgüç-Kunt et al. 2018; Ozili 2018: 329–40; Islam, Muzi, and Rodriguez Meza 2016). Owning a mobile phone can allow the unbanked and low-income people of rural areas to access formal bank accounts (Demirgüç-Kunt et al. 2018; Ouma, Odongo, and Were 2017: 29–35; Wyman 2016). Mostly, mobile banking now enables people to deposit, withdraw and transfer their money (Ouma, Odongo, and Were 2017: 29–35). DFSs also enable customers to handle their accounts with liberty in order to preserve and share their financial data for making payments and transferring funds (Duncombe 2014: 567–88).

Currently, sophisticated and updated digital technologies can be integrated with a mobile device to use financial services (Demirgüç-Kunt et al. 2018). Biometrics customers' information can ensure the authenticity of their identity when opening a bank account and authorising transactions that can mitigate the barriers to owning a bank account (Demirgüç-Kunt et al. 2018; Wyman 2016). Different innovative mobile applications can also offer micro-insurance for poor people in rural areas and facilitate social safety net transfers (Duncombe 2014: 567–88).

Prospects and challenges of digital finance in developing countries

Because of financial inclusion, digital finance facilitates low-income people to borrow from and save in formal financial channels, encouraging them to build good savings for earning a handsome return so that it can meet their consumption and investment demands (Ouma, Odongo, and Were 2017; Wyman 2016). This financial empowerment can improve their livelihoods, ensuring higher profits and increasing their ability to cope with negative income shocks (Islam, Muzi, and Rodriguez Meza 2016). Since digital finance provides smooth access to various financial instruments to the masses and firms and increases the volume of digital transactions, it is believed that it can also stimulate the total output of a digital economy (Ozili 2018: 329–40). However, digital finance alone is not sufficient to increase credit access and increase financial inclusion (Demirgüç-Kunt et al. 2018; Ozili 2018: 329–40). Thus, a few challenges of digital finance like strict regulations, awareness and trust and physical infrastructure should be addressed properly to enjoy the whole benefit of the digitalised financial system. Most importantly, it is also necessary to spread such beneficial services to needy people, for instance, women, rural and low–income people.

Conclusion

Adopting financial services using digital platforms can be a key step towards formalisation for the unbanked two-thirds of the global labour force involved in the economy's informal sector (International Labour Organization 2018). Mobile money services can be perceived as the first step towards social safety nets, quick and prompt access to finance and formalisation of small savings and micro-insurance, which, when aggregated, can provide a source of capital for SDG implementation on an expansive scale. Digitalisation of the financial sector not only offers easier access to credit but also tailored services that stimulate the advancement of micro, small and medium enterprises (MSMEs) and women as well as youth education and employment. At present, various startups, new business models and innovative ideas are the outcomes of rising digital finance.

In order to facilitate the advancement of SDGs, The Better Than Cash Alliance, which was formed by companies, governments and international organisations, is trying to accelerate the transition from cash payments to digital payments (Better Than Cash Alliance 2022). Even central banks are considering issuing their own digital currencies to support greater financial inclusion, financial stability, operational efficiency, monetary policy effectiveness and financial integrity (Griffoli et al. 2018).

Presently, digitised banks, mobile banking, digital platforms and fintech start-ups use big data to expand their access to finance and lower credit costs, reduce transaction times and offer existing debt refinancing substitutes (Evans 2019). Digitalisation in the financial sector, particularly in developing countries, increases people's savings behaviour (Barry 2019a, 2019b). In the case of developed countries, new fintech-enabled financial institutions offer considerably higher interest rates on customer deposits, even sometimes double or triple those offered by conventional banks (Watson 2020). Robot financial advisers have expanded people's financial access to well-diversified asset pools by lowering the capital thresholds and reducing the cost of expensive financial advisers (Das 2019: 981–1007).

In the future, digital finance will emerge in all countries and be available to the masses. Therefore, the tentative barriers and risks associated with digitalisation should be resolved and mitigated to get its full benefit and accelerate SDG financing. Digital financial services (DFS) have already become a proven tool to enhance and promote financial inclusion worldwide. Thus, DFS must be improved, advanced and regulated with proper measures and actions to safeguard against all odds or risks and secure consumer protection.

Both governments and the private sector should think of how the infrastructure of the financial sector should evolve and adapt to operate, regulate and encourage new DFS. With the combined and harmonised effort of businesses and government leaders, it is possible to achieve inclusive growth. Digital technologies and digital finance can open up new economic innovations and opportunities for billions of people, ensuring the achievement of SDGs.

References

Anton-Diaz, Pablo, and Amin Khairy.·2019. *Charting the Customer Journey in the Digital Age*, (Center for Financial Inclusion/Institute for International Finance), <https://content.centerforfinancialin clusion.org/wp-content/uploads/sites/2/2019/05/Charting-the-Customer-Journey-in-the-Digital-Age-_-Center-for-Financial-Inclusion_v6.pdf> [Accessed 11 October 2021].

Asian Development Bank Institute.·2014. *Low-Carbon Green Growth in Asia: Policies and Practices*, (Asian Development Bank), <http://www.adb.org/sites/default/files/publication/159319/adbi-low-carbon-green-growth-asia.pdf> [Accessed 20 August 2021].

Auer, R., G. Cornelli, and J. Frost.·2020. *Covid-19, Cash, and the Future of Payments*, (Bank for International Settlements), <https://www.bis.org/publ/bisbull03.pdf> [Accessed 4 January 2021].

Bangladesh Bank.·2021. *Mobile Financial Services (MFS) Data* <https://www.bb.org.bd/fnansys/paymentsys/mfsdata.php> [Accessed 11 October 2021].

Barry, N. 2019a 'After Access, What's the Impact of Digital Finance on Clients?' *Center for Financial Inclusion* <https://www.centerforfinancialinclusion.org/impact-of-digital-finance-on-clients> [Accessed 5 January 2022]

———. 2019b. *No Title After Access, What's the Impact of Digital Finance on Clients?*,

Beck, Thorsten, Asli Demirgüç-Kunt, and Ross Levine. 2007. 'Finance, Inequality and the Poor', *Journal of Economic Growth*, 12 (1), 27–49.

Better Than Cash Alliance. 2022. *Better Than Cash*, <https://www.betterthancash.org/> [Accessed 4 January 2022].

Bhakta, P. 2020. 'Coronavirus Pandemic: Mumbai Startup Riskcovry Launches New Insurance Cover' *Money Control* <https://www.moneycontrol.com/news/business/startup/coronavirus-pandemic-bengaluru-startup-riskcovry-launches-new-insurance-cover-5041921.html> [Accessed 11 October 2021]

Bruhn, Miriam, and Inessa Love. 2014. 'The Real Impact of Improved Access to Finance: Evidence from Mexico', *The Journal of Finance*, 69 (3), 1347–76.

BusinessWire. 2020. 'Supporting Small Businesses – Intuit Quickbooks Joins GoFundMe as Co-Founder of the Small Business Relief Initiative for Covid-19 Support'. <https://www.business wire.com/news/home/20200324005677/en/Supporting-Small-Businesses-%E2%80%93-Intuit-QuickBooks-Joins> [Accessed 11 October 2021].

Cecchetti, S.G., and E. Kharroubi.·2012. *Reassessing the Impact of Finance on Growth*, (Bank for International Settlements), <https://www.bis.org/publ/work381.pdf> [Accessed 11 October 2021].

Collins, Daryl, Morduch Jonathan, Rutherford Stuart, and O. Ruthven. 2009. 'Portfolios of the Poor: How the World's Poor Live on $2 a Day', *Development and Change*, 41 (1), 184–85.

Communications Commission of Kenya.·2020. *Annual Report for the Financial Year 2019–2020*, www.ca.go.ke/index.php/%0Aannual-reports> [Accessed 11 October 2021].

Cozzo, S. 2013. 'G2P Electronic Payments Leading to Increased Aid and Inclusion in LAC' *Center for Financial Inclusion/ACCION* <https://www.centerforfinancialinclusion.org/g2p-electronic-payments-leading-to-increased-aid-and-inclusion-in-lac> [Accessed 11 October 2021]

Das, Sanjiv R. 2019. 'The Future of Fintech', *Financial Management*, 48 (4), 981–1007.

DBS Bank.·2020. *Fact Sheet – DBS Initiatives for SMEs and Corporates – Covid-19*, https://www.dbs.com/iwov-resources/images/newsroom/DBS%20fact%20sheet_SMEs_corporates_Covid-19.pdf> [Accessed 4 January 2022].

Demirgüç-Kunt, A., L. Klapper, D. Singer, S. Ansar, and J. Hess. 2018. *Global Findex Database 2017: Measuring Financial Inclusion and the Fintech Revolution* (Washington, DC: World Bank).

Duberstein, B. 2020. 'A Fintech Is Buying a Bank for the First Time Ever, and It Could Change Everything' *The Motley Fool* <https://www.fool.com/investing/2020/02/23/a-fintech-just-bought-a-bank-for-the-first-time-ev.aspx> [Accessed 5 January 2022]

Duncombe, Richard A. 2014. 'Understanding the Impact of Mobile Phones on Livelihoods in Developing Countries', *Development Policy Review*, 32 (5), 567–88.

Ellis, K., A. Lemma, and J.P. Rud.·2010. *Financial Inclusion, Household Investment and Growth in Kenya and Tanzania*, (Overseas Development Institute), <https://www.files.ethz.ch/isn/121123/pb43.pdf> [Accessed 4 January 2022].

Evans, Lawrance L.·2019. *Financial Technology: Agencies Should Provide Clarification on Lenders' Use of Alternative Data: Testimony to Task Force on Financial Technology, Committee on Financial Services, House of Representatives*, (Washington DC: US Government Accountability Office), <https://www.gao.gov/assets/gao-19-694t.pdf> [Accessed 4 January 2022].

Financial Stability Board.·2019. *Fintech and Market Structure in Financial Services: Market Developments and Potential Financial Stability Implications*, https://www.fsb.org/wp-content/uploads/P140219.pdf> [Accessed 4 January 2022].

Fintech. 2021. *Fintech Open Source Foundation*, <https://www.finos.org/> [Accessed 4 January 2022].

Fintech News Malaysia. 2020. 'What Malaysia Can Learn from China in Battling Covid-19 Using Digital Technologies' <https://fintechnews.my/23137/digital-transformation/china-malaysiacovid-%0A19/> [Accessed 4 January 2022].

GMSA Intelligence.·2016. *GMSA Intelligence Database*, <https://www.gsmaintelligence.com/data/> [Accessed 4 January 2022].

Griffoli, T.M., M.S.M. Peria, I. Ari A. Agur, J. Kiff, A. Popescu, and C. Rochon.·2018. *Casting Light on Central Bank Digital Currency*, (International Monetary Fund), <https://www.imf.org/en/Publications/Staff-Discussion-Notes/Issues/2018/11/13/Casting-Light-on-Central-Bank-Digital-Currencies-46233> [Accessed 4 January 2022].

Han, R., and M. Melecky.·2013. *Financial Inclusion for Financial Stability: Access to Bank Deposits and the Growth of Deposits in the Global Financial Crisis*, (Washington, DC: World Bank), <http://documents.worldbank.org/curated/en/850681468325448388/Financial-inclusion-for-financial-stability-access-to-bank-deposits-and-the-growth-of-deposits-in-the-Global-Financial-Crisis> [Accessed 4 January 2022].

International Labour Organization.·2018. *Women and Men in the Informal Economy: A Statistical Picture*, <https://www.ilo.org/global/publications/books/WCMS_626831/lang–en/index.htm> [Accessed 4 January 2022].

International Telecommunication Union.·2016. *Digital Financial Inclusion*, Issue Brief Series, (Inter Agency Taskforce on Financing for Development), <https://www.un.org/esa/ffd/wp-content/uploads/2016/01/Digital-Financial-Inclusion_ITU_IATF-Issue-Brief.pdf> [Accessed 31 December 2021].

——.·2021. *International Telecommunication Union Database*<https://www.itu.int/en/ITU-D/Statistics/Pages/publications/wtid.aspx> [Accessed 5 January 2022].

Islam, Asif, Silvia Muzi, and Jorge Luis Rodriguez Meza.·2016. *Does Mobile Money Use Increase Firms' Investment?: Evidence from Enterprise Surveys in Kenya, Uganda, and Tanzania*, (Washington DC.: World Bank), <https://openknowledge.worldbank.org/handle/10986/25692> [Accessed 5 January 2022].

KPMG Fintech.·2019. *The Pulse of Fintech 2018 Biannual Global Analysis of Investment in Fintech*, https://assets.kpmg/content/dam/kpmg/xx/pdf/2019/02/the-pulse-of-fintech-2018.pdf> [Accessed 5 January 2022].

Kulish, N. 2020. 'People Need Immediate Relief', and Online Donors Make It Happen", *New York Times*, 16 March 2020. <https://www.nytimes.com/2020/03/16/business/coronavirus-bills-charity.html> [Accessed 5 January 2022].

Lund, S., O. White, and J. Lamb. 2017. 'The Value of Digitalizing Government Payments in Developing Economies.' in Sanjeev Gupta, Michael Keen, Alpa Shah and Geneviève Verdier (eds.), Digital Revolutions in Public Finance (Washington DC: International Monetary Fund), pp. 305–25

Lyman, T., and K. Lauer 2015 'What Is Digital Financial Inclusion and Why Does It Matter?' *Consultative Group to Assist the Poor (CGAP)* <https://www.cgap.org/blog/what-digital-financial-inclusion-and-why-does-it-matter> [Accessed 5 January 2022]

Manyika, J., Lund S., Singer M., White O., and C.C. Berry.·2016. *Digital Finance for All: Powering Inclusive Growth in Emerging Economies*, (McKinsey Global Institute), <https://www.mckinsey.com/~/media/mckinsey/featured%20insights/Employment%20and%20Growth/How%20digital%20finance%20could%20boost%20growth%20in%20emerging%20economies/MGI-Digital-Finance-For-All-Executive-summary-September-2016.ashx> [Accessed 5 January 2022].

Mas, Ignacio, and Amolo Ng'Weno. 2010. 'Three Keys to M-PESA's Success: Branding, Channel Management and Pricing', *Journal of Payments Strategy and Systems*, 4 (4), 352–70.

Organisation for Economic Cooperation and Development, and Selected Partner Economies. 2020. *Tax Policy Reforms 2020*. (Paris: OECD)

Ouma, Shem Alfred, Teresa Maureen Odongo, and Maureen Were. 2017. 'Mobile Financial Services and Financial Inclusion: Is It a Boon for Savings Mobilization?', *Review of Development Finance*, 7 (1), 29–35.

Ozili, Peterson K. 2018. 'Impact of Digital Finance on Financial Inclusion and Stability', *Borsa Istanbul Review*, 18 (4), 329–40.

Prasad, Eswar.·2010. *Financial Sector Regulation and Reforms in Emerging Markets: An Overview*, (Cambridge, MA: National Bureau of Economic Research), <http://www.nber.org/papers/w16428.pdf> [Accessed 5 January 2022].

PRNewswire. 2020. 'WeSure Launches Novel Coronavirus Pneumonia Insurance Covering 15 Million People against Outbreak of Covid-19', *PRNewswire*. <https://www.prnewswire.com/news-releases/wesure-launches-novel-coronavirus-pneumonia-insurance-covering-15-million-people-against-outbreak-of-covid-19-301005341.html> [Accessed 4 January 2022].

Scott, Susan V., John Van Reenen, and Markos Zachariadis. 2017. 'The Long-Term Effect of Digital Innovation on Bank Performance: An Empirical Study of Swift Adoption in Financial Services', *Research Policy*, 46 (5), 984–1004.

Telenor Group. 2016. *Telenor Announces 100% Ownership of Tameer Microfinance Bank*, <https://www.telenor.com/telenor-announces-100-ownership-of-tameer-microfinance-bank/#:~:text=Telenor%20announces%20100%25%20ownership%20of%20Tameer%20Microfinance%20Bank,Tameer%20a%20wholly%20owned%20entity%20within%20Telenor%20Group.> [Accessed 5 January 2022].

United Nations.·2014. *The Role of Business and Finance in Supporting the Post-2015 Agenda* (United Nations Global Compact), <https://d306pr3pise04h.cloudfront.net/docs/news_events%2F9.6%2FPost2015_WhitePaper_2July14.pdf> [Accessed 10 November 2021].

—— 2015 *General Assembly Resolution 69/313: Addis Ababa Action Agenda* United Nations (Addis Ababa, Ethiopia: Third International Conference on Financing for Development) <https://sustainabledevelopment.un.org/content/documents/2051AAAA_Outcome.pdf> [Accessed 24 January 2022].

——.·2019a. *Roadmap for Financing the 2030 Agenda for Sustainable Development 2019-2021*, (New York: United Nations Secretary General's Office), <https://www.un.org/sustainabledevel

opment/wp-content/uploads/2019/07/EXEC.SUM_SG-Roadmap-Financing-SDGs-July-2019.
pdf> [Accessed 10 July 2021].

——.·2019b. *The Sustainable Development Goals Report 2019*, (New York United Nations),
<https://unstats.un.org/sdgs/report/2019/The-Sustainable-Development-Goals-Report-2019.
pdf> [Accessed 24 January 2022].

United Nations Conference on Trade and Development.·2014. *World Investment Report – Investing
in the SDGs: An Action Plan*, (Geneva, Switzerland: United Nations), <https://unctad.org/sys
tem/files/official-document/wir2014_en.pdf> [Accessed 28 January 2022].

United Nations Development Programme.·2018. *Financing the 2030 Agenda – an Introductory
Guidebook for UNDP Country Offices*, (New York: United Nations), <https://www.uncclearn.
org/resources/library/financing-the-2030-agenda-an-introductory-guidebook-for-undp-
country-offices/> [Accessed 24 January 2022].

United Nations Secretary General's Task Force on Digital Financing of the Sustainable Development
Goals.·2020. *People's Money: Harnessing Digitalization to Finance a Sustainable Future*,
(United Nations), <https://unsdg.un.org/resources/peoples-money-harnessing-digitalization-
finance-sustainable-future> [Accessed 5 January 2022].

Watson, T. 2020. 'Neobank Report 2020: Digital Banking in a New Decade' *Mozo* <https://mozo.
com.au/neobanks/articles/neobank-2020-report-digital-banking-in-a-new-decade> [Accessed
5 January 2022]

Wood, C. 2020. 'Free Coronavirus Cover Offered by Insurtech WeSure', *Reinsurance News*
<https://www.reinsurancene.ws/free-coronavirus-cover-offered-by-insurtech-wesure/>
[Accessed 5 January 2022].

World Bank. 2014. *Digital Finance: Empowering the Poor Via New Technologies*, <https://www.
worldbank.org/en/news/feature/2014/04/10/digital-finance-empowering-poor-new-
technologies> [Accessed 5 January 2022].

——.·2017. *Global Financial Inclusion*, <https://databank.worldbank.org/reports.aspx?source=
1228> [Accessed 5 January 2022].

——.·2020. *States and Trends of Carbon Pricing 2020*, (Washington DC World Bank Group),
<https://openknowledge.worldbank.org/bitstream/handle/10986/33809/9781464815867.
pdf> [Accessed 10 September 2021].

Wyman, Oliver.·2016. *Accelerating Financial Inclusion in South-East Asia with Digital Finance*,
(Asian Development Bank), <https://www.oliverwyman.com/content/dam/oliver-wyman/v2/
publications/2017/jan/Accelerating-financial-inclusion-in-south-east-asia.pdf> [Accessed
5 January 2022].

Fitri Nurfatriani, Mimi Salminah and Dewi Ratna Kurniasari

Chapter 10
Fiscal governance to support post-COVID low-carbon development in Indonesia

Abstract: This paper outlines how fiscal instruments should be governed to support post-COVID low-carbon development. The investigation is focussed on Indonesia which has used fiscal instruments, including issuing economic recovery policies, to promote low-carbon development while dealing with deteriorating socioeconomic conditions due to the COVID-19 pandemic. The pandemic has affected the fiscal position of Indonesian government. The government's revenue in 2020 decreased by USD 16 billion compared to 2019 due to a decrease in tax revenue, while government spending increased by USD 20 billion to overcome impacts of the pandemic in various sectors. To cope with the challenges, the government has allocated around USD 27.84 billion for Indonesia's economic recovery programmes. Some other fiscal instruments that the government uses to promote low-deforestation risk investments are climate budget tagging and the green sukuk scheme. While they are currently still focussed on infrastructure development, non-infrastructure projects should be also addressed in the schemes with different prerequisites. This is because mitigation in the land-based sector are mostly non-infrastructure projects and do not have underlying assets as an investment guarantee. Therefore, the framework of the green finance should be further modified in order to ease land-based projects to access it.

Keywords: COVID-19, sustainable development, low-carbon development, deforestation, forest degradation, fiscal policy

Introduction

The coronavirus pandemic has plunged the world economy into recession. The situation may even exceed the severity of the global financial crisis during 2008–2009. The IMF reveals that the global economic growth during the pandemic outbreak in 2020 rapidly dropped to −3, compared to that during the global financial crisis which fell to −0.1. In Indonesia, the pandemic has affected every walk of life dimension including socioeconomics, environment and politics. It has also affected the implementation of Indonesian sustainable development agendas, particularly the target of better social, economic and environmental management, that have been mainstreamed into mid-term national development planning.

Indonesia's economic growth went through a slowdown, dropping to −2.07% while the poverty rate increased to around 10.2% in 2020. The government's revenue

https://doi.org/10.1515/9783110733488-010

in 2020 decreased by USD 16 billion compared to 2019 due to a decrease in tax revenue, while government spending increased by USD 20 billion to overcome impacts of the pandemic in various sectors. The private sector was significantly impacted since demand for goods and services decreased. Lockdown policy has resulted in high job losses and food shortages. Moreover, while environmental parameters have improved, fiscal capacity for environmental improvement continues to contract. The government lockdown policy during the pandemic temporarily reduced daily global emissions due to restricted human movement (Le Quéré et al. 2020). Nonetheless, when the lockdown policy was relaxed for economic recovery, the emission rate in most countries including Indonesia increased again (Wahidah and Antriyandarti 2020: 1).

The limited fiscal capacity forced the Indonesian government to slow its climate change mitigation actions. The government prioritised the budget allocation for economic recovery including health and social protection programmes. Most of the government budget for economic recovery was allocated for health and social assistance, business incentives and corporate financial support to keep the economy growing. Meanwhile, the government budget that was previously allocated for environment protection and management was reallocated to fight against the pandemic under the economic recovery programmes. As a result, the implementation of sustainable agendas in the environment aspect is likely to be hampered. This has further consequences, where a degraded environment, such as fragmented forests, may accelerate the spread of COVID-19, increasing the risk of its re-emergence, and worsen its impacts.

Some literature mentions that deforestation and habitat fragmentation contribute to the emergence and spread of zoonotic diseases such as COVID-19 (Rulli et al. In press; White and Razgour 2020; Rohr et al. 2019). Fragmented forest causes closer interactions between wildlife and humans and changes wildlife dynamics that increase the risk of transmitting the virus to humans. On the other side, the deforestation rate doubled following the policy taken by global and national governments to overcome the pandemic impacts on socioeconomics and health, which was associated with affected countries' capacity on conservation measures (Brancalion et al. 2020: 244).

Emission reduction is one of Indonesia's sustainable development commitments in the environmental aspect that has been confirmed by the Nationally Determined Contribution (NDC) of Indonesia. It is planned to be reached by implementing climate change mitigation actions in the four main sectors contributing to most emissions in Indonesia, which are forestry, energy, industry and waste. Forestry and energy are the two highest contributors to emissions so that mitigation actions in those sectors have become the focus of the sustainability agendas. Deforestation and land use changes contributes around 30% to current total emissions, while fossil fuel consumption is predicted to contribute around 57% to the total emissions by 2030 (Indonesia National Development Planning Agency 2020a). Green energy development and energy conservation are being implemented to reach the target in the energy sector, while the forestry sector rests on strategies such as reducing emissions from deforestation, implementing sustainable forest management, rehabilitating degraded forests, and restoring degraded peatlands (Indonesia Ministry of Environment and Forestry: Directorate General of Climate Change 2017: 12).

Local government and the private sector are the two key actors for implementing mitigation actions at the site level. Local governments are the authority to regulate and manage the operation of the mitigation actions in their region while the private sector is deemed to be a potential emitter. For instance, in the forestry sector, of the 96.6 million ha area of the REDD+ Performance Measurement Area (WPK REDD+), about 24.6 million ha is forest area that has been granted forest concession permits including logging concessions in native forests (IUPHHK-HA), logging concessions in plantation forests (IUPHHK-HT), restoration ecosystem concessions (IUPHHK-RE), and borrow-to-use area permits (IPPKH) (see Chapter Five regarding REDD+). Since the national target has been distributed to all provincial governments with different emission reduction allocations (cap) for each, the provincial governments in coordination with the central government need to regulate allowable emission for the potential emitters in order to reach their reduced emission target. The private sector is therefore the government's strategic partner to accelerate the implementation of mitigation actions.

Furthermore, strategies to implement emission reduction policies engender substantial costs. For the forestry sector alone, the government has estimated that the budget needed for climate change mitigation until 2030 is approximately USD 60 billion exceeding the available climate change budget of only USD 3.6 billion (Indonesia Directorate of Mobilization Sectoral and Regional Resources 2021: 10). Although funding for climate change mitigation actions in the forestry sector is also supported by international grants which reach USD 158.6 million, the total available budget still falls short of the requirements. Similar to the forestry sector, the energy sector also estimates that the available budget can only meet 20% of the need for climate change mitigation funding within the sector. This means that there is still a wide funding gap to achieve the sustainable development commitment for reducing emissions.

Given the risk of increasing emissions after the relaxed lockdown policy, the government needs to optimise the state budget allocated for post-COVID economic recovery programmes in order to anticipate more severe environmental degradation and unachievable emission reduction target. The government has currently allocated around USD 27.84 billion for Indonesia's economy recovery programmes, outside of health and social protection. One of the economic recovery focusses is to protect, maintain and improve the economic capabilities of business actors affected by the pandemic in running their businesses. It basically covers three clusters: business incentives mostly by reducing taxes; funds for small to medium enterprises, and corporate financing through investment schemes. Meanwhile, the economic recovery programmes for line ministries and local government are to improve public services and the local economy through several measures including labour-intensive programmes, housing incentives, support for tourism, provision of incentive fund, special allocation funds and loan facilities.

The programmes still apply conventional economic approaches nonetheless and have not unequivocally promoted green initiatives or addressed low-carbon pathways. No regulation states a requirement of a low-carbon pathway in using the budget for the economic recovery programmes. This might lead to an increase in the risk of the degraded environment as mentioned above. It is vital therefore to optimise the fiscal instruments in order to achieve a low-carbon development target. A low-carbon development approach could be a pathway for the private sector and local governments to align pandemic recovery and sustainable agendas by being used to maintain the national economic outlook and apply climate-friendly development at the same time. Optimising the value of ecosystem services, energy efficiency, renewable energy and green technology are among other instruments that can be used to promote low-carbon development.

Low-carbon development is a new development platform that aims to maintain economic and social growth through low greenhouse gas (GHG) emission development activities and minimise the exploitation of natural resources. Low-carbon development is one of the government's priority programmes. It is a derivation of national priority policies in the National Medium Development Planning (RPJMN), namely building the environment, increasing disaster resilience and climate change. The government of Indonesia has set out to transform the country's economy into one where progress is measured not only by GDP growth but also environmental sustainability, resource efficiency and social equity. The low-carbon development platform will require a series of policy adjustments to development policies in various sectors, especially those related to land, energy, biodiversity and water resources. The land sector is critical because it is the largest contributor to reducing the national carbon emissions. Achieving ambitious GHG reductions and sustainable development demands bold and permanent actions regarding forests and land use in Indonesia. The strategy of low-carbon development policies in the RPJMN 2020–2024 for sustainable land restoration is carried out through several activities, including a) peatlands restoration, b) forest and land rehabilitation, c) reducing deforestation rates, d) increasing agricultural productivity and efficiency towards sustainable agriculture. The future development pathway has to address post-COVID economic recovery and low-carbon development policy that reconcile environmental and economic purposes.

This paper outlines and analyses on how fiscal instruments should be governed to support post-COVID low-carbon development, using the theoretical basis of fiscal policy combined with empirical investigation.

Government fiscal structure for implementation of low-carbon development and post-COVID economic recovery

The discussion in this chapter will include an examination of the government's fiscal structure in terms of expenditures and revenues related to low-carbon development and post-COVID economic recovery.

Government budget

The government's budget structure for low-carbon development includes a budget for implementing low-carbon development, a budget for climate change, and a budget for post-COVID-19 recovery.

Budget for low-carbon development

As a developing country, Indonesia still relies on the exploitation of natural resources to grow economically. The average GDP growth rate in Indonesia from 2015 to 2019 was 5%, making the development pattern geared towards high-carbon development and causing environmental degradation. To mitigate this, Indonesia has set a low-carbon development programme in national policy planning. The programmes have been formulated especially for the land-based sector through a) peatland restoration, b) forest and land rehabilitation, c) reducing deforestation rates, d) increasing agricultural productivity and efficiency towards sustainable agriculture. However, the government needs to allocate a budget for supporting the low-carbon development programmes. The government has set the emission reduction target from low-carbon development activities higher than the NDC target at 43% by 2030 (Indonesia National Development Planning Agency 2019: 2). Hence, this chapter will outline the expenditures or budget allocation required to reach the low-carbon development target and the NDC target.

The Indonesian National Development Planning Agency (Bappenas) (2020a: 16) has mapped the need for low-carbon development funding of all central government expenditure to encourage environmentally friendly economic growth. The mapping was carried out over the ministerial budget allocated to reduce or control GHG emissions in the peatland and forestry sectors, agriculture, energy, transportation, industry and waste management, including coastal and marine areas. Based on Bappenas' mapping in 2020, the government has allocated a budget for low-carbon development funding in 2018, 2019 and 2020 of USD 2.38 billion, USD 2.41 billion, USD 1.62 billion, respectively. These amounts only constitute about

1.3% the average of the total government budget in 2018–2020. For the forestry and peatland sectors, low-carbon development funding in 2018 was USD27.5 million, while in 2019, it was increased to USD172.4 million. In 2020 it was USD89.7 million, resulting in an annual average of USD 96.5 million. This low-carbon development budget describes government spending as expenditure on mitigation action activities consisting of core and supporting activities. Core activities consist of development activities that directly impact reducing emissions while supporting activities support implementing core activities such as socialisation, research and development and capacity building.

In the peatland and forestry sectors, the budget of low-carbon development is spent mostly on peatland restoration, forest, land rehabilitation and avoiding forest degradation. In comparison, the budget for the agriculture sector is allocated more to develop fodder forums, organic agriculture and ex-mining rehabilitation programmes. The other sectors that used the highest budget among all sectors are transportation and energy. The construction of railway lines is the focus of the transportation sector, with an average of up to 75% of the total low-carbon development budget for transportation. For the energy sector, most the budget is allocated to natural gas network infrastructure for households, energy saving solar lamps in unelectrified areas and efficiency in public street lighting programmes (Indonesia National Development Planning Agency 2020a: 19).

Meanwhile, based on Bappenas' calculation, the total investment cost needed to implement low-carbon development to reach the emission reduction target is about USD 21 billion or 2% of total GDP. In order to achieve this target, the government budget would need to contribute 24–39% of investment costs. However, the budget only contributes 8–11%. Therefore, the gap needs to be filled from national and international funding mechanisms from private and philanthropic institutions and bilateral/multilateral cooperation (Nurfatriani and Satrio 2020: 37–38).

Climate budget tagging

Another milestone in low-carbon development funding governance in Indonesia is climate change budgeting (climate budget tagging, or CBT) system in the state budget. The government of Indonesia, via the Ministry of Finance, has conducted climate budget tagging since 2016. Climate budget tagging is a process of marking, tracking and identifying climate change outputs and budgets in planning and budgeting documentation. The implementation of CBT has resulted from the collaboration between the Ministry of Finance, Bappenas and the Ministry of Environment and Forestry and by involving several related ministries/institutions through the KRISNA system (Planning and Budgeting System Collaboration) (Indonesia Fiscal Policy Agency 2020a: 11). Since Indonesia has set the NDC to target that in 2030 Indonesia is determined to reduce its GHG emissions by 29% against the business-as-usual (BAU) scenario with Indonesia's efforts without support from international institutions and up to 41% against the BAU scenario with support from international institutions. This target has been broken down into targets per sector as described in Table 10.1.

Table 10.1: Emission reduction target per sector (MTonCO$_2$e).

Emission reduction target (%)	Emission reduction target per sector (MTonCO$_2$e)				
	Forestry	Energy and transportation	Waste	Agriculture	Industrial process and product use
29%	497	314	11	9	2.75
41%	650	398	26	4	3.25

Source: Indonesia Ministry of Environment and Forestry: Directorate General of Climate Change (2017: 9).

The total cost needed to fund the programmes and activities to reach GHG emission reduction targets was calculated by Indonesia's NDC in 2019. The energy and transportation sector requires the most funds to reach the emission reduction target, about USD 22 billion per year, with accumulative cost from 2020 to 2030 is about USD 241 billion. For land-based sectors, the forestry and land sectors need around USD 585 million per year with accumulative costs from 2020 to 2030, about USD 6.4 billion. The total cost needed from 2020 to 2030 to reach the NDC target for the agriculture sector is about USD 278 million. While industrial processes and product use need the smallest cost compared to other sectors, at USD 5.7 million per year with accumulative costs from 2020 to 2030 to about USD 63 million (Indonesia Fiscal Policy Agency 2020a: 4–5; Indonesia Ministry of Environment and Forestry 2019: 58). Several funding sources are needed to achieve the NDC target, one of which is from the government budget.

In the government budgeting system, the budget allocation is determined based on the government's work programme. In the National Medium Development Planning (RPJMN) 2020–2024, climate change control is included in the sixth National Policy Priority (PN-6). This priority policy is divided into three priority working programmes, namely (PP-1) Environmental Quality Improvement (PP-2) Improving Disaster and Climate Resilience and (PP-3) Low-Carbon Development. According to the Badan Kebijakan Fiskal Fiscal Policy Agency (BKF) (2020a), climate change budget tagging is a process to identify the budget used to finance specific outputs for climate change mitigation and adaptation activities. By tagging the climate budget, climate change funding needs can be identified and allocated effectively and efficiently. In addition, the tagging of climate change budgets aims to increase public transparency and accountability in the management of the state budget to fund climate change mitigation and adaptation activities within ministries and agencies.

Based on climate budget tagging results (Indonesia Fiscal Policy Agency 2020a: 15–17), in 2018–2020 the government allocated a climate change budget of USD 21.2 billion, with an average of USD 7.1 billion per year. In 2016, the climate change mitigation and adaptation budget was only USD 5.1 billion and increased in 2018 by 82.96% to USD 9.1 billion. The central government's climate change budget is mostly used for climate change mitigation activities, both in 2018 (66.2%) and 2019 (55.6%). Meanwhile, based on budget value, climate change spending is dominated to produce outputs of physical infrastructure development (waste, energy, transportation and agriculture sectors). In 2019, the climate change budget allocation was USD 6.7 billion, with budget realisation reaching USD5.8 billion (85.5%). Meanwhile, in 2020, amid the COVID-19 pandemic, the government allocated a climate change mitigation and adaptation budget of USD 5.7 billion. It shows that the commitment to promote low-carbon and climate-resilient development is maintained (see Figure 10.1).

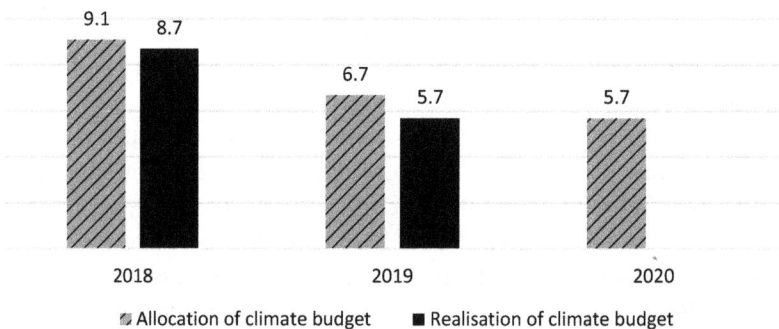

Figure 10.1: Allocation and realisation of climate budget 2018–2020 (USD billion).
Source: Indonesia Fiscal Policy Agency (2020a: 17). Reproduced with permission.

From 2018 to 2019, the climate change budget was mostly spent on the mitigation budget that reached USD 9 billion (consisting of 62% of total climate change budget realisation). It reflects the government's commitment to reduce GHG emissions through low-carbon development. In addition, the Indonesian government has committed through budget allocation for climate change adaptation activities within two years, in total reaching USD4.6 billion (31.8%) or with an average reach of USD 2.3 billion per year. The co-benefit activities programme from 2018 to 2019 accumulatively reached USD 0.9 billion (6.2%). While in 2020, the government allocated the climate change action budget of USD 5.4 billion with a composition mitigation budget of USD 2.9 billion (53.5%), adaptation budget of USD 2.3 billion (42.8%), and co-benefit budget reached USD 0.2 billion (3.7%).

The detailed climate budget spending is based on Indonesia's ministries, especially for the land-based sector, mostly spent by the Ministry of Environment and

Forestry (MoEF) from 2018–2020. The MoEF allocated for climate change mitigation activities an amount of USD 0.3 billion (47.2%). Accumulatively, the allocation of mitigation budget mostly came from the Directorate General of Climate Change Control, reaching USD 0.1 billion, used for peatland restoration in seven provinces prone to forest fires. Meanwhile, the Ministry of Agriculture spent USD 0.2 billion (67.2%) of their output and budget mostly for climate change mitigation activities over the past three years (2018–2020). Accumulatively, the allocation for mitigation budget, mostly from the Directorate General of Agricultural Infrastructure and Facilities, reached USD 0.1 billion used for land optimisation to make the agricultural land more productive and less emissions intensive (Indonesia Fiscal Policy Agency 2020a: 20–23).

The Ministry of Transportation accumulatively allocated USD 3.7 billion from their budget for climate change mitigation over the past three years in the transportation sector. On average, the Ministry of Transportation allocation reached USD 1.2 billion per year for the climate change budget. The Ministry of Transportation is one of the ministries in Indonesia that contribute to low-emission infrastructure construction in the climate change budget overall. Most of the climate change budget was spent in 2018 and 2019 to build sustainable transportation infrastructure and utilise renewable energy in the transportation sector, at USD 2.3 billion.

In the energy sector, the Ministry of Energy and Mineral Resources has allocated a climate change budget for mitigation (USD 0.5 billion; 95%) and adaptation with USD 0.5 billion accumulatively for the past three years. On average, the allocation of the climate change budget in the Ministry of Energy and Mineral Resources reached USD 0.2 billion per year. Most of the climate change mitigation budget in the Ministry of Energy and Mineral Resources is used to provide energy-efficient equipment, energy saving solar lamps, hydroelectric power plants, and natural gas infrastructure at household-scale as a substitute for kerosene (Indonesia Fiscal Policy Agency 2020a: 27–32).

Information on climate change spending can be used to develop innovative financing instruments for climate action refinancing such as green sukuk (sustainable development based on Islamic law principles), bonds and a reference for reporting to stakeholders at the national and international levels.

Budget for post-COVID-19 economic recovery

The low-carbon development and climate change budgeting has been affected by COVID-19 pandemic. The COVID-19 pandemic impacted many things in every aspect, which also impacts the government fiscal structures. The government's revenue in 2020 decreased by USD 22.3 billion compared to 2019 due to a decrease in tax revenue, while government spending increased by USD 19.3 billion to overcome the impacts of the pandemic in various sectors. Tax revenue also decreased significantly because of the pandemic, with the amount of USD 18.1 billion. While on the other hand, central government expenditure was increased significantly to USD 22.7 billion. However, the transfer from central government to regional government decreased USD 3.5 billion. The Indonesian fiscal structure figures from 2019 and 2020 can be seen in Table 10.2.

Table 10.2: Fiscal figures of Indonesia in 2019 and 2020.

Fiscal component	Amount (USD billion)		Change (2020–2019)
	2019	2020	
I. Revenue:	135.0	112.7	−22.3
a. Tax	106.6	88.5	−18.1
b. Non-tax state revenue	27.9	23.3	−4.6
c. Grant	0.5	0.8	0.4
II. Expenditure:	159.3	178.6	19.3
a. Central expenditure	103.4	126.0	22.7
b. Transfer to regional government	51.1	47.7	−3.5
c. Village fund	4.8	4.9	0.1
III. Deficit (I–II)	−24.3	−66.0	−41.6

Source: Indonesia Fiscal Policy Agency (2020b: 89–91; 2021: 151–53).

The government has allocated USD 47.94 billion for COVID-19 pandemic handling expenses. The COVID-19 pandemic handling expenses cover two aspects, the health programme and the national economic recovery programme. The budget for Indonesia's economic recovery programmes, outside of health and social protection programmes, is USD 27.84 billion. The economic recovery programmes aim to protect, maintain and improve the economic capabilities of business actors affected by the pandemic in running their businesses. It covers four clusters: business incentives mostly by reducing taxes, the fund for small to medium enterprises, corporate financing through investment schemes, and budget for line ministries and local government to improve public services and local economies. The budget for business incentives channelled through taxation facilities are USD 8.38 billion. It consists of income tax borne by government, exemption from import tax, reduction of income tax, value added tax return and corporate income reduction.

Meanwhile, the support for small to medium enterprises has allocated USD 8.51 billion for interest subsidies, credit fund remissions and job capital assurance. Another budget allocation is used for corporate financing through investments schemes at an amount of USD 3.69 billion. This budget is directed to corporations, especially for those which are labour-intensive. It also supports state-owned enterprises that have an important role in providing essential goods and services for the public in the form of state equity participation and government investment (through loans), credit guarantee for a labour-intensive private corporation and state-owned enterprises.

Another form of budget for handling the COVID-19 pandemic is through the provision of budget for line ministries and local government of USD 7.32 billion. Budget allocation was directed to support regional governments. Their role is to encourage the regional economy in the middle of the COVID-19 pandemic. One supporting form is for sectors impacted the pandemic, such as the tourism and housing sectors. Funding schemes may be transferred through fiscal transfer into regional governments, through the Special Allocation Fund (DAK), and Regional Incentive Fund (DID) scheme. In addition, the budget is also allocated for the ministries or departments that perform labour-intensive activities programmes (Novianti et al. 2020: 86–90).

In July 2021, the government revised the budget for handling COVID-19 and National Economic Recovery for the 2021 fiscal year, from USD 48.2 billion to USD 51.3 billion (Alaydrus and Pangestu 2021). The largest budget allocation is still for health, at USD 14.8 billion. This amount is an increase from the budget presented in the previous cabinet meeting of USD 13.4 billion. Meanwhile, the most significant increase occurred in the budget allocation for social protection. The total budget reached USD 12.9 billion, an increase of USD 2.3 billion from the previous USD 10.6 billion, which has accommodated additional estimates for the increase in claims for COVID-19 patients, the addition of emergency hospitals, to the acceleration of vaccinations related to the increasing implementation of restrictions on community activities, assistance and subsidies such as social assistance, rice subsidies, electricity bill subsidies and electricity subscriptions, to study quota subsidies. The budget allocation for business incentives is USD 4.3 billion, an increase of USD 62 million, bringing the total to USD 8.1 billion. Meanwhile, the budget for support for medium, small and micro enterprises and corporations was recorded to have decreased by USD 728.9 million to USD 11.1 billion. The addition to the COVID recovery budget is because of the surge in the number of COVID patients in Indonesia.

Sources of government revenue for the environment, forest and climate change

From the revenue side, the government obtains various funding sources for environmental conservation and to address the impacts of climate change, including reducing deforestation. These various funding sources can be grouped into:
1. Public funds, namely from Non-Tax State Revenue (NTSR), taxes, foreign grants, both bilateral and multilateral, with payments using the RBP mechanism for the attainment of reducing emissions from deforestation as well as in the form of technical aid and other finance

2. Philanthropic funds from civil society organisations and other institutions
3. Private funds from corporate social responsibility programmes and blending finance in green projects

The forestry fiscal instrument most widely used for the management and utilisation of forest resources in Indonesia is the tariff policy, such as levies on forestry business permit holders. The implementation of forestry tariff instruments is mostly realised in a form of NTSR for forest management activities, forest product utilisation, and forest land use (Cadman et al. 2019). The type of forestry NTSR from timber forestry business levies that are earmarked and returned for forest rehabilitation, is the Reforestation Fund. With the enactment of the Job Creation Law No. 11 of 2020 and its derivative regulations, there are types of NTSR, from fines for business activities that already occur in the forest area, such as plantation business activities and mining. This fine does not remove the obligation of the permit holder to return the area into a forest area to the government if the business is located in a protected or conservation forest area.

Another type of government revenue for environmental and forestry funding is international funding, both bilateral and multilateral. One of the current sources and instruments of public funding is the Environmental Fund Management Agency (BPDLH), formed by the government to optimally mobilise environmental funds from domestic and foreign sources, manage these funds in a transparent and accountable manner, distributing them effectively and efficiently. Currently, BPDLH will receive potential REDD+ funding, which will be managed by BPDLH as follows:
1. USD 56 million from the government of Norway for the period 2020–2030
2. USD 103 million from the Green Climate Fund for the period 2020–2023
3. USD 110 million from the Forest Carbon Partnership Facility (FCPF) World Bank for payment periods 2021, 2023 and 2025
4. USD 60 million from the BioCarbon Fund for the period 2023–2025

The funds will be paid using a RBP scheme for Indonesia's performance in REDD+) (Nurfatriani and Satrio 2020: 71).

Fiscal instruments to support post-COVID low-carbon development

Fiscal instruments are crucial to back up implementation of post-COVID low-carbon development pathways. They can be used to stimulate private sectors and local governments to carry through with low-carbon development. The pandemic has created momentum to convince all Parties of the importance of low-carbon pathways and to mobilise resources to advance green economy transformation and redirect development pathway from brown to green towards sustainable post-COVID development.

There are a range of current fiscal instruments that can be optimised to cope with COVID-19 impacts and recovery at the same time as advancing sustainable development at the same time towards sustainable COVID-19 recovery. COVID-19 recovery strategies present an opportunity to embark on low-carbon development scenarios as described in the RPJMN (GGGI, Global Green Growth Indonesia 2020). In order to achieve sustainable COVID-19 recovery, the post-COVID development strategy needs to better stimulate decarbonisation objectives, apply structural change towards a green economy transition, enhance society's resilience to any severe change and diminish risks in the future. Some strategies and fiscal instruments that can be explored to promote sustainable post-COVID development are explicated below.

Shifting from brown to green development

Long-term brown development has led to the depletion of natural resources. The brown development or the current business-as-usual approach tends to degrade natural resources, including carrying capacity, that threaten future economic productivity and growth. Since 2017, the government has been shifting from brown development towards a green economy by echoing the low-carbon development approach that aims to reconcile economic growth and environmental objectives through low-emission development activities. The policy has been internalised in the National Medium Term Development Plan 2020–2024 and is projected to trigger an increase in GDP growth.

Some of the activities have been carried out to demonstrate green development performance, and one of the remarkable efforts is launching a green finance facility platform to advance sustainable development by promoting sustainable green infrastructure projects to replace the grey ones. The definition of sustainable green infrastructure is based on environmental assessment.

Sustainable Development Goals (SDG) Indonesia One is a green finance facility platform was launched in October 2018, with more 30 partners generating almost USD 3 billion in funding. Asian Development Bank has been working with PT SMI (Sarana Multi Infrastruktur) using this platform. The SDG Indonesia One aims to offer innovative financial products to eligible green infrastructure projects (against green, financial, technical and environmental and social safeguards criteria), based and aligned with the needs and cash flows of the projects (Asian Development Bank 2020).

Another measure for implementing green development is Global Green Growth Indonesia (GGGI) which supports Indonesia to achieve green growth that is socially inclusive, environmentally sustainable and resource-efficient. A 2020 GGGI report shows that number of jobs in the green economy is higher than in brown economy projects. There are two to five times more jobs in renewable energy and energy efficiency than in brown jobs in fossil fuel projects for every USD invested (GGGI, 2020). Green jobs that are focussed on socioeconomic development, for example peatland and mangrove restoration, reforestation and afforestation, watershed management and social forestry, are able to contribute to nature-based solutions to mitigate and adapt to climate change (GGGI, 2020).

Efforts to reduce plastic waste are one of the government's programme goals. The Action Plan to Reduce Plastic Pollution in Indonesia was unveiled in April 2020 by the multi-stakeholder National Plastic Action Partnership, led by the government of Indonesia. The total capital investment of the action plan is USD 5.1 billion with a target of achieving systemic change from 2017 to 2025 and describes a roadmap to reduce plastic leakage by 70% into Indonesia's coastal waters by 2025 and is expected to be close to zero by 2040 through a circular economy approach (Asian Development Bank 2020: 22). The expectations of the programme is to include generating the economic impact of green initiatives that are sustainable for society. In addition investment can flow to small and medium enterprises as well as green and sustainable infrastructure for a variety of waste treatment activities, including recycling, new technologies for packaging and recycling, together with waste disposal facilities (Asian Development Bank 2020: 22).

Promoting innovative financing for land-based businesses

The government of Indonesia has undertaken a number of policies that open opportunities to increase diversification of finance sources from both national and international public and private sources. At the national-level, the opportunities to optimise state budgets are explored (e.g., using instruments of green sukuk or green bonds) and the draft of Presidential Regulation on Carbon Economic Value (NEK) on Carbon Pricing Instruments such as fees and carbon levies, instruments of intergovernmental fiscal transfer, instruments of local source revenue and other sources of income. Furthermore, Indonesia continues to mobilise international financial sources through bilateral, regional, and multilateral channels, including RBP for REDD+ under the Paris Agreement, grants and other potential sources and mechanisms (Government of Indonesia 2021).

Some of the innovative financing models include global green sukuk, retail green sukuk, Project Development Facility (PDF), Credit Enhancement Facility and Viability Gap Fund. The implementation of the PDF refers to Presidential Decree number 75/ 2014 concerning the Acceleration of Priority Infrastructure Provision; number 122/ 2016 concerning amendments to number 75 of 2014; the Minister of Finance Regulation number 73/2018 concerning Facilities for the Preparation and Implementation of Government Cooperation Project Transactions with Business Entities in the Provision of Infrastructure (Government of Indonesia 2014, 2016, 2018).

Optimising blended finance

The blended finance scheme was introduced in 2018, it is an example of innovative financing practice to support the fulfilment of SDGs financing, with a value USD 2.5 billion (Sustainable Finance Indonesia 2021: 19). The blended finance financing scheme developed by the Indonesian government focuses on combined funding from multilateral agencies, government or philanthropic organisations to overcome barriers to private investment in infrastructure projects. There are two key elements of blended finance principles: (1) Adapting blended finance solutions to the local context and (2) focussing on effective partnership (Indonesia National Development Planning Agency 2020b). There are some approaches for successful blended finance in Indonesia. Blended finance may be practiced in local, small and social projects to support the national or local government's development programmes. The government can initiate blended finance through facilitation of development cooperation or the official development funding scheme (Indonesia National Development Planning Agency 2020b).

An example of success in this scheme is the construction and revitalisation of the Power Plants Micro Hydro Power (PLTMH) in Jambi funded by donations and corporate social responsibility from the National Zakat Agency (BAZNAS), Jambi Bank, UN Development Programme, Ministry of Energy and Mineral Resources and the Jambi Provincial government (Indonesia National Development Planning Agency 2018).

Another initiative is The Tropical Landscapes Finance Facility (TLFF) that was established in 2016 by a multi-stakeholder group to provide affordable loans to smallholders, thereby improving their livelihoods, rehabilitating degraded lands and providing clean electricity in Indonesia (Louman et al. 2020). As blended finance, the purpose of establishing TLFF is to stimulate Indonesia's green growth and improve rural livelihoods by mobilising international capital for long-term financing for projects and companies, for example sustainable agriculture, forest conservation, renewable energy (Louman et al. 2020; Tropical Landscapes Finance Facility Indonesia 2021). TLFF projects also involve marginalised communities and have clearly defined gender targets to develop benefits for women (Hincks 2021).

Promoting green sukuk for the land-based sector

The government has released green sukuk since 2018 to support financial needs for sustainable development based on Islamic law principles. It is exclusively to finance green projects that correlate with the target of emission reduction and biodiversity conservation. Climate budget tagging as described in section A.2 serves as the basis for distribution of green sukuk proceeds since it draws on government priorities and supports for green projects.

In the first issuance, the government succeeded in raising green sukuk around USD 1.25 billion. This was followed by the second and third issuances in February 2019 and June 2020 with the total proceeds of USD 1.5 billion. In June 2021 the government returned to its annual global sukuk market and successfully booked sales transactions of USD 3 billion, consisting of USD 1.25 billion with a 5-year tenure, USD 1 billion with a 10-year tenure, and USD 1 billion with a tenure of 10 years, and USD 750 million with a tenure of 30 years. In this latest transaction, the government introduced the green sukuk format with a 30-year tenure for the first time, which is also the first in the world, which proves its dedication and long-term commitment to green and sustainable financing particularly in the fight against climate change.

These proceeds have been used to finance green projects implemented by several line ministries in the sectors of renewable energy, ecotourism development and waste management. Specifically, the green projects that have been financed through the green sukuk are flood and drainage management, as well as conservation of coastal areas under the Ministry of Public Works and Housing. Other projects are a railway support facility under the Ministry of Transportation, and renewable energy development under the Ministry of Energy and Mineral Resources.

Unfortunately, all projects financed by the green sukuk are still focussed on infrastructure projects, while green projects on land-based sectors particularly under the MoEF as the national focal point for climate change mitigation actions are still neglected. The project of ecotourism facility development in a national park is the only project implemented under the MoEF. The current framework of green sukuk set by the government has made it difficult for land-based sectors to access the scheme. The scheme requires an underlying asset as a guarantee, which is usually in a form of state-owned land, or a high-value construction built during the project. The requirement is difficult to meet since most land-based sector projects are not commercial construction projects, but social and ecological projects that have high-risk of uncertainty in theecondtation, such as forest rehabilitation, peatland restoration or forest fire prevention and suppression. The situation is exacerbated by an uncertain market of environmental services that usually constitute a primary product generated from the land-based projects, making it difficult generate returns from the investments.

Given that green finance has increased with greater awareness of sustainable development and a new niche of green investment has emerged, this opportunity should be mobilised to support projects for climate change mitigation. Some green investments are managed through the platform of SDG Indonesia One under the Ministry of Finance and PT SMI which manages public and private funds to be channelled into infrastructure projects related to the achievement of SDGs. It aims to raise funding from investors, donors and philanthropic organisations to be channelled into projects in Indonesia that support the achievement of SDGs.

However, the framework of the green finance should be further modified in order to improve land-based based projects to access it. The concept of sustainable land bonds as a modified green sukuk for land-based sectors has been discussed, proposing a scheme where the role of line ministries in guaranteeing all uncertainties of the projects are strengthened, such as providing carbon capitalisation mechanisms and acting as a guarantor for project failure when it occurs. It is also important to formulate agreed indicators applied to the monitoring, reporting and verification system for verifying projects. Furthermore, the green finance mechanism is proposed to be integrated with the RBP scheme that has been developing in Indonesia and managed by the Environmental Fund Management Agency (BPDLH). The financing scheme should be used to support forest protection or restoration and prioritised in rainforest-rich provinces that have performed well in forest sustainability.

Providing incentives for the private sector to invest in green projects through taxes and subsidies

The Indonesian government has implemented environmental taxes, levies and subsidies as part of environmental economic instruments. Its implementation refers to Government Regulation (PP) No. 46/2017 concerning environmental economic instruments, which aims to: (a) encourage the preservation of environmental functions; (b) provide monetary incentives to carry out activities that have a positive impact on natural resources and the environment; (c) provide a monetary burden to reduce activities that have a negative impact on natural resources and the environment.

Tax incentives as a fiscal instrument are used to assist national economic recovery and strengthening economic transformation. The government of Indonesia has regulated tax incentives as follows: (1) Accelerated VAT Return (preliminary return), to support companies' cash flow to resume business activities, (2) import tax Article 22, to stimulate industry to import raw materials for production, (3) tax borne by the government, to support competitiveness and the economy of targeted sectors, and (4) tax holidays and tax allowances, to attract capital to increase domestic investment to trigger the emergence of new industries, economic diversification, new job opportunities and accelerating regional growth (Directorate General of Budget 2021: 9). For example, tax holidays for the pioneering industries and a tax allowance, namely exemption from VAT and import duties for the renewable energy sector. The tax allowance is issued by the Investment Coordinating Board (BKPM) through an online single submission.

The regulations governing tax holidays are Minister of Finance Regulation No. 130/2020 concerning on Provision of Corporate Income Tax Reduction Facility. It explains that corporate taxpayers with a minimum capital value of USD 6.9 million who make new investments in pioneer industries can obtain corporate income tax deductions on income received or gained from the main business activities carried out.

The tax allowance is regulated in Government Regulation No. 78/2019 concerning income tax facility for investment in certain business fields in specific regions, and its derivatives through the Minister of Finance Regulation No. 11/2020, which was amended through the Minister of Finance Regulation No. 96/2020. The regulation explains that business fields that can receive tax facilitation include the following: (1) crop farming, animal husbandry, hunting and related activities; (2) forestry and harvesting of wood and non-timber forest products; (3) fisheries; (4) coal gasification; (5) exploitation of geothermal energy; (6) metal ore mining; (7) food industry; (8) water management; (9) wastewater management and waste recycling; (10) real estate, among others.

Optimising economic recovery programmes for labour-intensive green projects

The Indonesian government has two main strategies in dealing with the COVID-19 pandemic, namely maintaining life (health) and livelihoods. The strategy of maintaining livelihoods is implemented by the National Economic Recovery and Transformation Task Force, with several agendas: supporting and helping the community; supporting and helping affected business to reopen and expand; prioritising job creation assistance and upskilling; maintaining the availability of liquidity and financial system safety nets; and public infrastructure investment, both hard and network infrastructure (Bank Indonesia 2020: 9). The total National Economic Recovery Programmes (PEN) budget of USD 47.9 billion is intended for health, social protection, sectoral and regional government, business incentives, SMEs and corporate financing programmes. For labour-intensive programmes part of sectoral and regional government, USD 11.7 billion is allocated for PEN activities, and include: fund placement for labour-intensive restructuring, state equity participation (PMA) and debt securities to state-owned asset management companies lax incentives, labour-intensive programme, physical-specific allocation fund reserves and tourism incentives (Bank Indonesia 2020: 19)

Physical-specific allocation funds as part of fiscal transfer from central to regional government in 2020 will be used to finance three major programmes, namely poverty reduction, food security and sustainable economic infrastructure provision. Two main activities that will be financed by this fund are forest rehabilitation carried out by the community using agroforestry as a social safety net and facilitating productive economic development infrastructure for the Social Forestry Business Group (KUPS) with gold and silver criteria and/or Forest Farmers Group (KTH) (Saputra et al. 2020: 64). It indicates that the government has considered labour-intensive green projects in allocating its budget.

MoEF has reported that the ministry will continue to implement the national economic recovery policy through enhancing the role and community access in agroforestry practices (Antaranews.com 2021). This is one of the government programmes in addition to others such as maintaining productivity and business sustainability. The enhancement of the role and access of communities is carried out to increase forest productivity through social forestry programmes such as the Community Forest Plantation and Partnership that favour forest product industry and other industries.

Optimising ecological fiscal transfer from central to regional government

The government has implemented a decentralisation policy since 1999, in which some of the central government's authority (excluding for strategic issues) is transferred to local governments. The transfer of authority is supported by funding/government budget from the central government to enable local governments to exercise their new authority. The mechanism of the fund transfer from the central government to the regional government uses intergovernmental fiscal transfer, in which the funds are used to finance activities related to regional autonomy processes, particularly for activities that are under regional government authority and relevant to national priorities. The following table describes the 2016–2020 government budget, including central government spending and transfers from the central government to the regional government. It can be seen from Table 10.3 that the annual budget tends to increase every year.

Table 10.3: Indonesian government budget 2016–2020.

Government Budget	USD (billions)				
	2016	2017	2018	2019	2020
I Central government expenditure	91.42	90.72	100.31	112.71	116.10
– Ministry/institution expenditure	54.08	52.66	58.44	58.99	62.73
– Non-Ministerial/institution expenditure	37.34	38.07	41.87	53.72	53.37
II Transfers to the regional government and village funds	53.12	52.75	52.84	57.02	59.10
– Transfers to the regional government	49.88	48.61	48.70	52.19	54.13
– village funds	3.24	4.14	4.14	4.83	4.97
Total	144.53	143.48	153.15	169.73	175.20

Source: Indonesia Ministry of Finance (2016, 2017, 2018, 2019, 2020).

Fiscal transfer from central to regional government aims to fund some priority programmes these include development of the Ministry of Micro, Small and Medium Enterprises, food security and farmer/fishing workers welfare, tourism development, education and health reforms, improved infrastructure and connectivity and information communication technology development. Meanwhile, the Physical

Special Allocation Fund (DAK) – as one of the intergovernmental fiscal transfer schemes – has goals/targets for the environment and forestry in 2021 through budget allocation of 17 units of the construction of waste recycling centres and 16,750 ha community forests (Directorate General of Budget 2021: 22).

Ecological Fiscal Transfer in Indonesia was initiated by national and local governments. The implementation of this concept at the provincial level through the concept of Ecological-Based Provincial Budget Transfer (TAPE) and at the district level through the concept of Ecological-Based District Budget Transfer (TAKE). The TAPE concept can be implemented in a budget transfer scheme for the Regional Revenue and Expenditure Budget in the form of financial aid, social aid, grants, tax revenue-sharing and regional levies by including ecological indicators that are adapted to the characteristics of each region. The TAPE concept was initiated in North Kalimantan Province through Governor Regulation no. 6/2019 concerning Procedures for Provision, Distribution and Accountability of Financial Aid Expenditures for the North Kalimantan Provincial Government. Meanwhile, the TAKE concept was initiated by several regencies, namely Jayapura, Pidie and Nunukan. (Nurfatriani and Satrio 2020: 50).

At a national-level, there are two schemes of intergovernmental fiscal transfer that are considered the most appropriate for ecological-based fiscal transfers, these are the Special Allocation Fund (DAK) and regional incentive funds (DID). According to the Ministry of Finance Regulation No. 50/2017, regarding the management of transfers to regional governments and village funds (TKDD), DAK consists of physical DAK and non-physical DAK. Physical DAK is a fund allocated in the state budget (APBN) to certain regions with the aim of helping fund physical activities, which are regional affairs and in accordance with national priorities. Meanwhile, non-physical DAK is also allocated in the APBN with the aim of helping fund non-physical activities, which are also regional affairs. The physical DAK scheme aims to be ecologically based through the following activities: facilitation of waste management infrastructure, early warning systems for environmental disaster control, forest and land rehabilitation on critical land and facilitation of productive economic infrastructure. Another scheme is the non-physical DAK for the environment and forestry sector is designed to support physical activities in the form of capacity building and community empowerment: monitoring and monitoring of pollution, climate change, waste management, forestry technical personnel in Forest Management Units (FMUs), and social forestry assistance (Indonesia Ministry of Environment and Forestry 2021a). DID is a fund allocated in the APBN to certain regions based on certain criteria with the aim of rewarding certain performance improvements in the areas of regional financial governance, basic public services and community welfare. The DID mechanism has started to include the environmental indicator since 2019,using the waste management indicator. This incentive mechanism provides rewards to local governments that have performed well in reducing the amount of waste generated. Currently, the Ministry of Environment and Forestry

(KLHK) is drafting the concept of strengthening the DID scheme through the expansion of forestry and environmental criteria and indicators used in selecting the regional governments receive DID based on their performance (Indonesia Ministry of Environment and Forestry 2021b). The two concepts (non-physical DAK and DID) are being prepared by the MoEF and have been submitted to the Ministry of Finance and are expected to be included in the TKDD scheme for the 2022 fiscal year.

Figure 10.2 depicts the TKDD from 2015 to 2021 (which tend to increase).

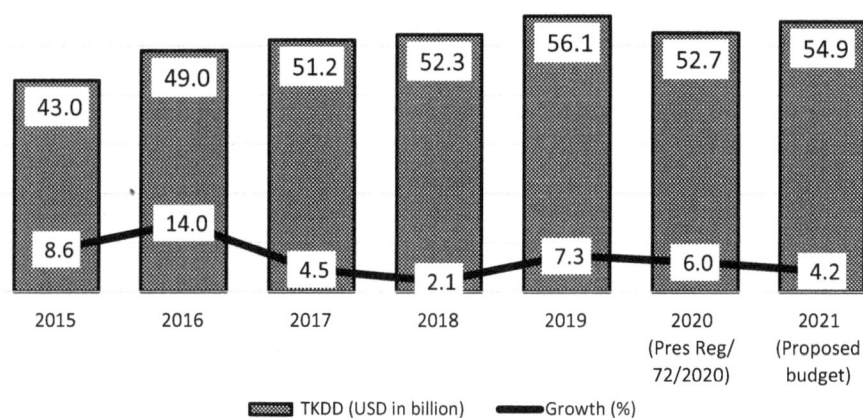

Figure 10.2: TKDD budget and growth in 2015–2021.
Source: Directorate General of Budget (2021: 21). Reproduced with permission.
Note: Government support to regions other than through TKDD is also provided through regional grants and regional loans. TKDD data converted from IDR (Indonesian rupiah) to USD (USD 1=IDR 14,500).

Improving governance of forest charges to support sustainable forest practices

Before the issuance of a new Government Regulation No 23/2021, most forest use activities attracting to private sector's interest are extractive activities, such as logging activities in native forests or plantation forests. With the emergence of markets for ecosystem services such as carbon trading and the decline of timber markets, the government has changed the regime of forest uses through a new Government Regulation No 23/2021 as implementing regulation of the Omnibus Law on Law creation No 11/2020. The government has started to facilitate the private sector to develop various businesses with only one permit, a forest utilisation permit. With the permit, the private sector granted the permit can optimise their area for both extractive and non-extractive businesses. For instance, a forest company that holds a forest utilisation permit can carry out logging activities in some parts of their area, while other parts can be used for business on forest ecosystem services, thus they can earn profit from both activities from one area but the transaction cost for the licensing arrangement is much reduced.

The new policy on the uses of forest area offers wide opportunities to increase government involvement in the forestry sector, not only from extractive forest uses but also from the use of forest ecosystem services. The policy is aims to boost business on forest ecosystem services, which can in turn increase government revenues from forestry sector. Some potential forest charges are the Forest Utilization Licensing Fee (Iuran Perizinan Berusaha Pemanfaatan Hutan), Forest Resource Provision (provisi sumber daya hutan), Reforestation Fund (Dana Reboisasi), fees for forest utilisation for ecotourism, water and energy, carbon and non-timber forest products.

Furthermore, the revenues from the forest charges could be utilised to support climate change mitigation actions in land-based sectors. Since the revenues derive from the authority of the central government, the central government has arranged the revenue distribution in order to favour mitigation actions. Some of the revenues from non-tax forest charges are basically redistributed to finance programmes and activities carried out by both the MoEF and regional governments where the forest operations take place. In order to support low-carbon development in the forestry sector as well as to cope with the COVID-19 pandemic, the government now has stipulated the use of the fund for climate change mitigation actions, such as forest fire prevention and suppression, forest rehabilitation, peatland restoration that promote community empowerment. All climate change mitigation actions carried out by line ministries and local governments have to be able to raise the community economy that has been severely impacted by the pandemic. This has been done through either involvement of the community as restoration workers or development of forest restoration-based small-scale community business.

Conclusion

The Indonesian government has demonstrated strong efforts to promote sustainable development pathways that are aligned with the handling of the COVID-19 pandemic. Low-carbon development initiatives to accelerate achievement of targeted emission reduction shows the government's strong commitment to shifting from brown to green development. Some fiscal policies have been used to enhance these efforts, such as the establishment of financing mechanisms for sustainable development and climate change. However, effectiveness of optimising the use of these funds remains to be seen. The government needs to take policy discretion, particularly for climate change mitigation actions in land-based sectors. Physical infrastructure should be not the only priority in development projects since most mitigation actions in land-based sectors which do not build physical infrastructure but encourage social-environmental improvements.

The COVID-19 pandemic has become a turning point for the government to rearrange conventional economic pathways to green economy in order to reach a sustainable post-COVID recovery. Even though some challenges are still faced, some instruments are potential to support the target; they are (a) shifting policy from brown to green development, (b) promoting innovative financing for land-based businesses, (c) providing incentives for the private sector to invest in green projects through taxes and subsidies, (d) optimising economic recovery programmes for labour-intensive green projects, I optimising EFT from central to regional government, and (f) improving governance of forest charges to support sustainable forest practices.

References

Alaydrus, Hadijah, and Wibi Pangestu. 2021. 'Utak-Atik Anggaran Pen 2021 Untuk Covid-19, Ini 4 Kebijakan Penting Sri Mulyani', *Bisnis.com*, July 19, 2021. <https://ekonomi.bisnis.com/read/20210719/10/1419225/utak-atik-anggaran-pen-2021-untuk-covid-19-ini-4-kebijakan-penting-sri-mulyani.> [Accessed 29 January 2022].

Antaranews.com. 2021. *KLHK Akan Tingkatkan Peran Dan Akses Masyarakat Terhadap Agroforestri*, <https://www.antaranews.com/berita/2312354/klhk-akan-tingkatkan-peran-dan-akses-masyarakat-terhadap-agroforestri> [Accessed August 4, 2021].

Asian Development Bank.·2020. *Green Finance Strategies for Post-Covid-19 Economic Recovery in Southeast Asia: Greening Recoveries for People and Planet*, (Manila: Asian Development Bank), <https://www.adb.org/sites/default/files/publication/639141/green-finance-post-covid-19-southeast-asia.pdf> [Accessed 29 January 2022].

Bank Indonesia. 2020. *Synergy to Drive National Economic Recovery, Mitigating Covid-19 Risk* (Jakarta: Investor Relations Unit – Republic of Indonesia).

Brancalion, P.H.S., E.N. Broadbent, S. De-miguel, A. Cardil, M.R. Rosa, C.T. Almeida, D.R.A. Almeida, S. Chakravarty, M. Zhou, J.G.P. Gamarra, Jingjing Liangg, Renato Crouzeilles, Bruno Hérault, Luiz E.O.C. Aragão, Carlos Alberto Silva, and Angelica M. Almeyda-Zambrano. 2020. 'Emerging Threats Linking Tropical Deforestation and the Covid-19 Pandemic', *Perspectives in Ecology and Conservation*, 18, 243–46.

Cadman, Tim, Tapan Sarker, Zahrul Muttaqin, Fitri Nurfatriani, Mimi Salminah, and Tek Maraseni. 2019. 'The Role of Fiscal Instruments in Encouraging the Private Sector and Smallholders to Reduce Emissions from Deforestation and Forest Degradation: Evidence from Indonesia', *Forest Policy and Economics*, 108, 101913.

Directorate General of Budget, Indonesia Ministry of Finance. 2021. *Proposed 2021 Budget: Accelerating Economic Recovery and Strengthening Structural Reforms* (Jakarta: Kemenerian Keuangan).

Global Green Growth Indonesia.·2020. *Achieving Green Growth Post-Covid-19 – GGGI Technical Report*, <https://gggi.org/site/assets/uploads/2020/07/GGGI-Technical-Report-Achieving-Green-Growth-and-Climate-Action-Post-COVID-19.pdf> [Accessed 28 July 2021].

Government of Indonesia. 2014. *Presidential Decree Number 75/2014 Concerning the Acceleration of Priority Infrastructure Provision*, <https://peraturan.bpk.go.id/Home/Details/41567/perpres-no-75-tahun-2014> [Accessed 10 January 2022].

——. 2016. *Presidential Regulation Number 122/2016 Concerning Amendments to Number 75 of 2014 on Acceleration of Priority Infrastructure Provision*, <https://peraturan.bpk.go.id/Home/Details/41026/perpres-no-122-tahun-2016.> [Accessed 10 January 2022].

——. 2018. *Minister of Finance Regulation Number 73/2018 Concerning Facilities for the Preparation and Implementation of Government Cooperation Project Transactions with Business Entities in the Provision of Infrastructure*, <https://jdih.kemenkeu.go.id/fullText/2018/73~PMK.08~2018Per.pdf> [Accessed 10 January 2022].

——.·2021. *Indonesia Long-Term Strategy for Low Carbon and Climate Resilience 2050*, (United Nations Framework Convention on Climate Change), <https://unfccc.int/sites/default/files/resource/Indonesia_LTS-LCCR_2021.pdf> [Accessed 29 January 2022].

Hincks, Joseph. 2021. *How Blended Finance Is Protecting Indonesia's Forests and Empowering Women at the Same Time*. (United Nations Indonesia) <https://indonesia.un.org/en/130274-how-blended-finance-protecting-indonesias-forests-and-empowering-women-same-time> [Accessed 29 January 2022]

Indonesia Directorate of Mobilization Sectoral and Regional Resources 2021 *Notes on Climate Change Finance for Forestry Sector* (Jakarta: The Green Finance Workshop)

Indonesia Fiscal Policy Agency. 2020a. *Laporan Anggaran Mitigasi Dan Adaptasi Perubahan Iklim Tahun 2018-2020*. (Jakarta: Badan Kebijakan Fiskal, (BKF))

——. 2020b. *Potret Ekonomi Indonesia 2019*. (Jakarta: Badan Kebijakan Fiskal, (BKF))

——. 2021. *Potret Ekonomi Indonesia 2020*. (Jakarta: Badan Kebijakan Fiskal, (BKF))

Indonesia Ministry of Environment and Forestry. 2019. *Peta Jalan Mitigasi Perubahan Iklim NDC* (Jakarta: Kementerian Lingkungan Hidup dan Kehutanan (KLHK)).

——. 2021a. *Kebijakan Dana Alokasi Khusus (DAK) Non Fisik Bidang Lingkungan Hidup Dan Kehutanan*. (Jakarta: Kementerian Lingkungan Hidup dan Kehutanan (KLHK))

——. 2021b. *Kebijakan Dana Insentif Daerah Bidang Lingkungan Hidup Dan Kehutanan*. (Jakarta: Kementerian Lingkungan Hidup dan Kehutanan, (KLHK))

Indonesia Ministry of Environment and Forestry: Directorate General of Climate Change. 2017. *Towards Operationalization of Climate Finance* (Jakarta: Direktorat Jenderal Pengendalian Perubahan Iklim).

Indonesia Ministry of Finance.·2016. *APBN 2016*, (Jakarta: Kemenerian Keuangan), <https://www.kemenkeu.go.id/apbn2016.> [Accessed 29 January 2022].

——.·2017. *APBN 2017*, (Jakarta: Kemenerian Keuangan), <https://www.kemenkeu.go.id/apbn2017.> [Accessed 29 January 2022].

——.·2018. *APBN 2018*, (Jakarta: Kemenerian Keuangan), <https://www.kemenkeu.go.id/apbn2018.> [Accessed July 30 2021].

——.·2019. *APBN 2019*, (Jakarta: Kemenerian Keuangan), <https://www.kemenkeu.go.id/apbn2019.> [Accessed 30 July 2021].

——.·2020. *APBN 2020*, (Jakarta: Kemenerian Keuangan), <https://www.kemenkeu.go.id/apbn2020.> [Accessed 30 July 2021].

Indonesia National Development Planning Agency. 2018. *KPBU, Pina, Dan Blended Finance: Instrumen Pemerintah Indonesia Capai Target Pembangunan Infrastruktur*, (Badan Perencanaan Pembangunan Nasional (Bappenas),), <https://www.bappenas.go.id/files/6715/4338/8360/Siaran_Pers_-_KPBU_PINA_dan_Blended_Finance_Instrumen_Pemerintah_Indonesia_Capai_Target_Pembangunan_Infrastruktur.pdf> [Accessed 28 July 2021].

——. 2019. *Low Carbon Development: A Paradigm Shift Towards a Green Economy in Indonesia* (Jakarta: Badan Perencanaan Pembangunan Nasional, (Bappenas)).

──── 2020a *Inisiasi Pemetaan Awal Pendanaan Pembangunan Rendah Karbon Versi 1.0*. (Webinar of Low Carbon Development Funding)

────. 2020b. *Promoting and Optimizing Blended Finance for Financing the National Development Programs*. (Jakarta: Badan Perencanaan Pembangunan Nasional (Bappenas))

Le Quéré, Corinne, Robert B. Jackson, Matthew W. Jones, Adam J.P. Smith, Sam Abernethy, Robbie M. Andrew, Anthony J. De-Gol, David R. Willis, Yuli Shan, Josep G. Canadell, Pierre Friedlingstein, Felix Creutzig, and Glen P. Peters. 2020. 'Temporary Reduction in Daily Global CO_2 Emissions During the Covid-19 Forced Confinement', *Nature Climate Change*, 10, 647–53.

Louman, Bas, Alexandre Meybeck, Gerhard Mulder, Michael Brady, L. Fremy, H. Savenije, V. Gitz, and E. Trines.·2020. *Innovative Finance for Sustainable Landscapes. Working Paper 7*, (Bogor, Indonesia: The CGIAR Research Program on Forests, Trees and Agroforestry (FTA)), <https://www.cifor.org/publications/pdf_files/FTA/WPapers/FTA-WP-7.pdf> [Accessed 29 January 2022].

Novianti, D.A., R. Saputri, I.K. Sari, W. Parasian, Wignyo, A.Y. Trihartanto, and A.H. Imaduddin. 2020. *Covid-19 Catatan Linimasa Para Analis Muda* (Jakarta: PT Gramedia Pustaka Utama).

Nurfatriani, F., and A.E. Satrio. 2020. 'Urgensi Pendanaan Pembangunan Berbasis Ekologi' in F Nurfatriani and I W S Darmawan (eds.), *Pendanaan Pembangunan Berbasis Ekologi Di Provinsi Kalimantan Timur-Tinjauan Atas Skema Result Based Payment Sebagai Insentif REDD+* (Bogor, Indonesia: IPB Press), pp. 37–38

Rohr, J.R., C.B. Barrett, D J Civitello, M.E. Craft, B. Delius, G.A. DeLeo, P. Hudson, N. Jouanard, K.H. Nguyen, R. Ostfeld, J.V. Remais, G. Riveau, S.H. Sokolow, and D. Tilman. 2019. 'Emerging Human Infectious Diseases and the Links to Global Food Production', *Nature Sustainability* 2(6),445–56.

Rulli, M.C., P. D'Odorico, N. Galli, and D.T.S. Hayman. In press. 'Land Use Change and Coronavirus Emergence Risk', *MedRxiv*.

Saputra, Wiko, Alin Halimatussadiah, Joko Tri Haryanto, Fitri Nurfatriani, and Mimi Salminah. 2020. *Rancangan Kebijakan Transfer Fiskal Berbasis Ekologi Di Indonesia: Dana Insentif Daerah (DID), Dana Alokasi Khusus (DAK) Bidang Lingkungan Hidup Dan Kehutanan, Dan Dana Desa (DD)* (Jakarta: Kemitraan bagi Pembaharuan Tata Pemerintahan Indonesia).

Sustainable Finance Indonesia. 2021. *Roadmap Keuangan Berkelanjutan Tahap II (2021–2025): The Future of Finance* (Jakarta: Otoritas Jasa Keuangan).

Tropical Landscapes Finance Facility Indonesia. 2021. *A Blended Finance Facility for Indonesia*, <https://www.tlffindonesia.org/about-us/> [Accessed July 28, 2021].

Wahidah, N.L., and E. Antriyandarti. 2020. 'Impact of Climate Change and Coronavirus Disease (Covid-19) on Inflation in Indonesia', *IOP Conference Series: Earth and Environmental Science* 724 (012105), 012105.

White, Rebekah J., and Orly Razgour. 2020. 'Emerging Zoonotic Diseases Originating in Mammals: A Systematic Review of Effects of Anthropogenic Land-Use Change', *Mammal Review*, 50, 336–52.

Zoltán Kun
Chapter 11
The EU renewable energy policy and its impact on forests

Abstract: The European Union's (EU) actions in increasing the use of renewable energy and decreasing greenhouse gas emission includes the Renewable Energy Directive, which defines the various Renewable Energy Sources (RES). The most important element of RES is wood-based biomass, which accounts for over 60% of all EU domestic biomass supplied for energy.

The sustainability and carbon neutrality of primary woody biomass for energy have recently been widely questioned. According to a group of plaintiffs, who took the EU to court, burning firewood shall not be treated as renewable energy, because it is not a solution leading to meet the climate and biodiversity targets. While the territory of forests increases in Europe, the area cover only measures the quantity of forest land use category. Even the EU's Joint Research Centre found significant problems with the conservation status and resilience of Europe's forests. It is these and other concerns that led a consortium of NGOs and policy think tanks to mount a legal challenge to the use of EU sustainable finance for forestry and bioenergy, claiming such funding was unscientific, contrary to the provision to avoid significant harm in the EU's own Taxonomy Regulation, and would increase rather than mitigate carbon emissions (Partnership for Policy Integrity 2022).

Harvesting that considers the growth of increment as the main indicator of sustainability is not a solution for considering forest biomass as renewable. This chapter looks at how the increasing use of forest biomass contribute to the current status and trends of forests in Europe and outlines policy recommendations to improve the situation.

Keywords: renewable energy, forest biomass, forestry, biodiversity, climate change, sustainability, public subsidy, carbon neutrality, European Union, COVID-19

Introduction

The European Union (EU) has committed to increasing the use of renewable energy in its energy mix and decreasing greenhouse gases, including carbon emission. The EU has constructed the Renewable Energy Directive (RED) to define and promote the various Renewable Energy Sources (RES). Wood-based biomass accounts for over 60% of all EU domestic biomass supplied for energy purposes, which is the most important element of the EU renewable energy mix. Its main use is in the

https://doi.org/10.1515/9783110733488-011

heating and cooling sector with an 83% relative share, but also growing in electricity generation.

The utilisation of firewood as the main form of solid biomass has received considerable attention in past years as a RES because of its potential to reduce dependence on fossil fuel-based energy. However, the sustainability of production and whether or not bioenergy from forests should be considered as zero carbon by RES has recently been widely questioned. The civil society sector has called for stopping subsidies for powerplants and an online petition calls for removing forest biomass from the RED. According to a group of plaintiffs, who took the EU to court, burning firewood should not be treated as renewable energy, because it is not a solution leading to meet the climate goals.

By simply looking at the land use statistics, an observer might think forests are doing well. On the contrary, the most recent research indicates that Europe's forests are in a dire condition. While the territory of forests is increasing in Europe, the area covered only measures the quantity of those land use category, which is statistically considered as forests. Reports coming from the European Commission's own research body, the Joint Research Centre, have found significant problems with the conservation status and health of EU forests without any evidence of improvement.

Less than 18% of the forests in Europe are made of more than three tree species. Combined with the significant proportion of evenly aged forest structure this indicates a huge challenge for the forests in terms of biodiversity protection and climate change resilience.

Sustainable harvesting is not a solution for considering forest biomass as renewable. Treating sustainable harvesting as equivalent to carbon neutrality assigns ongoing forest growth to offset emissions, and thus does not constitute increased carbon uptake. Therefore – if forest biomass is not removed from RED – the sustainability criteria must be so strict that hardly any woody biomass could qualify.

Such a move would practically mean that forest biomass be ineligible for public subsidies, so this funding could be reallocated for actions filling the gap in the energy mix. These actions could include the following: supporting the remaining, truly RES, improving energy efficiency including insulation, investing in energy storage and forest protection, all of which guarantee the protection of current carbon stock and increase carbon removal from the atmosphere.

Legislative pathway towards RES

From UNFCCC to Paris

This chapter of the handbook looks at what policies promote the utilisation of forest biomass for energy within the EU, how this utilisation influences the current status and future trends of forest habitats in the EU and finally concludes with a few key policy recommendations for the EU and beyond.

Due to the increasing scientific evidence about human-induced climate change (Rogers 1990), policy changes were initiated on a global and national levels in order to promote action by governments. As a first step, the United Nations Framework Convention on Climate Change (UNFCCC 1992) was agreed upon as a worldwide framework pact for coordinating international actions to combat climate change. Its central element was to limit average global temperature increases and the resulting climate change through forestalling the inevitable human-made intrusion into the global climate system.

In order to reinforce the global response to climate change, the negotiation of the Parties of the UNFCCC eventually led to the adoption of the Kyoto Protocol on 11 December 1997. The Kyoto Protocol legally binds developed countries that are party to the Convention to greenhouse gas (GHG) emission reduction targets. While the 37 industrialised countries had different national targets – for instance the EU aimed at 8% reduction – their different targets were intended to add up to a total reduction of 5.2% over the period of 20082012.

While the first commitment period fell between 2008 and 2012, the Conference of the Parties agreed to lengthen the life of the Protocol until 2020 at the 2012 United Nations Climate Change Conference in Doha. The second commitment period, in which the Parties agreed to reduce emissions by at least 18% below 1990 levels, began on 1 January 2013 and ended in 2020.

Following upon the protocol, the Paris Agreement was adopted in Paris on 12 December 2015 as the first ever international, legally binding treaty linked to climate change. This Agreement aims at keeping the global temperature rise below 2, but preferably 1.5, degrees Celsius compared to the pre-industrial level (UNFCCC 2015). Based on the Nationally Determined Contributions (NDCs), the Agreement also targets strengthening global actions to promote and increase investments needed for a sustainable low-carbon future. The Agreement also aims to improve the ability of countries to respond to the likely impacts of climate change through mitigation efforts.

The response of EU and member states

In the framework of the Paris Agreement, the European Union and its Member States (MSs) submitted their intended NDCs on 6 March 2015, which – as part of the EU's wider 2030 climate and energy actions – presented the commitment to reduce GHG emissions by at least 40% by 2030 compared to 1990 (Latvian Presidency of the Council of the EU 2015). Accordingly, the relevant key EU legislation for implementing this target was adopted by the end of 2018.

The EU Emission Trading System (ETS), non-ETS sectors under the Effort Sharing Regulation and land use related emissions and removals addressed by the regulation on emissions and removals from land use, land use change and forestry (LULUCF) are included in the EU climate pack. The block's emission reduction targets are separated between those sectors which are covered by these tools (EU 2020). For this chapter, the most pertinent regulatory tool is the latest, which is further described below.

Agriculture, forestry and other land use (AFOLU) are considered a significant net source of GHG emissions, contributing to about a quarter of anthropogenic sources (UNFCCC). LULUCF itself is accountable for 46% of the AFOLU emissions (Bertaglia et al. 2016). The EU LULUCF regulation (EU 2013) sets up the accounting methodology for GHG emission, establishes the procedure for monitoring for MSs to calculate emissions, as well as removals from actions in their forests, and finally increases the scope of accounting for all managed land in the EU. In order to support the regulation, the EC published a Delegated Act for the Forest Reference Levels which each MS must apply for the period between 2021 and 2025 (EU 2020b).

As part of the efforts to decrease GHG emissions, the EU has also committed to increasing the use of RES in its energy mix (EU 2020a). The EU constructed the RED (2009a) to define and promote the various RES. The RED established a mandatory 20% share of EU total energy consumption that must come from RES by 2020. The MSs were also required to acquire 10% of their transport fuel from RES by the same year. The directive also mapped out mechanisms like support schemes, guarantees of origin, joint projects and cooperation between MSs and third countries, which MSs might utilise in order to reach their targets (European Parliament n.d.). The directive was reworked in 2018 with special attention on certain sustainability criteria and the Revision of the Renewable Energy Directive (REDII) was approved by the European Parliament and the Council (European Parliament and Council 2018) and entered into force, as part of the 'Clean energy for all Europeans' package in December 2018. The revised directive established a new binding RES target for the EU: at least 32% of final energy consumption should come from renewable sources by 2030, with a clause for a possible upward revision by 2023.

Following upon this commitment, in December 2019 the European Council endorsed the objective of achieving a climate-neutral EU by 2050, in line with the Paris Agreement (European Union Council 2020b). Reflecting this climate neutrality objective, the Council of the EU adopted a long-term low GHG emission development strategy of the EU and its MSs on 5 March 2020. This long-term strategy was subsequently submitted to the UNFCCC Secretariat (EU 2020). During the German Presidency, the EU further boosted its ambition and the updated NDC, submitted in December 2020, increased the target to reduce net domestic GHG emissions by at least 55% by 2030 from 1990 levels (EU 2020).

The NDC referred to the earlier Council of the EU conclusion that covered the EU preparation of the post-2020 global biodiversity framework Convention on Biological Diversity. This conclusion highlights the important role what nature-based solutions play in responding to various global challenges such as biodiversity loss, ecosystems degradation, poverty, hunger, health, water scarcity and drought, gender inequality, disaster risk reduction and climate change (European Union Council 2019). In order to limit the temperature increase to 1.5 °C above pre-industrial levels, the document identified nature-based solutions as tool for climate change mitigation and adaptation.

The policies described above might send the right signals to the various actors within the EU, but there are still challenges in relation to national implementation. The proposed Delegated Act EU Sustainable Financial Taxonomy for instance resulted in an outcry among the civil society sector, which pointed out problems in the suggestion linked to forests and bioenergy. In a letter to Members of the European Parliament (MEPs) signed by over 90 organisations, including consumer protection organisations (BEUC: The European Consumer Organisation 2021), NGOs pointed out the controversy about the standards for forestry and bioenergy, which classify the burning of trees and in some cases crops, clearcutting of forests, intensive mono-species plantations, use of chemical fertilisers and pesticides in forestry and removal of stumps as green investment.

The impact of COVID-19 and financing economic recovery in the EU

The policy environment currently is unsteady in the EU. The revision of various legislation introduced earlier (LULUCF, RED, Biodiversity Strategy, Forest Strategy) and the development of new tools (e.g., binding Restoration Target) are happening at the same time and this process might result in very different policy circumstances by the end of 2021.

The COVID-19 pandemic situation has further complicated this complex situation. The impact of the pandemic was not only visible on the economy, but also on recognising how the intertwined biodiversity and climate crises impact people's lives directly in Europe. Therefore, green and digital growth were put into the centre of the EU economic recovery.

EU leaders agreed that the EU budget entitled the Multiannual Financial Framework (MFF) for 20212027 would be reinforced through a new EU recovery instrument referred to as the Next Generation EU (NGEU). The Council of the EU specifically proposed mainstreaming climate actions in programmes financed through the MFF and NGEU, with the concrete figure of 30% of the total amount of expenditure allocated for such activities (EU 2020c).

The MFF and the temporary financial instrument of the NGEU represents over 1,800 billion euros, so the funding dedicated to climate actions will be over 540 billion euros. This is a huge opportunity but might also be an equally huge threat depending on national plans to spend the funding. The MSs submitted their Recovery and Resilience Facility plans to the EC by 30 April 2021, which has yet to approve them.

The importance of woody biomass in Europe's energy mix

Clarifying the terminology

The utilisation of firewood as the main form of solid biomass has received consider-able attention in the past years as a RES, because of its potential to reduce depen-dence on fossil fuel-based energy. In order to get a clear picture about the status and trends of wood-based biomass for energy use, the terminology used in RED and the Eurostat database needs to be clarified. The RED defines biofuels as liquid fuel for transport produced from biomass (EU 2009a), while the Eurostat recognises and reports on the use of solid biofuels in its Shares dataset. Eurostat defines solid bio-fuels covering organic, non-fossil material of biological origin irrespective whether used for heat production or electricity generation (Eurostat 2013).

Other important definitions in the renewable energy dialogue include the following:
– Bioenergy: derived from organic materials, such as wood, agricultural crops or organic waste. It is obtained from recently grown organic material, known as biomass, as opposed to fossil fuel, which is ancient fossilised biomass. It can be used in electricity, heating, cooling and transport. It can be used in liquid forms such as biofuels, in gaseous forms like biogas, or in solid forms, as is the case when burning wood for energy (eubioenergy.com).
– Biomass: the biodegradable fraction of products, waste and residue from bio-logical origin from agriculture, including vegetal and animal substances, from forestry and related industries, including fisheries and aquaculture, as well as the biodegradable fraction of waste, including industrial and municipal waste of biological origin:
– Forest biomass: biomass produced from forestry
– Biomass fuels means gaseous and solid fuels produced from biomass (EU 2009a)

The classification of wood-based fuels varies within the EU MSs, but Eurostat recog-nises the following types of wood-based fuels (Eurostat 2013):
– Firewood originating from whole trees
– Non-standardised wood fuels
– Standardised wood fuels, which include pellets, briquettes and chips
– Used wood or demolition wood
– Wood fuels including all fuels consisting of wood materials
– Wood residue coming from the wood processing industry

Within this chapter, the terms of fuelwood, firewood, wood-based biomass are used interchangeably.

The users of wood-based biomass for energy

Wood-based biomass are the oldest form of providing heat to human society and has been a historic part of the energy mix in Europe.

Lots of attention is paid to burning wood in power plants, including carbon emissions, because information gathered about the use of solid biomass in powerplants is relatively well documented through the national energy agencies. The Environmental Paper Network for instance launched two online maps to show (a) bioenergy plants that have a capacity bigger than 20 MW and use woody biomass as their main fuel or co-fire biomass in coal power plants; (b) pellet mills that produce industrial or/and domestic pellets and have an annual production of 50 000 metric tonnes or more (Environmental Paper Network 2020). Power plants and industrial plants burning wood for heat and energy are often criticised as drivers behind the increasing demand for fuelwood, which creates a growing market for less valuable timber and results in intensification of forestry (Booth and Mitchell 2020).

It must be noted that MSs count residential wood burning toward renewables targets and in some cases are actively seeking to increase use of wood for heating. Eurostat admits in its manual that almost all solid biofuel uses in households are wood-based fuel. RESs including firewood are widely used in private households and are becoming increasingly important for fulfilling the EU's commitment on the renewable energy proportion in its energy mix. Wood burning by households is still widespread around the EU MSs (Lindroos 2011), but its impact receives much less attention than large-scale powerplants. As there is a lack of sustainability criteria in the REDII for the residential sector, this is important not only because of the question of considering wood burning as renewable, but also because of calculating the carbon sink within the LULUCF reporting and nature conservation, especially due to the influence of this usage on available biomass resources and biodiversity, such as on forest dwelling species.

When looking at the impact of wood burning on forests, the residential firewood usage in the EU MSs must thus be taken into account. Some MSs argue that firewood use of households might be a driver of illegally sourced wood, which will be further explained in the next section.

The proportion of wood-based biomass in the EU energy mix

Wood-based biomass accounts for over 60% of all EU domestic biomass supplied for energy purposes (EU 2009a), thus is still the most important element of the EU renewable energy mix. Its main use is in the heating and cooling sector with an 83% relative share, but its relevance also increases in electricity generation (European Environmental Agency 2020b).

In terms of the wood resource balance, the proportion of wood use by the energy sector in the EU-28 increased from 45.8% in 2009 to 48.9% in 2015. However, as wood pellet is used in the energy sector, its 4.1% share in 2015 should also be added to the energy use of wood. This means that 53% of energy production in the MSs comes from wood resources (Cazzaniga et al. 2019).

The data from Eurostat Shares show the proportion of solid biomass in EU-28 RES was 49.15% in 2015, with huge variation between MSs with 86.51% in Estonia as highest and 4.38% in Malta as lowest proportion (Eurostat 2021). This is a significant proportional decrease compared to the same data in 2004, when almost two thirds of RES (63.34%) in the EU-28 was solid biomass. This proportional decrease is due to the fact that other RES, e.g., photovoltaic and wind, increased significantly and not to the decreasing use of solid biomass. In terms of volume, the increase of energy use of wood is even more significant. The volume grew by 33% in volume from 337.7M m^3 to 435.9M m^3 between 2009, when the RED came into force, and 2015. The increase of timber volume for material use in the same period was less than half for energy use, at only 16%. When looking at a longer time scale, the volume of solid biomass burned in Europe has increased by 38% since 2004 when ten new MSs joined the EU (Cazzaniga et al. 2019). A further increase of 15% between 2015 and 2018 should be noted.

12.8% of all wood used in Europe came from unaccounted sources in 2015, which means no one knows how it entered into the EU market. The volume of this unaccounted wood on the EU market has increased by 35% between 2009 and 2015.

The solid biomass use is largely linked to heating and cooling (H&C) in the EU-28 (92%) with only 8% linked to electricity production in 2015.

The National Energy and Climate Plans (NECPs) developed by the MSs confirm that the volume of solid biomass use is likely to further increase in the energy mix (EC 2020d). While referring to air pollution control requirements, the Austrian NECP prioritises forming the necessary conditions for an increase in the use of domestic wood biomass for energy production, for instance through green electricity follow-up tariffs (Federal Ministry of Sustainability and Tourism Republic of Austria 2019).

In terms of future plans, the NECPs of 14 MSs mention the increase of biomass in the renewable energy package, while only 7 MSs indicate the decrease of the volume of solid biomass use. This information suggests that the volume of solid biomass use, including residential firewood for heating, is likely to continue growing to an EU-27 level by 2030.

Table 11.1: Projected solid biomass use tendencies in the NECPs in the 27 MSs.

Country	Tendency about solid biomass use	Note linked to the residential use of solid biomass
Austria	increase	no special focus
Belgium	decrease	the gradual reduction of solid biomass use is linked to public health concerns. In relation to the local supply of fuelwood, the proposal is to maintain the current status quo
Bulgaria	increase	the document predicts 11% increase of solid biomass use in the residential sector
Croatia	unclear	support for boilers in the residential sector is planned
Cyprus	unclear	the biomass opportunity is under investigation, but said to be on a decline
Czech Republic	increase	increase the share of biomass in final heat consumption, in the form of co-firing with coal, central heat sources and domestic biomass boilers
Denmark	decrease	solid biomass decreases by 2% from 2017 to 2030 and 12% from 2017 to 2040
Estonia	increase	11 TWh of the total heat demand will be met by biomass by 2030
Finland	increase	the biomass use is projected to increase by 14% in the electricity generation and by 11% in the H&C by 2030
France	increase	ensure the rapid replacement of inefficient independent wood burning appliances (fireplaces, stoves, heating inserts)
Germany	decrease	the expected trajectory for biomass demand indicates 5% decrease in solid biomass demand by 2030
Greece	increase	there is a project 4 times increase in biomass & biogas-based power generation, but this remains small proportion of total RES
Hungary	increase	the document identifies major potential for the efficient use of biomass in both individual heating equipment and in district heating
Ireland	increase	no special focus on solid biomass
Italy	stable	no increase projected but investment in higher efficiency boiler is planned
Latvia	decrease	the country wants to invest in increasing efficiency and expect lower total energy demand
Lithuania	increase	aiming at producing additional wood biofuels from logging waste

Table 11.1 (continued)

Country	Tendency about solid biomass use	Note linked to the residential use of solid biomass
Luxembourg	decrease	decrease of solid biomass use is projected in both the electricity and heat sector
Malta	minimal	the document clearly states that biomass production is not an option
Netherlands	increase	as a result of promoting co-fuelling and co-firing in coal-fired power plants the consumption of energy from biomass will continue to grow
Poland	stable	while RES is projected to increase from 32% to 40% by 2040, the volume of solid biomass remains the same with focus on offshore and onshore wind
Portugal	stable	very small projected increase indicated in NECP
Romania	decrease	while total RES is projected to increase solid biomass volume is expected to decrease
Slovakia	increase	8% increase is project
Slovenia	decrease	focus on using wood (forest) as aa climate mitigation tool rather than an energy source
Spain	increase	biomass will play an important role in increasing the total share of renewable energy
Sweden	increase	the NECP indicates a slight, 2.5% increase of biomass use in the total RES

Source: Compiled from Smith et al. (2021). See additional reference below.

Forests in the EU

Policies dedicated to forests in the EU

While section one introduced the range of legislation linked to the EU's climate commitments, the forest biomass use for energy requires also looking into those EU policies that directly influence the status of forests in the EU.

The EU Biodiversity Strategy for 2030 (EC 2020a) put special emphasis on forests through three calls:
1. Targeting the strict protection of the remaining primary and old-growth forests
2. Increasing the quantity of forests as well as their resilience
3. Aiming at planting 3 billion trees while respecting full ecological principles by 2030

The biodiversity strategy also promised to develop and publish a dedicated EU Forest Strategy in 2021. The post 2020 non-binding EU Forest Strategy is as part of the 'Fit for 55' climate package (Euractiv 2021). While the previous forest strategy (published on 20 September 2013) recognised the multifunctionality of forest, it largely focussed on ensuring the necessary raw materials for industry and energy through sustainable forestry. Protection of forest was practically linked to sustainable management of forests (EC 2013).

Following up on the biodiversity strategy, the European Parliament (EP) adopted a report entitled the EU's role on protecting and restoring the world's forest on 16 September 2020 (European Parliament 2020a). The resolution highlighted that assuming forest biomass harvesting for energy as climate-neutral is erroneous. The document also pointed out the shared responsibility between the EU and MSs in terms of forests. This shared competence is based on a decision of the European Court of Justice, which linked community competence to protecting forests against degradation and destruction as part of the EU's environmental action. Hence the EU competence is based on Article 130s of the EU Treaty (European Court of Justice 1999). The EU's Birds and Habitats Directives are the basis of protecting priority forest habitats and forest dwelling species across the EU (EU 1992, 2009b). These two binding sets of legislations establishes the Natura 2000 network, which the EC claims is the largest coordinated network of protected areas in the world (European Commission 2021). Despite the EP resolution, the clear ruling of the European Court of Justice and the two nature directives, the shared competence between the EU and MSs on forests is still widely questioned by MEPs and some MSs.

The most recent examples ahead of the publication of the post 2020 EU Forest Strategy are the resolution of the EP about the European Forest Strategy adopted on 8 October 2020 (European Parliament 2020b) and the Council's conclusion about the Perspectives for the EU forest-related policies and EU Forest Strategy post 2020 (European Union Council 2020a). These two legislative documents not only argue for MSs' competence over forests, but they turn the normal decision-making process and try to limit the EC's manoeuvring opportunity in terms of its communication about forests.

Finally, the EU Timber Regulation (EUTR) is another legally binding regulation, which aims at securing that only legally harvested wood can enter the EU internal market (EU 2010). The regulation uses three elements to legalise the timber market: prohibiting illegal timber, forcing due diligence process for traders and keeping a record of suppliers and customers. There are national Competent Agencies (CA) in each MS, which are responsible for the implementation. The proposal of the Hungarian CA, NÉBIH, suggests common irregularities and gaps in the EUTR (2018a). NÉBIH explained to the EC expert group that placing illegally harvested firewood is widespread and easy and it requested action from the EC to develop common standards. The CA document even includes an example of how to place illegal timber on the market through sourcing from both legal and illegal sources, while ensuring having no more firewood than the legally purchased amount in the storage yard at the same time. The non-compliant firewood should always be sold to final consumers or traders claiming themselves to be final consumer, which limits the monitoring opportunity.

Conservation status of EU forests

Forests are the largest terrestrial ecosystem in the EU, covering around 39% of the land area (European Environmental Agency 2020a). By simply looking at the land use statistics, one might think forests are doing well. On the contrary, the most recent research indicates that EU forests are in a dire condition. While the territory of forests increases in Europe, the area statistically considered to be forest is only measured by quantity, not quality. Reports coming from the EC's own research body, the Joint Research Centre, found significant problems with the conservation status and health of European forests without any evidence of improvement.

The current condition of forest ecosystems in the EU is the result of natural and human-induced disturbances that have been taking place since the mid-Holocene. An assessment on forest status in relation to the degradation of ecosystem integrity and the risk of approaching climate tipping points in the next decades under different climate change scenarios is badly needed. Due to legacies of past overexploitation, forests in many parts of Europe, for instance in the South-Eastern margins, are particularly exposed to such risk. This goes hand-in-hand with past soil erosion, depletion and its future restoration.

Based on Forest Europe's *Status of Europe's Forest* (SoEF) report, only 2.2% of forests remained undisturbed by humans by 2020, indicating significantly low natural conditions (ForestEurope 2020: 118). The recent EU Joint Research Centre (JRC) report on mapping old-growth and primary forest in Europe, which describes these places as the natural heritage of Europe, and the ancient temples of the culture, found 4.9 million hectares of old-growth forest which represented only 3% of the EU's total forested area and 1.2% of EU land. The report further argues that the protection of these places is essential for both preserving biodiversity and mitigating climate change (Barredo-Cano et al. 2021). These natural forests are substantially different ecosystems from human-disturbed forests (Ranius et al. 2018) and they provide much greater and more diverse ecosystem services, including a much more substantial contribution to mitigating the biodiversity and climate crises.

Other reports highlight significant problems with the ecosystem integrity, biodiversity status and resilience of EU forests and their conservation status (European Environmental Agency 2020c). While some indicators may be improving, such as forest area, growing stock and productivity, indicators of defoliation and species abundance and richness are declining, and these are critical to maintain ecosystem resilience and the provision of ecosystem services.

Although the SoEF reported 94% of Europe's forests as semi-natural, which is defined as 'neither undisturbed by man nor plantations but display some character-istics of natural ecosystems,' (ForestEurope 2020: 118) this is contradicted by other findings in the same document, which is that 33% of forests are dominated by sin-gle tree species, indicating higher proportion of planted tree monocultures. Hence, in reality a large proportion of European forests are not semi-natural, and this po-tentially undermines the understanding of the quantity and quality of benefits from forests.

Combined with the significant proportion of forests with even-aged structure (75%), the majority of forests are not capable of supporting the full complement of biodiversity for the ecoregion, are not resilient to climate change and other pertur-bations, and are not providing the high-quality benefits and ecosystem services of natural forests. Added to this is the fact that less than 18% of European forests are made of more than three tree species. Such contradictions in reported status and trends call into question the reliability of data about the definition and proportion of semi-natural forests and the appropriateness of characteristics under this classifi-cation. More precise data indicates a huge challenge for forests in terms of biodiver-sity protection and climate change resilience.

The overall assessment for EU forests shows poor conditions and there are seri-ous concerns regarding upwards trends of several pressures and degrading condi-tion indicators. The State of Nature in the EU report (European Environmental Agency 2020c: 41) actually shows a slight decline of their conservation status, resil-ience and the ecosystem services they are supposed to provide.

The Habitats Directive's EU level assessment of the conservation status of 81 for-est habitats, which covers 28% of the EU's forest area, concluded that 14% are in good (or favourable) conservation status (European Environmental Agency 2020c). The remaining habitats are in poor status (54%), bad status (31%) or unknown (1%). In terms of future trends, 26% of forest habitats have deteriorating status in the EU.

In addition, the assessment also indicates that forestry management for com-modity production is the dominant pressure reported for most of the forest habitat types, which suggests that reduction in logging is needed to improve the status of forest habitats and resilience. Removing dead and dying trees and clear cutting are the biggest threats to forests. JRC's scientists recently reported 49% increase in har-vested areas and 69% of biomass loss in Europe for the period of 2016–2018 relative to 2011–2015 (Ceccherini et al. 2020). Large losses have been reported on the Iberian Peninsula and in the Nordic and Baltic countries, which triggered heavy criticism, especially from Sweden and Finland. Critiques claimed JRC did not take official har-vesting statistics into account (Korhonen 2020; Swedish Forest Agency 2020). How-ever, a parallel study on the Mapping and Assessment of Ecosystem Services in Europe, which assesses the entirety of EU's forests, provides a potential explanation of the different between JRC's finding and official national statistics (Maes et al. 2020). The report found that tree cover loss, which is used as a metric to define the quality of forests, increased by 26% in the period 20012012, and by 74% in the period 20092018. Tree cover loss is a better indicator to capture local processes than the simple forest cover, which is measured in 500 x 500 m grids.

Exacerbating the current trends in forests are the interacting impacts of climate change, its indirect effects, the effects of pollutants and the constantly increasing demand for forest biomass driven by the demand for biomass-based energy (Camia et al. 2020; Camia et al. 2018) and the EU Bioeconomy Strategy (European Commission Directorate General Research and Innovation 2018). Growing demand for wood is likely to lead further increasing of forest area clear-cut, shorter rotation periods and greater use of exotic species. The trends are clearly worrying, because the increased area of tree plantations and natural reforestation cannot compensate for loss of natural forests, where natural disturbances are integral parts of the ecosystem dynamics.

The degradation in forest condition is of great concern and not only points to the need for policy and management reform, but also to utilise the full array of ecosystem services of forests. Europe's forests are becoming less natural, which makes them less resilient and more vulnerable to natural disturbances. This issue will be addressed through the Nature Restoration Plan, which the EU Biodiversity Strategy proposed as a new binding legislation. The plan is to be published by the end of 2021 as part of the EU's commitment to the UN Decade on Ecosystem Restoration and promoted as nature-based solution to the climate crises.

The challenges linked to forest biomass use for energy

The sustainability of production and whether or not bioenergy from forests should be considered as carbon zero RES is being widely questioned. According to a group of plaintiffs who took the EU to court, burning firewood should not be treated as renewable energy, because it is not a solution leading to meet the climate goals (eubiomasscase.org 2019).

NGOs also call on the EU and MSs to revisit the RED and remove primary forest biomass as an eligible renewable energy source. The campaign involves an online petition (WeMove 2021), has been signed by over 24,000 citizens as at 1 July 2021. The petition calls the attention of policymakers for the necessity to improve protection of forests in EU as a contribution to climate mitigation through protecting existing carbon stock and increasing carbon removal from the atmosphere. The protection of forest and removing forest wood from RED is said to contribute to the implementation of other important EU commitments beyond the climate target, namely the EU Green Deal and EU Biodiversity Strategy for 2030. According to the NGOs, the current regulation incentivises the burning of primary forest biomass, which results in increasing logging in the EU and beyond and eventually leads to degradation of forest health and resilience.

A key concept of the RED is that renewable energy supply must come from sustainable sources. Therefore, there were also sustainability criteria for biofuels established in the directive. The lack of sustainability criteria dealing with residential firewood use in the REDII must be specifically noted. The directive's sustainability criteria only apply above 20 MW energy output facilities. There are four points highlighted below as main challenges linked to the forest biomass use for energy:

1. Legal sourcing of forest biomass for energy linked to sustainability
2. The specific role and impact of residential firewood use
3. Data availability
4. Carbon neutrality

Sustainability and legality

A key element of sustainability is to ensure the legality of sourcing renewable energy. Illegal and inappropriately planned timber removals lead to degradation of forest ecosystems, which poses risks to both biodiversity protection and climate change mitigation. The current forest management practices in Europe involve overlogging, skidding damage to remaining trees and the soil, and a lack of replanting at critical sites. Despite potential negative effects on biodiversity the salvage logging, which typically follows natural disturbances, has become widespread across the continent (Thorn et al. 2017).

The REDII assumes that the EUTR, which aims to be properly enforced by the MSs and guarantees the legality of wood used for bioenergy. One of the measures of EUTR is indeed to prohibit placing illegally harvested timber or timber products including fuel wood on the internal market for the first time. However, the EU JRC (Cazzaniga et al. 2019) found clear evidence of significant underreporting of domestic timber removal in several countries.

The wood resource balance of the EU indicates about 12% of the wood coming from unaccounted sources, and this difference can unlikely be linked to either wood reuse or collecting forest residues by private households but suggests a significant underreporting of actual wood cut across the MSs.

The wood resource balance of the EU indicates about 12% of the wood comes from unaccounted for sources (Cazzaniga et al. 2019). It is unlikely that this can be linked to either wood reuse or collecting forest residues by private households but suggests a significant underreporting of actual wood cut across the MSs. JRC's report on the use of woody biomass for energy supports the NGOs' view of considering forest biomass as high-risk, because the document attributes the gap between reported uses and sources of woody biomass, which are mainly underestimated removals, largely to the energy sector (Camia et al. 2020). The document reported this removal under two different terms:

1. Unaccounted sources: amount of wood required to reach a perfect balance between sources and uses.
2. Unknown wood: woody biomass entering energy production from unknown sources.

The second term is clearly linked to the energy sector, while the first term might be divided between the two main wood use categories: material use (including wood pellet) and energy use. The report indicated an increasing volume and proportion of unaccounted and unknown wood in the sector between the period of 2009 and 2015. While the total unaccounted sources of wood increased in the seven-year period by 35.4%, the volume of unknown wood linked directly to energy use has increased even more, by 52.4% (see Table 11.2).

Table 11.2: The volume and proportion of unaccounted and unknown sources of wood in the EU wood resource balance between 2009 and 2015.

		2009	2010	2011	2012	2013	2014	2015	Volume increase %
Unaccounted sources of wood	1,000 m³	87,007	65,516	76,364	89,293	112,061	107,402	117,782	35.4%
	%		11.8%	8.3%	9.4%	10.7%	12.8%	12%	12.8%	
Unknown wood in energy sector	1,000 m³	41,247	48,255	45,021	47,596	60,965	63,529	62,864	52.4%
	%		5.6%	6.1%	5.6%	5.7%	7%	7.1%	6.8%	

Source: Cazzaniga et al. (2019).

Based on the above, EUTR does not seem to fulfil its main purpose, to prohibit placing illegally harvested timber on the EU market, which questions the overall sustainability of forest biomass sourcing for energy in the EU. Whether or not the fitness check of EUTR will lead to correcting the existing gaps in the legislation and its enforcement is yet to be revealed (EC 2020c).

The impact of firewood use in the residential sector

Based on the analysis of the EUTR biennial national reports, only two MSs paid special attention to issues linked to firewood (EC 2020b). The annual reports of the Austria and Hungary suggest that firewood use is high-risk due to illegal activity

As a consequence of the export ban for roundwood from Ukraine, Austria focussed its checks on products that were customs cleared under HS code 44,039 (wood in the rough) in Austria, but that had been exported under code 4,401 (fuel wood, in logs) or 4,407 (wood sawn or chipped lengthwise) from Ukraine. The responsible national authority also checked imports from EU candidate and potential candidate countries and high-risk imports with special focus on firewood (United Nations Environment Programme World Conservation Monitoring Centre 2018).

In 2016, Hungary focussed on the domestic firewood trade, because its internal stakeholder enquiry, which addressed forest managers, operators and owners, defined the firewood trade as the main driver of illegal logging (NÉBIH 2016). The annual report of the Hungarian CA admitted that the scale of illegal logging might be much higher than reported. NÉBIH's report is based on five primary statistical sources:
- The statistical information of NÉBIH (219 m³ wood was taken from illegal loggers)
- The criminal statistical record (average firewood stealing cases in 2016 and 2017)
- Forest Authorities of county administrative bodies (14,887 m³ wood stolen as average in 2016 and 2017)
- The Agriculture Ministry, based on the reports of state forest companies (5,655 m³ wood stolen from the state forest companies)
- National Wood Damage Registration System (the cases wood theft on average was 117)

Logging in those areas which fall under the jurisdiction of the national Forest Law, is only possible with the permission or at least advance information of the forestry authority. However, the implementation of permitted logging is monitored based on risk assessment and is hence incomplete. Only 10% of logged areas are actually checked through field visits annually, while the rest of harvested areas are checked randomly. During this monitoring, the volume of potential illegal logging is not recorded. Therefore, the CA assumes that the actual volume of illegal harvest is far bigger than the recorded 14,887 m³ in 2017 and wood theft is probably largely linked to residential fuelwood use (NÉBIH 2018b).

In conclusion, the experiences of National CAs and anecdotal stories suggest that the residential firewood market in the EU is not free from illegal activities, but tracking its exact scale is not possible, because of the nature of illegal logging. The biennial EUTR national reports also indicate that the National CAs lack the capacities to effectively carry out regular checks of the timber market on the national-level.

Data inaccuracy

Various evidence confirms that data linked to wood removal in the EU MSs are unreliable. The felling rates in Germany are based on different calculation approaches and the official felling statistics underestimate the actual rates considerably. In the years between 1995 to 2020 the mean underestimation was 15 million m^3 per year (ThünenInstitute 2020).

The National Forestry Accounting Plan of the Netherlands also admits underreporting of wood removal linked to fuelwood. Based on the knowledge about the underestimation of fuelwood harvested from the forest for the period 20032013, the plan considered the amount of fuelwood for the period 19902002 is likely an underestimate. The plan approximates the average amount of 399,000 m^3 wood fuel (under bark), which is 256,000 m^3 (279%) more compared to the reported amount of 143,000 m^3 (Arets and Schelhaas 2019).

Data inaccuracies are also notable for countries in the Carpathians mountain range, which is especially worrying as the Carpathian is considered as the last stronghold of temperate old-growth forests (World Wildlife Foundation 2014). Based on Eurostat Shares dataset, the use of primary solid biofuels for heating in Slovakia was between 15 and 20 peta joule (PJ) for the past decade. In 2019, the figure suddenly more than doubled the decade average from 17.7 PJ to 43.6 PJ, which indicates previous underreporting (Eurostat 2021).

A forest inventory commissioned by the Romanian government and leaked to the media last year showed that 20 million cubic metres of wood are cut illegally from the forests every year, while 19 million cubic metres are cut legally (Radio Free Europe 2020).

The anomalies in estimation of firewood use have also been reported from Hungary. The Regional Energy Research Centre's (REKK) Wood Market Analysis in 2009 found 45 times difference of residential firewood use between the calculation of the Hungarian National Statistical Office household survey and the forest harvesting data (Hungarian Regional Energy Centre 2009). According to the 2009 estimate, which became quasi-official with the recalculation of household firewood use in 2015, the illegally harvested wood was 33.5M m^3.

REKK's policy brief in 2017 highlighted that wood fuel use in residential heating increased massively when the survey approach changed from using forestry data to household survey (Mezősi, Pató, and Szabó 2017). See Table 11.3. This change of data reporting is based on the implementation of 431/2014 directive of the EU. The most interesting part of the report is the table, which showed similar increase not only in Hungary, but in seven additional EU MSs.

Based on the above evidence, the official data available on the Eurostat roundwood removal dataset are likely unreliable and there is significant under reporting of wood removal in several, if not all, EU MSs.

Table 11.3: Increase of residential firewood use in eight selected EU MSs after recalculation in 2015 based on the new reporting method.

Country	2011			Usage in 2015	
	Usage before recalculation, PJ	Usage after recalculation PJ	Difference %	Usage PJ	Increase compared to usage before recalculation %
Belgium	10	18	180%	21.8	118%
Croatia	16.1	48.3	300%	48.4	201%
Czech Republic	46.3	65.1	141%	73.4	59%
Hungary	30.3	76.2	251%	73.9	144%
Italy	146.3	190.6	130%	265.9	82%
Netherlands	12.5	17	136%	18.4	47%
Sweden*	25.9	49	189%	38.2	47%
UK	15	38.6	257%	67	347%

Source: Mezősi, Pató, and Szabó (2017). Reproduced with permission.
Note: The Swedish data is based on the 2010 figure.

Carbon impact of forest biomass burning

Even if the sourcing of forest biomass for energy is totally sustainable and legal, such sourcing is not the proxy for carbon neutrality. Unlike wood waste, harvesting additional wood just for burning is likely to increase carbon in the atmosphere for decades to centuries to come (Searchinger et al. 2018). Sustainable harvesting is not a solution for considering forest biomass as renewable.

A study commissioned by EC DG Clima found that the best outcome is to increase carbon stock in existing EU forests for GHG emission and removal in the EU-28, which increases the forest carbon sink over time to −340 Mt CO2e as of 2030 (Rüter et al. 2016). Another study commissioned by EC DG ENER concluded that deprioritisation of bioenergy consumption in the EU post 2020 achieves the biggest improvement for decarbonising the economy with total annual GHG emissions reductions by 3.4 Gt CO2e per annuum by 2050 (Matthews et al. 2015).

The European Academies Science Advisory Council (EASAC) have called the attention of policymakers to long carbon payback periods of forest biomass. EASAC stated (2018) that forest biomass burning could increase atmospheric CO_2 levels, putting Paris Agreement targets at risk. A Chatham House paper from 2017 also proposed not considering woody biomass for energy automatically as carbon neutral, because the combustion of woody biomass with the inclusion of its supply chain would emit more CO_2 and methane than the fossil fuels it replaces (Brack 2017).

Despite the repeated warning from the scientific sector and the findings of the EC's own studies, the EP, when adopting the revised RED on 13 November 2018, practically allowed countries, power plants and factories to claim that cutting down trees in order to burn them for energy fully qualifies as renewable energy (JRC: European Union Joint Research Centre 2019b). Sustainable harvesting is not equivalent to carbon neutrality, so – if forest biomass is not removed from RED – the sustainability criteria would be so strict that hardly any woody biomass could qualify.

Handling subsidies forest biomass for energy

Due to the current policy environment, firewood use for energy, including electricity, is expected to further increase in Europe (JRC 2019a), a trend which is fuelled by public subsidies. Environmental NGOs argue that subsidies contribute to the increasing volume of forest biomass burning, and eventually lead to creating a lucrative market for harvesting low-quality wood and burning stem wood. The EU Biodiversity Strategy for 2030 aims at minimising the use of whole trees for energy production from both domestic and imported sources (EC 2020a). Unfortunately, the term of whole tree is not defined in any legal document, so this statement drives further discussion about the ongoing recast of the REDD.

The removal of forest biomass from eligible RESs will practically mean that forest biomass will not be eligible for public subsidies, so the current subsidies could be reallocated to actions filling the gap in the energy mix. Natural Resources Defence Council (NRDC) commissioned an assessment of government subsidies and other forms of financial support offered to biomass energy producers in the 15 MSs (UK included) most heavily reliant on bioenergy. The report found only these 15 countries spent more than €18 billion to subsidise bioenergy production within the period of 2015 to 2017 (Smith, Smit, and Gardiner 2019). The analysed subsidies do not include energy and carbon tax exemptions. Carbon tax exemptions were excluded from the study because of the view by most tax offices that bioenergy is carbon neutral and therefore is exempt from carbon taxes levied on other fuels.

Decisions on reallocation of subsidies need to be underwritten with calculations addressing the various subsidies including those not included in the NRDC's assessment. First of all, the effectiveness and speed with which the forest bioenergy gap arising from subsidy removal, that likely leads to decreases in forest biomass energy production, could be filled by genuine alternative renewables, for given levels of subsidy reallocation.

Differential calculations should be made for different forms of energy by country and aggregated against an action plan timescale. Additional calculations should be made of the net impact from switching to genuine renewables, in terms of emissions saved for given levels of investment and energy output.

The respective industry representatives have much information, and it would be in their interests to cooperate in making this available and helping with calculations.

The relative role of nature-based solutions, especially carbon rich ecosystems, in emission reductions by habitat type, scale and conservation management must also be defined, because the subsidy reallocation might provide extra, and badly needed, finances for nature conservation activities. The net impact on emissions saved for given levels of funding can be cost-effective, from avoided habitat loss and increased sequestration to storage in different habitat situations.

This would give a guide to what are appropriate relative proportions of subsidy reallocation, but also needs to bear in mind the multiple benefits of nature-based solutions, which should attract higher levels of matched funding in their own right.

The relative cost-effectiveness of increased investment to reduce energy demand and emissions should initially focus should be on a set of relatively generalised macro calculations, with emphasis on individual illustrative examples. This would help inform an overall framework for subsidy reallocation and engagement of associated funding, drawing off existing information sources.

Industry representatives would, again, have an incentive to support these calculations. Collated calculations for return on investment (ROI) involving replacement of forest bioenergy, accounting for relative costs and increased net emission removals. These could be compared with current ROI scenarios for projected levels of forest bioenergy use.

In the case of subsidy reallocation, the actions filling the energy gap can include the following:

1. Supporting the penetration of remaining RESs into the total energy mix of the EU
2. Improving energy efficiency including insulation
3. Investing in energy storage capacities, which is high on the agenda for Horizon Europe (EC n.d.)
4. As a nature-based solution protecting carbon rich ecosystems including forest habitats across the EU, which guarantee the protection of current carbon stock and increase the carbon removal from the atmosphere

Key recommendations

The joint Intergovernmental Science-Policy Platform on Biodiversity and Ecosystem Services (IPBES) and Intergovernmental Panel on Climate Change (IPCC) workshop report pointed out that the biodiversity and climate crises are intertwined and the commitments to guarantee a habitable climate and preserving biodiversity are mutually beneficial goals (Pörtner et al. 2021). The five sections above are constructed along the concept of highlighting that climate actions are only credible if they also contribute to reaching biodiversity objectives. Promoting the increase of biomass harvesting in the EU's forests for questionable climate benefit results the degradation of forest resilience and blocks fulfilling biodiversity objectives.

Following the above logic, the recommendations of this chapter can be clustered in four larger groups: (a) further research requirements, (b) traceability of wood sources, (c) handling statistical data and monitoring, and (d) policy changes.

(a) Further research requirements
  – Further research is needed to investigate the exact scale of illegal logging linked to forest biomass burning with clear division of the various user groups (e.g., the residential sector).
  – While some of the recent reports, including the JRC's woody biomass for energy report, link the energy use to biodiversity outcomes, more research is needed on what exact impact the forest biomass use for energy has on habitats and species. In order to assess the impact of climate policy, special attention should be paid to tendencies since the adoption of RED.

(b) Traceability of wood sources
  – National reports for EUTR should look into the drivers and sources of illegal timber and what products are more likely to be illegal. National Competent Authorities (NCAs) must pay more attention to the residential fuelwood market in order to enforce EUTR.
  – NCAs should conduct a proper analysis of risk of illegality of sourcing forest biomass for energy.
  – The fuelwood market requires better control in order to reduce unaccounted wood entering the market and also to make consumers aware of their impact on biodiversity and protected areas through burning wood.

(c) Handling statistical data and monitoring
  – Statistical clarity is needed in relation to the various terminology.
  – Use of the same reporting format and terminology across the EU MSs.
  – Use of the same measurement, which would make the data comparable, so the EC can produce reports which actually support decision-making processes.

(d.1) Policy changes linked to energy
  – Although energy poverty still exists in the EU, national governments should not subsidise burning of forest biomass in the energy sector (including the residential sector), but support energy efficiency also at households, which would bring down the volume of wood use.
  – Policy development is needed to guarantee that it will not lead to illegal (or inappropriate) logging.
  – By removing forest biomass from RED, EU MSs must stop subsidising the burning of fuelwood as this practice provides a false solution to climate challenges and can lead to promoting illegal logging.
  – In supporting the proposal to establish 12M hectares of strict forest reserve (Nabuurs et al. 2017), the existing protected areas (national protected areas

as well as Natura 2000 sites) require more resources to stop illegal logging which might increase parallel with the increase of solid biomass use.

(d.2) Policy changes in relation to forests

- The EU Forest Strategy must establish priority actions which contribute to improving the ecosystem integrity and resilience of forests in the EU. These actions increase protection in order to improve the conservation status of forest habitats.
- For the benefits of forest to genuinely contribute to a greener economy – including the post-COVID-19 recovery – and a climate-neutral EU, the EU Forest Strategy must reflect the multiple benefits and the increasing societal concern about forests and recognise the full array of ecosystem services and benefits of forests.
- The consultation about the EU Forest Strategy must involve a wider range of sectoral actors than the traditional forest biomass-based industries.
- Clear statistical, EU-wide reporting is needed to differentiate between the various forest types from primary/old-growth forest, semi-natural forests to multi- or monoculture tree plantations.
- The EC and MSs must improve the consistency of reporting about the status and use of forests including the timber removal. This will help to decrease the current high volume of unaccounted sources within the EU Wood Resource Balances.
- Harmonised EU policies, including the EU Forest Strategy, should guarantee the protection and restoration of forests as a nature-based solution to the interrelated biodiversity and climate crises through lowering the economic pressure for forest biomass provisioning.
- Along with the EU Biodiversity Strategy for 2030, the EU Forest Strategy must recognise the shared policy competence on forests and contribute to an overall policy framework that guarantees improved protection and recovery of forest resilience across the EU and beyond.
- To reverse the worrying trends, the EU Forest Strategy must promote more resilient, functioning forest ecosystems by 2030, which can be attained through two strong interlinked elements:
  - 15% of the EU's forests need strict protection, including the immediate protection of primary and old-growth forests, with the concept of increased core protected areas surrounded by appropriate buffers that provide functional connectivity.
  - semi-natural forests under extractive forest management must have more biodiversity-friendly management practices delivering higher climate mitigation benefits.
- The new EU Forest Strategy must promote management practices that recognise strict protection with non-intervention also as a forest management choice delivering multiple benefits.

- The EU Forest Strategy must establish the framework for utilising payments for ecosystem services as an alternative to the direct market values.
Such a move will help to reward protection of carbon stocks for instance
in primary/old-growth forests, not only the gains from annual flows.
- The EU Forest Strategy must enforce legalising the MSs' wood resource balances and guarantee that the bioeconomy is not measured by the volume
of timber used in Europe but by the higher added value of the products.
This will contribute to securing more jobs, while protecting more forests.

References

Arets, Eric, and Mart-Jan Schelhaas.·2019. *National Forestry Accounting Plan, Submission of the
Forest Reference Level 2021-2025 for the Netherlands*, (Wageningen, The Netherlands: Dutch
Ministry of Agriculture, Nature and Food Quality), <https://english.rvo.nl/sites/default/files/
2019/12/National%20Forestry%20Accounting%20Plan.pdf> [Accessed 2 November 2021].
Barredo-Cano, Jose Ignacio, Cristina Brailescu, Anne Teller, Francesco Maria Sabatini, Achille Mauri,
and Klara Janouskova.·2021. *Mapping and Assessment of Primary and Old-Growth Forests in
Europe*, (Luxembourg: Publications Office of the European Union), <https://publications.jrc.ec.
europa.eu/repository/handle/JRC124671> [Accessed 2 November 2021].
Bertaglia, Marco, Pavel Milenov, Vincenzo Angileri, and Wim Devos.·2016. *Cropland and Grassland
Management Data Needs from Existing IACS Sources*, (Ispra, Italy: European Union),
<https://publications.jrc.ec.europa.eu/repository/handle/JRC102591> [Accessed 29 January 2022].
BEUC: The European Consumer Organisation. 2021. *Letter to MEPs*, <https://www.beuc.eu/publica
tions/beuc-x-2021-057_joint_letter_to_meps_on_eu_taxonomy_delegated_act.pdf> [Accessed
6 July 2021].
Booth, Mary S., and Ben Mitchell.·2020. *Paper Tiger – Why the EU's RED II Biomass Sustainability
Criteria Fail Forests and the Climate*, (Partnership for Policy Integrity), <http://eubiomasscase.
org/wp-content/uploads/2020/07/RED-II-biomass-Paper-Tiger-July-6-2020.pdf> [Accessed
16 July 2020].
Brack, Duncan.·2017. *Woody Biomass for Power and Heat Impacts on the Global Climate*, (London:
Chatham House), <https://www.chathamhouse.org/sites/default/files/publications/research/
2017-02-23-woody-biomass-global-climate-brack-final2.pdf> [Accessed 2 November 2021].
Camia, Andrea, Jacopo Giontoli, Klas Jonsson, Nicolas Robert, A Noemi Cazzaniga, Gediminas
Jasenivicius, Valerio Avitabile, Giacomo Grassi, Jose Ignacio Barredo Cano, and Sarah
Mubareka.·2020. *The Use of Woody Biomass for Energy Production in the EU*, (Luxembourg:
Publications Office of the European Union), <https://publications.jrc.ec.europa.eu/repository/
handle/JRC122719> [Accessed 2 November 2021].
Camia, Andrea, N. Robert, R. Jonsson, R. Pilli, S. García-Condado, R. López-Lozano, M. van der
Velde, T. Ronzon, P. Gurría, R. M'Barek, S. Tamosiunas, G. Fiore, R. Araujo, N. Hoepffner,
L. Marelli, and J. Giuntoli.·2018. *Biomass Production, Supply, Uses and Flows in the European
Union. First Results from an Integrated Assessment*, (Luxembourg: EU Joint Research Centre),
<https://publications.jrc.ec.europa.eu/repository/bitstream/JRC109869/jrc109869_biomass_
report_final2pdf2.pdf> [Accessed 2 November 2021].

Cazzaniga, N., K. Jonsson, R. Pilli, and A. Camia.·2019. *Wood Resource Balances of EU-28 and Member States*, (Luxembourg: Publications Office of the European Union), <https://publications.jrc.ec.eu ropa.eu/repository/handle/JRC114889> [Accessed 2 November 2021].

Ceccherini, Guido, Gregory Duveiller, Giacomo Grassi, Guido Lemoine, Valerio Avitabile, Roberto Pilli, and Alessandro Cescatti. 2020. 'Abrupt Increase in Harvested Forest Area over Europe after 2015', *Nature*, 583, 72–77.

Croation Presidency of the Council of the European Union. 2020. *Long-Term Low Greenhouse Gas Emission Development Strategy of the European Union and Its Member States*, <https://unfccc.int/sites/default/files/resource/HR-03-06-2020%20EU%20Submission% 20on%20Long%20term%20strategy.pdf> [Accessed 5 July 2021].

Environmental Paper Network. 2020. *Mapping the Biomass Industry*, <https://environmentalpaper. org/tools-and-resources/mapping-bioenergy/> [Accessed 18 July 2020].

EU, German Presidency of the Council of. 2020. *The Update of the Nationally Determined Contribution of the European Union and Its Member States*, (EU) <https://www4.unfccc.int/ sites/ndcstaging/PublishedDocuments/European%20Union%20First/EU_NDC_Submission_ December%202020.pdf> [Accessed 8 July 2021].

eubioenergy.com. *Most of Europe's Renewable Energy Is Bioenergy. That Means Burning a Lot of Biomass – but What Is Bioenergy Exactly?*, <https://www.eubioenergy.com/whatisbioenergy/> [Accessed 8 July 2020].

eubiomasscase.org. 2019. *EU Biomass Legal Case* <http://eubiomasscase.org> [Accessed 2 November 2021].

Euractiv 2021 'Europe's 'Fit for 55' Climate Package: What to Expect', (Euractive.com) <https://www. euractiv.com/section/energy-environment/news/europes-fit-for-55-climate-package-what-to- expect/> [Accessed 10 July 2021].

European Academies Science Advisory Council. 2018. *The EU's Renewable Energy Ambitions: Bioenergy from Forests Is Not Always Carbon Neutral – and May Even Increase the EU's Carbon Emissions* (EASAC), <https://easac.eu/fileadmin/PDF_s/reports_statements/Carbon_Neutrality/ EASAC_Press_Release_on_Carbon_Neutrality_15_June_2018.pdf> [Accessed 2 November 2021].

European Commission.·2013. *A New EU Forest Strategy: For Forests and the Forest-Based Sector*, <https://eur-lex.europa.eu/resource.html?uri=cellar:21b27c38-21fb-11e3-8d1c-01aa75ed71a1. 0022.01/DOC_1&format=PDF> [Accessed 8 July 2021].

——.·2020a. *EU Biodiversity Strategy for 2030*, (Brussels: European Commission), <https://ec.eu ropa.eu/info/sites/default/files/communication-annex-eu-biodiversity-strategy-2030_en.pdf> [Accessed 3 November 2021].

——. 2020b. *EUTR Reports and Reviews*, <https://ec.europa.eu/environment/forests/eutr_report. htm> [Accessed 21 June 2020].

——. 2020c. *Illegal Logging – Evaluation of EU Rules (Fitness Check)*, <https://ec.europa.eu/info/ law/better-regulation/have-your-say/initiatives/11630-Illegal-logging-evaluation-of-EU-rules- fitness-check-_en> [Accessed 2 November 2021].

——. 2020d. *National Energy and Climate Plans (NECPs)*, <https://ec.europa.eu/info/energy- climate-change-environment/implementation-eu-countries/energy-and-climate-governance- and-reporting/national-energy-and-climate-plans_en#final-necps> [Accessed 9 July 2021].

——. 2021. *Natura 2000 in a Nutshell*, <https://ec.europa.eu/environment/nature/natura2000/ index_en.htm> [Accessed 11 May 2021].

——. N d. *Horizon Europe Research and Innovation Grants*, <https://ec.europa.eu/info/funding- tenders/opportunities/portal/screen/how-to-participate/reference-documents> [Accessed 8 July 2021].

European Commission Directorate General Research and Innovation.·2018. *A Sustainable Bioeconomy for Europe: Strengthening the Connection between Economy, Society and the Environment*, DG

Research and Innovation (Luxembourg: Publications Office of the European Union), <https://op.
europa.eu/en/publication-detail/-/publication/edace3e3-e189-11e8-b690-01aa75ed71a1/
language-en/format-PDF/source-149755478≥

European Court of Justice. 1999. *Regulations on the Protection of Forests against Atmospheric
Pollution and Fire*, <https://eur-lex.europa.eu/legal-content/EN/TXT/PDF/?uri=CEL
EX:61997CJ0164_SUM&from=SK> [Accessed 2 November 2021].

European Environmental Agency. 2020a. *Forest Information System for Europe*, <https://forest.eea.
europa.eu> [Accessed 2 November 2021].

——. 2020b. *Share of Energy Consumption from Renewable Sources in Europe*, <https://www.eea.
europa.eu/ims/share-of-energy-consumption-from> [Accessed 18 July 2020].

——.·2020c. *State of Nature in the EU*, Results *from Reporting under the Nature* Directives *2013-
2018*, Report No 10/2020, (EEA), <https://www.eea.europa.eu/publications/state-of-nature-in-
the-eu-2020> [Accessed 12 May 2021].

European Parliament. 2020a. *The EU's Role in Protecting and Restoring the World's Forests*, P9_TA
(2020)0212 (European Parliament) <https://www.europarl.europa.eu/doceo/document/TA-9-
2020-0212_EN.pdf> [Accessed 3 November 2021].

——. 2020b. *The European Forest Strategy – the Way Forward*, <https://www.europarl.europa.eu/
doceo/document/TA-9-2020-0257_EN.html> [Accessed 9 October 2020].

——. N d. *Renewable Energy*, <https://www.europarl.europa.eu/factsheets/en/sheet/70/renew
able-energy> [Accessed 25 July 2020].

European Parliament and Council. 2018. *The Promotion of the Use of Energy from Renewable
Sources (Recast)*, DIRECTIVE (EU) 2018/2001 (European Union) <https://eur-lex.europa.eu/
legal-content/EN/TXT/?uri=uriserv:OJ.L_.2018.328.01.0082.01.ENG&toc=OJ:L:2018:328:TOC>
[Accessed 27 June 2021].

European Union. 1992. *Council Directive 92/43/EEC of 21 May 1992 on the Conservation of Natural
Habitats and of Wild Fauna and Flora*, (Council of the European Union) <https://eur-lex.eu
ropa.eu/legal-content/EN/TXT/?uri=CELEX:31992L0043> [Accessed 2 November 2021].

——. 2009a. *Directive 2009/28/EC of the European Parliament and of the Council of 23 April 2009
on the Promotion of the Use of Energy from Renewable Sources and Amending and
Subsequently Repealing Directives 2001/77/EC and 2003/30/EC*, (European Parliament and of
the Council) <https://eur-lex.europa.eu/legal-content/EN/ALL/?uri=CELEX%3A32009L0028>
[Accessed 2 November 2021].

——. 2009b. *Directive 2009/147/EC of the European Parliament and of the Council of
30 November 2009 on the Conservation of Wild Birds*, (European Commission) <https://eur-
lex.europa.eu/legal-content/EN/TXT/?uri=CELEX:32009L0147> [Accessed 2 November 2021].

——. 2010. *Regulation (EU) No 995/2010 of the European Parliament and of the Council of
20 October 2010 Laying Down the Obligations of Operators Who Place Timber and Timber
Products on the Market Text with EEA Relevance*, <https://eur-lex.europa.eu/legal-content/EN/
TXT/?uri=CELEX:32010R0995> [Accessed 2 November 2021].

——. 2013. *Decision No 529/2013/EU of the European Parliament and of the Council of 21 May 2013
on Accounting Rules on Greenhouse Gas Emissions and Removals Resulting from Activities
Relating to Land Use, Land-Use Change and Forestry and on Information Concerning Actions
Relating to Those Activities*, <https://eur-lex.europa.eu/legal-content/EN/TXT/?uri=celex%
3A32013D0529> [Accessed 8 July 2021].

——. 2020a. *Citizens' Summary EU Climate and Energy Package* (European Commission),
<https://ec.europa.eu/clima/system/files/2016-11/climate_package_en.pdf > [Accessed
18 July 2020].

——. 2020b. *Commission Delegated Regulation (EU) 2021/268*, (Official Journal of the European Union) <https://eur-lex.europa.eu/legal-content/EN/TXT/?uri=uriserv:OJ.L_.2021.060.01. 0021.01.ENG> [Accessed 8 July 2021].

——. 2020c. *Special Meeting of the European Council (17, 18, 19, 20 and 21 July 2020) – Conclusion*, <https://www.consilium.europa.eu/media/45109/210720-euco-final-conclusions-en.pdf> [Accessed 17 June 2021].

European Union Council. 2019. *Preparation of the Post-2020 Global Biodiversity Framework Convention on Biological Diversity (CBD) – Council Conclusion*, <https://www.consilium.eu ropa.eu/media/41924/st15272-en19.pdf> [Accessed 5 June 2021].

——. 2020a. *Council Conclusions on Perspectives for the EU Forest-Related Policies and EU Forest Strategy Post 2020*, <https://data.consilium.europa.eu/doc/document/ST-12695-2020-REV-1/ en/pdf> [Accessed 11 November 2020].

——. 2020b. *European Council Meeting (12 December 2019) – Conclusions*, <https://www.consi lium.europa.eu/media/41768/12-euco-final-conclusions-en.pdf> [Accessed 11 November 2020].

European Union Joint Research Centre. 2019a. *Brief on Biomass for Energy in the European Union*, <https://publications.jrc.ec.europa.eu/repository/bitstream/JRC109354/biomass_4_energy_ brief_online_1.pdf> [Accessed 30 July 2021].

——.·2019b. *Renewable Energy – Recast to 2030 (RED II)*, <https://ec.europa.eu/jrc/en/jec/renew able-energy-recast-2030-red-ii> [Accessed 30 July 2021].

Eurostat. 2013. *Manual for Statistics on Energy Consumption in Households*, p142. (Publications Office of the European Union)) <https://ec.europa.eu/eurostat/documents/3859598/ 5935825/KS-GQ-13-003-EN.PDF/baa96509-3f4b-4c7a-94dd-feb1a31c7291> [Accessed 8 July 2020]

——.·2021. *Shares Energy from Renewable Sources* <https://ec.europa.eu/eurostat/web/energy/ data/shares> [Accessed 8 July 2021].

Federal Ministry of Sustainability and Tourism Republic of Austria.·2019. *Integrated National Energy and Climate Plan for Austria 2021-2030 Pursuant to Regulation (EU) 2018/1999 of the European Parliament and of the Council on the Governance of the Energy Union and Climate Action*, (Vienna: Federal Ministry of Sustainability and Tourism Republic of Austria), <https://ec.europa.eu/energy/sites/ener/files/documents/at_final_necp_main_en.pdf> [Accessed 9 July 2021].

ForestEurope.·2020. *State of Europe's Forest*, (Bratislava: Forest Europe), <https://foresteurope. org/wp-content/uploads/2016/08/SoEF_2020.pdf> [Accessed 20 May 2021].

Hungarian Regional Energy Centre, REKK.·2009. *ErdéSzeti ES ÜLtetvéNy Eredetű FáS SzáRú Energetikai Biomassza MagyarorszáGon (Wood Market Analysis)*, https://rekk.hu/downloads/ projects/wp2009_5.pdf> [Accessed 29 October 2021].

Hungary National Food Chain Safety Office (NÉBIH). 2016. *Fighting against Illegal Logging with Timber Tracing*, <https://portal.nebih.gov.hu/-/faanyag-nyomon-kovetessel-az-illegalis-fakitermeles-ellen> [Accessed 29 October 2021].

——. 2018a. *Proposal to Improve the Implementation of EUTR*.

——.·2018b. *Summary of the Statistical Data of 2016-2017 About the Risk of Illegal Timber Harvesting and of the Implementation of Monitoring the Chain of Custody of Timber Trading in 2017*, <https://24d837a9-2fc9-cc62-72a3-c3c7d9956461 (gov.hu)> [Accessed 29 October 2021].

Korhonen, Kari T. 2020 'A New Article in the Journal Nature Overestimates the Increase of Forest Harvesting in Europe' *Luke Natural Resources Finland* <https://www.luke.fi/en/blog/a-new-article-in-the-journal-nature-overestimates-the-increase-of-forest-harvesting-in-europe/> [Accessed 30 July 2020]

Latvian Presidency of the Council of the EU. 2015. *Intended Nationally Determined Contribution of the EU and Its Member States*, (EU) <https://www4.unfccc.int/sites/ndcstaging/PublishedDo cuments/European%20Union%20First/LV-03-06-EU%20INDC(Archived).pdf> [Accessed 8 July 2021].

Lindroos, Ola. 2011. 'Residential Use of Firewood in Northern Sweden and Its Influence on Forest Biomass Resources', *Biomass and Bioenergy*, 35 (1), 385–90.

Maes, Joachim, Anne Teller, Markus Erhard, Sophie Conde, Sara Vallecillo Rodriguez, Jose Ignacio Barredo Cano, Maria-Luisa Paracchini, Dania Abdul Malak, Marco Trombetti, Olga Vigiak, Grazia Zulian, Anna Addamo, Bruna Grizzetti, Francesca Somma, Andrea Hagyo, Peter Vogt, Chiara Polce, Arwyn Jones, Ana Marin, Eva Ivits, Mauri Achille, Carlo Rega, Balint Czuch, Guido Ceccherini, Enrico Pisoni, Andrej Ceglar, Pierluca De Palma, Iacopo Cerrani, Michele Meroni, Giovanni Caudullo, Emanuele Lugato, Juergen Vogt, Jonathan Spinoni, Carmelo Cammalleri, Annemarie Bastrup-Birk, Jesus San-Miguel-Ayanz, Sonsoles San Roman, Peter Kristensen, Trine Chiristiansen, Nihal Zal, Arie De Roo, Ana De Jesus Cardoso, Alberto Pistocchi, Irene DelBarrio Alvarellos, Konstantinos Tsiamis, Eugenio Gervasini, Ivan Deriu, Alessandra La Notte, Vinas Abad, Raúl, Matteo Vlizzarri, Andrea Camia, Nicolas Robert, Georgia Kakoulaki, Eduardo Garcia Bendito, Panagiotis Panagos, Cristiano Ballabio, Simone Scarpa, Luca Montanarella, Alberto Orgiazzi, Oihane Fernandez Ugalde, and Fernando Santos-Martin.·2020. *Mapping and Assessment of Ecosystems and Their Services: An EU Ecosystem Assessment*, (Ispra, Italy: EU Joint Research Centre), <https://publications.jrc.ec.europa.eu/repository/han dle/JRC120383> [Accessed 29 Janaury 2022].

Matthews, Robert, Nigel Mortimer, Jan Peter Lesschen, Tomi J Lindroos, Laura Sokka, Allison Morris, Paul Henshall, Charlotte Hatto, Onesmus Mwabonje, Jeremy Rix, Ewan Mackie, and Marc Sayce.·2015. *Carbon Impacts of Biomass Consumed in the EU: Quantitative Assessment*, (Farnham, UK: Forest Research), <https://ec.europa.eu/energy/sites/ener/files/documents/ EU%20Carbon%20Impacts%20of%20Biomass%20Consumed%20in%20the%20EU%20final. pdf> [Accessed 29 January 2022].

Mezősi, András, Zsuzsanna Pató, and László Szabó.·2017. *Meg-Megújuló Statisztikák*, (Budapest: Regionális Energia- és Infrastruktúra-politikai Együttműködésért Alapítvány), <https://rekk. hu/downloads/academic_publications/rekk_policybrief_hu_2017_01.pdf> [Accessed 2 November 2021].

Nabuurs, Gert-Jan, Philippe Delacote, David Ellison, Marc Hanewinkel, Lauri Hetemäki, and Marcus Lindner. 2017. 'By 2050 the Mitigation Effects of EU Forests Could Nearly Double through Climate Smart Forestry', *MDPI Forests*, 8 (12), 484.

Partnership for Policy Integrity. 2022. *Challenging Greenwashing, NGOs Take Aim at Sweeping EU Finance Policy*, <https://www.pfpi.net/eutaxonomychallenge> [Accessed 5 February 2022].

Pörtner, Hans-Otto, Robert J. Scholes, John Agard, Emma Archer, Almut Arneth, Xuemei Bai, David Barnes, Michael Burrows, Lena Chan, Cheung Wai Lung (William), Sarah Diamond, Camila Donatti, Carlos Duarte, Nico Eisenhauer, Wendy Foden, Maria A. Gasalla, Collins Handa, Thomas Hickler, Ove Hoegh-Guldberg, Kazuhito Ichii, Ute Jacob, Gregory Insarov, Wolfgang Kiessling, Paul Leadley, Rik Leemans, Lisa Levin, Michelle Lim, Shobha Maharaj, Shunsuke Managi, Pablo A. Marquet, Pamela McElwee, Guy Midgley, Thierry Oberdorff, David Obura, Balgis Osman Elasha, Ram Pandit, Unai Pascual, Aliny P. F. Pires, Alexander Popp, Victoria Reyes-García, Mahesh Sankaran, Josef Settele, Yunne-Jai Shin, Dejene W. Sintayehu, Peter Smith, Nadja Steiner, Bernardo Strassburg, Raman Sukumar, Christopher Trisos, Adalberto Luis Val, Jianguo Wu, Edvin Aldrian, Camille Parmesan, Ramon Pichs-Madruga, Debra C. Roberts, Alex D. Rogers, Sandra Díaz, Markus Fischer, Shizuka Hashimoto, Sandra Lavorel, Ning Wu, and Hien Ngo.·2021. *Scientific Outcome of the IPBES-IPCC Co-Sponsored Workshop on Biodiversity and Climate Change*, (IPBES secretariat), <https://zenodo.org/record/5031995#.YOcTXhMzY_V> [Accessed 29 October 2021].

Radio Free Europe. 2020. 'EU Warns Romania over Illegal Logging', *Radio Free Europe*, 3 November 2021. <https://www.rferl.org/a/eu-warns-romania-over-illegal-logging/30431181. html> [Accessed 29 October 2022].

Ranius, Thomas, Aino Hämäläinen, Gustaf Egnell, Bengt Olsson, Karin Eklöf, Johan Stendahl, Jörgen Rudolphi, Anna Sténs, and Adam Felton. 2018. 'The Effects of Logging Residue Extraction for Energy on Ecosystem Services and Biodiversity: A Synthesis', *Journal of Environmental Management*, 209, 409–25.

Rogers, Peter. 1990. 'Climate Change and Global Warming: A New Role for Science in Decision Making', *Environmental Science and Technology*, 24 (4), 428–30.

Rüter, Sebastian, Anne-Laure Levet, Nicklas Forsell, Christopher Prins, Frank Werner, and Estelle Vial. 2016. *Climwood2030 Climate Benefits of Material Substitution by Forest Biomass and Harvested Wood Products, Perspective 2030: Final Report*, (Thünen Institute), <https://op.eu ropa.eu/en/publication-detail/-/publication/993ecb81-2e54-11e8-b5fe-01aa75ed71a1> [Accessed 29 October 2021].

Searchinger, Timothy D., Tim Beringer, Bjart Holtsmark, Daniel M. Kammen, Eric F. Lambin, Wolfgang Lucht, Peter Raven, and Jean-Pascal van Ypersele. 2018. 'Europe's Renewable Energy Directive Poised to Harm Global Forests', *Nature Communications*, 9 (1), 1–4.

Smith, Matthew, Tycho Smit, and Ann Gardiner. 2019. *Financial Support for Electricity Generation and CHP from Solid Biomass*, (Rotterdam, The Netherlands: Trinomics), <https://www.nrdc. org/sites/default/files/burnout-eu-clean-energy-policies-forest-destruction-ip.pdf> [Accessed 29 October 2021].

Smith, Matthew, Anna Kralli, Peter Lemoine. 2021. Analysis on biomass in National Energy and Climate Plans , available at: https://www.fern.org/fileadmin/uploads/fern/Documents/2021/ Fern_-_Biomass_in_NECPs_-_Final_report.pdf [Accessed 06/07/2022]

Swedish Forest Agency. 2020. *Forest Harvesting Development in Sweden*, <https://www.skogsstyr elsen.se/globalassets/statistik/bruttoavverkning/forest-harvesting-development-in-sweden. pdf:https://www.skogsstyrelsen.se/globalassets/statistik/bruttoavverkning/forest-harvesting-development-in-sweden.pdf> [Accessed 29 October 2021].

The German Presidency of the Council of the Eurpean Union. 2020. *The Update of the Nationally Determined Contribution of the European Union and Its Member States*, <https://www4. unfccc.int/sites/ndcstaging/PublishedDocuments/European%20Union%20First/EU_NDC_Sub mission_December%202020.pdf> [Accessed 5 June 2021].

Thorn, Simon, Claus Bässler, Roland Brandl, Philip J. Burton, Rebecca Cahall, John L. Campbell, Jorge Castro, Chang-Yong Choi, Tyler Cobb, Daniel C. Donato, Ewa Durska, Joseph B. Fontaine, Sylvie Gauthier, Christian Hebert, Torsten Hothorn, Richard L. Hutto, Eun-Jae Lee, Alexandro B. Leverkus, David B. Lindenmayer, Martin K. Obrist, Josep Rost, Sebastian Seibold, Rupert Seidl, Dominik Thom, Kaysandra Waldron, Beat Wermelinger, Maria-Barbara Winter, Michal Zmihorski, and Jörg Müller. 2017. 'Impacts of Salvage Logging on Biodiversity: A Meta-Analysis', *Journal of Applied Ecology*, 55 (1), 279–89.

ThünenInstitute. 2020. *Fellings and Use of Roundwood*, <https://www.thuenen.de/en/wf/figures-facts/fellings-and-roundwood-use/> [Accessed 29 January 2022].

Trinomics, 2021, Analysis on biomass in National Energy and Climate Plans, available at: https://www.fern.org/fileadmin/uploads/fern/Documents/2021/Fern_-_Biomass_in_ NECPs_-_Final_report.pdf (accessed 13/06/2022).

United Nations Environment Programme World Conservation Monitoring Centre. 2018. *Background Analysis of the 2015-2017 National Biennial Reports on the Implementation of the European Union's Timber Regulation (Regulation Eu No 995/2010)*, (Cambridge, UK: UNEP-WCMC), <https://ec.europa.eu/environment/forests/pdf/WCMC%20EUTR%20analysis%202017.pdf> [Accessed 29 October 2021].

United Nations Framework Convention on Climate Change. *Land Use, Land-Use Change and Forestry*, <https://unfccc.int/topics/land-use/workstreams/land-use–land-use-change-and-forestry-lulucf> [Accessed 2 November 2021].

——. 1992. *UN Framework Convention on Climate Change*, <https://unfccc.int/process-and-meetings/the-convention/what-is-the-united-nations-framework-convention-on-climate-change> [Accessed 8 July 2021].

United Nations Framework Convention on Climate Change (UNFCCC). 1997. *Kyoto Protocol Website*, <https://unfccc.int/kyoto_protocol> [Accessed 8 July 2021].

——. 2015. *Paris Agreement* <https://unfccc.int/process-and-meetings/the-paris-agreement/the-paris-agreement> [Accessed 8 July 2021].

WeMove. 2021. *Online Petition*, <https://you.wemove.eu/campaigns/the-eu-must-protect-forests-not-burn-them-for-energy> [Accessed 1 July 2021].

World Wildlife Foundation.·2014. *Preserving Carpathian Old Growth Forests*, <https://d2ouvy59p0dg6k.cloudfront.net/downloads/wwf_factsheet_carpathian_old_growth_forests_sep2014.pdf> [Accessed 2 November 2021].

Part 3: **Private finance**

Tapan Sarker and Timothy Cadman

Chapter 12
Private finance for sustainable development

Abstract: Private financing is an important aspect of sustainable finance for economic development and financial inclusion. Various forms of private sector financing need to be mobilised to achieve environmentally or socially sustainable outcomes as well as the United Nations' Sustainable Development Goals (SDGs). Strategically leveraging public finance through systemic change and stimulating private investment are both necessary to achieve a paradigm shift in the global economy (Clark, Reed, and Sunderland 2018). In the absence of the private sector progress will remain insufficient. A wide variety of impediments to incentivising private sector engagement persists. For private finance to make a positive contribution, fundamental systemic modifications and policy reforms are required to ensure that sustainable socioeconomic development happens within planetary boundaries (Steffen et al. 2015). This chapter consequently explores the unlocking of private sector finance to fulfil sustainability goals. However, not all is well in the private realm. Green bonds, while an innovative vehicle for investment, are problematic and wealth generation continues to be propped up by extreme poverty at the base of the economic pyramid. While new technologies, such as blockchain, offer a way forward for those at the base, progress will be limited unless and until the activities of all sectors are recognised and valued to the same extent as business as society emerges from the COVID-19 pandemic.

Keywords: artificial intelligence, base of the economic pyramid, green bonds, informal economy, private finance, voluntary sector, COVID-19

Background: Private finance and its role in achieving sustainability

The private financial sector is in control of significant power and resources to direct finance towards economic wealth creation that can meet public interest needs for long-term sustainability and social wellbeing. Mobilisation of economic and corporate constituents takes place within certain boundaries, national and institutional structures in the system of financial regulation and corporate law. The European Union (EU) mainstreaming agenda in sustainable finance, for instance, aims for ambitious outcomes, resulting from the simultaneous reorientation of investors as well as their investee companies and the prioritising of sustainable objectives. Private enterprises can optimise stakeholder' wealth, socioenvironmental responsibility and

https://doi.org/10.1515/9783110733488-012

fulfilment of SDGs (Chiu 2021). The private sector has thus been set the challenge of responding positively in support of the SDGs while at the same time acting in the interests of its stakeholders (Wynn and Jones 2020).

Corporate sustainability has become an increasingly important business imperative and if companies make contributions meaningfully to the SDGs, they will certainly need to integrate their achievements into their reporting processes. Corporations can be affected by resource constraints and may lack the managerial or structural capacity to respond to the sustainability challenges (Przychodzen and Przychodzen 2018). However, strategic innovations by corporations can develop a culture that may internalise new sustainability challenges positively and effectively (Fellnhofer 2017). Further, organisations can be externally influenced by stakeholder perceptions, industry trends and network collaborations in determining strategic and operational reforms to meet sustainability challenges (Frishammar and Parida 2019). A diverse approach and deliberate policy leadership can help achieve sustainability objectives effectively (Dudfield 2019).

The private sector is both a potential partner and key player and can contribute to development objectives in multiple ways for the achievement of the SDGs, such as stimulating healthy habits and job creation, providing investment opportunities and sharing the resources and knowledge required to shape innovative solutions to global" challenges (Killick and Wachenfeld 2015). Castro (2004) sought to lay the foundations for a more radical theory of sustainability by questioning the very possibility of sustainable development under neoliberalism and arguing that economic growth" relies upon the continuing and inevitable exploitation of both natural and social capital. These potentially irreconcilable objectives have resulted in trade-offs that may ultimately compromise environmental protection (Bernstein 2001). This has led to calls for a reorientation of capitalism", with an emphasis on quality, rather than quantity, a shift, which it is argued, is underway, but continually challenged by the dominance of the single bottom line ideology of profit maximisation and cost-externalisation (Cadman, Eastwood, et al. 2015).

Competition between varieties of capitalism notwithstanding, the SDGs have given new impetus to sustainability with a shift from viewing sustainability as a cost centre to recognising it as an opportunity (Clark, Reed, and Sunderland 2018). Private investment flows in this context may require public sector interventions and support. As in many nations, public sector resources are scarce and spread across many competing commitments, they need to be used judiciously and strategically to leverage sufficient private flows. At the same time, the involvement of the business community in the Millennium Development Goals was limited as they were aimed at emerging countries. However, with the arrival of the SDGs, sustainability is gradually shifting from the corporate sidelines into the mainstream (PricewaterhouseCoopers 2015).

The SDGs can be productively incorporated into business strategy and operations. Companies need to emphasise the importance of the creativity, strategic skills and global reach they bring to the SDGs and the continuing need to integrate the SDGs into corporate management strategies (Wynn and Jones 2020). Those that embrace the challenge to decarbonise their manufacturing operations, whether in response to regulation (or the threat of regulation) or market opportunities, invariably discover ways to improve their operations in the process. These discoveries can potentially enhance a company's ability to produce better products, through redesign, efficiency gains, as well as improved manufacturing processes. In doing so, a company can transform itself and reshape its industry sector (Hart 2013).

Ceres (2016), in proposing a roadmap for sustainability, suggested that the financial services sector also plays a key role in promoting sustainable financing and in supporting the move to a sustainable economy, via its influence on capital across global markets. Few financial services companies have demonstrated their commitment to sustainability. The challenge for today's financial businesses is to address sustainability in such a way that they meet the current and future expectations of their customers, employees, communities and the environment, across both the public and private sectors (Garetti and Taisch 2012). Companies within the financial services sector have begun to publicly report on how they plan to address a range of environmental, social and governance (ESG) challenges (Cadman 2011; Cadman 2012). Other companies, however, seem to be slow to commit themselves publicly to such targets as those contained within the SDGs.

Another important sector for private financing whose contribution to sustainable development is essential is the information and technology sector. Information and communications technologies are playing a significant role in facilitating the SDGs and this role undoubtedly gets greater approaching 2030. In addition, the outbreak of COVID-19 has provided an expanded role for Information and communications technology (ICT) in the economy. Unfortunately, the role of ICT in achieving the SDGs was largely overlooked by policymakers in the formulation of the SDGs (Unwin 2015) and is not mentioned in any of the 17 SDGs and only four of the 169 targets. Sachs et al. (2015) demonstrated the potential of ICT to drive progress on the SDGs in four major areas namely, financial services, education, health and energy and climate change. The ICT industry sees the SDGs as a major new business opportunity but the role and the impact of the ICT industry in contributing to the SDGs differ in various parts of the world (Wynn and Jones 2020). Nonetheless, ICTs are evolving in developing countries from being specialist tools to day-to-day utilities, with digital mediation emerging as the dominant mechanism for economic, political and cultural development, via distributed ledger technologies, electronic contracts and blockchain, to name but a few examples.

There are several examples of previously unsustainable private sector industries embracing sustainability objectives. The automotive sector has gradually incorporated SDGs into its business strategy and operations and developed evolving sustainability strategies. Petroleum or diesel engine-operated motor vehicles are being replaced by automated driving and electrification, transforming engine efficiency. Fuel efficiency regulations in countries like Japan and the United States are lending further impetus to change. Japanese automobile manufacturers are now leading actors in manufacturing fuel-efficient vehicles. Net-zero carbon power systems require yet further technological innovation and low-carbon fuels such as hydrogen are also becoming increasingly available, although more are needed (International Energy Agency 2020). It is not easy to eliminate emissions from specific subsectors and engage with consumers to ensure public acceptance and energy affordability at the same time. Total CO_2 emissions would need to fall by around 45% from 2010 levels by 2030. In addition, since 2020, due to the pandemic, there have been declines in global energy demand, energy-related CO_2 emissions, energy investment, oil as well as oil and coal consumption. Renewables, on the other hand, have been less affected than other fuels (International Energy Agency 2020) – an unforeseen transformative impact of COVID-19.

Similarly, the tourism industry can play a major role in contributing to the SDGs to promote a healthy environment (see Chapter Twenty-Four). Even the marketing and media industries have identified the importance to accommodate, if not yet fully embracing sustainability (Wynn and Jones 2020). Furthermore, the transition to a sustainable new principle has become a burgeoning advertising theme in the marketing and media industries and a new wave of creative agencies and practitioners has arisen in a time when the global advertising industry has encountered increasing criticism for promoting unsustainable consumerism (Mokoena et al. 2021). Pharmaceutical companies, according to Wynn and Jones (2020), have also adopted a more inclusive approach to the SDGs, recognising the value and need for partnerships. Eccles (2018) has suggested that the biotechnological and pharmaceutical industries are particularly important for progressing many of the SDGs, although a substantial variation in SDGs is observed within the healthcare sector, especially in developing countries. Antimicrobial resistance to drugs has also increased in recent years, increasing the significance of the pharmaceutical industry in advancing SDG3 (good health and wellbeing).

Retailers are the major actors between primary producers and consumers. These intermediaries also play a vital role in promoting more sustainable patterns of consumption. In Europe, the European Commission (2022) has recognised that retailers are in a singularly powerful position to drive sustainable consumption through their daily interactions with consumers and their partnerships with suppliers. The energy industry is in a similar position to contribute to the SDGs, although there are some tensions between immediate shareholder value and more altruistic aspirations. Wynn and Jones (2020) have noted that whatever companies might state regarding their alignment to SDGs, contradictions between their intent, action and impact remain.

In summary, meeting the SDGs can only be achieved if the private sector works alongside national governments, the United Nations system and other international institutions. It is often difficult for a single company or any single sector or industry alone to deliver a low-carbon future. Everyone, from consumers to corporations to governments, needs to take responsibility. Even a challenge as complex as climate change can be met and addressed if private sector works collectively (Hart 2013).

Shared value model and agency theory on sustainable behaviour of private institutions

Shared value can be understood as those corporate policies and practices that stimulate the competitiveness of a company while simultaneously enhancing socioeconomic conditions in the communities where it operates (Kramer and Porter 2011). This concept is important since businesses are continually having to defend themselves from the economic, social and environment-related claims and objections of stakeholders and shareholders (Steurer et al. 2005). Maintaining good stakeholder relations is an essential element of corporate practice, while sustainability itself is should be seen as making an important contribution to stakeholder theory (Wheeler, Colbert, and Freeman 2002). There are some weaknesses and shortcomings in the shared value model, however, as it can overlook the tensions between social and economic goals and does not always take into account business compliance challenges. It is also difficult to portray corporate responses concerning environmental and social problems as arising solely from good stakeholder relations, but rather as a consequence of continuous struggles between corporate bodies and their stakeholders (Crane et al. 2014). Whatever the cause, or origin, of corporate behaviour change, it is encouraging to see the greening of business practice at all levels, from the regional to the global, from certifying timber to emissions trading (Cadman and Hume 2012; Cadman, Hume, et al. 2015).

The use of executive stock options has long been encouraged by economists as a means of aligning the interests of managers with those of the firm's shareholder (Hirshleifer and Suh 1992; Hemmer, Kim, and Verrecchia 1999) and could be equally applied to changing sustainability-related behaviour. A large fraction of these remuneration packages come in the form of equity-based pay (van der Zee 2012). Equity-based compensation aligns the interests of managers with those of the shareholders. Agency theory argues that the outcome of a firm is visible on the observable indicators of performance (Holmström 1979). Agency problems arise when the interests of managers differ substantially from those of shareholders. It is impossible to build every action a manager should take in every possible scenario into their contract, so shareholders delegate some decision-making authority to the manager. However, the actions of managers cannot be judged and need not always be in the best interest of the shareholders, as managers are also rational human beings. Agency theory predicts that the interests of shareholders and managers will become more aligned when an executive's compensation package is linked to firm performance (Jensen and

Meckling 1976). Few studies disagree with the significant positive relationship between executive compensation and firm performance. When managers alter the payment setting process the relationship between executive pay and performance can be weakened (Bebchuk and Fried 2003). Consequently, building sustainability into contractual obligations and binding it to executive performance and remuneration methods could play a significant role in enhancing private sector support for, and implementation of, the SDGs.

Role of government policy in supporting private finance for sustainable development and technology

Continuing robust policy support is critical to achieving the levels of adoption necessary to successfully address SDGs. Market forces will not support technology adoption at the scale needed in the absence of policies to support private sector development, resulting in market failure. By providing a policy framework supportive of innovation and by removing barriers, the government has considerable leverage to encourage the private sector to deploy essential capital and technical capacity to scale up the economy. Leveraging private sector finance provides a good initial indication of the strength of the sustainability-related market signals, and the adaptability and potential effectiveness of sustainability policies. Policies that provide permanent and continuous incentives on an economy-wide basis, exert stronger leverage, as opposed to those which provide a temporary incentive or affect a limited segment of the economy. For example, a one-time grant to a specific firm favours that particular firm and does not provide an incentive for multiple actors within an industry. In contrast, a carbon tax applied economy-wide incentivises all firms to reduce emissions.

Governments should therefore adopt policies that complement desirable business characteristics, particularly regarding new technologies for combatting human-caused environmental problems such as climate change, desertification and deforestation. The EU and China have both set aggressive goals for increasing renewable energy and the adoption of clean energy technologies, which are supported by legislation providing financial incentives (Hart 2013). The EU has adopted ambitious new targets to curb climate change, with a pledge to make them legally binding. Under a new law agreed between Member States and the EU Parliament, the bloc will cut carbon emissions by at least 55% by 2030, compared with 1990 levels (BBC 2021). Despite being the world's biggest emitter, China is the biggest energy financier and biggest market, so its decisions play a major role in shaping how the rest of the world progresses with its transition away from the fossil fuels that are threatening the world climate. China has introduced various policies which aim to hit peak emissions before 2030 and for carbon neutrality by 2060. The current technological shift from the research and development stage toward commercialisation will require a change in the types of policies governments create to finance technological development. Ultimately, while it is the government" that makes these policy settings, it is the private sector that must implement them.

There have been multiple – albeit highly fragmented – efforts that ought to instil some optimism within the financial system that public and private initiatives are arising to help businesses transition to a sustainable footing. The Alliance for Financial Inclusion, the Green Infrastructure Investment Coalition, the Principles for Responsible Investment, the Principles for Sustainable Insurance, the Sustainable Banking Network, the Green Bond Principles, the Sustainable Stock Exchanges Initiative and the United Nations Environment Programme Finance Initiative, are just some of a few examples of standards for corporate responsibility (Hart 2013; Waddock 2008; Cadman and Maraseni 2014). However, the fragmented nature of these actions only further perpetuates the disconnect between various industries, even within the same sector, as well as current policy and legislation (Clark, Reed, and Sunderland 2018). The focus of international discourse and policy discussions should therefore make efforts to tap into private capital to address root causes creating current conditions that incentivise resource depletion and fail to recognise the true economicc value of natural capital.

Overview of chapters

Tackling the conditions that have resulted in economic systems incompatible with Earth systems could address the catastrophic implications of the current business-as-usual trajectory – although this is an extremely difficult endeavour, particularly in developing countries with weak political environments. In their chapter 'Green bonds: at the crossroads between finance, law, environment, and society' Tomaso Ferrando and colleagues investigate one of the latest financial instruments set to occupy an increasing role in financing the transition towards a green economy. Green Bonds (also referred to in Chapter One) are a new form of raising debt and are increasingly being promoted throughout the world as a low-cost and appealing way for public and private actors to access liquidity to finance activities or projects that contribute to climate change mitigation and adaptation (see Part 4 for a closer examination of climate finance). The more recent popularity of green bonds is exemplified by the central role attributed to them in the European Green Deal and by the establishment of a European taxonomy and standards (see Chapter Two), which aim to define the boundaries of what can be considered a green bond and thus provide investors and borrowers with a recognition of their commitment to greening the economy. In addition to the escalating climate emergency, the COVID-19 pandemic and the ensuing global recession have heightened mainstream political, academic and business interest in the role of private finance for green growth.

Green bonds are not only popular at the European level, but they are also increasingly issued by public and private actors in the Global South. At the crossroad between law, finance, society, and the environment, green bonds raise important questions about the consequences of adapting mainstream financial responses, that is, debt, to address the ongoing ecological crisis. Although still representing a small fraction of the global debt market, green bonds have experienced exponential growth with a significant diversification of issuers, relying mainly on financial arguments regarding the existence of a *greenium*: those who issue green bonds and those who invest in green bonds. As debt instruments whose proceeds are previously earmarked to environmentally beneficial projects, one central dimension of green bonds is the regulation of eligible green assets, with relevant standards being set at a transnational, private, self-regulatory level that, nonetheless, does not and should not forego public involvement. The background activity that precedes the landing of global standards in local contexts is important, as are the institutional aspects associated with the creation and expansion of green bonds, such as taxation.

Using concrete examples, the authors discuss the ways in which green bonds operate on the ground and the problems that can arise when local players (public or private) borrow green capital from the market in an unequal global economy and a context of intense political and environmental contestation. This bottom-up approach to the real life of green bonds is used to flag existing gaps in the scholarly discourse and to suggest that researchers pay more attention to green debt as a mechanism to financ the transition to a greener economy. The authors conclude that there are both possibilities and limits to relying on green bonds for the construction of a green and just future. In an attempt to counterbalance mainstream literature that praises almost any intervention that contributes to action on climate change, they explicitly question the role of the financial sector in supporting decarbonisation and the forms of debt instruments used.

Chris Dembek and Jodi York in their chapter 'Investing in sustainable business models at the base of the pyramid' explain how the SDGs were developed collaboratively by diverse stakeholders to secure a better, more sustainable future for everyone. The SDGs present sustainable development as the ability to meet basic human needs, while maintaining natural capital and slowing climate change – and these form the basis to empowering stakeholders in their implementation of the goals overall. The authors note that progress in one aspect of sustainable development, should it come at the expense of another, is temporary and illusory. The current unsustainable production and consumption patterns of wealthy countries are propped up by extreme poverty at the base of the economic pyramid (BoP), which forces people to make short-term, survival-based decisions with profoundly negative long-term environmental consequences to meet their basic needs. Post-COVID, the reinforcing cycle of extreme poverty and environmental degradation will only accelerate unless BoP business models take an innovative approach to facing the challenge.

Business models have long been a powerful tool for harnessing enterprise as an engine for poverty alleviation and will continue to do so in a green post-COVID recovery. Now more than ever, investments made to address extreme poverty through private enterprise must be made to embed environmental sustainability and climate resilience rather than simply reinforcing unsustainable patterns. For some years, private companies of all sizes have sought to develop business models that create shared or mutual value by generating profits while engaging the BoP as suppliers or employees. More recently development finance institutions have been directly supporting enterprises in developing countries through various initiatives and these approaches have often failed to deliver their intended outcomes, sometimes even creating significant harm for those they purported to help. This is because traditional short-term profit maximisation rarely addresses the underlying causes of poverty but has a high likelihood of reinforcing unsustainable development and environmental pollution that will disproportionately affect poor communities.

Responding to the need to promote and support the development of business models that effectively alleviate poverty in sustainable ways, the authors provide guidance for investors on how to assess BoP business models and choose those that are likely to alleviate poverty sustainably. They use the recent systems theory-based analysis of three types of sustainable BoP business models to provide insights into aspects such as poverty alleviation mechanisms, growth mechanisms and potential sustainability risks. Drawing on these insights they establish the requirements for investment and provide a framework to match the different types of capital with the right BoP initiatives and models.

Focussing on the world's second-most populous nation, Arnab Bose, Seema Sharma, and Amarender Reddy discuss the problem-solving capabilities of emerging financial technologies in their chapter 'AI and blockchain for sustainable development in India.' While artificial intelligence and blockchain are not without risks, their adaptability to decentralised and distributed networks, communities and businesses make them particularly suitable for India. While the country's Human Development Index value has increased considerably since the 1990s due to economic liberalisation and the inflow of private capital in various aspects of the economy, COVID-19 has taken a heavy toll on the nation's wellbeing.

Economic development in India confronts various inefficiencies in processes and system designs, referred to as micro-inefficiencies, which in the aggregate make the SDGs very difficult to achieve. The pandemic has highlighted the bureaucratic and systemic malaise in policy and governance and has exacerbated the crises in air quality, waste management and the inequalities suffered by those existing within the informal economy.

Against this background, new age technologies like AI and blockchain offer exciting possibilities to accelerate India's goals for sustainable development, with better forecasting and cost-effective tools for governance and management across various fields. The authors confront these challenges and present a framework for the effective management of AI- and blockchain-associated risks in the Indian context, particularly in the light of COVID-19. They put forward a range of methods for effective decentralised decision-making, comment on the nature and sources of finance to enable the transition to these technologies in India and provide a way out of the pandemic, to attain sustainable development.

In a stimulating chapter, 'Valuing civil society environmental engagement,' Tony Bradley questions traditional economic theory about what really counts in the so-called advanced countries. Although some thinkers have questioned whether the marketisation of social life has gone too far, the general assumption that Western economies are, essentially, market economies has gone relatively unchallenged. Yet, in reality, a significant amount of action on the environment, for example, has its origins in the voluntary sector. He makes the case for the recognition of the activity of households and civil society in conserving the environment and natural capital, that is, activity which takes place outside markets, price mechanisms and the formal economy. In 2014, for example, according to the UK Office of National Statistics, this non-market production was worth more than GBP 1 billion in value, or equivalent to over 60% of Gross Domestic Product – yet this activity was virtually invisible to conventional economics.

The application of measures for valuing the environmental related core economy and household production has hardly begun. While increasing attention is being paid to the valuations of natural capital and ecological services, little attention has been paid to the valuation of non-market environmental volunteering and action. The increasing use of satellite accounts to measure the value of domestic, informal, community-based and volunteer production has made it possible to estimate the levels of value to market economies – somewhere between 35 and 70% of GDP, according to the methodologies used to calculate these valuations. The chapter examines a range of dimensions of environmental core economic activity, including membership and time given to environmental groups, green activism, informal nature-based recreation and sport, non-market green household production, in the spheres of green energy, transport and food, unpaid work to mitigate the effects of climate and biodiversity crises, and the health benefits and savings to the NHS of informal environmental activity within the UK. The author concludes by looking at UK data on the contribution of radical environmental action to community resilience during the COVID-19 pandemic. This raises important questions over the connection of valuing environmental engagement in respect of overall sustainable development in society as a whole.

This chapter, and those which precede it, lend weight to the argument that informal, emerging, economies have a lot teach to teach the developed world about sustainability and post-COVID recovery.

References

BBC. 2021. 'Climate Change: EU to Cut Co$_2$ Emissions by 55% by 2030', *BBC News*, 21 April. <https://www.bbc.com/news/world-europe-56828383> [Accessed 6 February 2022].

Bebchuk, Lucian Arye, and Jesse M. Fried. 2003. 'Executive Compensation as an Agency Problem', *Journal of Economic Perspectives*, 17 (3), 71–92.

Bernstein, Steven. 2001. *The Compromise of Liberal Environmentalism* (New York: Columbia University Press).

Cadman, Tim. 2012. 'The Legitimacy of ESG Standards as an Analytical Framework for Responsible Investment.' in W. Vandekerckhove, J. Leys, K. Alm, B. Scholtens, S. Signori and H. Schäfer (eds.), *Responsible Investment in Times of Turmoil* (Springer), pp. 35–53.

Cadman, Tim, and Margee Hume. 2012. 'Developing Sustainable Governance Systems for Regional Sustainability Programmes and 'Green' Business Practices: The Case of 'Green' Timber.' in Marco Tortora (ed.), *Sustainable Systems and Energy Management at the Regional Level: Comparative Approaches* (Hershey, PA: IGI Global), pp. 365–82.

Cadman, Tim, Margee Hume, Tek Maraseni, and Federico Lopez-Casero. 2015. 'Developing Sustainable Governance Systems at the Regional Level: The Case of Emissions Trading.' in Ken D. Thomas (ed.), *Handbook of Research on Sustainable Development and Economics* (Hershey, PA: IGI Global), pp. 248–66.

Cadman, Tim, and Tek Maraseni. 2014. 'Addressing the Participation Gap in Institutional Investment: An Assessment Framework and Preliminary Results.' in James P. Hawley, Andreas G.F. Hoepner, Keith L. Johnson, Joakim Sandberg and Edward J. Waitzer (eds.), *Cambridge Handbook of Institutional Investment and Fiduciary Duty* (Cambridge UK: Cambridge University Press), Chapter 35.

Cadman, Timothy. 2011. 'Evaluating the Governance of Responsible Investment Institutions: An Environmental and Social Perspective', *Journal of Sustainable Finance and Investment*, 1 (1), 20–29.

Cadman, Timothy, Lauren Eastwood, Federico Lopez-Casero Michaelis, Tek Narayan Maraseni, Jamie Pittock, and Tapan Sarker. 2015. *The Political Economy of Sustainable Development: Policy Instruments and Market Mechanisms* (Edward Elgar Publishing).

Castro, Carlos J. 2004. 'Sustainable Development: Mainstream and Critical Perspectives', *Organization and Environment*, 17 (2), 195–225.

Ceres.·2016. *The Ceres Roadmap for Sustainability: A Strategic Vision and Practical Framework for Sustainable Corporations in* th*e 21st Century Economy*, <https://www.ceres.org/sites/default/files/2018-02/ceres-rfs-8.5x11-rd7-v1-1-sm_updated.pdf> [Accessed 6 February 2022].

Chiu, Iris HY. 2021. 'Regulating Sustainable Finance in Capital Markets: A Perspective from Socially Embedded Decentered Regulation', *Law and Contemporary Problems*, 84 (1), 75–93.

Clark, Robyn, James Reed, and Terry Sunderland. 2018. 'Bridging Funding Gaps for Climate and Sustainable Development: Pitfalls, Progress and Potential of Private Finance', *Land Use Policy*, 71, 335–46.

Crane, Andrew, Guido Palazzo, Laura J Spence, and Dirk Matten. 2014. 'Contesting the Value of "Creating Shared Value"', *California Management Review*, 56 (2), 130–53.

Dudfield, Oliver. 2019. 'Sdp and the Sustainable Development Goals.' in Holly Collison, Simon C. Darnell, Richard Giulianotti and P. David Howe (eds.), *Routledge Handbook of Sport for Development and Peace* (London: Routledge), pp. 116–27

Eccles, Robert G. 2018. 'The Importance of the Healthcare Sector to the Sustainable Development Goals', *Forbes*, July 1, 2018. <https://www.forbes.com/sites/bobeccles/2018/07/01/the-importance-of-the-healthcare-sector-to-the-sustainable-development-goals/?sh=349a000c67a3> [Accessed 6 February 2022].

European Commission. 2022. *Retail Forum*, <https://ec.europa.eu/environment/industry/retail/about.htm> [Accessed 6 Februaruy 2022].

Fellnhofer, Katharina. 2017. 'Drivers of Innovation Success in Sustainable Businesses', *Journal of Cleaner Production*, 167, 1534–45.

Frishammar, Johan, and Vinit Parida. 2019. 'Circular Business Model Transformation: A Roadmap for Incumbent Firms', *California Management Review*, 61 (2), 5–29.

Garetti, Marco, and Marco Taisch. 2012. 'Sustainable Manufacturing: Trends and Research Challenges', *Production Planning and Control*, 23 (2-3), 83–104.

Hart, Craig. 2013. *Climate Change and the Private Sector: Scaling up Private Sector Response to Climate Change* (New York: Routledge).

Hemmer, Thomas, Oliver Kim, and Robert E Verrecchia. 1999. 'Introducing Convexity into Optimal Compensation Contracts', *Journal of Accounting and Economics*, 28 (3), 307–27.

Hirshleifer, David, and Yoon Suh. 1992. 'Risk, Managerial Effort, and Project Choice', *Journal of Financial Intermediation*, 2 (3), 308–45.

Holmström, Bengt. 1979. 'Moral Hazard and Observability', *The Bell Journal of Economics*, 74–91.

International Energy Agency.·2020. *World Energy Outlook, 2020*, https://www.iea.org/reports/world-energy-outlook-2020> [Accessed 6 February 2022].

Jensen, Michael C, and William H Meckling. 1976. 'Theory of the Firm: Managerial Behavior, Agency Costs and Ownership Structure', *Journal of Financial Economics*, 3 (4), 305–60.

Killick, N, and M Wachenfeld. 2015. 'State of Play: Business and the Sustainable Development Goals: Mind the Gap–Challenges for Implementation', *London: Institute for Human Rights and Business*, IHRB State of Play Series: Volume Four.

Kramer, Mark R, and Michael Porter. 2011. 'Creating Shared Value', Harvard Business Review, 89 (1/2), 62–77.

Mokoena, Alistair, Johannes Jürgens Prinsloo, Remigiusz Gawlik, and Theuns Pelser. 2021. 'A Framework for the Sustainability of Advertising Agencies in an Emerging Economy: The Case of South Africa', *Journal of Marketing Communications*, 1–21.

PricewaterhouseCoopers.·2015. *Making It Your Business: Engaging with the Sustainable Development Goals*, (London: PwC), <https://www.pwc.com/gx/en/sustainability/SDG/SDG%20Research_FINAL.pdf> [Accessed 6 February 2022].

Przychodzen, Wojciech, and Justyna Przychodzen. 2018. 'Sustainable Innovations in the Corporate Sector–the Empirical Evidence from IBEX 35 Firms', Journal of Cleaner Production, 172, 3557–66.

Sachs, J.D., V. Modi, H. Figueroa, M.M. Fantacchiotti, K. Sanyal, F. Khatun, S.L. Ramos, E. Grunewald-Weidman, M.P. Scharp, and A. Shah.·2015. *ICT and SDGs: How Information and Communications Technology Can Achieve the Sustainable Development Goals*, (New York: Earth Institute and Ericsson), <https://www.ericsson.com/assets/local/news/2016/05/ict-sdg.pdf> [Accessed 6 February 2022].

Steffen, Will, Katherine Richardson, Johan Rockström, Sarah E Cornell, Ingo Fetzer, Elena M Bennett, Reinette Biggs, Stephen R Carpenter, Wim De Vries, and Cynthia A De Wit. 2015. 'Planetary Boundaries: Guiding Human Development on a Changing Planet', *Science*, 347 (6223), 1259855-1-10.

Steurer, Reinhard, Markus E Langer, Astrid Konrad, and André Martinuzzi. 2005. 'Corporations, Stakeholders and Sustainable Development I: A Theoretical Exploration of Business–Society Relations', *Journal of Business Ethics*, 61 (3), 263–81.

Unwin, T 2015 'ICTs and the Failure of the Sustainable Development Goals' *Tim Unwin's Blog* <https://unwin.wordpress.com/2015/08/05/icts-and-the-failure-of-the-sustainable-development-goals/> [Accessed 6 February 2022] van der Zee, Sjoerd. 2012. *The Relationship between Religious Beliefs, Equity-Based Remuneration and Firm Performance*, Tilburg University, 50pp.

Waddock, Sandra. 2008. 'Building a New Institutional Infrastructure for Corporate Responsibility', *Academy of Management Perspectives*, 22 (3), 87–108.

Wheeler, D, B Colbert, and RE Freeman 2002 *Focusing on Value: Reconciling Corporate Social Responsibility Academy of Management* (Denver, US: Sustainability and a Stakeholder Approach in a Network World)

Wynn, Martin, and Peter Jones. 2020. 'The Sustainable Development Goals, the ICT Industry and ICT4D Research.' in Tay Keong Tan, Milenko Gudić and Patricia M. Flynn (eds.), *Struggles and Successes in the Pursuit of Sustainable Development* (New York: Routledge), pp. 84–95.

Tomaso Ferrando, Gabriela Junqueira, Iage Miola,
Flavio Marques Prol and Diogo R. Coutinho

Chapter 13
Green Bonds: Debt at the crossroad between finance, law and ecology

Abstract: Green bonds are one of the latest financial instruments to join in the game of financing for climate change mitigation and adaptation. Presented as innovative, they are increasingly promoted throughout the world as a low-cost and appealing way for public and private actors to access liquidity to finance activities or projects that contribute to climate change mitigation and (although in a limited way) adaptation. However, they are just a specific way of for public and private actors to raise capital through debt. At the crossroads between law, finance, society and environment, green bonds raise important questions and offer a privileged entry point to discuss the implications of adapting mainstream financial responses, that is, debt, to address the ongoing ecological crises. This chapter provides a multi-disciplinary and critical overview of green bonds as a financial instrument that keeps together multiple actors and spaces and offers some reflections on specific cases that illuminate the manifold nature of this instrument and some of the most significant concerns that they raise. The aim is to draw an introductory framework to green bonds and enrich it with a critical assessment of green bonds' expansion, current uses and limitations.

Keywords: green bonds", debt, territories, financial accumulation, social impacts, COVID-19

Introduction: Debt for the green transition

For years, climate finance was considered a high-risk and niche territory for environmentalists and socially oriented enterprises. However, between 2010 and 2019, more than EUR 2.28 trillion went into building new renewable capacity globally, primarily solar and wind energy, demonstrating a new appetite for projects that contribute to climate change mitigation and, to a lesser extent, adaptation (United

Acknowledgements: This chapter draws on data collected in the research project 'Green Finance and the Transformation of Rural Property in Brazil: Building New Theoretical and Empirical Knowledge,' funded by the Newton Fund of the British Academy (Newton Fund Advanced Fellowships 2017 RD 03 −NAF2R2\100124). The authors want to thank Marcella Puppio and Marina Kitayama for their invaluable research assistance.

https://doi.org/10.1515/9783110733488-013

Nations Environment Programme 2021). More recently, the combination of the climate emergency, the COVID-19 pandemic and the global recession has strengthened the idea of privately financing green growth into mainstream political, academic and business spaces.

The normalisation and universalisation of sustainable finance is visible through the adoption of the multiple instruments and discourses that are mapped and discussed in this edited volume. All the available mechanisms, from environmental, sustainable and governance (ESG) guidelines to the EU Taxonomy on green investments, share the sense of climate urgency and the commitment to address decades of the destructive Anthropocene with the desire to maintain economic growth and the functioning of the structural premises of capitalism (Escobar 1994).

Of all the tools that green and sustainable finance uses to celebrate the marriage of decarbonisation, economic growth and finance, green bonds have been considered one of the most prominent (Park 2018). According to the definition that is adopted by most practitioners and academics working on the topic (e.g., Jones et al. 2020), green bonds are debt instruments whose proceeds are earmarked to fund projects that are associated with environmental benefits and have been described by academics and practitioners as a promising financial tool with the potential of being a straightforward and easy way of financing the low-carbon transition (Heine et al. 2019). In the year 2020, an estimated total of USD 290.1 billion was issued in green debt globally.

The most recent academic discussions about green bonds present them as a great candidate to fill the financial gap in the transition to a low-carbon economy (Campiglio 2016; Fabian 2015; Flammer 2018; Sachs et al. 2019; Weber and Saravade 2019) thanks to their potential to mobilise private capital into green investments and projects (International Financial Corporation 2016). Because bonds can be issued and bought by a multiplicity of actors (multilateral banks, states, subnational administrations, corporations, etc.), and because they constitute a safer form of investment than equity, the green bond market is thus increasingly seen as a natural fit for low-carbon and climate-resilient infrastructure (Organisation for Economic Co-operation and Development 2017).

For some authors, green bonds are also said to promote intergenerational fairness, since they allow the next generations, that is, those who are going to benefit from green investments realised today, to pay for the efforts of the current generation (Flaherty et al. 2017). Backed by this academic literature and by the work of key financial actors, green bonds now occupy a central place in the green economy narrative and political framework. Governments, cities, corporations, certifiers, institutional investors, international financial institutions and banks alike are increasingly convinced of the potential of green bonds and their markets are expanding all over the world.

In this chapter, the authors provide a general overview of green bonds as a popular and growing way of financing the green transition with the intention to highlight controversial issues that are currently dismissed by mainstream academic discussions. This is done by relying on a literature review of the most recent academic articles on green bonds, on public documents and on reports published by different actors engaged with the green bonds market. The chapter then illustrates contentious issues with the use of specific cases whose understanding has been deepened in the context of the research conducted by the Green Bonds from the South collective, of which all authors are part. Overall, the authors provide a critical sociolegal analysis of green bonds as a debt tool at the crossroads between law, finance, ecology, past, present and future.

The chapter is structured as follows. The first section describes the financial logic behind green bonds, their origins and structures of governance, as well as the processes and actors that have turned this financial instrument into a popular form of sustainable finance. Then, it discusses the way in which green bonds operate on the ground and introduces a set of five criticalities that should be considered when actors borrow green capital from the global market. With the use of concrete examples, the five subsections engage both with the relationship between green bonds and the mechanisms of the unequal global economy and with the way in which green debt deals with the social and environmental complexity of territories where projects are realised. This approach to the real life of green bonds is used to flag existing gaps in the academic discourse around green bonds and to suggest that more attention is paid to green debt as a mechanism to think about the future of society and the economy.

The origins, financial logic and governance structure of green bond

A bond is a contract between a debtor and a creditor through which the latter (the investor) lends money to the former (the issuer), who promises to repay the sum received (principal) along with an extra sum that can be variable or fixed (coupon or interests). In general terms, a green bond is no different from any other bond, apart from one aspect: when the issuer labels or designates the bonds as green it is signalling that the proceeds raised by that bond are earmarked to fund projects that are considered to have environmental benefits. The fact that the funds will be used for green purposes is thus what distinguishes this kind of bonds from vanilla bond, – that is, debt instruments that do not characterise nor restrict the destination of the money that is collected.

From multilateral development banks to municipalities, states and corporations

The idea of issuing bonds for environmental purposes was initially linked to the work of multilateral development banks. In 2007, the European Investment Bank issued a Climate Awareness Bond whose proceeds were dedicated to renewable and energy efficiency projects (International Financial Corporation 2016). Shortly after, the World Bank responded to the demand of a group of Swedish institutional investors and issued a US 290 million debt instrument that was the first to be labelled as green and whose purpose was to raise funds for projects seeking to mitigate climate change or help affected people adapt to it (World Bank 2019). According to the data elaborated by the Climate Bonds Initiative (CBI), development banks were not only responsible for the first issuances of green bonds worldwide but backed almost all the issuance throughout the first years of the expansion of the market, being the sole issuers up to 2012 and the leading issuers up to 2016 (Data available at: https://www.climatebonds.net/market/data/).

Since the early 2010s the use of the green bonds market has experienced remarkable growth (see Figure 13.1). In particular, the signing of the Paris Agreement in 2015 represented a landmark for the rapid expansion of the green bonds market, with the twenty-first Conference of the Parties (COP21) also becoming the stage for the issuance of the Paris Green Bond Statement by a group of global investors committed to supporting policies for the development of a long-term green bond market as a climate solution (Whiley 2015). Since then, green bonds have been thus recognised as a key player in the implementation of the Paris Agreement (OECD 2017; United Nations

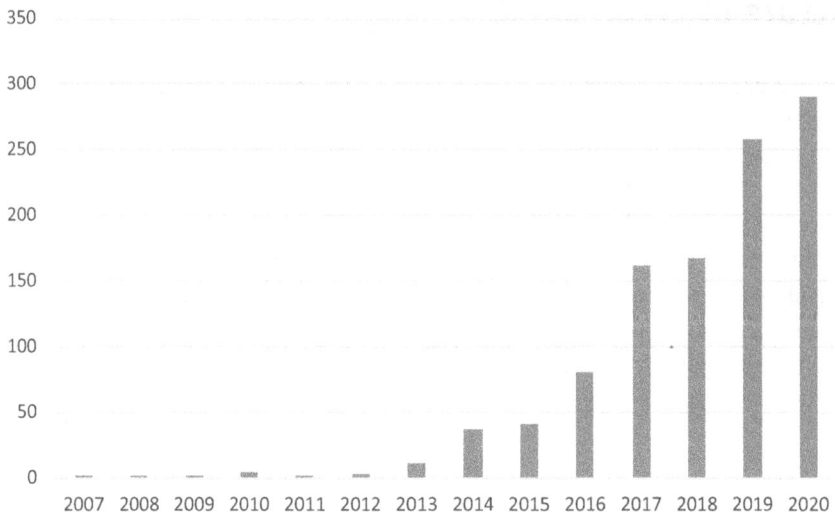

Figure 13.1: Based on data elaborated by the CBI.

2016) and, as a consequence, increasing attention has been paid to developing their normative horizon, standards and governance mechanisms (Bishop 2019).

The expansion of green bonds has occurred in tandem with the diversification of the players in the market. The year of 2013 was a hallmark in this sense. In October, the city of Gothenburg in Sweden became the first city to issue a green bond, with the proceeds being used to fund municipal projects in the areas of public transport, water management, energy and waste management projects (Nassiry 2018). In November of the same year, it was the time for the début of corporate issuers (Flammer 2018), with Vasakronan, Sweden's largest property company, issuing a green bond associated with its broader sustainability programme and commitment to reduce the company's carbon emissions and energy use (Nassiry 2018). A few years later, in 2016, Poland became the first country to issue a green sovereign bond (Whiley 2016) adding a new category of issuers and a new opportunity for the market to invest in the green transition. By now, all these broad categories of issuers – supranational developmental banks, subnational entities, corporate (financial and non-financial) and countries, – are issuing green debt with regularity and have thus contributed to the expansion of green bonds both in financial and political terms.

With the consolidation and diversification of the players, the importance of development banks has decreased. Green bonds are now a debt instrument mostly mobilised by corporations and governments (see Figure 13.2). At the same time, the consolidation of these forms of financing has proved to be appealing to public and private actors in the Global South, with an increasing share of green bonds issued in emerging markets (International Financial Corporation and Climate Bonds Initiative 2018). However, Europe and North America are still the leading regions in terms of issuance.

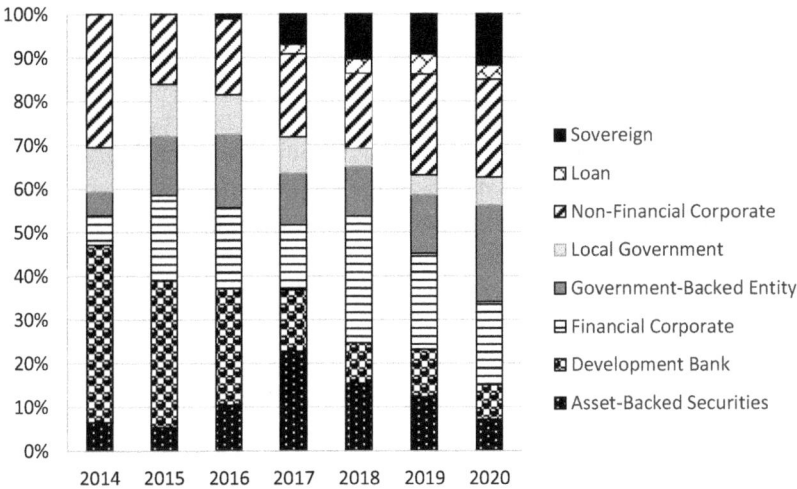

Figure 13.2: Issuer type 20142020.

By August 2021, the CBI reported that cumulative green bond issuance was US 1.3 trillion (CBI 2021a). European public and private actors had issued US 590 billion, North American US 294 billion, Asia-Pacific US 289 billion, supranational organisations US 100 billion, Latin American US 26 billion and African US 4 billion. Undoubtedly, each region has different issuers' profiles. For instance, the largest source of green debt in the US – with US 52.9 billion issued in 2020 – is represented by cities (CBI 2021c). On the contrary, in countries in the Global South, like Brazil, it is private debt that tends to occupy a higher share of the market for green bonds, with land use and forestry as two important destination for green bonds' proceeds (Miola et al. 2021).

Despite the geographical difference, green bonds issued in the North and in the South tend to share an element, that is that most of these instruments are issued in so-called hard currencies. In 2020, 85% of the issuances (in value) where done in hard currencies, with the euro as the leading currency, followed by USD and RMB (CBI 2021c). With the exception of China, one of the leaders in issuance and purchase of bonds with a green connotation, almost all of the green debt is issued and traded in the Global North, with the stock exchanges in Luxembourg, London and Amsterdam competing to become the main hub. As discussed in Section II, this poses relevant questions in terms of the legal structure of the bonds (i.e., the contracts will be submitted to a law and jurisdiction that are different from the ones of the country where the issuer is located), but also in terms of risk distribution, flow of capital and value distribution (Ferrando et al. 2021).

In terms of sectors, the CBI data platform (2021b) on climate bonds reports that green bonds have funded projects in areas such as clean energy (35%), low-carbon buildings (26%), low-carbon transportation (23%), and sustainable management of water resources (6%). Importantly, the destination of funds raised through this form of debt may not be the same of the place of issuance. An example developed in Section II is the issuance, in 2014, of a green bond by the French electric utility corporation GDF Suez to fund renewable energy which included projects in the Amazon region, something that was later criticised for its impacts on ecosystems and local Indigenous communities. As an increasingly popular thematic financial tool that is issued by a multiplicity of actors across the planet to finance projects in all continents, green bonds soon required new governance structures and, in some cases, judicial and financial arrangements that could bring new territories and actors within the sphere of finance (Ferrando et al. 2021; Miola et al. 2021).

Governance and (self)regulation of green bonds

The main difference between vanilla and green bonds is the contractual commitment by the issuer to use the proceeds to finance specific green projects. Ensuring the green nature of this commitment is, therefore, considered to be key. Although issuers can establish their own criteria and nominate as green whatever project they want, the most common mechanism to ensure the greenness of a bond is to subordinate the issuance to the application of private or public instruments of governance such as standards, procedures, taxonomies and assessment criteria.

Because the adoption of common and legitimate denominators provide standardisation, universalisation and reduce the asymmetry of information (Bishop 2019; Weber and Saravade 2019), standards on what counts as green occupy a central space in the governance apparatus of green bonds and in most of the academic literature on the topic. It is thus noteworthy that definitions of green and procedures for certification not only regulate a pre-existing market but constitute it from within and provide the conditions for its expansion and reproduction beyond its original boundaries. After all, without accepted definitions of greenness that transcend individual transactions, there could not be a global market for green bonds.

Currently, private governance mechanisms with a voluntary character (Park 2018) occupy a central role in the establishment and governance of green bonds. Under the private label, two regulatory strategies can be identified: on the one hand, there are standards set by third-party organisations which are not part of the issuer-buyer contractual relationship and provide guidelines for issuers based on steps that shall be followed, as well as on eligible assets that can be defined as green.

One of the most prominent standards used in the green bonds market is the Green Bond Principles (GBP) developed by the International Capital Market Association (ICMA). The GBP are purely procedural standards that concern the procedures to be followed by the issuer to ensure transparency of the commitment that is being made (Park 2018). According to the GBP, a bond may be considered green if the issuer complies to certain transparency criteria, describing (i) their use of proceeds; (ii) the process for project evaluation; (iii) the management of proceeds; and (iv) publicly reporting the use of proceeds (ICMA 2021) Therefore, they do not impose 'any substantive requirements regarding what should qualify as a "green" use of proceeds' (Bishop 2019: 381) and do not enter into the details of specific economic activities that can or cannot be labelled as green. Overall, the focus is on the reduction of greenhouse gases and contribution to climate change mitigation and adaptation.

On the other hand, there are governance regimes that offer substantive standards to green bonds and identify specific activities that can (and should) be financed through these tools. They comprise green taxonomies as 'a classification system identifying activities, assets, and/or project categories that deliver key climate, green, social or sustainable objectives with reference to identified thresholds and/or targets' (ICMA 2020: 5). This is the case, for example, of the Climate Bond Standard and Certification Scheme (CBS), that comprises (i) a broad taxonomy and (ii) sector eligibility criteria, both designed for 'contributing to the rapid transition to a low-carbon and climate-resilient economy in line with the goal of the Paris Climate Agreement' (CBI 2021b: 22). As private actors that compete for the same market, service providers attempt to establish their standards as universal not only by convincing private issuers to adopt them, but also by actively lobbying policymakers and participating in policy processes (Ferrando and Tischer 2020).

In this context, it is important to stress that second party opinion (SPO) providers often develop their own criteria and methodologies. For instance, the Centre for International Climate and Environmental Research (CICERO), the leading SPO provider in the global market, developed the shades of green methodology, which takes the GBP as an overall guide, but 'pushing much deeper on the definition of "green" to reveal potential climate and environmental risks' (2016: 3). CICERO provided the SPO for the first World Bank green bond in 2008, said to have stablished a blueprint for the market. In the operation, CICERO had an import role in translation of financial and scientific languages (World Bank 2019). In the Brazilian context, Sitawi is the most relevant SPO provider: it developed its own taxonomy which is applied whenever they are hired to assess green bonds' issuances (Sitawi 2018).

Along with *ex ante* definitions, the governance system is also composed by pre- or post-issuance reviews. Pre-issuance reviews analyse whether a specific project complies with the conditions and characteristics of a certain standard or with specific private criteria to be deemed as green. Types of pre-issuance reviews include third-party assurance, SPOs, green bond ratings and pre-issuance certifications. Post-issuance reviewing means checking whether or not the use of the proceeds effectively respected the green conditions that were assumed by the issuer. These kinds of reviews include second or third-party assurance reports, impact reporting and the post-issuance verification for the maintenance of a certification.

Although private and voluntary criteria and procedures to govern green bonds still predominate (Park 2018, 2019), public entities have slowly undertaken regulatory interventions in the area of green finance with the aim of promoting, streamlining and defining the boundaries of green bonds' issuance. This is reflected both in the adoption of public taxonomies and in the use of sovereign prerogatives to incentivise the issuance of green bonds, for example, by means of fiscal benefits (Park 2019). In Singapore and Malaysia, for instance, policies of subsidising extra costs in green bond issuance have been adopted, covering the costs of extra costs such as the cost of external reviews (Azhgaliyeva, Kapoor, and Liu 2020). In Brazil, a bill in the national congress provides fiscal benefits for certified green debentures.

For what concerns the introduction of public taxonomies, China was the precursor. Between 2015 and 2016, the People's Bank of China (PBoC) and the National Development and Reform Commission published two sets of green bond guidelines of a mandatory character (CBI 2021a). The latter applied to green domestic corporate bonds and offered several details about projects and areas to be considered as priorities for financing. The PBoC Green Bond Endorsed Projects Catalogue applied to financial entities and was less specific, but wider in reach (CBI 2019a), and was reviewed in April 2021 after critiques of greenwashing due to the reference to nuclear energy and the inclusion of clean coal, coal-fired power coal mining and coal washing (Baiyu 2020; Boren 2016). By 'regulating the domestic market of green bond,' the PBoC aims at giving 'full play to the role of green finance in promoting structural adjustment and transformation, accelerating the ecological civilisation construction and facilitating the sustainable development of the economy' (People's Bank of China 2020: 1).

In 2017, the Securities and Exchange Board of India (SEBI), the Ministry of Environment Japan and, at the international level, the ASEAN followed a similar path and introduced voluntary guidelines for the issuance of green bonds (ASEAN Capital Markets Forum 2018; Securities and Exchange Board of India 2017). Issuers of private governance schemes such as the IMCA played a crucial role in some of this emerging regulation, mainly because of the countries' intention to implement a regulation that was aligned with internationally accepted and widely used standards and facilitate and streamline national and cross-border issuances (Kawabata 2020).

The European Union, the leader in terms of annual issuances, is going its own way. On July 6, 2021, the European Commission proposed a regulation on a voluntary European Green Bond Standard (EUGBS) as part of recently approved EU Green Deal and directly linked with the content of the EU Green Taxonomy Regulation for sustainable finance, a piece of legislation issued in 2020 and directly linked with the work of the Technical Expert Group (TEG) on Sustainable Finance (European Commission 2020; EC Technical Expert Group on Sustainable Finance 2020). The purpose of the EUGBS is to create a European homogeneous standard available to all issuers of bonds interested in using the EU green label so to increase the effectiveness, transparency, comparability and credibility markets for green bonds with the aim of encouraging market participants both invest in and issue EU green bond related products (European Commission 2021).

Despite the voluntary character, the EUGBS competes for global relevance and aims at attracting investors' appetite by relying on standardisation by adherence to the EU Taxonomy, full transparency and the requirement of a third-party review conducted by external reviewers registered with and supervised by the European Securities Market Authority. In the intentions of the Commission, the voluntary nature of the standards should be balanced by its wide adaptation and recognition, as evidenced by the Commission's statement that new EUGBS will be open to any issuer of green bonds, including companies, public authorities, and also issuers located outside of the EU (European Commission 2021).

Public support for the market may also come in the form of technical assistance for potential issuers and governments". This is case, for instance, of the technical support provided by intergovernmental organisations such as the Inter-American Development Bank (IADB) and the Deutsche Gesellschaft für Internationale Zusammenarbeit (GIZ, a German development agency) for financial institutions and national development banks in modelling green bonds issuances. Through the Green Finance for Latin America and the Caribbean Platform (GFL) launched in 2016, the IADB offers informational support to promote greater transparency and comparability to investors, as well as financial support through anchor investments and guarantees to de-risk the issuance of thematic bonds and favour their adoption (Gabor 2021; GFL 2021).

A similar role is performed by national development banks that use official development aid money. A recent report by the Cities Climate Finance Leadership Alliance (2021) urges that national development banks help the development of sustainable urban projects. The report mobilises a specific example of Mexico's state-owned development bank Nacional Financiera (Nafin), which issued green bonds in 2015 and 2016 for wind and hydroelectric projects in the country and paved the way for the Mexico City issuance of green bonds. The Brazilian case appears similar, with the Brazilian Development Bank (BNDES) claiming to be the first Brazilian bank to have issued green bonds in the international market for the development of wind and solar projects in the country.

Along with the issuance of standards and taxonomies, these public interventions play a central role in structuring new markets and fostering their global reach. Moreover, they reinforce the idea that green bonds are not only a matter for the private sector, but that the public and private realm are co-constructing them, their market and the greenness of the activities that uphold them. Given that private and public actors are increasingly cooperating to put green bonds at the centre of the climate transition and given that mainstream and policy literature is generally enthusiastic about the potential of green bonds, the next section uses concrete case studies to highlight five reasons for critical scrutiny and reflection.

When green bonds touch base: Environmental and political contestation in the Global North and South

For the time being, most studies and reports around green bonds are dedicated to mapping and assessing the necessary measures to foster this market (Arruti and Bruzón 2018; Mathews and Kidney 2012). Another important stream of literature is interested in mapping the issuers, assessing the role of third-party verifiers and reflecting on yields, volatility and liquidity of green bonds (Bachelet, Becchetti, and Manfredonia 2019; Sanderson 2018). Other authors focus on the impact of issuing green bonds on firms' profitability and provide considerations on the link between credit rating and the use of this financial tool (Barua and Chiesa 2019).

Another area of intense academic debate is around the existence of the so-called greenium: the price differential between green bonds and plain vanilla bonds and the price reward for green bonds issuers who decide to commit to green debt rather than issuing plain vanilla bond. So far, the literature is not conclusive regarding this discussion and the financial case for these green instruments and whether or not going green is actually rewarding for issuers or buyers (or neither of them) (Larcker and Watts 2020).

Therefore, mainstream literature on green bonds is based on the assumption that green bonds as a financial product is desirable as well as effective in dealing with the imperatives of the climate emergency and hence has to be promoted and diffused. The question regarding which option would be best, whether change finance or less finance (Hache 2021), is seldom posed. On the contrary, green bonds tend to be characterised as an exclusively technical and unproblematic solution that has the merit to reconcile economic growth with climate change adaptation and mitigation.

A more critical literature is nevertheless emerging, one that take green bonds as a financial product that is embedded in the complexity of the socioenvironmental relationships and disputes that go beyond the contractual agreement between issuers and buyers. The next five subsections draw on the authors' own research and this emerging critical literature and illustrate key issues around the green bonds market that the authors hope will receive trans disciplinary academic attention. These five points of structural and immediate tension should be put at the centre of intellectual and political debates on the future relationship between finance, law, environment and society.

If everything can be green, what is green?

The key distinctive character of a green bond in respect to a vanilla bond is the qualification of the use of proceeds. Defining what activities or projects are green and can be eligible to be funded is a condition for a green bond to be borne and dealt with by the described governance regimes. Such definition, however, is as fundamental as potentially controversial.

In 2014, a EUR 2.5 billion green bond issued by the French electric utility corporation GDF Suez (renamed Engie in 2015) to fund renewable energy was rewarded with the Pinocchio Award (a prize promoted by Friends of the Earth, ActionAid France and CRID Research and Information Centre for Development) for the abusive and deceiving communication campaign on the environmental merits of the projects being funded. Among other projects, the proceeds had been used to finance the Jirau dam in the Madeira river in the Amazon, accused of being a destructive project with enormous and irreversible impacts on ecosystems and local Indigenous communities (Brightwell and Hurwitz 2014).

Public taxonomies can be equally problematic. In 2016, for instance, the Central Bank of China released its guidelines for establishing a green financial system, a taxonomy of project categories that could be considered green and, therefore, financed through green bonds (Yu 2016). Among the categories was the oxymoron clean coal, another way of justifying investments in coal-fired power. Not surprisingly, the guidelines were criticised for being irreconcilable with a horizon of a green economy.

According to Unearthed and Greenpeace (Boren 2016), six coal projects received roughly USD 300 million through the issuance of green bonds in China.

An equally controversial definition of green was adopted in 2017 by Repsol, the Spanish oil and gas giant when the company announced the issuance of green bonds worth 500 million euros to finance energy efficiency projects (Chasan 2017). In the issuance, Repsol explicitly endorsed the Green Bonds Principles and submitted the bond to the external review of an SPO (Repsol 2017). However, the proceeds were used in downstream activities, refineries and chemical facilities that were later criticised as being hardly compatible with a green economy (Viegas 2017).

These kinds of cases have opened the door for green bonds to be questioned as potential vehicles of greenwashing. After all, if industries such as oil and coal can be green or clean, then what is green? In response, the content of universal standards and the adoption of widely accepted definition of green have become key areas of debate. For some authors, they represent the primary challenge in ensuring the integrity of green bonds (Shishlov, Nicol, and Cochram 2018). For others, the process is central but is also characterised by risks and criticalities (Bishop 2019; Trompeter 2017).

Indeed, ensuring that a bond labelled green actually funds activities with environmental benefits has become a pivotal issue for policymakers, financial institutions and academics. One of the main practical challenges raised in the mainstream literature is precisely protecting product integrity (Jones et al. 2020) both for the planet and investors. As it is argued, if a certain level of environmental integrity is not guaranteed when a bond is qualified as green, issuers may be exposed to reputational damage, investors may turn away from them and, in the long-run, the market as a whole may not hold up and the opportunity for investors to participate in the green transition via buying lower risk tools and financially benefit from them will be reduced (Shishlov, Nicol, and Cochram 2018).

In addition, greenwashing through green bonds could be read as a breach not only of contractual clauses but also of the obligations that countries have assumed with the conclusion of the Paris Agreement. This becomes even more problematic in the case of issuances being made by public entities and of those with public benefits and subsidies.

In short, the green promise, if false, implies the financing of activities that will not reach objectives that are of public interest, having the potentially perverse effect of legitimising and facilitating environmentally harmful activities or a slow-paced transition that is incompatible with the urgency of the current situation. However, the possibility of green default, that is, that debtors are required to repay the whole sum received plus interest because of the breach of their contractual obligation to greenness and the legal relevance of green bonds *vis-à-vis* the obligations assumed by states in 2015 and with their national contribution plans are two unexplored legal terrains.

The funding of coal or oil projects may appear evidently incompatible with the layperson's notion of green, and indeed they are excluded by several of the governance regimes described above. Beyond that, however, the spectrum of greenness is a controversial space whose boundaries are defined by means of political pressure, economic strategies and visions of the future. For example, solar, wind and hydroelectric energy projects that may appear more in principle totally aligned with the notion of green may be linked with land grabbing, environmental disasters and deforestation, human rights violations and greenhouse gas emissions due to the extraction of the minerals needed for these technologies. The same issues are present in the forestry industry and other economic activities that may be generally associated with a notion of green but can be associated with several socioenvironmental problems. In Brazil, for example, several green bonds have been issued in this sector, including some that have been certified via the GBP principles and submitted to complex external reviews. This very sector, however, is subject to strong criticism by Indigenous people, civil society organisations and academics because of the promotion of detrimental monocultures, the change in use of the land, the extraction of water and the impact on Indigenous communities' rights.

What constitutes a green activity is not predetermined and should not be dissociated from territorial ecologies and dynamics. As a matter of fact, green is a social, political and cultural problem and not a mere technicality (Swyngedouw 2010). Efforts of standardisation and universalisation of green are thus facing inevitable conflicts: if a considerable degree of variation has to be accommodated, they reduce the universal nature of the standards and increase the costs of transaction. In contrast, if they endorse a standardised approach, they may lose sight with local specificities and histories. Similarly, if public and private setters of standards adopt a strict definition of what constitutes an environmentally sound activity, less activities may qualify, costs may be higher and financial returns may be limited; while a broader scope may represent an opportunity for this source of funding and investments to thrive.

Green without social: Saving an unequal planet?

A second key issue related with the global expansion of green bonds – barely touched by mainstream literature – regards their relationship with the impact that green debt has on people's livelihoods and human rights, both in terms of increasing debt and because of the materiality of the projects that are financed. In other words, the attention on the environmental character of the bonds is such that there is scarce attention to the way in which green bonds incorporate (or not) social considerations and on the social repercussions of the expansion of debt as an instrument for environmental transition.

Past work on the socioeconomic impact of debt and ongoing empirical research suggests that green bonds that are built around the urgency of addressing climate change without grasping the interconnection between environment and society and can reinforce social inequalities in the territories where the economic activities are undertaken or even generating more social and environmental conflicts on the ground. For Jenkins (2021), the history of municipal bonds in the United States is intertwined with the history of racial inequality. In particular, the subordination of the bonds' market to credit scorings and the assessment of economic and political risk meant that lending to majority-black cities was considered riskier and, as a consequence, less appealing to investors and less prone to be financed. According to Ponder and Omstedt (2019), such racialised disparity is still visible in the contemporary market of municipal bonds, with the individual median interest rates for the largest black-majority cities exhibiting a bias against these cities in comparison with the median of all municipal bonds issuers in the US. Higher interest rates mean more expensive credit and that black-majority cities still have to pay more to access funding for their basic infrastructure and for financing the green transition.

Looking at more recent situations, Bigger and Millington (2020) assess green municipal bonds issued in Cape Town and New York during the time of austerity, pointing out that they are largely associated with the recreation of existing inequalities as well as with the intensification of risk borne by poor people of colour. Similarly, Hilbrandt and Grubbauer (2020) show that the issuance of green municipal bonds in Mexico City did not have any positive effect on poor communities, thus did not address the underlying conditions of social injustice and marginalisation that make certain people more vulnerable to climate change.

Finally, Miola et al. (2021) develop a case study that goes beyond urban inequalities and looks at green bonds in the forestry sector in Brazil to argue that the construction of green bonds as merely environmental tools overlooks social and ecological struggles on the ground that cannot be ignored. In this case, the mechanistic approach behind green bonds tends to prioritise carbon dioxide reduction and transforms human rights into a risk that has to be minimised, thus ignoring the vast literature that has criticised the socioecological impact that the forestry sector has on the Brazilian territory as a complex interaction between people and nature. This is not only about excessive use of pesticides, the depletion and pollution of water resources and reduction of biodiversity that have been constantly emphasised as problematic implications of the forestry sector in the country, but about the inherent incompatibility between certain economic activities (i.e., the expansion of eucalyptus monoculture) and the lives and economies of people in those territories.

In order to avoid the reproduction of climate injustice through the expansion of green finance, it is thus essential to reflect on the capacity and will of green bonds actors (policymakers, issuers, third parties, buyers, etc.) to deal with the urgency of climate change without overlooking the social construction of the problem and the social implications of more debt as the proposed solution. For example, Paranque and

Revelli (2019) argue that green bonds must be part of a broader social project of collective governance and that finance must be re-embedded in society. Along similar lines, Tolliver, Keeley and Manangi (2019) argue for the broadening of the spectrum of green criteria to identify the role of green bonds in advancing Sustainable Development Goals and National Determined Contributions objectives.

Once more, this means that the decision of issuing green debt is not just a technical matter that depends on economic considerations and the work of engineers, but a deeply political question with potential long-term implications on livelihoods and human rights. More importantly, the emergency behind addressing climate change should not be such as to reproduce historical inequalities or sacrifice people and communities. Unless the goal is to save the planet but intensify existing socioeconomic inequality. If this is not the aim, the first step would be to subject the issuance of green bonds to social criteria that are more stringent than the mere principle of do not harm currently adopted by the European Union Green Bonds Standards. However, more is needed: climate finance should be disbursed in order to actively address socioeconomic disparity and inequality, in line with Sam Moyn's (2018) recognition that guaranteeing the bare minimum is not enough. Whether there is space for justice and equality in the vision of global private finance may be, however, no more than a rhetorical question.

Public universal standards as the solution to the privatisation of the market?

The first section discussed the existence of different standards, taxonomies, and criteria (Shishlov, Nicol, and Cochram 2018) that are at the disposal of issuers who want to characterise their bond as green (Laboratório de Inovação Financeira and Deutsche Gesellschaft für Internationale Zusammenarbeit 2021). Most of these regimes are private (e.g., see: Park 2018). These networks of private norms, largely dominated by financial actors, are currently performing crucial roles in the meaning-building of green activities (Manning and Reinecke 2016), as well as in the assessment of concrete projects being financed by green bonds.

For some, there are three main problems with the predominance of self-regulation and private standards: the privatisation of criteria away from democratic participation; the multiplication of standards and the risk of greenwashing. For these authors, the universal adoption of common public standards would represent the solution. The lack of public taxonomies or differences between jurisdictions are therefore identified as gaps to be filled. This subsection uses the example of the EUGBS to present some arguments to show how the intervention of the public sector can create other issues and, in some circumstances, intensify some of the problems that have been identified in the previous sections.

These considerations trigger three counterarguments. Firstly, public standards are not necessarily mandatory. The voluntary character of public standards, such as the EUGBS means that borrowers and investors could thus continue issuing and buying green bonds that are not aligned with the public criteria and still call them green. Secondly, a public taxonomy regulation for sustainable investments usually sets the boundaries between what can be considered green as a mere technical definition, ignoring its economic, social and political consequences. As an example, both the final report of the TEG (2020) and the first list produced by the European Commission (2021) present a taxonomy that merely clarifies what sustainable is and who are the winners (i.e., green projects that will receive funds) and losers (those who should not be funded). However, the definition of sustainability is a process that is neither neutral nor merely technical. As a matter of fact, the technical content of the taxonomy has already raised strong criticism from within the TEG that inspired the taxonomy (Ferrando and Cerrato 2020). In the last months, for example, an internal rupture within the EU sustainable finance expert groups has taken place due to the inclusion of controversial activities like wood burning for biomass (BEUC: The European Consumer Organisation 2021), while more than 250 organisations (including the CBI) signed a letter to ask for the exclusion of coal-to-gas and cogeneration (CHP) from the taxonomy.

In other words, the EUGBS example illustrates how public standards can translate the vision of a limited group of experts, in this case, the TEG, into clusters of sustainable economic activities that should be rewarded by investors and spared from criticisms. This is the vision where the urgent need for private funding, net-zero carbon emissions, decoupled growth and carbon neutrality are normalised and taken for granted. Moreover, this is the vision where the imminent character of climate change is used to justify the limited relevance of the social component of the people-nature relationship, as evidenced by the notion of do not harm rather than by more proactive considerations about fulfilling human rights and enhancing living conditions while making sure that the economy respects the planetary boundaries (Raworth 2017).

Thirdly, the adoption of public regulations by key jurisdictions like the EU or the US can have serious consequences in terms of the capacity of enterprises, cities and countries to have access to funds. Once again, the European case makes it clear: standards are not only aimed at EU players but can be applied also by issuers located outside of the EU. Therefore, the vision of sustainability suggested by the TEG and adopted by the taxonomy could progressively be transformed into a universal standard defining the activities of financial actors and the flow of resources. This has consequences in terms of competitiveness (with EU actors potentially having a comparative advantage as the first movers), but also in terms of capacity for smaller players and actors outside of the EU to adapt the standards that the TEG and the Commission have developed for EU economic activities. Of course, it could be said that high standards mean a quicker transition and the survival of the most virtuous enterprises. However, it is important to question whether the urgency of climate change should be transformed in a way for EU and larger companies to better access funds *vis-à-vis* issuers in third countries (especially in the Global South). Nor should this become an opportunity to universalise the European vision of what is green or sustainable.

Green dots in a brown sea

Another element that is seldom discussed is that green bonds are mostly issued to finance specific activities that are part of in the context of complex value chains that cut across multiple jurisdictions and that keep together (materially and immaterially) people, territories and economic activities. Eucalyptus plantations, for example, are just the first step in a long chain of paper and pulp that also includes the transformation, transport, consumption and disposal of the products created by the plant. Similarly, green bonds that finance the installation of solar panels or wind turbines often focus on the installation phase, without addressing the long chain of activities that is needed in order for these technologies to be realised and installed, nor the way in which the energy produced is going to be used.

It is by looking at the interaction between green bond and the complexity of global value chains that the authors encountered a case study that reveals the limits of contemporary approaches to green bonds as forms of financing specific economic activities. The case regards an infrastructural programme launched by the Brazilian Ministry of Infrastructure that is aimed at authorising the construction of three railroads by the private sector. In order to facilitate the attraction of global investors the CBI developed a green bond framework to prepare future concession holders to issue CBI-certified green bonds and raise the funds needed for the projects. The public-private framework was externally reviewed by Ernst Young (Empresa de Planejamento e Logística S.A. 2020) who attested the adherence to the climate bonds standard, including the low-carbon land transport eligibility criteria (Ernst and Young 2021).

Within the concession program, the first auction concerned the Ferrogrão railroad, an infrastructure ranging 933 kilometres from the city of Sinop, in the state of Mato Grosso, to the Miritituba port, in the state of Pará. Once finalised, the railroad promises to save 77% of CO_2 emissions currently produced by the system of road transportation (Ministério da Infraestrutura (Brazil) 2021). The railroad is supposed to integrate the *Arco Norte* (Northern Arch), a logistic plan that aims to improve the infrastructure needed for the increasing exports of the grains (especially soybeans) being produced in central and northern Brazil.

What is not discussed in the green standards nor assessed, is that the construction of the Ferrogrão railroad has already generated negative socioenvironmental consequences on the Tapajós river (Instituto de Estudos Socioeconômicos 2021).

More importantly, the idea that the railroad is green(er) than the roads completely obliterates the fact that the project is associated with the expansion of soy monoculture in Brazil and the connection between these territories and the international ports located along the Amazon River and the Atlantic coast. Moreover, the Ferrogrão project is going to affect Indigenous communities, that have voiced the complaint that they have not been granted the right to previous consultation (Instituto Socioambiental 2021). Finally, the existence of a logistics route has historically increased the likelihood of deforestation and the incentives towards producing tradable goods: Ferrogrão may not be any different.

In this disputed context, the Brazilian Supreme Court (2021) granted an injunction that suspended Ferrogrão's auction in March 2021 on the basis of one of these concerns. For the Court, the outline of the new railroad cuts through the domains of the National Park of Jamanxim, which was illegally altered by a provisional measure. The judgement has not been delivered yet and no action has been taken to challenge the greenness of the bonds on the basis of the overall environmental impact associated with the value chain in which the railroad would be a key component.

Even if the project is successfully barred by the coalition of actors that are fighting against it, the case of Ferrogrão reveals a very relevant risk behind green bonds, namely, the fragmentation of projects' concept, analysis and implementation. What is interesting and peculiar here is that even when a project is meeting the criteria regarding what counts as green, and even if it was taking into consideration social impacts, the issuance of green bonds can have environmental and social consequences at other levels of the value chain that should not be ignored. In the case of Ferrogrão, as can be the case in a lot of issuances, the willing dismissal of the broad picture and the slicing of the chain into a multiplicity of isolated economic activities made it possible to obtain the green label and attract global investors.

Like a green dot in brown sea, the Ferrogrão case in Brazil shows that green bonds can fund projects that – even when they formally comply with formal requirements – can be at odds with the overall goal to prevent climate change, restore biodiversity and finance the holistic achievement of the Sustainable Development Goals. From a developmental perspective, should private investors be allowed to strategically label green pieces of larger value chains that are scantly concerned with environmental and social impacts? Does a brown commodity like soybeans not affect the colour of the logistic system that is transporting it also? Should the reduction of GHG be promoted also when it affects Indigenous communities? The extent to which the use of green bonds in key infrastructure projects should be holistically compatible with environmental and social policy approaches and development strategies – based on ESG goals, for instance – is a controversial and still little discussed topic.

Indebting cities

By 2030, there will be 43 megacities with 10 million or more people, 66 cities of 5–10 million population, 597 medium-sized cities of 1–5 million and 710 cities of 500,000 to 1 million (UN Department of Economic and Social Affairs 2018). The link between cities, climate change and a socioenvironmentally just transition cannot be overlooked (Dawson 2017: 11). On the one hand, climate change is turning cities into ovens (Simon 2021) On the other hand, cities are currently 'shelters to more than half of the world population and responsible for three quarters of global" energy consumption and greenhouse gas' (Mi et al. 2019: 582).

In this context, a specific category of green bonds, that is, green city bonds or green municipal bonds, are promoted as opportunities for cities, as some of the most carbon-intense and climate-exposed areas in the world, to raise capital to reduce their impact (mitigation) and/or to finance projects that can increase the socioeconomic resilience *vis-à-vis* the intensification of climate events (adaptation). In conferences and online, the issuance of green municipal bonds is advertised as an opportunity for cities to send a strong signal of their sustainability commitment, contribute to the pathway towards Agenda 2030 and the Sustainable Development Goals", incentivise the collaboration between different agencies within the same administrations, increase their autonomy *vis-a-vis* the national-level and promote projects with increased proximity and limited scale.

As mentioned in the first section, green municipal bonds are particularly popular in the USA, where their diffusion is underpinned by the historical use of the debt market by municipalities. But this is not all. Cities and other local authorities in the Global South are also playing their part. In 2014, Johannesburg issued a US 136 million green bond, with Cape Town, Mexico City, and La Rioja Province in Argentina following right afterwards (CBI 2017). In 2019, Chinese local government financing vehicles contributed USD 6.2 billion (RMB 42.5 billion) to total issuance, while the provinces of Guangdong, Anhui, Hubei, Jiangsu and Shandong were the top five provinces for green issuance.

All over the world, municipalities are increasingly seeking to join this market, mostly because of a context characterised by the need for more investments in reducing emissions and adaptable infrastructures, the normalisation of the idea that financial markets have a central role to play in solving the climate crisis (Reyes 2016) and an increasing demand for ESG investments on the side of financers. This latter point is evidenced by the 2014 green bond programme for New York City, according to which

> through the issuance of green debt, cities would borrow for environmentally beneficial capital projects by tapping into the growing pool of "double bottom line" institutional and individual investors – investors who not only seek quality returns, but who also want to invest in particular types of environmentally friendly projects.   (New York City Comptroller 2014)

Green city bonds raise similar concerns as other green bonds when it comes to the definition of greenness, the involvement of development actors, the risk of privatisation and financialisaton of essential services, and the link between issuing green bonds and enhancing social inequality – a circumstance which has already happened in the past with municipal bonds that were mainly repaid by increasing the cost of services to African American communities in US cities (Jenkins 2021; Ponder and Omstedt 2019). In addition, the adherence of urban authorities to the green bonds market must also be analysed through the lenses of the urban-national relationship, that is, the fact that municipal finances are typically backed up by state funds, and through the inevitable competition for resources and infrastructure that they would generate not only within cities but among cities.

Leaving aside the problems that more debt may have on the budgets of cities, the question arises if those who are at the forefront of the climate emergency will have real and cheap access to climate finance through green city bonds or if their capacity to raise debt will be affected by the financial risk behind their condition of precarity? Will the mechanisms of climate finance and the vision adopted by financial investors be such to bear the risk of default in the name of the climate urgency, or will they opt for cities like Paris, Gothenburg, New York and San Francisco that are bankable and financially reliable? Or will the de-risking of buying municipal debt (Gabor 2021) and the higher costs of accessing debt be borne by public actors, such as multilateral development banks and national authorities, to the point that green city bonds become nothing else but a way to publicise losses and privatise rent? As in the previous cases, without adequate research and engagement, answers risk being merely rhetorical.

Conclusions: Indebting the green transition

Very few authors engage with the premise of relying on financial actors, and more precisely on debt, to deal with the ecological crises that finance has had a central role in creating (Quinson and Benhamou 2021) and that it continues to benefit from (Jones et al. 2020). Even if there was some agreement on granting some role to financial actors in the transition to a low-carbon economy (Castree and Christophers 2015) there are relevant shortcomings in the way in which green bonds are conceptualised, organised and governed, along with the implications that more debt can have on private and public finances. In the construction of a critical approach to the present and future of green bonds, some support is provided by Christophers et al. (2020), who discuss green bonds as a financial mechanism that relies on the shifting of risk and costs from individuals to a broader social constituency, that is, the sustainable environment, and the broader literature about green finance (Antal and Den Bergh 2016; Reyes 2016; Zhang, Zhang, and Managi 2019), and by more critical literature on the financialization of nature (Bracking 2019; Jessop 2012)and of development (Gabor 2021). Of relevance here is also the discussion regarding the governance structure of climate finance instruments (Bracking and Leffel 2021).

In the framework of sustainable finance, green bonds are increasingly popular and utilised. Their global expansion is based on the transplant/diffusion of institutional apparatus and governance structure that are thought and produced elsewhere (mainly in the European context), but also on their (more or less significant) territorialisation and adaptation to local contexts. As the authors discuss in this chapter, the production and circulation of the institutional apparatus and the way in which these abstract financial tools touch base into specific circumstances need particular attention. Green bonds are not a technical tool. They are political, social, legal and financial relationships that have to do with the definition of what is green, the need to holistically approach social and environmental implications, the complexity of value chains and the tensions between the urgency of climate change and the risk analysis of financial investors. But this is not all.

Academic research on green bonds should never be separated by the establishment of a debtor-creditor relationship and the way in which debt has historically been used to reproduce subordination and the unequal distribution of power, value and labour. The expansion of green bonds to finance the green transition is not only a way to bind future generations to pay for a climate emergency that they have not contributed to, but also a way to favour those players who can afford the repayments and disfavour those who are already burdened by decades of indebtedness. From the perspective of the Global South, the flow of capital from the North in the form of climate-linked debt rather than grants or reparation, is a dismissal of the historical responsibilities and a way of subordinating development to the wills of creditors and the continuous expansion of the economy. Green bonds may mobilise private capital and increase investments. But is it enough to prevent the climate catastrophe if this means a social disaster (Moyn 2018)?

References

Antal, M., and J. Den Bergh. 2016. 'Green Growth and Climate Change: Conceptual and Empirical Considerations', *Climate Policy*, 16 (2), 165–77.

Arruti, Fransciso Javier Garayoa, and Adrán García Bruzón. 2018. 'Bonos Verdes Y Bonos Sociales Como Motores De Cambio', *Boletín de Estudios Económicos*, 73 (224), 233–50.

ASEAN Capital Markets Forum. 2018. *ASEAN Green Bond Standards*, <https://www.theacmf.org/ini tiatives/sustainable-finance/asean-green-bond-standards#:~:text=The%20ASEAN%20Green %20Bonds%20Standards%20is%20an%20initiative,efforts%20in%20developing%20green% 20finance%20for%20the%20region.> [Accessed 8 October 2021].

Azhgaliyeva, D., A. Kapoor, and Y. Liu. 2020. 'Green Bonds for Financing Renewable Energy and Energy Efficiency in South-East Asian: A Review of Policies', *Journal of Sustainable Finance and Investment*, 10 (2), 113–40.

Bachelet, Maria Jua, Leonardo Becchetti, and Stefanio Manfredonia. 2019. 'The Green Bonds Premium Puzzle – the Role of Issuer Characteristics and Third-Party Verification', *Sustainability*, 11 (4), 1098.

Baiyu, Gao 2020 'China's New Green Bond Catalogue Could Be Greener', *China Dialogue* <https://chinadialogue.net/en/business/chinas-new-green-bond-catalogue-could-be-greener /#:~:text=China%E2%80%99s%20new%20green%20bond%20catalogue%20could%20be% 20greener.,or%20in%20print%2C%20under%20the%20Creative%20Commons%20license.> [Accessed 9 July 2020].

Barua, Suborna, and Micol Chiesa. 2019. 'Sustainable Financing Practices through Green Bonds: What Affects the Funding Size?', *Business Strategy and the Environment*, 28 (3), 1–17.

BEUC: The European Consumer Organisation. 2021. *BEUC Plus Scientists and Environmental Groups Denounce EU's Green Finance Labelling Plans*, <https://www.beuc.eu/press-media/news-events/beuc-plus-scientists-and-environmental-groups-denounce-eu%E2%80%99s-green-finance> [Accessed 15 October 2021].

Bigger, Patrick, and Nate Millington. 2020. 'Getting Soaked? Climate Crisis, Adaptation Finance, and Racialized Austerity', *Environment and Planning E: Nature and Space*, 3 (3), 601–23.

Bishop, Nathan. 2019. 'Green Bond Governance Structure and the Paris Agreement', *New York University Environmental Law Journal*, 27 (2), 377–411.

Boren, Z. 2016. 'China Green Bonds Funnel Money to Coal Projects', *Unearthed and Greenpeace*, 01/09/2016. <https://unearthed.greenpeace.org/2016/09/01/g20-china-gives-green-bonds-clean-coal-projects/> [Accessed 12 October 2021].

Bracking, Sarah. 2019. 'Financialisation, Climate Finance, and the Calculative Challenges of Managing Environmental Change', *Antipode*, 51 (3), 709–29.

Bracking, Sarah, and Benjamin Leffel. 2021. 'Climate Finance Governance: Fit for Purpose?', *WIREs Climate Change*, 12 (4), e709.

Brazil Superior Tribunal Federal. 2021. *Ação Direta De Inconstitucionalidade (ADI) 6553. Injunction fºm 15th March 2021,*

Brightwell, R., and Z. Hurwitz 2014 'Green Bond Issue Risks Raising Finance for Destructive Dams' *Banktrack* <https://www.banktrack.org/blog/green_bond_issue_risks_raising_finance_for_de structive_dams> [Accessed 10 October 2021]

Campiglio, Emanuele. 2016. 'Beyond Carbon Pricing: The Role of Banking and Monetary Policy in Financing the Transition to a Low-Carbon Economy', *Ecological Economics*, 121, 220–30.

Castree, Noel, and Brett Christophers. 2015. 'Banking Spatially on the Future: Capital Switching, Infrastructure, and the Ecological Fix', *Annals of the Association of American Geographers*, 105 (2), 378–86.

Center for International Climate and Environmental Research Oslo.·2016. *Framework for CICERO's 'Second Opinions' on Green Bond Investments*, (Oslo: CICERO), <https://www.cicero.oslo.no/ en/posts/single/CICERO-second-opinions> [Accessed 12 October 2021].

Chasan, Emily 2017 'First Green Bonds Sold by an Oil Giant Find Willing Investors' *Bloomberg NEF* <https://about.bnef.com/blog/first-green-bonds-sold-by-an-oil-giant-find-willing-investors/> [Accessed 12 October 2021]

Christophers, Brett, Patrick Bigger, and Leigh Johnson. 2020. 'Stretching Scales? Risk and Sociality in Climate Finance', *Environment and Planning A: Economy and Space*, 52 (1), 88–110.

Cities Climate Finance Leadership Alliance.·2021. *Leveraging National Development Banks to Enhance Financing for Climate-Smart Urban Infrastructure*, <https://www.climatepolicyinitia tive.org/wp-content/uploads/2021/03/Policy-Brief-l-Directed-to-National-Development-Banks.pdf> [Accessed 12 October 2021].

Climate Bonds Initiative (CBI).·2017. *Bonds and Climate Change. The State of the Market*, (London: CBI), <https://www.climatebonds.net/resources/reports/bonds-and-climate-change-state-market-2018> [Accessed 12 October 2021].

——.·2019. *China Green Bond Market. 2019 Research Project*, (London: CBI), <https://www.climate bonds.net/resources/reports/china-green-bond-market-2019-research-report> [Accessed 12 October 2021].

——. 2021a. *Homepage*, <https://www.climatebonds.net/> [Accessed 15 November 2021].

——. 2021b. *Interactive Data Platform*, <https://www.climatebonds.net/market/data/> [Accessed 12 October 2021].

——.·2021c. *Sustainable Debt Global State of the Market 2020*, (London: CBI), <https://www.clima tebonds.net/resources/reports/sustainable-debt-global-state-market-h1-2020#:~:text=Sus tainable%20Debt%20Global%20State%20of%20the%20Market%20H1,our%20series%20of% 20the%20State%20of%20the%20Market.> [Accessed 12 October 2021].

Dawson, A. 2017. *Extreme Cities: The Peril and Promise of Urban Life in the Age of Climate Change* (London and New York: Verso).

EC Technical Expert Group on Sustainable Finance.·2020. *Taxonomy: Final Report of the Technical Expert Group on Sustainable Finance*, (Brussels: EC), <https://ec.europa.eu/info/sites/de fault/files/business_economy_euro/banking_and_finance/documents/200309-sustainable-finance-teg-final-report-taxonomy_en.pdf> [Accessed 15 October 2021].

Empresa de Planejamento e Logística S.A. 2020. *Green Bonds: EPL Assina Acordo Para a Realização De Estudos Verdes Para Concessões De Ferrovias*, <https://www.epl.gov.br/green-bonds-epl-assina-acordo-para-realizacao-de-estudos-verdes-para-concessoes-de-ferrovias-> [Accessed 12 October 2021].

Ernst and Young.·2021. *Independent Limited Assurance Report on the Green Bond Framework for the New Railway Concessions Program of Brazilian Ministry of Infrastructure*, (London: EY), <https://www.gov.br/infraestrutura/pt–br/assuntos/sustentabilidade/EPLGreenBondsAssur anceStatement_Publicversiondraft_ENG_02.Feb.2021.pdf> [Accessed 12 October 2021].

Escobar, A. 1994. *Encountering Development – The Making and Unmaking of the Third World* (Princeton: Princeton University Press).

European Commission.·2020. *Sustainable Europe Investment Plan European Green Deal Investment Plan Com/2020/21 Final*, (Brussels: EC), <https://www.eumonitor.eu/9353000/1/j9vvik7m1c3 gyxp/vl5bgbajymzx> [Accessed 15 October 2021].

——. 2021. *Taxonomy, Corporate Sustainability Reporting, Sustainability Preferences and Fiduciary Duties: Directing Finance Towards the European Green Deal*, <https://www.european sources.info/record/communication-on-eu-taxonomy-corporate-sustainability-reporting-sustainability-preferences-and-fiduciary-duties-directing-finance-towards-the-european-green-deal/> [Accessed 15 October 2021].

Fabian, Nathan. 2015. 'Support Low-Carbon Investment', *Nature*, 519, 27–29.

Ferrando, Tomaso, and Davide Cerrato. 2020. 'The Financialization of Civil Society Activism: Sustainable Finance, Non-Financial Disclosure and the Shrinking Space for Engagement', *Accounting, Economics, and Law: A Convivium*, 10 (2), 28.

Ferrando, Tomaso, Gabriela De Oliveira Junqueira, Marcela Vecchione-Gonçalves, Iagê Miola, Flávio Marques Prol, and Hector Herrera. 2021. 'Capitalizing on Green Debt: A World-Ecology Analysis of Green Bonds in the Brazilian Forestry Sector', *Journal of World-Systems Research*, 27 (2), 410–38.

Ferrando, Tomaso, and Daniel Tischer 2020 'How Banks Are Trying to Capture the Green Transition', *The Conversation* <https://theconversation.com/how-banks-are-trying-to-capture-the-green-transition-142458#:~:text=How%20banks%20are%20trying%20to%20capture% 20the%20green,Research%20Institute%20at%20the%20London%20School%20of%20Eco nomics.> [Accessed 15 Juy 2020].

Flaherty, Michael, Arkady Gevorkyan, Siavash Radpour, and Willi Semmler. 2017. 'Financing Climate Policies through Climate Bonds – a Three Stage Model and Empirics', *Research in International Business and Finance*, 42, 468–79.

Flammer, C. 2018. 'Corporate Green Bonds', *Global Development Policy Center* Working Paper 023.

Gabor, Daniela. 2021. 'The Wall Street Consensus', *Development and Change*, 52 (3), 429–59.

Green Finance for Latin America and the Caribbean (GFL) 2021. *Green, Social and Thematic Bonds*, <https://greenfinancelac.org/our-initiatives/green-social-and-thematic-bonds/#scope-of-activities> [Accessed 12 October 2021].

Hache, F. 2021 *Change Finance or Less Finance?* (Vienna: AEMS summer school) <https://greenfinanceobservatory.org/wp-content/uploads/2021/08/Speech-vienna-clean-2.0.pdf> [Accessed 12 October 2021].

Heine, Dirk, Willi Semmler, Mariana Mazzucato, João Paulo Braga, Michael Flaherty, Arkady Gevorkyan, Erin Hayde, and Siavash Radpour.·2019. *Financing Low-Carbon Transitions through Carbon Pricing and Green Bonds*, (Washington DC: World Bank Group), <https://documents1.worldbank.org/curated/en/808771566321852359/pdf/Financing-Low-Carbon-Transitions-through-Carbon-Pricing-and-Green-Bonds.pdf#:~:text=To%20finance%20the%20transition%20to%20low-carbon%20economies%20required,effects%20that%20result%20from%20these%20different%20policy%20instruments.> [Accessed 15 October 2021].

Hilbrandt, Hanna, and Monika Grubbauer. 2020. 'Standards and SSOs in the Contested Widening and Deepening of Financial Markets: The Arrival of Green Municipal Bonds in Mexico City', *Environment and Planning A: Economy and Space*, 52 (7), 1415–33.

Instituto de Estudos Socioeconômicos.·2021. *Enquanto a Soja Passa: Impactos Da Empresa Hidrovias Do Brasil Em Itaituba, Pará*, https://www.inesc.org.br, (Brasilia: INESC), <https://www.inesc.org.br/wp-content/uploads/2021/02/DossieHidrovias-RESUMO2.pdf> [Accessed 12 October 2021].

Instituto Socioambiental. 2021. *Indígenas Exigem Direito À Consulta Previa Na Fase Do Planejamento Da Ferrogrão*, <https://www.socioambiental.org/pt-br/noticias-socioambientais/indigenas-exigem-direito-a-consulta-previa-na-fase-do-planejamento-da-ferrograo> [Accessed 12 October 2021].

International Capital Market Association (ICMA). 2020. *Sustainable Finance – High-Level Definitions*. <https://www.greenfinanceplatform.org/sites/default/files/downloads/resource/Sustainable-Finance-High-Level-Definitions-May-2020-110520v4.pdf> [Accessed 12 October 2021]

——. 2021. *Green Bond Principles – Voluntary Process Guidelines for Issuing Green Bonds*. <https://www.icmagroup.org/assets/documents/Sustainable-finance/2021-updates/Green-Bond-Principles-June-2021-140621.pdf > [Accessed 12 October 2021]

International Financial Corporation.·2016. *Mobilizing Private Climate Finance – Green Bonds and Beyond*, (London: IFC), <https://www.ifc.org/wps/wcm/connect/2996f197-a75b-422a-9e2f-cdc022d8ea96/EMCompass+Note+25+Green+Bonds+FINAL+12-5.pdf?MOD=AJPERES&CVID=lzgXSmr> [Accessed 12 October 2021].

International Financial Corporation, and Climate Bonds Initiative.·2018. *Creating Green Bond Markets – Insights, Innovations, and Tools from Emerging Markets*, (London: IFC and CBI), <https://www.ifc.org/wps/wcm/connect/37797d8b-c7c1-4361-9183-1e038b225b5a/SBN+Creating+Green+Bond+Markets+Report+2018.pdf?MOD=AJPERES&CVID=mqtaapl> [Accessed 12 October 2021].

Jenkins, Destin. 2021. *The Bonds of Inequality: Debt and the Making of the American City* (Chicago: The University of Chicago Press).

Jessop, Bob. 2012. 'Economic and Ecological Crises, Green New Deals and No-Growth Economies', *Developments*, 55 (1), 17–24.

Jones, Ryan, Tom Baker, Katherine Huet, Laurence Murphy, and Nick Lewis. 2020. 'Treating Ecological Deficit with Debt: The Practical and Political Concerns with Green Bonds', *Geoforum*, 114, 49–58.

Kawabata, Toyo. 2020. 'Private Governance Schemes for Green Bond Standard: Influence on Public Authorities' Policy Making', *Green Finance*, 2 (1), 35–54.

Laboratório de Inovação Financeira, and Deutsche Gesellschaft für Internationale Zusammenarbeit. 2021. *Taxonomia Em Finanças Sustentáveis: Panorama E Realidade Nacional*. <http://www.la binovacaofinanceira.com/wp-content/uploads/2021/04/Taxonomia-em-finan%C3%A7as-sustent%C3%A1veis-Panorama-e-Realidade-Nacional.pdf> [Accessed 12 October 2021]

Larcker, David F., and Edward M. Watts. 2020. 'Where's the Greenium', *Journal of Accounting and Economics*, 69 (2–3).

Manning, Stephan, and Juliane Reinecke. 2016. 'A Modular Governance Architecture in-the-Making: How Transnational Standard-Setters Govern Sustainability Transitions,' *Research Policy*, 45.

Mathews, John A., and Sean Kidney. 2012. 'Financing Climate Friendly Energy Development through Bonds', *Development Southern Africa*, 29 (2), 337–49.

Mi, Zhifu, Dabo Guan, Zhu Liu, Jingru Liu, Vincent Viguié, Neil Fromer, and Yutao Wang. 2019. 'Cities: The Core of Climate Change Mitigation', *Journal of Cleaner Production*, 207, 582–89.

Ministério da Infraestrutura (Brazil). 2021. *Certificação Pela CBI Do Programa De Novas Concessões Ferroviária*, <https://www.gov.br/infraestrutura/pt-br/assuntos/sustentabilidade/certifica cao-pela-cbi-do-programa-de-novas-concessoes-ferroviarias> [Accessed 12 October 2021].

Miola, Iagê, Gabriela de Oliveira Junqueira, Flávio Prol, Marcela Vecchione-Gonçalves, Tomaso Ferrando, and Héctor Herrera. 2021. 'Bonos Verdes En La Ecología-Mundo: Capital, Naturaleza Y Poder En La Expansión Financiarizada De La Industria Forestal En Brasil', *Relaciones Internacionales (1699–3950)* 46 (2021).

Moyn, Samuel. 2018. *Not Enough: Human Rights in an Unequal World* (Cambridge, UK: Cambridge University Press).

Nassiry, D. 2018. 'Green Bond Experience in the Nordic Countries', *ADBI Working Paper Series*, Working Paper n. 816.

New York City Comptroller. 2014. *A Green Bond Programme for New York City*, <https://comptroller. nyc.gov/reports/a-green-bond-program-for-new-york-city/#:~:text=The%20City%E2%80%99s %20Green%20Bonds%20program%20would%20reinforce%20New,demand%20strict%20ac countability%20in%20project%20selection%20and%20expenditures.> [Accessed 12 October 2021].

Organisation for Economic Co-operation and Development.·2017. *Mobilising Bond Markets for a Low-Carbon Transition*, (Paris: OECD), <https://www.oecd.org/env/mobilising-bond-markets-for-a-low-carbon-transition-9789264272323-en.htm> [Accessed 12 October 2021].

Paranque, Bernard, and Christophe Revelli. 2019. 'Ethico-Economic Analysis of Impact Finance: The Case of Green Bonds', *Research in International Business and Finance*, 47, 57–66.

Park, S.K. 2018. 'Investors as Regulators: Green Bonds and the Governance Challenges of the Sustainable Finance Revolution', *Stanford Journal of International Law*, 54, 1–47.

⸺. 2019. 'Green Bonds and Beyond: The Regulatory and Corporate Governance Dimensions of Debt Financing as a Sustainability Driver.' in, *Cambridge Handbook of Corporate Law, Corporate Governance and Sustainability* (Cambridge, UK: Cambridge University Press), pp. 596–610

People's Bank of China. 2020. *Green Bond Endorsed Projects Catalogue (2020 Edition) (Draft for Consultation)* [Unofficial translation by Climate Bonds Initiative]. <https://www.climatebonds. net/files/files/China-Green-Bond-Catalogue-2020-Consultation.pdf> [Accessed 15 October 2021]

Ponder, C.S., and Mikael Omstedt. 2019. 'The Violence of Municipal Debt: From Interest Rate Swaps to Racialized Harm in the Detroit Water Crisis', *Geoforum, 132*, 271–280.

Quinson, Tim, and Mathieu Benhamou. 2021. 'Banks Always Backed Fossil Fuel over Green Projects – until This Year', *Bloomberg*, 19/05/2021. <https://www.bloomberg.com/graphics/2021-wall-street-banks-ranked-green-projects-fossil-fuels/#:~:text=Banks%20Always%20Backed%20Fossil%20Fuel%20Over%20Green%20Projects%E2%80%94Until,Tim%20Quinson%20and%20Mathieu%20Benhamou%20May%2019%2C%202021> [Accessed 12 October 2021].

Raworth, Kate. 2017. *Doughnut Economics: Seven Ways to Think Lik^e a 21st-Century Economist* (White River Junction, VT: Chelsea Green Publishing).

Repsol. 2017. *Repsol Green Bond Framework*, <https://www.repsol.com/content/dam/repsol-corporate/es/accionistas-e-inversores/pdf/repsol-greenbond-framework-investors-presentation.pdf#:~:text=Repsol%20Green%20Bond%20Framework%20has%20been%20developed%20with,Repsol%C2%B4s%20Green%20Bond%20%E2%80%93%20is%20available%20at%20https%3A%2F%2Fwww.repsol.energy> [Accessed 12 October 2021].

Reyes, C. 2016 'Cities and Climate Change – the Funding Gap', *Environmental Finance* <https://www.environmental-finance.com/content/analysis/cities-and-climate-change-the-funding-gap.html> [Accessed 26/08/2016].

Sachs, Jeffrey D., Wing Thye Woo, Naoyuki Yoshino, and Farhad Taghizadeh-Hesary 2019 'Why Is Green Finance Important?', *ADBI Working Paper 917* (Tokyo: Asian Development Bank Institute) <https://papers.ssrn.com/sol3/papers.cfm?abstract_id=3327149> [Accessed January 2019].

Sanderson, Owen. 2018. 'How to Trust Green Bonds: Blockchain, Climate, and the Institutional Bond Markets.' in Alastair Marke (ed.), *Transforming Climate Finance and Green Investments with Blockchains* (Cambridge, MA: Academic Press), pp. 273–88

Securities and Exchange Board of India.·2017. *Disclosure Requirements for Issuance and Listing of Green Debt Securities*, <https://www.bseindia.com/downloads/whtsnew/file/SEBI%20_Cir_Green_Debt_Securities.pdf> [Accessed 12 October 2021].

Shishlov, I., M. Nicol, and I. Cochram.·2018. *Environmental Integrity of Green Bonds: Stakes, Status and Next Steps*, Green Bonds Research Program Work Package 2, (Paris: Institute for Climate Economics), <https://www.i4ce.org/wp-core/wp-content/uploads/2018/03/I4CE-GreenBondsProgram-Environmental-Integrity-web.pdf> [Accessed 5 November 2021].

Simon, M. 2021. 'Climate Change Is Turning Cities into Ovens', *Wired*, 01/07/2021. <https://www.wired.com/story/climate-change-is-turning-cities-into-ovens/> [Accessed 12 October 2021].

Sitawi.·2018. *Não Perca Esse Bond: Ativos E Projetos Elegíveis À Emissão De Títulos Verdes Em Setores-Chave Da Economia Brasileira*, (Rio de Janiero: Sitawi), <https://www.sitawi.net/publicacoes/nao-perca-esse-bond/> [Accessed 12 October 2021].

Swyngedouw, E. 2010. 'Trouble with Nature: Ecology as the New Opium for the Masses.' in, *The Ashgate Research Companion to Planning Theory*, Hillier, Jean, and Patsy Healey (New York: Routledge), pp. 299–318.

Tolliver, C., A.R. Keeley, and S. Managi. 2019. 'Green Bonds for the Paris Agreement and Sustainable Development Goals', *Environmental Research Letters 14*, 6, 064009.

Trompeter, Luke. 2017. 'Green Is Good: How Green Bonds Cultivated into Wall Street's Environmental Paradox', *Sustainable Development Law and Policy*, 17 (2), 4–9.

United Nations Department of Economic and Social Affairs, Population Division.·2018. *The World's Cities in 2018 – Data Booklet* (New York UN), <https://www.un.org/development/desa/pd/content/worlds-cities-2018-data-booklet> [Accessed 5 November 2021].

United Nations. 2016. *Green Bonds a Low Carbon Economy Driver after COP21*, <https://unfccc.int/news/green-bonds-a-low-carbon-economy-driver-after-cop21> [Accessed 12 October 2021].

United Nations Environment Programme.·2021. *Adaptation Gap Report 2020 – Executive Summary*, (Nairobi: UNEP), <https://wedocs.unep.org/bitstream/handle/20.500.11822/34726/AGR_en. pdf?sequence=35> [Accessed 5 November 2021].

Viegas, Marcio 2017 'Repsol's Green Bond: Exploring the Controversy', *Environmental Finance* <https://www.environmental-finance.com/content/analysis/repsols-green-bond-exploring-the-controversy.html> [Accessed 19/05/2017].

Weber, O., and V. Saravade. 2019. 'Green Bonds: Current Development and Their Future', *Center for International Governance Information Paper* (210).

Whiley, A. 2015. *Today at COP21: Global Investors Representing $11trn AUM Back 'Paris Green Bond Statement*, <https://www.climatebonds.net/2015/12/today-cop21-27-global-investors-representing-11trn-aum-back-paris-green-bonds-statement> [Accessed

——. 2016. *Poland Wins Race to Issue First Green Sovereign Bond. A New Era for Polish Climate Policy?*, <https://www.climatebonds.net/2016/12/poland-wins-race-issue-first-green-sovereign-bond-new-era-polish-climate-policy> [Accessed 26 February 2022].

World Bank. 2019. *10 Years of Green Bonds: Creating the Blueprint for Sustainability across Capital Markets*, 10 Years of Green Bonds: Creating the Blueprint for Sustainability Across Capital Markets (worldbank.org) [Accessed 26 February 2022].

Yu, K. 2016 'Green Bonds, Green Boundaries: Building China's Green Financial System on a Solid Foundation' *International Institute for Sustainable Development* <https://www.iisd.org/ar ticles/green-bonds-green-boundaries-building-chinas-green-financial-system-solid-foundation> [Accessed 12 October 2021]

Zhang, Dayong, Zhiwei Zhang, and Shunsuke Managi. 2019. 'A Bibliometric Analysis on Green Finance: Current Status, Development and Future Directions', *Finance Research Letters*, 29, 425–30.

Krzysztof Dembek and Jodi York

Chapter 14
Investing in sustainable business models at the base of the pyramid

Abstract: Using entrepreneurship and market forces is seen as one of the key ways to achieve poverty eradication, the first Sustainable Development Goal (SDG). Pursuing SDG1, many companies have applied traditional, narrowly focussed business models, often pursuing short-term profit maximisation. Such a narrow approach tends to create no or negative impacts on poverty and result in negative environmental impacts. If poverty is alleviated in ways that reinforce unsustainable consumption patterns, any positive effects on poverty are likely to be erased by the advancing effects of climate change that are foreseen to affect poor countries the most. It is therefore necessary to promote and support the development of business models that alleviate poverty effectively in sustainable ways. Responding to this need, this chapter provides guidance for investors on how to assess BoP business models and choose those that are likely to alleviate poverty sustainably. It uses recent analysis of three types of sustainable BoP business models to provide insights into aspects such as poverty alleviation mechanisms, growth mechanisms and potential sustainability risks. Drawing on these insights this chapter establishes investment requirements and provides a framework for matching the different types of capital with the right BoP initiatives and business models.

Keywords: sustainable poverty alleviation, systemic change, financing impact, sustainable business models, base of the pyramid, impact investing, sustainable development goals, COVID-19

Introduction: Systems thinking for sustainable development

The Sustainable Development Goals (SDGs) were developed collaboratively by diverse stakeholders over decades to settle on the set of 17 interlinked global goals adopted in 2017 as a 'blueprint to achieve a better and more sustainable future for all' (United Nations 2017: 1). These represent 17 success indicators of a densely interconnected and complex system of people, environment and economy collectively termed development. To the degree that all of those indicators progress without compromising their continued ability to do so in the future, development is termed sustainable. While beautiful in their simplicity, the interlinking of the goals can

https://doi.org/10.1515/9783110733488-014

make them surprisingly difficult to use for strategic investment decision-making. Many investments either do not deliver the intended outcomes or they deliver significant unintended consequences.

To conceptualise why this is, it can be useful to think of the 17 interconnected goals in five actionable and investable themes within sustainable development (Morgan Stanley Capital International 2017): basic needs (SDGs 13, 6, 11), empowerment (SDGs 45, 810), natural capital (SDGs 12, 14, 15), climate change (SDGs 7, 13) and governance (SDGs 1617). See Figure 14.1 for a graphical representation.

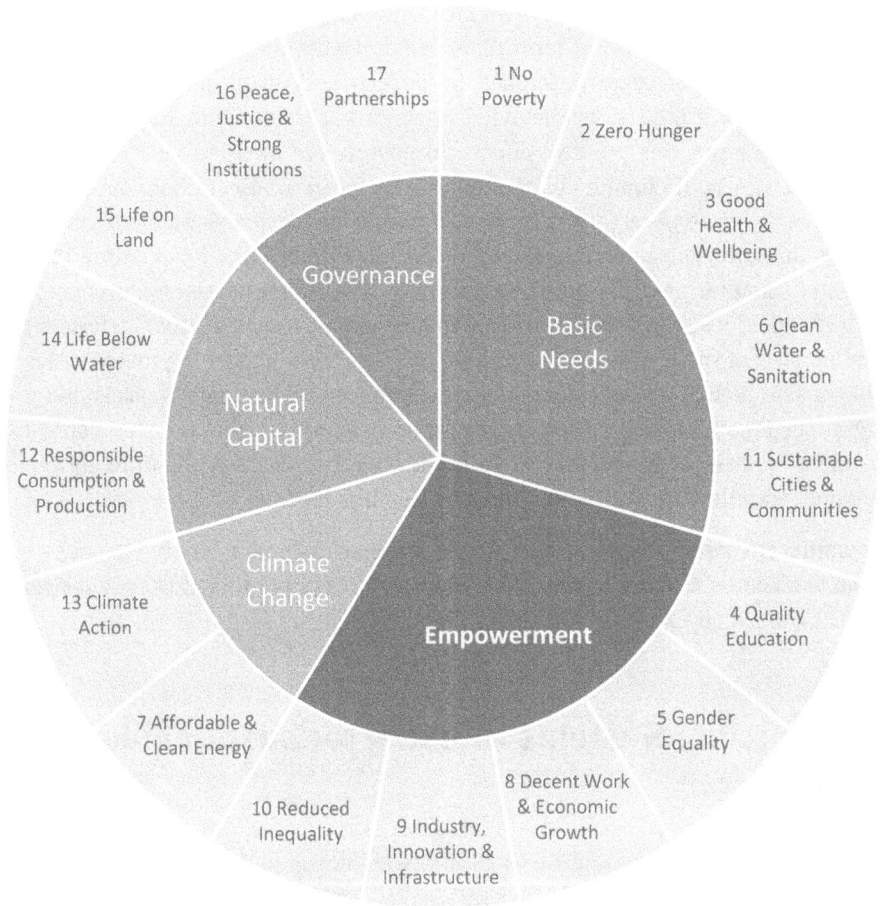

Figure 14.1: 17 interconnected SDG goals in five themes.

The ability to meet basic human needs while maintaining natural capital and slowing climate change forms the guardrails or boundaries within which the empowerment goals can be pursued. Progress in any one of these themes that comes at the expense of another is temporary and illusory. It is reasonably well understood that people whose basic human needs are unmet receive minimal value on empowerment efforts that sidestep that problem; hence the importance of childhood health and nutrition to education (Behrman 1996), of basic physical safety to women's workforce partici- pation (Verick 2014; Jayachandran 2019) and of housing and the resolution of chronic health problems (Larimer et al. 2009). Similarly, investors must adopt the position that investing in so-called solutions for meeting basic needs that degrade natural cap- ital (which this chapter will term environmental degradation for simplicity) and cli- mate resilience are long-term ineffective and simply dangerous.

Environmental degradation and climate change are driven by both unsustain- able patterns of production and consumption in higher income countries and ex- treme poverty at the base of the global economic pyramid (BoP). Extreme poverty – defined here as the inability to consistently meet the basic needs of food, water, shelter, health and safety named in SDG 13, 6 and 11 – forces people to make short- term, survival-based decisions with profoundly negative long-term environmental consequences. Sometimes this is direct and obviously linked to subsistence, like clearing forest to plant crops. More frequently it is to satisfy unsustainable global supply chains and the trade-offs are less visible at the individual level, for instance, overfishing (Cinner et al. 2009) and overproduction of clothing to meet the relent- less global appetite for fast fashion (Niinimäki et al. 2020).

The visible acceleration of climate change impacts over the last decade has under- scored the need for urgent action to avert environmental disaster and the integral role poverty alleviation must play in those efforts (Intergovernmental Panel on Climate Change 2014, 2018). The confluence of climate change, conflict and COVID-19 are forc- ing a reassessment of how to eradicate poverty while addressing overlapping planetary emergencies. On the one hand, addressing these problems is understood to be mutu- ally reinforcing – eradicating extreme poverty is critical to addressing climate change and environmental degradation and a healthy environment is critical to addressing poverty (Organisation for Economic Co-operation and Development 2006; OECD Devel- opment Co-operation Directorate 2006; Heger, Zens, and Bangalor 2018). At the same time, successful poverty alleviation at scale is itself fraught, as improving standards of living (i.e., more people meeting basic needs and seeking empowerment) increases the rate at which natural capital is drawn down, measured as per capita environmental footprint (World Bank 2015). Thus, the application of systems thinking – actively seek- ing out interconnection, emergence and feedback loops – has become critically im- portant to making investment decisions that deliver their intended outcome while minimising unintended consequences. Understanding of the inextricable linkage be- tween these problems is now woven into policy and guidance from the UN (United Na- tions High Level Panel 2013; United Nations Development Programme 2020), the World Bank and other international bodies.

Private investors have been slower to embed a systems lens into their approaches. Sustainable investment is a large and rapidly growing force in the market – measured as USD 30.7 trillion at the beginning of 2018, up 34% from 2016 (Global Sustainable Investment Alliance 2019) with the potential to catalyse the types of change the world needs to ensure ongoing prosperity for all in a green post-COVID-19 recovery. However, few sustainable finance initiatives can offer compelling answers to the qualitative questions raised by Climate-KIC in their recent white paper: 'What exactly does it mean to deploy capital in service of reduced emissions and increased equity, and in the context of sustainable development and efforts to eradicate poverty, as the Paris Agreement demands?' (Hofstetter 2020: 8). The narrow focus on single outcomes divorced from their systemic context can blind investors and lead to unintended consequences. This chapter uses prior research on sustainable business models designed to alleviate extreme poverty to illustrate how applying a systems lens can help investors identify and avoid some of the common traps that can derail well-intentioned sustainable investments.

Business models are critically important for building sustainable livelihoods, as they are the vehicles through which most investments are transformed into target outcomes. They are engines for value and impact creation and an important tool for achieving systemic change, but they can both impede and support sustainable development. Hence, the following question is asked here: How can investors finance business models that alleviate poverty sustainably? This chapter has two key objectives. First, it synthesises the findings of the authors' prior research on different types of business models designed to alleviate BoP poverty (York and Dembek 2021; Dembek and York 2020, 2019; Dembek, York, and Singh 2018) and to identify the risks and opportunities for alleviating poverty and advancing sustainability offered by different types of BoP business models. Please, note this part of based on the previous research as referenced and draws in particular on the presentation of this research and ideas published in York and Dembek (2021). Following York and Dembek (2021), the concept of system traps is used to identify these risks and opportunities and to understand what determines sustainable outcomes. System traps is the term coined by environmental scientist Donella Meadows (Meadows and Wright 2008) for common patterns or archetypes of system structures that lead to problematic system behaviour over time. Once recognised, common system traps can be avoided by altering the structure of the system, for example by reducing delays and feedback loops. Second, the chapter explores the capital requirements of different models and recommendations that can help investors catalyse sustainable development and avoid unintended negative consequences.

To address the above objectives, the following section discusses general business model approaches to poverty alleviation. Next, three distinct types of business models: delivering, sourcing and reorganising and their roles in sustainable poverty alleviation are explained, followed by the system traps into which they can fall and the enablers that can be built into them to help avoid these traps, thus increasing their chances of sustainable outcomes. The chapter uses this alignment of business models, system traps and enablers to provide a framework outlining what investors need to know about responsibly and sustainably matching appropriate investment capital and other support with BoP business models.

Market-based approaches to poverty alleviation

Enterprise has been used as a tool for social uplift and poverty alleviation throughout the modern era (e.g. poor farms), but the rise of management as a discipline in the late twentieth century crystalised focus on the business model as an abstraction and object of innovation (Amit and Zott 2011). Prahalad and Hart (2002: 1) drew attention to business models for poverty alleviation proposing that multinational corporations can help the poor 'improve their lives by producing and distributing products and services in culturally sensitive, environmentally sustainable and economically profitable ways.' This proposition initiated three waves of BoP-specific business models. The first one based on the original proposal focussed on selling to the poor. The second, called BoP 2.0, sought to engage the poor in the co-creation of products, services and business ventures as clients, entrepreneurs and employees (Simanis, Hart, and Duke 2008). BoP 3.0 approaches adopt holistic and collaborative approaches to sustainably developing out of poverty rather than just income growth (Chmielewski, Dembek, and Beckett 2020; Dembek, Sivasubramaniam, and Chmielewski 2019; Caneque and Hart 2017).

Business models are without a doubt a critical tool for poverty alleviation, but their likelihood of advancing sustainable development without serious unintended consequences is determined in large part by how they integrate the guardrails of environmental degradation and basic needs satisfaction discussed above. They can help meet basic needs and advance empowerment – with or without advancing environmental degradation – or they can work against sustainable development by contributing to entrenching impoverishment and/or environmental degradation (see Figure 14.2). Those that focus solely on income generation are likely to be ineffective long-term if they do not address the root causes of poverty that affect all aspects of basic needs and drive environmental degradation.

Some BoP-specific business models are outright unsustainable and are likely to result in a net value destruction and even in harm to communities, ultimately reinforcing the problems faced by BoP communities (Hall et al. 2012). These are, for example, business models that focus exclusively on empowering the poor by increasing their ability to consume while failing to address the underlying causes of poverty and environmental degradation. Since these models do not consider the guardrails of meeting basic needs without advancing environmental degradation, they are highly unlikely to deliver sustainable development and should be avoided by investors.

Business models that increase BoP income without seeking to understand how this impacts the underlying causes and effects of poverty that made it difficult for a

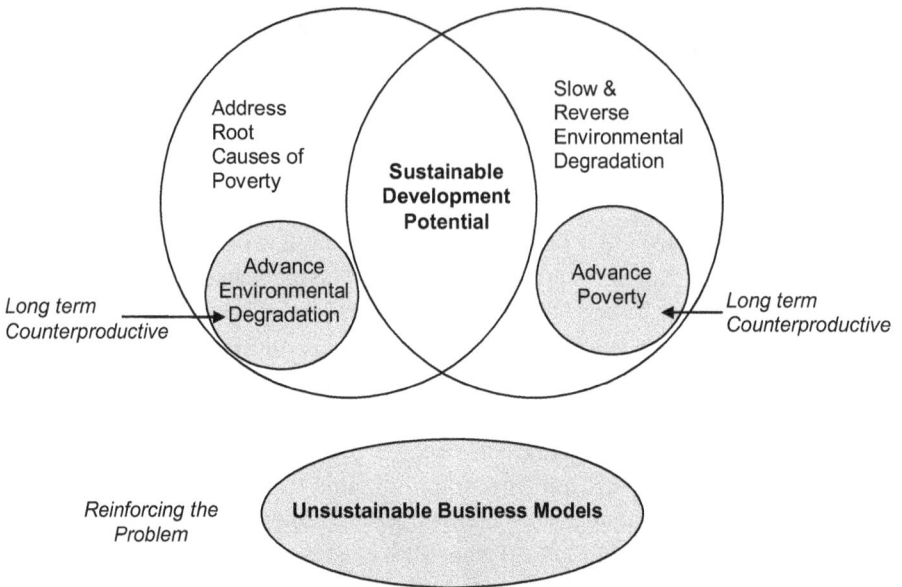

Figure 14.2: How BoP business models can contribute to sustainability.
Source: adapted from York and Dembek (2021).

BoP community to meet their basic needs in the first place, are also likely to generate unintended consequences. Similarly, business models that increase income of the poor but at the same time advance environmental degradation (such as unsustainable primary production) and those that aim to slow environmental degradation at the cost of local livelihoods are counterproductive in the long-term, even if they can create short-term benefits. Like the creation of conservation areas that displace forest-based farmers without alternative homes or livelihoods, these initiatives merely push the poor to other locations, where the environmental consequences of meeting basic needs may be as bad or worse (Peluso and Watts 2001; York 2002).

To drive sustainable development outcomes through BoP business models, investors should seek out business models that actively seek to address extreme poverty while actively avoiding exacerbating environmental degradation. Sustainable investors should take particular care to avoid investing in business models that are counterproductive. That is, they address the causes of poverty but advance exacerbating environmental degradation or develop environmentally sustainable initiatives but have little understanding of how they may exacerbate extreme poverty. Business models of the same general type (e.g., providing access to products and services for underserved communities) can be sustainable or unsustainable, depending on what activities are included and how they are connected. The next section offers a deeper dive into three specific types of business models identified by the authors, and how they can advance sustainable development.

Understanding sustainable BoP business models and their mechanisms

The authors have identified three types of BoP business models: delivering models, sourcing models, and reorganising models based on their exploration of 55 organisations addressing poverty in Indonesia and the Philippines (Dembek, York, and Singh 2018). Understanding and recognising these can be critical in helping capital providers identify models with better chances of progressing sustainable development or to anticipate and mitigate pitfalls for existing investments. See Table 14.1.

Table 14.1: Sustainable development opportunities and risks for BoP business model types.

BoP business model type	Potential role in sustainable development	
	Opportunities for advancing sustainable development	**Risks for hindering sustainable development**
Delivering – Provide access to products or services to the BoP communities – Address single needs within BoP community (e.g., lighting)	– Introduce innovation to BoP communities – Sustainably meet genuine and previously unmet BoP community needs – May transmit innovations developed for BoP to be used in other locations.	– Promote BoP overconsumption – Create dependency on unsustainable production. – Shift focus away from genuine and unmet needs to those that are most economically exploitable – Contribute to unmanaged solid waste, especially plastic
Sourcing – Source materials, products and services from BoP communities for sale to non-BoP customers – Address a defined set of needs within the BoP community (e.g., skills development, income and access to market)	– Introduce innovation to BoP communities – Develop BoP capacities, ability to meet basic needs and economic" resilience.	– Create economic dependency on unsustainable production (e.g., agriculture) practices or overproduction of low-value goods in exploitative conditions – Observed potential to cause conflict and disruption in BoP communities

Table 14.1 (continued)

BoP business model type	Potential role in sustainable development	
	Opportunities for advancing sustainable development	Risks for hindering sustainable development
Reorganising – Create new or modify existing systems and ways of life to benefit BoP communities – Community wellbeing comprised of interconnected needs that change over time	– Introduce innovation to BoP communities – Develop BoP capacities, ability to meet basic needs, and economic resilience.	– Attach livelihood to environmentally unsustainable production and consumption or to exploitative social relations

Source: adapted from York and Dembek (2021).

Delivering models

Delivering models can meet BoP needs by providing access to new, adopted or existing technologies, services and livelihood solutions such as solar lamps or micro-insurance (Elango, Chen, and Jones 2019; Joshi et al. 2019). The key mechanism in delivering models is focussed on increasing consumption and based on innovation in multiple areas including product or service design, packaging, outbound logistics and/or revenue collection.

Delivering models can advance sustainable development when they enable BoP communities to consume more sustainably and meet their 'genuine unsatisfied needs without creating negative social or environmental externalities' (York and Dembek 2021: 141; Elango, Chen, and Jones 2019; Joshi et al. 2019). They can, however, also create harm and be unsustainable by providing access to unneeded, harmful or less sustainable goods and services. Examples include whitening cream that, although profitable, advances harmful racial stereotypes or promoting baby formula in the place of breast feeding (Ims and Zsolnai 2014; Karnani 2007).

Sourcing models

Sourcing models engage BoP communities as suppliers of materials, products and/or services, which tend to then be sold in non-BoP markets (Dembek and York 2020; Dembek, York, and Singh 2018). The main poverty addressing mechanism in sourcing models is income generation for the BoP individuals and communities. As much as this seems right and beneficial, sourcing models can advance community development and sustainability or create harm.

In order to be beneficial and alleviate poverty, sourcing models often need to include broad support mechanisms such as financial training and even conflict resolution. As previous research has found, increased income may create different problems in BoP communities including substance abuse, violence and more (Dembek and York 2020). These problems are due to deeply rooted effects of poverty, such as living with a lack of hope (Dembek and York 2020). Investors should be aware of this risk and ensure there are appropriate mechanisms in place to avoid them. Investors should also ensure that sourcing models treat BoP communities fairly and provide dignifying conditions, as they may easily become extractive and abusive, instead of building economic resilience.

Also, the long-term impact of sourcing models depends on what is and how it is sourced. If for example, sourcing models that involve BoP communities in unsustainable farming practices that damage their natural environment, the benefits of any economic advancement is likely to be wiped out by the effects of environmental destruction. Hence, to be beneficial, sourcing models should create products and involve production practices that do not cause negative social and environmental externalities (York and Dembek 2021).

Reorganising models

Reorganising models create system level change or replace systems that maintain poverty and other problems. This often involves addressing environmental degradation. Examples include redeveloping the disrupted economies of conflict-affected communities, removing economic dependence on illegal logging or formalising transport systems around electric vehicles to replace abusive and environmentally damaging ones (Dembek, York, and Singh 2018; York and Dembek 2021). Unlike delivering and sourcing, reorganising models do not focus on one specific need or set of needs, but rather rely on a mechanism of iterative experimentation to combine multiple activities, products, services and solution ideas in a comprehensive system that takes on complex system level problems (Dembek, York, and Singh 2018; York and Dembek 2021).

By definition, reorganising models take on a challenge to create a long-lasting environmental and social improvements. Due to the complexity of this challenges and of the models themselves, an important determinant of whether a reorganising business model delivers on its intention, is the ability to be responsive to changes and address pitfalls that occur in complex systems. To understand these, the next section looks at the concept of system traps (Meadows and Wright 2008).

System traps for BoP business models

All systems, from software to politics, economics and development, can be abstracted to sets of information flows with feedback loops and delays. Meadows and Wright (2008) defined system traps as common patterns in systems that lead to problematic system behaviour. System traps are archetypes of the ways in which systems go wrong, generating unintended and undesired results that can be difficult to trace. System traps are caused by the structure of the system, resulting from the interaction of feedback channels and information flows. Thus, system traps can be anticipated, leverage points identified and addressed in the design and implementation of business models.

The first common system trap is called shifting the burden. In this trap, repeated application of quick fixes to address symptoms of a problem diverts attention away from the underlying causes of the problem. Over time, this undermines the ability to address the true causes, creating a downward spiral in the larger system (Meadows and Wright 2008). For instance, intensification of agriculture supported with synthetic fertilisers drives soil erosion and degradation and overfishing leads to the collapse of fishing stocks and loss of biodiversity. By temporarily masking the symptoms of the real problems of climate change and natural capital degradation, these short-term actions draw resources away from actions that could directly address the underlying problem, deteriorating the capacity to solve the bigger problem.

Delivering models can fall into the shifting the burden trap when they (1) promote overconsumption or consumption of goods like skin whitening creams that do not address a genuine BoP community need, (2) lead to dependency on products with unsustainable supply chains such as palm oil or cacao, or (3) fail to consider the negative social and environmental consequences of the product offered (York and Dembek 2021). A highly topical manifestation of this system trap is the challenge of unmanaged plastic waste in developing and emerging economies. The same single-use plastics that have made fast moving consumer goods like cleaning products accessible to BoP markets now threaten to overwhelm these communities with waste (Nulkar 2016; Prahalad and Hart 2002).

Sourcing and reorganising models fall into the shifting the burden trap when they incorporate BoP communities into unsustainable production practices, thus creating economic dependency on the thing that is making their lives worse over time (York and Dembek 2021). This production might be environmentally unsustainable in a direct sense because it is toxic, or indirectly through the overproduction of goods destined for landfill after minimal use (e.g., fast fashion) and/or harmful to BoP health and wellbeing because they are produced in exploitative conditions like sweatshops. The effect is intensified when the mass-produced, low-end goods require high production volumes to meet basic income needs for the BoP communities involved (York and Dembek 2021).

The wrong goal system trap occurs when a system is set up to target the wrong success indicators and usually generates a lot of effort but does not deliver the desired results. This can affect delivering models when they are optimised to maximise only producer profit, without regard for whether goods improve the BoP consumer's quality of life or help them realise their human potential (York and Dembek 2021). Focus on profit maximisation also incentivises businesses to encourage overconsumption.

The wrong goal trap can affect sourcing and reorganising models in two different ways (York and Dembek 2021). First, they can focus on satisfying only the BoP community's instrumental need for income (e.g., to meet basic needs and pursue empowerment), without consideration of the associated social and environmental consequences. Increasing disposable income does not necessarily lead to wellbeing in terms of a BoP community's ability to meet basic needs and pursue empowerment. Instead, abrupt increases in income for some members of the BoP community can have negative unintended consequences, disrupting communities with increased alcohol consumption, gambling, interpersonal conflict or family violence (York and Dembek 2021; Dembek, York, and Singh 2018).

Sourcing and reorganising models can also fall into the wrong goal trap when they optimise the production of low-cost goods that require environmentally unsustainable high production volume, rather than producing higher value added and more sustainable goods that satisfy genuine needs and generate more value for the BoP communities involved in the model (York and Dembek 2021). This scenario can trigger another system trap, known as drift to low performance. In this trap, the feedback loop between past performance and present performance standards locks the community into a downward spiral of unambitious and uncritical production of low-quality goods not really valued in the market.

Another trap is known as the tragedy of the commons. In this trap, each user of a collective resource benefits entirely from using it, but as more and more users join, the cost of overusing the resource is distributed across all of them. This misalignment of feedback reduces the disincentive for overusing the resource for individual benefit. For instance, if most BoP community members engage in a small amount of illegal logging, eventually everyone suffers from the collapse of the forest. Reorganising models are especially vulnerable to this trap, as they depend on careful coordination and timing of activities to break down the forces that maintain social and environmental problems in place and then to reorient the complex systems to support new solutions. If there is too little oversight of or stakeholder buy-in to the development of a balanced and self-reinforcing model, individual component activities of the business model overgrow at the expense of developing the whole system (York and Dembek 2021).

In the success to the successful trap, the structure of a system consistently rewards winners with the means to win again, resulting in growing inequality over time. For instance, farmers with larger trucks are able to transport more produce to market each week, enabling them to afford better trucks, widening the gap between them and the other farmers. The success to the successful system trap affects reorganising models when a powerful family or community faction captures coordination of the model and begins to reorganise systems to their benefit, to the detriment of the long-term interests of the community as a whole (York and Dembek 2021).

To help avoid the above system traps it is possible to build particular enablers into BoP business models. These enablers were identified by York and Dembek (2021) and are addressed in the following section.

Identifying BoP business models with appropriate sustainability enablers

A series of sustainability enablers can both help BoP business models avoid systems traps and increase their potential for delivering sustainable poverty alleviation (York and Dembek 2021). All BoP business models benefit from three enablers: (1) an embedded, inclusive process to identify BoP community needs and monitor impact, (2) a network of aligned and collaborative stakeholders, and (3) deep consideration of long-term, net environmental footprint and social consequences of production and consumption. Due to their additional complexity, reorganising models in particular benefit from continued iteration to include diversified business model activities. Table 14. 2 summarises for each BoP business model type the sustainability enablers that can be embedded into the BoP business model to help avoid the system traps identified in the previous section and fulfil the model's potential in advancing sustainable development.

Table 14.2: Sustainability alignment enablers for different BoP business model types.

BoP business model type	Key principle or enabler to look for or commit to developing	How this addresses system traps
All types	Embedded, inclusive process to identify BoP community needs and monitor impact	At outset, this process identifies genuine BoP community needs to avoid the wrong goal trap. As ongoing monitoring, enables early identification and mitigation of emerging challenges such as entry into shifting the burden, success to the successful or tragedy of the commons traps.

Table 14.2 (continued)

BoP business model type	Key principle or enabler to look for or commit to developing	How this addresses system traps
All types	Network of aligned and collaborative stakeholders	Avoid the shifting the burden trap, which deteriorates the ability to solve problems while reinforcing them through ongoing and focussed attention on ways to: 1. address genuine BoP needs with sustainably produced products and services in delivering models 2. improve performance, product quality and sustainability within sourcing and reorganising models where deteriorating product quality or BoP community issues undermine the ability to bring in the income on which they depend (stakeholder input helps address problems identified by the BoP community) 3. avoid unwittingly attaching livelihood to environmentally unsustainable production and consumption or to exploitative social relations within sourcing and reorganising models. 4. guide the timing of business model activities to be reinforcing within reorganising models 5. Avoid a tragedy of commons trap by ensuring that no component activities of the business model overgrow at the expense of the system as a whole due to weak coordination and institutions.
Delivering models	Deep consideration of long-term social and environmental consequences of goods sold	Explicit consideration helps avoid the wrong goal trap in which delivering business model delivers producer profits without meeting genuine BoP needs and helps avoid unintended environmental consequences like unmanaged plastic waste.

Table 14.2 (continued)

BoP business model type	Key principle or enabler to look for or commit to developing	How this addresses system traps
Sourcing models & Reorganising models	Deep consideration of long-term, net environmental footprint and social consequences of production	Explicit consideration helps avoid two versions of the wrong goal trap: 1. addressing the instrumental need for BoP income, rather than the underlying inherent needs, and 2. optimising for lowest cost rather than high-value creation, leading to drift to low performance through unambitious and uncritical production. Explicit consideration also helps avoid the shifting the burden trap by unwittingly creating economic dependency on unsustainable production practices (e.g., palm oil production) or overproduction of low-value goods in exploitative conditions.
Reorganising models	Continued iteration to include diversified business model activities	If a success to the successful or tragedy of the commons trap emerges, diversification ensures that opportunities still exist rather than allowing the process to be captured by powerful community members to their benefit or to exhaust shared resources.

Source: adapted from York and Dembek (2021).

Framework: Investing in sustainable BoP business models

Forming investment relationships that meet the needs of both investors and BoP business models delivering sustainable poverty alleviation requires patience, communication and creativity. Some of the challenges faced by investors seeking to invest in BoP businesses include higher perceived credit risk, lower potential returns, longer time horizons, harder and slower path to scale, fewer exit opportunities as well as higher transaction and other costs. BoP businesses and communities, for their part, have a longer-term commitment to their enterprise and its complex operating environment that leave them less concerned about exits and more concerned about preserving mission and avoiding failure (Armeni and Ferreyra de Bone 2017).

Adapting capital to create alignment with the needs of BoP businesses

Traditional debt and equity capital may not fit the needs of BoP business models delivering sustainable poverty alleviation. Studying emerging markets of Latin America, Armeni and Feyerra de Bone (2017) found that despite their demonstrable social and economic contributions, viable impact enterprises often struggle to access growth stage capital appropriate to the needs of their business. There is a financial valley of death that many such businesses fail to survive because they fall outside of the expectations of the conventional debt and equity financiers that make up most of the capital supply. These businesses are unlikely to meet the return expectations of private equity investors on the one hand or the expected risk profile of traditional debt providers on the other.

For this reason, investors and entrepreneurs are encouraged to consider the full range of financial and non-financial capital that can potentially be brought to bear, as well as alternative financing structures that have emerged in recent years to address the central challenge of creating a path to liquidity that will distribute cash back to investors while providing enough breathing room for the BoP business. These paths are explicitly structured into the deal terms of alternative structures, rather than relying on an as yet unidentified acquisition or an initial public offering opportunity that may never emerge in a form appropriate to the business. A non-exhaustive list of these is presented in Table 14.3 at the bottom of this section.

Debt minimises dilution of ownership and governance and may be preferred by BoP businesses on this basis. Alternative debt structures tend to offer investors predictable cash returns, but over an unpredictable return period and with less reliance on traditional forms of collateral. These can be well-suited to BoP businesses that have activities generating predictable cashflow and can be structured around seasonality, long-tail costs and similar. Uncommitted finance facilities are another format, which varies the amount of capital available without adding debt burden to the BoP business.

Equity offers a BoP business maximum liquidity, but also maximum dilution of governance. It is often impractical for both investees and investors because of the lack of exit opportunities. Alternative equity structures tend to focus on predetermined liquidity mechanisms like selling back to the company rather than another investor.

In addition to the basic categories of financial funding – grants, debt and equity – investors are encouraged to consider potential roles for human capital, social capital and capacity building. Human capital – that is, skills, experience and key competencies – can be brought by an investor to a BoP business or developed within the BoP business and its value chain by funding education, skill development and training, as well as activities that shape the values, mindsets, confidence and time horizons of BoP communities. Social capital, the personal relationships

Table 14.3: Matching capital to the needs of Sustainable BoP business models.

	Value	Growth mechanism	Critical alignment needed	Potentially appropriate investments
Delivering – Provide access to products or services to the BoP communities – Address single needs within the BoP community (e.g., lighting)	Source of value Ongoing utility of product or service meeting specific needs BoP value capture Appropriate pricing Capacity for post-sale service	Identifying new markets (scaling) or new products/ services for existing market (depth)	Commitment to shared vision of delivering only sustainable products that meet genuine community needs, rather than just most profitable products	Equity (where exits are possible), Debt, Facility Direct, via fund or blended finance structure Can be institutional
Sourcing – Source materials, products and services from BoP communities for sale to non-BoP customers – Address a defined set of needs within the BoP community (e.g., skills development, income and access to market)	Source of value Scale of modelNetwork size & content BoP value capture Capacity development Mindset shift	Identifying new markets (scaling) or new needs within the existing community (deepening)	Slow growth of operations cannot outpace community preparedness Profits as a tool of community development rather than investor wealth creation	Patient capital only Equity (where exits are possible), Debt, Facility Responsible exits are critical Direct, via open-end fund or blended finance structure Requires technical assistance

Table 14.3 (continued)

	Value	Growth mechanism	Critical alignment needed	Potentially appropriate investments
Reorganising – Create new or modify existing systems and ways of life to benefit BoP communities – Community wellbeing comprised of interconnected needs that change over time	Source of value complementarities between activities and value creation logics BoP value capture Capacity development Mindset shift Creation of new more sustainable systems (e.g., more sustainable agriculture, transport system etc)	Process replication	Slow growth of operations cannot outpace community preparedness Growth of system as a whole rather than individual components in isolation Profits as a tool of community development rather than investor wealth creation Evolution of the business model as the reorganisation happens	Patient capital only with minimal liquidity requirement Equity (where exits are possible), Debt, Facility Direct co-investment in small tranches Requires technical assistance

and networks that can contribute to an organisation's success, can be invested by leveraging the investors' own social capital for the benefit of the BoP business model or it can be developed in the business by funding the intentional growth of trust, mutual respect and shared values within and between investee organisations and their value chains.

Capacity building support is non-financial, or technical, assistance that supports the investee's operations, strategy or impact (Pineiro and Bass 2017). This support can be provided directly by the investor or through a third-party and can encompass general upskilling, specific activities such as project preparation and implementation or enhancing the broader business environment and strengthening markets. For example, by improving the legal environment, building the capacity of local stakeholders and broadly supporting the local enabling environment.

Alternative deal structures can be used across a portfolio of investments that is set up as a traditional closed-end fund, thus allowing a fund manager to have a broader set of structures available, while the fund structure remains familiar to potential limited partners. However, the exit-oriented timeline of these structures can put pressure on otherwise financially viable enterprises that are necessarily slow to mature. Hence, holding companies and open-ended funds can provide attractive alternatives that do not compromise the BoP business' mission or natural growth trajectory (Armeni and Ferreyra de Bone 2017).

BoP businesses are also well-suited to structuring approaches that bring multiple capital types together. Blended finance uses funds from a donor (like a development finance institute) or a philanthropic source (like a foundation) to attract funds from a private sector investor and using these blended funds to help solve a development problem (Covergence n.d.). By crowding in private sector funds that would not otherwise have been devoted to a development problem, blended finance can mobilise more financial resources to solve sustainable development challenges.

BoP businesses and communities may also benefit from conservation finance, which is a set of approaches through which conservationists utilise a range of funding and financing options, leveraging government and traditional philanthropic resources in combination with other capital sources to the support conservation of land, water and resources (Schuyler 2005). These can include debt financing, emerging tax benefits, private equity investments and project financing. One example is debt-for-nature swaps that allow for public and private interests to purchase debt from a developing country, which is discharged to free up capital to fund environmental sustainability efforts in those nations. Another example is payment for ecosystem services, in which a private investor financially incentivises local communities to conserve and restore ecological systems. However, it is likely that an approach would have to be designed around the needs of specific BoP communities as well as ecosystems to succeed in serving both needs.

Any BoP-focussed investment is best approached with two critical principles that can be used throughout the investment process; these can guide appropriate growth. First, understand that both poverty and environmental degradation are complex problems that evolve over time and manifest differently in different locations. BoP business models require active engagement from investors and are not appropriate for set and forget approaches. Investment managers and asset owners must be alert to the potential shifts of all BoP business models into unsustainable activities, which can be picked up through ongoing impact monitoring. Doing so allows for addressing the complexities of poverty and adjusting the initiative to the changing needs of the communities and, as a result, for embedding the business model in the local ecosystem (Dembek and York 2020). It is good practice to consider in advance how unsustainable performance will be managed, under what conditions the investor will exit and how that exit will be managed responsibly (Schiff and Dithrich 2018).

Secondly, investments in BoP poverty alleviation should be approached with the understanding that profits are a tool for BoP community development rather than the *raison d'etre* of the business or a way to build investor wealth (Dembek and York 2020). This is an important filter to help screen out candidates with weak mission alignment and identify those investees for whom financial and sustainable development outcomes share the same drivers.

To understand the implications for capital of each of the BoP business model types above, it is useful to consider in abstract terms how they work and the circumstances under which they succeed and fail in driving sustainable development as conceptualised in Figure 14.2. The section below addresses, for each model type in turn: the factors necessary to create and capture value for the company and its target stakeholders, sustainable and unsustainable growth paths and the implications for capital requirements of these characteristics.

What investors need to know: Delivering models

In a delivering model, the target stakeholder for the poverty alleviation is the customer (and by extension their household or community) and the focus is on satisfying one or more discreet needs within BoP communities. Thus, the enduring utility of the products or services delivered is as important a source of value in delivering models as the pricing and design that makes the product accessible and appropriate for the BoP community. Once a good is consumed or when a durable good, such as a solar light breaks, the value created within the community is no longer sustained (Dembek and York 2019). For this reason, the provision of post-sale service, or capacity development, in repair and maintenance are critical to creating enduring value and sustainable development through delivering models (Dembek, York, and Singh 2018).

Delivering models can be grown by scaling through product line expansion and/or market expansion (Dembek, York, and Singh 2018). Product line expansion can be in goods and services that complement the initial offering, such as training in equipment repair and maintenance to complement the development of electrical microgrids. Product expansion can also be into other needs identified by the target community, such as solar powered fans as well as clean cookstoves. Alternatively, delivering models can scale by delivering the same goods and services into different communities.

Delivering models are the least complex BoP business model for investors. Thus, making them the easiest for institutional investors to access (generally through specialist fund managers rather than directly). They are suitable for equity (where exit paths exist) and debt investments (such as funding microfinance) made directly or through funds. Blended finance, which is a structuring approach that uses catalytic capital from public or philanthropic sources to increase private sector investment in sustainable development (Covergence n.d.), can be a very effective way to invest in delivering models. This allows organisations with different objectives to invest alongside each other while achieving their own objectives (whether financial return, social impact or a blend of both).

Delivering models cease to be vehicles for advancing sustainability when they cease to serve a genuine basic need or empowerment goal. They become actively unsustainable when they begin to do harm to people and planet by damaging community wellbeing (e.g., gambling), and/or advancing environmental degradation (e.g., by delivering unsustainably produced goods or by creating unmanaged plastic waste).

What investors need to know: Sourcing models

In sourcing models, the target stakeholder for poverty alleviation are employees or suppliers creating the product or service (and their communities), while the product or service is sold to a customer who must also be satisfied if the model is to remain commercially viable. Sourcing models address a defined set of basic needs or empowerment goals within the BoP community (e.g., skills development, income and access to market). Because the ability to address these needs is determined by the commercial success of the model, the size and mix of the customer network that consumes the goods and services is a critical source of value. Sourcing models grow by scaling the size and quality of this customer network (which also requires development of the BoP provider base) or by deepening the impact within the community by sourcing higher value intermediate goods and service (Dembek, York, and Singh 2018). For instance, a model that starts out by sourcing basic inputs from the BoP community may over time identify and grow skills such as design, logistics or management within the same community, as Habi Footwear did in Manila (Dembek and York 2020).

Sourcing models are more complex for investors than delivering models because the complex challenges of BoP poverty are in the upstream value chain of the business, rather than downstream, difficulties can threaten the financial viability of the entire business. These models are suitable for equity (where exit paths exist) and debt investments made directly, through open-ended funds and through co-investment in blended finance structures. These models are best suited to investors willing to engage in high-touch and high-trust relationships that include co-investors. Prior research suggests that long-term viable sourcing models are often accompanied by social support or capacity development programmes of various sorts (Dembek et al 2018); these elements are critical to the long-term sustainability of the model but may not be directly tied to income generation. While the conditions above are best suited to patient capital, investors with higher requirements for predictable short-term liquidity may be able to support these models through co-investment in working capital or supplier development finance facilities that are accessed by the business or BoP community to support these needs.

The systems lens is critical to sustainable investing in sourcing models, which cannot be based on reductionist expectations that income generation will eradicate poverty (Chmielewski, Dembek, and Beckett 2020) or that the choices and values of the BoP community members will align to the expectations of investors. It is characteristic of those living in extreme poverty to have very short-term perspectives and focus on the immediate at the expense of longer-term considerations (Mani et al. 2013; Mullainathan and Shafir 2013; Shah, Mullainathan, and Shafir 2012). Mental timeframes, sense of empowerment and sense of self-efficacy within BoP communities develop slowly over time, given predictable conditions and appropriate opportunities to do things like build financial literacy and planning capacity or fund education for children. Failing to allow time for this development can prevent BoP communities from deriving value from engagement with BoP business models and constrain the likelihood of delivering the target social outcomes (Beckett, Chmielewski, and Dembek 2020).

Direct investing in BoP sourcing models requires an open mind, flexibility, patience and a great deal of listening. Investors and their representatives should commit to an ongoing process of identifying and resolving problems. With patience, this can guide innovation and design around the strengths and resources of a given BoP community (Dembek and York 2020).

A long-term commitment to slow growth should underpin the development of BoP sourcing models if they are to remain sustainable (Dembek and York 2020). Community development and empowerment in BoP communities (the target outcome of the investment, for which profits are a tool) proceeds on its own timeline, which must be the limiting factor on growth if the model is to contribute to sustainable development (Beckett, Chmielewski, and Dembek 2020).

The right mix and amount of capital can be critical in balancing long-term vision and community development with the shorter-term business requirements of sourcing models. For instance, a business may balance retained earnings with equity (where exits are available) and debt investment from patient investors who understand and are committed to the development of the community. Care must be taken not to inject too much capital into the business, which might force it into unsustainable growth. This approach demonstrates an investor's ongoing commitment to working with and supporting BoP communities, setting them apart from the investors, companies and non-profit organisations that come and go rapidly (Dembek and York 2020). A long-term and slow growth approach is critical for delivering the model's social mission, and also drives financial sustainability because it allows time for BoP communities to develop human capital – the skills and capacities that underpin high-quality, reliable production.

Sourcing models cease to be vehicles for advancing sustainable development when they cease to benefit stakeholders or begin to harm people and planet. In environmental terms, this happens when sourcing models tie BoP communities' ability to meet basic needs to unsustainable production practices such as destructive agriculture practices like palm oil or overproduction of low-value goods (often in exploitative conditions like sweatshops). In social terms, the sustainability of sourcing models drops off rapidly when scaling of the business model exceeds the speed at which the BoP community can develop capacities to deliver quality products and/or adapt to the change in community structure and power dynamics that inevitably accompany development (Dembek and York 2020).

What investors need to know: Reorganising models

Reorganising models target the wellbeing of BoP communities as a whole, which is comprised of interconnected needs that evolve over time. The critical source of value in reorganising models is design – not just of products and services, but of the complementarities between activities and value creation logics of the reorganising model itself. Just as all BoP communities are unique, all reorganising models are unique. These models grow not through replication of the model itself, but of the process of identifying and targeting leverage points for change – initially within the problem facing the BoP community, and later the opportunities for building reinforcing connections between elements of the solution that comprises the new economic model (York and Dembek 2021).

Reorganising models have enormous transformative potential but are also highly complex for investors. As for sourcing models, the right mix and amount of capital is an important part of balancing long-term vision and community development with the shorter-term business requirements. As reorganising models can encompass multiple business entities, some entities within mature reorganising models may be suitable for direct equity (where exits are possible) or debt investments. However, these investments generally emerge from ongoing, high-trust relationships between highly aligned investors and organisation sponsors.

Investment is best undertaken in small tranches into areas specified by the stakeholders. Care must be taken not to add too much capital, which could force the business into unsustainable growth, or to add capital too quickly or to the wrong elements of the model, which can upset the balance between different elements of the model. As with sourcing models, capital with higher requirements for predictable short-term liquidity may be able to support these models through co-investment in working capital or community development finance facilities that are accessed by the component businesses or BoP community to support their development.

The ongoing process of iteratively identifying and resolving problems is the core of a sustainable reorganising model. The process can also be a crucial mechanism for lengthening timeframes, allowing businesses and community members to identify which specific activities are appropriate at a given time. This process also builds the in-depth understanding of how the community's perception of value and planning horizons co-evolve over time (Beckett, Chmielewski, and Dembek 2020), which are critical to the success of reorganising models.

Reorganising models cease to be vehicles for advancing sustainability when they cease to benefit stakeholders or begin to harm stakeholders. The paths by which this happens are similar to sourcing models: tying BoP communities' ability to meet basic needs to unsustainable production practices, such as destructive agriculture practices or overproduction of low-value goods, and scaling at a rate that exceeds the rate of BoP community adaptation.

Table 14.4 summarises the content laid out above.

Table 14.4: Types of capital.

Type of Capital	Description	Considerations
Grants	Cash that is directed toward a charitable purpose, and never has to be repaid no financial return for investment no impact on ownership or governance	Good for early phases when there is a clear need for research and development into a business model, and for any new effort that has high degree of uncertainty or risk (e.g., new product, new service or new region). Also needed for activities related to community development and support without which commercial activities often do not work. Sources include foundations, donor advised funds, government development agencies, competitions, etc. Highly relationship dependent.
Recoverable Grant (also, Repayable grant; Forgivable loan)	Loan that is either paid back or written off as a grant by a certain date under certain conditions. Generally made at lower interest rates than other loans because the lender intends to help the enterprise show it can service debt.	Useful where the proposed project or activity does not have a sufficient track record to assess risk and receive a more conventional investment vehicle. when the enterprise needs risk tolerant and inexpensive capital but has a route to positive cash flow. Testing business feasibility, developing financial discipline within the organisation, and demonstrating to future investors an ability to pay back debt.

Table 14.4 (continued)

Type of Capital	Description	Considerations
Loan guarantee (also, Credit guarantee; Loss layer; Letter of credit)	Third-party capital to protect an investor in the case that investee does not pay back in full. This can take the form of a grant held in escrow, a letter of credit that will repay the lender in the case of loan default, as a co-guarantor agreeing to repay the lender in the case of default, or as subordinate loan in case of loss.	Letters of credit and loss layers in a loan with capital from different investors with different terms (called a multi-layered or stacked deal) can help attract sources of capital to the deal that would otherwise consider it too risky. They can also be an attractive development finance tool because they optimise the use of public resources, as these resources are only disbursed in the case of losses, can be partial guarantees or full, and address credit and political risk. Sources include foundations, governments and public charities
Concessional capital (Also, first-loss debt or equity, investment-stage grants)	Debt or equity that bears risk at below-market financial returns to mobilise private sector investment.	Public or philanthropic investors may provide funds on below-market terms within the capital structure to lower the overall cost of capital or to provide an additional layer of protection to private investors.
Program-Related Investments (PRI) (also mission-related investments)	An investment made by private foundations in order to achieve its philanthropic goals. PRIs are expected to be repaid, often with at least a modest financial return.	PRIs are generally made as deposits, lines of credit, debt or equity investments. Useful for those looking for capital as a step in between grants and commercial investment.

Table 14.4 (continued)

Type of Capital	Description	Considerations
Committed and Uncommitted Facilities	An agreement between a lender and a borrower wherein the lender agrees to make short-term funding available to the borrower. A committed facility involves clearly defined terms and conditions set by the lender. An uncommitted facility can include a working capital facility, also known as an overdraft, and is payable on demand.	A revolving loan facility provides the borrower with the ability to draw down or withdraw, repay and withdraw again. Term loans are a common committed facility, which can include equipment, working capital and equipment loans. Uncommitted facilities are used to finance seasonal or temporary needs of businesses with fluctuating revenues, such as paying creditors to earn trade discounts, single or one-off transactions and meeting payroll obligations.
Variable Repayment loan (Also, Revenue-based financing; Demand dividend; Quasi-equity; Structured Exit)	A loan given with customised repayment terms that relate to the operations of the company. Investors may add upside provisions, or rights to convert loans to equity. Low impact on ownership and governance	Variable repayment, especially revenue-based financing, is a common tool for later stage investing, and is being used more and more for impact enterprises, including in developing markets where traditional exit options are less common. Useful for companies that need a more flexible and/or less risky option for debt capital, that lack hard assets to collateralise a loan. Useful in situations with long-tail costs before revenues kick in or with lumpy, seasonal or hard to predict revenues and those operating in geographies or sectors where there are not yet good equity exit possibilities.

Table 14.4 (continued)

Type of Capital	Description	Considerations
Debt	Debt can be asset-based or cashflow based, depending on company size. No ownership or governance dilution, but interest rate exposure if not fixed.	Debt financing takes a variety of forms, each with its own underwriting standards: working capital lines of credit, asset-based loans (secured by account receivables, inventory, or other assets), equipment loans, mortgages, etc. Useful when activities generating regular and predictable cash flow that can be used to make interest payments. Can be an attractive tool for expansion, inventory purchasing or to smooth out seasonal fluctuations in revenue
Convertible Debt	A loan that that will convert into equity on pre-established conditions, usually when future equity investment rounds are raised. Often used as a bridge to provide cash in between equity rounds.	Quasi-debt; Convertible note; Convertible loan
Mezzanine Capital	Flexible hybrid instruments that can combine debt and equity. While mezzanine debt is more expensive than bank debt, it is not as rigid. Maximises total leverage with little to no equity dilution.	Takes many forms, including Pay in Kind notes, bonds with warrants, profit participating rights, participating loans, silent participation, subordinated debt.
Redeemable equity	Similar in its terms to traditional equity, except the investor's exit is back to the company, not to another equity investor.	Allows for equity-like terms without the need for a liquidity event. May be implemented through mandatory repurchase of the shares via a percentage of revenue set aside over time, or recapitalisation of the company.

Table 14.4 (continued)

Type of Capital	Description	Considerations
Mandatory dividends	Similar to a preferred equity model, under a mandatory dividend structure the company pays the investor a percentage of profits in the form of a dividend for a specified period, or until a target is achieved. offer partial payments to the investor, generally based on measuring the company's financial performance.	The variability avoids the burden on the enterprise that would come from predetermined repayments during low revenue periods. Generally executed through percentage-based dividends until a specified multiple is reached
Equity	Selling shares in the company's ownership to individuals or institutions. Equity investors depend on an exit event to sell their shares and reap a financial return.	Achieves maximum liquidity with higher dilution. Typically funded by a private equity investor or institutional investor. Only available to some legal structures. Useful where cash flow is uncertain in early stages, or when there is significant growth potential for the venture and a financial exit scenario is plausible. Typical exit options are later stage investors, IPO (initial public offering), acquisition or management buy-out. In some impact sectors, the exit market may be nascent or non-existent Best for businesses with high growth trajectories operating in markets or industries where rapid scaling is required to compete

Source: composited from Armeni and Ferreyra de Bone (2017); Clark (2017).

Matching capital to the needs of BoP business models – when to back and when to balk

Investing in BoP business models can be high-impact and extremely rewarding, but it should not be entered into lightly. An investor interested in sustainable poverty alleviation must consider their requirements and capacity as an engaged investor, the specifics of the BoP business model they are considering and the alignment between the two prior to entering into an investment relationship.

The capacity of private investors to finance sustainable BoP poverty alleviation is determined to a large extent by their own constraint or flexibility in terms of timeline, liquidity requirements, risk tolerance and willingness to explore alternative deal or co-investment structures. Possibilities exist along the entire continuum of capital and investors are encouraged to learn more about innovation in this space through sources like Armeni and Ferreyra de Bone (2017), Shankar et al. (2021), Collaboration for Frontier Finance (2019), Dutch Good Growth Fund (2019) and Pacific RISE (2021).

For those wishing to progress to screening candidate investees, the authors have identified four key principles that support the success of a BoP business model that should be reflected in the structure of a BoP business model as well as its interactions with funders.

- BoP communities are complex adaptive systems, and as such require ongoing engagement and monitoring.
- Profits are a means to community development and empowerment, rather than the entire goal of business model.
- Sustainable BoP business models require long-term commitments and (often slow) growth that is limited by the rate of community development and empowerment.
- Sustainable BoP business models must incorporate value capture mechanisms for BoP participants.

This highlights several key things that investors in BoP business models should not target if they wish to drive sustainable development: short-term profit maximisation, rapid scaling, set and forget approaches and fixed timeframes. The paragraphs below summarise why that is.

Short-term profit maximisation does not align with – and is unlikely to generate – poverty alleviation and may actually create harm (Dembek, Sivasubramaniam, and Chmielewski 2019). Profits are best viewed as tool to be tailored to the BoP sustainable development challenge at hand as part of a long-term, slow growth investment strategy rather than something to be maximised through the investment. When used in combination with a systems lens, in-depth knowledge of and relationships with communities, as well as substantial effort and time dedicated to community development, this approach can generate sustainable positive development outcomes and appropriate returns. Without these efforts, and without providing BoP communities mechanisms for value capture, interventions targeting BoP income generation may still have severe unintended negative consequences for them.

Focus on scale and rapid growth is not a universal path to success for BoP business models. Many BoP businesses intend to see their companies grow organically over the long-run and do not prioritise rapid growth, creating potential a mismatch of time-horizon and growth expectations with potential investors expecting rapid business growth (Armeni and Ferreyra de Bone 2017; Hilton, Saif, and Khan 2021;

Hornberger and Chau 2018). If communities are not prepared for the economic development, pursuing scale and growth may harm both communities and the company. In these cases, slower growth and replicating the community development process may be much more effective than scaling universal solutions. BoP ventures require continuous practice on the ground with care around power relationships with and within poor communities (Arora and Romijn 2012). Additionally, not all BoP ventures need to scale large and attract big investment to create mutual value, some BoP sourcing initiatives may be more suitable for smaller investors looking for impactful investment opportunities (London 2016).

Another important practical implication from this research is the importance of engaged and value-aligned investment capital in a structure appropriate to the investees short-term needs and long-term trajectory. Identifying the right investment capital means, in particular, ensuring that the investors' goals and values are aligned with the objective of creating mutual value and community wellbeing. An important role of capital in BoP venture development is to help manage tensions between the short and long-term needs of the business. Investment approaches should be tailored to the needs of the business to ensure that they help businesses address short-term needs to allow them to focus on long-term goals of sustainable poverty alleviation (Shankar, Jones, and York 2021).

Finally, there must be mechanisms present through which BoP communities can lengthen their time horizons and experience empowerment. These value capture mechanisms are critical to ongoing success of the business model as a vehicle for sustainable development, even though they may not directly generate revenue. For instance, Habi Footwear developed a dual business model structure which linked a value chain dedicated predominantly to creating economic and environmental benefits, with a value shop dedicated mostly to creating social benefits (Dembek and York 2020).

Community development requires time, dedication and long-term commitment. Mutual value creation requires designing business models that incorporate a process dedicated to identifying and addressing problems and concerns in community on an ongoing basis. Investors who are not prepared to commit substantial time and resources into ensuring that appropriate structures exist should reconsider their plans to invest in BoP business models or seek out communities that are well-prepared for collaboration. That is, those with the mindset, means and skills needed to capture value created by participating in economic activity and preferably are already involved in such activity. One solution for doing so is following companies that are open to connecting new organisations to the communities in which significant groundwork and supplier development has already taken place and where the monitoring of impact is implemented. Past experiences show that not following these principles carries serious risks of harming communities and the company (Varman, Skålén, and Belk 2012).

Conclusion

Forward-looking opportunities in BoP business models

The problems of poverty and environmental degradation are closely entwined for world's poorest people in the Global South and every effort to alleviate poverty that expands and reinscribes the currently unsustainable modes of production and consumption is in the long-term counterproductive to sustainable development. BoP business models can reinforce or break down currently unsustainable models of production and consumption that are edging the planet toward environmental disaster.

It will take some time to sort out exactly how catastrophic COVID-19 has been across the BoP. In March 2020, the International Monetary Fund reported that investors had already 'removed US$83 billion from emerging markets since the beginning of the crisis, the largest capital outflow ever recorded' (IMF 2020: 1). The Organisation for Economic Co-operation and Development reported in June 2020 that external private finance inflows to developing economies could drop by USD 700 billion in 2020 compared to 2019 levels, exceeding the immediate impact of the 2008 financial crisis by 60% (OECD 2020). Oxfam reported that six to eight percent of the global population could be forced into poverty due to COVID-19 and anti-poverty efforts could be set back by a decade and up to 30 years in some regions. Its worst projections were that over half the global population could be living in poverty as a result of COVID-19 and that years of donor progress promoting economic growth, supporting entrepreneurs and small and medium business and fostering job growth could be wiped away (Oxfam 2020).

While much of the developed world struggled with isolation, BoP communities have had to rely even more on face-to-face interaction. Limited access to technology restricts the ability of most micro-entrepreneurs and BoP customers to pivot to e-commerce. Similarly, e-learning is not an option for students who cannot afford a computer, a smart phone or an internet connection (Geaneotes and Mignano 2020).

This has implications for all BoP business model types. Many have had to adapt rapidly, which requires engaged, flexible and responsive finance. Delivering models have had to shift to alternate distribution methods to reach their BoP customers, as well as adjusting pricing and payment methods and even adapt product offerings (Geaneotes and Mignano 2020). Delivering models also had the opportunity to shine: the Center for Financial Inclusion highlighted the critically important role played by robust digital payment infrastructures, micro-insurance and working capital facilities for food producers (El-Zoghbi 2020).

COVID-19 has laid bare how little resilience the very poor have in the face of systemic disruption: by March 2020, 50% of respondents across seven countries had no emergency funds, and another ~1530% had already tapped into the funds they had (except India, where ratios are reversed) (BFA Global 2020). Even with modest savings or remittance networks, BoP communities struggle to survive widespread loss of income opportunities. The most vulnerable groups within BoP communities – women, children, people with disabilities and other stigmatised populations – bear these consequences the hardest. This underscores how critical it is that BoP sourcing and reorganising models should develop not just income streams, but the safety nets, human capital, natural capital and social capital that underpins financial resilience.

The global community has been presented with an opportunity to focus on rebuilding better, stronger, more sustainable and more resilient systems in a green post-COVID-19 recovery. This has implications for how actors work together across the system, including the importance of blended finance approaches. As Naveen Rao of the Rockefeller Foundation observed, 'the private sector can't tackle COVID-19 by itself, and neither can the public or NGO sectors. We all need to come together' (Sinclair 2020: 2). This has implications, for instance for how investors think about risk and undertake due diligence, which may be much more difficult than before in a world of restricted travel. For instance, development technical assistance provider, LINC, has asked:

> Can the donor community leverage the capabilities and tools they have developed doing remote monitoring of aid delivery in conflict or other non-permissive environments (third-party monitoring, GIS-tagged images, etc) and share them with the private sector investment community? (LINC 2020: 2)

Sustainable development is a system-based process. All systems have leverage points for change, which include slowing feedback loops that hold the problem in place, cultivating alternative pathways and putting in place feedback loops to reinforce nascent solutions (Meadows and Wright 2008). Leverage points can and should be used in the design of business models and sustainable finance initiatives to maximise their potential for swift change to more sustainable production and consumption patterns and reduced poverty in a post-COVID-19 world.

References

Amit, Raffi, and Christopher Zott. 2011. 'The Business Model: A Growing Domain of Scholarly Inquiry.' in Gideon D. Markman and Phillip H. Phan (eds.), *The Competitive Dynamics of Entrepreneurial Market Entry* (Cheltenham, UK: Edward Elgar Publishing), pp. 465–67.

Armeni, Andrea, and Miguei Ferreyra de Bone.·2017. *Innovations in Financing Structures for Impact Enterprises: Spotlight on Latin America*, (Transform Finance), <http://transformfinance.org/briefings/2017/9/1/innovations-in-financing-structures> [Accessed 15 Jun 2021].

Arora, Saurabh, and Henny Romijn. 2012. 'The Empty Rhetoric of Poverty Reduction at the Base of the Pyramid', *Organization*, 19 (4), 481–505.

Beckett, Jennifer R., Danielle A. Chmielewski, and Krzysztof Dembek. 2020. 'Taking the Time to Understand Time at the Bottom/Base of the Pyramid', *Business and Society*, 1–32. https://doi.org/10.1177/0007650320927332

Behrman, Jere R. 1996. 'The Impact of Health and Nutrition on Education', *The World Bank Research Observer*, 11 (1), 23–37.

BFA Global.·2020. *Covid-19 and Your Finances – BFA Global Worldwide Survey* BFA Global <https://datastudio.google.com/u/0/reporting/1yyG5QHGV-v-bxw6pJNZvwtqnIfCLj-7q/page/kJOKB> [Accessed 15 Jun 2021].

Caneque, F.C., and S.L. Hart. 2017. *Base of the Pyramid 3.0: Sustainable Development through Innovation and Entrepreneurship* (Milton Park, UK: Taylor and Francis).

Chmielewski, Danielle A., Krzysztof Dembek, and Jennifer R. Beckett. 2020. "Business Unusual': Building BoP 3.0', *Journal of Business Ethics*, 161 (1), 211–29.

Cinner, Joshua E., Timothy R. McClanahan, Tim M. Daw, Nicholas A.J. Graham, Joseph Maina, Shaun K. Wilson, and Terence P. Hughes. 2009. 'Linking Social and Ecological Systems to Sustain Coral Reef Fisheries', *Current Biology*, 19 (3), 206–12.

Clark, C.·2017. *Types of Capital Comparison*, (Durham, NC: CASE Smart Impact Tools) <https://sites.duke.edu/casei3/case-smart-impact-capital/> [Accessed 16 January 2022].

Collaboration for Frontier Finance.·2019. *Closing the Gaps – Finance Pathways for Serving the Missing Middles*, https://dalberg.com/wp-content/uploads/2020/01/ClosingtheGaps_FullReportvF.pdf> [Accessed 1 September 2021].

Covergence. N d. *Blended Finance*, <https://www.convergence.finance/blended-finance> [Accessed 15 Jun 2021].

Dembek, Krzysztof, Nagaraj Sivasubramaniam, and Danielle A. Chmielewski. 2019. 'A Systematic Review of the Bottom/Base of the Pyramid Literature: Cumulative Evidence and Future Directions', *Journal of Business Ethics*, 165 (3), 365–82.

Dembek, Krzysztof, and Jodi York. 2019. 'Sustainable Business Models: Rethinking Value and Impact.' in Thomas Wunder (ed.), *Sustainable Strategic Management* (New York: Springer), pp. 131–48.

———. 2020. 'Applying a Sustainable Business Model Lens to Mutual Value Creation with Base of the Pyramid Suppliers', *Business and Society*, 1–36.

Dembek, Krzysztof, Jodi York, and Prakash J. Singh. 2018. 'Creating Value for Multiple Stakeholders: Sustainable Business Models at the Base of the Pyramid', *Journal of Cleaner Production*, 196, 1600–12.

Dutch Good Growth Fund.·2019. *Scaling Access to Finance for Early-Stage Enterprises in Emerging Markets: Lessons from the Field*, <https://g4aw.spaceoffice.nl/files/files/G4AW/resource%20page%20-%20recommended%20publications/Acces%20to%20capital/2019%20MoFA%20DGGF%20Study+on+scaling+access+to+finance+for+early-stage+enterprises.pdf> [Accessed 1 September 2021].

El–Zoghbi, Mayada 2020 'Covid-19 Reveals the Limits of Individual Action and Market-Based Solutions' *Center for Financial Inclusion* <https://www.centerforfinancialinclusion.org/covid-19-reveals-the-limits-of-individual-action-and-market-based-solutions> [Accessed 15 Jun 2021]

Elango, B., Stephen Chen, and Jim Jones. 2019. 'Sticking to the Social Mission: Microinsurance in Bottom of the Pyramid Markets', *Journal of General Management*, 44 (4), 209–19.

Geaneotes, Alexis, and Kathleen Mignano.·2020. *Leveraging Inclusive Business Models to Support the Base of the Pyramid During Covid-19*, EMCompass, (Washington DC: International Finance Corporation), <https://openknowledge.worldbank.org/handle/10986/34307> [Accessed 27 Jun 2021].

Global Sustainable Investment Alliance.·2019. *Global Sustainable Investment Review 2018*, (GSIA), <http://www.gsi-alliance.org/wp-content/uploads/2019/06/GSIR_Review2018F.pdf?mc_cid=11eda827b4&mc_eid=cea61a254b> [Accessed 3 November 2021].

Hall, Jeremy, Stelvia Matos, Lorn Sheehan, and Bruno Silvestre. 2012. 'Entrepreneurship and Innovation at the Base of the Pyramid: A Recipe for Inclusive Growth or Social Exclusion?', *Journal of Management Studies*, 49 (4), 785–812.

Heger, Martin, Gregor Zens, and Mook Bangalor.·2018. *Does the Environment Matter for Poverty Reduction?: The Role of Soil Fertility and Vegetation Vigor in Poverty Reduction.*, Policy Research Working Paper, (Washington DC: World Bank), <http://hdl.handle.net/10986/30227> [Accessed 30 January 2022].

Hilton, Tom, Syeda Samira Saif, and Jawad Khan.·2021. *Pacific RISE Final Evaluation*, (Canberra: Department of Foreign Affairs and Trade (Australia)), <https://www.pacificrise.org/wp-content/uploads/2021/06/Pacific-RISE-Final-Evaluation.pdf> [Accessed 1 September 2021].

Hofstetter, Dominic.·2020. Transformation Capital – Systemic Investing for Sustainability, (Amsterdam: EIT Climate-KIC), <https://www.climate-kic.org/wp-content/uploads/2020/08/Transformation-Capital-Systemic-Investing-for-Sustainability.pdf> [Accessed 3 November 2021].

Hornberger, K., and V. Chau.·2018. *The Missing Middles: Segmenting Enterprises to Better Understand Their Financial Needs*, (Dalberg Advisors, supported by the Collaborative for Frontier Finance: Omidyar Network/Dutch Good Growth Fund.), <https://static1.squarespace.com/static/59d679428dd0414c16f59855/t/5c5b4b38e5e5f0051af084a0/1549486917983/Missing_Middles_CFF_Report.pdf> [Accessed 1 September 2021].

Ims, Knut J., and Laszlo Zsolnai. 2014. 'Ethics of Social Innovation', *Society and Business Review*, 9 (2), 186–94.

Intergovernmental Panel on Climate Change.·2014. *Climate Change 2014: Impacts, Adaptation, and Vulnerability. Part A: Global and Sectoral Aspects. Contribution of Working Group II to the Fifth Assessment Report of the Intergovernmental Panel on Climate Change*, (Cambridge, UK: Cambridge University Press), <https://www.ipcc.ch/site/assets/uploads/2018/02/WGIIAR5-FrontMatterA_FINAL.pdf> [Accessed 3 November 2021].

———.·2018. *Global Warming of 1.5 °C. Special Report*, (IPCC), <https://www.ipcc.ch/sr15/> [Accessed 21 July 2019].

International Monetary Fund. 2020. *The Great Lockdown: Worst Economic Downturn since the Great Depression* (IMF), <https://www.imf.org/en/News/Articles/2020/03/23/pr2098-imf-managing-director-statement-following-a-g20-ministerial-call-on-the-coronavirus-emergency> [Accessed 27 Jun 2021].

Jayachandran, Seema.·2019. *Social Norms as a Barrier to Women's Employment in Developing Countries*, WIDER Working Paper Series, (Helsinki: World Institute for Development Economic Research), <https://ideas.repec.org/p/unu/wpaper/wp-2019-74.html> [Accessed 29 October 2021].

Joshi, Lalita, Deepak Choudhary, Praveen Kumar, Jayendran Venkateswaran, and Chetan S. Solanki. 2019. 'Does Involvement of Local Community Ensure Sustained Energy Access? A Critical Review of a Solar PV Technology Intervention in Rural India', *World Development*, 122, 272–81.

Karnani, Aneel. 2007. 'Doing Well by Doing Good—Case Study:'Fair & Lovely'whitening Cream', *Strategic Management Journal*, 28 (13), 1351–57.

Larimer, Mary E., Daniel K. Malone, Michelle D. Garner, David C. Atkins, Bonnie Burlingham, Heather S. Lonczak, Kenneth Tanzer, Joshua Ginzler, Seema L. Clifasefi, William G. Hobson, and G. Alan Marlatt. 2009. 'Health Care and Public Service Use and Costs before and after Provision of Housing for Chronically Homeless Persons with Severe Alcohol Problems', *Journal of the American Medical Association*, 301 (13), 1349–57.

LINC.·2020. *Covid-19 and Blended Finance: Five Ways to Adaptively Respond*, (Washington DC: LINC), <https://linclocal.org/wp-content/uploads/2020/04/COVID-and-Blended-Finance_FINAL_formatted.pdf> [Accessed 27 June 2021].

London, T. 2016. *The Base of the Pyramid Promise: Building Businesses with Impact and Scale* (Redwood City, CA: Stanford University Press).

Mani, Anandi, Sendhil Mullainathan, Eldar Shafir, and Jiaying Zhao. 2013. 'Poverty Impedes Cognitive Function', *Science*, 341 (6149), 976–80.

Meadows, Donella H., and Diana Wright. 2008. *Thinking in Systems: A Primer* (White River Junction, VT: Chelsea Green Pub).

Morgan Stanley Capital International. 2017. *The SDGs and Sustainable Impact: A Practical Guide for Investors*, <https://www.msci.com/documents/10199/3995bb20-a1ec-4cf7-9fe7-8b80b12ed0c9> [Accessed 12 February 2021].

Mullainathan, S., and E. Shafir. 2013. *Scarcity: Why Having Too Little Means So Much* (New York: Times Books).

Niinimäki, Kirsi, Greg Peters, Helena Dahlbo, Patsy Perry, Timo Rissanen, and Alison Gwilt. 2020. 'The Environmental Price of Fast Fashion', *Nature Reviews Earth and Environment*, 1 (4), 189–200.

Nulkar, Gurudas. 2016. 'The Environmental Costs of Serving the Bottom of the Pyramid', *Sustainability*, 9 (1), 31–38.

Organisation for Economic Co-operation and Development Development Co-operation Directorate.·2006. *Why a Healthy Environment Is Essential to Reducing Poverty*, (Paris: OECD), <https://www.oecd.org/dac/environment-development/36348154.pdf> [Accessed 15 Jun 2021].

Organisation for Economic Co-operation and Development.·2006. *Why a Healthy Environment Is Essential to Reducing Poverty*, (Paris: OECD Development Co-operation Directorate), <https://www.oecd.org/dac/environment–development/36348154.pdf> [Accessed 15 Jun 2021].

———.·2020. *The Impact of the Coronavirus (Covid-19) Crisis on Development Finance*, OECD Policy Responses to Coronavirus (COVID-19), (Paris: OECD), <https://read.oecd-ilibrary.org/view/?ref=134_134569-xn1go1i113&title=The-impact-of-the-coronavirus-(COVID-19)-crisis-on-development-finance&_ga=2.64940719.1206669990.1625563628-2020439747.1624771576> [Accessed 27 Jun 2021].

Oxfam.·2020. *Dignity Not Destitution: An 'Economic Rescue Plan for All' to Tackle the Coronavirus Crisis and Rebuild a More Equal World*, Oxfam media briefing, <https://oxfamilibrary.openrepository.com/bitstream/handle/10546/620976/mb-dignity%20not%20destitution-an-economic-rescue-plan-for-all-090420-en.pdf> [Accessed 29 October 2021].

Pacific RISE.·2021. *Pacific Possibilities*, (Canberra: Australian Department of Foreign Affairs and Trade), <https://www.pacificrise.org/wp-content/uploads/2021/07/Pacific-RISE-Pacific-Possibilities.pdf> [Accessed 1 September 2021].

Peluso, N.L., and M. Watts. 2001. *Violent Environments* (Ithaca, NY: Cornell University Press).

Pineiro, Aliana, and Rachel Bass. 2017. *Beyond Investment: The Power of Capacity Building Support*, GIIN Issue Briefs, (Washington DC: Global Impact Investing Network), <https://thegiin.org/assets/GIIN_issuebrief_capacitybuilding_finalwebfile_101217.pdf> [Accessed 29 October 2021].

Prahalad, C.K., and Stuart L. Hart. 2002. 'The Fortune at the Bottom of the Pyramid', *Strategy+Business*, 26 (1), 55–67.

Schiff, Hannah, and Hannah Dithrich.·2018. *Lasting Impact: The Need for Responsible Exits*, GIIN Issues Briefs, (Washington DC: Global Impact Investing Network), <https://thegiin.org/research/publication/responsible-exits> [Accessed 30 January 2022].

Schuyler, Kevin W. 2005. 'Expanding the Frontiers of Conservation Finance.' in James N. Levitt (ed.), *From Walden to Wall Street: Frontiers of Conservation Finance* (Washington: Island Press), pp. 109–23.

Shah, Anuj K., Sendhil Mullainathan, and Eldar Shafir. 2012. 'Some Consequences of Having Too Little', *Science*, 338 (6107), 682–85.

Shankar, Shravan, Ian Jones, and Jodi York.·2021. *Demand-Led Investment: A New Perspective on Approaches to Adapting Capital and Bridging the Missing Middle in Southeast Asia*, (Frontiers Lab Asia), <https://fla.yourcreative.com.au/wp-content/uploads/2021/10/Report_on_De mand-led_Investment_for_the_Missing_Middle_2021.pdf> [Accessed 1 October 2021].

Simanis, Erik, Stuart Hart, and Duncan Duke. 2008. 'The Base of the Pyramid Protocol: Beyond "Basic Needs" Business Strategies', *Innovations: Technology, Governance, Globalization*, 3 (1), 57–84.

Sinclair, Matt 2020 '5 Questions for . . . Naveen Rao, Senior Vice President, Health Initiative, Rockefeller Foundation' *Philanthropy News Digest* <https://philanthropynewsdigest.org/5-questions-for/naveen-rao-senior-vice-president-health-initiative-rockefeller-foundation> [Accessed 29 October 2021]

United Nations. 2017. *Work of the Statistical Commission Pertaining to the 2030 Agenda for Sustainable Development*, A/RES/71/313 (United Nations) <https://undocs.org/A/RES/71/313> [Accessed 3 November 2021].

United Nations Development Programme.·2020. *Human Development Report 2020 the Next Frontier: Human Development and the Anthropocene*, (New York: UNDP), <http://hdr.undp.org/en/2020-report> [Accessed 3 November 2021].

United Nations High Level Panel.·2013. *A New Global Partnership: Eradicate Poverty and Transform Economies through Sustainable Development*, The Report of the High-Level Panel of Eminent Persons on the Post-2015 Development Agenda, (New York: United Nations), <https://www.post2020hlp.org/wp-content/uploads/docs/UN-Report.pdf> [Accessed 29 October 2021].

Varman, Rohit, Per Skålén, and Russell W. Belk. 2012. 'Conflicts at the Bottom of the Pyramid: Profitability, Poverty Alleviation, and Neoliberal Governmentality', *Journal of Public Policy and Marketing*, 31 (1), 19–35.

Verick, Sher.·2014. *Female Labor Force Participation In developing Countries*, (Bonn, Germany: IZA World of Labor), <https://wol.iza.org/articles/female-labor-force-participation-in-developing-countries/long> [Accessed 29 October 2021].

World Bank. 2015. *Climate Change Complicates Efforts to End Poverty*, <https://www.worldbank.org/en/news/feature/2015/02/06/climate-change-complicates-efforts-end-poverty> [Accessed 29 October 2021].

York, Jodi. 2002. 'Forests for Whom? Ethnic Politics of Conservation in Northern Thailand 1996-2001', *Berkeley Journal of Sociology: A Critical Review*, 46, 132–54.

York, Jodi, and Krzysztof Dembek. 2021. 'Building BoP Business Models for Sustainable Poverty Alleviation: System Tips and System Traps.' in Annabeth Aagaard, Peter Wells and Florian Ludeke-Freund (eds.), *Business Models for Sustainability Transitions: How Organisations Contribute to Societal Transformation* (London: Palgrave Macmillan), pp. 123–59

Arnab Bose, Seema Sharma and A. Amarender Reddy

Chapter 15
AI and blockchain for sustainable development in India

Abstract: AI (artificial intelligence) and blockchain are promising technologies for all countries, including India. While these two technologies have a landscape of associated risks, there are distinct aspects like decentralisation and distribution, which make these technologies particularly suitable for India. It seems that the promise of technology could not come any sooner, especially as India faced the COVID-19 crisis in 2021. With this in mind, the chapter will do three things. First, the chapter will draw out a framework of effective risk management of AI and blockchain and put forward methods of effective decentralised decision-making. Second, the chapter will comment on the nature and sources of finance in this technology transition in India with empirical evidence. Third, the chapter will trace policy feedback and suggest a way forward with a focus on the COVID-19 crisis. Thus, the chapter will seek to draw out a meaningful narrative about the landscape of AI and blockchain in India particularly in its use to attain effective local governance and sustainable development.

Keywords: artificial intelligence, blockchain, sustainable development, COVID-19, India

Introduction

It might seem that AI, blockchain or distributed ledger technologies, sustainable development and poverty alleviation all are disparate items which do not fit into any coherent narrative. However there has been an effort from various stakeholders to align various technological progress to work towards achieving the compelling challenges of sustainable development and poverty alleviation in the world today (World Economic Forum (WEF) 2020; National Institution for Transforming India 2021). The Indian case is a particularly suitable case for discussion. First, it is an argumentative democracy with more than a billion people of various hues; second, in terms of sensory appeal India seems far too chaotic for any meaningful development to take place. However, third, there are signs that show technological progress can be dovetailed towards some poverty alleviation action like the direct transfer benefits, etc. Given this tough terrain this chapter sets out to align fledgling technologies like AI and blockchain to achieving the objectives of sustainable development and poverty alleviation for a country like India. To do this, the chapter utilises

https://doi.org/10.1515/9783110733488-015

uses various forms of qualitative techniques including participant observation, interviews, discourse analysis, case studies and field trips over an extended period of time in India at various locations from 2015 to 2021, and in Berlin, Germany in 2018/19 during the winter break. The questions what, why and how are answered particularly in the context of India. The field study in Germany is being included to broaden the scope and adding to the knowledge of this research. The discourse and field trips both point towards a missing element of effective local governance. This can also be interpreted a non-effective implementation of various policies and programmes. An exemplar of this is that at onset of the COVID-19 crisis in India, large numbers of ventilators were distributed across numerous hospitals in India in both urban and rural areas (The Times of India 2021). However, when the second wave hit these ventilators could not be used as there were missing elements or lack of trained personnel to run them. The entire financial allocation on such machines was wasted. While such wastage can be attributed to public finance in India, private finance will not entertain such wastage. There will be due diligence and other processes in private firms where such process mistakes will not happen. This attribute of the divergence between public and private finance is not true only in India, various other countries have similar features. However private finance has its own risks and so do new fledgling technologies like AI and blockchain.

AI, through new age technologies like AI and blockchain, offers exciting possibilities to accelerate India's goals for sustainable development and poverty alleviation, there has to be an effective strategy to align the technologies with requirements and local realities. The strategy will be to first understand the nature of the problem, both for sustainable development and the technologies. One efficient method to get the feel of the nature of the problem is to look at the interplay of technology and ground realities through lens of associated risks. Surveying and understanding concepts in risks will become pertinent. The second part of the strategy will be to delineate an effective framework to mitigate the risks associated with using technologies like AI and blockchain to attain sustainable development. And finally, the third part of the strategy will be to find out how palatable the framework to mitigate risks will be to the prevalent policy paradigm in India.

Given this scenario, the chapter will seek to do three things. First, the chapter will draw out a framework to portray risks of AI and blockchain in the Indian context amid the present COVID-19 crisis and put forward methods of effective decentralised decision-making. Here the known, unknown, unknowable (KuU) framework (Diebold et al. 2010) will be used. In fact in the portrayal of risks, not only will this research touch upon AI (Scherer 2015) and blockchain risks (Supreme Court of India 2020), but also of the risks of carrying out interventions in sustainable development for a country like India (Bose et al. 2012b). COVID-19 risks are also brought in the narrative (Fronteira et al. 2021).

Second, the chapter will comment on the nature and source of finance in this technology transition in India. Financial gradients (Bose 2011: 57–58) will be used to construct the discourse in this section. Financial gradients are already a financial strategy for sustainable development action, however in this research an extension is made to the framework of financial gradients to include the discourse on risks of technologies such as AI and blockchain. This extension of the framework will help the financial gradients concept to be used as a risk mitigation tool of using technologies such as AI and blockchain for achieving goals for sustainable development.

Third, the chapter will trace the policy feedback and a way forward with a focus on the COVID-19 crisis. Therefore, first, the chapter will draw out a theoretical construct, second it will bring out empirical evidence, and third it will recommend a policy as a way forward. Thus, the chapter will seek to draw out a meaningful narrative about the landscape of AI and blockchain in India particularly in its use to attain sustainable development.

The COVID-19 crisis in India

According to the COVID-19 Data Repository by the Center for Systems Science and Engineering (CSSE) at Johns Hopkins University (2021), the second wave in India can be seen as a typical bell curve with a peak of daily 391,232 cases on 8 May 2021.

India was doing relatively well in managing the COVID-19 crisis up until 15 April 2021. It seems there was a change in circumstances thereafter (Bhowmick 2021a). The New York Times (2021), using official Indian Government sources (Indian Ministry of Health and Welfare 2021), reported that the average number of new cases were around 9,000 per day on 15th February 2021, moving up to approximately 24,000 on 15 March 2021, and to 217,000 per day on 15 April 2021. And finally, a new global record of new cases was created on 23 April 2021 with the number of cases surpassing 330,000 surpassing the US which held the previous one-day record with 300,669 new cases as recorded on 8 January, 2021 (Bhowmick 2021a).

Though the scale of the second surge was ghastly (The Lancet COVID-19 Commission India Taskforce 2021), there were signs which should have been noted and precautionary measures should have been taken but were missed (Biswas 2021). Also, the Lancet COVID-19 Commission (2021) notes that the second wave was different from the first wave in ways that the infection rate was higher (which became later known as the Delta variant) and the spread in tier two and tier three cities were higher.

Another thing to note is that while the Lancet COVID-19 Commission (2021) mentioned the role of decentralised decision-making processes and community action, the international media focussed on the central leadership, as if changing the leader would cure the problem. Why changing the leader in this context would work, when other sustainability or inclusion issues have also not been solved, is not clear. It is important that the arguments to put India in the right direction is not merely getting a certain kind of people into government. In fact, it is important to put in processes and systems which will work for effective community-based neighbourhood solutions and increasing capacity at the level of the community or the neighbourhood.

Summarily, two things come to light as the cause of the spectacular onset of the second wave of the COVID-19 crisis in India. First, the COVID-19 variant now known as the Delta variant is far more virulent and infectious than the variants first seen such as the Alpha variant. Second, there were inherent flaws in processes in managing and implementing governmental orders. When it comes to implementation failure it will affect the vast majority of the population in India, who do not have effective community-based or neighbourhood-based solutions, in a greater magnitude than those who do. Again, going back to the case of non-functional ventilators in the hospital (The Times of India 2021), the implications of this meant that while there were ventilators in the district hospital because no one could operate them the family of the COVID-19 patient would have to travel to urban areas with the same equipment with personnel to operate a ventilator. This is just one case of the ventilators, and if other resources, like oxygen (Sharma 2021b), medicines and even vaccines (Sharma 2021a) are brought into the narrative of micro-inefficiency in each process, then the adversity starts snowballing to enormous proportions. Then more families with COVID-19 patients would need to travel, requiring more ambulances. In fact, there were cases in which ambulances had to stand still because of a lack of drivers (News18 2021). This is all in a country of more than 1.3 billion people.

The need for instilling and installing local effective governance

India's Human Development Index (HDI) value for 2019 was 0.645 (United Nations Development Programme (UNDP) 2021a); this was a 50.3% increase from 1990 (UNDP 2021a 2021). This period is important as post 1991 India liberalised its economy considerably and paved the way for the inflow of private capital in various aspects of the economy. The discourse on private capital becomes important in this research as the funding of technology-based interventions using AI and blockchain happen primarily via private capital. The interpretation of private capital means sources of finance which seek returns on investment (Bose 2011: 57–58). Private capital is different from public finance, where the latter normally refers to government expenditure which does not seek an explicit return on capital. However, to say that the advent of private capital has led to an increase in the quality of life as evident from the HDI might not be easy. Albeit that there are signs of increased industrial productivity (Majumdar 1996), the terrain is difficult with various non-linear manifestations (Kohli 2006) and the argument of private capital or investment grade finance creating efficiencies (Bose 2011: 57–58) might not happen as a particular eco-system needs to be instilled and installed.

In the discourse on poverty alleviation, in India the population headcount on the Multidimensional Poverty Index (MPI) is 27.9% as per the last record (UNDP 2021). To quote the United Nations report on multidimensional poverty on India, the statement reads – 'four countries halved their MPI value. India (2005/20062015/2016) did so na-tionally and among children and had the biggest reduction in the number of multi-dimensionally poor people (273 million). Ten countries, including China, came close to halving the MPI value' (UNDPa 2021: 3). The pandemic of course will affect these trends in disparate ways, however the pre-pandemic efforts to reduce poverty has been in line with the task at hand. However, given the population size is there a need to accelerate the process of poverty alleviation? Yes, for sure (NITI Aayog 2021: 4). Is there a need to accelerate the process using technologies like AI and blockchain? Yes, for sure (WEF 2020: 8). If there is a need to accelerate to human development goals of poverty alleviation and the overall Sustainable Development Goals (SDG) technology may well be helpful in creating a more coherent narrative on how to instil and install the various actors to achieve the goals.

The problems of development have been studied using various economic lenses, whether crafting randomised control trials (Banerjee et al. 2016) or looking at the problem of development from understanding institutions (North 1991). While these endeavours are promising, often they run into problems. As Kabeer (2020: 104809) has pointed out 'that the theoretical model of causal inference underpinning RCTs (randomised control trials) is frequently undermined by the failure of different actors involved in their implementation to behave in ways required by the model.' This statement alone points towards the wicked problems (Head 2008) that sound meth-ods like RCTs face in a very complex and dynamic system.

While the construct of formal and informal institutions (North 1991) is helpful, also useful are ideas of Banerjee and Duflo (2011) on crafting interventions which minimise inefficiencies or wastage, yet RCTs may just add to the complexity to an already difficult terrain than mitigate it. To, however, sense the discourse better one might analyse the terrain using politics in India. To be more precise the dis-course on Prashant Kishore may be used to possibly to understand instil and install better.

Prashant Kishor (Goyal 2020) is not a politician but a strategist, who in 2021 in India is seen as a very powerful and possibly the only challenger to Prime Minister Modi. It can be noted that Prashant Kishor started his political career assisting Prime Minister Modi in the 2014 general elections in India (Jaffrelot 2015). And many agree that Kishor and Modi concurred on the general direction on the imme-diate priorities that needed to be addressed in the Indian context, principle among them was the need for effectiveness in governance (Kishor 2019), or what in this research is being called instil and install. Prashant Kishor does not fight elections himself but strategises for various other political parties (Haq 2017). He has a near unblemished record in the very uncertain and nebulous political terrain of India (Goyal 2020). His only condition for help is that he would have his way holistically during a political campaign and be in direct liaison with the leader of the political party, as happened in the vigorously contested West Bengal state elections in 2021 (Oxford Analytica 2019; Bhowmick 2021b). This discussion may seem like a digression, however how Prashant Kishore is able to deliver as they understand the prevailing misalignment of relevant stakeholders in implementing anything, especially at the level of local governments. He wants a free hand during campaigns because they want to deliver a message or implement a programme which in the traditional set up is quite difficult. In West Bengal, apart from political messaging, they helped in implementing various programmes including Duare Sarkar (2021). Duare Sarkar means the government at your doorstep (West Bengal Government 2021), which envisages a plethora of activities very specific to the district or sub-district (municipality or sub-municipality). Duare Sarkar (2021) can be construed as a mechanism to instil and install effective governance. Similar mechanisms have been adopted by Kishore in the many other political campaigns they had assisted in. The case of Prashant Kishore in this research highlights the power of bringing in local governance effectively. Effectively implies delivery of the programme as intended, and this is possible due to the fact the relevant actors work in a non-conflicting, constructive manner. The control which Prashant Kishore wants is to enforce the effectiveness of the planned programmes. This argument seems to the missing in the discourse of political analysis as seen in the observations of the 2021 West Bengal state elections. The question of stakeholder alignment is not only an anthropological, social or political question, it is an economic question too (Kishor 2019).

It might be opportune now, having used this part as a segue, to start the discourse on the landscape of risks and the financial framework to mitigate the risks to align technologies like AI and blockchain to achieve sustainable economic development. To reiterate, this research endeavours to bring the attention towards the need to align stakeholders (instil) and form processes (install), particularly at the local level, to achieve the goals of sustainable development and poverty alleviation. However, it should be noted that this research does not seek to bring any radical change. Instead, these should be noted as minor, incremental changes which happen in day-to-day governance in any case. The research notes the importance and presence of both formal and informal institutions (North 1991). Given the institutions of the market economy present in India, the goals can be attained within this framework. This will help use the entrepreneurial animal spirits (Akerlof and Shiller 2010) to achieve the human development goals.

Key risk concepts in the discourse on AI, blockchain, sustainable development and COVID-19 in India

The known, the unknown and the unknowable, or simply referred to as KuU, (Diebold et al. 2010) is a risk management framework in finance (Nigbur 2010). The impact of the KuU framework may be far-reaching even outside of the finance world and can be looked upon as a governance tool in scenarios where diverse kinds of uncertainty and complexity play an important role.

Diebold et al. (2010), building upon Gomory (1995) delineate that knowledge is both measurement and theory. The following is a summary of the work by Diebold et al. (2010) for the benefit of the reader.

KuU, when looked upon in the knowledge as measurement realm where a probability distribution as a could be said to be a complete and exhaustive set of outcomes, together with associated probabilities, that may befall some variable of interest, then:

a. K is when the distribution is completely specified.
b. u is when the probabilities cannot be assigned to at least part of the event space.
c. U corresponds to a situation where even the events defining the space cannot be identified in advance.

KuU, when looked upon as knowledge as theory, is a conceptual model that helps to understand the underlying structure of the phenomenon of interest.

a. K is when the underlying model is well understood by most stakeholders. An analogy is made to Darwin's model, where there is a broad agreement even if granular details are not universally accepted. K therefore is a short form of the existence of a theory or theory itself.
b. u refers to a situation where there is more than one model competing with each other, none of which has ascended to the status of a paradigm. If K is theory, then u is hypothesis, or conjecture.
c. U is where there is no describing or underlying model (or no model with scientific credibility yet). Here the attribute is not yet studied or detected yet.

However, it is important to note the two taxonomies are complementary (Diebold, Doherty, and Herring 2010: 4). The complementariness of the taxonomies and the general understanding that the movement from U to u to K under both taxonomies is the journey that humankind should take should not be amiss to anyone. This broad understanding of the requirements of the knowledge sets to mitigate uncertainty by all stakeholders should be an agreed objective. This broad understanding will be more relevant in the discourse of the COVID-19 crisis in India and the requirement to scale existing technology will be quite explicit in the vignettes.

In order to get to a working framework for risk management of AI and blockchain, it will be important to create a narrative of the landscape of the perceived risks for both AI and blockchain. This is to understand what are the knowns, unknowns and unknowables (Ks, us, Us) in the paradigm of AI and blockchain. This will set the base of how the journey from unknowable to unknown to known can take place for AI and blockchain based interventions.

It is interesting to note that AI has a wider range of perceived risks, as they can be in the range of the known, the unknown and of course even the unknowable risks. AI has perceived systematic as well as systemic risks. It can be understood that some systemic risks can become systematic as in the financial crisis of 2008 (Bose 2011: 57–58). From that crisis it has been learnt that nebulous concepts have inherent systemic risks to start with and when there is worldwide usage or acceptance of these practices there is a systematic risk created for the world; and if the systemic risk has countrywide usage, then that would translate to a countrywide systematic risk. Unlike the wide-ranging plausibly unfathomable manifestation of risks associated with AI, blockchain and the perceived risks right now are possibly mostly systemic in nature. These risks can also be addressed within a country especially as blockchain is subject to country specific regulation as is the case with India. Therefore, the discourse on AI has to be broad-based, whereas the discourse on blockchain can be country specific (as with this chapter). It should be understood that the systemic and systematic risks are concepts borrowed from finance where systemic risks are risks mostly as a result of incorrect rules, regulation or policy; whereas systematic risks are those risks like the pandemic which have a market-wide effect.

In the case of AI, there are several discourses on the perceived risks, from corporate notes to academic journals; however, a succinct analysis can be found in Scherer (2015: 353–400).

Scherer (2015: 362) notes that several characteristics of artificial intelligence will make it more difficult to regulate AI as compared to other sources of public risk, as has been found that in the case of blockchain for instance. Scherer (2015: 353–400) divides the risks into two categories one, *ex ante* and the other *ex post*. *Ex ante* challenges of AI are to do with the research and development stage of AI, and *ex post* is to do with the challenges once AI is created and implemented.

The *ex ante* challenges are described as discreetness, diffuseness, discreteness and opacity. Discreetness refers to the fact that AI projects can be created without large-scale institutional support or infrastructure. Individuals, startups to large corporations can create their own AI projects or interventions. Diffuseness refers to the fact that the AI projects can happen anywhere. It mostly requires very basic computing and the internet. Discreteness refers to the fact that AI projects may be very nebulous and vague to start with, but once the ecosystem is completed possibly to do with the requirements of data, software or hardware the full potential will be realised. Opacity refers to the fact that the underlying concepts will be unknowable to various practitioners and regulators for a long time. In fact, what is also known as the black box problem (Cress 2019), such as how deep neural networks can make decisions: while the inputs and outputs are understood, the complexities within the neural network are not.

The *ex post* challenges are described as the foreseeability problem, narrow control and general control problems. Foreseeability refers to the situation that the AI may act and operate in a manner which is unforeseen even by the original programmers themselves, possibly much like the AI AlphaGo's triumphant game move 37, much described by commentators, after they had recovered from the shock, which was both creative and beautiful left its human opponent utterly flummoxed (Bailey 2019).

The narrow control problem refers to a situation when personnel legally responsible for the AI system are not in a position to control the AI system, and the general control problem is when the AI system is no longer in control within the entirety of the human civilisation, which is what has been described as superintelligence (Bostrom 1998). It can be inferred here that the range of problems in AI spread across the unknowable (e.g., general control, foreseeability or opacity problems), unknown (e.g., discreetness) and known (e.g., diffuseness, narrow control problems).

With respect to blockchain the discussion is substantially less complicated. It is said that the perceived risks are systemic in nature which possibly for blockchain can be located in a specific country, such as India, which is pertinent. A good summative discourse can be obtained from the judgement of the Supreme Court of India on virtual currencies (Supreme Court of India 2020). It can be inferred from the reading of the judgement that while the landscape of the risks is less, going into the granular details to explain the intricacies of the complications and how each possible systemic risks associated with unproven technology on one side and balancing it with fiduciary duty in the banking environment on the other side, opens up a Pandora's box, so to speak. However, from the Supreme Court (2020) it can be inferred, especially from an Indian context, that the risks with blockchain are within the known and unknown realms, never at the high-risk unknowable realm.

On 4 March 2020, a three-judge bench of the Supreme Court of India partially struck down a 2018 circular of the Reserve Bank of India (RBI), which directed banks and institutions regulated by the RBI not to deal in cryptocurrencies. The Court (2020) observed that as of that date the virtual currencies were not banned, but trading in virtual currencies and functioning of virtual currencies exchanges has nevertheless been severely impacted, as the interface with the regular banking sector was disconnected by RBI. The reading of the judgement may give rise to the following questions, which will plausibly provide guidance towards delineating the nature of the systemic risk at hand.

For instance, why did the RBI find virtual currencies so problematic? How much did the Financial Action Task Force (FATF, which is the global money laundering and terrorist financing watchdog. This intergovernmental body sets international standards that aim to prevent these illegal activities and the harm they cause to society) or Bank for International Settlements (BIS, which is an international financial institution that aims to promote global monetary and financial stability through the coordination of global central banks and their monetary policy efforts) affect the regulatory space in India via the RBI, which is the central bank of India). The RBI indicated the FATF documents saying that crypto assets can play a nefarious role in money laundering or even finance terror activities. It noted the BIS correspondence regarding risks with respect to money supply. The judgement also shed light on the policy process with the inter-ministerial policy meetings. It is perhaps that the institutions did not have the power to recognise the power of this new technology for India. Also, the heavy dependence on non-India actors like FATF and BIS for the RBI, and therefore in the inter-ministerial committees, is an important aspect where it can be seen that Indian institutions are unable to create emic understanding of technology aspects for better governance of India. It is perhaps due to various historical reasons including the Bhopal tragedy, that Indian policy circles are reticent towards foreign technology transfers (Sriramachari 2005). However, the preparedness of India with respect to technology adoption was at fault across institutions however the Achilles' heel in the given circumstance can be that of the Institute for Development and Research in Banking Technology (IDRBT, established by RBI in 1996 as an institution to work at the intersection of banking and technology). IDBRBT submitted a white paper on *Applications of blockchain technology to banking and financial sector in India* (2017). The white paper listed the advantages and disadvantages of digital currency; however, the institution did not play any further role in creating an appropriate discourse. It is here that the NITI Aayog (National Institution for Transforming India Policy Commission) takes over. But the NITI Aayog is a national-level think tank, which already has a lot on its plate, the IDRBT could have given more credible advice so that the amount of time wasted and opportunities lost for India, its entrepreneurs and the ecosystem would not have happened.

Vignettes: AI and blockchain use case analysis for COVID-19 in India

This section will try to look into the problem of the second COVID-19 surge in India. While this will be a huge expanse of a topic to study, the idea here will be to look into the risks that played out in this second surge, which is described as a syndemic (Fronteira et al. 2021). As pointed out in Fronteira et al. (2021), the current pandemic has affected communities, populations and countries throughout the world. In the second wave in India the magnitude is overwhelming.

As the current pandemic developed, 'the extent to which the disease interacted with already existing endemic, non-communicable and infectious diseases became evident, hence deeply influencing health outcomes' (Fronteira et al. 2021: 1). In addition, a synergistic effect and therefore a syndemic, has been manifesting with 'various socioeconomic, cultural, and contextual determinants of health which seem to contribute to poorer health and accumulating social disadvantages' (Fronteira et al. 2021: 1). Fronteira et al. (2021: 1) also point out that the failure to acknowledge this syndemic contributes to 'weakened policymaking processes and public health responses and ineffective health policies and programmes.'

The section will try to find out the nature of the risks, how this syndemic is playing out in India in the second surge and in what way can AI or blockchain help or how can they be related. However, the main focus in this section will be to see how the risk as seen in the second surge in India can be categorised, especially in the KuU framework.

An appropriate method of delving into the problem will be to construct vignettes, which are short case studies. The cases are drawn from the discourse of using AI and blockchain for solving typical COVID-19 related problems in India towards the nature of the risk (AI School of India 2021). These vignettes will also draw upon the financial and legal structure of the AI and blockchain based interventions or projects undertaken in India. These vignettes are captured in Table 15.1, COVID-19 centric interventions or projects using AI or blockchain in India.

Table 15.1: COVID-19 centric interventions or projects using AI or blockchain in India.

Name of the project	Purpose	Actors	Financing method
1. Atman AI (a deep learning application indigenously developed by CAIR-DRDO for COVID-19 screening using digital chest X-Rays) (Arakal 2021)	Detection of COVID-19 infection	CAIR (Centre for AI and Robotics), DRDO (Defence Research and Development Organization) with the support of 5C network and HCG educators	Public finance
2. COVIRAP (India Science Wire 2020)	A new diagnostic test for COVID-19	IIT Kharagpur	Grant, public finance

Table 15.1 (continued)

	Name of the project	Purpose	Actors	Financing method
3.	Qxr (a chest X-ray screening tool that functions on deep learning algorithms) (Qure.ai 2021)	Automated tool to identify abnormal findings in the chest X-ray within a minute.	Qxr.ai startup with the support of NITI Aayog and the Piramal Foundation.	Equity, public finance, philanthropic grant
4.	AI-powered surveillance tool (Cyient 2020)	AI-based system to identify and catch hold of people who are violating the law by not wearing a mask on the road	Cyient (formerly Infotech Enterprises Limited) with Telangana Police	Equity, public finance
5.	AI analytics device to alert retailers and shops to identify people not wearing masks and not following social distancing norms (Glimpse Analytics 2020)	To identify people not wearing masks and not following social distancing norms	Glimpse Analytics (a Pune based startup)	Equity
6.	Yellow Messenger Cares (a conversational AI platform) (Yellow Messanger 2020)	To develop COVID-19 related cross-channel help chatbots for hospitals, NGOs, medical and healthcare support groups and businesses to boost their health management efforts	Yellow Messenger	Equity
7.	MyGov Saathi (an AI-powered chatbot) (Arzo 2020)	AI-powered chatbot that helps to provide precise and latest information related to COVID-19 to the users. It is capable of handling 300,000 users each day	Accenture and Microsoft with the Government of India's Digital India Corporation	Equity, public finance
8.	WhatsApp-based chatbot named Introbot (Bhavani 2021)	Provides users with an evolving and verified database of beds, oxygen cylinders, plasma and other sources through WhatsApp	Startup by Divyaansh Anuj and Utkarsh Roy	Equity

Table 15.1 (continued)

Name of the project	Purpose	Actors	Financing method
9. AI model for drug repositioning in the treatment of COVID-19 (Indo-Asian News Service 2020).	Use AI to prune massive database and select a handful (5 to 10) of drugs that have better chances of succeeding. This would allow more concerted effort/trials on this handful of prospective treatment regimes.	Indraprastha Institute of Information Technology (IIIT-Delhi) in collaboration with IPGME&R Kolkata and INRIA, Saclay, Paris, France.	Public finance
10. VaccineLedger (a first of its kind initiative in air cargo industry in India). (Chakravarthy 2018)	It allows for end-to-end tracing of vaccines from manufacturers to the end customers	GMR Hyderabad Air Cargo in partnership with Singapore-based technology startup StaTwig	Equity

Sources: Arakal (2021); Arzo (2020); Bhavani (2021); Chakravarthy (2018); Cyient (2020); GlimpseAnalytics (2020); India Science Wire (2020); Indo-Asian News Service (2020); Qure.ai (2021); Yellow Messenger (2020).

Financial gradients as a risk mitigation strategy for AI and blockchain based interventions in India

Financial gradients can be described as a method to analyse financial flows in sustainability projects, or projects which involve a level of complexity which traditional financial analysis cannot gauge. Also, sustainability projects or any project where the outcome is more complex, financial flows to the project have to be stable. Purely grant-based or purely investment grade financing is not a stable method of financing such projects. Financial gradients as an approach can help in aligning these two sources of financing, that is grant (non-investment grade) based and investment grade in order to achieve a stable financial flow to the project. In summation, it can be said that financial gradients are a long-term strategic decision-making tool to ensure completion, maintenance and survival of complex sustainability centric projects.

This research uses the framework of financial gradients as a strategy for achieving long-term sustainable development targets especially for a country like India (Bose et al. 2012) and then extends it to include technology-based interventions via using the KuU strategy (Diebold et al. 2010). Bose et al. (2012) empirically validated the theory of financial gradients (Bose 2011: 57–58) and this research extends the framework to technology-based interventions like AI and blockchain. Bose et al.

(2012: 154–155) state there is a risk construct for action for sustainable development itself. While the landscape of risk was constructed for climate adaptation-based interventions, the context of risks related to sustainable development is given below.

Primary risk: in short this is the risk taken when a project is envisaged for the first time and there are no precedents. Such risks are normally borne by non-investment grade or grant finances. It should be noted that public finance is a grant-based financing method.

Implementation risk: This risk is activated as a part of simply implementing the project. Projects with primary risks have higher implementation risk and higher costs. Iterative process design is a method to control and manage risks. Such iterative designs, though expensive initially, will minimise losses for all stakeholders in the long-run. Investment grade financing will be a better method to finance such risks.

Consequential risk: This is the risk of the consequences of implementing a particular project. Just to reiterate that projects with primary risks have higher implementation risks and the feedback of the project can go awry. As pointed out earlier, iterative process design can help in such situations. There is a substantial non-linear cause and effect with such risks. Public finance can be used to mitigate such risks, also modern day financial derivative instruments can also add value to mitigate such risks (Bose 2011: 57–58).

It can be understood, that primary risk is an unknown risk, implementation risk is a known risk, and consequential risk is an unknown or unknowable risk (Diebold et al. 2010, Bose, Wolf, and Sharma 2012).

The manifestation of the risks for sustainable development action itself came about as a result of the enquiry into the framework of financial gradients (Bose et al. 2012a, 2012b),; and now this research traces them into the KuU framework (Diebold et al. 2010). This activity was necessary to put the risks of sustainable development (Bose 2011; Bose et al. 2012b), and AI risks (Scherer 2015), blockchain risks (Supreme Court of India 2020) and COVID-19 risks (Fronteira et al. 2021) to a single paradigm of financial (Bose 2011: 57–58) risk (Diebold et al. 2010) framework. This manifestation is represented in Tables 15.2a, 15.2b, 15.2c and 15.2d. The tables depict the financial gradients framework to how it can manage risks and are adapted from Bose (2011).

In Table 15.2a, the various kinds of finance are depicted, in Table 15.2b key attributes associated with the kind of finance is given. And in Tables 15.2c and 15.2d which kind of finance manages what risk are depicted. The notion is that if the AI or blockchain intervention is sourced with a financing mechanism which has the attributes of a pure grant, research grant, public finance, debt and equity then the various kinds of risks emanating from the sustainable development side, technology side and COVID-19 side are managed, accounted for or strategically mitigated. From Table 15.1 on COVID-19 centric interventions or projects using AI or blockchain in India it can be deciphered that the following financial narrative will emerge using the financial gradients method.

Financial gradients can be summarised as in the Table 15.2b on financial gradients. This will ensure continuity, efficiency, innovation and better risk management.

Table 15.2a: Financial gradients.

Category	Definition	Known for
Pure grant	Funds given as a part of philanthropic activity (tax benefits possible)	Philanthropy
Research grant	Funds given as a part of research activity (can also be seed financing)	Innovation
Public finance	Government funds with fiscal objectives	Social dividend
Debt	Funds from typically commercial (or even multilateral) banks	Continuity
Equity	Shareholder contribution with expectation of returns	Efficiency

Table 15.2b: Financial gradients, attributes.

Category	Known for	Accountability	Monitoring cost	Perversity	Motivation
Pure grant	Philanthropy	Lowest	Highest	Possible	High
Research grant	Innovation	Moderate	High	Rare	High
Public finance	Social dividend	Moderate	High	Possible	Low
Debt	Continuity	High	Low	Rare	Low
Equity	Efficiency	Highest	Lowest	High	High

Therefore, it can be said that interventions or projects using AI or blockchain with non-negative feedback will have elements of:
1. Equity
2. Debt
3. Public finance
4. Research grants
5. Grants

Table 15.2c: Financial gradients, risk management.

Category	Known for	Risk managed	Key stakeholder
Pure grant	Philanthropy	Unknown, Unknowable, Systemic	Multiple
Research grant	Innovation	Unknown, Unknowable, Systemic	Academia
Public finance	Social dividend	Unknown, Unknowable, Systematic	Government
Debt	Continuity	Known, Unsystematic	Financial Institutions
Equity	Efficiency	Known, Unsystematic	Entrepreneurs

Diverse inclusion in types of share capital (equity to grants) are a better method to manage risks making the intervention:
- long-term
- environmentally sustainable
- socially acceptable
- better work availability

Risks managed are:
- systemic (e.g., financial crisis, 2008)
- systematic (e.g., pandemics, COVID-19)
- unsystematic (e.g., competition)

And also, as per the KuU framework (K = knowable, u = unknown, U = unknowable)

Table 15.2d: Financial gradients.

Category	Source	Private
	Government	Companies
Pure grant	Substantial	Possible
Research grant	Substantial	Possible
Public finance	Substantial	No
Debt	Possible	Possible
Equity	Possible	Substantial

Policy implications of financial gradients

This research has so far done two things. It has primarily laid the landscape of risks in technology and in implementing action on sustainable development. It has also given a narrative on the COVID-19 situation, particularly the second wave in India. Then the research articulated a method to manage and mitigate the risks by using a financial framework called financial gradients. In India philosophy what financial gradients has done is articulated the *guna* (virtues) of each kind of finance depending on their nature and source. Financial gradients (Bose 2011: 57–58) suggest a diffused financing method such that the *gunas* of each source can be present while implementing the project. So, the elements of equity will bring in efficiency, then, elements of public finance will bring in social dividends. The question is for this section – what policy set up can bring about a situation under which all the *gunas* can be realised. One suggestion is that the project should be financed in a diffused fashion (Bose 2011: 57–58). However, as the vignettes section of this research shows, in some cases this might be possible, in other cases this might not be simple to achieve. In cases when diffused financing is difficult to achieve then the project document should have the elements or *gunas* encapsulated. In case the project using AI or blockchain is being carried out by a private company completely funded via equity the *gunas* can be brought in via parts of the company law like memoranda of association or articles of association. This method might better than the legislation (or legislative) method as advocated in Scherer (2015: 393–398). In fact, the suggestion here is minimally invasive and in sync with NITI Aayog (2021) recommendations on technology policy on issues involving AI and blockchain.

Conclusion

In the present COVID-19 crisis, the technologies of AI and blockchain have been conspicuous by their absence (Kahn 2021). In fact, some have quipped the next pandemic will most likely be solved by AI, but not this one (Kahn 2021). This is not to say that AI and blockchain were completely absent, as this research has shown there were use cases affecting various people in welcome ways. However, the scale required to help combat the virus was not reached. It might be that the ecosystem has not been developed yet. For that ecosystem to develop multiple narratives may be needed. This research has been an attempt to create one of those. This chapter offers stakeholders to come into conversation with others, from technology makers to agencies working on achieving SDGs. The framework suggested here can be developed further to create a toolbox for managing risks while creating or implementing programmes or projects for sustainable development using AI or blockchain for a country like India.

References

AI School of India. 2021. *How Are AI-Based Solutions Being Used to Combat Covid-19?*, <https://indiaai.gov.in/article/how-are-ai-based-solutions-being-used-to-combat-covid-19> [Accessed 20 June 2021].

Akerlof, George A., and Robert J. Shiller. 2010. *Animal Spirits: How Human Psychology Drives the Economy, and Why It Matters for Global Capitalism* (Princeton, NJ: Princeton University Press).

Arakal, Ralph Alex. 2021. 'DRDO Develops Artificial Intelligence Algorithm to Detect Covid-19 Presence from Chest X-Rays', *Indian Express*. <https://indianexpress.com/article/india/drdo-develops-artificial-intelligence-algorithm-to-detect-covid-19-presence-from-chest-x-rays-7305758/> [Accessed 20 June 2021].

Arzo, Tamanna Farooque. 2020. 'Saathi Chatbot by Mygov Launches for Indian Citizens to Provide Correct Info', *TechGenyz*. <https://www.techgenyz.com/2020/04/24/saathi-chatbot-by-mygov/> [Accessed 30 January 2022].

Bailey, C. 2019. *Was Alphago's Move 37 Inevitable?*, < https://katbailey.github.io/post/was-alphagos-move-37-inevitable/> [Accessed 15 May 2021].

Banerjee, Abhijit, and Esther Duflo 2011 *The Authors of 'Poor Economics' on Ending Poverty* (Knowledge@Wharton: The University of Pennsylvania) <https://knowledge.wharton.upenn. edu/article/the-authors-of-poor-economics-on-ending-poverty/> [Accessed 30 July 2021].

Banerjee, Abhijit Vinayak, Esther Duflo, and Michael Kremer 2016 *The Influence of Randomized Controlled Trials on Development Economics Research and on Development Policy* (Washington DC: The State of Economics, The State of the World)

Bhavani, Divya Kala. 2021. 'Conversational AI Becomes the Unlikely Hero During the Covid-19 Pandemic', *The Hindu*. <https://www.thehindu.com/sci-tech/technology/coronavirus-covid19-chatbots-covidindresbot-introbot-ai-for-oxygen-cylinders-hospital-beds-medical-resources/ar ticle34533822.ece> [Accessed 20 June 2021].

Bhowmick, Nilanjana. 2021a. 'How India's Second Wave Became the Worst Covid-19 Surge in the World', *National Geographic*, 26 April 2021 <https://www.nationalgeographic.com/science/ar ticle/how-indias-second-wave-became-the-worst-covid-19-surge-in-the-world> [Accessed 5 May 2021].

Bhowmick, Soumya.·2021b. *Battle for Bengal 2021: Political Themes and Electoral Dynamics* (New Delhi: Observer Research Foundation), <https://www.orfonline.org/research/battle-for-bengal-2021-political-themes-and-electoral-dynamics/> [Accessed 30 June 2021].

Biswas, Soutik. 2021. 'Covid-19: How India Failed to Prevent a Deadly Second Wave', *BBC News*, 19 April 2021. <https://www.bbc.com/news/world-asia-india-56771766 > [Accessed 6 May 2021].

Bose, Arnab. 2011. 'Climate Finance and Financial Gradients: Perspectives and Methods', *International Journal of Regulation and Governance*, 11 (2), 57–76.

Bose, Arnab, Aditya Ramji, Jarnail Singh, and Dhairya Dholakia. 2012a. 'A Case Study for Sustainable Development Action Using Financial Gradients', *Energy Policy*, 47, 79–86.

Bose, Arnab, Jedamiah Wolf, and Seema Sharma. 2012b. 'The Future of Adaptation Finance: Methods and Perspectives', *International Journal of Regulation and Governance*, 12 (2), 145–72.

Bostrom, Nick. 1998. 'How Long before Superintelligence?', *International Journal of Futures Studies*, 2.

Chakravarthy, Siddhartha 2018 'StaTwig: Improving Food and Vaccines Distribution Systems More Efficiently through Blockchain', (UNICEF Office of Innovation) <https://www.unicef.org/innova tion/stories/statwig-improving-food-and-vaccines-distribution-systems-more-efficiently-through> [Accessed 30 January 2022].

Cress, M. 2019 'The Black Box Problem' *Artificial Intelligence Mania* <http://artificialintelligencemania.com/2019/01/10/the-black-box-problem/ > [Accessed 30 January 2022]

Cyient. 2020. *AI-Powered Surveillance Tool*, <https://www.cyient.com/> [Accessed 20 June 2021].

Diebold, Francis X., Neil A. Doherty, and Richard J. Herring. 2010. *The Known, the Unknown, and the Unknowable in Financial Risk Management: Measurement and Theory Advancing Practice* (Princeton, NJ: Princeton University Press).

Fronteira, Inês, Mohsin Sidat, João Paulo Magalhães, Fernando Passos Cupertino de Barros, António Pedro Delgado, Tiago Correia, Cláudio Tadeu Daniel-Ribeiro, and Paulo Ferrinho. 2021. 'The Sars-Cov-2 Pandemic: A Syndemic Perspective', *One Health*, June 12, 2021, 100228.

GlimpseAnalytics. 2020. *Covid19-Toolkit – Glimpse Analytics*, <https://glimpseanalytics.com/ covid-19-toolkit/> [Accessed 20 June 2021].

Gomory, Ralph E. "The known, the unknown and the unknowable." *Scientific American* 272.6 (1995): 120–120.

Goyal, Shikha. 2020. *Prashant Kishor, an Indian Political Strategist: Biography – Early Life, Family, Education, and Works*, <https://www.jagranjosh.com/general-knowledge/prashant-kishor-biography-1582723444-1 > [Accessed 31 July 2021,].

Haq, Noorul. 2017. 'Dimensions of Political Marketing in India', *International Journal of Engineering and Management Research* 7(3),532–36.

Head, Brian W. 2008. 'Wicked Problems in Public Policy', *Public Policy*, 3 (2), 101–18.

India Science Wire. 2020. 'ICMR Certifies 'Economical' Covid-19 Test COVIRAP', *Down to Earth*. <https://www.downtoearth.org.in/news/science-technology/icmr-certifies-economical-covid-19-test-covirap-73895> [Accessed 30 January 2022].

Indian Ministry of Health and Welfare. 2021. *Homepage*, <https://www.mohfw.gov.in/> [Accessed 6 May 2021].

Indo-Asian News Service. 2020. 'AI Model for Drug Repositioning in the Treatment of Covid-19', *Economic Times Healthworld.com*. <https://health.economictimes.indiatimes.com/news/medical-devices/iiit-delhi-develops-ai-model-to-repurpose-existing-drugs-to-treat-covid-19/76939010> [Accessed 20 June 2021].

Institute for Development and Research in Banking Technology.·2017. *Applications of Blockchain Technology to Banking and Financial Sector in India*, (New Delhi: Reserve Bank of India), <https://idrbt.ac.in/assets/publications/Best%20Practices/BCT.pdf> [Accessed 30 December 2021].

Jaffrelot, Christophe. 2015. 'The Modi-Centric BJP 2014 Election Campaign: New Techniques and Old Tactics', *Contemporary South Asia*, 23 (2), 151–66.

Johns Hopkins University. 2021. *Covid-19 Data Repository by the Center for Systems Science and Engineering (CSSE)* <https://github.com/CSSEGISandData/COVID-19 > [Accessed 30 July 2021].

Kabeer, Naila. 2020. "Misbehaving' RCTs: The Confounding Problem of Human Agency', *World Development*, 127, 104809.

Kahn, Jeremy 2021. 'Vaccinating the World against Covid Is Off to a Slow Start, These Firms Think A.I. And Blockchain Could Help', *Fortune*, 12th May 2021 <https://fortune.com/2021/01/06/covid-vaccine-rollout-distribution-vaccination-coronavirus-ai-blockchain/ > [Accessed 30 January 2022].

Kishor, Prashant 2019 *Prashant Kishor Is in Conversation with Prof Ashutosh Varshney* (Harvard University, Cambridge MA: India Conference 2019) <https://www.youtube.com/watch?v=RCbQzFcAtnE > [Accessed 31st July 2021].

Kohli, Atul. 2006. 'Politics of Economic Growth in India, 1980-2005: Part II: The 1990s and Beyond', *Economic and Political Weekly* (April 8, 2006), 1361–70.

Majumdar, Sumit K. 1996. 'Fall and Rise of Productivity in Indian Industry: Has Economic Liberalisation Had an Impact?', *Economic and Political Weekly*, 31 (48), M46-M53.

National Institution for Transforming India.·2021. *SDG India Index and Dashboard 2020-21*, (New Delhi: Government of India), <https://www.niti.gov.in/writereaddata/files/SDG_3.0_Final_04.03.2021_Web_Spreads.pdf> [Accessed 30 July 2021].

New York Times. 2021. *India Coronavirus Map and Case Count*, <https://www.nytimes.com/interactive/2021/world/india-covid-cases.html?searchResultPosition=1> [Accessed 6 May 2021].

News18. 2021. 'War of Words between Pappu Yadav, Bihar BJP MP over Ambulances 'Lying Unused' on Parliamentarian's Plot', *News18*. <https://www.news18.com/news/politics/war-of-words-between-pappu-yadav-bihar-bjp-mp-over-ambulances-lying-unused-on-parliamentarians-plot-3718004.html> [Accessed 30 January 2022].

Nigbur, Tobias. 2010. 'Francis X. Diebold, Neil A. Doherty, and Richard J. Herring: The Known, the Unknown, and the Unknowable in Financial Risk Management', *Financial Markets and Portfolio Management*, 24 (4), 453.

North, Douglass C. 1991. 'Institutions', *Journal of Economic Perspectives*, 5 (1), 97–112.

Oxford Analytica. 2019. 'Modi's Party Will Grow Stronger in West Bengal', *Emerald Expert Briefings* <https://www.emerald.com/insight/content/doi/10.1108/OXAN-DB245910/full/html> [Accessed 30 January 2022].

Qure.ai. 2021. *Automated Chest X-Ray Interpretation – QXR*, <https://www.ai4hlth.org/product-profiles/Qure.ai> [Accessed 20 June 2020].

Scherer, Matthew U. 2015. 'Regulating Artificial Intelligence Systems: Risks, Challenges, Competencies, and Strategies', *Harvard Journal of Law and Technology*, 29, 353–400.

Sharma, Harikishan. 2021. 'Covid Second Wave: On the Ground, Oxygen SOS but on the Record, Zero Deaths', *Indian Express*, 30 July 2021. <https://indianexpress.com/article/india/second-wave-on-the-ground-oxygen-sos-but-on-the-record-zero-deaths-7414439/ > [Accessed 8 November 2021].

Sriramachari, S. 2005. 'Bhopal Gas Tragedy: Scientific Challenges and Lessons for Future', *Journal of Loss Prevention in the Process Industries*, 18 (4-6), 264–67.

Supreme Court of India. 2020. *In the Supreme Court of India Civil Original Jurisdiction Writ* Petition *(Civil) No.528 of 2018 Internet and Mobile Association of India, Petitioner, Versus, Reserve Bank of India, Respondent with Writ Petition (Civil) No.373 of 2018*. <https://main.sci.gov.in/supremecourt/2018/19230/19230_2018_4_1501_21151_Judgement_04-Mar-2020.pdf> [Accessed 15 May 2021]

The Lancet COVID-19 Commission India Taskforce.·2021. *Managing India's Second Covid-19 Wave: Urgent Steps*, <https://static1.squarespace.com/static/5ef3652ab722df11fcb2ba5d/t/6076f57d3b43fb2db4a7c9c9/1618408831746/India+TF+Policy+Brief+April+2021.pdf> [Accessed 6 May 2021].

The Times of India. 2021. 'Covid-19: In Many States, Ventilators Lie Unused and Defunct', *The Times of India*, May 16, 2021. <http://timesofindia.indiatimes.com/articleshow/82672053.cms?utm_source=contentofinterest&utm_medium=text&utm_campaign=cppst > [Accessed 30 July 2021].

United Nations Development Programme (UNDP) 2021a. *United Nations Development Program, Human Development Index Ranking and Country Profile of India*, (New York: UNDP), < http://hdr.undp.org/en/countries/profiles/IND > [Accessed 30 July 2021].

——.·2021b. *United Nations Development Programme, Multidimensional Poverty Index*, (New York: UNDP), <http://hdr.undp.org/en/2020-MPI > [Accessed 30th July 2021,].

West Bengal Government, India. 2021. *Duare Sarkar*, < https://wb.gov.in/duare-sarkar.aspx> [Accessed 17 July 2021].

World Economic Forum.·2020. *Unlocking Technologies for Global Goals*, (Geneva: WEF), <http://www3.weforum.org/docs/Unlocking_Technology_for_the_Global_Goals.pdf > [Accessed 30 July 2021].

Yellow Messenger. 2020. *Yellow Messenger Cares (a Conversational AI Platform)*, <https://get.yellowmessenger.com/yellowmessengercares/> [Accessed 20 June 2021].

Tony Bradley
Chapter 16
Valuing civil society environmental engagement

Abstract: Much voluntary environmental action originates from civil society move-ments. This chapter will connect the environmental sustainability activity of house-holds and civil society, to core economics: productive activity which sustains society but takes place outside markets and price mechanisms.

Conventional finance assumes that Western economies are market economies. Consequently, the application of measures for valuing environmental related house-hold production has hardly begun. While increasing attention is being paid to the valuations of natural capital and ecological services, little attention has been paid to valuing non-market environmental volunteering and action.

The increasing use of satellite accounts – to measure the value of domestic, in-formal, community-based and volunteer production – has made it possible to esti-mate their levels of value and reciprocity to market economies. The current chapter examines a range of domains of environmental core economic activity, from mem-bership and time given to environmental groups, through non-market green house-hold production, in the spheres of energy, transport and food, to the health benefits of informal environmental activity.

Important methodological issues surrounding measurement are raised. The pre-dominate methodologies, of replacement and time-based opportunity cost valua-tions are utilised. This raises significant questions about valuing environmental engagement, in respect of overall societal sustainable development.

Keywords: civil society, core economics, satellite account valuations, environmen-tal engagement, integrated financial reporting, COVID-19

Introduction

This might sound like a curious activity in relation to a handbook on sustainable development and finance. It is neither a regular topic in relation to sustainable de-velopment, usually associated with the action of states, nor one of formal financial analysis. The primary challenges of the climate and biodiversity catastrophes are understood as resting with governments, as in the case of the Conference of the Par-ties (COP) process, such as COP26, in Glasgow, during November 2021. The chief concern lies with the Nationally Determined Contributions (NDCs) of greenhouse gas (GHG) emissions that states sign up to.

https://doi.org/10.1515/9783110733488-016

That said, a moment's thought reveals that states need their citizens to change their behaviour, act differently and reproduce alternative forms of societal engagement, if these NDCs are to be met, or even, exceeded. As this chapter is being written, the world has reached 100 days prior to COP26. Caroline Lucas, the UK's only Green Party Member of Parliament, marked this milestone, by commenting that policy needed to be tailored to local needs, addressed by local authorities and involve the actions and values of local citizens (Lucas 2021).

Yet, to date, most examinations of civil society engagement in hastening environmental responsiveness, have focussed on the role of civil society organisations (CSO), in lobbying both the state and corporations to make policy shifts to lower GHG emissions (Newell 2008; Bernauer et al. 2016; Jacobs 2016; Jacquet and Jamieson 2016). Even standard texts on change management for environmental sustainability, often overlook the citizenship role of civil society, outside of CSOs, as a vital part of the transition towards emissions reduction economies and society (Doppelt and McDonough 2017).

There has, however, been some research over the past 20 years, in seeking to connect civil society consumption patterns, in terms of formal market behaviour, to understanding mechanisms for reducing carbon emissions (Nonhebel and Moll 2001; Spaargaren and Mol 2013; Bjørn et al. 2018; Wynes et al. 2018; Lucas 2021). Even so, such work does not engage with the informal, everyday non-market, or, rather, extra-market productive activity, that individuals and households engage in, as part of their participation in environmental engagement. In fact, it might be assumed that such activities, within largely capitalist market-oriented societies, such as the UK, are marginal, not measurable and, largely, archaic, predating the irresistible rise of the marketized society (Sandel 2012; Chang 2014; Raworth 2017). But the rationale of this chapter is to present evidence on the value of civil society environmental engagement which takes place, primarily, outside markets. However, it will be necessary to use some market price mechanisms to estimate certain valuations.

In consequence, it is important to know what level of engagement people are making to reduce their carbon footprint and mitigate the environmental costs of everyday life. In the glossaries to the various IPCC reports, the distinction between mitigation and adaptation is: 'Mitigation (of climate change): A human intervention to reduce emissions or enhance the sinks of greenhouse gases (Intergovernmental Panel on Climate Change 2018: 554).' 'Adaptation: In human systems, the process of adjustment to actual or expected climate and its effects, in order to moderate harm or exploit beneficial opportunities (IPCC 2018: 542)'.

The focus of this chapter is on civil society actions towards mitigation, rather than adaptation.

There are many sources of data on aspects of these behavioural changes, such as rates of waste recycling (Department for Environment Food and Rural Affairs UK 2019), participation in environmental groups (Cracknell, Miller, and Williams 2013), changing behaviour in respect of energy use, transport and food purchasing (Kronberg and Weekes 2018), together with other forms of ethical consumption (The Cooperative Wholesale Society 2019), *inter alia*. Equally, although some of this is, necessarily, measured in respect of market activity, it reflects behavioural choices that are made beyond markets.

Journeying to the core of the economy

How households interact with markets, both in terms of consumption spheres and the labour market are the subject of considerable research, not least in relation to the ethics of business. But this is far from the whole story. Alongside the relative transparency of open markets are less visible ones. These can be in such spheres as the direct investments of hidden asset classes, such as securitised financial instruments, the advanced use of ICT and digital platforms, for-profit, in industries such as higher education (Komljenovic 2021), the spread of alternative labour markets in the online platform gig economy (Kässi and Lehdonvirta 2018) and a whole range of informal and, even, black economy practices (Walker-Munro 2021). According to (Knobel 2019) the total value of securities processed in the US, in 2018, was US1.85 quadrillion, which was almost 100 times the entire US GDP, for 2017. The role of securitised credit default swaps in hastening the 2008 financial crash is well understood.

But, in addition to these more occluded aspects of capitalism, there are alternative economic systems operating within capitalist societies. It is, usually, assumed that these were features of earlier social formations, but became overtaken by markets, under capitalist conditions. In his classic text, *The Great Transformation* (Polanyi 1944/2002) – which is becoming increasingly reappraised currently (Dale 2016) – Karl Polanyi, writing at the end of WWII, wrote about the three economic systems of reciprocity, redistribution and markets. In discussing these, they distinguished between them according to the extent to which these economic systems were either embedded or dis-embedded, in respect of social relations.

The first two (reciprocity and redistribution) they described as characteristic of embedded economies, wherein social practices (reciprocity) or the need to maintain and reproduce social relations (redistribution) conditioned the operation of the economic system. Polanyi contrasted these embedded economic systems with market-based societies, which they saw as dis-embedded, so that social relations were submerged beneath the dominant activities of market forces. These economies represented a great transformation away from the historical dependence of the economic on the nature of social structures, towards the reverse. Political and social structures became dependent upon the functioning and relative efficiency of market economics.

It is a widespread assumption that reciprocity, as an economic system, which is not based in the use of monetary exchange, belongs to either historic social formations or the situation of contemporary groups of Indigenous peoples, in exotic locations, where global market penetration has yet to permeate. It is this latter assumption that needs addressing from contemporary secondary empirical sources, in respect of environmental engagement. Specifically, how significant is non-monetary (reciprocity-based) production, connected to environmental and sustainable development, within the contemporary economy of the UK?

To answer this question it is possible to turn to the construction, in an increasing number of advanced societies, of household satellite accounts (HHSAs) (see: Payne and Vassilev 2018). How do households contribute to the formation of non-monetary economy domestic production that relates to environmental activity? As such, this chapter raises four sets of considerations. These are:

(a) Theoretical issues regarding: what is the significance of non-monetary reciprocity in respect of environmental engagement?
(b) Some of the main methodological issues that confront any calculations of the non-monetary economy, generally and environmental engagement, particularly.
(c) Presentation of data, from a wide range of secondary sources, together with its interpretation, on this theme.
(d) The way in which such data, particularly in disaggregated, local, form, can be used to shape policy responses of the local state, and the activities of CSOs and ordinary citizens, to mitigate the environmental emergency.

How significant is the non-monetary economy in Western societies?

In the ancient Greek *Oikonomika*, the economics of the household is described as a second economy, alongside that of the city-state (Brodersen 2007). Later economists have subordinated this by referring to it as the non-market economy, as if markets were the only things that mattered economically. By contrast, the heterodox economist Neva Goodwin (2018) has turned the distinction between a primary – industrial production, consumption and distribution market economy – and a secondary – household and communal reciprocity economy – upside down.

They refer to the latter, household economy, as the core economy and the preceding, market economy, as the peripheral economy. The core economy amounts to those resources which comprise and sustain social life (Goodwin et al. 2019). According to Mira Luna (Cahn 2009), this economy of family and neighbourhoods accounts for approximately 4050% of productive activity. Even so, such statistics do not convey the significance of an economy that is largely ignored.

To identify this significance Anna Coote and Neva Goodwin (2010), express the social fact that the core economy is a crucial part of the lives of all people. It involves the use of time, experience, skills, knowledge and wisdom. And it reflects relationships, of love, empathy, responsibility, care, learning and mutualism. It is central to sustaining society, through the care of children, the elderly and the frail, as well as building intimacy, social networks and civil society. Equally, it is crucial for safeguarding nature and environmental capital.

In other words, the core sphere undergirds all market-based systems to the extent that the embeddedness of reciprocity is a central feature of capitalist societies. The core-periphery reversal is akin to the challenge that ecological economists make to conventional economics, in respect of the relationships between natural capital, society and the economy. As the eminent ecological economist Herman Daly (1991), pointed out, the economic system exists within and is dependent upon the ecological system, not the other way around.

That is the view of Mark Carney (2020), former Governor of the Bank of England and, currently, UN Special Envoy on Climate Action and Finance. Economists have woken up to ecological crisis. And they are beginning to wake up to the core sphere economy, as well. In other words, it is necessary to be able to place financial valuations on non-market economic activity, both in terms of planetary costs, and, as here, in terms of civil society accruals.

The development of household production measurement towards household satellite accounts

So, how have heterodox economists begun to measure the scale of the core economy? More conservatively than Mira Luna, economist Edgar Cahn (2009), as early as 1998, estimated that the value of household work in the United States came to total US 1.911 trillion – about one quarter of the size of the US Gross Domestic Product that year. But Cahn's estimate was only for household work. It did not account for the value of community networking, such as giving gifts of time, domestic work in other households, the value of visiting friends and neighbours, running unpaid youth, sport and community facilities. Nor did it account for taking the kids and their friends to activities, including football, supporting the physically and mentally sick and disabled outside of formal healthcare services, and a host of other, supposedly trivial, activities that are invisible to most monetised economic analysis. When, in a later study, Cahn added these activities in, they came to a very similar estimate as Mira Luna, of 40% of GDP.

But, in addition to these household production functions, it is possible to add the value of civil society environmental engagement. This is, also, linked to other forms of core economic activity, beyond markets. During the coronavirus pandemic, for example, it has been evident, from research that is yet to be published, that the presence of radical environmental groups, in UK localities, has been one of the most determinate factors in the formation of COVID-19 Mutual Aid Groups. The core economy connects several facets of mutualism and reciprocity together.

The measurement and estimation of the scale and extent of the core economy has developed considerably, in recent years. The work of pioneers, such as Margaret Reid (1934), Colin Clark (1958), Oli Hawrylyshyn (1976) and Edgar Cahn (2009) were methodologically relatively unrefined. But, the fundamental work of Gary Becker (1965), the work of Ann Chadeau (1992), Aurelien Poissonier and Delphine Roy (2017), and, particularly, Duncan Ironmonger (2001, 1972, 1989, 1995), at the Households Research Unit, Melbourne, together with Faye Soupourmas (2012), have developed far more sophisticated methodologies for assessing the value of household and other non-market production in developed economies. Nevertheless, it has taken some time for those who compile national income accounts to wake up to the scale of the core economy, not least in respect of environment-related activity.

In fact, the inadequacy of measurements of national income accounts, in terms of excluding household production, was recognised in a major conference as early as 1971, (see: Atkinson and Bourguignon 2015; Poissonnier and Roy 2017; Ponthieux and Meurs 2015). By 1993, the System of National Accounts indicated the need for extending income accounts to include household production. But even more than 40 years on from the original call to adequately account for household production, the debate about the inclusion of non-market work and leisure, in national income accounts, remains unsettled. Even so, a major step was taken in the Commission for the Measurement of Economic Performance and Social Progress (Stiglitz, Sen, and Fitoussi 2009), in using a broader measure of income, including non-market household production, to provide a better account of economic, as well as social, wellbeing.

As a result, further steps to develop official statistics have been taken over recent years. An increasing number of national statistical services, such as the UK's Office for National Statistics (ONS), have begun compiling what are known as household satellite accounts (HHSA). These are accounts that cover activities linked to the economy but not part of the central UK national accounts, which include environmental and tourism accounts, alongside those for household production.

The first attempt at a national income account of non-market production was conducted in the UK, by Holloway, Short & Tamplin (2002), for the ONS. They produced an experimental methodology for constructing a national HHSA. The following year Eurostat (2003) produced their first attempt at an experimental methodology, for all the countries of the EU. In the same year, the US American Time Use Survey (United States Department of Labor. Bureau of Labor Statistics 2006) began to collect continuous annual data on households' use of time. But the fact that market money values for household production do not exist generates a range of methodological issues.

Methodology, general considerations: Estimating the scale of the civil society environmental core economy

There are considerable methodological challenges associated with seeking to calculate the value of the core economy. These are magnified when attempting to apply such measurements to the environmental engagement of citizens and households. As with many aspects of the analogous field of welfare economics, considerable reliance needs to be placed on the use of indicative measures. Even so, there are a wide range of available data sets that allow for the construction of precise measures of some aspects of the core economy. These need to be understood in relation to two basic methodological questions. Firstly, should the inputs or outputs of households and others in non-market production be measured? And, secondly, what accounting assumptions should be applied to these measurements?

In standard core economy household production calculations, the primary consideration is whether time inputs or productive value outputs are being measured. Essentially, the most favoured use of time survey data is to ascribe a generalised substitution wage rate, such as the National Living Wage, to each hour spent in household production. This is, often, referred to as the housekeeper rate. Of course, using time taken in domestic work does not account for differences of Gross Value Added, the standard measure of productivity. Some households do the laundry faster than others.

The main alternative to using time-input calculations is to apply an output replacement model of valuation. These assess the cost of replacing a household activity, such as doing the laundry, with the price that such an activity would generate in a marketplace. But, measuring outputs, as separate activities, may result in considerable double-counting; suggesting that the time-input measure is preferable. Overall, the evidence indicates that using a generalised substitution (housekeeper) wage rate, applied to time inputs, is a reasonable basis for valuations, albeit producing much lower estimates of the total value of the core economy than those based on calculating replacement output values. Charging the time that you spend doing the laundry, at home, at a housekeeper rate, is significantly below the price you would pay for sending all your laundry to a local high street launderer.

Even so, as will be evident from this analysis, calculation of time inputs, for some aspects of environmental engagement, are, either, extremely difficult or nonsensical. For example, while it makes sense to use time inputs for membership and volunteering in environmental organisations, calculating estimates of ethical consumption are not time dependent. These are more concerned with the choices that households make between different types of purchases. Similarly, choices in respect of substituting plant-based for meat-based diets are less time-input dependent, than chosen on the basis of a wide range of other considerations, to do with health, animal welfare, GHG emissions, land use, lifestyle preferences and so on.

As such, in the valuation cases included below, the following analysis uses a mixed-methods approach, whereby different valuations of outputs are applied to some variables, whereas standardised time-input valuations are used in others. In general, a housekeeper rate (at National Living Wage) for time inputs has been used. These produce considerably lower valuations that those which seek to measure the value of specific substitution outputs. Where the use of time inputs is not appropriate, two, alternative, ways of assessing output valuations have been used, one giving lower (opportunity cost) valuations and the other giving higher (substitution output) estimates. Furthermore, although the goal is to calculate non-market household production, in respect of environmental engagement, some of the best data relates to the use of market price valuations, for certain activities, such as estimates of energy efficiency and usage. Alternatively, other variables, such as time spent walking, have been estimated according to calculated health benefits, rather than the housekeeper rate, for the time taken, regarding the valuations produced by applying standardised hourly rates – which are in the high £billions – to be implausible, as estimates of the value of walking. In this respect it becomes important to be clear about the assumptions being made, in relation to specific data, on each domain used in the calculus.

In effect, the analysis and commentary presented here is only an initial attempt. It is one that others will be able to critique, build on and develop. But it is offered as a first attempt, that can be substantially revised by further work. Equally, the approach adopted is one of parsimony, to avoid some of the wilder claims that could be made for civil society environmental engagement. The figures produced are at the lower end of the range, even when considering the substitution values of outputs. When compared with some estimates of environmental engagement, such as ethical consumerism, the valuations used here are a fraction of those included in standard sources, such as the annual reports of Ethical Consumer.

Methodology, specific considerations: Identifying data, assumptions and measurement criteria

Given the variety of different activities which are included in this assessment, and the methodological expediency operated, it is important to be clear, at each stage, in respect of a range of different considerations of how to estimate valuations. Equally, an attempt has been made to be precise about the various assumptions adopted. See Table 16.1.

Given the impact of the COVID-19 pandemic within the UK, it was decided to collect data and use a housekeeper rate (National Living Wage, outside London, the 2021 rate was used, even though the data analysed relates to 2018, to make the

Table 16.1: Decisions made in respect of domain variables for calculating aggregate UK environmental engagement.

Choice of variables	Reasons for choice/ understanding of the field
Methodological basis	Which methods of measurement criteria are used in estimations (see above discussion)
Data sources	Authoritative empirical data sets e.g., based on official sources, credible surveys or best sources (seeking to avoid, in most cases, in-house estimates from CSO)
Assumptions made regarding data use	Credible basis for assumptions

estimates relevant to contemporary income accounts), where applicable, together with the baseline adult population of the UK (53,812,795) for the (calendar) year 2018 or (academic or tax) year 201819. This was the latest year for which accurate data was available, which was unaffected by the influence of the virus. The range of domains, indicator variables, summary definitions and brief account of data sources used in the estimates are listed in Table 16.2.

The following section includes greater detail on each of the domains included in the estimation of values, together with summary tables of the figures derived from the various calculations.

Results: Valuation tables and details of the calculations

The domains selected and operated here are neither comprehensive nor devoid of methodological challenge. Indeed, it would be surprising if trenchant arguments were not made for including other fields, variables, definitions and data sources. Consequently, it is important to be as transparent as possible about how these calculations were derived. That is the objective of this section.

Membership of environmental organisations

The most authoritative and comprehensive survey of UK environmental organisations, hitherto, is Cracknell, Miller, and Williams (2013). These authors identified 25 organisations as making the most significant contribution to the field of environmental engagement in Britain. On that basis, data was collated for each of these 25, with a further three organisations added, which were considered to have become

Table 16.2: Domains, indicator variables, summary definitions and sources used in estimating civil society environmental engagement.

Domain	Indicator variable (s) selected	Summary definitions (for opportunity cost measurements)*	Source(s) of data
1. Formal membership of environmental organisations	Membership data on 25 top UK environmental organisations identified in Cracknell, Miller and Williams (2013), plus an additional three prominent organisations that have emerged since that survey.	Data collected from membership records of each organisation.	2018 Annual Reports and websites for each organisation.
2. Volunteering through environmental organisations	As above	Organisational data on volunteering numbers/ estimates of social value or use of estimated rates.	As above or estimated on the basis of calculations of volunteering rates (volunteers estimated at 1% of membership).
3. Informal environmental activity	Walking and cycling, for travel and leisure	Official data from (Kronberg and Weekes 2018) and the Active Life Survey (Sport England 2020). Describing patterns of walking and cycling. Estimated on the basis of health benefits A quality adjusted life years (QALY) approach, as utilised by the National Institute for Health and Clinical Excellence (NICE) (2021) for length of time in activity.	*UK Government Walking and Cycling Statistics*, 2018 (Department for Transport UK 2019).

4.	Amateur (non-professional) formal outdoor sporting activity	Participation in football (soccer), rugby union, rugby league, cricket, tennis, running, coarse angling (fishing), rowing, other outdoor water sports and golf (cycling data included in previous domain).	Size of population engaged in the average time given to each sporting activity, measured according to health benefits (physical and mental health, QALYs), subtracting the average costs of GHG emissions from car transport to sports venues based on (Dosumu 2016).	Most data on participation rates from Statista (Lange 2020), surveys of involvement in amateur sports, augmented by data from bodies representing particular sports.
5.	Housing (household) energy/ carbon savings and domestic energy generation	Property classes for each main energy saving installation: cavity wall and loft insulation; installation of new boilers. Household revenue from various Feed-in Tariff (FiT) capacity generation.	The value of GHG emission efficiency savings, calculated as metric tonnes, at average % reductions, according to mid-point carbon trading values, normalised by behavioural rebound effects see (Adan and Fuerst 2016).	*Household Energy Efficiency National Statistics: detailed report 2018* (Oxley 2019). This data augmented by material from the Grantham Institute of the London School of Economics, (McCoy 2017) on the real-world impact of energy efficiency measures.
6.	Transport savings (carbon emissions) through public transport and new Electric Vehicle (EV) usage.	Estimates of the savings in GHG emissions for population usage of each major form of public transport, when compared with average petrol engine car usage, over the same aggregate distances. In respect of switching to hybrid and electric vehicles (HEV and EV) the difference in GHG emissions against conventional petrol engine vehicles was calculated.	The value of GHG emission savings, when compared with distances travelled by petrol engine vehicle equivalents, calculated as Metric tonnes, at mid-point carbon trading prices.	Main source: Kronberg and Weekes (2018). Other sources include: European Union statistics on GHG emissions (European Commission 2020), modified by Transport & Environment/ Greenpeace (Archer 2020; Department for Environment Food and Rural Affairs UK 2020) evidence on the real levels of GHG emissions from plug-in hybrid cars and Statista data on average miles travelled by car in 2018 (Statista Research Department 2020).

(continued)

Table 16.2 (continued)

Domain	Indicator variable (s) selected	Summary definitions (for opportunity cost measurements)*	Source(s) of data
7. Food savings, on meat-free food shopping by dedicated meat-free consumers.	Estimate of the average purchase price savings made by vegans, when compared with non-vegan food purchases.	Low estimate of numbers of vegans in the UK, in 2018, from The Vegan Society. The average annual reduction in meat-free shopping basket purchases, compared with shopping baskets including meat purchases.	Sources include: Department for Environment Food and Rural Affairs UK Department for Environment Food and Rural Affairs UK (2020) and The Vegan Society (2018).
8. Recycling and reuse.	Aggregate value of civil society recycling, particularly in relation to Materials Recovery Facilities (MRF).	Application of WRAP (Waste and Resources Action Programme) (Dick and Scholes 2018) measurement of the value of MRF to British recycling statistics, and savings on the costs of waste treatment.	Two main sources: Department for Environment Food and Rural Affairs UK (2019) on Britain's recycling statistics and Dick and Scholes (2018), from WRAP.

9.	Ethical purchasing.	Some use of data from Ethical Consumer, related to Green Home, Ethical Clothing and Ethical Cosmetics purchasing.	Inclusion of some items of ethical purchasing e.g., energy-efficient light bulbs; ethical cleaning products. Cautious use of data on ethical clothing and cosmetics purchasing, as a result of further research.	Baseline source: (The Cooperative Wholesale Society 2019) *Ethical Consumer Report, 2019.* The evidence from this report was modified in respect of a range of other sources, which pointed to the limitations of evidence on various items of ethical purchasing, such as energy-efficient appliances, ethical clothing and ethical cosmetics' (see: Cerri, Testa, and Rizzi 2018; Reimers, Magnuson, and Chao 2016), *inter alia*). Other fields of ethical consumption, such as local shopping, were excluded on *prima facie* grounds.

Sources: (Adan and Fuerst 2016; Archer 2020; Cerri, Testa, and Rizzi 2018; Cracknell, Miller, and Williams 2013; Department for Environment Food and Rural Affairs UK 2020; Department for Transport UK 2019; Dick and Scholes 2018; Dosumu 2016; European Commission 2020; Kronberg and Weekes 2018; Lange 2020; McCoy 2017; National Institute for Health and Clinical Excellence 2021; Oxley 2019; Reimers, Magnuson, and Chao 2016; Sport England 2020; Statista Research Department 2020; The Cooperative Wholesale Society 2019; The Vegan Society 2018).

Note: The alternative (higher) substitution methodology definitions and calculations are explained in the more detailed text relating to each domain, below.

equally significant between 2013 and 2018. The decisions made for the calculations are laid out here, as for each subsequent domain, as in Table 16.1.

Volunteering through environmental organisations

Other assumptions needed to be made, in addition to those included in Table 16.3, in respect of volunteering through environmental organisations. An increasing number of CSOs produce estimates of the value of their volunteers in societal environmental engagement. For example, The Woodland Trust comment that their volunteers gave time worth £2.7million in 2018 (2019). Other organisations state their volunteer hours, without estimating their value, e.g., Groundwork (2019). Yet others comment that making such valuations are inherently difficult (Environmental Investigation Agency UK 2019).

Table 16.3: Decisions on calculations in respect of membership and volunteering through environmental organisations.

Membership of environmental organisations	A key aspect of civil society environmental engagement is through the membership of environmental CSO.
Methodological basis	Calculation of time given to these organisations, by virtue of membership, accounted for at the housekeeper rate.
Data sources	Each organisation's annual report, website and other, additional, academic sources, related to these organisations, were searched, to get an accurate estimate of their membership (the sites and reports visited are included in the reference list).
Assumptions made regarding data use	Each organisations' members gave no more than 1 hour per year, on average, to their environmental engagement. This was reduced to 10 minutes per year, for some organisations, such as the campaigning group 38 Degrees, where a small fraction of their membership was estimated to be involved in environmental lobbying. Certain assumptions were made in respect of the higher replacement/ substitution method, where organisations were staff-only pressure groups, without a wider membership list. The Replacement Income hourly rate was based on the standard salary of a junior conservation ranger in 2018 of £13.33 per hour (UK National Careers Service 2019). It was assumed that staff working in the pressure groups listed (Client Earth, Environmental Investigations Agency, FERN, Global Witness, E3G and Forum for the Future) gave 10 days per year, calculated at junior/ early career rates for their type of work e.g., Junior Solicitor, £32k pa; early years NGO worker £36.5K pa, &c.

On this basis the housekeeper rate was used for the lower estimate and the junior conservation ranger rate for the higher, substitution valuation. But while some organisations quote their volunteer numbers and the average numbers of hours volunteering per year e.g. The National Trust (2019) – 65,000 volunteers (1.1% of 5,600,000 members) giving an average of 0.86 hrs per week volunteering, others simply describe volunteering activities. It was estimated that, on average, 1% of members volunteer and give an average equivalent of one working week per year.

Informal nature-based recreation and travel – walking, cycling and outdoor sports

Calculating walking and cycling as environmental pursuits raised a range of methodological issues and decisions, as identified in Table 16.4.

Table 16.4: Decisions on calculations in respect of informal recreation, travel and sports.

Informal nature-based recreation and travel – walking and cycling	Most policies to encourage walking and cycling focus on their health benefits, although these do not always lead to behavioural change (Pooley et al. 2013). Even so, support for walking and cycling does, frequently, lead to environmental benefits, according to UK government ministers, as affirmed in the support for these activities announced in respect of the new highway code (Lee 2021).
Amateur sporting activities	The same *prima facie* logic was applied to participation in amateur sporting activities, although it was recognised that travel to such activities will often be by vehicles, causing GHG emissions. In addition to direct health benefits to participants, the provision of public and private open spaces, improvements in air quality and protection of green spaces can be seen as resulting from informal sports activities. No attempt was made to estimate these precise benefits, apart from the overall health-based environmental engagement. Equally, it is recognised that some sports, such as golf, coarse angling and other water sports are seen as generating serious environmental costs. But, in the case of golf, the evidence is highly contested (Balogh et al. 2020; Minoli and Smith 2011; Wheeler and Nauright 2006).

Table 16.4 (continued)

Methodological basis	Using calculations of time-use, at alternative wage rates, did not make sense and gave astronomical estimates (e.g., £137BN for recreational walking alone). Consequently, a health benefits approach was adopted. A QALY approach, as utilised by NICE (2021) yielded the most credible results. An alternative, of using population attributable fractions, for health benefits over a single year (£8.17 per person QALY) gave a value of 0.002 pence per minute (ppm) walked, which was considered to be infinitesimally low. A similar QALY-based approach was used to calculate the benefits from participation in amateur sporting activities.
Data sources	The main data sources used were: (Department for Transport UK 2019 Walking and Cycling Statistics, England 2018), which divided these activities between work and leisure. These were augmented with data from Statista (Wagner 2021). The health benefit ppm walked/cycled was applied to the aggregate lengths of time in these activities, for different fractions of the population. For each sporting activity, the main data sources were Statista estimates of participation rates, compiled by e.g., for football (soccer): (Lange 2020).
Assumptions made regarding data use	According to the Ramblers Association/NHS *Walking Works* (2014) report, lack of walking and informal outdoor recreation shortens life expectancy by an average of four years. NICE estimates that social prescribing walking and cycling interventions cost less than £10k pa, well below the £20K threshold, for NICE prescribing approval. On this basis the health benefits of walking throughout any year can be assessed as £40,000, or the equivalent value of 4.58 ppm walked. This only takes physical health into account, as the NICE data is based on reducing the impact of four physical conditions. The mental health and wellbeing benefits of walking are, increasingly, well understood, both in terms of recreational walking in natural environments (Barton, Hine, and Pretty 2009; Mutz and Müller 2016) and during commuting and other instrumental activities (Singleton 2019). Additionally, there is evidence that simply staring at the ocean has significant health benefits (Hall 2019). As such, the 4.58 ppm to account for mental health and wellbeing was doubled, to 9.16ppm.

Table 16.4 (continued)

The replacement income rate was based on the health benefits attributable to extending life to average life expectancy (81.5 years) beyond retirement age (66 years) i.e., 15.1 extra years, calculated on the basis of 34.6ppm walked or cycled (£151,000 compared to £40,000 QALY benefits). It was considered to have some health justifications and was an estimate between the astronomical and infinitesimal ranges.
For sporting activities, the QALY benefit was reduced from four years to one year, on the basis that participation for many sports would be for shorter periods of life, compared to walking or cycling. Some sports e.g., football and rugby are mainly confined to younger life periods, while other sports, such as fishing and golf may be taken up later in life, although it was recognised that these are gross generalisations. This gave a benefit value estimate of 2.29ppm (£1.37 phr). But, this was reduced by 41pphr – using the calculations of (Dosumu 2016), for the average GHG emissions generated by travel to amateur sporting activities, calculated at the 2018 mid-point carbon trading price (£12.76 per tCO2e). The resultant value was estimated at 96pphr. This was applied to the aggregate lengths of time for population fractions participating in each sporting activity, in 2018. Each sport was assessed on average numbers of hours engagement per week, for the number of months played outdoors, at each valuation rate e.g., soccer at one hour per week, for 10 months.
The replacement income rate was based on the National Living Wage (UK Government 2019) phr rate of £8.91, with 41p subtracted for GHG emissions resulting from travel to and from activities = £8.50 phr. These calculations need to be seen in the light of official economic estimates, such as that for the value of coarse angling, in England, of £1.4BN pa (Mawle 2018).

Sources: Balogh et al. (2020); Barton, Hine, and Pretty (2009); Department for Transport UK (2019); Dosumu (2016); UK Government (2019); Hall (2019); Lee (2021); Mawle (2018); Minoli and Smith (2011); Mutz and Müller (2016); National Institute for Health and Clinical Excellence (2021); Pooley et al. (2013); Ramblers Association (2014); Singleton (2019); Wheeler and Nauright (2006).
Note: ppm = pence per minute; pphr = pence per hour; phr = per hour.

The big three: Energy, transport and food

In terms of the environmental engagement activities of civil society households in reducing GHG emissions, there are three sectors that have, arguably, greatest signif-icance, according to the US Environmental Protection Agency (Environmental Pro-tection Agency US 2021): home energy usage and efficiency savings; transportation shifts from cars and planes (the impact of airline travel and flights reduction was not included in this evaluation) to public transport and low emissions vehicles (LEVs); and food consumption, related to alternative agricultural systems. Together these account for *circa* 55% of emissions, if agriculture is added to the domestic sec-tor, in respect of food consumption (Waite 2021). Consequently, a goal was to include estimates of the value of environmental engagement by households in emissions re-duction, for these three sectors.

There were considerable methodological issues in deciding which evaluative criteria to use in respect of these three sectors, as laid out in Table 16.5.

Table 16.5: Decisions on calculations in respect of household energy efficiency, use of transportation and food consumption.

Residential energy efficiency	For the estimation of residential energy saving, the value of carbon emissions saved from cavity wall and loft insultation, and the installation of energy-efficient boilers was used. These are the three most important sources of residential home emissions, where efficiency saving measures have not been introduced.
Transportation emissions reduction	A similar approach was adopted in respect of transportation. The primary assumption was that travel by public transport results in a per capita reduction in GHG emissions and environmental benefits, compared with travel by petrol engine vehicles. This is sometimes disputed (Davis and Boundy 2021), as some forms of public transport can be more polluting than standard cars per capita (Rowlatt 2009). Even so, the kms travelled by the main forms of public transport: trains, buses, light rail and underground tube trains were compared to the emissions generated by standard petrol engines.
Food consumption	Food is one of the most fraught areas to attempt to assess. The goal was to compare plant-based and meat-based food purchasing. Simply calculating the aggregate amounts of plant to meat-based food purchases produces enormous figures. Vegan and vegetarian purchases for 2018 were calculated in some sources as in excess of £1.3BN (Ubamarket 2019). But this was a market research survey of 2005 UK adults, many of whom were flexitarian shoppers, whose purchasing decisions were based on a wide variety of factors, not necessarily concerned with environmental considerations. Equally, *Ethical Consumer* (The Cooperative Wholesale Society 2019)

Table 16.5 (continued)

	estimated meat-free food purchasing to be in the order of £1BN. By contrast, the Vegan Society calculated the number of vegans at a low figure of c 600,000, in 2018 (The Vegan Society 2018). This figure was used in calculations by Statista (Wunsch 2021), as the most reliable figure for UK adult food purchasing of meat-free shopping baskets.
Methodological basis	In respect of household energy savings and efficiency, official data on cavity wall and loft insulations and installations of new low emissions boilers was used to calculate aggregate reductions in carbon emissions. Official BEIS data on the numbers of property installations for each measure were used (Department for Business 2019). Again, the value of these reductions was established using the mid-point carbon trading price, in 2018, of £12.76 per Mt. Research from the Grantham Institute (McCoy 2017) indicates that real-world GHG emissions reductions are about 50% of those reported, compared with engineered installations (the so-called rebound effect). Consequently, the values in the BEIS official statistics were halved. A small amount was added for the level of FiT household micro-generation, mainly from solar panels, calculated at the average pence per KwH, available for solar and wind FiT, in 2018. Transportation savings were estimated from the relative levels of GHG emissions for each mode of public transport, when compared with the emissions, for the same scale of journeys, by petrol engines, at average emission rates. Again, the mid-point carbon trading price was deployed. For example, average UK train emissions, in 2018, were 90g/km, over 67BN kms. This method was preferable to calculating the time-use, in aggregate travel by different modes (taking average mode speeds into account), which, once again, resulted in unfeasibly high figures e.g., £7.5BN for the opportunity cost of rail travel, alone. For the numbers of LEVs used in 2018, the carbon price of emissions saved, when compared with standard petrol engines, was calculated. Similar to the FiT figures for micro-generation, this produced a fractional increase in the valuation estimate. Several different methodologies were tried for estimating green food purchasing and consumption. Initially, generalised estimates of vegetarian food purchases and takeaways, plus the opportunity cost time-use in cooking were used. Once again, these produced unfeasibly large estimates. Data from the government's family food shop, for both meat-based and plant-based food baskets, together with the data from the Vegan Society on the numbers of vegans, in the UK was used. On this basis, the saving for these consumers, of cutting meat out of their food purchases was estimated. While this produced a figure in the high £Ms, it was far below the billions of UK pounds for the preceding methodology.

Table 16.5 (continued)

	The replacement rate energy savings were calculated using market price estimates, rather than carbon savings, based on data from the Energy Savings Trust (Energy Saving Trust 2021), reduced by 50% to account for the rebound effect. The market rate per KwH of generation (mid-point) was added for micro-generation at the replacement rate. Replacement rate transportation savings aggregated all the petrol engine equivalent emissions for all public transport journeys travelled, including in respect of LEVs. Food consumption replacement rate was calculated by all vegans replacing their food basket with the inclusion of meat products.
Data sources	Data relating to household energy, efficiency savings and carbon budgets came from the Department of Business, Energy and Industrial Strategy (BEIS) (2019), Oxley (2019), the government's response to the Committee on Climate Change (Energy and Industrial Strategy Great Britain 2016), Adnan and Fuerst (2016), Buchs and Scneph (2013) and McCoy (2017). The main transportation data source used was: Kronberg and Weekes (2018), for the Department of Transport, Transport Statistics, Great Britain. GHG emissions for transport modes were taken from the above source and European Union estimates (European Commission 2020). Main food consumption data came from the UK government's national statistics in *Family Food, 2018–19* (Department for Environment Food and Rural Affairs UK 2020), augmented by information from the Vegan Society (2018).
Assumptions made regarding data use	The primary assumption surrounding household energy budgets was to measure reductions in the costs of GHG emissions related to residential properties. On the basis of previous evidence, official estimates were halved, while using the mid-point carbon trading price as a benchmark valuation figure. A similar assumption was made in respect of transportation, as above. Valuations of reductions in emissions between public transport and LEVs were used, when compared with conventional vehicle emission levels. There is wide variation in figures quoted for emissions savings, with, for example *Ethical Consumer* (The Cooperative Wholesale Society 2019) quoting a higher level of emissions for hybrid vehicles (100g CO_2/ Km) than the UK government's estimate of standard saloon petrol engine vehicles (95g CO_2/ km) (Kronberg and Weekes 2018). The principle of parsimony pertained. As discussed above, the replacement rate valuations considered the substitution effect, in each case, according to market prices.

Table 16.5 (continued)

Then, in relation to food purchasing, the objective was to estimate the difference between a plant-based consumption regime, when compared with one that included meat purchases. This was on the environmental basis that even within the UK – where there has been a considerable drive to reduce GHG emissions from British agriculture – the pattern for much livestock production, over the 10 years to 2017, was largely in reverse, compared with substantial advances in mitigation for crop production (Wray 2017). More extravagant estimates of ethical consumption purchases, from some lobby CSOs, were eschewed, reporting, instead, for figures for a relatively small population of 600,000 vegans.

Sources: Adan and Fuerst (2016); Buchs and Schnepf (2013); Davis and Boundy (2021); Department for Business (2019); Department for Environment Food and Rural Affairs UK (2020); Energy and Industrial Strategy Great Britain (2016); Energy Saving Trust (2021); European Commission (2020); McCoy (2017); Oxley (2019); Rowlatt (2009); The Cooperative Wholesale Society (2019); The Vegan Society (2018); Ubamarket (2019); Wray (2017); Wunsch (2021).

Recycling and ethical consumption

The final domains concerned two of the topics that are most readily associated with civil society environmental engagement: recycling and ethical consumption. Recycling rates vary considerably across Britain's local authorities, ranging from 17–65% of material waste, in 2018/19 (Department for Environment Food and Rural Affairs UK 2019). This does not, necessarily, reflect variations in the marginal propensities of households to recycle, but, rather, the capacities of local councils to do so. Future research should account for these local variations. Indeed, as commented in the conclusions, one of the most important aspects of developing this research area is to move from aggregate, national household satellite accounts, to ones that enable comparisons and, hence, policy decisions to be taken, at a local level. As such, the evaluation, at this stage, only accounts at a national scale.

There is a wealth of information available on ethical consumption, through Ethical Consumer's magazines and reports. Some of the authors' previous research has placed this in the context of the greening of markets and governance in Britain, as a whole (Bradley and Ziniel 2017). This points to the almost exponential growth in the UK's moral markets since the turn of the millennium. Nevertheless, changes in definitions from year to year, and the lack of detail about how data sources have been used, does cast doubt on some of the more extravagant figures quoted in that source's annual reports.

Consequently, the use of such data was deliberately limited; only including some items of green home, clothing and cosmetics purchasing. All data on local purchasing was excluded, as, although this can be seen as contributing to environmental engagement, it, equally, embraces a wide range of other considerations. Ethical Consumer provides a figure of almost £4BN for the value of local shopping in the UK, in 2018 (The Cooperative Wholesale Society 2019). But it is considered that only a fraction of this figure represents environmental decision-making and engagement. The methodological issues addressed are outlined in Tables 16.6 and 16.7; the summary of overall values are contained in Table 16.8.

Table 16.6: Decisions on calculations in respect of recycling and ethical consumption.

Recycling	Official estimates of recycling of waste collections and deliveries to local authorities, in the UK, for 2018–19, range from 43.5–44.7% (Department for Environment Food and Rural Affairs UK 2019)*. Individual local authority figures were aggregated.
Ethical consumption	Despite the reservations expressed above in respect to Ethical Consumer reporting, this is regarded as the most reliable summary guide to the scale of ethical purchasing and decision-making in the UK. Even so, most categories of purchasing were excluded from the analysis.
	Energy-efficient boilers and feed-in tariffs were excluded, as these are included in previous calculations. Furthermore, the categories of energy-efficient appliances, and sustainable timber and paper products had too many caveats associated with them. By contrast, the purchase of energy-efficient light bulbs did reflect an ethical purchasing decision. Equally, it was assumed that the same was true in respect of ethical cleaning products, clothing and cosmetics, each of which represent distinct niche markets within far larger, globally produced and distributed industries.
Methodological basis	In respect of recycling, decisions were made on the method of waste management to consider as most reflective of the environmental decision-making of households. WRAP (Dick and Scholes 2018) produces an annual report on gate fees (at waste and recycling centres) for various methods of waste disposal. The figures for MRF, on the extent of recycled materials, for the year, were applied.
	The figures from Ethical Consumer were used as the basis for the calculations. These were in respect of energy-efficient light bulbs, ethical cleaning products, clothing and cosmetics, as each of these product ranges are effectively green labelled, in the UK. Even so, evidence from (Reimers, Magnuson, and Chao 2016; Cerri, Testa, and Rizzi 2018), suggests that ethical consuming generally, and clothing, specifically, can be over-estimated by a factor of two. Based on this evidence, the figures quoted by Ethical Consumer for these product lines were halved.
	Replacement rates for recycling were based on the cost of landfill taxes (Department for Environment Food and Rural Affairs UK 2019). For ethical purchasing, the full figures from Ethical Consumer were used, independent of the modifications indicated in the literature.

Table 16.6 (continued)

Data sources	As indicated above, data was sourced from DEFRA, WRAP and Ethical Consumer, as the basis for these valuations.
Assumptions made regarding data use	See above.

Sources: Cerri, Testa, and Rizzi (2018); Department for Environment Food and Rural Affairs UK (2019); Dick and Scholes (2018); Reimers, Magnuson, and Chao (2016).
Note: DEFRA's statistics only relate to England.

Table 16.7: Detailed estimates of environmental engagement.

1. Organisational membership and volunteering

Name of organisation	Estimate of time-use opportunity cost valuation (£1,000s) membership	Estimate of time-use replacement/ substitution rate valuation (£1000s) membership	Estimate of time-use opportunity cost valuation (£1,000s) volunteers	Estimate of time-use replacement/ substitution rate valuation (£1000s) volunteers
Greenpeace	1,158	1,732	434.4	649.8
Friends of the Earth	58.75	87.9	22	33
RSPB	9,801	14,663	3,675.4	5,498.6
WWF UK	4,018.4	6,011.5	1,506.9	2,254.3
The National Trust	49,896	74,644.4	42,768	63,980.9
Buglife	243.2	363.8	91.2	136.4
Butterfly Conservation	356.4	533.2	133.6	199.9
Client Earth	N/A	N/A	8.3	17.0
The County Wildlife Trusts	7,573.5	11,330	11,694.4	17,494.8
Marine Conservation Society	5,766	8,626	384.1	574.7
Green Alliance	3.6	5.3	1.3	2
Sustrans	267.3	400	1,219.5	1,824.5
The Woodland Trust	2,575	3,852.2	2,833.4	4,235.9
Environmental Investigations Agency	N/A	N/A	9.2	20.5

Table 16.7 (continued)

FERN	N/A	N/A	4.7	10.6
Global Witness	N/A	N/A	26.7	55.5
38 Degrees	2,970	4,443.1	1.67	2.5
Fauna & Flora International	4,740.1	7,091.2	112.9	169
Forum for the Future	N/A	N/A	10	45.6
Groundwork	N/A	N/A	3,564	5,791.7
New Economics Foundation	333.2	498.5	N/A	N/A
Soil Association	8.9	13.3	N/A	5,136.3
Wildfowl & Wetlands Trust	1,532.5	2,292.6	668.2	999.7
Wildlife & Countryside Link	71,280	106,634.9	58,137.7	86,974.1
Transition Towns#	89.1	133.3	33.4	50
Extinction Rebellion	66.8	100	250.6	374.9
Environmental School Strikes	N/A	N/A	1,443.3	2,159.2
Total valuations: organisational membership and volunteering	162,737.75	243,460.94	129,034.87	192,907.13

2. Walking, cycling and participation in amateur and informal sporting activities

Activity	Opportunity cost environmental health benefit (QALYs) rate (£1000s)	Replacement cost environmental health benefit (QALYs) rate (£1000s)
Walking for leisure	231,674.8	874,572.5
Walking for travel	157,243.1	593,592.8
Cycling for leisure	54,283.4	204,919.8
Cycling for travel	21,257.4	80,246.7
Football (soccer)	80,482.6	712,606
Rugby Union	8,284	73,348.2
Rugby League	2,032.1	17,992.8
Cricket	11,209	99,246
Tennis	29,037.3	257,101.2
Running	170,556.7	1,510,137

Table 16.7 (continued)

Coarse angling (fishing excl. hunting)	158,208	1,400,800
Rowing	19,699.2	174,420
Swimming (wild) and other outdoor water sports	61,900.8	548,080
Golf	68,090.4	602,883.7
Total valuations: walking, cycling and outdoor sports	1,073,958.8	7,149,946.7

3. GHG emissions savings in residential home improvements, use of public transport, switching to LEVs and adopting plant-based food consumption.

Activity	Opportunity cost reductions in GHG emissions (carbon pricing) (£1000s)	Replacement cost market substitution prices (£1000s)
Cavity wall insulation	3,640.1	17,505.2
Loft insulation	368.1	2,334
Energy-efficient boilers	6,026	4,668
FiT micro-generation	366.3	23,749.2
Rail transport	4,274.6	28,212.4
Bus transport	7,372.7	48,659.8
Underground transport	7,145.6	47,161
Light railway transport	1,212.2	8,000.5
LEV emissions savings	237.2	3,982.2
Meat-free food basket savings	383,400	978,432
Total valuations: energy, transport and food	414,042.8	1,162,704.3

4. Recycling and ethical purchasing.

Activity	Opportunity cost Materials Recovery Facility and modified Ethical Consumer rates (£1000s)	Replacement cost Landfill taxes and full Ethical Consumer rates (1000s)
Recycling	484,000	1,956,900
Ethical purchasing – energy-efficient lighting and cleaning products	104,000	208,000

Table 16.7 (continued)

Ethical purchasing – clothing	50,000	25,000
Ethical purchasing – cosmetics	832,000	416,000
Total valuations: recycling and ethical purchasing	1,470,000	2,605,900

Source: Valuations calculated by the author. Details of data sources are contained in the above explanatory tables and references.
Notes: 1) The Soil Association volunteers are local farmers for whom a housekeeper rate is not applicable. The valuation for substitution rate is based on average farm income salaries for 2018; 2) Transition Towns, Extinction Rebellion and Environmental School Strikes were added to the 2013 list.

Table 16.8: Summary of overall valuations table.

Summary activity	Opportunity cost valuations (GBP M)	Replacement cost valuations (GPB M)
Membership of organisations	162.74	243.46
Volunteering through organisations	129.03	192.90
Walking, cycling and outdoor sports	1,073.96	7,149.95
The big three: energy, transport and food	414.04	1,162.70
Recycling and ethical purchasing	1,470.00	2,605.9
Total overall valuations	3,249.77 (c £3.25BN)	11,354.91 (c £11.35BN)
Mid-point between these two aggregate estimates: £7,302.34M (c £7.3BN) compared with UK GDP, 2018 = c £2,200BN		

Source: Summary of calculated valuations, by author.

Discussion and conclusion

The objective of this chapter has been to sketch out a methodology and some re-sults for valuing aggregate civil society engagement in environmental activity, for a single year (2018), in the UK. Considerable limitations surround the evaluation presented here. Arguments can be made for the choice of other domains of envi-ronmental engagement. The methodologies used for calculating the valuations of each domain have partly connected with more recent household satellite account approaches, in relation to the use of time-use data, but some market shadow pricing costings have been deployed.

Furthermore, the data sets relied upon have revealed the partial and, sometimes, suspect nature of such information, from both official and CSO sources. Equally, the relationship between opportunity cost and replacement value methods has, in some instances, veered away from the way these economic valuation terms are, generally, understood. A considerable number of assumptions concerning how to use various data sets, in relation to these methodologies – to arrive at some sort of estimated values of civil society environmental engagement – have been made. As such, it will not be difficult for other social economy researchers to challenge and improve on the evaluations that are presented here.

But that is to miss the point. If there is any merit in the approach adopted here and, even, in the valuation results that given, it is in the attempt to do so. These valuations are, undoubtedly, at the low-end of the possible range, even when considering the replacement rate totals. At the higher estimate they represent approximately 1% of the household satellite account evaluation for the entire UK, in all spheres of the core economy, as published by the ONS (Payne and Vassilev 2018). Even so, despite all these caveats, the main purpose of this chapter has been to open a conversation and debate about civil society environmental engagement.

Why? Because the relationship between the financial system and sustainability goals demands it. Asset and investment managers need to be increasingly able to understand how to maximise returns to their clients and investors, while managing risk and securing defined benefits, in an era of climate and biodiversity catastrophe. Whether a three-capitals (finance, human and natural capital, see (Bose, Dong, and Simpson 2019)) is taken or a six capitals (adding in manufactured, intellectual and social-relational, (Integrated Reporting 2021)) model of the relationships between planet, people and profit, there is a need to understand what the main stocks and flows are, in the system.

One of the most critical stocks, in relation to human and social-relationship capital, is the aggregate activity of civil society. And, a vital flow, to understand, is its actions in respect of the transfer of revenue, from this capital stock, towards the creation, preservation and mitigating the erosion of natural capital. The task of this chapter has been to put some numbers to the value of that revenue flow, which takes place in the currency of volunteering, agency and behaviours, rather than through money transfers. This environmental engagement is a function of non-market (core) economic allocations, made by ordinary people, some more intentional than others, towards the sustainability of natural capital and ecological services.

Even so, the aggregate numbers are, possibly, the least important aspect of this endeavour. To be able to, increasingly, integrate the activities of public policy, the requirements of corporate and private sector business and the role of NGOs and CSOs, with the demands of the UN Sustainable Development Goals (SDGs) some basis for an integrated reporting framework is needed. The International Integrated Reporting Council framework has seven guiding principles (Integrated Reporting 2021: 7), which can be related to the analysis presented here:

- Strategic focus and orientation – exemplified by the purpose of this chapter.
- Connectivity of information – bringing together a wide range of data sets and measurement criteria.
- Stakeholder relationships – using the approaches, information and internal valuations of the most significant environmental CSO, together with those of government and other agencies, in the UK.
- Materiality – seeking to compare lower level (opportunity cost) and higher level (replacement/ substitution rate) valuations of civil society engagement.
- Conciseness – attempting to present the valuations in as succinct a way as possible.
- Reliability and completeness – showing the methodology in a transparent and unvarnished way.
- Consistency and comparability – opening the debate for this to happen.

It is in regard of the final principle that this chapter is offered. The intention is to open the debate about which domains, data sets, measurement criteria and assumptions to make, about the environment engagement of households and the core economy. If some consistency and comparability can be arrived at on these, both in relation to localities, within a country such as the UK, and between societies, that gives further opportunities for policy, philanthropy and impact investment decisions to be directed towards, both motivating enhanced and new core economic household production, in relation to environmental engagement.

Klaus Radunsky (see Chapter Nineteen), suggests that, in respect of the UNFCCC Adaptation Fund, methodologies, such as the one deployed here, can be applied to assess adaptation needs, together with their suitability and efficacy. Following COP26 (November 2021) such approaches remain under discussion. But a breakthrough took place at Glasgow in the provision of arrangements for non-market approaches (Paris Protocol, Article 6.8) for cooperation on adaptation, paving the way for new methodologies, such as the one outlined in this chapter, to be utilised, particularly for supporting finance for developing countries.

It should be noted that the analysis presented here is more relevant to policies related to climate change mitigation, rather than adaptation. In this respect, the linkage to Klaus Radunsky's chapter will be best made through further research into the ways in which environmental engagement more specifically targets climate adaptation practices

The consistent operation of comparable data sets, methodologies and assumptions related to the activity of civil society environmental engagement, will enable such, more detailed, valuations to be made. These are, equally, vital for developed, mid-developing and less developed countries, alike. The types of valuations indicated here – as a model of alternative financial analysis – can drive the ability of policy-makers to target their strategies more tightly, but only if this type of analysis is operationalised in a comparative way – between localities within a country and between entire countries.

Research needs to be developed along the lines adopted here, that can be utilised in a consistent way: the right domains, methodology, sources of data and accounting principles. But, arguably, the non-monetary financial transactions of citizens, in the core economy, must be taken seriously. Failure to do so will mean missing one of the most significant aspects of mitigating the ecological crises of the twenty-first century.

References

Adan, Hassan, and Franz Fuerst. 2016. 'Do Energy Efficiency Measures Really Reduce Household Energy Consumption? A Difference-in-Difference Analysis', *Energy Efficiency*, 9 (5), 1207–19.

Archer, G. 2020. *UK Briefing: The Plug-in Hybrid Con*, (Transport and Environment), <https://www.transportenvironment.org/sites/te/files/publications/2020_09_UK_briefing_The_plug-in_hybrid_con.pdf> [Accessed 9 October 2021].

Atkinson, A., and F. Bourguignon (eds.) 2015. *Handbook on Income Distribution*, (Amsterdam: Elsevier).

Balogh, J.C., V.A. Gibeault, W.A. Walker, M.P. Kenna, and J.T. Snow. 2020. *Golf Course Construction and Management: Environmental Perspectives* (Boca Raton, FL: CRC Press).

Barton, J., R. Hine, and J. Pretty. 2009. 'The Health Benefits of Walking in Greenspaces of High Natural and Heritage Value', *Journal of Integrative Environmental Sciences*, 6 (4), 261–78.

Becker, Gary S. 1965. 'A Theory of the Allocation of Time', *The Economic Journal*, 75 (299), 493–517.

Bernauer, Thomas, Robert Gampfer, Tianguang Meng, and Yu-Sung Su. 2016. 'Could More Civil Society Involvement Increase Public Support for Climate Policy-Making? Evidence from a Survey Experiment in China', *Global Environmental Change*, 40, 1–12.

Bjørn, Anders, Pradip Kalbar, Simon Elsborg Nygaard, Simon Kabins, Charlotte Louise Jensen, Morten Birkved, Jannick Schmidt, and Michael Zwicky Hauschild. 2018. 'Pursuing Necessary Reductions in Embedded GHG Emissions of Developed Nations: Will Efficiency Improvements and Changes in Consumption Get Us There?', *Global Environmental Change*, 52, 314–24.

Bose, Satyajit, Guo Dong, and Anne Simpson. 2019. *The Financial Ecosystem: The Role of Finance in Achieving Sustainability* (Cham, Switzerland: Springer International Publishing).

Bradley, Tony, and Curtis Ziniel. 2017. 'Green Governance? Local Politics and Ethical Businesses in Great Britain: Bradley and Ziniel', *Business Ethics (Oxford, England)*, 26 (1), 18–30.

Brodersen, K.A.I. 2007. *Aperghis (G.G.) the Seleukid Royal Economy. The Finances and Financial Administration of the Seleukid Empire* (Cambridge, UK: Cambridge University Press).

Buchs, M., and S.V. Schnepf. 2013. 'UK Households' Carbon Footprint: A Comparison of the Association between Household Characteristics and Emissions from Home Energy, Transport and Other Goods and Services', *SSRN*, IZA Discussion Paper No. 7204.

Cahn, Edgar 2009 'It's the Core Economy Stupid: An Open Letter to the Non-Profit Community' *Time Banks* <https://timebanks.blogspot.com/2007/12/welcome-to-priceless-money.html> [Accessed 10 November 2021]

Carney, M. 2020. *Lecture 1: From Moral to Market Sentiments, Reith Lectures 2020 – How We Get What We Value?*, 57 minutes. (United Kingdom: BBC Radio 4) <https://www.bbc.co.uk/pro grammes/m000q3sp> [Accessed 9 October 2021]

Cerri, Jacopo, Francesco Testa, and Francesco Rizzi. 2018. 'The More I Care, the Less I Will Listen to You: How Information, Environmental Concern and Ethical Production Influence Consumers' Attitudes and the Purchasing of Sustainable Products', *Journal of Cleaner Production*, 175, 343–53.

Chadeau, Ann. 1992. 'What Is Households' Non-Market Production Worth?', *OECD Economic Studies*, 18, 85–103.

Chang, H-J. 2014. *Economics: The User's Guide* (London: Pelican-Penguin Books).

Clark, C. 1958. 'The Economics of Housework', *Bulletin of the Oxford Lnstitute of Statistics* 20 (2), 205–11.

Coote, A., and N. Goodwin. 2010. *The Great Transition: Social Justice and the Core Economy*, (New Economics Foundation), <https://neweconomics.org/uploads/files/82c90c4bb4d6147dc3_1fm6bxppl.pdf> [Accessed 9 October 2021].

Cracknell, J., F. Miller, and H. Williams. 2013. *Passionate Collaboration: Taking the Pulse of the UK Environmental Sector*, (Greenfunders.org), <http://www.greenfunders.org/wp-content/up loads/Passionate-Collaboration-Full-Report.pdf> [Accessed 9 October 2021].

Dale, G. 2016. *Reconstructing Karl Polanyi: Excavation and Critique* (London: Pluto Press).

Daly, H.E. 1991. *Steady-State Economics: With New Essays* (Washington DC: Island press).

Davis, S., and R.G. Boundy. 2021. *Transportation Energy Data Book: Edition 39*, (Oak Ridge, TN: Oak Ridge National Lab), <https://www.ornl.gov/publication/transportation-energy-data-book-edition-39> [Accessed 30 January 2022].

Department for Business, Energy and Industrial Strategy UK. 2019. *Household Energy National Statistics: Detailed Report, 2019*, Energy and Industrial Strategy Business (London: Office for National Statistics), <https://www.gov.uk/government/statistics/household-energy-efficiency-statistics-detailed-report-2019> [Accessed 9 October 2021].

Department for Environment Food and Rural Affairs UK. 2019. *Statistics on Waste Managed by Local Authorities in England in 2018/19*, DEFRA (London: Office for National Statistics), <https://assets.publishing.service.gov.uk/government/uploads/system/uploads/attach ment_data/file/918853/201819_Stats_Notice_FINAL_accessible.pdf#:~:text=The%20official%20England%20%E2%80%98waste%20from%20households%E2%80%99%20recycling%20rate,percentage%20points%20to%20the%20recycling%20rate%20in%202018.> [Accessed 9 October 2021].

——. 2020. *Family Food, 2018-19: Annual Report on Household Purchases of Food and Drink*, DEFRA (London: Office for National Statistics), <https://www.gov.uk/government/statistics/family-food-201819> [Accessed 9 October 2021].

Department for Transport UK. 2019. *Walking and Cycling Statistics, England: 2018, Statistical Release*, (London: Department of Transport), <https://assets.publishing.service.gov.uk/gov ernment/uploads/system/uploads/attachment_data/file/821842/walking-and-cycling-statistics-2018-accessible.pdf> [Accessed 9 October 2021].

Dick, H., and P. Scholes. 2018. *Gate Fees 2017-18 Final Report: Comparing the Costs of Alternative Waste Treatment Options*, (Banbury, UK: WRAP), <https://archive.wrap.org.uk/sites/files/wrap/WRAP%20Gate%20Fees%202018_exec+extended%20summary%20report_FINAL.pdf> [Accessed 9 October 2021].

Doppelt, B., and W. McDonough. 2017. *Leading Change toward Sustainability: A Change-Management Guide for Business, Government and Civil Society* (London: Routledge).

Dosumu, A.A. 2016. *The Environmental Impacts and Wellbeing Benefits of Sport: Assessing Spectator and Participant Dominated Sports in England*, University of Essex.

Energy and Industrial Strategy Great Britain.·2016. *Government Response to the Committee on Climate Change: Progress on Meeting Carbon Budgets*, (London: Department of Business, UK Goverment), <https://assets.publishing.service.gov.uk/government/uploads/system/up loads/attachment_data/file/559954/57204_Unnumbered_Gov_Response_Web_Accessible. pdf> [Accessed 30 January 2022].

Energy Saving Trust.·2021. *Reducing Home Heat Loss: Cavity Wall Insulation*, <https://energysavingtrust.org.uk/advice/cavity-wall-insulation/> [Accessed 9 October 2021].

Environmental Investigation Agency UK.·2019. *Annual Report and Accounts 2019*, <https://eia-international.org/wp-content/uploads/UK-2019.pdf> [Accessed 9 October 2021].

Environmental Protection Agency US.·2021. *Sources of Greenhouse Gas Emissions*, (Washington DC: EPA.gov), <https://www.epa.gov/ghgemissions/sources-greenhouse-gas-emissions> [Accessed 9 October 2021].

European Commission. 2020. *Co$_2$ Emissions Performance Standards for Cars and Vans*, <https://ec.europa.eu/clima/policies/transport/vehicles/regulation_en> [Accessed 9 October 2021].

Eurostat.·2003. *Eurostat Yearbook 2003: The Statistical Guide to Europe*, (European Commission), <https://ec.europa.eu/eurostat/documents/3217494/5640993/KS-CD-02-001-EN.PDF.pdf/ c19a6c90-f1e4-47f1-aa52-18333c9aea47?t=1414770954000> [Accessed 31 December 2021].

Goodwin, Neva. 2018. 'There Is More Than One Economy', *Real-World Economics Review*, 84, 16–35.

Goodwin, Neva, Jonathan M. Harris, Julie A. Nelson, Pratistha Joshi Rajkarnikar, Brian Roach, and Mariano Torras. 2019. *Principles of Economics in Context* (New York: Routledge).

Groundwork.·2019. *Our Impact in 2018*, <https://www.groundwork.org.uk/about-groundwork/our-impact/our-impact-in-2018/> [Accessed 9 October 2021].

Hall, K. 2019. 'Coastal Living Linked with Better Mental Health', *Blue Health*. <https://bluehealth2020.eu/news/coast-health/> [Accessed 30 January 2022].

Hawrylyshyn, Oli. 1976. 'The Value of Household Services: A Survey of Empirical Estimates', *Review of Income and Wealth*, 22 (2), 101–03.

Holloway, S., S. Short, and S. Tamplin. 2002. *Household Satellite Account (Experimental) Methodology.* (London: Office for National Statistics)

Integrated Reporting.·2021. *International <IR> Reporting Framework January 2021*, (Integrated Reporting.org), <https://integratedreporting.org/wp-content/uploads/2021/01/Internationa lIntegratedReportingFramework.pdf> [Accessed 9 October 2021].

Intergovernmental Panel on Climate Change.·2018. *Glossary*, https://www.ipcc.ch/site/assets/up loads/sites/2/2019/06/SR15_AnnexI_Glossary.pdf> [Accessed 10 November 2021].

Ironmonger, D.S. 1972. *New Commodities and Consumer Behaviour* (Cambridge: Cambridge University Press).

⸻. 1989. 'Research on the Household Economy.' in D.S. Ironmonger (ed.), *Household Work* (Sydney: Allen and Unwin),

⸻. 1995. 'Modelling the Household Economy.' in M. Dutta (ed.), *Economics, Econometrics and the Link: Essays in Honour of Lawrence R Klein*. (Amsterdam: Elsevier),

⸻. 2001. *Household Production and the Household Economy*, Department of Economics Household Research Unit Research Papers. (Melbourne: University of Melbourne)

Ironmonger, D.S., and F. Soupourmas 2012 *Output-Based Estimates of the Gross Household Product of the United States 2003-2010: And Some Interactions of GHP with Gross Market Product During the Great Financial Crisis (2008-2009)* (Boston, MA: 32nd General Conference of the International Association for Research in Income and Wealth)

Jacobs, M. 2016. 'High Pressure for Low Emissions: How Civil Society Created the Paris Climate Agreement', *Juncture*, 22 (4), 314–23.

Jacquet, J., and D. Jamieson. 2016. 'Soft but Significant Power in the Paris Agreement', *Nature Climate Change*, 6 (7), 643–46.

Kässi, O., and V. Lehdonvirta. 2018. 'Online Labour Index: Measuring the Online Gig Economy for Policy and Research', *Technological Forecasting and Social Change*, 137, 241–48.

Knobel, Andres, Beneficial Ownership in the Investment Industry: A Strategy to Roll Back Anonymous Capital (October 7, 2019). Available at SSRN: https://ssrn.com/abstract=3470358 or http://dx.doi.org/10.2139/ssrn.3470358

Komljenovic, J. 2021. 'The Rise of Education Rentiers: Digital Platforms, Digital Data and Rents', *Learning, Media and Technology*, 46 (3), 320–32.

Kronberg, Nick, and Shawn Weekes.·2018. *Transport Statistics Great Britain, 2018: Moving Britain Ahead*, Department for Transport (London: Office for National Statistics), <https://assets.pub lishing.service.gov.uk/government/uploads/system/uploads/attachment_data/file/787488/ tsgb-2018-report-summaries.pdf> [Accessed 9 October 2021].

Lange, D.·2020. *Number of People Participating in Football in England from 2016 to 2020* Statista. com <https://www.statista.com/statistics/934866/football-participation-uk/> [Accessed 9 October 2021].

Lee, J. 2021. 'Walking and Biking Prioritised in New Highway Code', *BBC News* <https://www.bbc. co.uk/news/uk-58021450> [Accessed 19 August 2021].

Lucas, C. 2021. 'Net Zero by 2050 Is Far Too Late to Avert Climate Catastrophe', *The Independent*, 22 July 2021. <https://www.independent.co.uk/climate-change/opinion/climate-crisis-boris-johnson-cop26-b1888067.html> [Accessed 9 October 2021].

Mawle, G.·2018. *A Survey of Freshwater Angling in England*, (London: UK Goverment Environment Agency), <https://www.gov.uk/government/publications/a-survey-of-freshwater-angling-in-england/a-survey-of-freshwater-angling-in-england-phase-1-summary> [Accessed 30 January 2022].

McCoy, D.·2017. *Heating Homes: Do Energy Saving Measures Reduce Energy Consumption in Social Housing?*, (London: Granthan Research Institute on Climate Change and the Environment, London School of Economics), <https://www.lse.ac.uk/granthaminstitute/news/heating-homes-do-energy-saving-measures-reduce-energy-consumption-in-social-housing/> [Accessed 30 January 2022].

Minoli, D.M., and M.T. Smith. 2011. 'An Exploration of Golf and Voluntary Environmental Programmes', *Journal of Environmental Planning and Management*, 54 (7), 871–89.

Mutz, M., and J. Müller. 2016. 'Mental Health Benefits of Outdoor Adventures: Results from Two Pilot Studies', *Journal of Adolescence*, 49, 105–14.

National Institute for Health and Clinical Excellence. 2021. *Glossary Q*, <https://www.nice.org.uk/ Glossary?letter=Q> [Accessed 28 December 2021].

National Trust.·2019. *Annual Report 2018-19*, National Trust Annual Reports, (Swindon: The National Trust), <https://nt.global.ssl.fastly.net/documents/201819-annual-report.pdf> [Accessed 9 October 2021].

Newell, P. 2008. 'Civil Society, Corporate Accountability and the Politics of Climate Change', *Global Environmental Politics*, 8 (3), 122 53.

Nonhebel, S., and H.C. Moll. 2001. 'Evaluation of Options for Reduction of Greenhouse Gas Emissions by Changes in Household Consumption Patterns', *IVEM OR*, 106, 136.

Oxley, S.·2019. *Household Energy Efficiency National Statistics: Detailed Report 2018.*, Energy and Industrial Strategy Department for Business (London: Office for National Statistics), <https://assets.publishing.service.gov.uk/government/uploads/system/uploads/ attachment_data/file/795929/Detailed_Release_-_HEE_stats_18_Apr_2019.pdf> [Accessed 9 October 2021].

Payne, C., and G. Vassilev.·2018. *Household Satellite Account, UK: 2015 and 2016*, (London: Office for National Statistics) <https://www.ons.gov.uk/economy/nationalaccounts/satelliteac counts/articles/householdsatelliteaccounts/2015and2016estimates> [Accessed 9 October 2021].

Poissonnier, A., and D. Roy. 2017. 'Household Satellite Account for France: Methodological Issues on the Assessment of Domestic Production', *Review of Income and Wealth*, 63 (2), 353–77.

Polanyi, K. 1944/2002. *The Great Transformation: The Political and Economic Origins of Our Time*. (Boston, MA.: Beacon Press).

Ponthieux, S., and D. Meurs. 2015. 'Gender Inequality.' in A. Atkinson and F. Bourguignon (eds.), *Handbook on Income Distribution* (Amsterdam: Elsevier), pp. 981–1146.

Pooley, C.G., D. Horton, G. Scheldeman, C. Mullen, T. Jones, M. Tight, A. Jopson, and A. Chisholm. 2013. 'Policies for Promoting Walking and Cycling in England: A View from the Street', *Transport Policy*, 27, 66–72.

Ramblers Association.·2014. *Walking Works: Making the Case to Encourage Greater Uptake of Walking as a Physical Activity to Reduce the Burden of Long-Term Health Conditions on the Nhs*, Walking for Health, (London: Walking for health.org.uk), <https://www.walkingforhealth. org.uk/sites/default/files/HCP_walkingworks_download.pdf> [Accessed 9 October 2021].

Raworth, K. 2017. *Doughnut Economics: Seven Ways to Think L^{ik}e a 21st-Century Economist* (White River Junction, VT: Chelsea Green Publishing).

Reid, M.G. 1934. *Economics of Household Production* (New York: J. Wiley and Sons).

Reimers, V., B. Magnuson, and F. Chao. 2016. 'The Academic Conceptualisation of Ethical Clothing: Could It Account for the Attitude Behaviour Gap?', *Journal of Fashion Marketing and Management: An International Journal*, 20 (4), 383–99.

Rowlatt, J. 2009 'Why Cars Are Greener Than Buses (Maybe)' *BBC News Blogs Ethical Man* <https://www.bbc.co.uk/blogs/ethicalman/2009/11/why_cars_are_greener_than_buses. html> [Accessed 9 October 2021]

Sandel, M.J. 2012. *What Money Can't Buy: The Moral Limits of Markets* (London: Macmillan).

Singleton, A. 2019. 'Walking (and Cycling) to Well-Being: Modal and Other Determinants of Subjective Well-Being During the Commute', *Travel Behaviour and Society*, 16, 249–61.

Spaargaren, G., and A.P.J. Mol. 2013. 'Carbon Flows, Carbon Markets, and Low-Carbon Lifestyles: Reflecting on the Role of Markets in Climate Governance', *Environmental Politics*, 22 (1), 174–93.

Sport England.·2020. *Active Lives Adult Survey: November 2018/19 Report*, <https://sportengland-production-files.s3.eu-west-2.amazonaws.com/s3fs-public/2020-04/Active%20Lives% 20Adult%20November%2018-19%20Report.pdf?BhkAy2K28pd9bDEz_NuisHl2ppuqJtpZ> [Accessed 28 December 2021].

Statista Research Department.·2020. *Distribution of the Average Annual Mileage of All Motorists in the United* Kingdom *(UK) in 2017 and 2018*<https://www.statista.com/statistics/513456/an nual-mileage-of-motorists-in-the-united-kingdom-uk/> [Accessed 30 January 2022].

Stiglitz, J.E., A. Sen, and J-P. Fitoussi.·2009. *Report by the Commission on the Measurement of Economic Performance and Social Progress*, (Commission on the Measurement of Economic Performance and Social Progress), <https://ec.europa.eu/eurostat/documents/8131721/ 8131772/Stiglitz-Sen-Fitoussi-Commission-report.pdf> [Accessed 10 November 2021].

The Cooperative Wholesale Society.·2019. *Twenty Years of Ethical Consumerism: Ethical Consumer Report, 2019*, Ethical Consumer Reports, <https://assets.ctfassets.net/5ywmq66472jr/ 5hkc6bA1y2eNRGsHJzyvX2/14449115fafac1c02cf4f9fd5a52b13b/Twenty_Years_of_Ethical_ Consumerism_2019.pdf> [Accessed 9 October 2021].

The Vegan Society. 2018. *Further Information: Key Facts*, <https://www.vegansociety.com/about-us /further-information/key-facts> [Accessed 30 August 2021].

Ubamarket. 2019. *The Flexitarian Shopper*, <https://ubamarket.com/the-flexitarian-shopper/>
    [Accessed 9 October 2021].
UK Government. 2019. *National Minimum Wage Rates and Living Wage Rates*, <https://www.gov.
    uk/national-minimum-wage-rates#!> [Accessed 28 December 2021].
UK National Careers Service. 2019. *Contryside Ranger Job Profile*, <https://nationalcareers.service.
    gov.uk/job-profiles/countryside-ranger> [Accessed 28 December 2021].
United States Department of Labor. Bureau of Labor Statistics.·2006. *American Time Use Survey
    (ATUS), 2003*<https://www.icpsr.umich.edu/web/ICPSR/studies/4186> [Accessed
    31 December 2021].
Wagner, I.·2021. *Prevalence of Walking and Cycling in England 2018/19 by Region* Statista.com
    <https://www.statista.com/statistics/376189/prevelance-of-walking-and-cycling-in-england-
    uk-by-region/> [Accessed 30 December 2021].
Waite, C.·2021. *UK Greenhouse Gas Emissions: Final Figures*, Energy and Industrial Strategy
    Department for Business (London: Office for National Statistics), <https://assets.publishing.
    service.gov.uk/government/uploads/system/uploads/attachment_data/file/957887/2019_
    Final_greenhouse_gas_emissions_statistical_release.pdf
Walker-Munro, B. 2021. 'Tax Enforcement in the Black Economy: Tackling Disruptive Challenge.'
    in A. Rafay (ed.), *Handbook of Research on Theory and Practice of Financial Crimes* (Hershey,
    PA: IGI Global), pp. 356–80.
Wheeler, K., and J. Nauright. 2006. 'A Global Perspective on the Environmental Impact of Golf',
    Sport in Society, 9 (3), 427–43.
Woodland Trust.·2019. *Our Year in the Woods*, Annual Reports, https://www.woodlandtrust.org.
    uk/media/48770/annual-review-2019.pdf> [Accessed 9 October 2021].
Wray, A.·2017. *Agricultural Statistics and Climate Change*, (London: UK Department for
    Environment, Food and Rural Affairs), <https://assets.publishing.service.gov.uk/government/
    uploads/system/uploads/attachment_data/file/666073/agriclimate-8edition-8dec17.pdf>
    [Accessed 9 October 2021].
Wunsch, N-G.·2021. *Number of Vegans in Great* Britain *2014-2019* Statista.com <https://www.sta
    tista.com/statistics/1062104/number-of-vegans-in-great-britain/> [Accessed
    30 December 2021].
Wynes, S., K.A. Nicholas, J. Zhao, and S.D. Donner. 2018. 'Measuring What Works: Quantifying
    Greenhouse Gas Emission Reductions of Behavioural Interventions to Reduce Driving, Meat
    Consumption, and Household Energy Use', *Environmental Research Letters*, 13 (11), 113002.

Part 4: **Climate finance**

Timothy Cadman and Tapan Sarker

Chapter 17
Climate finance for sustainable development

Abstract: Finance is one of the central aspects necessary for combatting climate change and is covered by a wide range of mechanisms, institutional arrangements and governing bodies with the United Nations Framework Convention on Climate Change (UNFCCC), validating claims that the Convention is indeed both a regime complex and a complex regime. The chapter begins by outlining those arrangements historically and how they, and the responsibilities pertaining to them, have evolved over time. It continues with a summary of some of the main points of contention, not the least of which have been disputes over the provision of resources from developed to developing countries, which have served to reinforce the North/South divide, notably in the context of climate finance. The remainder of the chapter summarises the key themes and findings of the contributing authors to this section of the Handbook, who discuss the strengths and weaknesses of some of the central mechanisms for financing climate action within the UNFCCC, and beyond. They provide recommendations as to how the integrity of finance can be safeguarded, both within the Convention and beyond, where the impacts of poverty – and COVID-19 – make resilience in the face of the escalating climate emergency especially difficult.

Keywords: clean development mechanism, climate finance, contributor parties, Kyoto protocol, North/South divide, paris agreement, recipient parties, UNFCCC, COVID-19

Sustainable development, climate finance and the climate convention

All of the Rio conventions are oriented toward sustainable development and the United Nations Framework Convention on Climate Change (UNFCCC) is no exception, although this priority and focus have evolved over time. In the Paris Agreement (PA) for example, all activities are couched under the broader governing principle of sustainable development and poverty alleviation (UNFCCC 2015a). With several hundred subcomponents, and a Secretariat of over four hundred staff (UNFCCC 2022a), the Convention is one of the most complex regimes in the UN system and has been understood and analysed a regime complex by scholars for some time (Keohane and Victor 2011; Breakey, Cadman, and Sampford 2016). Readers are advised that this

https://doi.org/10.1515/9783110733488-017

introductory section is rife with acronyms and are encouraged to consult https://cli materegimemap.net/ to assist them in keeping track of all elements mentioned.

Institutional arrangements for climate change management and finance

The involvement in, and the contribution of, country Parties to the UNFCCC depends on their development status. Financial support is expected to be provided via the Convention's policy instruments (such as the PA, and before it the Kyoto Protocol KP) from better-resourced countries to those with less capacity and which are most vulnerable to climate change. The allocation of such resources is facilitated through what is referred to as the Financial Mechanism, which under the Article 11 of the Convention is delegated to third parties (United Nations 1992b), including the Global Environment Facility (GEF) and the Green Climate Fund (GCF). The Financial Mechanism is answerable to COP and it is this body which determines its policies, programmes and funding priorities with an emphasis on developing country Parties to the Convention (United Nations 2022).

There are two principal financial arrangements under the FM – finance mechanisms which are formally under the UNFCCC and those mechanisms which contribute to financing under the FM but are not formally part of the Convention. In the case of the former, there are institutions and arrangements that have been created over the life of the Convention at various COPs, or at other official climate-related meetings, designed to meet specific tasks for set periods, and others which continue to facilitate finance. One such example of a now concluded finance agenda, designed to feed into what ultimately became the PA, was the work programme on long-term climate finance (LTF), which was initiated at COP 17 and concluded at COP 19 in Warsaw, although some of its deliberations on how to scale up LTF pre-2020 and subsequently have continued (UNFCCC 2022d). Other aspects of the FM are more permanently embedded. The Standing Committee on Finance (SCF) was established at COP 16 (Cancun, 2010) by the Parties to assist COP (essentially the supreme decision-making body under UNFCCC, comprised as it is of all Member States who are party to the Convention) in fulfilling Parties' roles in relation to the FM. Cancun was also important for a series of agreements regarding long-term cooperative actions necessary for managing the impacts of climate change, including finance and set an ambitious target of USD 100 billion a year by 2020 to meet the needs of developing countries, a target that has not yet been reached (United Nations 2021). The SCF's roles include coordinating the delivery, mobilisation, rationalisation and monitoring of financial resources, coordinating with other bodies of the Convention, as well as undertaking any other tasks as they arise (UNFCCC 2022f). Various funds exist and are managed under the auspices of the Convention, one of the most notable being the Adaptation Fund (discussed by Klaus Radunsky in Chapter Nineteen below). As indicated above, the GEF has an important role to play, not the least of which is overseeing a range of funds allocated to adaptation and mitigation activities under the Convention, including the Least Developed Countries Fund (LCDF) and the Special Climate Change Fund (SCCF). The GCF is a more recent addition to the instrumentalities of the FM, with its governing arrangements formalised at COP 17 (Durban, 2011). The GCF might be seen as a next generation fund manager, with a greater level of independence from the Parties than the GEF and, it has been suggested, stronger governance arrangements (Elges 2016). The GCF might be seen as a challenger to GEF in the environmental funding space and certainly the climate finance space (Cadman 2014), but the two funds managers seems to have reached an accommodation, with the GEF maintaining some of its traditional funds, and the GCF taking more financing responsibility for some of the later Convention initiatives, most notably forests, and REDD+ in particular (Reducing emissions from deforestation and forest degradation and the role of conservation, sustainable management of forests and enhancement of forest carbon stocks in developing countries – also a negotiating theme in the climate talks). Since its inception, the GCF has financed 52 forest projects to the tune of USD 1.5 billion (Green Climate Fund 2022).

Forests, part of the PA under Article 5, are a responsibility shared in part with the World Bank's Forest Carbon Partnership Facility (FCPF 2017) and the UN-REDD programme, a collaboration between the UN Development Programme (UNDP), the UN Environment Programme (UNEP) and the Food and Agriculture Organization (FAO) (UN-REDD 2022). These sorts of bodies are particularly important in climate finance and include governmental agencies in collaboration with other non-state partners, such as the Global Energy Efficiency and Renewable Energy Fund (GEEREF), which seeks to use public finance to leverage private investment in renewable energy, advised by the European Investment Bank (EIB) (GEEREF 2022).

Responsibilities for climate finance

Different actors have different responsibilities for finance under the Convention. One of the principal agents for climate finance is the contributing (developed country) Parties. These used to be called Annex II countries (UNFCCC 2014a), in the old language of the Convention, in the days of the KP and prior to the PA, when language and policy, shifted to the notion of Nationally Determined Contributions (NDCs) to reduce emissions, which made emissions reduction a collective effort (UNFCCC 2022e), rather than one belonging to the historical – largely developed country – emitters (Maguire 2015). These contribute either through unilateral, bilateral, multilateral or regional institutions (UNFCCC 2022b), an example of which is the Asian Development Bank, which has been funding carbon investments for some time and launched a new carbon fund to incentivise investment at COP 26 (Glasgow

2021). Private donors in climate finance, whether they be commercial banks issuing green bonds (see Chapter Thirteen), insurance companies or pension funds, have been actively encouraged since 2014 to play a role in, contribute to or pledge to commit to such funds as the GCF (UNFCCC 2014b).

Recipient Parties are the beneficiaries of climate finance and were previously referred to as the non-Annex I countries. Resources are generally allocated to a national climate fund (NCF) or similar nationally-managed arrangement as a means of aggregating various sources of finance (domestic and international, public and private) (Flynn 2011), and are directed to mitigation and adaptation activities managed by an implementing agency or agencies (IA). Activities have often focussed on technology or capacity building, both of which have their own specific negotiating streams, as well as a Technology Mechanism (TM) and capacity building framework (CBF) under the Convention (UNFCCC undated, 2022c) and are covered by Articles 10 and 11 of the PA.

Implementers of climate finance can be governmental, intergovernmental, nongovernmental or combinations thereof. Finance post-PA still relates largely to adaptation and mitigation. In the lead up to, and immediately after, the PA was ratified, most national-level projects were still mitigation-dominated, a legacy from the KP, which was itself largely focussed on mitigation, through the Clean Development Mechanism (CDM). This is likely to be the case going forward as the CDM has largely been superseded by the new sustainable development mechanism (SDM), which combines compliance and voluntary markets, covers transferrable mitigation outcomes between countries (ITMOs), carbon trading and non-market mechanisms as well as grants, loans, payments, etc. This is discussed in more detail in Chapter Twenty.

Reporting of climate finance by contributor and recipient Parties is covered under Article 13 of the PA. Developed country Parties and other Parties providing support are expected to report on financial, technology transfer and capacity building support provided to developing countries under Articles 9, 10 and 11 (UNFCCC 2015b: 17). Developing countries are under less obligation, but are also expected to report against the provision of those resources under the same articles (UNFCCC 2015b: 18).

Historical and current tensions around climate finance

In the early-stage of the climate negotiations, the division between developed and developing countries was formalised and institutionalised through the designation of countries as being either Annex I (developed) or non-Annex I Parties (i.e., developing countries) The Berlin Mandate (1995) and the ratification of the KP (1997) mark a period of the hegemony of the neoliberal market order during the collapse of Communism in the East. The next phase, starting with the first dialogue in Montreal in 2005, focussed on determining what arrangements would be put in place once the KP commitment period finished in 2012. There was a great deal of collaboration between Parties, culminating in the Bali Road Map. Tensions arose when climate change mitigation was seen as an obligation of both developed and developing countries (Abreu Mejía 2010).

Agenda 21 (United Nations 1992a) recognises non-state participation in international environmental policymaking and non-state interests in environmental decision-making. But citizen involvement has led to some tensions between state and non-state actors in how climate change management should be governed, and the geo-political or sectoral interest, all of which is happening at both the local and international levels, and influencing both, most notably in the role of local government. While the nation-states ultimately still have control, the KP, for example, commodified climate change mitigation through market mechanisms requiring cooperation between state and non-state actors. Sustainable development has the potential to integrate climate change and development policies. This proved to be important in the pre-PA arrangements, especially in the provision of financial and technical support. Much of the debate focussed on the argument that approaches such as carbon offsets were a cheap way to avoid action, exploiting the global commons, subordinating nature to the dictums of private property and the market and externalising the needs of the poor for basic resources. On the sustainability side of the scale, the CDM facilitates North/South transferral of technologies, a cost-effective and efficient way of dealing with emissions. Developing Southern countries insisted that the developed world take action; they didn't start the process, merely came in later, so why should they bear the same burden of responsibility? The KP-related framework and its North to South models resulted in an uneven spread of development (Cadman 2013).

Relying only on Northern countries' obligations to reduce emissions and not including countries who changed their development statuses, such as India and China, was a design flaw in the KP since it was these two countries that benefitted most from the CDM to the almost complete exclusion of other countries (Cadman et al. 2015). COP 15 (Copenhagen 2010) did not deliver a legally binding instrument but it did result in a shared approach to reducing emissions via the NDCs (Radunsky and Cadman 2017) and by 2012 the CDM had lost much of its impetus and prospects for a global carbon market were in danger of evaporating (Clean Development Mechanism Policy Dialogue 2012). The COP 18 Doha Amendment (DA) later in the year succeeded in extending the life of the KP, although it only represented only 15 per cent of total global emissions and several of the original KP countries did not sign up (Maguire 2015: 38).

Negotiations before COP 21 (Paris, 2015) over market mechanisms were protracted, creating a great deal of uncertainty in climate finance (Cadman 2014). These discussions continued afterward to COP 24 in Katowice, Poland in 2018. The conflict between developed and developing countries was largely over their differentiated responsibilities under previous arrangements, notably the KP, but with the rise of the NDCs as a way forward, enabling emissions reduction (mitigation) activities and adaptation.

This was largely because of the unresolved tensions underpinning the finalisation of the Paris Rulebook, which took place during COP 22 (Marrakech, 2016), COP 23 (Bonn, 2017) and in Katowice, 2018 (COP 24), where the negotiations were expected to be concluded (Cadman et al. 2018). COP 25 (Madrid, December 2019) saw ongoing arguments about who was to pay for the loss and damage brought about by climate change and market-based mechanisms for sustainable development (Timperley 2019). Language within Article 6 at that time did not include human rights or social and environmental safeguards, issues that had been contested in previous negotiations (Cadman et al. 2018). At that time, with no clear path for emissions trading, geoengineering started to gain traction as a possible policy alternative (Harvey 2019).

COP 26 (Glasgow, 2021) was held after a twelve-month pause due to COVID. It was at that point Article 6 negotiations were finalised (even if the exact mechanisms and their modalities were not). Financing and investing in climate change action, whether through non-market measures such as grants, subsidies and loans or market mechanisms, notably carbon offsets, are not without their detractors. The environmental NGO sector, one of sustainable development's core constituents, is at best ambivalent towards such measures, at worst hostile, and various groups asserted during COP 26 'there is no carbon budget left to continue discussions around "offsetting" emissions' (Climate Ambition and Rights Alliance 2021: 1).

Overview of chapters

The authors in this section write from their research on, and participation in, the climate change deliberations. In Chapter Eighteen 'Financing emission reductions: ODA-driven climate finance and beyond,' Hitomi Roppongi provides a comprehensive overview and analysis of the sources and institutions of both public and private climate finance inside and outside UNFCCC. In a broad sense, climate finance is the provision of funds to target actions aimed at addressing climate change mitigation and adaptation and may not exactly fit the criteria required in the Official Development Assistance (ODA) framework used by governments for international reporting purposes. In addition, there are other international funding obligations, such as those associated with SDGs, resulting in a further lack of clarity over which countries have received what, and to what ends. Determining how funds are spent is important, not only for transparency purposes, but also to determine whether financial allocations have risen or fallen, particularly in the context of the economic downturn created by the pandemic, or whether funds have been repurposed to meet other needs (again, potentially, for pandemic support). This part therefore makes an important contribution not only by identifying the data gap in climate finance flows hitherto overlooked in the current system, but also by investigating the difficulties associated with expanding climate finance globally.

The Cancun Agreement is now aligned with the Paris Agreement, and there is an expectation that both the public and private sectors will contribute. However, there is limited guidance on how to achieve these targets, no clear methodologies for how these contributions are to be counted and no comprehensive or comparable data to determine how much climate finance is flowing to developing countries overall. Here, the pandemic offers a unique opportunity to restructure global finance to support climate change adaptation and mitigation, and the goals of sustainable development, while also reforming the financial system itself.

In the context of decades of experience as an EU negotiator, Klaus Radunsky provides an in-depth commentary on one of the most important intergovernmental vehicles for financing adaptation to climate change under UNFCCC in Chapter Nineteen, 'The Adaptation Fund.' The chapter begins by describing the historical, political and financial background to the Fund and compares the levels of financing for mitigation and adaptation, noting that the taxonomy of mitigation action is far more developed than adaptation, reflecting the historical precedence of reducing emissions, rather than dealing with their consequences. This has arisen as a consequence of the original focus of the Kyoto Protocol on mitigation, while negotiations by the Parties regarding adaptation have been more protracted, due to changing circumstances, as the real-time impacts of climate change have become more pressing.

The Fund's rules of procedure (always complex in the UN system), have also impacted the levels of funding provided for addressing climate change, as the fund has been largely dependent on the proceeds arising from the CDM (a vehicle designed specifically to deliver mitigation outcomes). This approach to funding differs from the older, more established Global Environment Facility, and the newer, Green Climate Fund. As a result, funding for adaptation has fluctuated over time, as have the voluntary contributions from donor to recipient countries. After providing an overview of funded projects relative to the GDP and adaptation investments of the recipient country, they reflect on the performance of the Fund and comments on and how it could be better managed, notably in relation to sustainable development and poverty alleviation, the stated objectives of the Paris Agreement. COVID-19 has revealed the frailties in the existing economic system and impacted climate finance. However, there is much to be gained from learning the lessons of funding for adaptation in the light of the pandemic, and vice-versa, like climate change, if not tackled, will be far worse. The top priority should be to build back better in order to put the world on a development path that is more sustainable, inclusive and resilient. Funding adaptation to climate change is vital. If the gap between financing mitigation and adaptation continues, the worse it will be for humanity, as the success of adaptation is measured by the reduction in loss and damage from the impacts of climate change, not their escalation.

Rob Hales tackles the ethics of carbon offsets in Chapter Twenty, 'An analysis of the global carbon market post COP26: How fossil fuel emission reductions and offset integrity must guide carbon market operation.' Offsets are contentious from a number of perspectives, including problems associated with carbon accounting, such as double-counting (by a company for its corporate responsibility obligations, or a government for its national greenhouse gas reporting requirements, when there has only been one activity). There can be a failure to deliver the promised outcomes (such as genuinely reducing emissions through a specific project) or not targeting the primary cause of CO_2e emissions (the combustion of fossil fuels for energy and transport). Or the reverse: that is, claiming emissions reductions which would have happened in any case, known as additionality (such as counting a forest as an offset which was not threatened by clearing). Offsets can also outsource the moral responsibility of the primary emitter to reduce emission to other actors in the market, while the primary emitter continues business-as-usual, nor can offsets alone ensure countries reach their net-zero emissions targets. Lastly, carbon markets can also lead to further externalities such as transferring negative social, economic or ecological costs elsewhere (through building a dam on First Nations' land for clean energy, for example, thereby inundating special places and sources of income generation or impacting threatened species' habitat).

With these problems in mind, the chapter details how the various elements of the market need to come together to produce an economic system where costs are internalised at the appropriate location in the global offset supply chain. However, even with the apparent agreement about an international carbon market as a consequence of the COP 26 negotiations, there will be continuing issues about implementation. There will be risks associated with the movement of carbon trading from the dual model of compliance and voluntary markets to a more unified system. Historically there have been integrity and transparency issues associated with the transfer of emissions-reducing activities from developed to developing countries. These may be repeated in the international transfer of mitigation outcomes from one country to meet the NDCs to global emissions reduction in another. Although reducing carbon is the aim, offsetting how markets are constructed and used will determine their social, environmental and economic impacts.

Interestingly, COVID-19 has not impacted carbon markets, and the greater levels of certainty arising from COP 26 means that emerging approaches to offsetting (such as nature-based solutions) are likely to continue and increase. Consequently, the chapter provides a series of criteria and indicators for government and companies seeking to maximise emissions reduction activities and achieve socially and ecologically informed development. Such standards will be essential in safeguarding the needs of rights holders and stakeholders and ensuring the effectiveness of emissions reductions.

The reality for much of the Earth's population, poor as they are, is that they have little influence over the climate negotiations, are unlikely to benefit from carbon markets, will bear the brunt of climate change impacts and are among those most affected by COVID-19. In the Chapter Twenty-one, the final in this section 'Financing climate resilience: New opportunities and challenges,' Andrea Young investigates disaster risk reduction and climate change management in the light of COVID-19 to determine whether climate finance and business can learn anything from the global responses to the pandemic.

The current crisis has shown that sustainable development cannot avoid material concerns related to social and environmental conditions. On the one hand, the pandemic has brought with it a cascade of problems, including the contraction of key economic sectors and increase of public debt. On the other hand, it has also provided a rare opportunity to look into the future and understand the potential impacts that a shock to the climate-based system might bring. The stark reality of COVID-19 has, if anything, reinforced the need for investment to be based on principles of sustainable development.

This chapter reinforces previous observations that the many different social and economic sectors currently being affected by the pandemic, and likely to be impacted in the future by climate change, need strong public fiscal management processes to encourage responsible private investment. In both public and private contexts, well-governed institutions are needed to foster resilience in the face of societal shocks. Systemic change is also necessary to tackle the interconnected and complex global challenges of climate change, poverty, inequality and biodiversity loss.

References

Abreu Mejía, Daniel. 2010. 'The Evolution of the Climate Change Regime: Beyond a North-South Divide?', *International Catalan Institute for Peace, Working Paper* (2010/6).

Breakey, Hugh, Tim Cadman, and Charles Sampford. 2016. 'Governance Values and Institutional Integrity.' in Tim Cadman, Rowena Maguire and Charles Sampford (eds.), *Governing the Climate Change Regime* (London and New York: Routledge), pp. 34–62.

Cadman, Timothy. 2013. 'Introduction: Global Governance and Climate Change.' in Timothy Cadman (ed.), *Climate Change and Global Policy Regimes* (New York: Palgrave Macmillan), pp. 1–16.

⸺. 2014. 'Climate Finance in an Age of Uncertainty', *Journal of Sustainable Finance and Investment*, 4 (4), 351–56.

Cadman, Timothy, Lauren Eastwood, Federico Lopez-Casero Michaelis, Tek Narayan Maraseni, Jamie Pittock, and Tapan Sarker. 2015. *The Political Economy of Sustainable Development: Policy Instruments and Market Mechanisms* (Cheltenham: Edward Elgar Publishing).

Cadman, Timothy, Klaus Radunsky, Andrea Simonelli, and Tek Maraseni. 2018. 'From Paris to Poland: A Postmortem of the Climate Change Negotiations', *The International Journal of Social Quality*, 8 (2), 27–46.

Clean Development Mechanism Policy Dialogue.·2012. *Climate Change, Carbon Markets and the CDM: A Call to Action*, (Luxembourg: CDM), <http://www.cdmpolicydialogue.org/report/rpt110912.pdf.> [Accessed 11 September 2017].

Climate Ambition and Rights Alliance, CLARA. 2021. *CLARA Recommendations for Article 6 of the Paris Agreement*, <https://static1.squarespace.com/static/610ffde0dd5c39015edc6873/t/

6152350fc789cd311ee73cf5/1632777487736/CLARA+Minimum+requirements+for+Article+6+ of+the+Paris+Agreement+FINAL+5.+Dec.pdf> [Accessed 5 February 2022].

Elges, Lisa. 2016. 'Climate Governance Accountability Challenges: Lessons from Multilateral Climate Finance.' in Timothy Cadman, Rowena Maguire and Charles Sampford (eds.), *Governing the Climate Change Regime* (Routledge), pp. 215–29.

Flynn, Cassie 2011 *National Climate Funds: Designing and Establishing a National Fund to Achieve Climate Change Priorities* (Durban, South Africa: UNFCCC Climate Change Conference,) <https://unfccc.int/files/press/media_outreach/application/pdf/111130_mw_undp_cf.pdf> [Accessed 8 February 2022].

Forest Carbon Partnership Facility. 2017. *About FCPF*, <https://www.forestcarbonpartnership.org/ about-fcpf-0 > [Accessed 8 September 2017].

Global Energy Efficiency and Renewable Energy Fund, GEEREF 2022. *What GEEREF Is*, <https://geeref.com/about/what-geeref-is.html> [Accessed 7 February 2022].

Green Climate Fund. 2022. *Forests and Land Use*, <https://www.greenclimate.fund/results/ forests-land-use> [Accessed 7 February 2022].

Harvey, Fiona. 2019. 'UN Climate Talks Failing to Address Urgency of Crisis, Says Top Scientist', *The Guardian*, 9 December 2019. <https://www.theguardian.com/environment/2019/dec/08/ un-climate-talks-are-failing-to-see-urgency-of-crisis-says-scientist> [Accessed 11 February 2022].

Keohane, Robert O., and David G. Victor. 2011. 'The Regime Complex for Climate Change', *Perspectives on Politics*, 9 (1), 7–23.

Maguire, Rowena. 2015. 'Mapping the Integrity of Differential Obligations within the United Nations Framework Convention on Climate Change.' in Vesselin Popovski and Rowena Maguire. Hugh Breakey (ed.), *Ethical Values and the Integrity of the Climate Change Regime* (Farnham: Ashgate), pp. 31–42 3.

Radunsky, Klaus, and Timothy Cadman. 2017. 'Afterword: The Long Road to Paris: Insider and Outsider Perspectives.' in Timothy Cadman, Rowena Maguigre and Charles Sampford (eds.), *Governing the Climate Change Regime: Instituional Integrity and Integrity Systems* (Abingdon, UK: Routledge), pp. 250–65 Afterword.

Timperley, Jocelyn. 2019. 'Cop25: What Was Achieved and Where to Next? ', *Climate Home News*. <https://www.climatechangenews.com/2019/12/16/cop25-achieved-next/> [Accessed 3 January 2022].

United Nations.·1992a. *Agenda 21*, <https://sustainabledevelopment.un.org/content/documents/ Agenda21.pdf> [Accessed 11 February 2022].

——.·1992b. *United Nations Framework Convention on Climate Change*, <http://unfccc.int/files/ essential_background/background_publications_htmlpdf/application/pdf/conveng.pdf> [Accessed 11 February 2022].

——. 2021. *UN Climate Chief Urges Countries to Deliver on USD 100 Billion Pledge*, <https://unfccc.int/news/un-climate-chief-urges-countries-to-deliver-on-usd-100-billion- pledge> [Accessed 5 February 2022].

——. 2022. *Climate Finance in the Negotiations*, <https://unfccc.int/topics/climate-finance/the- big-picture/climate-finance-in-the-negotiations> [Accessed 7 February 2022].

United Nations Collaborative Programme on Reducing Emissions from Deforestation and Forest Degradation in Developing Countries, UN-REDD. 2022. *The Programme*, <https://www. un-redd.org/about/programme> [Accessed 7 February 2022].

United Nations Framework Convention on Climate Change. 2014a. *Parties and Observers*, <http://unfccc.int/parties_and_observers/items/2704.php> [Accessed 28 September 2017].

——. 2014b. *UN Climate Summit: Finance Results*, <https://newsroom.unfccc.int/news/un- climate-summit-financing> [Accessed 7 February 2022].

——. 2015a. *Conference of the Parties Serving as the Meeting of the Parties to the Paris Agreement (CMA)*, <http://unfccc.int/bodies/body/9968.php> [Accessed 28/09/2017].

——.·2015b. *Paris Agreement as Contained in the Report of the Conference of the Parties on Its Twenty-First Session*, https://unfccc.int/sites/default/files/english_paris_agreement.pdf > [Accessed 05/02/2022].

——. 2022a. *About the Secretariat*, <https://unfccc.int/about-us/what-is-the-unfccc-secretariat> [Accessed 7 February 2022].

—— 2022b 'Bilateral and Multilateral Funding' <https://unfccc.int/topics/climate-finance/resources/multilateral-and-bilateral-funding-sources> [Accessed 07/02/2022]

—— 2022c 'Building Capacity in the UNFCCC Process' <https://unfccc.int/topics/capacity-building/the-big-picture/capacity-in-the-unfccc-process> [Accessed 08/02/2022]

——. 2022d. *Long-Term Climate Finance (LTF)*, <https://unfccc.int/topics/climate-finance/workstreams/long-term-climate-finance-ltf> [Accessed 7 February 2022].

—— 2022e 'The Paris Agreement' <https://unfccc.int/process-and-meetings/the-paris-agreement/the-paris-agreement> [Accessed 07/02/2022]

——. 2022f. *Standing Committee on Finance (SCF)*, <https://unfccc.int/SCF> [Accessed 7 February 2022].

——. undated. *Technology Mechanism*, <https://unfccc.int/ttclear/support/technology-mechanism.html> [Accessed 8 February 2022].

Hitomi Roppongi

Chapter 18
Financing emission reductions: Official development assistance (ODA)-driven climate finance and beyond

Abstract: The Cancun Agreement of USD 100 billion is often referred to as a symbol of international cooperation on climate action and the Paris Agreement reaffirmed the stance to strengthen the global response to climate change by aligning global finance flow. Although the so-called 'Paris alignment' has become a new target for both the public and private sectors, little guidance is provided under the agreed international framework. Counting methods are yet to be standardised and more comprehensive and comparable data is needed to understand the broader picture of climate finance flows. Climate finance in a broad sense is a type of fund provision that targets actions to tackle climate change mitigation and adaptation, which may not necessarily meet the existing criteria of climate finance reporting largely driven by the development finance framework. The aim of this study is two-fold: 1) to identify the data gap of climate finance flows not recognised in the current system; and 2) to discuss challenges of expanding climate finance globally.

Keywords: climate finance, mitigation finance, Paris alignment, climate fund, development bank, private finance, data governance, COVID-19

Introduction

Since the first World Climate Conference in 1979, climate change has officially been discussed at the global-level for over four decades. The United Nations Framework Convention for Climate Change (UNFCCC) is the first international agreement dedicated to climate change, which still functions as the primary forum to discuss and negotiate global responses to climate change and its impacts. Although climate change was not addressed in the Agenda 21, it is now recognised as 'one of the greatest challenges of our time' (United Nations 2015b: 5) and combatting climate change and its impacts is one of the 17 Sustainable Development Goals (SDGs) stipulated in the 2030 Agenda for Sustainable Development (United Nations General Assembly 2015). It is widely acknowledged that climate change presents widespread impacts everywhere and is a serious threat to sustainable development (United Nations Framework Convention on Climate Change 2021a). Meeting the global agendas

https://doi.org/10.1515/9783110733488-018

requires a significant shift in investment and mobilisation of finance, which is yet to be materialised sufficiently.

Article 4.3 of the UNFCCC sets out that the Annex II developed countries are required to provide financial resources to developing countries to undertake mitigation actions (UNFCCC 1992: 13–14). This defines the foundational framework and narrowly defines climate finance as financial transfer from developed countries to developing countries for mitigation purposes. This has since been extended to cover climate change adaptation, though the idea of developed countries providing financial support to developing countries remains the same. Under the UNFCCC context, the traditional definition classifies the Annex II developed countries as donors and developing countries as recipients. Article 9 of the Paris Agreement reiterates this by defining climate finance as provision and mobilisation of financial resources by developed countries to developing countries in order to fund climate mitigation and adaptation (United Nations 2015b: 13). After the negotiation at the 2009 Copenhagen Conference, developed countries agreed in the 2010 Cancun Conference to mobilise USD 100 billion annually to developing countries for the purpose of financing mitigation actions by 2020 (UNFCCC 2010: 17). Experts have warned that insufficient funds have been mobilised to meet the target and climate finance needs to be scaled-up and transformed including an extensive change in private finance (Bhattacharya et al. 2020). Although the annual USD 100 billion pledge made in the Cancun Agreement has been extended through to 2025 (United Nations 2021: 2), it is a floor rather than an ultimate goal and international climate finance needs to work alongside private and other sources of finance. The Cancun Agreement is considered to be the bedrock of international climate finance that represents a symbol of trust and international cooperation on climate action, however, counting methods are yet to be standardised (Bhattacharya et al. 2020: 6). Article 2.1c of the 2015 Paris Agreement reaffirmed the stance to strengthen the global response to climate change by aligning global finance flow with a pathway towards low-emission and climate-resilient development (United Nations 2015b). Although the Paris alignment has become a new target for both public and private sectors, little guidance is provided under the agreed international framework and a more comprehensive and comparable data is needed to understand the broader picture of climate finance flows.

Underpinned by these arrangements under the international frameworks, climate finance is often understood as a subset of development finance or Official Development Assistance (ODA). According to the Organisation for Economic Co-operation and Development (OECD), ODA is defined as government aid that promotes and targets the economic development and welfare of developing countries, which is more broadly referred to as development aid or development finance (OECD 2021c). The progress is overseen by the Development Assistance Committee (DAC) of the OECD, known as the OECD DAC, which compiles and discloses statistics of climate-related development finance annually and publishes reports periodically to analyse the development of climate finance. Existing studies led by public bodies largely focus on financial flows that meet the methodologies that focus on finance mobilised by or through public finance actors (OECD 2020; UNFCCC 2016; UNFCCC 2018). Such methods cannot capture and track the development in private investments outside of the public finance system. It was acknowledged and agreed in the Addis Ababa Action Agenda (AAAA) that funding from all sources including public, private, bilateral, multilateral and alternative sources of finance need to be scaled-up to invest in climate-focussed development and more transparent reporting is necessary (United Nations 2015a: 29). Climate finance in a broad sense is a type of fund provision that targets actions to tackle climate change mitigation and adaptation, which may not necessarily meet the existing criteria of climate finance reporting. The methodologies to capture climate finance flow is still in the process of development and the global effort accelerated after the adoption of AAAA and the Paris Agreement in 2015.

The aim of this study is two-fold: 1) to identify the data gap of climate finance flows not recognised in the current system; and 2) to discuss challenges of expanding climate finance globally, see Chapter Nineteen on the Adaptation Fund (AF) for adaptation-related discussions of climate finance. This chapter provides and overview with a focus on climate change mitigation. Particular attention is drawn here to mitigation actions, though some overarching analysis may cover climate finance as a whole due to the nature of the discussion. In so doing, the study provides an overview of the existing framework under the UNFCCC by describing the key actors, available data, financing mechanisms and instruments to mobilise climate finance. Classifications and definitions developed by the leading official agencies are used in this research to understand the core methodology of data collection and analysis in order to highlight the potential for expansion beyond the traditional development aid framework. Finally, challenges to scale up climate finance are discussed followed by a concluding paragraph.

Key actors of climate finance

Climate finance under the UNFCCC system is characterised by donor-recipient relationship with supporting entities to operate, collect data and provide various services necessary for operation and facilitation. Its key players can broadly be classified into providers, recipients and operating entities. Financial support from donor countries may be arranged bilaterally, multilaterally or through third-party entities in the form of loans, grants, equity and other financial instruments with or without utilising financing mechanisms (see below for details). The provider and recipient perspective employed by the OECD DAC guides the description of actors and financial flow amongst them.

Donors

Traditionally, climate finance donors are Annex II developed countries defined under the UNFCCC, who have the obligations to provide financial resources and environmentally friendly technologies to developing countries and economies in transition (EIT). According to the 2020 OECD report, climate finance provided and mobilised by developed countries reached USD 78.9 billion in 2018, of which USD 62.2 billion is attributed to public climate finance (OECD 2020: 14). The donor base has been expanding, and developing countries such as Indonesia, Vietnam and Chile in receipt of climate finance have also pledged funds (Green Climate Fund 2021b).

The private sector also has a growing role to play in climate finance. In spite of year to year fluctuation and difficulty in data collection, private climate finance reached 34% of total private finance, or USD 14.6 billion out of USD 42.6 billion mobilised to developing countries in 2018 (OECD 2020: 31–32). Private finance analysed using the OECD methodology is mobilised either by bilateral or multilateral public finance. Note the majority of climate finance captured by leading international analysis is provided for mitigation purposes, particularly for private finance where 93% of funds focussed on mitigation between 2016 and 2018 (OECD 2020: 33). In regard to defining climate finance, a clear definition is not indicated within the UNFCCC. This has caused confusion and inconsistencies when understanding the climate finance flows, especially involving private finance. Likewise, climate finance can also be provided domestically to fund actions locally both from public and private sources, but these are often not captured in data, including the above-mentioned OECD report. It is also not clear whether domestic sources to fund in-country climate actions are categorised as climate finance; this depends on the definition employed.

Recipients

Most of the developed country-led climate finance was allocated directly to individual countries (79%) between 2016 and 2018, while the rest was provided at regional level or to a group of countries (OECD 2020: 7). It is found that 64% of environment and climate-related investment is distributed to cities and regions (Organisation for Economic Co-operation and Development, The World Bank, and United Nations Environment Programme 2018: 122–23), yet only a small proportion of climate finance is directed to the local level (Soanes et al. 2017). Internationally agreed climate finance commitments, where negotiations are usually made between national governments in absence of local actors, have led to gaps between the providers and local actors in need of finance. Growing research interest in this knowledge gap has led to methodological development to analyse the domestic landscape of climate finance, such as the attempts by the Institute for Climate Economics (I4CE) to track domestic climate finance through the Landscape of Climate Finance initiative (Hainaut and Cochran 2018; WiseEuropa, NewClimate Institute, and Institute for Climate Economics (I4CE) 2019). The Climate Policy Initiative (CPI) has been developing a method to analyse climate finance flows along their life cycle, where the funds are classified according to sources and intermediaries, instruments, uses and sectors.

Operating entities

There are a range of operating entities that implement and administer global financial assistance related to climate change. Various types of public intermediary organisations are involved to mobilise and distribute funds from donors to recipients. The key climate-focussed operating entities are summarised below, including a note on the entity that complements and assists the work of operating entities under the UNFCCC.

Global Environmental Facility Trust Fund (GEF)

The GEF was established in 1992 ahead of the Rio Summit to provide funds to developing or EIT countries to meet objectives of international environmental agreements. GEF funds are provided to different kinds of government and non-governmental agencies, institutions and partners (known as GEF agencies) to implement climate-related projects in recipient countries (Global Environment Facility 2021b). It was initially created as a pilot programme in the International Bank for Reconstruction and Development (IBRD under the World Bank Group) involving interagency arrangements between the United Nations Development Programme (UNDP), the United Nations Environment Programme (UNEP) and the World Bank. The World Bank is the GEF trustee, which is responsible for mobilising resources, distributing funds, preparing reports and monitoring budgets and project funds (The World Bank Group 2021). As of July 2021, the GEF has 184 member countries of which 40 are donor countries, with a fund balance exceeding USD 5.7 billion (Global Environment Facility 2021a). See Chapter Seventeen on the Adaptation Fund (AF) for adaptation-related functions of GEF.

The operation of the UNFCCC's financial mechanisms is partly entrusted to the GEF under the Article 11 of the UNFCCC and the GEF has thus been a central operating entity to fund mitigation projects. According to GEF reports, the share of climate-related financing within the GEF-7 has continued to exceed the target level of 60% as summarised in Table 18.1. Although a slight decline has been observed since June 2020, the total amount of climate-related finance has increased steadily and the share continues to exceed the target by more than 20%.

Table 18.1: Breakdown of GEF-7 financing related to climate change mitigation.

	2019 Jun		2019 Dec		2020 Jun		2020 Dec		2021 Jun	
	mil USD	% total	mil USD	% total	mil USD	% total	mil USD	% total	mil USD	% total
Share of climate finance in GEF-7	349	73%	722	72%	2,138	85%	2,607	84%	2,892	82%
GEF-7 contribution for mitigation (1)+(2)	209	60%	385	53%	1,538	72%	1,796	69%	1,963	68%
Not Targeted (0)	140	40%	337	47%	600	28%	811	31%	929	32%
Significant (1)	165	47%	275	38%	1,054	49%	1,237	47%	1,397	48%
Principal (2)	44	13%	110	15%	484	23%	559	21%	566	20%

Source: Global Environment Facility Secretariat (2019b, 2019a, 2020b, 2020a, 2021).

Green Climate Fund (GCF)

The GCF is the world's largest climate fund and was established in 2010 at COP16 as a financial mechanism of the UNFCCC. It was designated as an operating entity in accordance with the Article 11 of the UNFCCC at COP 17. Developing countries receiving the funds take ownership of the GCF financing decisions and a capacity building support programme (Readiness Programme) is available to all developing countries. Recipient countries work with over 200 accredited entities and delivering partners for design and implementation of GCF projects. Financial support is structured with a flexible combination of grant, concessional debt, guarantees and equity instruments. The GCF allocates the funds between mitigation and adaptation equally in grant equivalent, which is in contrast from the GEF climate finance predominantly allocated to mitigation (Green Climate Fund 2021a). The Private Sector Facility (PSF) within the GCF is a division specifically designed to mobilise private sector actors. PSF structures a range of instruments across practices including investing in high-impact climate technologies and innovations, developing carbon markets that require bespoke structuring options, anchoring investments in funds, financial institutions to mainstream climate change in the financial system and tailoring life cycle of concessional finance (Green Climate Fund n.d.).

As of 30 April 2021, 80% of the USD 10.3 billion pledged (USD 8.31 billion) in the initial resource mobilisation (IRM) period has been officially confirmed and USD 9.52 billion out of USD 9.99 billion pledge for the first replenishment (GCF-1) has been confirmed. There are pledges confirmed by climate finance recipients such as Vietnam (USD 1 million), Chile (USD 0.3 million) and Indonesia (USD 0.3 million) in the IRM period (Green Climate Fund 2021b: 2). Note while China has made no pledge for the GCF, the country has been leading cooperation amongst developing countries to support climate actions with a pledge of USD 3.1 billion to the South-South Cooperation Climate Fund (Weigel 2016: 8).

Development finance institutions (DFI)/multilateral development banks (MDBs)

DFIs are specialised development banks typically owned by national governments and financed by national or international development funds to foster private sector investment in developing countries. Bilateral DFIs implement their own government's development and cooperation objectives and multilateral DFIs are established by multiple counties such as MDBs. Examples of multilateral DFIs include the African Development Bank (AfDB), the Asian Development Bank (ADB), the Asian Infrastructure Investment Bank (AIIB), the European Investment Bank (EBI), the Inter-American Development Bank Group (IDBG), the Islamic Development Bank (IsDB) and the New Development Bank (NDB). Adoption of SDGs and global challenges such as financial crises and the COVID-19 pandemic have led to growing interest in and expectations of DFIs among academia and policymakers (Usher et al. 2019; Runde, Bandura, and Ramanujam 2019; Xu, Ren, and Wu 2019). The International Development Finance Club (IDFC) consists of 26 leading national and regional development banks, which prides itself as the largest provider of climate finance (USD 150 billion) and public development globally (The International Development Finance Club 2019).

MDBs are the exclusive allocator of funds under the Climate Investment Fund (CIF), a multilateral climate fund established in 2008 to scale up mitigation and adaptation actions in developing and middle-income countries. As of 30 December 2020, 14 donor countries have contributed USD 8.54 billion to the CIF. Contributions from donor countries are held in trust by the World Bank, and are allocated exclusively by MDBs in the forms of grants, concessional loans and risk mitigation instruments (Climate Investment Funds 2012). The Clean Technology Fund (CTF) is one of the largest sources of international public finance for climate mitigation in developing countries, which is implemented through DFIs including the Asian Development Bank (ADB), the African Development Bank (AfDB), European Bank of Reconstruction and Development (EBRD) and International Development Bank (IDB) alongside the World Bank (Watson and Schalatek 2020: 2). Note the literature often uses MDBs to refer to MDBs and other DFIs, given the majority of central players are MDBs. For the purpose of this chapter, a broader definition of DFI is introduced here to discuss MDBs and other DFIs in climate finance

MDBs and other DFIs are expected to play a critical role in blending public and private finance to accelerate development finance. According to the Joint Report by MDBs and other DFIs, they mobilised USD 63.6 billion of private finance to middle and low-income counties in 2019 and positive correlation between mobilisation from private sector and developmental impact has been observed in early data (MDB Task Force on Mobilization, 2021). The private sector has also started to join the effort to mobilise development-oriented finances to developing countries, as seen in the establishment of the JP Morgan DFI that aims to build development finance as a traded asset class (JP Morgan Chase and Co. 2020).

Standing Committee on Finance (SCF)

The SCF was established in 2010 to assist the implementation of financial mechanisms under the UNFCCC and to improve the coordination amongst climate finance actors. The functions of SCF in supporting COP include improving coordination and coherence in the delivery of climate finance, analysis and presentation of data related to implementation, mobilisation of financial resources for climate finance and measurement, reporting and verification (MRV) of financial support provided to recipient developing countries via Biennial Assessments (BA) (UNFCCC 2021c: 1). The SCF closely collaborates with various international, regional and national financial institutions, intergovernmental organisations, think tanks and stakeholders specialising in tracking and reporting of climate finance flows and producing information on developing countries' needs for implementation (UNFCCC 2021h: 8).

Data on climate finance flow

The OECD DAC and the SCF are the key global players collecting and analysing international climate finance flows. Methodologies understandably differ between the two approaches due to the difference in the data provided by Member States. The OECD primarily focusses on what the donating Member States provide to developing countries while the SCF is mandated to produce reports for the COP that also includes recipient developing countries under the UNFCCC framework. A brief summary of the analytical frameworks employed by the two data providers are introduced in this section.

OECD DAC

Data reported by donor countries to the OECD DAC are analysed specifically for climate finance in OECD publications. The recent climate finance report by the OECD includes four components of climate finance, which are bilateral public, multilateral public, export credits and mobilised private funds, as explained in the following paragraphs (OECD 2020). Note that while the report takes donor approach, the

OECD DAC database discloses data analysed from both recipient and provider per-spectives (OECD n.d.).

Bilateral contribution is made by the donating developed countries to the recipi-ent developing countries, most notably between governments and other entities in-cluding NGOs, research institutes, the private sector and networks. Finance provision by donor countries to trust funds, special purpose programmes and multilateral or-ganisations are considered as the donor countries' bilateral public climate finance under the OECD DAC reporting. Bilateral climate finance flows are reported to the UNFCCC using a common format, based on the climate-related development finance data reported to the OECD DAC. However, data reported to the UNFCCC is not as de-tailed or standardised as the ones reported for OECD DAC statistics and there is leeway in UNFCCC reporting. Significant inconsistencies in methodologies, categorisations and definitions across Annex II countries are identified (OECD 2020: 40–41).

Multilateral public climate finance covers climate-related financial flows by MDBs, multilateral climate funds and other multilateral organisations. Their ordi-nary capital or funds that originally come from developed countries are considered as bilateral climate finance inflow to multilateral organisations under OECD DAC reporting. Funds from trust funds and special purpose programmes operated via multilateral organisations are currently not included in this category, even those for climate-related projects. Note that multilateral finance outflow data is limited to countries and territories included in the DAC List of ODA Recipients (OECD 2021b), which are not identical to the non-Annex I countries under the UNFCCC. Multilat-eral organisations report to the OECD DAC statistical system based on the Rio marker methodology that monitors development finance flow according to objec-tives of the Rio Conventions (OECD 2016) and the MDB methodology based on a list of GHG reducing activities that are also compatible with low-emission development (African Development Bank et al. 2020: 9–10).

Officially supported export credit under the OECD framework applies to official supports of goods, services and financial leases that have repayment terms of two or more years (OECD 1998: 6). It can take the form of direct credits, direct financing, refinancing, interest rate support, aid financing through credits and grants, export credit insurance and guarantees. There are limitations on terms and conditions, in-cluding minimum premium benchmarks, minimum initial cash payment, maximum payment terms and minimum interest rates. Some products such as military equip-ment and agricultural commodities are excluded and special guidelines apply to ships, nuclear power plants and aircraft (OECD 1998: 4). Export credit data is sourced from the OECD Export Credit Group database and complementary data pro-vided by some countries like Canada, Japan and Switzerland. Reported data mainly relates to renewable energy and activities submitted to the UNFCCC are excluded from the bilateral public finance component of the OECD database to avoid double-counting (OECD 2020: 46).

Private finance mobilised by official climate finance intervention covers the finance flows through the mechanisms (see below) used by development finance providers. When multiple donors invest in the same project or vehicle with the private sector, an instrument-specific approach is used to avoid double-counting. DAC members and multilateral agencies that report to the OECD DAC provide information on the mechanisms used, source of funds and amount mobilised from the private sector, although the identity of private financiers and terms and conditions of the finance are not disclosed (OECD 2020: 47).

SCF

The SCF produces Biennial Assessments (BAs) of climate finance flows every two years, aiming to understand climate-related financial flows between developed and developing countries, South-South flow amongst developing countries and domestic flows. The 2018 BA provides an overview of climate finance flow from Annex II developed countries to non-Annex I countries as reported in the UNFCCC biennial reports (BRs), with a breakdown of flow through multilateral climate funds and MDBs, private climate finance provided and reports on recipients.

Annex II countries are required to submit information on finance provided to developing countries in their national communications and UNFCCC BR's common tabular format (BR-CTF) tables, which are used for analysis in the BAs. In line with the reporting style of the BR-CTF tables, flows through the MDBs are distinguished from that of the multilateral climate funds, unlike the OECD DAC. Data on private climate finance is compiled by MDBs and OECD, however, the 2018 BA points out uncertainty and lack of available data for private finance sources (UNFCCC 2018: 7). In regard to the data on recipient institutions, according to the 2016 BA, data is available for only 50% of the bilateral finance reported to the OECD DAC. Only 40% of total flow was received by developing country governments, which means finance channelled through other intermediaries is not captured in the data (UNFCCC 2016: 57). Although an improvement to data collection was suggested in the 2016 BA, adequate data was not complied for the 2018 BA to make meaningful analysis. The 2018 BA also analyses methodological challenges in the MRV of data and makes recommendations for future improvements.

Financing mechanisms and instruments

This section introduces financing mechanisms and instruments used to provide funds for climate-related purposes. The term mechanism is used in various contexts without a clear definition, which in some contexts have been used interchangeably with instruments. This section summarises international mechanisms mentioned in the international climate agreements and financing mechanisms available to mobilise private finance through public interventions, followed by a list of key instruments mentioned in the reports.

Kyoto mechanisms

The 1997 Kyoto Protocol under the UNFCCC laid out binding targets for emission reduction for Annex II developed countries and introduced flexible mechanisms to deliver the broad, collective obligations through the Clean Development Mechanism (CDM), Joint Implementation (JI) and International Emission Trading (IET). These mechanisms are dedicated to mitigation actions are available to Annex I Parties that meet eligibility criteria such as ratification of the Kyoto Protocol, calculation of assigned amount in terms of tonnes of CO_2 equivalent emissions, a national system to estimate emissions and removals of GHGs are in place, existence of national registry to record and track emission reduction units and annual reporting to the secretariat (UNFCCC 2007).

CDM

The CDM enables public and private entities to produce certified emission reductions (CER) units by investing in developing countries' mitigation projects and programmes. The CER credits can be traded and used to meet the GHG emission targets of developed countries that have invested in the projects and programmes. Emission reductions can only be certified if they meet the additionality criteria, where the CDM project or programme provides emission reductions in addition to what would have occurred in the absence of the activities (UNFCCC 2006: 16). CER credits can be removed or cancelled from the system when the owner of the credit finances the additional emission reduction that the CER represents. According to the latest report, 8,181 activities have been registered and 3,324 activities have been issued with CERs since the inception of the CDM and more than 2 billion CERs were issued between 2008 and 2020. Some countries have started to use the CDM for domestic mitigation efforts and the private sector has purchased CERs to address their own climate or sustainability goals (UNFCCC 2021b: 6). CER credits can be accessed directly through the CDM Registry or by contacting a broker. As of 1 July 2021, 93% of the current CDM projects are live and the average issuance success of CER is 80.6% (United Nations Environment Programme Technical University of Denmark (DTU) Partnership 2021). There are currently 30 designated operational entities accredited to validate activities under the CDM (UNFCCC 2021e).

This mechanism is aimed at providing flexibility for developed countries to achieve emission reduction targets while also benefitting developing nations through technology transfer and investment for sustainable development. Despite the intentions, it has faced criticisms of inequality amongst host countries, actual contribution to sustainable development, difficulty to test and capture additionality and high transaction costs (Cadman et al. 2015; Michaelowa and Jotzo 2005; Nussbaumer 2009; Olsen and Fenhann 2008; Paulsson 2009; Sutter and Parreño 2007; Watts, Albornoz, and Watson 2015; UNFCCC 2021d). In June 2021, it was discussed by the Subsidiary Body for Scientific and Technological Advice (SBSTA) that 'the CDM was not successful at limiting climate change' and therefore the CERs from the mechanism cannot be used in the Paris Agreement mechanisms (UNFCCC 2021g: 2).

JI

The JI is a mechanism available to invest in mitigation projects in Annex I developed countries. Emission reduction units (ERUs) are produced from emission-reducing or emission-removing projects as inscribed in Annex B, for investing countries with reduction or limitation commitments under the Kyoto Protocol. As in the case of the CDM, credits are only produced if the activities meet the additionality criteria. Cancellation of ERUs equivalent to the net emissions of GHG is possible under the JI, in a similar manner to the cancellation of CERs under the CDM. Projects verified by the host Annex I countries are referred to as track one projects as per the paragraph 23 of the JI guidelines, which is also known as the simplified JI procedure. If the host country does not meet the eligibility requirements, the verification of emission reductions needs to be done through the procedure under the JI Supervisory Committee, which is known as track two or independently verified projects as per the JI guideline (UNFCCC 2006: 41). The majority of JI activities ceased at the end of the first commitment period in 2021; the last issuance of ERU was recorded in August 2015 and no country has yet issued ERUs in the second commitment period (UNFCCC 2019: 4).

IET

Developed countries with emission reduction commitments can obtain ERUs to partially fulfil reduction targets. The creation of IET has led to the establishment of emission trading systems (ETSs) at regional, national and subnational levels and, according to the International Carbon Action Partnership (ICAP), as of July 2021 there are 24 in operation, nine under development and 12 under consideration globally. An ETS could be set up involving multiple jurisdictions from the onset, as seen in the EU ETS and the Regional Greenhouse Gas Initiative in the United States. Each ETS has flexibility to form linkages with another ETS regardless of national jurisdiction. For instance, the EU ETS and Swiss

ETS have linked as of January 2020 and cap-and-trade schemes of Quebec (Canada) and California (USA) linked in January 2014. Provincial pilot ETSs in China are in the process of transitioning into the China National ETS, the world's biggest ETS. On the contrary, there are cases of terminated linkage or abolishment of ETS, such as the termination of Ontario system in Canada (2018) and the New Zealand ETS's transformation into a domestic-only system since 2015 (International Carbon Action Partnership 2021).

Mechanism under article 6 of the Paris agreement

The Paris Agreement demonstrates the global consensus that it is necessary to go beyond zero-sum offsetting mechanisms to drastically reduce emissions by 2030 to remain within the 1.5 degrees temperature limit. Article 6.2 of the Paris Agreement introduced the concept of internationally transferred mitigation outcomes and cooperative approaches to reduce GHG emissions on voluntary basis. The 6.4 mechanism is stablished in the Article with the newly introduced concept of overall mitigation in global emissions (OMGE) to strengthen global effort to mitigate GHG emissions alongside the promotion of sustainable development. The Article 6.4 stipulates that participation of both public and private entities to mitigate GHG emissions be facilitated and emission reduction by one country could be used in another country to fulfil its Nationally Determined Contribution (NDC) (United Nations 2015b: 7).

While the 6.4 mechanism is sometimes seen as the successor of the CDM, no pre-2020 CERs or other Kyoto units can be used towards NDCs. Compromises may only be found for the CERs that meet certain conditions such as registration date, use by date, implementation methods specified by the meeting of the Parties to the Paris Agreement, reporting in accordance with the enhanced transparency framework and the cases of CDM hosts using CERs from their own country. There is no automatic transition of financial mechanisms from the Kyoto Protocol to Paris Agreement, as they are treated as two distinct frameworks, particularly if the OMGE concept is to be applied. Conformity of the OMGE to the Article 6.2 cooperative approach is still under discission by the SBSTA, in order to avoid disincentivising participation in the Article 6.4 mechanism (UNFCCC 2021f).

Mechanisms used to mobilise private finance by official climate finance interventions

Finance mechanisms and instruments are often used interchangeably in the context of private climate finance. Under the OECD framework, financing instruments gather investments and mechanisms structure or intermediate instruments to mobilise capital (OECD 2018). Six categories of financial mechanisms used to mobilise private climate finance are introduced in the OECD classification, which are direct investment or special purpose vehicles (SPVs), guarantees, syndicated loans, credit lines, simple cofinancing and shares in collective investment vehicles (CIVs) as summarised in Table 18.2 (OECD 2018: 80). This is followed by brief explanations of typical instruments used by the providers with latest figures in. The mechanisms classified and examples of instruments introduced in the OECD climate finance report (2020) are used for analysis here, complemented by the documents on DAC methodologies (Organisation for Economic Co-operation and Development Development Assistance Committee 2020) and blended finance (Habbel et al. 2021; OECD 2018).

Table 18.2: An overview of financing mechanisms to mobilise private finance.

Mechanisms	Description	Private finance 2016–18	Instruments used by private finance providers
Direct investment (SPVs)	On-balance sheet investment in corporate entities without intermediaries	43%	Common equity, mezzanine finance, standard loans, bonds and other debt instruments
Guarantees	Guarantor agrees to pay any outstanding amount on the instrument in case of non-payment	23%	Common equity, CIVs, mezzanine finance, standard loans, bonds and other debt instruments
Syndicated loans	A group of investors (syndicates) act together to fund a single borrower	14%	Standard loans, subordinated loans
Credit lines	Standing credit can be drawn at any time up to a specific amount within a given period of time	10%	Standard loans, subordinated loans to the local finance institution; equity of the end-borrowers
Simple cofinancing	Joint or parallel financing by official institutions in association with other providers	6%	Standard grants, standard loans
Shares in CIVs	Investing in entities that allow investors to jointly invest in a portfolio of companies	4%	CIVs, debt instruments and mezzanine finance

Source: OECD (2020); Organisation for Economic Co-operation and Development Development Assistance Committee (2020).

Blended finance, defined as the strategic use of development finance for the mobilisation of additional finance towards sustainable development in developing countries, was agreed on for use to strengthen development aid by OECD countries in 2017 (OECD 2018: 22). Additional finance in this context refers to commercial capital, which are public and private sources of capital, whose primary motivation is commercial and not development related. This is applicable to gather finance for climate mitigation as a cross-cutting and overarching theme of sustainable development. There are four mechanisms categorised specifically for blended finance, to bring together development related and commercial investments through official intervention (See Table 18.3).

Table 18.3: Mechanisms of blended finance.

Mechanisms	Description
Funds / CIVs	Different actors gather resources to own equity
Syndication	A group of investors pool resources together to reduce transaction cost and share risk
Securitisation	Originators transfer ownership of assets in their balance sheet to raise capital
PPPs	Governments and private partners cooperate to combine financial instruments to provide public services for a financial return

Source: OECD (2018); Habbel et al. (2021).

Instruments used to mobilise climate finance

Loans

A loan involves lending of the loan principal amount to the borrower and repayment occurs in the future with interest or financing charges added to the principal amount. According to the OECD report, the growth of public climate finance between 2013 and 2018 was largely driven by development loans (USD 19.8 billion in 2013 to USD 46.3 billion in 2018) and nearly three quarters of the analysed public climate finance took the form of loans in 2018 (USD 46.3 billion out of 62.6 billion). The majority of the loan between 2016 and 2018 targeted mitigation objectives (75%) while the share of loans for mitigation finance decreased from 79% in 2016 to 70% in 2018 (OECD 2020: 17–19).

Concessional loans offer terms that are substantially more generous and preferential than those available on the market according to the OECD DAC definition. For lending by major development banks, the International Monetary Fund (IMF) and the World Bank, concessionality is determined by each institution (International Monetary Fund 2014: 46). There is no clear definition of concessional loans or what constitutes as ODA and therefore it has historically been open to interpretation. It has been agreed to modernise the reporting system of concessional loans to improve comparability and data quality of ODA figures (Organisation for Economic Co-operation and Development Development Assistance Committee 2014). Concessionality for DAC members is assessed through the grant element calculation, based on the interest rate, the grace period, the maturity and the discount rate. Eligibility to qualify as ODA depends on the level of concessionality for DAC members. On average, between 2016 and 2018 72% of bilateral climate finance loans committed by DAC members were concessional and the share grew from 65% to 80% in the same period. For multilateral climate loans, 22% of MDB loans were concessional and 54% of loans by multilateral climate funds were concessional between 2016 and 2018 (OECD 2020: 17).

Syndicated loans are provided by a group of lenders known as syndicates, which act together to fund a single borrower. Syndication allows borrower default risk to be diversified among lenders, which encourages private participation. Lead or official arrangers of syndicated loans, who typically involve MDBs, may negotiate terms with the borrower and retain a portion of the loan for its own account (A loan) and sell the remaining portion to other syndicates also known as junior participants (B loan). Alternatively, the lead arranger could seek to syndicate parallel loans from other participants. In this case, the lead arranger identifies potential participants, including those not eligible for B loans, structures the deal and coordinates with all parallel lenders to negotiate with the borrower (Organisation for Economic Co-operation and Development Development Assistance Committee 2020; Habbel et al. 2021). Subordinated loans are also known as junior loans, which rank below other loans. This structure shields investors from losses in tranches with different levels of seniority (OECD 2018).

Grants

A grant is a direct monetary contribution given to a project or fund that typically does not need to be repaid. It usually aims to incentivise performance or to facilitate achievement of specific goals. Thirty-three percent of climate finance grants between 2016 and 2018 targeted mitigation and 29% had a cross-cutting focus (OECD 2020: 19).

Bonds/purpose-driven development bonds

A bond is a debt instrument that involves periodical interest payments made to the investor in exchange for the issuer borrowing the principal amount. At the maturity date of the bond, the principal amount needs to be paid back in full to the investor. Governments at all levels, corporations and project companies use bonds to borrow money to raise funds to finance certain projects or to grow their business. Many bonds are publicly traded and some are available over the counter or privately between the borrower and the lender. Bonds can be traded in the primary market upon issuance or in the secondary market where bonds are sold by the initial holder to other investors before the maturity date. Bonds are favoured by commercial investors due to the marketable and liquid nature of the asset and bonds enable large-scale commercial investment (OECD 2018).

Purpose-driven development bonds, such as green bonds, are issued when the proceeds are used to fund climate and environmentally friendly projects as per the contract. It is a useful instrument to raise private funds for climate change mitigation and many other environment-related projects. The green bond market is growing in developed and emerging economies thanks to increased awareness of investors, but market remains incipient in developing countries (Banga 2018: 17). In the face of growing interest to meet the sustainability agenda, the market has diversified and now includes sustainability bonds, social bonds, green loans and sustainability-linked loans.

Equity instruments

Equity finance is categorised into public or listed and private or unlisted equities. Public equity relates to investment in companies, funds or assets that are traded in stock exchange and private equity involves capital provision to unlisted companies (OECD 2015: 19). Equity was a marginal instrument to mobile climate finance in the period between 2013 and 2018, fluctuating at around USD 1 billion per year. Eighty-nine percent of equity investments between 2016 and 2018 targeted mitigation (OECD 2020: 19).

Mezzanine finance

Mezzanine instruments are a hybrid of debt and equity instruments that are subordinate to senior debt in the priority of repayment. It is a higher risk form of debt in exchange of higher yields and often includes equity participation (OECD 2015: 30). First capital loss is an important mezzanine instrument used for-purpose-driven credit enhancement provided by investors who agree to bear first losses in an investment in order to catalyse co-investor participations who would not participate otherwise (Habbel et al. 2021: 15).

Challenges

Data collection: comparability, consistency, gaps

The 2018 BA finds that collecting, aggregating and analysing information from diverse sources remains a challenge and a lack of clarity in definitions limits the comparability of data. Data uncertainty and gaps are also identified in the 2018 BA, due to lack of consistent, reliable and transparent methods used to collect data and inadequate understanding of the investment environment and instruments used (UNFCCC 2018). The CPI report finds that the annual flow of climate finance reached USD 540 billion in 2018 (Climate Policy Initiative 2019: 6). This result is in sharp contrast to the USD 78.9 billion mobilised in 2018 presented in the OECD climate finance report (OECD 2020: 14). According to the GEF, 82% of financing in GEF-7 is climate-related where USD 698 million financed mitigation projects are under the OECD DAC Rio Marker methodology. Officially supported export credits have fluctuated on an average of USD 2 billion annually since 2013, a trend that may have been caused by difficulties in comprehensively tracking the data, especially projects beyond renewable energy (OECD 2018). As the Cancun Accord did not specify what types of funding count towards the climate finance target, it is not possible to objectively examine if the target has been met (Roberts et al. 2021). Data gaps in the coverage of sectors and sources of finance remain significant and both public and private sources of climate-related investments and instruments behind them are still inadequately understood (UNFCCC 2018: 5).

Moreover, distinction of public and private finance is not straight forward in the current international climate framework. Private finance mobilised through public finance interventions is a distinct component analysed by the OECD DAC and subsequently the SCF under the UNFCCC. Public intervention is still a mainstream approach to understand private capital in climate finance. Private finance mobilised outside of public intervention is not included in the data and likewise public finance embedded in private sector instruments is not included in the figures. The concept of blended finance is a promising development in this regard, as it classifies the outflows based on purposes (development-oriented or commercial) rather than the public-private division. The Total Official Support for Sustainable Development (TOSSD) statistical framework was launched as a response to the AAAA, in order to provide a comprehensive, coherent, comparable and unified system to track SDG-related financial flows (TOSSD 2021b). While attempts have been made to fill the knowledge gap beyond ODA and TOSSD data has captured 60,000 activities and USD 76 billion in addition to the OECD statistics on development finance (TOSSD 2021a), the data is presented from the SDGs perspective and mitigation activities are not distinguished from adaptation. The question is how to filter out the data dedicated to climate purposes from the data collated for the purpose of broader development goals. It is a methodological challenge to distinguish financial flow related to a cross-cutting theme like climate change, needless to mention the additional difficulty of differentiating adaptation and mitigation within the new development aid strategy.

Not only are the data governance challenges found at national and international levels, but also at the local level and in the private sector. Monitoring of domestic climate investment have been patchy in both developed and developing countries and there is a lack of empirical evidences to better understand the climate finance in domestic contexts (Hainaut and Cochran 2018). While there is a possibility to improve the situation by clarifying nationwide definition and accounting methodologies, resources and capacities to deliver remain a big challenge, especially in the face of pandemic-induced fiscal constraints. In spite of decisions made at the national-level, implementation varies according to the division of power and responsibilities between national and subnational governments. Private donors may also have conflicting interests to favour confidentiality over data transparency for their own climate-related investments. Constraints over confidentiality upon reporting private finance mobilisation to the OECD have been indicated by some MDBs. A working group by the MDBs, DAC members and the OECD Secretariat was launched in 2019 to address the confidentiality issues and agree on a data disclosure rules that reflect interests of all involved parties while meeting information needs and preserving data integrity (OECD 2020: 48).

The business sector also needs transparent, standardised and reliable methods to understand and compare sustainability performances of investing entities. The rise of environmental, social and governance (ESG) assessment, green taxonomies in the world (e.g., EU, China, Malaysia, South Korea), climate bond standards, CDP Scores and the Task Force on Climate-related Financial Disclosures to standardise climate-related financial risk disclosures are responding to the knowledge and data gap. Creating a common, standardised methodology to comprehensively assess sustainability performance and mainstreaming it to investment strategies would unlock the unrevealed opportunities for investors to participate in climate finance.

Beyond ODA-driven climate finance for Paris alignment

The understanding of climate finance is still contested as to whether it falls under the definition of ODA or is considered a separate commitment (Warren 2019). Conceptual understanding has impacts on the analytical framework and data collection methods that have been developed the past decades. Application of blended finance to climate finance is a promising strategy as it builds onto the existing institutions and frameworks to fill the gap by welcoming commercial investors that are traditionally not included in development finance. What constitutes as financing for development is also a subject for debate, given the widening use of the term in light of evolving global challenges and complex frameworks around development finance. Climate change is no doubt a distinctive and overarching theme within the global agenda for sustainable development, yet climate finance should be mobilised alongside with other development related goals rather than at an expense of other investment opportunities.

According to a report cosponsored by the People's Bank of China and the United Nations Environment Programme Inquiry into the Design of a Sustainable Financial System (UNEP Inquiry), China is estimated to spend at least USD 320 billion to achieve green goals and over 85% of the total green investment will need to be financed by private capital (Green Finance Task Force 2015: 5). This is more than three folds of the Cancun pledge needed in a single, biggest climate finance recipient country and the expected role of private finance does not match the existing global financing situation. The flagship report by the Business and Sustainable Development Commission (2017) estimates that sustainable and inclusive business models could unlock at least USD 12 trillion of opportunities annually by 2030 for the private sector. An estimated additional investment of USD 2.4 trillion a year from both public and private sectors is needed to achieve the global sustainability goals. Taking action on climate change is the new normal for investors and calls for standardisation of measuring sustainability performances for business (Business and Sustainable Development Commission 2017: 70). Demand and untapped potential for private finance to grow are thus very clear. Methods and metrics to access the financial flows need to be developed further to accurately understand the current landscape beyond the traditional ODA framework and more so for private finance. MDBs, financial sectors and think tanks are actively developing new methodologies such as the 'building block' approach (African Development Bank et al. 2019: 3) and use of green taxonomies and ESG metrics to accelerate Paris alignment in both the public and private sectors. While these initiatives are encouraging, development in methods and metrics to align finance flows and asset allocation for private finance must be done in the context of transforming financial system and the MDB Building Block approach needs to embed the alignment of financial flows in a comprehensive strategy (Rydge 2020: 29). It is hoped that common methodology for Paris alignment will foster system transformation in the world for Paris alignment and achievement of SDGs.

Policy prioritisation in light of evolving global challenges

Global public debt stocks are projected to reach a record high 100% of global GDP in 2020, which is a sharp increase from 83% in 2019 and fiscal balances of developing countries are expected to turn negative. Vulnerabilities of sovereign debt that existed prior to the pandemic have exacerbated globally, with the public debt amongst the G20 reaching 240% of GDP in 2019 and 54% of low-income countries are deemed to be in or at high-risk of debt distress as of September 2020 (International Monetary Fund 2020: 1). The COVID-19 pandemic has led to serious debt distress for developing countries, which has consequently altered policy priorities for many in the face of the public health crisis. Emerging markets and developing economies have been particularly vulnerable to extreme events, suffering from severe damage to their economy and hence their fiscal and debt positions. Their ability to set and deliver ambitious recovery plans is extremely constrained due to lack of financial resources. It is a big challenge for developing countries to create and execute strong climate finance goals and action plans amid crisis at home. Even within developed countries, local government finances have been seriously affected by the global crisis and need to increase tax to fill the lost revenue and/or rely on aid from their national governments (Gudde et al. 2021; Institute for Fiscal Studies 2020). The future capacity for local governments to fund and deliver mitigation actions is in question regardless of donor-recipient status of climate finance at the national-level.

While the threat the global crisis has brought to the world is enormous, experts have called for a one-off, last-chance opportunity to restructure economies to integrate climate action into economic recovery. It is essential to align the funds from recovery and stimulus packages towards climate goals and many EMDEs would need extensive supports to deliver the transformation. Debt-for-climate and debt-for-nature swaps by donor countries are suggested by experts as a promising systemic approach to poor and climate-vulnerable countries already in debt distress (Bhattacharya et al. 2020: 38).

ODA supports by DAC members for inclusive global recovery increased the total ODA in 2020 by 3.5% from 2019, reaching record high level. DAC countries are estimated to have spent USD 12 billion in 2020 on pandemic related activities. The preliminary finding is that ODA remains resilient to global crisis, providing the highest level ever recorded without discontinuing existing programmes (OECD 2021a: 5). Experts warn that although MDBs have committed more than USD 230 billion to respond to the pandemic, it has not yet increased lending for all institutions and some MDBs will have to reduce financing as early as 2020 due to their own financial capacity (Bhattacharya et al. 2020: 47).

Conclusion: A financing model for a sustainable future

The world has seen the pressing challenges of climate finance sustainability in the light of global crisis. The pandemic has exacerbated global debt, caused fiscal constraint in both developing and developed countries and multilateral institutions are not immune from this either. While efforts have been made to improve frameworks and methodologies to mobilise finances for a bigger cause, institutional constraints and conflict of interest are yet to be overcome to tackle climate crisis. There is an urgent need to fundamentally shift the financial system and business models to better align the financial flow towards climate-aligned goals. Much potential is identified in this study for improving the system and expanding the finance pool to meet the Paris alignment and SDGs. It is hoped that the world can capitalise on the one-and-only opportunity in the context of the post-pandemic recovery to comprehensively change the financial system.

References

African Development Bank, Asian Development Bank, Asian Infrastructure Investment Bank, European Bank for Reconstruction and Development, European Investment Bank, Inter-American Development Bank, Islamic Development Bank, and World Bank Group.·2020. *2019 Joint Report on Multilateral Development Banks' Climate Finance*, <https://publications.iadb.org/en/2019-joint-report-on-multilateral-development-banks-climate-finance> [Accessed 30 January 2022].

African Development Bank, Asian Development Bank, European Bank for Reconstruction and Development, European Investment Bank, Inter-American Development Bank, Islamic Development Bank, and World Bank Group.·2019. *2018 Joint Report on Multilateral Development Banks' Climate Finance*, <https://documents1.worldbank.org/curated/en/247461561449155666/pdf/Joint-Report-on-Multilateral-Development-Banks-Climate-Finance-2018.pdf> [Accessed 18 August 2021].

Banga, J. 2018. 'The Green Bond Market: A Potential Source of Climate Finance for Developing Countries', *Journal of Sustainable Finance and Investment*, 9 (1), 17–32.

Bhattacharya, A., R. Colland, A. Averchenkova, L. Gonzalez, L. Martinez-Diaz, and J. van Rooij.·2020. *Delivering on the $100 Billion Climate Finance Commitment and Transforming Climate Finance*, (Independent Expert Group on Climate Finance), <https://www.un.org/sites/un2.un.org/files/100_billion_climate_finance_report.pdf> [Accessed 18 August 2021].

Business and Sustainable Development Commission.·2017. *Better Business, Better World: The Report of the Business and Sustainable Development Commission*, <https://sustainabledevelopment.un.org/content/documents/2399BetterBusinessBetterWorld.pdf> [Accessed 18 August 2021].

Cadman, T., L. Eastwood, F. L-C. Michaelis, T. N. Maraseni, J. Pittock, and T. Sarker. 2015. *The Political Economy of Sustainable Development: Policy Instruments and Market Mechanisms* (Chelthenham, UK: Edward Elgar Publishing).

Climate Investment Funds. 2012. *Donors and MDBs*, <https://www.climateinvestmentfunds.org/finances> [Accessed 17 September 2021].

Climate Policy Initiative.·2019. *Updated View on the Global Landscape of Climate Finance 2019*, <https://www.climatepolicyinitiative.org/wp-content/uploads/2020/12/Updated-View-on-the-2019-Global-Landscape-of-Climate-Finance-1.pdf> [Accessed 18 August 2021].

Global Environment Facility. 2021a. *Countries (Participants)*, <https://www.thegef.org/partners/countries-participants> [Accessed 18 August 2021].

——. 2021b. *GEF Agencies*, <https://www.thegef.org/partners/gef-agencies> [Accessed 18 August 2021].

Global Environment Facility Secretariat.·2019a. *GEF-7 Corporate Scorecard December 2019*, <https://www.thegef.org/publications/gef-7-corporate-scorecard-december-2019> [Accessed 18 August 2021].

——.·2019b. *GEF-7 Corporate Scorecard June 2019*, <https://www.thegef.org/sites/default/files/publications/gef7_corporate_scorecard_june_2019.pdf> [Accessed 18 August 2021].

——.·2020a. *GEF-7 Corporate Scorecard December 2020*, <https://www.thegef.org/sites/default/files/publications/GEF%20Scorecard_2020_December_CRA_bl2.pdf> [Accessed 18 August 2021].

——.·2020b. *GEF-7 Corporate Scorecard June 2020*, <https://www.thegef.org/sites/default/files/publications/gef7_corporate_scorecard_june_2020_v1.pdf> [Accessed 18 August 2021].

——.·2021. *GEF-7 Corporate Scorecard June 2021*, <https://www.thegef.org/sites/default/files/publications/GEF%20Scorecard_2021_June_CRA_bl2.pdf> [Accessed 18 August 2021].

Green Climate Fund. 2021a. *GCF: Financing Climate Action*, <https://www.greenclimate.fund/document/financing-climate-action> [Accessed 18 August 2021].

——.·2021b. *Status of Pledges and Contributions (Initial Resource Mobilisation)*, <https://www. greenclimate.fund/sites/default/files/document/status-pledges-irm-gcf1_7.pdf> [Accessed 30 January 2022].

——. n.d. *Private Sector Financing*, <https://www.greenclimate.fund/sectors/private> [Accessed 18 August 2021].

Green Finance Task Force.·2015. *Establishing China's Green Financial System. Report of the Green Finance Task Force April 2015*, <Establ'shing China's Green Financial System: Final Report (unep.org) > [Accessed 18 August 2021].

Gudde, P., J. Oakes, P. Cochrane, N. Caldwell, and N. Bury. 2021. 'The Role of UK Local Government in Delivering on Net Zero Carbon Commitments: You've Declared a Climate Emergency, So What's the Plan?', *Energy Policy*, 154, 112245.

Habbel, V., E. Jackson, M. Orth, J. Richter, and Harten S.·2021. *Evaluating Blended Finance Instruments and Mechanisms: Approaches and Methods*, OECD Development Co-operation Working Papers, <https://www.oecd-ilibrary.org/docserver/f1574c10-en.pdf?expires= 1629274090&id=id&accname=guest&checksum=B1930857B0C854062D4168E962D18FB5> [Accessed 18 August 2021].

Hainaut, H., and I. Cochran. 2018. 'The Landscape of Domestic Climate Investment and Finance Flows: Methodological Lessons from Five Years of Application in France', *International Economics*, 155, 69–83.

Institute for Fiscal Studies.·2020. *The Financial Risk and Resilience of English Local Authorities in the Coronavirus Crisis*, IFS Briefing Note, <https://ifs.org.uk/uploads/BN296-The-financial-risk-and-resilience-of-English-local-authorities-in-the-coronavirus-crisis.pdf> [Accessed 18 August 2021].

International Carbon Action Partnership.·2021. *ETS Detailed Information: Nova Scotia, Canada*, <https://icapcarbonaction.com/en/?option=com_etsmap&task=export&format=pdf&layout= list> [Accessed 18 August 2021].

International Monetary Fund.·2014. *External Debt Statistics: Guide for Compilers and Users*, <http://tffs.org/pdf/edsg/ft2014.pdf> [Accessed 17 September 2021].

——.·2020. *Fiscal Monitor, Policies for the Recovery*, <https://www.imf.org/en/Publications/FM/Is sues/2020/09/30/october-2020-fiscal-monitor> [Accessed 30 January 2022].

JP Morgan Chase and Co. 2020. *Development Finance Institution: Financing Opportunities with Anticipated Development Impact in Emerging Economies*, <https://www.jpmorgan.com/solu tions/cib/investment-banking/2020-dfi-announcement>

Michaelowa, A., and F. Jotzo. 2005. 'Transaction Costs, Institutional Rigidities and the Size of the Clean Development Mechanism', *Energy Policy*, 33 (4), 511–23.

Nussbaumer, P. 2009. 'On the Contribution of Labelled Certified Emission Reductions to Sustainable Development: A Multi-Criteria Evaluation of CDM Projects', *Energy Policy*, 37 (1), 91–101.

Olsen, K. H., and J. Fenhann. 2008. 'Sustainable Development Benefits of Clean Development Mechanism Projects a New Methodology for Sustainability Assessment Based on Text Analysis of the Project Design Documents Submitted for Validation', *Energy Policy*, 36, 2819–30.

Organisation for Economic Co-operation and Development.·1998. *The Arrangement on Guidelines for Officially Supported Export Credits*, <https://doi.org/10.1787/9789264189874-en> [Accessed 4 November 2021].

——.·2015. *Infrastructure Financing Instruments and Incentives*, <https://www.oecd.org/finance/ private-pensions/Infrastructure-Financing-Instruments-and-Incentives.pdf> [Accessed 18 August 2021].

——.·2016. *Annex 18. Rio Markers*, <https://www.oecd.org/dac/environment-development/Annex% 2018.%20Rio%20markers.pdf> [Accessed 18 August 2021].

——.·2018. *Making Blended Finance Work for the Sustainable Development Goals*, <https://doi.org/10.1787/9789264288768-9-en> [Accessed 18 August 2021].

——.·2020. *Climate Finance Provided and Mobilised by Developed Countries in 2013-18*, <https://doi.org/10.1787/f0773d55-en> [Accessed 18 August 2021].

——.·2021a. *Covid-19 Spending Helped to Lift Foreign Aid to an All-Time High in 2020*, <https://www.oecd.org/dac/financing-sustainable-development/development-finance-data/ODA-2020-detailed-summary.pdf> [Accessed 18 August 2021].

——.·2021b. *DAC List of ODA Recipients. Effective for Reporting on 2021 Flows*, <https://www.oecd.org/dac/financing-sustainable-development/development-finance-standards/DAC-List-ODA-Recipients-for-reporting-2021-flows.pdf> [Accessed 18 August 2021].

——. 2021c. *Official Development Assistance (ODA)*, <https://www.oecd.org/dac/financing-sustainable-development/development-finance-standards/official-development-assistance.htm> [Accessed 30 January 2022].

——. n.d. *Climate Change: OECD DAC External Development Finance Statistics*, <https://www.oecd.org/development/stats/climate-change.htm> [Accessed 30 January 2022].

Organisation for Economic Co-operation and Development, The World Bank, and United Nations Environment Programme.·2018. *Financing Climate Futures: Rethinking Infrastructure*, <https://www.oecd-ilibrary.org/environment/financing-climate-futures_9789264308114-en> [Accessed 18 August 2021].

Organisation for Economic Co-operation and Development Development Assistance Committee 2014 *DAC High Level Meeting: Final Communiqué* (Paris: DAC High Level Meeting) <https://www.oecd.org/dac/OECD%20DAC%20HLM%20Communique.PDF> [Accessed 18 August 2021].

——.·2020. *DAC Methodologies for Measuring the Amounts Mobilised from the Private Sector by Official Development Finance Interventions*, <https://www.oecd.org/dac/financing-sustainable-development/development-finance-standards/DAC-Methodologies-on-Mobilisation.pdf> [Accessed 18 August 2021].

Paulsson, E. 2009. 'A Review of the CDM Literature: From Fine-Tuning to Critical Scrutiny?', *International Environmental Agreements: Politics, Law and Economics*, 9, 63–80.

Roberts, J. T., R. Weikmans, S. Robinson, D. Ciplet, M. Khan, and D. Falzon. 2021. 'Rebooting a Failed Promise of Climate Finance', *Nature Climate Change*, 11, 180–82.

Runde, D. F., R. Bandura, and S. R. Ramanujam.·2019. *The Role of Development Finance Institutions in Enabling the Technology Revolution*, CSIS Briefs, <https://csis-website-prod.s3.amazonaws.com/s3fs-public/publication/190617_RundeRominaRamanujam_DFI_v3.pdf> [Accessed 18 August 2021].

Rydge, J.·2020. *Aligning Finance with the Paris Agreement: An Overview of Concepts, Approaches, Progress and Necessary Action*, (London: Grantham Research Institute on Climate Change and the Environment and Centre for Climate Change Economics and Policy, London School of Economics and Political Science), <https://www.lse.ac.uk/granthaminstitute/wp-content/uploads/2020/12/Aligning-finance-with-the-Paris-Agreement-3.pdf> [Accessed 18 August 2021].

Soanes, M., N. Rai, P. Steele, C. Shakya, and J. Macgregor.·2017. *Delivering Real Change: Getting International Climate Finance to the Local Level*, Working Paper, International Institute for Environment and Development), <https://pubs.iied.org/sites/default/files/pdfs/migrate/10178IIED.pdf> [Accessed 18 August 2021].

Sutter, C., and J. C. Parreño. 2007. 'Does the Current Clean Development Mechanism (CDM) Deliver Its Sustainable Development Claim? An Analysis of Officially Registered CDM Projects', *Climate Change*, 84, 75–90.

The International Development Finance Club. 2019. *A Global Network for Sustainable Development Investment: Mission and Vision*, <https://www.idfc.org/mission-vision/> [Accessed 18 August 2021].

The World Bank Group. 2021. *Global Environmental Facility Trust Fund (GEF)*, <https://fiftrustee. worldbank.org/en/about/unit/dfi/fiftrustee/fund-detail/gef> [Accessed 18 August 2021].

Total Official Support for Sustainable Development. 2021a. *TOSSD 2019 Data: The First TOSSD Data Collection*, <https://www.tossd.org/docs/2019-data-collection.pdf> [Accessed 18 August 2021].

———. 2021b. *TOSSD Reporting Instructions May 2021*, <https://tossd.org/docs/reporting-instructions.pdf> [Accessed 18 August 2021].

United Nations Framework Convention on Climate Change.·2006. *Report of the Conference of the Parties Serving as the Meeting of the Parties to the Kyoto Protocol on Its First Session, Held at Montreal from 28 November to 10 December 2005. Addendum Part Two: Action Taken by the Conference of the Parties Serving as the Meeting of the Parties to the Kyoto Protocol at Its First Session. Decisions Adopted by the Conference of the Parties Serving as the Meeting of the Parties to the Kyoto Protocol*, <https://unfccc.int/resource/docs/2005/cmp1/eng/08a02. pdf#page=2> [Accessed 11 October 2021].

United Nations. 2015a. *Addis Ababa Action on Agenda of the Third International Conference of Financing for Development (Addis Ababa Action Agenda). The Final Text of the Outcome Document Adopted at the Third International Conference on Financing for Development (Addis Ababa, Ethiopia, 13–16 July 2015) and Endorsed by the General Assembly in Its* Resolution *69/ 313 of 27 July 2015*, <https://sustainabledevelopment.un.org/content/documents/2051AAAA_ Outcome.pdf> [Accessed 18 August 2021].

———. 2015b. *Paris Agreement*, <https://unfccc.int/files/essential_background/convention/applica tion/pdf/english_paris_agreement.pdf> [Accessed 18 August 2021].

———.·2021. *Background Note on the USD 100 Billion Goal in the Context of UNFCCC* Process, *in Relation to Advancing SDG Indicator 13.A.1*, <https://unstats.un.org/sdgs/tierIII-indicators/ files/13.a.1_Background.pdf> [Accessed 18 August 2021].

United Nations Environment Programme/Technical University of Denmark (DTU) Partnership. 2021. *Welcome to the UNEP DTU CDM/JI Pipeline Analysis and Database*, <https://cdmpipeline.org/> [Accessed 18 August 2021].

United Nations Framework Convention on Climate Change. 1992. *United Nations Framework on Climate Change*, <https://unfccc.int/files/essential_background/background_publications_ htmlpdf/application/pdf/conveng.pdf> [Accessed 18 August 2021].

——— 2006 *Report of the Conference of the Parties Serving as the Meeting of the Parties to the Kyoto Protocol on Its First Session, Held at Montreal from 28 November to 10 December 2005. Addendum. Part Two: Action Taken by the Conference of the Parties Serving as the Meeting of the Parties to the Kyoto Protocol at Its First Session* (Montreal: Conference of the Parties) <https://unfccc.int/resource/docs/2005/cmp1/eng/08a03.pdf> [Accessed 18 August 2021].

———. 2007. *The Kyoto Protocol Mechanisms*, <https://unfccc.int/resource/docs/publications/ mechanisms.pdf> [Accessed 18 August 2021].

———. 2010. *Decision 1/CP.16 the Cancun Agreements: Outcome of the Work of the Ad Hoc Working Group on Long-Term Cooperative Action under the Convention*, <https://unfccc.int/sites/ default/files/resource/docs/2010/cop16/eng/07a01.pdf> [Accessed 18 August 2021].

———.·2016. *2016 Biennial Assessment and Overview of Climate Finance Flows Report*, https://unfccc.int/files/cooperation_and_support/financial_mechanism/standing_commit tee/application/pdf/2016_ba_technical_report.pdf> [Accessed 18 August 2021].

———.·2018. *2018 Biennial Assessment and Overview of Climate Finance Flows. Technical Report*, <https://unfccc.int/sites/default/files/resource/2018%20BA%20Technical%20Report% 20Final%20Feb%202019.pdf> [Accessed 18 August 2021].

——.·2019. *Annual Report of the Joint Implementation Supervisory Committee to the Conference of the Parties Serving as the Meeting of the Parties to the Kyoto Protocol*, <https://unfccc.int/sites/default/files/resource/cmp2019_02E.pdf> [Accessed 18 August 2021].

——. 2021a. *Action on Climate and SDGs*, <https://unfccc.int/topics/action-on-climate-and-sdgs/action-on-climate-and-sdgs> [Accessed 18 August 2021].

——.·2021b. *Annual Report of the Executive Board of the Clean Development Mechanism to the Conference of the Parties Serving as the Meeting of the Parties to the Kyoto Protocol*, <https://unfccc.int/sites/default/files/resource/cmp2020_01_adv.pdf> [Accessed 18 August 2021].

——.·2021c. *Background Document on the Fourth (2020) Biennial Assessment and Overview of Climate Finance Flows*, <https://unfccc.int/sites/default/files/resource/BN_BA_SCF%2024.pdf> [Accessed 18 August 2021].

——.·2021d. *Chair's Summary, Informal Consultations/Informal Technical Expert Dialogue on Article 6 of the Paris Agreement. Clean Development Mechanism Activity Transition to the Article 6.4 Mechanism*, <https://unfccc.int/sites/default/files/resource/IN.SBSTA2021.i15b.pdf> [Accessed 18 August 2021].

——. 2021e. *List of DOEs*, <https://cdm.unfccc.int/DOE/list/index.html> [Accessed 18 August 2021].

——.·2021f. *SBSTA Chair's Summary, Informal Consultations/Informal Technical Expert Dialogue on Article 6 of the Paris Agreement. Implementing Overall Mitigation in Global Emission in the Article 6.4 Mechanism*, <https://unfccc.int/sites/default/files/resource/IN.SBSTA2021.i15b.2.pdf> [Accessed 18 August 2021].

——.·2021g. *SBSTA Chair's Summary, Informal Consultations/Informal Technical Expert Dialogue on Article 6 of the Paris Agreement. Use of Kyoto Protocol Units Towards NDCs*, <https://unfccc.int/sites/default/files/resource/Inf_note04_Article%206.pdf> [Accessed 18 August 2021].

——.·2021h. *Summary of Cooperative Activities with United Nations Entities and Other International Organizations That Contribute to the Work under the Convention*, <https://unfccc.int/sites/default/files/resource/sbsta2021_inf01.pdf> [Accessed 18 August 2021].

United Nations General Assembly. 2015. *Resolution Adopted by the General Assembly on 25 September 2015. 70/1. Transforming Our World: The 2030 Agenda for Sustainable Development*, (UNGA) <https://www.un.org/ga/search/view_doc.asp?symbol=A/RES/70/1&Lang=E> [Accessed 18 August 2021].

Usher, A., A. Lemma, C. V. Nygaard, C. Isaac, C. Rudolph, D. W. te Velde, E. Maliepaard, J. Kwakkenbos, J. van Seters, J. Uusihakala, J. Frede, K. T. Blystad, K. Newitt, M. R. Romero, M. Gouett, M. W. Hansen, M. Liesner, P. Carter, P. Forestier, R. Kim, S. Attridge, S. Bilal, S. P. Andreasen, T. Nenova, and W. Loewenstein.·2019. *Impact of Development Finance Institutions on Sustainable Development*, An essay series, (London: Overseas Development Institute, Association of European Development Finance Institutions), <https://cdn.odi.org/media/documents/12892.pdf> [Accessed 18 August 2021].

Warren, P. 2019. 'The Role of Climate Finance Beyond Renewables: Demand-Side Management and Carbon Capture, Usage and Storage', *Climate Policy*, 19 (7), 861–77.

Watson, Charlene, and Liane Schalatek.·2020. *Climate Finance Thematic Briefing: Mitigation Finance (2020)*, (Overseas Development Institute/Heinrich Böll Stiftung Washington, DC), <https://climatefundsupdate.org/publications/climate-finance-thematic-briefing-mitigation-finance-2020/> [Accessed 30 January 2022].

Watts, D., C. Albornoz, and A. Watson. 2015. 'Clean Development Mechanism (CDM) after the First Commitment Period: Assessment of the World's Portfolio and the Role of Latin America', *Renewable and Sustainable Energy Reviews*, 41, 1176–89.

Weigel, M.·2016. *More Money, More Impact? China's Climate Change South-South Cooperation: Track Record and Future Direction*, (United Nations Development Programme), <https://www.cn.undp.org/content/china/en/home/library/south-south-cooperation/more-money–more-impact–china-s-climate-change-south-south-coop.html> [Accessed 30 January 2022].

WiseEuropa, NewClimate Institute, and Institute for Climate Economics (I4CE).·2019. *Domestic Landscape of Climate Finance: Why Systemic Approach to Climate Finance Matters?*, <https://www.i4ce.org/wp-core/wp-content/uploads/2019/02/WE-NCI-I4CE-Domestic_Landscape_Climate_Finance_policy_paper-2.pdf> [Accessed 18 August 2021].

Xu, J., X. Ren, and X. Wu.·2019. *Mapping Development Finance Institutions Worldwide: Definitions, Rationales, and Varieties*, NSE Development Financing Research Report, (Beijing: Institute of New Structural Economics Peking University), <https://www.idfc.org/wp-content/uploads/2019/07/nse_development_financing_research_report_no-1-2.pdf> [Accessed 18 August 2021].

Klaus Radunsky
Chapter 19
The adaptation fund (AF)

Abstract: One of the two main approaches to address the risks of climate change is adaptation. Parties to the Kyoto Protocol agreed in 2001 in Marrakesh at the 7th Conference of the Parties (COP 7) to the United Nations Framework Convention on Climate Change to establish the Adaptation Fund. This chapter provides insights into the history of this fund, which spans now 20 years, and offers information on its achievements addressing rules of procedures, sources of funding, disbursement and its relevance in the broader context of financial support for adaptation to the impacts of climate change; information about the outcome of an independent evaluation of the AF is also provided. Finally, the need is highlighted to speed up adaptation action in particular in the most vulnerable developing countries as there is broad agreement in the literature about the growing adaptation gap – the reason for this being that climate change risks are becoming larger faster than the adaptive capacity is being developed. Furthermore, some opportunities are identified to add momentum to adaptation.

Keywords: adaptation fund, AF board, evaluation, performance, options, projects, programmes; adaptation gap, COVID-19

Introduction: Milestones in establishing the AF

The Adaptation Fund (AF) is a financial instrument under the United Nations Framework Convention on Climate Change (UNFCCC) and the Kyoto Pr"otocol (KP) and was established to finance concrete adaptation projects and programmes in developing country Parties to the KP, in an effort to reduce the adverse effects of climate change facing communities, countries and sectors.

This chapter describes the development of the AF, highlighting the milestones achieved in chronological order and the accomplishments of the AF. In parallel, the change in climate risks is also highlighted, in order to better understand the adaptation gap which has been identified (United Nations Environment Programme 2021: vi–vii, Executive summary).

In order to better sense of the relevance of the AF, other options to finance adaptation to climate change are also described. However, this chapter cannot provide a comprehensive and complete overview over all areas of work related to adaptation under the UNFCCC. Institutions such as the Technology Executive Committee or the Nairobi Work Programme (NWP) and the Standing Committee on Finance

https://doi.org/10.1515/9783110733488-019

have relevance for adaptation but not directly for the AF. Finally, financing adaptation is compared to financing mitigation of greenhouse gas (GHG) emissions in developing countries.

In 2001 the COP to the UNFCCC met for the seventh time (COP 7, Marrakesh, Morocco) and laid the foundation for the AF through decision 10/CP.7 (UNFCCC 2002: 52, Addendum 1). After six years of negotiations, it was in 2007 at COP 13 in Bali (Indonesia), that the AF was operationalised and its Board established. The details of the outcome of those negotiations can be found in decision 1/CMP.3 (UNFCCC 2007: 3–9, Addendum 1). In 2010, the Adaptation Fund Board (AFB) approved the first two projects (in Honduras and Senegal) and in 2017 the AF celebrated its tenth anniversary. In March 2017 the AFB approved a record USD 60.3 million in new project funding and received another record USD 219.4 million in new funding requests for consideration at the AFB meeting in October 2017. In 2015, the first phase of an independent evaluation of the AF was concluded and in 2018 its second phase.

The approach for this examination of the AF used mainly official and publicly available documents of the UNFCCC. Additional sources included reports from other international organisations, for example, the Organisation for Economic Co-operation and Development (OECD), the Intergovernmental Panel on Climate Change (IPCC), the Earth Negotiations Bulletin and, if available, scientific studies on financing adaptation or on the AF. It did not include interviews e.g., of representatives of Parties or members of the AFB or non-governmental organisations (NGOs).

Background

In 2001, in decision 10/CP.7, Parties agreed for the first time on issues related to the AF. The draft decision on funding under the UNFCCC FCCC/CP/2001/L.14) states that there is a need for funding that is new and additional to the Global Environment Facility (GEF) and multilateral and bilateral funding, and that predictable funding should be available to non-Annex I Parties.

Another decision of COP 7 (FCCC/CP/2001/L.4/Rev.1) states that the GEF should provide financial resources to developing country Parties, in particular to the Least Developed Countries (LDCs) and Small Island Developing States (SIDS), including for implementing adaptation activities and establishing pilot or demonstration projects to show how adaptation planning and assessment can be translated into projects.

COP 7 also welcomed the joint political declaration made by some Annex I countries to provide USD 410 million annually in financial support to developing countries for climate change mitigation and adaptation by 2005, with this level to be reviewed in 2008.

In 2009, an assessment on delivering on this support by the European Union was published (Pallemaerts and Armstrong 2009). The conclusion was that the average annual level of financial support to developing countries, collectively provided by the 15 EU Member States that subscribed to the Bonn Declaration, through specific multilateral climate change-related funding channels falls well short of the level of USD 369 million to which they committed themselves. Whether or not the EU was complying with its political commitment under the Bonn Declaration could not be assessed in a robust fashion due to limited quality and consistency of information (Pallemaerts and Armstrong 2009: 1–23).

In 2007, six years after the establishment of AF, decision FCCC/SBI/2007/L.30 set out the functions of the AFB. Those include the development of strategic priorities, policies and guidelines, deciding on projects and the development of rules of procedure. On composition, the decision stipulates that the AFB shall comprise 16 members representing Parties to the Protocol, with two representatives from each of the five UN regional groups (African Group, Asia and the Pacific Group, Eastern European Group, Latin American and Caribbean and Western European and Others Group), one from SIDS, one from LDCs, two non-Annex I Parties and two Annex I Parties. In this way, developing countries usually have 69% of seats on the AFB. Decision-making is to be by consensus, and, in the event of non-agreement, by two-thirds majority. Decision 1/CMP.3 included an invitation to the GEF to provide secretariat services to the AFB on an interim basis, and an invitation to the World Bank to serve as a trustee on an interim basis.

In its early years, the AF thrived under an innovative market platform to receive a share of Certified Emission Reduction (CER) credits from the KP Clean Development Mechanism (CDM). Since the carbon market dropped in 2011–2012, the AF has relied mostly on generous public contributions. To meet this rising demand, the AF has striven to tap public, private and innovative sources of international climate finance.

The AF pioneered direct access and the fund has adopted several other innovative policies. Among them are progressive environmental and social policies, which promote human rights, gender equality and conservation principles in AF projects, and its Alternative Streamlined Accreditation Process for smaller entities – many of which would likely be unable to access climate finance otherwise. This process is designed to open up possibilities for smaller National Implementing Entities (NIE) to access the resources of the AF while taking into account the limited capacities of these entities.

Seven years after the establishment of the AFB, in 2014, the AFB introduced the streamlined accreditation process. This process officially initiates when the applicant NIE sends the Secretariat an official letter of agreement to pursue the streamlined process. The streamlined process aligns the AF's accreditation process further with the Paris Declaration on Aid Effectiveness (2005) and the Accra Agenda for Action (2008) as well as the Paris Agreement (2015).

The Paris Agreement (PA) emphasises the importance of efficient access to financial resources through simplified approval procedures and enhanced readiness support for developing country Parties, in particular for LDCs and SIDS, in the context of their national climate strategies and plans (AF 2021, see streamlined accreditation process).

In 2015, the PA was adopted. Article 6 (Cooperative Approaches) provides that Parties recognise that some Parties choose to pursue voluntary cooperation in the implementation of their National Determined Contributions (NDCs) to allow for higher ambition in their mitigation and adaptation actions and to promote sustainable development, environmental comparability and consistency and ensure integrity. Such cooperation is similar to the CDM agreed under the KP but these decisions did not include any linkage to the AF.

Issues related to the AF were addressed in decision FCCC/KP/CMP/2015/L.3/Rev.1 (CMP 11). This decision requests *inter alia*, that the AFB continues efforts to simplify accreditation procedures for NIEs. With respect to funding the AF, this decision urges Parties that responded to the fundraising target of the AFB but have not yet made financial contributions to do as soon as possible. The decision also encourages the other Parties to provide voluntary support that is additional to the share of proceeds from CDM activities to support resource mobilisation of the AFB. In terms of the future of the AF, the decision recommends that the COP serving as the meeting of the Parties to the PA (CMA) considers that the AF may serve the PA and invites COP 22 to request the Ad Hoc Working Group on the PA (SPA) to undertake necessary preparatory work and was to forward a recommendation to the CMP for adoption no later than CMP 15, in 2019.

In 2018, at the first session of the COP serving as the meeting of the Parties to the PA (CMA 1) and CMP 14, through decisions 13/CMA.1 and 1/CMP.14, Parties decided that the AF serve the PA, effective 1 January 2019. At these sessions, Parties also decided that the AF exclusively serve the PA, and no longer serve the KP once the share of proceeds under Article 6, paragraph 4, of the PA becomes available. However, the AF shall continue to receive the share of proceeds, if available, from activities under Articles 6, 12 and 17 of the KP. CMA one also decided that when the AF serves the PA, it is to be financed from the share of proceeds from Article 6, paragraph 4 of the PA (which establishes a mechanism to contribute to the mitigation of GHG emissions and support sustainable development) and from a variety of voluntary public and private sources.

In 2019, at CMP 15, Parties adopted amended and restated terms and conditions of services to be provided by the World Bank as an interim trustee of the AF. Parties did this also regarding the memorandum of understanding between the CMP and the GEF Council regarding secretariat services to the AF.

At COP 26 (Glasgow, November 31 – December 13) Article 6 negotiations around the 'sustainable development mechanism' for market and non-market mechanisms for emissions reduction activities were largely completed, but its operating modalities remain unclear. While countries can start to cooperate on carbon market instruments today, the development of bilateral and multilateral approaches and mechanisms would benefit from a clear international framework. Hampered by the sheer complexity of the issues, and recently also delayed by the pandemic, implementation of Article 6 will still take some time.

This delay is both a blessing and a curse. On the one hand, it means that stakeholders that want to engage in the new carbon market will not have regulatory certainty regarding some of the key issues. This is, above all, a challenge for the new mechanism under Article 6.4, which will not be operational until there is a decision on Article 6 including the establishment of a supervisory body. On the other hand, the delay has given countries and stakeholders time to digest and discuss technical and political issues of Article 6 before the resumption of the negotiations, and before countries begin detailed preparations for participating in Article 6 approaches (Asian Development Bank 2020).

The Green Climate Fund (GCF) and the AF are exploring options for whether the AF can implement projects funded by the GCF through modalities which are yet to be defined by the GCF Board and the AFB (GCF2019: 41f, Annex III). It seems that the Secretariat of the GCF had prepared the relevant information in October 2019 for a GCF Board meeting in November 2019 but that neither during the that meeting nor during 2020 has this issue been further considered by the GCF Board as reported by the AFB Secretariat during the October 2020 meeting of the AFB (2020: 35–36).

Activities under the AF

Overview

Before highlighting the activities which have been supported by the AF, information on the rules of procedure of the AF is provided. Information on the structure of donors and recipients as well as on the performance of the AF is also included.

Rules of procedure

The composition of the AFB has already been described above. A comparison with the Board of the GCF, which was established by decision 1/CP.16 at the COP in Cancun (2010), shows that the Board of the GCF is much larger (24 vs. 16 members) and that the Board of the GCF comprises an equal number of members from developing and developed country Parties whereas the AFB always has a majority of members from developing country Parties (UNFCCC 2011: 17–18).

Key governance arrangements elements informing the activities of the AFB are the rules of procedure, while substantive discussions are based upon the strategic priorities, policies and guidelines of the AF. Those were adopted by the Parties in Poznan, Poland in 2008, through decision 1/CMP.4 (AFB 2021, Annex I).

The strategic priorities require Parties to link projects and programmes funded under the AF *inter alia*, to national sustainable development and poverty reduction strategies, national communications and national adaptation programmes of action and other relevant policy instruments. Such other relevant instruments definitely include the National Adaptation Plan (NAP). The NAP's process was established under the Cancun Adaptation Framework (COP 16 in 2010),it invites Parties to formulate and implement NAPs as a means of identifying medium and long-term adaptation needs and developing and implementing strategies and programmes to address those needs. The NAP is understood to be a continuous, progressive and iterative process which follows a country-driven, gender-sensitive, participatory and fully transparent approach (UNFCCC 2021a).

According to the strategic priorities, Parties should also consider the guidance provided in decision 5/CP.7, paragraph 8, and, where necessary, further information included in reports from the IPCC and information generated under the NWP on impacts, vulnerability and adaptation to climate change.

Decision 5/CP.7 paragraph 8 (COP in Marrakesh, 2001) identified the following four activities to be supported by the AF: (i) Starting to implement adaptation activities where sufficient information is available to warrant such activities, *inter alia*, in the areas of water resources and land management, agriculture, health, infrastructure development, fragile ecosystems, including mountainous ecosystems, and integrated coastal zone management; (ii) improving the monitoring of diseases and vectors affected by climate change, and related forecasting and early warning systems, and in this context improving disease control and prevention; (iii) supporting capacity building, including institutional capacity, for preventive measures, planning, preparedness and management of disasters relating to climate change, including contingency planning, in particular, for droughts and floods in areas prone to extreme weather events; and (iv) strengthening existing and, where needed, establishing national and regional centres and information networks for rapid response to extreme weather events, utilising information technology as much as possible (UNFCCC 2001).

The AF provides funding on a full adaptation cost basis of projects and programmes that address the adverse effects of climate change. Full cost of adaptation means the costs associated with implementing concrete adaptation activities that address the adverse effects of climate change. The project proponent has to provide justification of the extent to which the project contributes to adaptation and climate resilience (AFB 2021: 3).

Decisions on the allocation of resources of the AF take into account criteria such as level of vulnerability, level of urgency and risks arising from delay, but also ensures access to the fund in a balanced and equitable manner. In order to confirm the latter, a cap in resource allocation per eligible host country, project and programme is agreed by the AFB based on a periodic assessment of the overall status of resources in the AF and with a view to promoting equitable distribution (AFB 2021: 4).

The AF allows international access through Multilateral Implementing Entities (MIE) and pioneered fully operational and direct access to climate finance through NIE and Regional Implementing Entities (RIE). Once accredited, NIE and RIE are allowed direct access financing and to manage all aspects of climate adaptation and resilience projects. For international access, countries access AF financing through an international intermediary organisation. Accreditation is valid for a five-year period with the possibility for renewal through reaccreditation. The Accreditation Panel reviews and assesses the application based on fiduciary standards (Heinrich Böll Stiftung 2020). The AF was the first climate fund to implement this direct access modality which is allowing national institutions to take on the implementation role typically undertaken by UN organisations and multilateral development banks.

By 2020 under the AF 32 NIEs have been established, 50% (or 16) of them in LDCs or SIDS (14) and with 32 approved projects in 22 LDCs or SIDS countries. Their directly accessed overall funding volume has been about USD 180 million (AF 2020b). It is expected that 2.4 million people will benefit from those projects. An assessment of the South African National Biodiversity Institute on the description of the projects supported by the AF states: 'The projects are localised. It is about making a difference on the ground. They are replicable, scalable and it is also about catalysing much bigger things. It enables local actors and can be transformational.' (Quoted in: AF 2020b: 1).

The AF's Readiness Programme is helping NIEs to efficiently navigate the accreditation process, to strengthen their capacity to design and implement climate adaptation projects and programmes and to build capacity and share lessons through workshops, communities of practice, webinars, field visits and readiness grants, including South-South cooperation and technical assistance (AF 2020b)

The project cycle of the AF for any project or programme size begins with a proposal submission to the Secretariat by the NIE/MIE chosen by the government of the recipient country or countries. The submission is followed by an initial screening, project review and approval, all by the AFB (AF 2020b).

All regular projects and programmes that complete implementation will be subject to terminal evaluation by an independent evaluator selected by the NIE. The AFB reserves the right to submit small projects and programmes to terminal evaluation when deemed appropriate (AF 2020b).

The AF is managed by the AF Board Secretariat, which provides research, advisory and administrative services, as well as an array of other services to the AFB. The Secretariat is based in Washington, D.C. and is comprised of a staff of 15-20 professionals. Every proposal for funding must be endorsed by the requesting government and thus each Party has to designate and communicate to the Secretariat of the AF the authority that endorses on behalf of the national government the projects and programmes proposed by the NIE. The Party might also choose to use the services of MIEs (AFB 2021: 2–16).

Furthermore, the guidelines differentiate between projects and programmes that are small in size (requesting up to USD 1 million) and regular projects and programmes (requesting over USD 1 million) (AFB 2021: 14).

Sources of funding

Funding for the AF comes from two main sources: proceeds from the CDM and voluntary contributions, both of which fluctuate over time (TANGO International 2018: 63).

The AF was originally financed with a share of proceeds from the CDM project activities. The share of proceeds amounts to 2% of CERs issued for a CDM project activity. That source has slowed to a trickle since the carbon market dropped in 2011–2012 and the AF has since this time increasingly depended on generous developed country government contributions (AF 2017).

An article from November 2017 (AF 2017) points to this issue of the financial sustainability of the AF. Financial sustainability of the AF is understood in this chapter as financial resources being in a balance with the adaptation needs in terms of eligible projects approved for funding. The problem: the AF raised USD 81.4 million in 2016 but approved USD 104.6 million in new projects during the following year. The demand for support by the AF for projects that meet the eligibility criteria was significantly larger compared to the financial resources available.

The AFB set in its Medium-term Strategy 2018 to 2022 an annual resource mobilisation target of USD 100 million per year for the years 2018 to 2020 in order to meet the increasing demand for adaptation project financing (AF 2016: 5–6).

The AFB decided at its meeting in October 2020 to approve a new resource mobilisation target of USD 120 million per year for the biennium 2020–2021, with the understanding that this is an indicative target and that support exceeding it would be welcome (AF 2020: 18).

As of November 2020, the Fund's total financial contributions received over time amounts to approximately USD 1.05 billion. CER sales have contributed about USD 208 million, voluntary contributions, primarily from Annex I countries, USD 842 million. For further details on the financial contributions to the AF see Climate Funds Update (Heinrich Böll Stiftung 2020).

Disbursement

With respect to the overall approval and disbursement time the following can be said (TANGO International 2018: 23):

> The AF's project cycle management is efficient, but increasingly tested by the expanding portfolio and new standards. Project approvals have taken longer, particularly those for two-step

projects in Fiscal Year (FY) 2016, which exceeded 31 months; in contrast, the approval time for one-step projects dropped dramatically from over 21 months in FY 2016 to just seven months in FY 2017.

In terms of project approval efficiency, the AF has a clear advantage over other climate funds. The AF averaged 8.1 months to approve one-step projects and 12.6 months for two-step projects; however, this figure is rising (Cordes and Christensen 2019). This is much faster than the Least Developed Countries Fund (LDCF) and Special Climate Change Fund (SCCF), which take an average 19 months to approve and implement projects of similar scale (TANGO International 2018: 26).

Other features of the AF

According to stakeholders, the AF adds value as being the only fund dedicated to adaptation because countries are able to prioritise and finance adaptation without any pressure to decide over the trade-offs of adaptation versus mitigation (Cordes and Christensen 2019: 20–25).

The secretariat of the AFB also conducted a survey of the effects of the COVID-19 pandemic on the projects supported by the AF before the meeting of the AFB in October 2020. It identified that 78% of the Implementing Entities had reported that they expected the pandemic to have a moderate-to-high impact on their portfolios that would extend beyond the period of the pandemic, with NIEs expecting an even greater impact. They also reported that monitoring and evaluation had been particularly difficult during the pandemic. According to the secretariat of the AFB, project delivery had already been delayed before the survey was conducted. The respondents also considered that the pandemic had increased the vulnerability of communities to climate change and had compounded their vulnerability to economic and social risks. In closing, the Secretariat stated that the survey also found that the support of the AF had remained relevant and had suggested new ways in which the AF could provide such support (AFB 2020: 3).

The AFB has defined the AF's mission as being to serve the PA by accelerating and enhancing the quality of adaptation action in developing countries (Grimm, Weischer, and Eckstein 2018: 13). In this context it is important to assess the overall relevance, effectiveness, efficiency, broader progress to and sustainability of results (technical, institutional, and financial) of the AF's portfolio of projects and programmes.

TANGO International (an organisation located in the US that provides institutional and technical support to organisations working to alleviate hunger and poverty among vulnerable populations around the world), performed an evaluation of the long-term outcomes, impacts and sustainability of AF interventions, focussing on its portfolio of funded projects from the beginning of its operations until March 2017 (TANGO International 2018: 16). According to this evaluation, the majority of Implementing Entities survey respondents strongly agreed that AF projects contribute to

Sustainable Development Goals implementation and that 14% of AF approved projects contribute to ending poverty.

Relevance

In the ten years from when operations of the AF were launched in 2007 to 2017, the AF has, allocated more than USD 460 million to 70 concrete projects in 58 countries – directly benefitting nearly 5.5 million people (AF 2017).

This means on average, from 2010 to 2017, the AF approved ten projects and allocated about USD 85 million per year. Demand for the AF has risen rapidly with record numbers of proposals received the last couple of years. In 2017 alone the AF received 54 funding proposals totalling over USD 350 million, a one-third increase from the previous year. In March 2017, the AF could approve only USD 60.3 million in new project funding, due to the limited financial resources available.

This comparison demonstrates that the role of the AF has been increasing over time. A briefing note, originally developed in 2018 and updated in July 2020, includes the information (AF 2020a) that 105 adaptation projects have been approved up to July 2020. This is an increase of 35 approved projects compared to the level reported in 2017. The increase in demand of support by the AF over the period 2019–2020 is also reflected by record highs of USD 268 million across 40 proposals, as well as USD 188 million in new projects approved by the AFB and 18 submissions received during intersessional review. Of those 105 adaptation projects, about half have requested funding below USD one million, with the highest being about USD 14 million so far. In total, USD 745 million has been allocated by the AF up to July 2020 for climate adaptation projects and programmes, project formulation activities, South-South cooperation grants for accreditation support and environmental and social policy technical assistance grants. In a total of 102 countries, the majority of projects are now in the implementation stage (AF 2020a). Of the 102 countries that have received funding, 28 countries are LDCs and 18 SIDS. By July 2020, 51 Implementing Entities have been accredited by the AF, of which 32 are NIEs in Africa, Latin America and the Caribbean, and the Asia-Pacific that have direct access to adaptation financing.

According to the briefing note (AF 2020a), disaster risk reduction was addressed the most (19.2% of the AF investments), followed by food security (15.8%), agriculture (13.2%), water management (12.8%) and rural development (12.1%). Multi-sector projects, coastal management, ecosystem-based adaptation, urban development and forests have been the other sectors that have received funding so far.

In the briefing note (AF 2020a) the AF claims to be one of the most innovative and unique climate funds, that has achieved impressive progress in just a few years and that the AF has proven its effectiveness as a highly efficient and transparent framework for directly channelling adaptation finance to developing countries.

Furthermore, the AF claims to be the only climate adaptation fund that includes the most vulnerable communities as a strategic priority.

Independent evaluation

An independent evaluation of the AF, conducted by TANGO International, in association with the Overseas Development Institute (an independent think tank on international development and humanitarian issues, founded in 1960 and based in London), was published in 2018 (TANGO International 2018). With respect to the relevance of the AF, the evaluation concluded that its design is coherent with and complementary to other adaptation efforts under the UNFCCC. It contributes directly to various adaptation work streams and complements the role of other climate funds by extending access to all developing countries. Though small in size, the AF is increasing financial support to developing countries and helping close the adaptation finance gap. The AF's design is appropriate to generating timely lessons about effective approaches to adaptation finance, especially with regards to direct access and scalable and replicable action benefitting the most vulnerable communities and social groups. The AF's design supports pilot activities with substantial potential for scaling-up impact at subnational, national and regional levels (TANGO International 2018: 20–30).

The AF is strong on transparency. Stakeholders are provided with the opportunity to read and comment on project proposals before they are presented to the Board for consideration. As an example, for the thirty-fourth AF Board meeting, the AF Secretariat published 33 project proposals and concepts for comment and review. The NGO Germanwatch is very active in promoting participation of the international NGO community and is also producing written assessments of each Board meeting (Cordes and Christensen 2019).

A study with a focus on projects funded by the AF has been recently published, assessing the role of the access modality to multilateral climate funds in enhancing the local inclusiveness of international adaptation finance. The result showed that the access modality has limited impact, but the study delivered other interesting insights (Manuamorn 2020: 265).

It is the Fund's tangible actions to the most vulnerable and its flexibility and willingness to innovate that have led to its achievements until now and will help lead to many more to come (AF 2016: 6).

A study by Norwegian NGOs (Dejgaard and Hattle 2020: 46) made a recommendation that Norway increase its contributions to the AF together with other like-minded donors.

Funding of adaptation beyond the AF

This section will provide some information related to other institutions financing adaptation, eligible countries and evaluation modalities. Additional information on various aspects of international climate finance has been published by the NGO Heinrich Böll Stiftung North America (2011–2021)

Global Environmental Facility (GEF)

The GEF plays a key role in financing adaptation as an operating entity of the financial mechanism to the UNFCCC. The GEF was the first global source of funds for adaptation, and channels support for climate adaptation mainly through the LDCF and the SCCF. The two funds also have an important role in serving the PA. As such, the GEF has been at the forefront of international efforts to strengthen the resilience of developing countries to climate change.

The GEF was established on the eve of the 1992 Rio Earth Summit to help tackle the planet's most pressing environmental problems. It has become not only the financial mechanism to the UNFCCC but also of the Convention on Biodiversity, the Stockholm Convention, the United Nations Convention to Combat Desertification and other international environmental agreements.

The GEF's approach to adaptation is based on the recognition that climate change affects all aspects of human, social and economic development. The GEF has supported the integration of appropriate adaptation measures into development plans, policies, programmes and projects at the regional, national, subnational and local level, with the ultimate aim of achieving climate-resilient development. Innovation, partnership and gender mainstreaming are also key to GEF's adaptation and resilience support.

The LDCF and SCCF are well-suited to help countries respond to the COVID-19 crisis, through enhancing resilience, creating buffers and applying nature-based solutions. Initiatives supported by the two funds have the potential to contribute to economic resilience and health, and the overall recovery efforts of affected countries, communities and sectors. For example, they are strengthening income generation and diversification, building supply chain resilience, aiding local food security and access to basic services, and targeting support to the vulnerable ecosystems and people that are likely to be hardest hit by the COVID-19, climate and biodiversity crises.

The GEF has been collaborating closely with the GCF through the coordinated engagement initiative and encouraging joint GEF-GCF country dialogues and programming. A number of projects are building on outcomes of GCF readiness support to address identified priorities, while other GEF projects are expected to be scaled-up with GCF support (GEF 2016).

Since 2001, the GEF has provided close to USD 2 billion in grant financing and mobilised more than USD 13 billion from other sources for 386 adaptation projects in 130 countries, including all LDCs and 33 SIDS. These projects are expected to directly reduce the vulnerability of approximately 30 million people.

These projects also ensure that more than 7.2 million hectares of productive and natural landscapes are better managed to more effectively withstand the effects of climate change. Importantly, GEF investments to date are preparing the ground for effective adaptation at a larger scale by providing various forms of adaptation training to more than 900,000 people.

The GEF, through the LDCF and the SCCF, has financed 119 projects supporting the development of hydro-meteorological and climate information services, while delivering technical assistance to integrate climate risks and adaptation into 2,500 key policymaking and planning processes at the regional, national and subnational level and across the most vulnerable sectors in developing countries (GEF 2016).

The goal of the GEF-7 adaptation strategy is to strengthen resilience and reduce vulnerability to the adverse impacts of climate change in developing countries and support their efforts to enhance adaptive capacity. These objectives are intended to be achieved through innovation and technology transfer for climate change adaptation, by mainstreaming climate change adaptation and resilience for systemic impact and by fostering enabling conditions for effective and integrated climate change adaptation. Thus, the GEF continues to support countries as they develop NAPs under the UNFCCC (GEF 2016).

With respect to evaluation, the SCCF implements a results framework that is structured to correspond to the three strategic objectives, with associated outcomes and indicators. These indicators are monitored at the portfolio level, drawing on project-level information received at CEO endorsement or approval stage, and through mid-term reviews and terminal evaluations. The results framework for 2018 to 2022 has been streamlined to consist of three core indicators for all LDCF and SCCF projects, along with several additional indicators aligned with the three strategic objectives. To enhance complementarity, some indicators are aligned with those tracked by the GCF and the Pilot Program for Climate Resilience where possible. In particular, the ongoing effort of the GCF in developing indicators for climate resilience will continue to inform the approach of the LDCF and SCCF (GEF 2020: xi–xiii, 36–42)

Green climate fund (GCF)

In 2010, at COP 16 held in Cancun, by decision 1/CP.16, Parties established the GCF as an operating entity of the Financial Mechanism of the Convention under Article 11. In 2011, at COP 17 held in Durban, Parties adopted decision 3/CP.17 and approved the Governing Instrument for the GCF. The GCF is governed by the GCF

Board and it is accountable to and functions under the guidance of the COP to support projects, programmes, policies and other activities in developing country Parties using thematic funding windows (GCF 2020).

When the PA was reached in 2015, the GCF was given an important role in serving the agreement and supporting the goal of keeping climate change well below 2 °C. The GCF is based in Incheon in South Korea and launched its initial resource mobilisation in 2014 (GEF 2020: 12–20).

The GCF helps developing countries to limit or reduce their GHG emissions and adapt to climate change. It seeks to promote a paradigm shift to low-emission and climate-resilient development, taking into account the needs of countries that are particularly vulnerable to climate change impacts. The GCF aims to deliver equal amounts of funding to mitigation and adaptation, while being guided by the UNFCCC's principles and provisions (GEF 2020: 12–20).

The GCF is a legally independent institution with a fully independent secretariat headed by an executive secretary. The World Bank serves as the interim trustee of the GCF, and the GCF functions under the guidance of and remains accountable to the UNFCCC Conference of Parties. At the July 2019 Board meeting, a decision-making mechanism in the absence of consensus was again discussed, as the Board has operated solely on the basis of consensus (which has delayed decision-making considerably) (GEF 2020: 12–20).

According to the portfolio dashboard (GCF 2021b), as of May 2021 the GCF has committed USD 7.2 billion, disbursed USD 1.7 billion and is supporting 158 projects. Among the supported countries are 62 LDCs and 62 African countries as well as 33 SIDS. The funding amount by theme is 64% mitigation and 36% adaptation (GCF 2021b).

The GCF has also developed the option of direct access; it describes a modality where national or regional entities become accredited to receive finance directly from climate funds. It does not require finance to be channelled through an international organisation, such as a UN agency or multilateral development bank. The objective is to promote recipient countries' ownership of climate finance and ensure that funding is aligned with national priorities such as national adaptation plans, NDCs and other national strategies (GCF 2021a: 3). According to the brief, 'The GCF's Direct Access Modality is not perfect. Stakeholders identified a number of challenges to direct access. These included the GCF's complex project cycle, lengthy timelines and limited capacity' (GCF 2021a: 2).

Climate technology centre and network (CTCN)

The CTCN is the operational arm of the UNFCCC Technology Mechanism, hosted by the UN Environment Programme and the UN Industrial Development Organization. The Centre promotes the accelerated transfer of environmentally sound technologies for low-carbon and climate-resilient development at the request of developing countries.

Requests can be made by all countries that have identified National Designated Entities (NDE), at present161 countries worldwide. The request is quite simple and must be forwarded via the NDE to the CTCN. Countries are making more and more use of this option, in the last 24 months (May 2019 to April 2021) more than 220 requests have been made, 26% being focussed on adaptation and 23% combining adaptation and mitigation.

Upon receipt of such requests, the Centre quickly mobilises its global network of climate technology experts to design and deliver a customised solution tailored to local needs. The CTCN does not provide funding directly to countries, but instead supports the provision of technical assistance provided by experts on specific climate technology sectors. Thus, the CTCN supports the development of bankable projects. The technical support includes technical assessments, technical support for policy and planning documents, training, tools and methodologies as well as implementation plans. Costs of up to USD 250,000 in support is free of charge (CTCN 2021).

Climate finance provided by developed countries

The information included in this section is extracted from a report published by the OECD in November 2020.

This report provides insights on the evolution of the following four distinct components of climate finance provided and mobilised: bilateral public climate finance, multilateral climate finance provided to developed countries, climate-related officially supported export credits and private finance mobilised by bilateral and multilateral public climate finance, provided to developed countries.

Total climate finance provided and mobilised by developed countries for developing countries reached USD 78.9 billion in 2018. Within this total, public climate finance provided USD 62.2 billion and private climate finance mobilised USD 14.6 billion in 2018.

Finance for adaptation reached USD 16.8 billion in 2018, or 20%, and cross-cutting projects represented 9% of the total. The share of adaptation finance was most prominent in the water and sanitation, and agriculture sectors.

Financing for LDCs and SIDS represented respectively 14% and 2% of the total.

In terms of climate finance provided per capita, SIDS and other countries with relatively small populations were the highest recipients in 2016–2018. Out of the top 25 per capita recipients, 21 were SIDS.

Private climate finance mobilised by developed countries during 2016–2018 focussed almost exclusively on climate mitigation (93%), targeted mainly the energy sector (60% of the total) and in the most part benefitted middle-income countries (69%).

On the 100 billion USD climate finance commitment

The starting point of this section is the COP 16 Accord, adopted in 2010 in Cancun (Mexico), which states that:

> Developed country Parties commit, in the context of meaningful mitigation actions and transparency on implementation, to a goal of mobilizing jointly USD 100 billion /yr by 2020 to address the needs of developing countries. (UNFCCC 2011: 17)

The synopsis from *Delivering on the USD 100 billion climate finance commitment and transforming climate finance* (Independent Expert Group on Climate Finance 2020) provides very clear language with respect to the impact of the COVID-19 pandemic on this commitment. To summarise: the COVID-19 pandemic has worsened the fiscal and debt positions significantly for emerging markets and developing economies (EMDEs) as well as for many climate-vulnerable middle-income countries. Thus, the COVID-19 crisis has shown that the old normal was deeply fragile. Experts agree that the harm finally caused by climate change and biodiversity loss will be much greater and longer-lasting compared to the impacts induced by COVID-19. The top priority should be to build back better in order to put the world on a development path that is more sustainable, inclusive and resilient (Independent Expert Group on Climate Finance 2020: 6–7).

The crisis presents an enormous threat but also a chance to restructure economies at the pace and scale that climate science requires by integrating climate action into the economic recovery from COVID-19.

Poor countries are much more constrained in their ability to respond due to lack of fiscal space and reduced access to external finance. No African country has been able to access the sovereign debt market since February 2020 and there have been more downgrades in credit ratings in 2020 than in any other previous year in history.

If EMDEs are unable to put in place recovery packages that are strong and sustainable, it will put the climate goals irrevocably beyond reach. EMDEs already account for two-thirds of global emissions and many are also the most vulnerable in the face of climate change. Support to tackle their debt and financing needs is a win-win proposition for the global economy and for the climate.

International public climate finance will have a crucial role to play in supporting a better recovery and transformation to low-carbon and climate-resilient growth. As the bedrock of international public finance, the USD 100 billion commitment should work in concert with all pools of finance including the large, and so far, untapped pools of private finance.

Since 2017 the Adaptation Committee, a constituted body under the UNFCCC, has published the Adaptation Finance Bulletin (AC 2017), the most recent being at the time when this chapter was prepared (March 2021), issue 7 from December 2020 (AC 2021c). This bulletin provides the latest news and updates to Parties and other interested stakeholders on adaptation finance-related information from funds, UNFCCC bodies and negotiations, as well as an overview of relevant upcoming events.

Adaptation gap report

The information included in this section is extracted from a report jointly published by the United Nations Environment Programme (UNEP), UNEP DTU Partnership and the World Adaptation Science Programme in 2021 (UNEP 2021).

Chapter four of that report describes the global progress on financing of adaptation. One key message of this chapter is that albeit international public adaptation finance is slowly rising, there is insufficient evidence that this increase over time is narrowing the distance to meet the growing adaptation costs. The reason for this being that there is not enough data to identify such a trend in domestic public or private finance flows. A recent approach is to design public adaptation finance as a catalyst for attracting private adaptation finance. The idea is to create new solutions and financial instruments such as insurance and results-based finance. It remains to be seen whether those efforts to expand the instruments, actors and approaches through which adaptation finance is delivered will be successful. New impetus for adaptation may be provided by the increasing momentum to ensure a sustainable financial system. This momentum is underpinned by growing recognition that both material physical risks and the risks introduced during the shift to a climate-resilient economy, impact company returns, asset values and, ultimately, financial stability. New tools should be used to identify and factor in these risks in investment decision-making and financial stability monitoring.

The Network for Greening the Financial System (NGFS) has recently concluded that it is 'within the mandates of central banks and supervisors to ensure the financial system is resilient to these risks' (NGFS 2019: 1) Stringent climate disclosure and climate risk management requirements – based on solid taxonomies – across the financial sector can help to monitor finance flows that contribute to adaptation, and also have the potential to stimulate an increase in investments in climate resilience and direct finance away from investments that increase vulnerability. Monitoring and impact assessment of sustainable finance measures are central to capitalising on their potential. However, the scale and scope of the effects of sustainable finance regulation are not yet fully understood, as qualitative assessments and quantitative indicators are at an early-stage of development, particularly those concerning adaptation (UNEP 2021: 30–31).

Discussion: Current challenges in funding adaptation

Countries adopted the Climate Convention in 1992 in Rio. Nine years later, in 2001 and informed by the Third Assessment Report of the IPCC, adaptation gained traction and Parties agreed on a process to address adverse effects and to establish funding arrangements for adaptation – the GEF got the mandate to establish the LDCF and the SCCF and the AF was created. Under the AF, concrete projects have received funding since 2010 and up to 2020 adaptation projects total funding by the AF, the LDCF and the SCCF have amounted to about USD 2.6 billion. The GCF, established in 2010, has also committed as of November 2020 about USD 2.6 billion to adaptation activities (AC 2021c).

There is some expectation that the finalisation of negotiations around Article 6 of the PA at COP 26 may help in the medium-term to meet the increasing demand for finance from the AF by the share of proceeds of emission reductions created under Article 6.4. The draft decision text already contained important details (Grimm, Weischer, and Eckstein 2018: 22–23) and was further elaborated at COP 25 in Madrid (2019), but despite agreement at COP 26, much will still have to be decided by a supervisory body later on. Given the funding resulting from shares of proceeds under the KP in the past, the ongoing existence of the CDM in some form or other, and in consideration of the different character of the PA compared to the KP in general, it is possible that the mechanism under Article 6.4 might contribute to reducing the adaptation gap in developing countries, although Article 6 overall is still largely focussed on mitigation.

An important question is whether those adaptation projects, which have been carefully planned and assessed against the criteria developed by the various funds, could demonstrate how to successfully enhance resilience to climate change of vulnerable communities, create enough capacity and raise enough awareness, in order to avoid maladaptation caused by ongoing investments, be it by the private or public sector. One important principle in this context is to build back better. This is a holistic concept using post-disaster reconstruction and recovery as an opportunity to improve a community's physical, social, environmental and economic conditions to create a more resilient community in an effective and efficient way (Build Back Better 2021). In the past finance provided by the AF was particularly relevant for the most vulnerable and poor people in the most vulnerable countries. Other constraints on funding for supporting adaptation have been identified under the GCF. Currently, there is more funding for projects available than there are proposals available. The reasons identified included the GCF's complex project cycle, lengthy timelines and limited capacity (GCF 2021a: 8). If the international community in cooperation with national authorities and stakeholders fail to enhance the resilience to a level that allows people to sustain themselves, the displacement of people and permanent migration driven by increasing climate risks becomes more likely (IPCC Core Writing Team 2001: 29–31).

The adaptation gap is mainly driven by increasing global warming. At the time when the Third Assessment Report (TAR) of the IPCC was written in 2001, Earth's surface temperature had increased over the record of direct temperature measurements (1860–2000) by about 0.6 °C, and now amounts to about 1.1 °C (Kappelle 2020: 8). This increase in Earth's surface temperature will continue until countries manage to reach net-zero emissions (IPCC Core Writing Team 2014: 56–74).

The Synthesis Report of the TAR, published in 2001, provided very clear and alarming messages. One being that the Earth's surface temperature had increased by about 0.6 °C – a rise that has been unprecedented over the last millennium; another that fossil fuel burning released on average $5.4 \cdot Gt \cdot C \cdot yr^{-1}$ during the 1980s, increasing to $6.3 \cdot Gt \cdot C \cdot yr^{-1}$ during the 1990s (IPCC Core Writing Team 2001: 2–34, SPM). Furthermore, the IPCC also informed in 2001 that adaptation has the potential to reduce adverse effects of climate change and can often produce immediate ancillary benefits but will not prevent all damage. Thus, according to the TAR, adaptation was recognised as a necessary strategy at all scales to complement climate change mitigation efforts. In this context, it is worth noting that it took nine years from 2001 to 2010 for the international community to move from recognising the need for adaptation to taking action on the ground, namely, to provide support to enhance resilience in developing countries. A key question is whether support is delivered fast enough and becomes large enough to be adequate to the increasing risks related to climate change.

The increase of climate risks is strongly dependent on the anthropogenic GHG emissions and the point in time by when humanity achieves net-zero global emissions (and even net negative emissions thereafter in order to address overshooting). The IPCC provides regular assessments of the changes already experienced as well as of the expected changes in the short, medium and long-term. The sixth assessment report is scheduled to be published in 2022 (information as of March 2021).

With respect to the support for developing countries to address those climate change risks, the PA has acknowledged the importance of the recognition of adaptation efforts of developing country Parties. This includes greater coherence in adaptation-related institutional arrangements under the Convention, of methodologies for assessing adaptation needs with a view to assisting developing Parties and of methodologies on taking the necessary steps to facilitate the mobilisation of support for adaptation in developing countries and to review the adequacy and effectiveness of adaptation and support provided for adaptation (UNFCCC 2015: 7–8).

The above-mentioned Adaptation Finance Bulletin reported in its third issue (March 2019) on the progress made during COP 25 in Katowice (2018) with respect to paragraphs 41, 42 and 45 of decision 1/CP.21 which address methods for increasing support for adaptation in developing countries (AC 2019). This important work has been delayed due to the COVID-19 pandemic. In March 2021, these issues were considered by the Adaptation Committee during its nineteenth meeting (AC 2021a) and a comprehensive stocktake has been prepared to inform that discussion of adaptation needs (AC 2021b). The modalities with respect to the cooperation between the GCF and the AF also had not been agreed on by March 2021 although a lot of preparatory work has already been done. Those decisions have to be made primarily by the boards of the GCF and of the AF. It has already become evident that the COVID-19 pandemic has some significant impact on adaptation to the impacts of climate change. Examples are a delay in decisions under the UNFCCC and of actions on the ground. But it seems even more important that a concerning body of evidence already indicates that climate hazards are likely to intersect with the COVID-19 outbreak. These compound risks will be exacerbated by the unfolding economic crisis and other longstanding disparities, both within countries and across regions. One consequence will be that specific populations are exposed to heightened risk. This poses a huge challenge: while keeping climate goals and pandemic containment in sight, countries will face a drumbeat of climate adaptation crises (Phillips et al. 2020: 586).

Conclusion

The AF was established to finance concrete adaptation projects and programmes in developing country Parties. A task that is becoming more important year by year because of the ongoing anthropogenic GHG emissions which drive global warming. This is also indicated by the finding that the adaptation component of NDCs receives greater focus, particularly adaptation planning and national adaptation plans (UNFCCC 2021: 6–7). Another important indicator for the expected trend is the social cost of carbon. Those have been recently estimated by the Biden administration to be USD 51 per tonne of CO_2 and are expected to rise by 2050 to USD 85 or by 66% (Chemnick 2021).

Also, methodologies to assess the needs, adequacy and effectiveness of adaptation and support are still under development. The chapter *Valuing civil society environmental engagement* of this Handbook by Tony Bradley might offer valuable information on new and promising approaches that could help prioritise adaptation action, in particular in developing countries. Nevertheless, analysts agree despite the shortcomings of the current approaches, that more funding is required to meet the adaptation costs, in particular in developing countries. Private finance contributes only very little when it comes to adaptation in the most vulnerable countries which can be found among LDCs and SIDS in particular.

Though small in size, the AF is increasing financial support to developing countries and helping close the adaptation finance gap. The AF's design is appropriate to generating timely lessons about effective approaches to adaptation finance, especially with regards to direct access and scalable and replicable action benefitting the most vulnerable communities and social groups.

There is the expectation that the cooperation of the AF and the GCF will broaden the financial basis of the AF. However, the exploration of the GCF and the AF on options for whether the AF can implement projects funded by the GCF through modalities which are yet to be defined by the GCF Board and the AFB is still ongoing and has not yet been concluded. Moreover, agreement on Article 6 will contribute to the sustainability of funding for the AF. The annual resource mobilisation target as set by AFB for the years 2018 to 2020 is USD 100 million in order to meet the increasing demand for adaptation project financing. It seems important to also develop rules that make it attractive for the private sector to contribute to the resources available for the AF.

Unfortunately, the decisions required to make funding of the AF more robust have also been hampered by the COVID-19 pandemic. As there is quite some uncertainty about the future impact of the pandemic on the relevant processes under the UNFCCC, it seems important that, in spite of the crisis, the funding for the AF continues in order to allow support for all the eligible and approved projects. Delaying adaptation action might enhance significantly the risk of loss and damage as well as of migration and social unrest.

There is a significant systemic risk that the adaptation gap further widens in the coming decades. One driver is the slow speed of the international response under the UNFCCC to mobilise support in terms of finance, capacity building and technical support to help vulnerable countries and people to enhance their resilience. The other reason is the growing risk associated with global warming – as stated in AR5: every 0.1 °C is counting and the warming is still speeding up and risks associated with each 0.1 °C warming are also increasing. Unfortunately, the COVID-19 pandemic has been further exaggerating this systemic risk described above. The pandemic further enhances vulnerability of already vulnerable people and is also further slowing down the processes under the UNFCCC. These facts require mobilisation efforts even more than before to make closing the adaptation gap a top priority for all countries by speeding up mitigation action and by becoming carbon neutral as quickly as possible and to enhance support for the most vulnerable countries and most vulnerable people – now and into the future.

Support of developing countries by developed countries, be it financial, building capacity or technical, helps to avoid maladaptation, which is very important in being efficient and effective in adaptation. This is particularly relevant for transformative adaptation activities. Institutions, such as the AF but also the other funds, are thus essential to help manage climate change risks better. Given that adaptation activities are much more context specific than issues related to decarbonisation for example, institutions that specialise in adaptation such as the AF have a role to play – in the future even more than until now.

Further ramping up finance for adaptation to impacts of climate change must not reduce financing of mitigation of GHG emissions in order to avoid further increase of climate change risks and to compromise on the goals to become carbon neutral.

In this context, further strengthening of international cooperation seems to be pivotal. This is quite similar to the most recent initiative of countries to strengthen international cooperation to prevent and combat future pandemics (Frankfurter Allgemeine Zeitung 2021), triggered by the COVID-19 crisis. Governments should improve their risk management, building on the lessons learnt from the COVID-19 pandemic to improve their management of compound risks.

In order to avoid a further increase of the adaptation gap, every effort should be made to reach meaningful decisions under the UNFCCC despite the COVID-19 pandemic in 2021. Parties should focus on a limited number of decisions – those that are essential to enhancing support for the most vulnerable and to further enhance momentum in addressing climate change risks.

The need to address the adaptation gap has also been recognised by United Kingdom Research and Innovation (UKRI). An international event series hosted by UKRI and partners has been taking place as the UK prepares for the UN Climate Change Conference (COP 26) in Glasgow in November 2021. One element will be to address questions such as: what research is needed to respond to the adaptation gap? Or how to evaluate the feasibility of adaptation options and outcomes for resilient and sustainable development? (UKRI 2021).

Hopefully, the decisions made by COP 26 will be informed by the outcome of this event series and thus speed up the support for those most vulnerable to the escalating impacts of climate change.

In this context, mixed signals from the government of the United Kingdom before the meeting of the G7 in Cornwall in June 2021 have raised concerns. While the UK government on one hand had promised earlier in 2021 to double its international climate finance to 11.6 billion GBP by 2025/26, it also faces accusations of hypocrisy after cutting back international aid by 4 billion GBP during the global pandemic (DeSmog 2021). The goal for adaptation should be that it has only been adequate if loss and damage is negligible. This will require the addressing of both at the same time: the adaptation gap as well as the mitigation gap. The more humanity fails to close those gaps the more people will suffer. Everyone should be encouraged to contribute to closing those gaps.

References

Adaptation Committee.·2017. *Adaptation Finance Bulletin: Issue 1, 2017*, (UNFCCC Adaptation Committee), <https://unfccc.int/sites/default/files/adaptation_finance_bulletin_no._1_august_2017.pdf> [Accessed 30 October 2021].

——.·2019. *Adaptation Finance Bulletin: Issue 3, March 2019*, (UNFCCC Adaptation Committee), <https://myemail.constantcontact.com/UNFCC-Adaptation-Finance-Bulletin—Issue-3—March-2019.html?soid=1117347475566&aid=M6YkYg_eSII> [Accessed 30 October 2021].

——. 2021a. *Nineteenth Meeting of the Adaptation Committee (AC19): UNFCCC*. <https://unfccc.int/event/nineteenth-meeting-of-the-adaptation-committee-ac19>

——.·2021b. *Possible Themes for the Second Report of a Series of Biennial Synthesis Reports in the Context of the Recognition of Adaptation Efforts of Developing Countries: Concept Note*, (UNFCCC Adaptation Committee), <https://unfccc.int/sites/default/files/resource/ac19_6d_recognition.pdf> [Accessed 30 October 2021].

——. 2021c. *UNFCCC Adaptation Finance Bulletin (Issue 7, December 2020)*. <https://myemail.con stantcontact.com/UNFCCC-Adaptation-Finance-Bulletin—Issue-7—December-2020-.html?soid=1117347475566&aid=zsmUJfe61mg>

Adaptation Fund.·2016. *Medium-Term Strategy 2018-2022* (UNFCCC Adaptation Fund), <https://www.adaptation-fund.org/wp-content/uploads/2018/03/Medium-Term-Strategy-2018-2022-final-03.01-1-1.pdf> [Accessed 30 October 2021].

——.·2017. *Adaptation Fund at 10 Years: Pioneering Action, Innovation and Learning* (UNFCCC Adaptation Fund), <https://cop23.unfccc.int/news/adaptation-fund-at-10-years-pioneering-action-innovation-and-learning> [Accessed 30 October 2021].

——. 2020a. *Briefing Note*. <https://www.adaptation-fund.org/wp-content/uploads/2018/08/AF-Informational-Briefing-July-2020-web.pdf> [Accessed 26 February 2022]

——.·2020b. *Climate Finance Adaptation: Direct Access*, (UNFCCC Adaptation Fund), <https://www.adaptation-fund.org/wp-content/uploads/2019/11/Direct-Access-June-2020.pdf> [Accessed 30 October 2021].

——. 2021. *Accreditation*, <https://www.adaptation-fund.org/apply-funding/accreditation/> [Accessed 2 October 2021].

Adaptation Fund Board.·2020. *Techreport of the Second Session of the Thirty–Fifth Meeting of the Adaptation Fund Board*, (UNFCCC Adaptation Fund Board), <https://www.adaptation-fund.org/wp-content/uploads/2020/12/AFB.B.35.b.8-Report-of-the-second-session-of-the-thirty-fifth-meeting-of-AFB.pdf> [Accessed 30 October 2021].

——.·2021. *Operational Policies and Guidelines for Parties to Access Resources from the Adaptation Fund*, (UNFCCC Adaptation Fund Board), <https://www.adaptation-fund.org/wp-content/uploads/2017/08/OPG-amended-in-October-2017-1_para41-corrected.pdf> [Accessed 30 October 2021].

Asian Development Bank.·2020. *Decoding Article 6 of the Paris Agreement-Version II*, (Manila, Philippines: Asian Development Bank), <https://www.adb.org/publications/decoding-article-6-paris-agreement-v2> [Accessed 30 October 2021].

Build Back Better. 2021. *About Us*, <https://buildbackbetter.co.nz/about-us/> [Accessed 2 October 2021].

Chemnick, Jean. 2021. 'Cost of Carbon Pollution Pegged at $51 a Ton ', *Scientific American* <https://www.scientificamerican.com/article/cost-of-carbon-pollution-pegged-at-51-a-ton/> [Accessed 30 October 2021].

Climate Technology Centre and Network. 2021. *About the Climate Technology Centre and Network (CTCN)*, <https://www.ctc-n.org/about-ctcn> [Accessed 29 October 2021].

Cordes, Amalie Kongsted, and Emil Hageman Christensen.·2019. *Assessment of Climate Finance Channels for Increase in Norwegian Government Support – Annexes*, (Oslo: Norwegian Forum for Development and Environment), <https://www.forumfor.no/assets/docs/Annexes-to-Norwegian-study-of-finance-channels-INKA-24-November-2019.pdf> [Accessed 29 October 2021].

Dejgaard, Hans Peter, and Andrew Hattle.·2020. *Funding What Counts – Assessment of Channels for Increasing Norwegian Climate Finance*, (Oslo: The Norwegian Forum for Development and

Environment), <http://forumfor.no/nyheter/2020/fundingwhatcounts> [Accessed 4 November 2021].

DeSmog 2021 'World Leaders Met beneath Sunny Skies' <https://desmogblog.cmail20.com/t/ViewEmail/t/3D815467BEEDCF9D2540EF23F30FEDED/F3F4AA3A2281D2CEDDA3541AF197FE1F> [Accessed 30 January 2022]

Frankfurter Allgemeine Zeitung. 2021. 'Lehren Aus Covid-19: Ein Großer Vertrag Zur Bekämpfung Von Pandemien', *Frankfurter Allgemeine Zeitung* 29/03/2021. <https://www.faz.net/1.7269543> [Accessed 30 October 2021].

Global Environment Facility. 2016. *Climate Change Adaptation*, <https://www.thegef.org/topics/climate-change-adaptation> [Accessed 30 October 2021].

——. 2020. *Techreport of the Global Environment Facility to the Twenty-Sixth Session of the Conference of the Parties to the United Nations Framework Convention on Climate Change*, https://unfccc.int/sites/default/files/resource/cp2020_01E.pdf> [Accessed 30 October 2021].

Green Climate Fund. 2019. *GCF/B.24/Inf.08: Techreport on the Activities of the Secretariat*, (Green Climate Fund), <https://www.greenclimate.fund/document/gcf-b24-inf08> [Accessed 30 October 2021].

——. 2020. *Green Climate Fund*, <https://www.greenclimate.fund/> [Accessed 30 October 2021].

——. 2021a. *GCF Insight #17 Stakeholder Views on the Green Climate Fund's Direct Access Modality*, <https://www.ecoltdgroup.com/wp-content/uploads/2021/03/GCF-insight-17.pdf> [Accessed 30 October 2021].

——. 2021b. *Portfolio Dashboard*, <https://www.greenclimate.fund/projects/dashboard> [Accessed 30 October 2021].

Grimm, Julia, Lutz Weischer, and David Eckstein. 2018. *The Future Role of the Adaptation Fund in the International Climate Finance Architecture*, (Bonn, Germany: Germanwatch), <https://newclimate.org/wp-content/uploads/2018/10/The-future-role-of-the-Adaptation-fund-in-the-internatinal-climate-finance-architecture.pdf> [Accessed 30 January 2022].

Heinrich Böll Stiftung. 2011-2021. *Climate Funds Update*, (Washington DC: Heinrich Böll Stiftung), <https://climatefundsupdate.org/about-climate-finance/climate-finance-fundamentals/> [Accessed 30 October 2021].

——. 2020. *Climate Funds Upyear – Adaptation Fund*, (Washington DC: Heinrich Böll Stiftung), <https://climatefundsupdate.org/the-funds/adaption-fund/> [Accessed 30 October 2021].

Independent Expert Group on Climate Finance. 2020. *Delivering on the $100 Billion Climate Finance Commitment and Transforming Climate Finance*, (Independent Expert Group on Climate Finance), <https://www.un.org/sites/un2.un.org/files/100_billion_climate_finance_report.pdf> [Accessed 30 October 2021].

Intergovernmental Panel on Climate Change Core Writing Team. 2001. *TAR Climate Change 2001: Synthesis Techreport*, (Cambridge, UK: IPCC), <https://www.ipcc.ch/report/ar3/syr/> [Accessed 30 October 2021].

——. 2014. *AR5 Synthesis Techreport: Climate Change 2014*, (IPCC), <https://www.ipcc.ch/report/ar5/syr/> [Accessed 29 October 2021].

Kappelle, Maarten. 2020. *United in Science 2020: UN Climate Report*, (Geneva: World Meteorological Organization), <https://www.researchgate.net/publication/344176836_United_In_Science_2020_-_UN_Climate_Report> [Accessed 30 October 2021].

Manuamorn, Ornsaran. 2020. *Governance of International Adaptation Finance for Local Climate Change Adaptation: An Analysis of Adaptation Fund Projects*, Doctoral thesis, Maastricht University.

Network for Greening the Financial System. 2019. *A Call for Action: Climate Change as a Source of Financial Risk*, (NGFS), <https://www.ngfs.net/sites/default/files/medias/documents/ngfs_first_comprehensive_report_-_17042019_0.pdf> [Accessed 30 October 2021].

Pallemaerts, Marc, and Jonathan Armstrong. 2009. 'Financial Support to Developing Countries for Climate Change Mitigation and Adaptation: Is the European Union Meeting Its Earlier Commitments?', *Studia Diplomatica*, 62 (4), 24.

Phillips, Carly A., Astrid Caldas, Rachel Cleetus, Kristina A. Dahl, Juan Declet-Barreto, Rachel Licker, L. Delta Merner, J. Pablo Ortiz-Partida, Alexandra L. Phelan, Erika Spanger-Siegfried, Shuchi Talati, Christopher H. Trisos, and Colin J. Carlson. 2020. 'Compound Climate Risks in the Covid-19 Pandemic', *Nature Climate Change*, 10 (7), 586–88.

TANGO International.·2018. *Overall Evaluation of the Adaptation Fund*, (Evaluation Team), <https://www.adaptation-fund.org/wp-content/uploads/2018/06/AF_Phase2_Eval_4June.pdf> [Accessed 30 October 2021].

United Kingdom Research and Innovation. 2021. *UKRI Prepares for COP26 with Global Climate Change Events: Cambridge Network*, <https://www.ukri.org/news/ukri-prepares-for-cop26-with-global-climate-change-events/> [Accessed 30 January 2022].

United Nations Environment Programme.·2021. *Adaptation Gap Techreport 2020*, <http://www.unep.org/resources/adaptation-gap-report-2020> [Accessed 30 October 2021].

United Nations Framework Convention on Climate Change 2001 *Decision 5/CP.7 Implementation of Article 4, Paragraphs 8 and 9, of the Convention (Decision 3/CP.3 and Article 2, Paragraph 3, and Article 3, Paragraph 14, of the Kyoto Protocol)* (Marrakech, Morocco: UNFCCC Conference of the Parties 7) <https://unfccc.int/sites/default/files/13a01p32.pdf> [Accessed 30 October 2021].

—— 2002 *Techreport of the Conference of the Parties on Its Seventh Session Held at Marrakesh from 29 October to 10 November 2001* (Marrakesh, Morocco: UNFCCC Conference of the Parties 7) <https://unfccc.int/resource/docs/cop7/13a01.pdf> [Accessed 30 October 2021].

—— 2007 *Techreport of the Conference of the Parties Serving as the Meeting of the Parties to the Kyoto Protocol on Its Third Session, Held in Bali from 3 to 15 December 2007* UNFCCC Conference of the Parties (Bali, Indonesia) <https://unfccc.int/resource/docs/2007/cmp3/eng/09a01.pdf> [Accessed 30 October 2021].

—— 2011 *Techreport of the Conference of the Parties on Its Sixteenth Session, Held in Cancun from 29 November to 10 December 2010* (Cancun, Mexico: UNFCCC Conference of the Parties 16) < https://unfccc.int/resource/docs/2010/cop16/eng/07a01.pdf> [Accessed 30 October 2021].

—— 2015 *Techreport of the Conference of the Parties on Its Twenty-First Session, Held in Paris from 30 November to 11 December 2015. Addendum. Part Two: Action Taken by the Conference of the Parties at Its Twenty-First Session* (Paris: UNFCCC Conference of the Parties 21) <https://unfccc.int/sites/default/files/13a01p32.pdf> [Accessed 30 October 2021].

——.·2021. *National Adaptation Plans: UNFCCC*, https://unfccc.int/topics/adaptation-and-resilience/workstreams/national-adaptation-plans> [Accessed 30 October 2021].

Robert Hales
Chapter 20
An analysis of the global carbon market post COP26: How fossil fuel emission reductions and offset integrity must guide carbon market operation

Abstract: Carbon markets have developed into an international market mechanism based on the agreements reached at COP26 in Glasgow in 2021. Carbon market development and the agreement at COP26 are not without their problems. Examining the history of the development of the agreement reveals many issues which are still relevant today. The main issues include the capacity of the market to deliver large-scale and rapid fossil fuel emissions reductions, the integrity of the accounting framework, potential impacts on biodiversity and natural capital and risks around the delivery of co-benefits and the failure of robust mechanisms for the rights of Indigenous people. The most pressing issue is that the agreed market mechanism will not deliver a rapid reduction in fossil fuel emissions. Hope exists in that Nationally Determined Contribution (NDCs) and the transparency around the carbon markets process can be strong enough to reduce the risks of carbon market failure. There are principles that can be applied to carbon trading and emissions reductions. The carbon integrity movement can adopt such principles and guide the carbon market. The carbon market mechanism in place cannot deliver required emissions reductions unless carbon integrity principles are adopted.

Keywords: carbon markets, paris agreement, carbon integrity, COP26, paris rulebook, climate finance, carbon offsets, COVID-19

Introduction: Climate change, market failure and carbon markets

Climate change has been described as the largest externality of the world economy (Nordhaus 2019). If climate change is treated as an externality how then might the costs that are external to economic production, in its various forms, be included in that production? Who will pay the cost? How will this cost be determined? Will there be a valid system of accounting for the true costs? What happens if this system fails to deliver its promise? The debate over financing the cost of climate change has been a central feature of national climate change politics and a sticking

https://doi.org/10.1515/9783110733488-020

point of global negotiations for decades (Hijam 2021: 10). Recent outcomes at COP26 have cemented much of the process of how carbon is traded. There are still issues regarding the implication and consequences of the rulebook of the Paris Agreement (Nieto 2022). This chapter is about how the market approach of climate change mitigation includes carbon within the means of a global system of production and explores issues with the integrity of the system.

The Paris Agreement is more than an agreement on targets for a net-zero world. Critical to the agreement is the rulebook (Rajamani and Bodansky 2019) which was the topic of negotiations at COP26 in Glasgow. The rulebook contains Article 6 – which includes measures to implement an international carbon market and other mechanisms to assist reduction in emissions (Edmonds et al. 2021). ITMOs provide the framework for a carbon market. The following excerpt from Article 6 outlines how ITMOs not only assist in NDC (i.e., net-zero emission targets of nations) but also aim to assist in sustainable development. It also indicates the potential issues around the accounting process.

> Parties shall, where engaging on a voluntary basis in cooperative approaches that involve the use of internationally transferred mitigation outcomes towards Nationally Determined Contributions, promote sustainable development and ensure environmental integrity and transparency, including in governance, and shall apply robust accounting to ensure, *inter alia*, the avoidance of double-counting, consistent with guidance adopted by the Conference of the Parties serving as the meeting of the Parties to this Agreement.
>
> (United Nations Framework Convention on Climate Change 2015: 4)

Within Article 6 there is guidance on a mechanism to contribute to the mitigation of greenhouse gas emissions and support sustainable development. In particular, at COP26 much of the rulebook was agreed upon to incentivise and facilitate participation in the mitigation of greenhouse gas emissions by public and private entities. The aim of the rulebook is to create tradable credits that will contribute to the reduction of emission in the host country, which will also benefit another country to fulfil its NDC (Rajamani and Bodansky 2019).

Prior to the agreement around points within Article 6, many local jurisdictions, nations and regional collectives have implemented their own carbon trading systems. There is also a strong international voluntary carbon trading system that is growing in several trading mechanisms and volume of emissions covered by carbon taxes and trading mechanisms. When both these types of carbon markets – official country and regional markets, and voluntary markets are totalled, the volume and number of markets are considerable.

The implementation of these markets is already influencing the global political economy as the costs of the goods and services in one particular carbon market are being transferred to other countries markets by adding the cost of carbon through trade regulations at the national or regional boundary (Neuhoff and Ritz 2019). Not only are there costs for polluters but there are significant risks for many stakeholders in the implementation of the carbon market. The purpose of this chapter is to examine the risks involved in the emerging global carbon markets and how agreement on Article 6 still has carbon integrity issues. This chapter will outline the basic elements of a carbon market, the trend in the global carbon market, the issues and risks of carbon markets and the inclusion of sustainable development into the agreement on carbon markets. Lastly, principles will be offered to guide the carbon market and promote the integrity of social and ecological informed development are provided.

The carbon market

Carbon markets across the world have several common features. The components of a carbon market include carbon credits, baselines, cap-and-trade, financial incentives and allowances. To understand carbon markets the elements of the market need to be understood.

Carbon credit – A carbon credit is the cornerstone of the carbon market. These credits are tradable entities that can be represented in the market in two ways: permits or certificates. They are both related to a project. A permit gives the permit holder the right to emit a certain amount of greenhouse gas into the atmosphere. Whereas a certificate refers to a project that represents the removal or avoidance of one tonne of greenhouse gas from the atmosphere.

Compliance market – A compliance market is created by an entity (either government or government backed) to regulate a carbon market. These markets usually adopt a cap-and-trade emissions reductions model where carbon traders buy and sell carbon credits to comply with a limit (cap) imposed on their emissions. The cap is key to reducing emissions. The company may breach the carbon pollution cap imposed on them, but they are then buying certified carbon credits in the market.

Voluntary market – A voluntary carbon market functions outside of compliance markets. Voluntary carbon credits are traded by businesses, governments, NGOs and individuals to offset their emissions by purchasing carbon credits. The carbon credits may or may not be certified by the government through a regulatory authority. The Gold Standard (2021a) and Verified Carbon Standard (Verra 2022) are two examples of voluntary offset standards.

Scaling-up to a global market

The international carbon emissions trading scheme under Article 6 of the Paris Agreement has been in the spotlight at the UN climate talks for many years. The debate around Article 6 at the COPs (Conference of Parties) has focussed on how the activities under Article 6 will be regulated and monitored. Some countries have wanted strict rules whereas others wanted more flexibility. Some countries also wanted a central authority while others wanted a non-centralised regulatory framework.

Despite there being no agreement on the matters within Article 6 for the 4 years leading up to COP26, many countries had already designed and implemented mitigation actions that align with the cooperative measures' mechanism of Article 6. Three areas categorise mitigation actions under Article 6. These are regulations, carbon markets and price instruments. Figure 20.1 represents these three elements of the cooperative mechanism of Article 6.

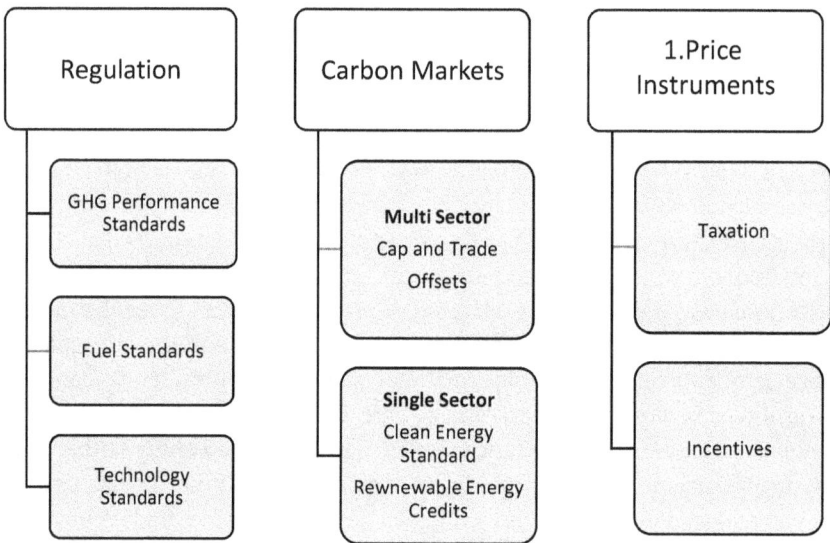

Figure 20.1: Elements of the cooperative mechanism of Article 6.

The major focus of the three areas has been the development of the cooperative arrangement of carbon markets.

Within the carbon market deliberations, three features received attention at COP26. The first is an agreement on ITMOs – internationally transferred mitigation outcomes – which are, in essence, a form of carbon credit that is traded between countries. The second area of deliberation is the trading platform which the United Nations would oversee to facilitate carbon trading involving the public and private sector (while fostering sustainable development). The third area is the acknowledgement of non-market cooperation. In practice, this means foreign aid for addressing such matters as assisting emissions reduction (mitigation), climate change adaptation, finance, technology transfer and capacity building.

Despite the longstanding disputes over Article 6 it is interesting to note that at the time of writing there were 64 carbon pricing initiatives across the world and of these 45 covered the whole country where they were initiated and 36 subnational jurisdictions had carbon markets in operation (World Bank 2021a). See Figure 20.2 for the share of greenhouse gas emissions under carbon trading systems.

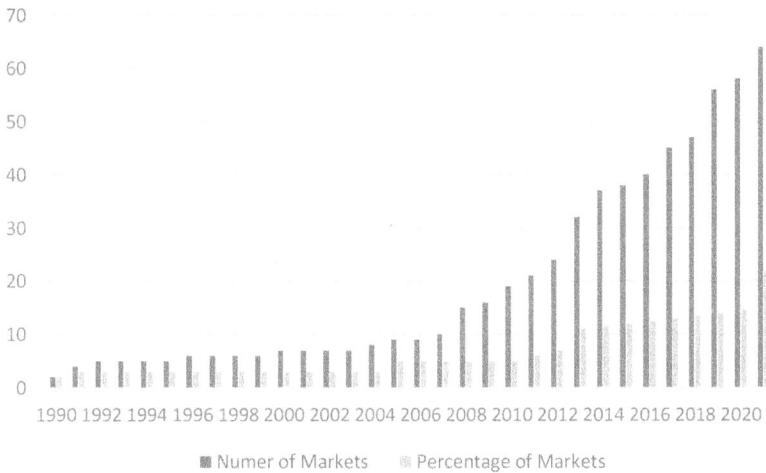

Figure 20.2: Share of global GHG emissions under emissions trading systems.
Source: The World Bank State and Trends of Carbon Pricing (2021b).

International pressure on countries without a carbon market is growing, with the EU announcing to protect domestic industry from goods and services outside of the EU that have not included the cost of carbon. The EU intends on taxing imports based on the greenhouse gases emitted during the manufacture of the import. A primary reason for this is the EU wants to halt polluting industries from shifting production outside the EU to avoid carbon costs and then exporting back into the EU (International Institute for Sustainable Development 2021).

Despite historic disagreements over the global mechanism to reduce carbon through Articles 6 there was momentum towards the global market for carbon prior to COP26, as indicated by an increasing number of large corporations committing to carbon emissions reduction in line with Paris commitments (Environment Defense Fund 2021). There was increased attention by companies directed toward achieving carbon neutrality sooner and to address scope three emissions (emission in their value chain outside their direct operation, e.g., supply chains). The adoption of a global standard for net-zero emissions through the Science Based Targets Initiative signifies the growing trend towards businesses becoming net-zero (Science Based Targets Initiative 2021). Companies committing early to net-zero emission can buy time to develop technologies to decarbonise their operations especially in sectors that do not yet have innovations to reduce emissions of their operations (airline industries being the most obvious in their pursuit of non-fossil fuel power aircraft).

Issues involved in adopting a carbon market

There are several issues surrounding carbon markets. The issues relate to inherent problems of carbon markets and then there are the problems associated with the application of the carbon market at an international, cooperative level. These issues can be examined from four perspectives: the non-linear nature of the carbon system, accounting problems and gaming, environmental and social justice issues and carbon market inefficiencies (Sovacool 2011). These issues apply to the emerging international carbon market after agreement on Article 6 at COP26 in Glasgow in 2021.

Non-linear nature of climate change

Calculating carbon credits faces systematic issues due to the inherent problems of constructing a system that attempts to repair human's negative impact on the complex cycle of carbon in the world. These relate to how carbon from fossil fuel is accounted for in present 'natural' carbon cycles and the problem of timescales of carbon and the difficulty in accounting for carbon credits over time. These problems can be conceived in two ways: non-natural/natural carbon divide and carbon across time.

Non-natural carbon

The source of carbon emitted into the atmosphere matters. Carbon that has been stored in the ground and then used as fossil fuels has a different overall effect compared to the emissions from the natural stock of carbon in the Earth's biosphere. Additionally, the anthropogenic types of carbon including chlorofluorocarbons, hydrochlorofluorocarbons, and bromofluorocarbons produced from burning fossil fuels have increased warming effects compared to the carbon emitted from biogenic sources. Thus, one tonne of carbon emitted from burning fossil fuels can have greater effects than one tonne of carbon from burning vegetative matter. Despite carbon accounting measures adopted to decrease the risks of underestimating the impact, problems persist regarding accounting for the impact of emissions from fossil fuels (Bebbington and Larrinaga-Gonzalez 2008; Bebbington et al. 2020; Gonzalez Moguel et al. 2021). To keep within a 1.5 °C carbon budget, almost 60% of oil and fossil methane gas, and 90% of coal must remain unextracted (Welsby et al. 2021). Offsets need to address this core problem to be an effective solution to climate change mitigation.

Carbon across time

Carbon markets must contend with the problem of time and carbon sequestration. The trading of carbon occurs at one time (the exchange of money for carbon credits) but the life of carbon continues past the moment of the trade. There are multiple issues with the unpredictability of longevity and quality of forests as carbon sinks (Pugh et al. 2019; Qubaja et al. 2020). There is also the issue of the time scale of carbon residing in the atmosphere. Some carbon is expected to remain in the atmosphere for 1,000 years (Shaffer 2010).

Imperfect markets and gaming in accounting

Carbon markets have problems associated with gaming and accounting issues. The pressure to promote high volumes of credit at low costs creates a range of problems. These are outlined below.

Additionality is a major issue in carbon markets. This refers to the counting of offsets which would have happened because the project would have proceeded in any case. To count as an offset a project needs to be added to normal or planned activity to count as an offset. A project is used in the broadest sense here as it may involve no activity as in the case of conservation of forests or other biological offsets. This is the area in which the most significant issue can occur around additionality. It is particularly common with forest conservation (Campbell, Herremans, and Kleffner 2018). If a forest is counted as an offset but was not threatened by future clearing, then the offset should not be counted as the amount of carbon is not additional. The offset is not adding to a reduction in carbon emissions. In such instances, it is difficult to determine the baseline.

In addition to this problem of what is the baseline of activity, the issue of non-natural carbon is an issue. Even if, for example, a forest is initially planned to be cleared but is then halted using a carbon offset project intervention, the carbon offset relates to stopping a loss of carbon in natural a system and does not address the issue of reducing the primary cause of climate change/fossil fuel emissions.

Double-counting

A significant risk in carbon markets is double-counting. A country selling a carbon credit might claim the underlying emissions reduction for itself, while at the same time the country buying the credit also claims the same emissions reduction. Any international transfer of emission reductions should account for the flow of carbon across borders. Importantly in the context of Article 6 and the outcomes COP26, an international system of accounting is needed in which the country selling carbon credits adjusts its emissions upwards, and the country acquiring the carbon credits adjusts, by the same amount, downwards (Schneider et al. 2019; Schneider and La Hoz Theuer 2019).

Perverse incentives leading to low ambition

Prior to COP26 there was concern that Article 6 needed to develop mechanisms to improve the integrity of global carbon markets. The concern centred on the fact that a country may not set ambitious targets for an emissions sector and the market or selling credits in another sector may push seller countries not to include certain sectors in their NDCs. Thus, strong ambition in a sector needed to meet the Paris commitments may not occur (Martínez-Serrano and Cuerdo-Mir 2021). In some cases, the sale of carbon credits has led to increased emissions as a result of the financial incentives in the carbon market (Haya et al. 2020).

Low prices for carbon

To drive long-term investment and development carbon needs to be priced at levels strong enough to drive down emissions to meet agreed targets. It is one thing to have a market but the ambition behind the market needs to be strong for the mechanism to effectively reduce emissions. The first global stocktake under the Paris Agreement is in 2023 and this can be used in conjunction with a global carbon market system to translate high ambition NDCs into a reduction in emissions through strong (high) prices. Having a reserve baseline price that is high is critical to send the signal for the effectiveness of the mechanism (Hofbauer Pérez and Rhode 2020).

Environmental and social justice

Transaction costs

The costs of carbon trading include contracting, monitoring, reporting and verification of offset projects. These costs are borne by the project developers (sellers of carbon offsets) and associated Parties (consultants) and can be a considerable obstacle if the project does not have economies of scale. There are also costs to buyers of carbon offsets which includes evaluating the proposed project, making transaction and monitoring outcomes. Additionally, the type of offset project can lead to higher transaction costs. Biomass and soil carbon have high transactions costs due to difficulty in measurement, problems with establishing baselines and uncertainty of carbon stock (sequestration) maintained over time (Cacho, Lipper, and Moss 2013).

The effect of high transaction costs has an impact on project feasibility and particularly at smaller-scale projects and thus have a disproportionate impact at the local level. Offset projects may not deliver expected outcomes which in turn has consequences for smaller project owners (e.g., landholders) who may not have the means to adequately develop projects but are escapable of absorbing costs for project failures. High transaction costs favour larger project developers and therefore justice issues arise if sustainable development is another outcome of the trading of carbon.

Externalities still exist at the site of emissions

Carbon is not the only externality involved with burning fossil fuels. Carbon trading aims to include the externality of carbon within the market but the industries that are carbon polluters cannot assume that trading carbon decreases the impact on local communities at the site of emissions. Other pollutants have an impact on communities and thus carbon markets do not capture this and include communities into the market (Lejano, Kan, and Chau 2020).

Privatising carbon and excluding communities

The practice of enclosure of commons is a significant issue for Indigenous and traditional communities that are not part of a system of land tenure which is based on private property. The market-based approach to reducing emissions through trading carbon has come about through a dynamic interplay between corporate interests, NGOs, governments and multilateral financial institutions. As a result of the economies of scale inherent in the international trade of carbon, this combination will invariably lead to exclusion of Indigenous people and other marginalised groups. The inclusion of lands within carbon markets systems have led to privatising forests and other lands where sequestration can occur and excluding Indigenous people from the lands which their traditionally own (Cabello and Gilbertson 2012).

The Paris Agreement only asks Parties to respect promote and consider the rights of Indigenous people and other groups listed. It also states that Indigenous knowledge is appropriately integrated into adaptation. Indigenous rights are not legally binding.

Absent sustainable development goals

Article 6 contains a reference to sustainable development and positions the trading of carbon credits within this concept. However, there is little practical guidance on how this should occur in the text of Article 6. The transactions in a carbon market can bypass local communities and have a little positive effect on the local economy (Michaelowa 2011). The SDGs can offer some guidance on the co-benefits to Article 6 implementation (Olsen et al. 2019). However, SDGs were not included in the rule-book development of Article 6, and it will be up to each government to set requirements for project proponents to deliver co-benefits that contribute towards the achievement of SDGs. There was only mention of sustainable development – 'To promote the mitigation of greenhouse gas emissions while fostering sustainable development.' (UNFCCC 2015: 24) Without clear direction, there is a risk of poor outcomes for the local communities which include Indigenous communities.

Carbon market inefficiencies

A sufficient degree of standardisation is needed to ensure objectivity and keep transaction costs to a minimum. A lesson from the Clean Development Mechanism (CDM) is that standardisation can increase the objectivity of assessments and regulatory decisions on emission-reducing activities, enhance the simplicity of the regulatory system and the predictability of mitigation outcomes, and contribute to major reductions in transaction costs. Justice problems involve issues of dependency and the concentration of wealth among the rich, meaning carbon trading often counteracts attempts to reduce poverty. The issues are explored further in the literature on the problems of carbon markets (see Aldred 2012; Carton, Lund, and Dooley 2021; Pearse and Böhm 2014; Watt 2017).

Principles to guide and assess the article 6 international carbon market

Key features for the development of an effective market mechanism within Article 6 has been extensively examined (Edmonds et al. 2021; Greiner et al. 2019; Müller and Michaelowa 2019; Obergassel and Asche 2018; Schneider and La Hoz Theuer 2019). The issues regarding carbon markets have been largely translated into a set of principles as a result of COP25 deliberations on Article 6 of the Paris Agreement. A set of principles, known as the San José Principles for High Ambition and Integrity in International Carbon Markets was agreed upon by 32 countries in the lead up (and more countries subsequently) to COP 25 in Madrid. The principles constitute the basis upon which a fair and robust carbon market should be built.

The countries pledged to implement a framework for the Article 6 mechanism that, at a minimum, incorporates these 11 principles:

1. Maintain high ambition: Ensures environmental integrity and enables the highest possible mitigation ambition.
2. Push for progressive reduction: Delivers overall mitigation in global emissions, moving beyond zero-sum offsetting approaches to help accelerate the reduction of global greenhouse gas emissions.
3. No carry-over credits: Prohibits the use of pre-2020 units, Kyoto units and allowances and any underlying reductions toward achieving the goals of the Paris Agreement and other international goals.
4. No double-counting/balanced system: Ensures that double-counting is avoided and that all use of markets toward international climate goals is subject to corresponding adjustments (i.e., that a traded reduction counts toward the goals of the transferee country but against those of the transferor country).
5. Meet the Paris Agreement global goal: Avoids locking in levels of emissions, technologies or carbon intensive practices incompatible with the achievement of the Paris Agreement's long-term temperature goal.
6. Meet the Paris Agreement national commitments: Applies allocation and baseline methodologies that support the domestic achievement of the transferring countries' Nationally Determined Contributions (i.e., their commitments under the Paris Agreement) and contribute to the achievement of the Paris Agreement's long-term temperature goals.
7. Count CO_2 appropriately: Uses CO_2-equivalence in reporting and accounting for emissions and removals, fully applying the principles of transparency, accuracy, consistency, comparability and completeness.
8. Track and share information centrally: Uses centrally and publicly accessible infrastructure and systems to collect, track and share the information necessary for robust and transparent accounting.
9. Incentivise progress: Ensures incentives to progression and supports all Parties in moving toward economy-wide emission targets.
10. Financially support developing countries: Contributes to quantifiable and predictable financial resources to be used by developing country Parties that are particularly vulnerable to the adverse effects of climate change to meet the costs of adaptation to those effects.
11. Build capacity to participate: Recognises the importance of the capacity building to enable the widest possible participation by Parties under Article 6 (Ministry of Environment and Energy of Costa Rica 2019).

Known as the Unconventional Group, the countries that have been working since the Pre-COP25 in San José, Costa Rica, provide a principled approach to developing international carbon markets. It is hoped that these principles can be used in making an agreement on the details of implementing Article 6 of the Paris Agreement. The difficulty of reaching agreements relate to carry-over credits from the previous agreements (Kyoto Agreement) codifying aid to developing countries in the agreement and ultimate agreement on governance arrangement.

The lessons of the CDM can be used to improve scalability, reduce inefficiencies and deal with justice issues in development through an international cooperative market-based instrument. Operationalising Article 6 as agreed during COP26 needs to use lessons from the past.

> The CDM already possesses key tools that can be used to target emissions of full sectors, including SBLs [standardised baselines], performance benchmarks, positive lists, PoAs [programme of activities] and other measures to enable a scaled-up approach. . . . . Importantly, they still allow credits to be issued for individual activities, and in doing so they maintain a clear link and incentive between the effectiveness of the activities and the credits they receive.
> (European Bank for Reconstruction and Development, 2017: 22)

Lessons learnt from the CDM have been translated into the intent of the San Juan Principles (Ministry of Environment and Energy of Costa Rica 2019). The combination of this provides a number of imperatives that need to be considered in developing Article 6. There needs to be an effective price on carbon drive long-term investment and technology change, to drastically lower emissions. There should be a standardisation measure for the determination of emission reductions (e.g., baseline setting, MRV procedures) to have an equitable system. An efficient process needs to be developed for carbon trading to decrease transaction costs. Standardised and objective approaches to additionality and estimation of emission reductions are needed. The governing body needs to have exercise power for overseeing the process of the international market. Ensuring carbon markets foster projects that are relevant to the sustainable development priorities of countries is an important principle to prioritise in the framework of the mechanism. Also providing capacity for developing countries to develop projects and trading capacity at the local level is important. A single currency needs to be adopted to enable ITMOs to be traded and a central transaction log needs to be developed that is transparent for all interested Parties, not just the Parties trading. The principle of seller liability is important so that carbon credits cannot be reclaimed if, for example, that country fails to meet its NDC. A standard process of environmental integrity for project design, implementation and monitoring is needed. The SDGs are an important tool in this regard. A no harm safeguard needs to be part of traded credits to avoid negative environmental and social impacts. The San José Principles can be used a critical lens to view the outcomes of COP26 and agreement on the Article 6 mechanism.

Article 6 agreement at COP26

After four years of protracted negotiations, agreement on Article 6 was reached at COP26 (UNFCCC 2021). The outcomes of COP26 and the agreement on how carbon can be traded between countries is offered below with analysis of key issues that impact on effectiveness and equity in reducing emissions.

The matter of governance and oversight was agreed. Disputes around carbon offsetting projects has oversight through the agreement. In independent grievance process was developed to satisfy key Indigenous and environmental groups.

A major issue in the agreement on Article 6.2 is around how fossil fuel pollution may not be reduced as there are no limits on carbon trade of emissions derived from fossil fuel burning. Article 6.2 governs bilateral cooperation via ITMOs. In this section of the agreement the guidelines will see countries link their emissions trading schemes, for example, or buying offsets towards their national climate goals. This is a good outcome. However, no limits on how much could be traded was stipulated in the agreement thus fossil fuel pollution could be traded without any (or limited) reduction in overall emissions from fossil fuels being made in the source country. The carbon market can enable continued fossil fuel carbon pollution with nature-based solutions to offset the emissions. While this may sound acceptable, this trade does not have mechanisms to reduce fossil fuel emissions and thus does not take into account for the absolute carbon budget of burnable fossil fuel to keep warming well below 2 degrees.

Double-counting at the country-level was also addressed to some degree. Corresponding adjustments are to be made under Article 6.2 in relation to bilateral trade between countries. In effect carbon sequestered in one country can offset emission through trade in another country. In reality, this may be difficult to achieve from an accounting perspective because of timelines of target years being different in multiple traded communities.

Voluntary markets are cause for greater concern. Under the other international mitigation purposes there is the inclusion of voluntary carbon markets. This may sound like a good development but there are problems with allowing for non-authorised credits not being adjusted in the country where carbon offset is purchased. In this instance a corporation could purchase an offset in another country and count it as their net-zero emissions targets but the country where the purchase is made needs to apply a corresponding adjustment to its own carbon accounting inventory to reflect the transaction. However, the country may choose to count this as a non-authorised credit and thus does not need to be counted in its national inventory. Thus, double-counting is still possible in the systems of trade.

This issue was debated at COP26, but a solution was not adopted. Previous Article 6 drafts had included the option to explicitly manage this issue, via the creation of second-tier Paris Agreement Support Units. These units would have to be compulsorily adjusted by the host country so double-counting could be avoided. Not having this adjustment is a major loophole as countries can keep credits and still profit from the sale of non- Paris Agreement aligned carbon trading.

The biggest issue regarding Article 6 was subparagraph 4. The section allows for the creation of a centralised hub replacing the CDM. The CDM (through the Kyoto Protocol) created millions of carbon credits through thousands of emissions reduction projects. As outlined earlier in this chapter, these credits are of low integrity. In other words, they may not have mitigated their espoused reductions and most of the projects they financed would have happened anyway without support through this system. This old system has not been completely scrapped in the Article 6 agreement at COP26. The agreement will most likely allow around 300 million of these zombie credits to be transferred within the new Article 6 agreement of the Paris Agreement. Although the Article 6 rulebook (Rajamani and Bodansky 2019) has excluded the use of national credits generated between 2015 and 2021 under the UN scheme known as REDD+ (Reducing Emissions from Deforestation and Forest Degradation), the carry-over credit problem means that countries do not have to set ambitious national emissions reduction targets.

Another important failure of Article 6 agreement is the low-level commitment to reducing the zero-sum game of offsetting. As argued earlier in this chapter offsetting can be used as a licence to keep polluting. The way to reduce this perverse impact of a credit system where the same unit of carbon can be repeatedly traded is to cancel each batch of credits that is traded. Under the Article 6 agreement only a mandatory 2% cancellation of each credit traded is needed under Article 6.4. This is too low for meaningful reductions in absolute fossil fuel emissions reductions. Additionally bilateral agreement for trade in carbon remains exempt from the mandatory 2% cancellation of traded carbon.

Lastly there are human rights issues which have not been addressed in Article 6 agreements. There is wording in the final text, but it did not include important mechanisms to ensure these rights are upheld. The text overlooks Indigenous peoples' right to free, prior and informed consent. On the (slightly) positive side there is a body which will oversee grievances from Indigenous people and communities which is independent from the body setting and administering carbon trading. This is a good outcome despite not having a robust mechanism to examine and procedurally address concerns.

Politics of sustainable development and risks in international carbon markets

Sustainable development can be strengthened within Article 6 of the Paris Agreement. Lessons learnt under the CDM about sustainable development can be applied to future progress on carbon market mechanisms. Sustainable development issues in multilateral instruments and institutions outside the UNFCCC is also important to consider the development of the mechanism for carbon trading in the Paris Agreement.

These experiences with the CDM and other instruments and institutions can help inform future Article 6 development post initial agreement. Important references in the Paris Agreement on sustainable development and safeguard provisions are vital to ensure sustainable development is a primary outcome of carbon trading. It would be ironic if the international carbon market adopted under the Paris Agreement produces an externality of increased harm on sustainable development as measured by the SDGs.

Political and technical barriers have prevented the integration of sustainable development impact assessment and safeguards under Article 6 market mechanisms. Provisions on enhancing sustainable development have been contested during the negotiations of Article 6 of the Paris Agreement up to and including COP26. This is due to the lack of specific text on the promotion of sustainable development in Article 6. Despite the lack of positive outcomes concerning sustainable development, it is not a technical issue that is the roadblock for the inclusion of sustainable development in carbon market mechanisms but rather a political constraint.

The significant reason for including nature-based solutions is as a mitigation strategy for emission reductions is because of co-benefits. Although there is a need for a drastic reduction in fossil fuel, the extra positive impacts of nature-based solutions in addition to emissions reductions is a significant consideration in determining the benefits of an offset. Investments in nature-based solutions can generate significant co-benefits for the local communities, ecosystem services and biodiversity conservation. Based on this rationale, greenhouse gas mitigation must not be the sole reason for adopting an international carbon market under Article 6 of the Paris Agreement.

Other existing procedures can be applied to safeguard sustainable development outcomes within a globally agreed carbon market. The Green Climate Fund's Environmental and Social Policy and the Adaptation Fund's Environmental and Social Policy (Adaptation Fund 2013; Green Climate Fund 2019) are existing and agreed set of rules for explaining global financial instruments. This type of policy could be useful in guiding sustainable development policy safeguards in the global carbon market. Many countries have already adopted these in national legislation so the adoption of such frameworks may be more achievable.

The Green Climate Fund stipulates that initiatives are 'designed and implemented in a manner that will promote, protect and fulfil universal respect for, and observance of, human rights for all recognised by the United Nations' (Green Climate Fund 2019: 7). The Green Climate Fund investment criteria indicators provide a robust framework for building safeguards for sustainable development outcomes with an international carbon market. These criteria are:

- Potential indicators to assess environmental co-benefits: Degree to which the project or programme promotes positive environmental externalities such as air quality, soil quality, conservation, biodiversity, etc.;
- Potential indicators to assess social co-benefits: Potential for externalities in the form of expected improvements, for women and men as relevant, in areas such as health and safety, access to education, improved regulation and/or cultural preservation;
- Potential indicators to assess the gender-sensitive development impact: Explanation of how the project activities will address the needs of women and men to correct prevailing inequalities in climate change vulnerability and risks;
- Potential indicators to assess economic co-benefits: Potential for externalities in the form of expected improvements in areas such as expanded and enhanced job markets, job creation and poverty alleviation for women and men, increased and/or expanded involvement of local industries; increased collaboration between industry and academia; growth of private funds attracted; contribution to an increase in productivity and competitive capacity; improved sector income-generating capacity; contribution to an increase in energy security; change in water supply and agricultural productivity in targeted areas, etc. (Green Climate Fund 2019).

There is a real risk of the future carbon market under Article 6 of not adopting guidance on sustainable development. This risk is real as there is concern that the same mistakes will be repeated as in the CDM mechanisms, which failed to deliver sustainable development outcomes (Asian Development Bank 2020). The matters raised above in the points within the Green Climate Fund relate to projects and it is at this level that assessment should be made about the co-benefits of any credit being traded in a carbon market.

There has been some progress on a mechanism for assessing sustainable development in the international carbon market development in the Paris Agreement. A methodology to assess the transformational impact of policies and actions has been developed through the Initiative for Climate Action Transparency Transformational Change Methodology. This guidance document attempts to provide assessment procedures and measures to seek synergies for climate action and sustainable development (see Initiative for Climate Action Transparency 2020). While this guidance is appropriate for the level of NDCs – that is, national-level – this guidance document does not provide adequate guidance on the project-level or relate that to a carbon credit or ITMO. Sustainable Development Goals metrics are mentioned as a measure for example, but this level of goal is difficult to translate into the project-level where the co-benefits is disbenefits are likely to exist. Extensive guidance materials on the impact of the project and social impact assessment have been published by the International Association of Impact Assessment (Vanclay 2003). The processes of evaluation and the development of indicators for co-benefits of carbon credits still require further development before the concerns raised above can be fully satisfied.

Principles to maximise emissions reduction activities and guide the integrity of social and ecological informed development

Principles for real emissions reduction carbon integrity within carbon markets are provided here for the purpose of guidance on maximising emissions reduction activities in line with the 1.5-degree target of the Paris Agreement as well as achieving the integrity of social and ecological informed activities. The principles to guide the offset hierarchy are outlined below. The principles have been informed by the arguments and discussion presented above. Key documents that have informed the principles include:

- *Net-Zero Emissions Standards* from Science Based Targets (2021)
- *Voluntary Carbon Market Integrity Consultation Feedback Report* (2021)
- *Consideration of Nature-Based Solutions as Offsets in Corporate Climate Change Mitigation Strategies* from the World Resources Institute (Seymour and Langer 2021)
- *Above and Beyond Carbon Offsetting* from Carbon Market Watch (2020)

Principle 1: Nature-based offset solutions should only be used for abating 10% of an organisation's operational emissions. This is based on the new Science Based Targets Standard announced in 2021.

Principle 2: For organisations that have fossil fuel emissions of greater than 10% of emissions that cannot be abated through present technology then rapid fossil fuel emissions reduction in existing, easy to abate emissions should be implemented.

Principle 3: Nature-based offset solutions should not be used in the abatement of an organisation's fossil fuel emissions if an alternative abatement action presently exists. Rapid reductions in fossil fuel emissions are the imperative.

Principle 4: An offset must be used in real-time and future unproven offset abatement strategies such as carbon capture and storage should not be used in net-zero emission planning.

Principle 5: Offsets should include measurable co-benefits to local communities if the offset occurs within the locality of the community. Literature on a just transition should inform best practice.

Principle 6: Where Indigenous communities are involved in offsets then the principle of Free Prior Informed Consent should govern the inclusion (or not) of Indigenous people in the offset project.

Principle 7: Offsets should be reported with robust transparency and accountability processes at the organisation level.

Principle 8: Carbon offsets used in once country by a country cannot be used in other countries – offsets need to be cancelled upon initial trade. The use of offsets should support high ambition NDCs.

Principle 9: Nature-based solution used as offsets need to have positive conservation and biodiversity benefits.

Principle 10: Offsets should have adaptation benefits as well as mitigation benefits.

The principles can be applied the way in which carbon markets evolve under the implementation Article 6 of the Paris Agreement as agreed at COP26 Glasgow. The new rules under Article 6 will guide the private sector or voluntary carbon market activities however the rules have been criticised as insufficient to limit fossil fuel emissions and give a licence for companies and countries to continue polluting. Already there are responses to the problems and concerns inherent in Article 6. Gold Standard have indicated problems with the dual system of credits aligned with country NDCs and the voluntary market (Gold Standard 2021b). In effect there are two systems of carbon markets which present considerable challenges of potential double-counting. The Voluntary Carbon Market Integrity (VCMI) Initiative (2021) will likely provide more direction to the offset market on how credits should not be double counted and assist in how the market system can contribute the Paris aligned targets. A focus on fossil fuels and the carbon budget will ensure carbon integrity in the future

Carbon offsets post-COVID-19 pandemic

The COVID-19 crisis has impacted economies across the globe. Previously economic shocks have impacted on carbon markets as indicated by significant decreases in the price of carbon during the financial crisis of 2008 (Koch et al. 2014). However, during the COVID-19 crisis prices of carbon increased. For the G20 countries over the period 20182021 there was an average increase of 18% across all sectors in the price of carbon (Organisation for Economic Cooperation and Development 2021). The causes of this most likely include the following. Project scale has increased since 2008 and these projects have long development and implementation pathways. Second, demand has increased with continued ambition on international climate change targets. Third, irrespective of the Article 6 agreement at COP26 there have been a number of countries that have initiated carbon markets – the notable one being China in July 2021. Then there was the agreement of Article 6 at COP26 which acknowledges two markets – Voluntary markets and the country-based markets which are linked to ITMOs. The effect of the acknowledgement of two types of markets within the agreement provides confidence on carbon as a tradable commodity.

Additionally, climate finance initiatives such as The Glasgow Financial Alliance for Net-Zero (GFANZ) continue to build momentum and provide market confidence (2021). The commitment of GFANZ is an agreement by the financial services sector to align their activities and deliver more than $100 trillion investments to achieve net-zero by 2050. The alliance covers 40% of the world's total financial assets. Additionally, companies in the alliance have committed to set science-based targets to achieve net-zero in their companies. Future climate finance targets under the Paris Agreement through are also in play. At COP26 countries agreed to a process to develop a larger climate finance target to come into effect in 2025 with agreements to be made by 2024.

The effect of the COVID-19 crisis has not adversely affected carbon prices. Thus, the price of carbon will likely encourage the uptake of low-carbon emissions technology through placing higher costs on carbon intensive activities and burning fossil fuels. Additional benefits aligning with post-COVID-19 recovery are also possible through an effect of coordinated regional action and wider international coordination. A uniform carbon market approach across multiple country boundaries reduces the risk of carbon leakage and displaced production in the pursuit of finding cheap non-carbon tax locations. The revenue from carbon pricing must be used to invest in-country economies otherwise carbon is costly from a social and emissions perspectives. Some green investment occurred during the COVID-19 recovery investments phase which also stimulated markets in general and also provided confidence in carbon markets. On average, in OECD countries 2.5% of all spending and 18.0% of recovery spending was likely to reduce emissions (O'Callaghan and Murdock 2021). Despite the relatively small proportion of recovery expenditure targeting green initiatives the investment has provided support for carbon markets.

Conclusion

The agreement on Article 6 will have a long-lasting effect on developing the global carbon market. Major issues exist in the way in which the rulebook governs the trade of carbon and its social and environmental consequences (Rajamani and Bodansky 2019). The most pressing issue in terms of the integrity of the evolving carbon market after COP26 is the fundamental features of the market mechanism will lead to a slower than needed reduction in fossil fuel emissions. Hope exists in that NDCs and the transparency around this process can be strong enough to reduce the risks of carbon market failure. There are principles which can be applied to carbon trading and emissions reductions, and standards that can be developed. There is hope in this, that the carbon integrity movement can adopt such principles, develop legitimate and robust standards on the basis of those principles, and guide the carbon market. The carbon market mechanism in place cannot deliver required emissions reductions unless carbon integrity principles are adopted, and standards developed.

References

Adaptation Fund.·2013. *Environmental and Social Policy*, <https://www.adaptation-fund.org/wp-content/uploads/2015/09/Environmental-Social-Policy-approved-Nov2013.pdf> [Accessed 7 October 2021].

Aldred, Jonathan. 2012. 'The Ethics of Emissions Trading', *New Political Economy*, 17 (3), 339–60.

Asian Development Bank.·2020. *Decoding Article 6 of the Paris Agreement Version II*, <https://www.adb.org/publications/decoding-article-6-paris-agreement-v2> [Accessed 28 December 2021].

Bebbington, Jan, and Carlos Larrinaga-Gonzalez. 2008. 'Carbon Trading: Accounting and Reporting Issues', *European Accounting Review*, 17 (4), 697–717.

Bebbington, Jan, Thomas Schneider, Lorna Stevenson, and Alison Fox. 2020. 'Fossil Fuel Reserves and Resources Reporting and Unburnable Carbon: Investigating Conflicting Accounts', *Critical Perspectives on Accounting*, 66, 102083.

Cabello, Joanna, and Tamra Gilbertson. 2012. 'A Colonial Mechanism to Enclose Lands: A Critical Review of Two REDD+-Focused Special Issues', *Ephemera: Theory and Politics in Organization*, 12.

Cacho, Oscar J, Leslie Lipper, and Jonathan Moss. 2013. 'Transaction Costs of Carbon Offset Projects: A Comparative Study', *Ecological Economics*, 88, 232–43.

Campbell, Jessica, Irene M Herremans, and Anne Kleffner. 2018. 'Barriers to Achieving Additionality in Carbon Offsets: A Regulatory Risk Perspective', *Journal of Environmental Planning and Management*, 61 (14), 2570–89.

Carbon Market Watch.·2020. *Above and Beyond Carbon Offsetting: Alternatives to Compensation for Climate Action and Sustainable Development*, <https://carbonmarketwatch.org/wp-content/uploads/2020/12/AboveAndBeyondCarbonOffsetting.pdf> [Accessed 1 January 2022].

Carton, Wim, Jens Friis Lund, and Kate Dooley. 2021. 'Undoing Equivalence: Rethinking Carbon Accounting for Just Carbon Removal', *Frontiers in Climate*, 3, 30.

Edmonds, James, Sha Yu, Haewon Mcjeon, Dirk Forrister, Joseph Aldy, Nathan Hultman, Ryna Cui, Stephanie Waldhoff, Leon Clarke, and Stefano De Clara. 2021. 'How Much Could Article 6 Enhance Nationally Determined Contribution Ambition toward Paris Agreement Goals through Economic Efficiency?', *Climate Change Economics*, 12 (02), 2150007.

Environment Defense Fund.·2021. *Trends in Voluntary Carbon Markets*, <https://www.edf.org/sites/default/files/documents/trends-voluntary-carbon-markets_1.pdf> [Accessed 20 October 2021].

Glasgow Financial Alliance for Net Zero. 2021. *Homepage*, <https://www.gfanzero.com/> [Accessed 18 December 2021].

Gold Standard. 2021a. *Homepage*, <https://www.goldstandard.org/> [Accessed 1 January 2022].

——. 2021b. *Reflections on Article 6 Outcomes*, <https://www.goldstandard.org/blog-item/post-cop26-%E2%80%93-reflections-article-6-outcomes> [Accessed 15 December 2021].

Gonzalez Moguel, Regina, Felix Vogel, Sébastien Ars, Hinrich Schaefer, Jocelyn Turnbull, and Peter Douglas. 2021. 'Using Carbon-14 and Carbon-13 Measurements for Source Attribution of Atmospheric Methane in the Athabasca Oil Sands Region', *Atmospheric Chemistry and Physics Discussions*, 22, no. 3 (2022): 2121–2133.

Green Climate Fund.·2019. *Environmental and Social Policy*, <https://www.greenclimate.fund/sites/default/files/document/environment-social-policy.pdf> [Accessed 10 October 2021].

Greiner, Sandra, Thiago Chagas, Nicole Krämer, Axel Michaelowa, Dario Brescia, Stephan Hoch, and CF Climate Focus. 2019. 'Moving Towards Next Generation Carbon Markets: Observations from Article 6 Pilots' *Zurich Open Repository and Archive* <ZORA17360.pdf (uzh.ch)> [Accessed 26 February 2022].

Haya, Barbara, Danny Cullenward, Aaron L Strong, Emily Grubert, Robert Heilmayr, Deborah A
    Sivas, and Michael Wara. 2020. 'Managing Uncertainty in Carbon Offsets: Insights from
    California's Standardized Approach', *Climate Policy*, 20 (9), 1112–26.
Hijam, Liza Dallo Rihmo. 2021. *International Climate Negotiations: Processes and Politics*. (Oxford:
    Oxford University Press).
Hofbauer Pérez, Maria, and Carla Rhode. 2020. 'Carbon Pricing: International Comparison', *IFO
    DICE Report*, 18 (01), 49–59.
Initiative for Climate Action Transparency. 2020. 'Transformational Change Methodology:
    Assessing the Transformational Impacts of Policies and Actions.' in K.H. Olsen and N. Singh
    (eds.), *Initiative for Climate Action Transparency (ICAT)*, (Copenhagen: UNEP DTU Partnership
    and World Resources Institute),
Integrity Council for the Voluntary Carbon Market. 2021. *Homepage*, <https://icvcm.org/>
    [Accessed 16 December 2021].
International Institute for Sustainable Development. 2021. *EU Unveils Planned Carbon Tax on
    Imports Amid USA/Japanese Concerns*, <https://sdg.iisd.org/commentary/policy-briefs/eu-
    unveils-planned-carbon-tax-on-imports-amid-u-s-japanese-concerns/> [Accessed
    11 October 2021].
Koch, Nicolas, Sabine Fuss, Godefroy Grosjean, and Ottmar Edenhofer. 2014. 'Causes of the EU ETS
    Price Drop: Recession, CDM, Renewable Policies or a Bit of Everything?—New Evidence',
    Energy Policy, 73, 676–85.
Lejano, Raul P, Wing Shan Kan, and Ching Chit Chau. 2020. 'The Hidden Disequities of Carbon
    Trading: Carbon Emissions, Air Toxics, and Environmental Justice', *Frontiers in Environmental
    Scienc*e, 8 (2020): 593014.
Martínez-Serrano, Josu, and Miguel Cuerdo-Mir. 2021. 'Governance, Sustainability and Carbon
    Markets under the Paris Agreement', *International Journal of Innovation and Sustainable
    Development*, 15 (2), 206–22.
Michaelowa, Axel. 2011. 'Failures of Global Carbon Markets and CDM?', *Climate Policy*, 11 (1),
    839–41.
Ministry of Environment and Energy of Costa Rica. 2019. *San Jose Principles*,
    <https://cambioclimatico.go.cr/sanjoseprinciples/about-the-san-jose-principles/> [Accessed
    28 December 2021].
Müller, Benito, and Axel Michaelowa. 2019. 'How to Operationalize Accounting under Article 6
    Market Mechanisms of the Paris Agreement', *Climate Policy*, 19 (7), 812–19.
Neuhoff, Karsten, and Robert Ritz. 2019. 'Carbon Cost Pass-through in Industrial Sectors',
    Cambridge Working Papers in Economics, 1988.
Nieto, Maria. 2022. 'Whatever It Takes to Reach Net Zero Emissions around 2050 and Limit Global
    Warming to 1.5 C: The Cases of United States, China, European Union and Japan', *BAFFI
    CAREFIN Centre Research Paper* (2022–170).
Nordhaus, William. 2019. 'Climate Change: The Ultimate Challenge for Economics', *American
    Economic Review*, 109 (6), 1991–2014.
O'Callaghan, Brian J, and Em Murdock.·2021. *Are We Building Back Better? Evidence from 2020 and
    Pathways for Inclusive Green Recovery Spending*, (Oxford: United Nations Environment
    Programme), <https://wedocs.unep.org/bitstream/handle/20.500.11822/35281/AWBBB.pdf>
    [Accessed 28 December 2021].
Obergassel, Wolfgang, and Friederike Asche.·2018. *Shaping the Paris Mechanisms Part III: An
    Update on Submissions on Article 6 of the Paris Agreement*, (Wuppertal Institut für Klima,
    Umwelt, Energie), <https://epub.wupperinst.org/frontdoor/deliver/index/docId/6987/file/
    6987_Paris_Mechanisms.pdf> [Accessed 31 January 2022].

Olsen, Karen Holm, Fatemeh Bakhtiari, Virender Kumar Duggal, and Jørge Villy Fenhann. 2019. 'Sustainability Labelling as a Tool for Reporting the Sustainable Development Impacts of Climate Actions Relevant to Article 6 of the Paris Agreement', *International Environmental Agreements: Politics, Law and Economics*, 19 (2), 225–51.

Organisation for Economic Cooperation and Development.·2021. *Carbon Pricing in Times of Covid-19: What Has Changed in G20 Economies?*, <https://www.oecd.org/tax/tax-policy/carbon-pricing-in-times-of-covid-19-what-has-changed-in-g20-economies.htm> [Accessed 16 October 2021].

Pearse, Rebecca, and Steffen Böhm. 2014. 'Ten Reasons Why Carbon Markets Will Not Bring About Radical Emissions Reduction', *Carbon Management*, 5 (4), 325–37.

Pugh, Thomas AM, Mats Lindeskog, Benjamin Smith, Benjamin Poulter, Almut Arneth, Vanessa Haverd, and Leonardo Calle. 2019. 'Role of Forest Regrowth in Global Carbon Sink Dynamics', *Proceedings of the National Academy of Sciences*, 116 (10), 4382–87.

Qubaja, Rafat, José M Grünzweig, Eyal Rotenberg, and Dan Yakir. 2020. 'Evidence for Large Carbon Sink and Long Residence Time in Semiarid Forests Based on 15 Year Flux and Inventory Records', *Global Change Biology*, 26 (3), 1626–37.

Rajamani, L., and D Bodansky. 2019. 'The Paris Rulebook: Balancing International Prescriptiveness with National Discretion', *International and Comparative Law Quarterly*, 68 (4), 1023–40.

Schneider, Lambert, Maosheng Duan, Robert Stavins, Kelley Kizzier, Derik Broekhoff, Frank Jotzo, Harald Winkler, Michael Lazarus, Andrew Howard, and Christina Hood. 2019. 'Double Counting and the Paris Agreement Rulebook', *Science*, 366 (6462), 180–83.

Schneider, Lambert, and Stephanie La Hoz Theuer. 2019. 'Environmental Integrity of International Carbon Market Mechanisms under the Paris Agreement', *Climate Policy*, 19 (3), 386–400.

Science Based Targets Initiative. 2021. *Launching the SBTi Net-Zero Standard*, <https://sciencebasedtargets.org/net-zero> [Accessed 11 October 2021].

Seymour, Frances, and Paige Langer.·2021. *Consideration of Nature-Based Solutions as Offsets in Corporate Climate Change Mitigation Strategies*, (World Resources Institute), <https://files.wri.org/d8/s3fs-public/consideration-nature-based-solutions-offsets-corporate-climate-change-mitigation-strategies.pdf> [Accessed 1 January 2022].

Shaffer, Gary. 2010. 'Long-Term Effectiveness and Consequences of Carbon Dioxide Sequestration', *Nature Geoscience*, 3 (7), 464–67.

Sovacool, Benjamin K. 2011. 'Four Problems with Global Carbon Markets: A Critical Review', *Energy and Environment*, 22 (6), 681–94.

United Nations Framework Convention on Climate Change. 2015. *Paris Agreement*. <https://unfccc.int/files/meetings/paris_nov_2015/application/pdf/paris_agreement_english_.pdf> [Accessed 1 January 2022]

—— 2021 *Decision -/CP.26: Glasgow Climate Pact* (Glasgow: COP26) <https://unfccc.int/sites/default/files/resource/cop26_auv_2f_cover_decision.pdf> [Accessed 1 January 2022].

Vanclay, Frank. 2003. 'International Principles for Social Impact Assessment', *Impact Assessment and Project Appraisal*, 21 (1), 5–12.

Verra. 2022. *Verified Carbon Standard*, <https://verra.org/project/vcs-program/> [Accessed 1 January 2022].

Voluntary Carbon Markets Integrity Initiative.·2021. *Feedback on VCMI Consultation Report*, <https://vcmintegrity.org/wp-content/uploads/2021/10/Synthesis-Report_Final.pdf> [Accessed 1 January 2022].

Watt, Robert. 2017. *The Moral Economy of Carbon Offsetting: Ethics, Power and the Search for Legitimacy in a New Market*: The University of Manchester (United Kingdom)).

Welsby, Dan, James Price, Steve Pye, and Paul Ekins. 2021. 'Unextractable Fossil Fuels in a 1.5 C
    World', *Nature*, 597 (7875), 230–34.
World Bank. 2021a. *Carbon Pricing Dashboard*, <https://carbonpricingdashboard.worldbank.org/>
    [Accessed 6 December 2021].
——.·2021b. *State and Trends of Carbon Pricing 2021* (Washington, DC: World Bank),
    <https://openknowledge.worldbank.org/handle/10986/35620> [Accessed 31 January 2022].

Andrea Ferraz Young

Chapter 21
Financing climate resilience: New opportunities and challenges

Abstract: In recent years, distinct financial instruments have been proposed to create incentives for investment in climate resilience, which include those based on environmental, social, and governance (ESG) principles. However, these include high upfront costs, investments in infrastructure, uncertain benefits, competition for budgetary priorities and data availability. These requirements are particularly challenging in developing countries often dealing with fiscal reforms and difficulties in accessing private finance. In addition, the pandemic has brought risks to public finance given its extent, the inability of national and subnational governments to absorb the fiscal costs and the asymmetric regional ability to struggle against its effects. It is essential to understand the context, identify the mechanisms for sustainable development and the effectiveness of climate resilience finance. In the following sections will discuss the growing need for resilience investments, different mechanisms and instruments that have been proposed to provide more adequate funding for investments, the challenges and recently aligned market incentives. Some brief cases are used to provide empirical background and discussion on the opportunities. The chapter also addresses equity and fairness concerns and focusses on pre-disaster resilience investments rather than finance for post-disaster recovery and reconstruction. Finally, the chapter offers some conclusions based on lessons from financing climate resilience experiences.

Keywords: disaster, socioenvironmental and economic support, urban resilience, sustainable development goals, COVID-19

Introduction

This chapter is intended to provide some preliminary reflections on financing climate resilience. Initially, three research questions are framed: What preliminary lessons from the pandemic can be drawn in terms of financial support to climate change resilience What is needed to support disaster risk reduction and to manage multiple and distinct interconnected aspects related to climate change and COVID-19? With climate change already threatening livelihoods, economies and societies, how should business change after the coronavirus crisis? It is argued that this linkage exposes once again the population vulnerability that calls for a substantive rethink of disaster prevention to acknowledge and take on this interconnectedness with investments.

https://doi.org/10.1515/9783110733488-021

The Sustainable Development Goals (SDGs) are becoming increasingly important for investors, as they represent the materiality of the socioenvironmental perspectives that have been recently taken into account for the generation of portfolios with a competitive advantage. The Environmental Social Goals (ESG) principles, established over 20 years ago, have gained traction as a means to support investments and as criteria for reporting sustainability performance.

Basically, it is all about using resources for economic growth, improved livelihoods, health and to promote job opportunities, while preserving the environment. For this reason, there is a significant global trend toward the adoption of ESG-related regulations targeting institutional investors, corporate issuers (bonds) or both. Actually, the resurgence of initiatives for sustainable development has reinforced ESG regulations across the world. The concept of sustainable development is gaining a new momentum. Since the beginning of the pandemic, scientists around the world have constantly been fighting to identify mechanisms to restrict the spread of coronavirus. However, the pandemic has brought with it a sequence of problems that go beyond those related to health systems, including broken supply chains and business models, contraction across key sectors and increasing debt of governments and businesses that invest to remain solvent. This situation has increased the risks to public finance given its extent, the inability of subnational governments to absorb the fiscal costs and due to the asymmetric regional ability to struggle against its effects. This circumstance can be aggravated by the non-fulfilment of carbon-reduction targets and by the coincidences of extreme events and pandemics.

This chapter presents some of the major elements for sustainable development and finance. In the following sections, there is an examination of the growing need for resilience investments, the different mechanisms and instruments that have been proposed to provide more adequate funding for resilience investments, the challenges and recent aligned market incentives. Brief cases are used to provide empirical background and discussion on the potential windows of opportunity for financing climate resilience. The chapter also addresses equity and fairness concerns and focuses on pre-disaster resilience investments rather than finance for post-disaster reconstruction. Finally, the chapter offers some conclusions based on lessons from financing climate resilience experiences.

Much of what has been learnt about assumes that despite of relative delay, the coronavirus has led countries to take drastic policy and legal measures to address what has been described as a kind of warlike situation. These circumstances contrast sharply with governments' initial approach to tackling climate change, in which both prevention action and adaptive response have fallen short of what has been specified by international agreements and are still needed to prevent an even greater global shock. Although significant attention has been paid to how COVID-19 and climate change are related, their financial interconnections and logistical supports are still unclear.

Pandemic lessons for action on climate change

It has for than two years since the first report of COVID-19 emerged from Wuhan, China. The consequences are complex and occur on a wide range of scales such as small- and medium-sized business interruption. About 92% of global enterprises have been negatively affected by COVID-19, which have shown some common characteristics: (1) reduced consumer demand due to economic shock; (2) reduced access to credit and outside investments, partners and networks; (3) disruptions of supply chains and logistics; (4) barriers to or higher costs of accessing inputs; (5) higher costs of distribution; (6) interruptions of operating licences and authorisations; (7) necessity to reduce the number of staff in workplace or dismissal of employees, care burden, sickness and deaths. Particularly, governments have had problems related to unemployment rates, income decrease, suspension of tourism and trade, disruptions of supply chains and logistics, migration difficulties and tax revenue reduction, among other interconnected aspects.

The interdependence of a globalised world brought to the surface the fragility of the social, economic, financial and political system. Since the early days of the pandemic, nations have constantly struggled to solve issues such as the rapid spread of the virus, the socioeconomic impacts, the necessary socioenvironmental transition and adaptation plans. COVID-19 has drastically altered the near-term prospects of the global economy and the results have not yet reached their full depth because a global recession could still occur in the event of a prolonged and uncontrolled pandemic scenario (e.g., in poor countries and with new strains).

The consequences of the pandemic invite reflection on how disastrous events are framed and dealt with. It can be observed that pandemics and climate risks share many attributes. Both are systemic, and their direct manifestations and indirect effects spread quickly in an interconnected world. Even though the virus is considered a natural phenomenon its spread is no more natural than disasters caused by tsunamis, hurricanes, floods or droughts. What the pandemic has shown is that focussing only on natural perspectives and seeing an event as an exogenous representation, outside the social context, people tend to hide different ways of thinking about what is happening. Events of this nature can only be assimilated by understanding and addressing the physical and social causes. Actually, the pandemic has forced the consideration of disasters from an 'endogenous' perspective, as a product of society itself (Revet 2020).

The effects of the pandemic and climate risks are similar, both represent shocks to existing structures, which translate into a series of socioeconomic impacts in a chain. The rapid spread of COVID-19 has exposed some of the old problems caused by longstanding structural inequalities (Kihato and Landau 2020) proving to be a significant obstacle for the current economic system (Barouki 2021). The long-term shutdowns have had negative impacts on economies. In terms of financial decisions, there is always a loss of confidence in the operating system and the fear of the consequent loss of value or liquidity. Whether in the public or private sector, decisions are normally shaped by financial, not structural, aspects. Nevertheless, the current pandemic reveals that if the structure is affected (e.g., public sector bodies were not sufficiently equipped to effectively respond to this health emergency) and an interruption in the global production networks occurs, which affects all interconnected mechanisms, showing their weakness to optimise costs and efficiency when the risks become reality (Tille et al. 2021: 49).

Both the pandemic and climate change disasters have non-linear consequences, as their socioeconomic impacts grow disproportionately, violating certain limits such as the collapse of health systems, discontinuity of supply chains and loss of the informal economy. Both are risk multipliers, as they highlight and exacerbate vulnerabilities hitherto not commonly tested in the financial sector. The need to address climate change comes from multiple risks. For example, it should be considered that widespread water shortages could have a similar impact as a pandemic, with an aggravating factor, the effect of climate change occurs gradually and is cumulative and does not go away with a vaccine. The drought in California has emphasised the need to consider water stress that spreads from the agricultural sector to semiconductor manufacturing with loss of job positions, creating feedback loops that accelerate the problem exponentially. In particular, rapid global warming produces gradual effects such as desertification, decrease in agricultural production and reduction of habitable land. These include the diversity of animals, plants and microorganisms at the genetic, species and ecosystem level that sustain structures, functions and processes in and around production systems and provide food and non-food agricultural products.

Both are non-stationary as past probabilities and occurrence distributions change rapidly and become insufficient for future projections. In 2011, an earthquake generated waves several metres high off the coast of Fukushima. The tsunami triggered the worst nuclear accident since Chernobyl, and ten years later, the region is still far from normal. In the same way, the new strains of coronavirus can prolong the fight against the pandemic. Since the beginning, more variants have emerged, and it is clear that strategy against coronavirus will have to be nimble in anticipating and responding to an evolving foe.

Likewise, both are regressive in a world where risks and disasters affect everyone, but at the same time exacerbate existing inequalities and disproportionately affect the poorest people, revealing direct relationships with vulnerable populations (e.g., Afro-descendants, people living in slums, seniors, women, refugees, Indigenous people). The challenges posed by coronavirus and climate change are, of course, different. COVID-19 is potentially acute and relatively short-term, while climate change is chronic and long-term. Managing complex and interconnected risks, such as climate change, pandemics, ecosystem degradation and biodiversity loss represent some of the most pressing global challenges. However, poor urban planning (e.g., poor infrastructure, lack of sewage, water supply and access to technology), along with other types of social exclusion, requires attention mainly when the scope is disaster risk reduction. Although scientists have consistently warned against these risks over the years, it must be considered whether peoples are equally well-prepared to prevent or deal with any of them.

The social challenge in times of COVID-19

The pandemic has exposed and exacerbated pre-existing inequalities between countries just as it has within countries (Bailey et al. 2020: 1164). Differences in the intensity of the effects of COVID-19 are evident with asymmetrical impacts across territories (Organisation for Economic Co-operation and Development 2020: 3). These differences are due, in part, to the timing of policy responses and the fact that people live in circumstances that make them more vulnerable to the coronavirus. Less developed economies have more precarious health conditions and health systems, which are not prepared to deal with the consequences of the pandemic (Stiglitz 2020: 8). The COVID-19 pandemic is far more than a health crisis (United Nations Sustainable Development Group 2020: 3). The impacts vary with regional conditions and developing countries simply do not have the same resources that advanced economies have to respond to the economic aftermath (Bailey et al. 2020: 1164). The disease revels social vulnerability through absence of concrete actions that ensure social equality (racial, gender, elder rights), economic balance (job losses, income decrease) and environmental justice (healthiness of urban spaces) (Sharifi and Khavarian-Garmsir 2020: 6). Across the world, there are marked differences in how countries have maintained the health of their citizens and the economy and in how the pandemic has been managed to reduce the magnitude of inequalities (Stiglitz 2020: 2). In addition, there are adverse and destructive political attributes that can weigh on society, strongly divided, leading to less inclusion and more discordance (Bailey et al. 2020: 1166). The regional and local impact of COVID-19 is highly significant with deep implications for dwellers of segregated and disfranchised neighbourhoods, which are disproportionately exposed to environmental and health risks (Sharifi and Khavarian-Garmsir 2020: 7). There are some reasons for these differences: the pre-existing state of healthcare and health inequalities; the preparedness of a country and the resilience of the economy; the quality of public response, including confidence in science; citizens' trust in government guidance; and how citizens balance their free will to do what they want without disrespecting others. It is risky separating disasters from social frameworks that take into account how hazards affect populations, recognising that any decision can generate externalities (Stiglitz 2020: 2).

In this sense, the alternative solution appears to be one where everyone has been considered. Years can be spent analysing the strength of its effects, but the pandemic will not be brought under control until it is controlled everywhere and the economic crisis will not be tamed until there is a global recovery (Stiglitz 2020: 8). In fact, the pandemic highlights a fundamental aspect of vulnerability in periods of economic recession. A pertinent example is that COVID-19 was a setback for the goals of the SDG, which sought to eradicate food insecurity by 2030. Last year, at least 118 million people entered the list totalling 768 million malnourished people one year before. Likewise, global food security may be at risk due to increasing pressures on natural resources and climate change, which threaten the sustainability of food systems (United Nations Food and Agriculture Organization et al. 2021: 10). Planetary borders may well be crossed with large-scale human displacement and migration if current trends continue (United Nations Food and Agriculture Organization et al. 2021: 65). From a sustainability perspective, COVID-19 is a vivid example of systemic compound risk, it is not possible separate economic vulnerability from social and environmental dimensions. Actually, they are all part of the same framework that has an undeniable spatial component or a strong territorial dimension (OECD 2021: 1–2). This shows that the very nature and scale of vulnerability has changed to the point where it has the potential to overwhelm conventional risk management approaches and the reach of institutions (United Nations Economic Commission for Latin America and the Caribbean/Office for Disaster Risk Reduction 2021: 3). For instance, urban density when associated with poverty, racial discrimination, lack of sanitation and limited access to work and healthcare can amplify hazards, manifesting in an array of non-linear effects. COVID-19 mortality rates can exhibit a strong regional concentration that should be considered and managed, otherwise it spreads by causing its effects to be diffuse, variable and uncertain (Kim and Bostwick 2020: 512). The same perspective could be considered for climate change effects.

As governments try to respond to the pandemic by seeking to return to the status quo, the unsustainability of underlying conditions suggests that things will never be the same again. The reason is simple, COVID-19 will remain until a cure is discovered or a burn out occurs. Unfortunately, however bad the inequality was before the pandemic, and however vigorous the pandemic has exposed the inequalities in society, the post-pandemic world may experience even greater inequalities, and the fear of another pandemic will persist (Stiglitz 2020: 4).

It is now critical that the public and private sectors take risks seriously. Naturally, as modern civilisation has not taken any significant action to address the multiple impacts of disasters, it is possible that certain economic activities, certain goods and services and certain production processes are seen as riskier and more expensive. The pandemic highlights the importance of structural and social positioning factors such as local investments, racial minorities considered as citizens in developing responses, community and institutional level and how this can provide different opportunities. It is necessary to take action now with long-term priorities to increase the responsiveness of socioeconomic systems. This recognition would benefit both the effectiveness of the decisions made and the legitimacy of those decisions (García-Sánchez et al. 2020: 6–7).

The short-term answer is to accelerate qualification and training in conjunction with changes in the labour market to rebuild the economy. But there is good reason to believe that this answer alone will not be enough. A comprehensive programme to reduce income inequality will be needed. It must first recognise that the competitive equilibrium model (through which producers maximise profit, job precariousness, and prices are determined in competitive markets that match demand and supply), that has dominated economists' thinking by more than a century, does not provide a good picture of the economy today and neither of the future, especially when it comes to understanding the growth of inequality, or even innovation-driven growth without considering social and environmental aspects that have been knocking on the door for decades (Stiglitz 2020: 5). Regulations and restrictions are needed that define how economic expansion can operate because the weakening of environmental constraints and limitless social exploitation will create a worse-performing economy, marked by unprecedented inequality.

Resilience

The current pandemic has shed new light on old problems with respect to resilience (Diffenbaugh et al. 2020: 470). While it is true that pandemic has affected everyone in some way, the proportion of the impact is unequal (Kim and Bostwick 2020: 509). The spread of the pandemic and the spatially differentiated effects emphasise the importance of contextual knowledge (Herrero and Thornton 2020: e174). How it is possible to talk about sustainable development or resilience without supporting citizens to play a responsible role in the development of their daily lives? If the political-economic model restricts urban development, perpetuating inequality of living conditions, why the insistence in outdated discourses that will never meet a common purpose? In fact, there is little coherence between institutions across policy domains on socioenvironmental approaches to urban development (Motta 2020: 1–5; van der Maesen 2012: 3). This has resulted in urban fragmentation and consequent loss of cities' identities, which is a vital factor to build a close relationship between citizens and essential to social development (Motta 2020: 5–10). The social concept is precisely defined as being realised through human interdependence and the interaction between individuals, in the realisation of the individual as a social being through social cohesion (van der Maesen and Walker 2013: 7).

What is so striking about these observations is their relevance for understanding contemporary life. Actually, humanity is living in a constitutive interdependency of processes that are disarticulated by current political ideologies such as lack of financing policies in strategic areas including health, education and sustainability, and clean technologies have had little penetration. With the compartmentalisation of the scientific and technological perspective, human beings are seen as individualised beings who basically pursue their own particular interests (Beck, van der Maesen, and Walker 2012: 44–54; Herrmann 2015: 198). No matter the threats of climate change, common sense has not changed yet and has created a chasm between humans and nature (Hamilton 2017: 1). In the same way, because of the self-centred perspective aimed at its own benefit, the set of identities has been lost and with them the identities of cities (Motta 2020: 5–10). Thus, the virus becomes just a detail and deaths are accepted naturally, practically without empathy, as there is practically no identity in terms of context, that is, of the whole.

The pandemic, as disastrous as it is, provides a unique opportunity to rethink decision-making process and policy responses (Hulme et al. 2020: 3–5). Starting from the premise that social and environmental problems and the pandemic are linked by their nature, that is, resilience which is connected to sustainable development and environmental justice (Menton et al. 2020: 1622). Indeed, the vulnerability is embedded in social structures (Chan et al. 2014: 456–66; Cutter et al. 2008: 598–99; Cutter, Boruff, and Shirley 2003: 242–43; Bracken-Roche et al. 2017: 2) that determine not only the risk exposure but also the capacity to deal with, respond to, and recover from disasters (Haque and Etkin 2007: 271–72; Kuhlicke 2013: 61–69). Since the early 80s, vulnerability continues to be a key concept for understanding of risk exposure (Burton 2015; Cutter, Boruff, and Shirley 2003) and responsiveness (Hagelsteen and Becker 2013: 4–5; Hagelsteen and Burke 2016: 43–45). The capacity response is normally applied to describe the ability to withstand disastrous circumstances (Alexander 2013: 2714; Greene et al. 2003: 1–2; Hoffman 2008: 1516; Patterson and Patterson 2001: 50–51) or to adapt to changing circumstances (Greene et al. 2003: 2–3); or such as the strength needed to recover from disastrous events (Burton 2015: 69; Kuhlicke 2013: 61–70). Actually, it can serve as a paradigm to understand how different strategies are implemented to reduce population vulnerability (Hagelsteen and Becker 2013: 4–10; Hagelsteen and Burke 2016: 43–44). The pandemic increases social vulnerability in several ways (Thomas, Jang, and Scandlyn 2020: 209–11), there is an unequal distribution of the resources that increase difficulties in capacity response (e.g., decreased income caused by insecurity or job loss, decreased informal activities due to lockdowns, population densification in unhealthy settlements). Normally, Afro-descendants suffer its consequences most severely because these current conditions add to existing inequalities depending on class, gender and ethnicity (Kim and Bostwick 2020: 509).

Resilience is a process linked to a network of adaptive capabilities with dynamic attributes capable of withstanding disturbance or adversity (Keck and Sakdapolrak 2013: 5–10). It emerges from primary sets of adaptive capacities: economic development, social capital, clear information and communication with competence, which together provide a state of disaster readiness (Gaillard, Cadag, and Rampengan 2019: 863–70). Actually, the concept highlights the complexity of dynamic vulnerability and responsiveness in global and local contexts (Kelman 2015: 117–20; Shepherd 2008: 2–3). Although this concept is widely discussed in the literature (Adger 2018: 1–13; Estrella and Saalismaa 2013: 26–28; Folke 2006: 254–55; Kelman 2015: 117–21; Levine 2014: 10–13; Renaud, Sudmeier-Rieux, and Estrella 2013: 140), covering a wide range of subjects, its application is limited in terms of scope and scale, making it a challenge that cannot be overcome with theoretical research alone (Mustafa et al. 2011: 62–65; Sheridan 2008: 418–20). Global resilience has its roots in coordination through multilateralism, which can be represented by regional and local structures (United Nations Covention on Biological Diversity 2010: 1–6; United Nations 2015: 9–12). In this case, it is necessary to overcome the hindrances of traditional agendas for those based on SDGs (Greene et al. 2003: 1–5; Griggs et al. 2014: 22–23).

Resilience consists of three necessary basic principles: (1) analysing the investments applied, taking into account a range of projects implemented within a system approach; (2) monitoring and including feasible data on the legal instruments and indicators through a long-term process; and (3) assessing the capacity response to change. It requires not only improvement of existing infrastructure but also creating and consolidating specific legal apparatus (Adger 2018: 1–10) needed to overcome obstacles (McEntire 2012: 294–99; Perry and May 2007: 1039–41) to include vulnerable populations in prevention and response plans (Weichselgartner and Pigeon 2015: 114–16). In fact, with appropriate investments in dwelling, wide education, health and technological support communities have the potential to function effectively and adapt successfully (Norris et al. 2008: 127–28). To build collective resilience, governments must reduce risk and social inequalities and involve local people in mitigation (Tierney 2012: 341–45). This would include creating organisational linkages, boosting and protecting social supports, and waiting for unforeseen events (Li, Wang, and Xie 2019: 2,11). Such an approach requires flexibility, decision-making skills, and trusted sources of information to face unknown events (Birkmann 2007: 21–23; Birkmann et al. 2013: 193–99).

As was realised through the pandemic, there is still a highly fragile institutional agenda and little linked to the concept of resilience. In general, the decision-making process focusses on post-disaster (i.e., recovery and reconstruction) rather than prevention (Sheridan 2008: 420). The traditional mechanisms do not operate to preserve the basic principles of resilience (Tierney 2006: 210). Normally, they used to depreciate them, managing disasters from a short-term perspective (Ulmer, Seeger, and Sellnow 2007: 130–34). For example, there is still limited knowledge on how much is invested to reduce urban inequalities and how the investments are taking place (Jones et al. 2014: 79–90; Okamuro and Nishimura 2020: 5–7).

Undoubtedly, the first two decades of the 21st century have foreshadowed the future of natural disasters unleashed against densely populated centres and it is incontrovertible that they have highlighted the importance of disaster risk reduction (Mercer 2010: 248–60). The disaster risk reduction was considered in the context of monitoring capacities to increase the prospects of higher accountability, recognised by several global initiatives, from the formulation of the Millennium Development Goals to the 2030 Agenda for Sustainable Development (New York, 2015).

However, if people live in so intricate a social framework with multi-criteria involved (Carreño, Cardona, and Barbat 2007: 2) and complex environments (Klenert et al. 2020: 756) with different levels of exposure (Hoffman 2008: 1501–02), why so little attention has been paid to disaster response in the past decades? Obviously, this is a tricky question about how to coordinate disaster risk reduction institutionally in national and subnational contexts (Mercer 2010: 248–61). This task becomes extremely necessary since budgets for disaster risk reduction are insufficient (Jones et al. 2014: 79–80) and there are still uncoordinated and poorly dimensioned measures that can result in ineffective actions (Holand and Lujala 2013: 313–14). There is no doubt that this can represent a significant obstacle to resilience, as the lack of specificity of the implemented measures can reduce accountability for results (Sorg et al. 2018: 275), masking the extent of population exposure levels (Myers and Patz 2009: 241). Monitoring systems are needed based on representative indices with emphasis on local spheres, where intra-urban inequalities are associated with specific sociospatial variations (Hagelsteen and Burke 2016: 43–45).

Making transition and supporting resilience: Measures to manage multiple and interconnected challenges

Given the magnitude of the disaster caused by COVID-19 and the long shadow it will cast, the world cannot afford not to pay attention to climate change and the need for a more sustainable economic system with a broader agenda based on ecological systems. Climate change will remain critical for the next decade, so the transition to a low-carbon future with investments in green and blue infrastructure can drive significant job creation while assisting economic and environmental recovery. Accordingly, transition and resilience plans need to reflect a substantive and credible budget with respective investment efforts. Both must be coherent and adequately address the challenges imposed by COVID-19 and climate change. Actually, the consequences of COVID-19 extend beyond public health and dealing with the pandemic requires an optimisation of a large part of social structures for better performance, as it demands an immediate recovery but at the same time ensuring that this system becomes resilient in the long-term.

Thinking in terms of economic means, the recent pandemic has shown that sustainable development cannot avoid concerns related to disaster risk reduction and the related social and environmental aspects with focus on goals, principles and outcomes. The first step in supporting disaster risk reduction and managing the multiple interconnected aspects would be to answer how this framework is established by different sectors. The question is no longer whether the disaster will occur or when, but what will be done through structural measures aimed at reducing the socioeconomic system fragility. While the world is at the middle of a fast-unfolding disaster, it can already be seen how the pandemic may influence the pace and nature of climate action, and how climate action could accelerate the transition by increasing economic resilience.

If on the one hand, the pandemic has brought a sequence of problems, including contraction across key sectors and increasing of public debt, it also offers a rare opportunity to look to the future and understand the potential impacts that a climate disaster can bring (Sharifi and Khavarian-Garmsir 2020: 2). This perspective includes investments on a wide range of levers, from expanding the renewable energy grid to implementing technologies to decarbonise the agricultural sector and heavy industries, favouring the ESG issues. Common themes used to define ESG include low-carbon development, macroeconomic growth, social inclusion, environmental sustainability and climate resilience by introducing considerations of resource efficiency, transforming energy systems, valuing natural capital in the economic return and pricing environmental externalities. In general, the objective of policies and regulations related to ESG is to ensure that environmental factors are taken into account when making social and economic decisions to become more resilient.

Decision-making and the efficient allocation of public resources to reduce the impact of disasters requires, among other things, an understanding of the social and environmental aspects that normally make the system's reaction extremely difficult. In this sense, the concept of resilience is praiseworthy when it defines the ability of a given system to persist when impacted by one or more events, which can be summarised through some of the basic aspects: (1) how long a system can withstand and remain despite changes caused by an event; (2) responsiveness (3) cross-disciplinary work between the natural and social sciences (4) and the ability to adapt more and more quickly by understanding and facing problems related to poverty, vulnerability, social exclusion and risk (Alexander 2013: 2714; Brown 2014: 2–4; Carpenter et al. 2001: 779; Folke 2016: 2). It represents a particular set of measurable resources and capacities to prepare for and respond to a disturbance caused by an event (Bélanger and Pilling 2019: 24–35). Actually, resilience is the way to reestablish socioecological function when exposed to adversities. Building resilience through an integrated analysis of vulnerability and responsiveness can be a significant alternative (Folke 2016: 2). Currently, public funds are not always invested to reduce local vulnerabilities and new prospects are needed to elucidate where the responsiveness is non-existent, deficient or may be improved.

Nevertheless, it is important to realise that each system has its own way to cope with adversities. A continued commitment to scaling-up climate finance is needed for both political and practical reasons. From a global perspective, it is important for governments to maintain commitments to climate finance to ensure the essence of mutual responsibility. This will be fundamental to secure a more ambitious global agreement on climate change. Furthermore, these investments can create opportunities for local development with new business, socioeconomic policies and interventions that support decent work, produce and sustain productive natural capital and assets (along with physical capital). In many cases, they also represent a low-cost investment option to boost jobs and to increase productivity and economic activity.

Moving towards a low-carbon economy despite major challenges

Despite the fact that SDGs have given a new momentum to include ESG alternatives, it is important to understand that the fragility of these options refer mainly to a low-income country, characterised by weak state capacity and/or weak state legitimacy, leaving citizens vulnerable to a range of shocks (e.g., social, health, environmental). In particular, in poor regions the impacts of climate change on water, food and land multiply existing pressures, where inequality persists and the population has limited capacity to address these pressures. The discourse on ESG issues is based on the premise that environmental and social issues do not receive sufficient consideration in investment decision-making. A number of reasons are offered to explain why: (1) it is difficult to assign a monetary value to ESG and to integrate them into quantitative models; (2) ESG-related disclosure by companies may be limited, unverified, and non-standardised; (3) ESG tends to influence financial performance over the long-term, while many investors have relatively short-term horizons; (4) there is some criticism regarding to such voluntary consideration of ESG results with reclassification of the assets under management without a substantive change in how investment decisions are made.

Despite the difficulties, there has been a slow but visible evolution in recent years in the way programmes and policies are designed, due in part to the renewed debate on the effectiveness of interventions. The introduction of SDGs mainly emphasises mechanisms that enable practical implementation, such as clean and affordable energy (SDG 7). These mechanisms have faced many challenges such as defining strategies, coordinating sectors, convening stakeholders and partnerships as well as follow-up and accountability. In the same way, environmental conservation and protection of biodiversity are the largest areas of funding, with objectives closer to private sector development, such as carbon–reduction, water supply and agriculture production. Nowadays, considering carbon-reduction, the market incentive to industrial sectors is greater than in the past, ensuring that carbon transition can happen more efficiently. The timing is particularly favourable because carbon prices have more immediate effects when they tip the balance between two available technologies. In the past, this could not happen because prices could not consolidate a cleaner energy advantage over dirtier energy, renewable technologies were too immature to benefit from any advantage. But in the last decade, the costs of wind and solar energy, for example, have plummeted and become more affordable.

Although some sectors dispute this and claim that the production of certain goods cannot be easily changed, governments in Europe and the US are promoting the possibility of direct government investment and establishing subsidy schemes to ensure that companies implement the technologies that the legal instruments will encourage. The EU and US are planning an expansion of their carbon pricing schemes, and China is instituting a brand new one. There may never have been a time when carbon-reduction instruments could achieve so much. The current reality has reinforced the need for investments based on sustainable development. However, it is important to stress that there are different types of financing. For instance, green financing is a specific instrument for green investment strategies (e.g., energy transition, global warming reduction, low-carbon strategy) (Wang and Zhi 2016). The Green Bond market has also arisen to enable and develop the key role that debt markets can play in funding projects that contribute to environmental sustainability-based on the Principles for Responsible Investment. Taken together, these principles suggest clear guidelines for a process which requires modifications of the original perception of economic growth and development considering the socioenvironmental interface based on socially responsible investments (SRI) (Dörry and Schulz 2018).

In contrast, ESG does not demand any specific requirement for allocation of financing proceeds. The main feature of such instruments is a price incentive offered if the purpose meets predefined requirements, such as environmental and social governance; gender diversity; percentage of people with disabilities; healthy living conditions, among others included in the Paris Agreement and the United Nations SDGs for low-carbon transition assessment. Enthusiasts often cite the proliferation of ESG implementation schemes as evidence of the popularity of the movement, but the actual result has been one of the confusing elements. The competing frameworks sometimes agree on what topics should be considered, for example, limiting and mitigating the impacts of anthropogenic climate change, but they rarely provide any useful guidance for which goals to prioritise as the most important or how to reconcile the conflicting demands of multiple stakeholders. This is not surprising, because the concept of ESG means different things for different people. Some legal representatives want to come up with specific results for environmental or labour policies. Some are individual investors who want a competitive rate of return in addition to minimising their carbon footprint. Others are professionals looking to sell ESG themed financial products and consulting services or to create a profitable niche for themselves in an expanding field.

Indeed, the lack of strict agreement on what is really needed and what is sought to achieve has made its meaning subject to different interpretations by different constituencies. For example, many countries claim that creating a carbon tax on imported products would only serve to protect the local industry from foreign competitors who are not subject to the same environmental standards. On the other hand, more than 95% of industrial emissions and about half of aviation emissions are currently covered by free emission allowances that can delay decarbonisation. In the rare cases where specific goals and outcomes are specified, these specifics are often highly controversial, applicable only to a certain set of circumstances, or so obvious as to be conventional wisdom.

With a wide spectrum of major public policy issues potentially coming under the umbrella of ESG, it also should not be surprising that implementing such a management and investment strategy yields mixed results. Proponents routinely refer to research findings that claim to validate ESG as a comprehensive theory, but detailed analysis reveals that only governance reforms – the most traditional and least controversial – generally yield improved business performance. However, even those findings are suspect, given the inability of professional research firms to agree on what constitutes compliance with ESG goals in the first place. Auditing the results of leading finance ratings firms reveals a shockingly low level of agreement, even when the topics being examined are objective and specific. For this reason, market regulation and proper adjustments are extremely necessary to prevent costs of inaction due to the existing deadlocks.

Although in the history of the European Union, the regulation of common policies for the entire set of countries has been configured through a lack of enthusiasm from the Member States, the pandemic gave urgency to the coordination of the economic challenges. Many countries are improving their regulatory processes by proposing a series of instruments to align monetary and fiscal policies to a new economic model based on greater use of renewable sources. By 2021, an entire secondary industry of finance research, ratings and investment products has grown up, with several hundred mutual funds and exchange-traded funds claiming to have an ESG focus. A similar regulatory and review process is taking place in the United States, which faces additional challenges caused by partisan division, without complete unity among the states. Globally, investments were managed by firms that have signed on to the United Nations' Principles for Responsible Investment (United Nations Conference on Trade and Development 2020: 5–6). There is no doubt that the COVID-19 pandemic is an alarm signal that draws attention to the fact that a return to the previous normal will be detrimental to the environment and ecosystems. The transition, planned and implemented in the long-run, it is the only way to build a resilient society. Among the priorities are transition efforts for sustainable development after the pandemic which include innovation, resource efficiency and compatible production, water management and energy supply, disaster prevention and reduction in social inequality.

Beyond COVID-19: How should business change after coronavirus?

For a significant advance away from high-carbon investments, it is important to develop and invest in climate finance plans, making strategic use of multilateral and bilateral channels and institutions. This can help local businesses implement effective measures to reduce emissions, protect critical ecosystems, build resilience against the impacts of climate change and promote the flow of capital toward climate-aligned investments. Briefly, it will be necessary to invest in a wide range of sustainability levers, including building renewable energy infrastructure, expanding the capacity of the electricity grid and increasing its resilience to support the deployment of technologies to decarbonise diverse industrial sectors.

In addition, it is necessary to be able to assess the development of an economic system-based on long-term green investments, providing insightful information for transition programmes, updating and improving the historical models that are used for infrastructure planning and allowing the use of climate parameters in financing mechanisms. Over time, competing interests, resource constraints and legacies from past conflicts and weak perspectives in the intergovernmental arrangements are likely to create significant tension. In the short and long-term, they include mobility control, international and domestic trade, supply chains, as well as income security measures for citizens (Paquet and Schertzer 2020). It is important not to lose sight of the progress made in these efforts and the distance from goals ahead. Tools to assess responsiveness to manage investments can help identify gaps and ensure that there is sufficient capacity available to carry out deployment operations effectively. Understanding how the local structure, norms, relationships and processes of the intergovernmental system are helping or hindering the transition is central to explaining policy outputs and the outcomes associated to new investments.

As highlighted before, although the COVID-19 affects all, the impacts have been worse for the elderly, essential workers, racialised populations, people with disabilities and women. There is a need to improve the health, social and economic conditions of these populations to achieve equity and protect people from the threats of pandemics and those caused by climate change. The decisions require high levels of coordination and collaboration among interconnected governments (Paquet and Schertzer 2020), which includes analysis and input from relevant executive departments and agencies, as well as appropriate outreach to local stakeholders.

Conclusion

The challenges currently being faced by distinct sectors highlight the need for greater clarity in three basic pillars of investments: (1) clarity on revised aspects about the carbon market; (2) the nature of the investment; (3) to evaluate the innovativeness and transformative potential of business models; and (4) the establishment of fiscal institutions to widen accountability over the rules. Systemic change is needed to tackle the complex global challenges of pandemics and climate change interconnected with poverty, social inequality and biodiversity loss.

Governments and civil society must use this moment to raise awareness of the impact of climate events, which can ultimately create disruptions of great magnitude and duration. Mechanisms can be applied to accelerate the recovery from pandemic, although there is a recognition that isolated strategies are insufficient to achieve the SDGs and both investments and control measures are important to mediate the investments for transition to a decarbonised scenario. Regulations can provide valuable support to provide incentives for investments based on ESGs, among other principles and instruments.

Nevertheless, although it has proven effective in recent years, the mechanisms were not designed to deal with current or potential shocks (linked to COVID-19, economic slowdown, increasing global poverty, etc.). Achieving climate neutrality will require more funding for climate action, including industrial innovation. Therefore, policymakers and stakeholders must use this opportunity wisely and make the carbon market an instrument to drive effective industrial transformation.

References

Adger, W. N., Brown, I., Surminski, S. 2018. 'Advances in Risk Assessment for Climate Change Adaptation Policy', *The Royal Society Publishing*, 376, no. 2121 (2018): 20180106.

Alexander, David E. 2013. 'Resilience and Disaster Risk Reduction: An Etymological Journey', *Natural Hazards Earth System Science*, 13, 2707–16.

Bailey, D., J. Clark, A. Colombelli, C. Corradini, L. De Propris, B. Derudder, U. Fratesi, M. Fritsch, J. Harrison, M. Hatfield, T. Kemeny, D. F. Kogler, A. Lagendijk, P. Lawton, R. Ortega-Argilés, C. Iglesias Otero, and S. Usai. 2020. 'Regions in a Time of Pandemic', *Regional Studies*, 54 (9), 1163–74.

Barouki, R.; Kogevinas, M.; Audouze, K.; Belesova, K.; Bergman, A.; Birnbaum, L.; Boekhold, S.; Denys, S.; Desseille, C.; Drakvik, E.; Frumkin, H.; Garric, J.; Destoumieux-Garzon, D.; Haines, A.; Huss A.; Jensen, G.; Karakitsios, S.; Klanova, J.; Koskela IM.; Laden, F.; Marano, F.; Franziska Matthies-Wiesler, E.; Morris, G.; Nowacki, J.; Paloniemi, R.; Pearce, N.; Peters, A.; Rekola, A.; Sarigiannis, D.; Šebková, K.; Slama, R.; Staalsen, B.; Tonne, C.; Vermeulen, R.; Vineis, P. 2021. 'The Covid-19 Pandemic and Global Environmental Change: Emerging Research Needs', *Environment International*, 146 (2021 Jan), 106272.

Beck, W., L. J. G. van der Maesen, and A. Walker. 2012. 'Chapter 2: Theorical Foundations.' in Laurent J. G. van der Maesen and Alan Walker (eds.), *Social Quality: From Theory to Indicators* (Palgrave Macmillan: New York), pp. 44–69.

Bélanger, J., and D. Pilling 2019. *The State of the World's Biodiversity for Food and Agriculture*, (Rome: Food and Agriculture Organization of the United Nations Commission on Genetic

Resources for Food and Agriculture Assessments), <http://www.fao.org/3/CA3129EN/ca3129en.pdf> [Accessed 12 July, 2021].

Birkmann, Joern. 2007. 'Risk and Vulnerability Indicators at Different Scales: Applicability, Usefulness and Policy Implications', *Environmental Hazards*, 7 (1), 20–31.

Birkmann, Joern, Omar D Cardona, Martha L Carreño, Alex H Barbat, Mark Pelling, Simon Schneiderbauer, Stefan Kienberger, Margreth Keiler, David Alexander, and Peter Zeil. 2013. 'Framing Vulnerability, Risk and Societal Responses: The Move Framework', *Natural Hazards*, 67 (2), 193–211.

Bracken-Roche, Dearbhail, Emily Bell, Mary Ellen Macdonald, and Eric Racine. 2017. 'The Concept of 'Vulnerability' in Research Ethics: An in-Depth Analysis of Policies and Guidelines', *Health Research Policy and Systems*, 15 (1), 1–18.

Brown, Katrina. 2014. 'Global Environmental Change I: A Social Turn for Resilience?', *Progress in Human Geography*, 38 (1), 107–17.

Burton, Christopher G. 2015. 'A Validation of Metrics for Community Resilience to Natural Hazards and Disasters Using the Recovery from Hurricane Katrina as a Case Study', *Annals of the Association of American Geographers*, 105 (1), 67–86.

Carpenter, Steve, Brian Walker, J Marty Anderies, and Nick Abel. 2001. 'From Metaphor to Measurement: Resilience of What to What?', *Ecosystems*, 4 (8), 765–81.

Carreño, Martha Liliana, Omar Darío Cardona, and Alex H Barbat. 2007. 'A Disaster Risk Management Performance Index', *Natural Hazards*, 41 (1), 1–20.

Chan, Emily YY, Jean H Kim, Cherry Lin, Eliza YL Cheung, and Polly PY Lee. 2014. 'Is Previous Disaster Experience a Good Predictor for Disaster Preparedness in Extreme Poverty Households in Remote Muslim Minority Based Community in China?', *Journal of Immigrant and Minority Health*, 16 (3), 466–72.

Cutter, Susan L, Lindsey Barnes, Melissa Berry, Christopher Burton, Elijah Evans, Eric Tate, and Jennifer Webb. 2008. 'A Place-Based Model for Understanding Community Resilience to Natural Disasters', *Global Environmental Change*, 18 (4), 598–606.

Cutter, Susan L, Bryan J Boruff, and W Lynn Shirley. 2003. 'Social Vulnerability to Environmental Hazards', *Social Science Quarterly*, 84 (2), 242–61.

Diffenbaugh, Noah S, Christopher B Field, Eric A Appel, Ines L Azevedo, Dennis D Baldocchi, Marshall Burke, Jennifer A Burney, Philippe Ciais, Steven J Davis, and Arlene M Fiore. 2020. 'The Covid-19 Lockdowns: A Window into the Earth System', *Nature Reviews Earth and Environment*, 1 (9), 470–81.

Dörry, S., and C. Schulz. 2018. 'Green Financing, Interrupted. Potential Directions for Sustainable Finance in Luxembourg', *The International Journal of Justice and Sustainability*, 23, 717–33.

Estrella, M., and N. Saalismaa. 2013. 'Ecosystem-Based Drr: An Overview.' in F. Renaud, Sudmeier-Rieux and Estrella K., M. (eds.), *The Role of Ecosystems in Disaster Risk Reduction* (Tokyo: United Nations University Press), pp. 26–47

Folke, C. 2016. 'Resilience (Republished)', *Ecology and Society*, 21 (4), 44.

Folke, Carl. 2006. 'Resilience: The Emergence of a Perspective for Social–Ecological Systems Analyses', *Global Environmental Change*, 16 (3), 253–67.

Gaillard, JC, Jake Rom D Cadag, and Mercy MF Rampengan. 2019. 'People's Capacities in Facing Hazards and Disasters: An Overview', *Natural Hazards*, 95 (3), 863–76.

García-Sánchez, Isabel-María, Nicola Raimo, Arcangelo Marrone, and Filippo Vitolla. 2020. 'How Does Integrated Reporting Change in Light of Covid-19? A Revisiting of the Content of the Integrated Reports', *Sustainability*, 12 (18), 7605.

Greene, R. R., A. P. Conrad, N. C. Livingstone, W. H. Barton, M. L. Watkins, R. Blundo, and J. G. Riley. 2003. *An Integrated Approach to Practice, Policy, and Research* (Washington DC: National Association of Social Workers Press).

Griggs, David, Mark Stafford Smith, Johan Rockström, Marcus C Öhman, Owen Gaffney, Gisbert Glaser, Norichika Kanie, Ian Noble, Will Steffen, and Priya Shyamsundar. 2014. 'An Integrated Framework for Sustainable Development Goals', *Ecology and Society*, 19 (4), 49.

Hagelsteen, Magnus, and Per Becker. 2013. 'Challenging Disparities in Capacity Development for Disaster Risk Reduction', *International Journal of Disaster Risk Reduction*, 3, 4–13.

Hagelsteen, Magnus, and Joanne Burke. 2016. 'Practical Aspects of Capacity Development in the Context of Disaster Risk Reduction', *International Journal of Disaster Risk Reduction*, 16, 43–52.

Hamilton, C. 2017. 'The Great Climate Silence: We Are on the Edge of the Abyss but We Ignore It', *The Guardian*, 5 May 2017. <https://www.theguardian.com/environment/2017/may/05/the-great-climate-silence-we-are-on-the-edge-of-the-abyss-but-we-ignore-it> [Accessed 1 April 2021].

Haque, C Emdad, and David Etkin. 2007. 'People and Community as Constituent Parts of Hazards: The Significance of Societal Dimensions in Hazards Analysis', *Natural Hazards*, 41 (2), 271–82.

Herrero, Mario, and Philip Thornton. 2020. 'What Can Covid-19 Teach Us About Responding to Climate Change?', *The Lancet Planetary Health*, 4 (5), e174.

Herrmann, P. 2015. 'Chapter 7: Social Empowerment and Its Indicators.' in Laurent J. G. van der Maesen and Alan Walke (eds.), *Social Quality: From Theory to Indicators* (Palgrave Macmillan: New York), pp. 198–223

Hoffman, Sharona. 2008. 'Preparing for Disaster: Protecting the Most Vulnerable in Emergencies', *University of California Davis Law Review*, 42, 1491–547.

Holand, Ivar Svare, and Päivi Lujala. 2013. 'Replicating and Adapting an Index of Social Vulnerability to a New Context: A Comparison Study for Norway', *The Professional Geographer*, 65 (2), 312–28.

Hulme, Mike, Rolf Lidskog, James M White, and Adam Standring. 2020. 'Social Scientific Knowledge in Times of Crisis: What Climate Change Can Learn from Coronavirus (and Vice Versa)', *Wiley Interdisciplinary Reviews: Climate Change*, 11 (4), 1–5.

Jones, Samantha, Katie J Oven, Bernard Manyena, and Komal Aryal. 2014. 'Governance Struggles and Policy Processes in Disaster Risk Reduction: A Case Study from Nepal', *Geoforum*, 57, 78–90.

Keck, Markus, and Patrick Sakdapolrak. 2013. 'What Is Social Resilience? Lessons Learned and Ways Forward', *Erdkunde*, 67 (1), 5–19.

Kelman, Ilan. 2015. 'Climate Change and the Sendai Framework for Disaster Risk Reduction', *International Journal of Disaster Risk Science*, 6 (2), 117–27.

Kihato, C. W., and L. B. Landau. 2020. 'Coercion or the Social Contract? COVID-19 and Spatial (in) Justice in African Cities', *City and Society*, 32 (1).

Kim, SJ, and W Bostwick. 2020. 'Social Vulnerability and Racial Inequality in Covid-19 Deaths in 508 Chicago', *Health Education and Behavior: The Official Publication of the Society for Public Health*, 509, 509–13.

Klenert, David, Franziska Funke, Linus Mattauch, and Brian O'Callaghan. 2020. 'Five Lessons from Covid-19 for Advancing Climate Change Mitigation', *Environmental and Resource Economics*, 76 (4), 751–78.

Kuhlicke, Christian. 2013. 'Resilience: A Capacity and a Myth: Findings from an in-Depth Case Study in Disaster Management Research', *Natural Hazards*, 67 (1), 61–76.

Levine, Simon. 2014. *Assessing Resilience: Why Quantification Misses the Point*, (London: Overseas Development Institute), <https://odi.org/en/publications/assessing-resilience-why-quantification-misses-the-point/> [Accessed 8 October 2021].

Li, Tongtong, Qi Wang, and Zheng Xie. 2019. 'Disaster Response Knowledge and Its Social Determinants: A Cross-Sectional Study in Beijing, China', *PloS One*, 14 (3), e0214367.

McEntire, David. 2012. 'Understanding and Reducing Vulnerability: From the Approach of Liabilities and Capabilities', *Disaster Prevention and Management: An International Journal*, 21 (2), 206–25.

Menton, Mary, Carlos Larrea, Sara Latorre, Joan Martinez-Alier, Mika Peck, Leah Temper, and Mariana Walter. 2020. 'Environmental Justice and the SDGs: From Synergies to Gaps and Contradictions', *Sustainability Science*, 15 (6), 1621–36.

Mercer, Jessica. 2010. 'Disaster Risk Reduction or Climate Change Adaptation: Are We Reinventing the Wheel?', *Journal of International Development: The Journal of the Development Studies Association*, 22 (2), 247–64.

Motta, Paolo. 2020. 'Urbanization and Sustainability after the Covid-19 Pandemic', *The International Journal of Social Quality*, 10 (1), 1–28.

Mustafa, Daanish, Sara Ahmed, Eva Saroch, and Heather Bell. 2011. 'Pinning Down Vulnerability: From Narratives to Numbers', *Disasters*, 35 (1), 62–86.

Myers, Samuel S, and Jonathan A Patz. 2009. 'Emerging Threats to Human Health from Global Environmental Change', *Annual Review of Environment and Resources*, 34, 223–52.

Norris, Fran H, Susan P Stevens, Betty Pfefferbaum, Karen F Wyche, and Rose L Pfefferbaum. 2008. 'Community Resilience as a Metaphor, Theory, Set of Capacities, and Strategy for Disaster Readiness', *American Journal of Community Psychology*, 41 (1), 127–50.

Okamuro, Hiroyuki, and Junichi Nishimura. 2020. 'What Shapes Local Innovation Policies? Empirical Evidence from Japanese Cities', *Administrative Sciences*, 10 (1), 11.

Organisation for Economic Co-operation and Development.·2020. *Cities Policy Responses*, *13 May*, <https://www.oecd.org/coronavirus/policy-responses/cities-policy-responses-fd1053ff/> [Accessed 8 October 2021].

──.·2021. *OECD Policy Responses to Coronavirus (Covid-19). The Territorial Impact of Covid-19: Managing the Crisis and Recovery across Levels of Government*, <https://www.oecd.org/coronavirus/policy-responses/the-territorial-impact-of-COVID-19-managing-the-crisis-across-levels-of-government-d3e314e1/> [Accessed 8 October 2021].

Paquet, M., and R. Schertzer. 2020. 'Covid-19 as a Complex Intergovernmental Problem', *Canadian Journal of Political Science*, 53, 1–5.

Patterson, J., and J. H. Patterson. 2001. 'Resilience in the Face of Imposed Changes', *Principal Leadership*, 16, 50–55.

Perry, Beth, and Tim May. 2007. 'Governance, Science Policy and Regions: An Introduction', *Regional Studies*, 41 (8), 1039–50.

Renaud, Fabrice G, Karen Sudmeier-Rieux, and Marisol Estrella. 2013. *The Role of Ecosystems in Disaster Risk Reduction* (Tokyo: United Nations University Press).

Revet, Sandrine. 2020. *Disasterland: An Ethnography of the International Disaster Community* (Berlin: Springer Nature).

Sharifi, Ayyoob, and Amir Reza Khavarian-Garmsir. 2020. 'The Covid-19 Pandemic: Impacts on Cities and Major Lessons for Urban Planning, Design, and Management', *Science of the Total Environment*, 749, 142391.

Shepherd, G. 2008. *The Ecosystem Approach: Learning from Experience* (Gland, Switzerland: International Union for Conservation of Nature).

Sheridan, Thomas B. 2008. 'Risk, Human Error, and System Resilience: Fundamental Ideas', *Human Factors*, 50 (3), 418–26.

Sorg, Linda, Neiler Medina, Daniel Feldmeyer, Arlex Sanchez, Zoran Vojinovic, Jörn Birkmann, and Alessandra Marchese. 2018. 'Capturing the Multifaceted Phenomena of Socioeconomic Vulnerability', *Natural Hazards*, 92 (1), 257–82.

Stiglitz, Joseph. 2020. 'Point of View: Conquering the Great Divide', *Finance and Development*, 57 (003), 17–19.

Thomas, Deborah SK, Sojin Jang, and Jean Scandlyn. 2020. 'The CHASMS Conceptual Model of Cascading Disasters and Social Vulnerability: The Covid-19 Case Example', *International Journal of Disaster Risk Reduction*, 51, 101828.

Tierney, Kathleen. 2006. 'Foreshadowing Katrina: Recent Sociological Contributions to Vulnerability Science', *Contemporary Sociology*, 35 (3), 207–12.

——. 2012. 'Disaster Governance: Social, Political, and Economic Dimensions', *Annual Review of Environment and Resources*, 37, 341–63.

Tille, Florian, Dimitra Panteli, Nick Fahy, Ruth Waitzberg, Navad Davidovitch, and Alexander Degelsegger-Márquez. 2021. 'Governing the Public-Private-Partnerships of the Future: Learnings from the Experiences in Pandemic Times', *Eurohealth*, 27 (1), 49–53.

Ulmer, Robert R, Matthew W Seeger, and Timothy L Sellnow. 2007. 'Post-Crisis Communication and Renewal: Expanding the Parameters of Post-Crisis Discourse', *Public Relations Review*, 33 (2), 130–34.

United Nations.·2015. *Sendai Framework for Disaster Risk Reduction 2015-2030*, (Sendai, Japan: United Nations), <https://www.unisdr.org/files/43291_sendaiframeworkfordrren.pdf> [Accessed 8 October 2021].

United Nations Conference on Trade and Development 2020 *Leveraging the Potential of ESG ETFs for Sustainable Development* <https://unctad.org/system/files/official-document /diae2020d1_en.pdf> [Accessed 8 October 2021].

United Nations Covention on Biological Diversity 2010 *The Strategic Plan for Biodiversity 2011-2020 and the Aichi Biodiversity Targets* (Nagoya, Japan: Conference of the Parties to the Convention on Biological Diversity, Number 10)

United Nations Economic Commission for Latin America and the Caribbean/Office for Disaster Risk Reduction.·2021. *The Coronavirus Disease (Covid-19) Pandemic: An Opportunity for a Systemic Approach to Disaster Risk for the Caribbean*, <https://www.cepal.org/sites/default/files/publi cation/files/46732/S2000944_en.pdf> [Accessed 8 October 2021].

United Nations Food and Agriculture Organization, International Fund for Agricultural Development, United Nations Children's Fund, World Food Programme, and World Health Organization.·2021. *The State of Food Security and Nutrition in the World 2021: Transforming Food Systems for Food Security, Improved Nutrition and Affordable Healthy Diets for All*, (Rome: UN Food and Agriculture Organization), <https://www.fao.org/publications/sofi/2021/ en/> [Accessed 31 January 2022].

United Nations Sustainable Development Group.·2020. *A UN Framework for the Immediate Socio-Economic Response to Covid-19*, <https://unsdg.un.org/resources/un-framework-immediate-socio-economic-response-covid-19> [Accessed 8 October 2021].

van der Maesen, L.J.D. 2012. '*The Functions of Social Quality Indicators.*' in Laurent J. G. van der Maesen and Alan Walker (eds.), Social Quality: From Theory to Indicators (New York: Springer), pp. 224–49

van der Maesen, L.J.D., and A. Walker.·2013. *Four Stages of Social Quality Thinking*, (European Foundation on Social Quality and the International Association on Social Quality), <https://www.oasisociale.it/wp-content/uploads/2013/11/Social-Quality.pdf> [Accessed 8 October 2021].

Wang, Y., and Q. Zhi. 2016. 'The Role of Green Finance in Environmental Protection: Two Aspects of Market Mechanism and Policies', *Energy Procedia*, 104, 311–16.

Weichselgartner, J., and P. Pigeon. 2015. 'The Role of Knowledge in Disaster Risk Reduction', *International Journal of Disaster Risk Science*, 6 (2), 107–16.

Part 5: **The blue economy**

Timothy Cadman, Tapan Sarker, Sikha Karki
and Rebecca Marshallsay

Chapter 22
Sustainable ocean development
and the blue economy

Abstract: Part 5 of this Handbook begins with a general introduction to the concepts
and definitions underlying the notion of the blue economy and continues with an
exploration of challenges and controversies confronting the sustainable development of the marine environment. The tensions inherent in the idea that the marine
environment can be both exploited for human use and protected for its intrinsic
natural values, reflect the origins of the concept of sustainable development itself
and these are explored in the chapters presented in this section. These cover an examination of the ethics and values underpinning the blue economy, the role that
blue finance can play in advancing sustainable development, particularly for tourism and local communities dependent on the oceans for their wellbeing. The views
of various stakeholders on the quality and legitimacy of the governance of a range
of blue economy initiatives are also explored, as is the extent to which, philosophi-
cally speaking, ocean development can be understood as genuinely sustainable,
whatever the rhetoric may be. A concluding chapter from practitioners of marine
permaculture completes the perspectives of the contributing authors on the complexities and contradictions within humanity's use of the many and various resources of the world's oceans and in the wake of COVID-19.

Keywords: blue economy, blue finance, coastal and marine tourism, ethics, governance, marine permaculture, ocean energy, seafood, sustainable ocean development, COVID-19

Background: Concepts and definitions
of the blue economy

The ocean, the world's largest ecosystem, covering 71% of the Earth's surface area,
supports humans by providing essentials like food, materials, energy and transportation. It offers civilisation a variety of vital functions. Over 40% of the world's population currently lives within 200 kilometres of the ocean. Out of 15 megacities in
the world, 12 are on the coast. The rising human population, industrial growth and
the resulting pollution, loss of habitat, climate change and unsustainable extraction
of resources have put pressure on the ocean and altered its health and production

https://doi.org/10.1515/9783110733488-022

(Visbeck et al. 2014; Visbeck 2018). Recent years have witnessed increased awareness and initiatives among various stakeholders and countries regarding the use of ocean space and resources while maintaining the health of the ocean; from this has arisen the notion of the blue economy; more recently still, the impacts of COVID-19 have affected various sectors of the hitherto rapidly-expanding blue economy (Okafor-Yarwood et al. 2020; Brears 2021).

The concept of the blue economy has been gaining ground over the last decades. blue economy complements the green economy concepts while fostering improved stewardship/management of ocean or blue resources. The United Nations defines the blue economy as an ocean economy that strives for the 'improvement of human wellbeing and social equity, while significantly reducing environmental risks and ecological scarcities' (United Nations Conference on Trade and Development 2014: 2) in a concept paper issued in 2014. According to the World Bank (2017: 6), the blue economy is defined as 'the sustainable use of ocean resources for economic growth, improved livelihoods and jobs while preserving the health of ocean ecosystem.' There are several definitions of the blue economy (see, e.g., Everest-Phillips 2014; World Wildlife Foundation 2015; National Maritime Foundation 2017; National Marine Science Committee 2015; Whisnant and Reyes 2015). These definitions of the blue economy vary with respect to the context in which it is defined and actors who define them (Wenhai et al. 2019; Silver et al. 2015; Choi 2017) and so do the discourses around its concept, highlighting the lack of universally accepted definition of the blue economy (Garland et al. 2019).

The blue economy paradigm portrays the ocean in two ways: one as a space for wealth creation in response to global poverty and inequality and the other as a fragile and vulnerable ecosystem in need of conservation in response to dramatic changes caused by climate change, pollution, overfishing and habitat destruction (Midlen 2021). The concept creates two conflicts of interest. Those tied to economic growth and development on the one hand and those linked to conserving and protecting the ocean's resources on the other (Martínez-Vázquez, Milán-García, and de Pablo Valenciano 2021). The interpretation of the blue (or ocean) economy resonates with discussions on trickle-down versus bottom-up development. The bottom-up approach appears to be central to the original blue economy proposal highlighting consequences of unequal economic development, such as historical marginalisation, the extraction of benefits from local resources away from local communities and long-term environmental impacts as industries depleted resources and left. The trickle-down theory on the other hand highlights that prosperous ocean industries will eventually benefit all of society, even if the majority of the benefits will go to a small segment of the population or private businesses. While environmental effects are likely to occur, they will be mitigated over time when new technologies are developed (Cisneros-Montemayor 2019).

While there is both agreement and disagreement on how the blue economy concept has developed and is being implemented, the concept's intrinsic ambiguity can be adopted as its scope for flexibility and adaptability while focussing on handling and managing conflicts between the various blue economy lenses in a way that reflects the diverse priorities (Voyer et al. 2018). The concept reflects the teetering balance between socioeconomic progress and irresponsible environmental destruction (Smith-Godfrey 2016). The blue economy strategy should be viewed as a chance to make a significant change towards ambitious social and environmental goals (Cisneros-Montemayor 2019). Improved awareness is critical for facilitating communication among colleagues and across disciplines, as well as convergence towards an operational definition of blue growth to develop comprehensive science-based policy that promotes and benefits both the social and economic sectors and the aquatic environment, mainly marine systems (Eikeset et al. 2018).

Issues and origin of the idea

The first proposal on blue economy formulation was the report to the Club of Rome by Pauli (2010) named *The Blue Economy: 10 years, 100 innovations, 100 million jobs.* Although the origins of the blue economy may be traced back to 1992 at the Rio Earth Summit (Voyer et al. 2018), the term blue economy came to light at Rio+20. The term was used at Rio 20 by several participants to highlight the significance of conservation and development of oceans amongst the wider environmental governance stakeholders as well as back-burning problems, associated solutions and actors (Silver et al. 2015). Even within the single summit, the Rio+20 summit, blue economy was recognised in various ways such as livelihood sources and natural capital, vital to Small Island Developing States and good business (Silver et al., 2015).

Challenges in the blue economy around sustainable development

The blue economy is associated with the utilisation of the ocean and its resources for sustainable economic growth. The blue economy supports all of the Sustainable Development Goals (SDGs), particularly SDG14 – 'Life below water,' and is included in the 2030 Agenda for Sustainable Development (United Nations 2021). The United Nations has designated the years 2021 to 2030 as the 'Decade of Ocean Science for Sustainable Development' (United Nations n.d.), to promote efforts to reverse the downward trend in ocean health and bring ocean stakeholders from around the world together under a single framework. This framework intends to ensure that ocean science can fully assist countries in improving circumstances for the ocean's long-term growth (United Nations n.d.). Nevertheless, there are challenges in the blue economy around sustainable development.

The scope and limitations of the blue economy in accordance with the UN's SDGs are ambiguous and difficult to define, as are the key stakeholders' interests and roles in the blue economy (Lee, Noh, and Khim 2020). Setting goals with targets and indicators that require productive, healthy and resilient oceans is critical (Martínez-Vázquez, Milán-García, and de Pablo Valenciano 2021). The achievement of the 17 SDGs targets will necessitate a global shift in economic strategy with multi-stakeholder consensus among countries and governments (Choudhary et al. 2021). Integration of ocean and terrestrial solutions into a comprehensive climate change policy is essential to attain sustainable targets, which will involve multi-government commitment and developed finance innovations (Choudhary et al. 2021). There is still no common strategy or framework that has been agreed upon. There is a lack of guidance, in particular, on relevant governance structures, such as how to adapt existing governance systems to enable the sustainable development of the blue economy. Therefore, countries need to review their policies and emphasise filling policy gaps and fixing flaws in the current governance system (Voyer et al. 2020). A more adaptable and flexible policymaking strategy that takes into account shifting environmental social, and economic circumstances is needed to achieve sustainable growth of the blue economy as synergies and tensions across sectors, as well as political decisions, may have an impact on the blue economy's long-term viability (Hoerterer et al. 2020). Several factors, such as inequitable outcomes, lack of infrastructure and technology to support expanding offshore sectors, poor awareness of environmental implications and a lack of planning and governmental control impede the attainment of a sustainable future in the blue economy. Therefore, social attitudes must evolve, money for offshore activities must be more evenly distributed, information sharing across companies and between nations must be transparent and international legal and institutional processes must be adjusted (Novaglio et al. 2021).

Controversies surrounding market-based approaches to sustainable ocean development

Consumers are becoming increasingly aware of the environmental implications of the marine products they consume and are more inclined to use their purchasing power to support businesses that are perceived to be eco-friendly. Directly linked to this, businesses are concerned about the commercial implications of not being perceived to be eco-friendly. Ironically, however, the desire to appeal to the consumer and the perceived threat of loss of businesses can sometimes drive corporate behaviour rather than a sense of corporate social responsibility and can ultimately lead to corruption and greenwashing (or rather, blue washing) rather than improved practices. This can be exacerbated by governments, who, in the presence of weak or ineffective environmental legislation are more concerned with meeting the needs of industry than consumers. This has led to the rise of third parties, such as environmental non-governmental organisations (ENGOs) entering the marketplace in an attempt to encourage sustainable business by seeking partnerships with industry through such approaches as certification and eco-labelling of businesses doing the right thing. However, the relationship is not one of independent oversight but rather a commercial relationship and, as has been shown in the commercial farmed salmon industry, can undermine an ENGOs' ability to sanction wrongdoing when it occurs, thereby potentially, defrauding the public. Consequently, without some form of independent oversight and governmental regulation, companies functioning with the blue economy can still engage in unsustainable practices, even if they are supported by environmental groups (Bleakley 2020).

In many instances where the use of ocean resources falls outside state jurisdictions, and relies on non-state legitimation, the notion of continuous improvement – that is, that a company constantly strives to do better than previous performance – can be used as a demonstration of a commitment to sustainability. However, unless private governance systems explicitly build this requirement and provide extra formal recognition, there is little incentive for companies to go beyond basic good practice. This, and the failure to include small-scale fisheries from local, often developing, countries in systems of private environmental governance, has favoured only large industrial-scale players (Bush et al. 2013).

Regrettably, when many of these approaches to demonstrating sustainability are challenged by community groups for failing to protect the natural resources of the oceans, the private governance systems which have accredited their members' activities refuse to act on such complaints. Examples from locations as diverse as Northern Australia, Alaska and the Faroe Islands reveal that eco-labelling organisations are reluctant to make findings against their members. In these cases, companies have sought to use the social licence implicit in certification as a shield against claims of malpractice and the schemes of which they were members dismissed all allegations, despite the impacts on endangered species or stocks (Hadjimichael and Hegland 2016).

Marine governance, by virtue of the space and resources being transnational commons, faces enormous challenges, as do the industries which are active in the oceans; indeed, even the notion of sustainable seafood is complex. Species, or areas of operation, may pose other challenges. This means that where broad terminology is used such as biodiversity, environmental protection or sustainability, there is considerable scope for interpretation or measuring the outcome. Attempts to design detailed standards that accurately reflect the complex nature of the field often become compromised with respect to feasibility and there are claims that no market-based efforts to deliver sustainable ocean development have been effective. As with forest management (a topic discussed earlier in Chapter Six), competition, rather than collaboration, between rival schemes has created uncertainty over what the standards they promote actually stand for (Wijen and Chiroleu–Assouline 2019).

The commercial prospects associated with the ocean are numerous and considerable. These include transportation, seafood production, ocean energy, mineral extraction, biotechnology, human settlements, tourism and recreation and exploration of the sea (Kaczynski, 2011). In the case of the blue economy, there are both governmental, public, processes regulating activities in the world's oceans, as well as private governance systems, based on certification of activities against a set of standards, such as the Marine Stewardship Council. There are a number of reasons for going beyond the purely compliance-based approach, whether it is to get a market edge or to have some kind of differential branding (Gunningham, Kagan, and Thornton 2004). However, there must be meaningful participation of social, environmental and economic stakeholders and rights holders in decision-making, particularly First Nations, especially if legitimacy or endorsement is one of the desired outcomes (Gray and Purdy 2018; Boutilier and Zdziarski 2017; Vince 2018; Breakey, Cadman, and Sampford 2016). Without it, these non-state governance systems become little more than decoy institutions (Dimitrov 2020), with all the appearance of adhering to the norms of global environmental governance and none of its governing values.

Overview of chapters

In this section's foundational chapter, 'Ethics in the blue economy,' Hugh Breakey interprets the blue economy as comprising marine industries, ostensibly operating in sustainable ways. It reviews the main ethical challenges arising in the blue economy and then explores the values and concepts at work in responding to these challenges. First, due to an array of factors (including being a quick-moving industry driven by developing technology operating on public spaces with only nascent regulation processes), what has been termed as the social licence to operate stands as an important factor in shaping blue economy ethical discourse. This significance of the social licence can have advantages when the process empowers ethical considerations and stakeholder involvement in industry activity. Equally though, it can pose risks where the social licence replaces or stymies the development of stronger ethical and governance practices, such as free, prior and informed consent. The chapter then explores the relevant ethical values (governing values) that undergird the ethical challenges and discusses the way these appear in the scholarly literature and social licence discourses. These values may be supplied by ethical principles and theory or by official instruments – of which the UN SDGs are a prime example. SDG 14 ('Conserve and sustainably use the oceans, seas and marine resources for sustainable development') is of particular importance, but many SDGs are relevant for the blue economy, impacting as it does on employment, food security, sustainable energy production and more. Some of these values are directly relevant to finance, with contested concepts of blue growth, green growth and de-growth aiming to define the proper role of finance and development in the blue economy.

Next, attention turns to governance values at work in the blue economy, noting that these can come in a spectrum running from thin (limited to transparency, accountability, and compliance practices) to thick (involving more robust mechanisms for democratic and deliberative processes, and effective problem-solving outcomes). Governance values can be employed to answer to the achievement of governing values (such as improving sustainability or promoting human rights). However, they also contribute to legitimacy in their own right, especially if thick governance values are employed.

The following section focusses on institutional integrity, considering where an organisation or system defines and lives up to its stated values or mission (its public institutional justification). Institutional integrity has both instrumental and intrinsic ethical significance. The section considers the presence or absence of institutional integrity in the blue economy as a whole, in key industries and for specific organisations, inquiring into when institutions have developed public institutional justifications (such as mission statements or values statements) and how they have done so and then explores the devices through which these values are pursued by the organisation.

The final section then draws upon all these distinct but interrelated ethical phenomena (social licence, governing values, governance values, and institutional integrity) as they interact together to deliver a full picture of the ethics and legitimacy of the blue economy. In the light of the COVID-19 pandemic, it is the good that a sustainable blue economy fosters, namely food security, basic employment and the support of livelihoods – especially of marginalised communities – notably small-scale fisherfolk, that stands in stark contrast to the large-scale, industrial enterprises, which have suffered a far greater economic shock. Here a lesson can be learnt, which applies equally on land as it does at sea.

In their chapter 'Financing sustainable coastal and maritime tourism in the blue economy of the Asia-Pacific,' Md. Wasiul Islam and Tapan Sarker explore the economic, environmental and social realities confronting coastal and marine tourism in the emerging economies of the Asia-Pacific region. Balanced and sustainable development, they argue, is essential for both the terrestrial and blue economies to foster national development. However, the coastal and marine environment is facing many challenges from human and natural causes. The region is a popular tourist destination and has a well-developed coastal and maritime tourism (CMT) subsector in the broader tourism industry and makes a substantive contribution to the global economy. Their study focusses on an in-depth case study of Bangladesh, which has great potential for CMT due to its unique biodiversity, strategic location in the Bay of Bengal, comfortable weather and hospitable people living around the country's coastal and marine areas. Bangladesh provides an excellent case study for two reasons. First, CMT has not yet been well-developed despite expectations and the sector's potential. Second, there are institutional and cultural barriers to accessing the finance necessary for developing CMT. The authors explore these, as well as the various impacts (both positive and negative) of CMT in the Asia-Pacific. The chapter provides a conceptual framework linking blue finance and sustainable development by strengthening the emerging blue economy through sustainable coastal and marine tourism built on the conservation of the coastal and marine environment and creating resilient coastal communities. Blue finance is an emerging class of sustainable investment and there is significant, but as yet unrealised role conservation-oriented projects as a means of both stimulating sustainable local, low-carbon economies and providing a basis for genuine ecotourism. Such investment can alleviate poverty and encourage sustainable development by promoting green energy projects, building capacity in locally based guiding enterprises, marine and coastal conservation projects, waste disposal management and sustainable food production.

In their chapter 'Evaluating the governance of sustainable development: The quality and legitimacy of the blue economy' Tek Maraseni and colleagues provide a broad overview of several of the major initiatives currently occurring in the intergovernmental policy arena, and beyond, seeking to promote, generate sustainable investment for, trade in services derived from, and certify, activities within the blue economy. In an empirical study, they investigate the views of multi-stakeholders from both developed and developing countries on the governance and sustainability of the different blue economy initiatives, based on research conducted in 2020. The seven initiatives under investigation included the blue economy generally, The Sustainable Ocean Initiative of the Convention on Biological Diversity (CBD), The Sustainable Blue Economy Finance Initiative (UNEP), The Blue Carbon Initiative, The Marine Stewardship Council, marine permaculture and other global, regional, national or local activities. Using an anonymous online survey, and applying an analytical method based on principles, criteria and indicators, stakeholders from both developed and developing nations rated the quality of these initiatives on a Likert scale (1-5) based on 11 indicators of governance quality. According to the findings, the Sustainable Ocean Initiative was rated the highest of all (a total score of 36.1 out of 55), while marine permaculture scored the lowest (32.3). Similarly, among all the governance indicators, inclusiveness received the highest scores and resources received the lowest scores (< 50% or < 2.5 out of 5) indicating that while the data indicates that respondents might be satisfied with their level of inclusion, they felt that the level of resources allocated in these initiatives for stakeholders to participate meaningfully in decision-making and implementation of the activities and outcomes of these initiatives were limited. Sector-wise, respondents from the environment sector gave higher scores for all the initiatives and indicators, while government respondents gave the lowest scores. In comparison to the Global North (developed countries), respondents from the Global South (developing countries) generally rated all indicators and initiatives higher than their developed country counterparts. This might be a consequence of the fact that these initiatives are largely occurring as sustainable development-oriented programmes from the Global North to the Global South (Maraseni and Cadman 2015), which is generally the prime beneficiary of these programmes and receive more funding for projects and capacity building activities, reflecting a potential South/North, rather than North/South Divide (Cadman and Maraseni 2013).

The findings of this study are important if sustainable outcomes in blue economy initiatives are to be achieved for all participants in this emerging economic and policy arena. The blue economy is an expanding frontier with a high potential for sustainable development; however, there are various challenges impeding its progress. Oceans and coasts which have already been harmed by climate change and increasing unsustainable use of marine resources for economic activities have been further impacted by the COVID-19 pandemic. Whether there is room for marginalised communities in the blue economy space (such as First Nations people or local-scale, community-based enterprises) or whether perceptions regarding the inherent sustainability of current ocean development implicit in this study are true, remain to be seen.

In an aptly juxtaposed chapter relating to the question, 'How green is the blue economy?,' Graham Wood confronts the potential contradictions with the blue economy by comparing the longstanding terrestrial economy with the emerging blue economy. Although there have long been marine dimensions to the terrestrial economy, the terrestrial economy as it is understood today, they argue, commenced with the resource surpluses produced with the start of the agricultural revolution to the present day's globalised economy. The history of the terrestrial economy has been one of trial and error in terms of how sustainable or green it may be characterised as being. Lessons have been learnt over the years, and hopefully, the terrestrial economy is heading in a more sustainable direction.

Keeping the lessons learnt within the terrestrial economy in mind, they make a comparison with the current state of the blue economy. The oceans as a whole are yet to go through what might be called the aquacultural revolution, so much so that much of the current exploitation of the ocean can be reasonably called a hunting and gathering economy. But presumably the coming years of human activity will see extensive exploitation of the ocean as a domesticated space. What lessons, they ask, can be learnt from the trial and error of the terrestrial economy, and can they be applied now before similar mistakes are made, and the oceans are depleted? The ensuing analysis is a discussion of the concepts of planetary boundaries, ecosystem services and natural capital and explores the contrasts between domesticated and non-domesticated space, strong and weak sustainability, intrinsic and instrumental environmental values, shallow and deep environmental ethics and biocentric versus. anthropocentric conceptual frameworks. Drawing on a number of approaches, including those motivated by the Brundtland definition of sustainable development, as well as other approaches, the concepts central to sustainability are also identified, including the resilience of systems to shocks, such as the impacts on and threats to Small Island Developing States from COVID-19.

Ultimately, the intent of the chapter is not to provide a single truth or a definitive response. Indeed, it is still too early to tell which route the blue economy will take: one based on the integration of sustainability-oriented values into social, economic and environmental activities; the (somewhat compromised) models of terrestrial sustainability; or outright business-as-usual. Rather, the point of the chapter is to provide those active in, and cognisant of, the blue economy with the tools necessary to ensure the role they play is beneficial, not harmful to the marine environment and all life that depends on it.

In the final chapter of this section 'Approaches to Finance in support of social enterprise, non-profits and for-purpose organisations: A marine permaculture case study,' the authors, coming from diverse non-governmental, scientific and entrepreneurial backgrounds, confront and discuss the realities of implementing sustainable ocean development from the perspective of an emerging enterprise within the blue economy. Sam Zak of the Climate Foundation and co-authors see a key role for decentralised finance in sustainable development, particularly for innovative solutions for markets and services that are still forming, such as carbon markets or public goods. The Climate Foundation has leveraged non-profit finance over more than a decade to support trials of marine permaculture (MP), an emerging technology and currently an industry focussing on a blue economy concentrated on the regeneration of the marine environment and sustainable development. The chapter begins by describing a long-term vision for MP and how it can help contribute to eight of the 17 SDGs. The chapter discusses how deep-water irrigation provided by MP could be crucial in building climate resilience, thereby helping tropical seaweed-growing communities adapt to climate change. The authors continue by presenting their insights from successful fundraising initiatives and other philanthropic fundraising options in the emerging fields of financial technology (fintech) innovation that have arisen in the MP space and outline the effective elements that contribute to successful philanthropic crowdfunding campaigns. The chapter, essential reading for those seeking to enter into the blue economy with new, sustainable, business ventures, concludes with reflections on how innovative fintech can boost startups and generate employment in the regenerative, circular, economy, in the challenging investment climate of COVID-19 and in the decades to come.

References

Bleakley, Paul. 2020. 'Big Fish, Small Pond: NGO–Corporate Partnerships and Corruption of the Environmental Certification Process in Tasmanian Aquaculture', *Critical Criminology*, 28 (3), 389–405.
Boutilier, Robert G., and Michal Zdziarski. 2017. 'Managing Stakeholder Networks for a Social License to Build', *Construction Management and Economics*, 35 (8–9), 498–513.

Breakey, Hugh, Tim Cadman, and Charles Sampford. 2016. 'Governance Values and Institutional Integrity.' in Tim Cadman, Rowena Maguire and Charles Sampford (eds.), *Governing the Climate Change Regime* (New York: Routledge), pp. 34–62.

Brears, Robert C. 2021. *Developing the Blue Economy* (Cham, Switzerland Springer Nature).

Bush, Simon R., Hilde Toonen, Peter Oosterveer, and Arthur P.J. Mol. 2013. 'The 'Devils Triangle'of MSC Certification: Balancing Credibility, Accessibility and Continuous Improvement', *Marine Policy*, 37, 288–93.

Cadman, Timothy, and Tek Maraseni. 2013. 'More Equal Than Others? A Comparative Analysis of State and Non-State Perceptions of Interest Representation and Decision-Making in REDD+ Negotiations', *Innovation: The European Journal of Social Science Research*, 26 (3), 214–30.

Choi, Young Rae. 2017. 'The Blue Economy as Governmentality and the Making of New Spatial Rationalities', *Dialogues in Human Geography*, 7 (1), 37–41.

Choudhary, Poonam, Monika Khade, Sandip Savant, Amar Musale, Meenakshi Sundaram Chelliah, and Santanu Dasgupta. 2021. 'Empowering Blue Economy: From Underrated Ecosystem to Sustainable Industry', *Journal of Environmental Management*, 291, 112697.

Cisneros-Montemayor, Andrés M. 2019. 'A Blue Economy: Equitable, Sustainable, and Viable Development in the World's Oceans.' in W. Cheung, Y. Ota and A. Cisneros-Montemayor (eds.), *Predicting Future Oceans* (Elsevier), pp. 395–404.

Dimitrov, Radoslav S. 2020. 'Empty Institutions in Global Environmental Politics', *International Studies Review*, 22 (3), 626–50.

Eikeset, Anne Maria, Anna B. Mazzarella, Brynhildur Davíðsdóttir, Dane H. Klinger, Simon A. Levin, Elena Rovenskaya, and Nils Chr Stenseth. 2018. 'What Is Blue Growth? The Semantics of "Sustainable Development of Marine Environments', *Marine Policy*, 87, 177–79.

Everest-Phillips, Max. 2014. Small, So Simple?: Complexity in Small Island Developing States (Singapore: UNDP Global Centre for Public Service Excellence).

Garland, Michaela, Stephen Axon, Marcello Graziano, John Morrissey, and C. Patrick Heidkamp. 2019. 'The Blue Economy: Identifying Geographic Concepts and Sensitivities', *Geography Compass*, 13 (7), e12445.

Gray, Barbara, and Jill Purdy. 2018. *Collaborating for Our Future: Multistakeholder Partnerships for Solving Complex Problems* (Oxford: Oxford University Press).

Gunningham, Neil, Robert A. Kagan, and Dorothy Thornton. 2004. 'Social License and Environmental Protection: Why Businesses Go Beyond Compliance', *Law and Social Inquiry*, 29 (2), 307–41.

Hadjimichael, Maria, and Troels J. Hegland. 2016. 'Really Sustainable? Inherent Risks of Eco-Labeling in Fisheries', *Fisheries Research*, 174, 129–35.

Hoerterer, Christina, Maximilian F. Schupp, Andreas Benkens, Dustin Nickiewicz, Gesche Krause, and Bela H. Buck. 2020. 'Stakeholder Perspectives on Opportunities and Challenges in Achieving Sustainable Growth of the Blue Economy in a Changing Climate', *Frontiers in Marine Science*, 6, 795.

Kaczynski, Wlodzimierz. "The future of blue economy: lessons for European Union." *Foundations of Management* 3, no. 1 (2011): 21–31.

Lee, Ki-Hoon, Junsung Noh, and Jong Seong Khim. 2020. 'The Blue Economy and the United Nations' Sustainable Development Goals: Challenges and Opportunities', *Environment International*, 137, 105528.

Maraseni, Tek Narayan, and Tim Cadman. 2015. 'A Comparative Analysis of Global Stakeholders' Perceptions of the Governance Quality of the Clean Development Mechanism (CDM) and Reducing Emissions from Deforestation and Forest Degradation (REDD+)', *International Journal of Environmental Studies*, 72 (2), 288–304.

Martínez-Vázquez, Rosa María, Juan Milán-García, and Jaime de Pablo Valenciano. 2021.
'Challenges of the Blue Economy: Evidence and Research Trends', *Environmental Sciences Europe*, 33 (1), 1–17.

Midlen, Alex. 2021. 'What Is the Blue Economy? A Spatialised Governmentality Perspective',
Maritime Studies, 20, 423–448 (2021). https://doi.org/10.1007/s40152-021-00240-3.

National Marine Science Committee.·2015. *National Marine Science Plan 2015–2025: Driving the Development of Australia'S Blue Economy*, (Townsville, Australia: National Marine Science Committee), <https://www.marinescience.net.au/wp-content/uploads/2021/08/NMSP-2015-2025-reportREDUCED.pdf> [Accessed 20 January 2022].

National Maritime Foundation 2017 *The Blue Economy: Concept, Constituents and Development* (New Delhi, India: Annual Maritime Power Conference)

Novaglio, Camilla, Narissa Bax, Fabio Boschetti, Gholam Reza Emad, Stewart Frusher, Liam Fullbrook, Mark Hemer, Sarah Jennings, Ingrid Van Putten, and Lucy M. Robinson. 2021.
'Deep Aspirations: Towards a Sustainable Offshore Blue Economy', *Reviews in Fish Biology and Fisheries*, 1–22.

Okafor-Yarwood, Ifesinachi, Nelly I. Kadagi, Nelson A.F. Miranda, Jacqueline Uku, Isa O. Elegbede, and Ibukun J. Adewumi. 2020. 'The Blue Economy–Cultural Livelihood–Ecosystem Conservation Triangle: The African Experience', *Frontiers in Marine Science*, 7 (586).

Pauli, Gunter A. 2010. *The Blue Economy: 10 Years, 100 Innovations, 100 Million Jobs*: (Paradigm Publications).

Silver, Jennifer J., Noella J. Gray, Lisa M. Campbell, Luke W. Fairbanks, and Rebecca L. Gruby. 2015.
'Blue Economy and Competing Discourses in International Oceans Governance', *The Journal of Environment and Development*, 24 (2), 135–60.

Smith-Godfrey, Simon. 2016. 'Defining the Blue Economy', *Maritime Affairs: Journal of the National Maritime Foundation of India*, 12 (1), 58–64.

United Nations.·2021. *The Sustainable Development Agenda*, (New York: United Nations), <https://www.un.org/sustainabledevelopment/development-agenda/> [Accessed 20 January 2022].

——. N d. *Decade of Ocean Science for Sustainable Development*, <https://www.oceandecade.org/> [Accessed 19 January 2022].

United Nations Conference on Trade and Development.·2014. *The Oceans Economy: Opportunities and Challenges for Small Island Developing States*, (Geneva: UNCTAD), <https://unctad.org/system/files/official-document/ditcted2014d5_en.pdf> [Accessed 19 January 2022].

Vince, Joanna. 2018. 'Third Party Certification: Implementation Challenges in Private-Social Partnerships', *Policy Design and Practice*, 1 (4), 323–36.

Visbeck, Martin. 2018. 'Ocean Science Research Is Key for a Sustainable Future', *Nature Communications*, 9 (1), 1–4.

Visbeck, Martin, Ulrike Kronfeld-Goharani, Barbara Neumann, Wilfried Rickels, Jörn Schmidt, Erik van Doorn, Nele Matz-Lück, Konrad Ott, and Martin F. Quaas. 2014. 'Securing Blue Wealth: The Need for a Special Sustainable Development Goal for the Ocean and Coasts', *Marine Policy*, 48, 184–91.

Voyer, Michelle, Anna K. Farmery, Lana Kajlich, Astrid Vachette, and Genevieve Quirk. 2020.
'Assessing Policy Coherence and Coordination in the Sustainable Development of a Blue Economy. A Case Study from Timor Leste', *Ocean and Coastal Management*, 192, 105187.

Voyer, Michelle, Genevieve Quirk, Alistair McIlgorm, and Kamal Azmi. 2018. 'Shades of Blue: What Do Competing Interpretations of the Blue Economy Mean for Oceans Governance?', *Journal of Environmental Policy and Planning*, 20 (5), 595–616.

Wenhai, Lu, Caroline Cusack, Maria Baker, Wang Tao, Chen Mingbao, Kelli Paige, Zhang Xiaofan, Lisa Levin, Elva Escobar, Diva Amon, Yin Yue, Anja Reitz, Antonio Augusto Sepp Neves,

Eleanor O'Rourke, Gianandrea Mannarini, Jay Pearlman, Jonathan Tinker, Kevin J. Horsburgh, Patrick Lehodey, Sylvie Pouliquen, Trine Dale, Zhao Peng, and Yang Yufeng. 2019. 'Successful Blue Economy Examples with an Emphasis on International Perspectives', *Frontiers in Marine Science*, 6 (261).

Whisnant, Ryan, and Antonia Reyes. 2015. *Blue Economy for Business in East Asia: Towards an Integrated Understanding of Blue Economy* (Quezon City, Philippines: Partnerships in Environmental Management for the Seas of East Asia (PEMSEA)), <http://pemsea.org/sites/default/files/PEMSEA%20Blue%20Economy%20Report%2011.10.15-2.pdf> [Accessed 20 January 2022].

Wijen, Frank, and Mireille Chiroleu-Assouline. 2019. 'Controversy over Voluntary Environmental Standards: A Socioeconomic Analysis of the Marine Stewardship Council', *Organization and Environment*, 32 (2), 98–124.

World Bank. 2017. *The Potential of the Blue Economy: Increasing Long-Term Benefits of the Sustainable Use of Marine Resources for Small Island Developing States and Coastal Least Developed Countries* (Washington DC: World Bank), <https://openknowledge.worldbank.org/bitstream/handle/10986/26843/115545.pdf?sequence=1&isAllowed=y> [Accessed 20 January 2022].

World Wildlife Foundation. 2015. *Principles for a Sustainable Blue Economy* (Switzerland: WWF Global), <https://wwfint.awsassets.panda.org/downloads/15_1471_blue_economy_6_pages_final.pdf> [Accessed 20 January 2022].

Hugh Breakey

Chapter 23
Ethics in the blue economy

Abstract: This chapter explores the ethics in the blue economy – understood as marine industries ostensibly operating in sustainable ways. The ethics of the blue economy is highly complex, a result of covering an ever-increasing multitude of overlapping activities, some with long supply chains and many with significant social, economic and ecological impacts, occurring in dynamic environments often hidden from the view of communities and regulators, and by industries expanding rapidly in scale and technology. In unpacking this complexity, this chapters consider the types of (governing) values that the blue economy should aim to achieve, including both humanist and ecocentric values, and with a particular focus on sustainable development and finance. It also explores the types of (governance) values that the blue economy should employ as it pursues these larger values. It further examines how the ideas of institutional integrity and multidimensional legitimacy can help the blue economy garner stakeholder and community support.

Keywords: blue economy, sustainable development, ethics, eco-centrism, multidimensional legitimacy, institutional integrity, COVID-19

Introduction

This chapter explores the ethics in the blue economy – understood as marine industries ostensibly operating in sustainable ways. The ethics of the blue economy is highly complex, a result of covering an ever-increasing multitude of overlapping activities, some with long supply chains and many with significant social and ecological impacts, occurring in dynamic environments often hidden from the view of communities and regulators, and by industries expanding rapidly in scale and technology. In unpacking this complexity, this chapter will consider the types of (governing) values that the blue economy should aim to achieve and the types of (governance) values that it should employ as it does so. It will further examine how the ideas of institutional integrity and multidimensional legitimacy can help it garner stakeholder and community support.

The chapter proceeds as follows. It begins by defining some key terms, before reviewing the main ethical challenges arising in the blue economy. It then explores

Acknowledgements: Thanks to Rebecca Marshallsay, Alex Naraniecki and Melea Lewis for background research that informed this chapter.

https://doi.org/10.1515/9783110733488-023

the role of stakeholders and communities, including through the social licence to operate. The chapter then explores the relevant ethical values (governing values) that undergird the blue economy's ethical challenges. Next, attention turns to governance values at work in the blue economy, noting that these can come in a spectrum running from thin (limited to transparency, accountability and compliance practices) to thick (involving more robust mechanisms for democratic and deliberative processes, and effective problem-solving outcomes). The following section focuses on institutional integrity, considering where an organisation or system defines and lives up to its stated values or mission (its public institutional justification). The final section draws upon all these distinct but interrelated ethical phenomena (the social licence, governing values, governance values and institutional integrity) as they interact together to deliver a full picture of the ethics and legitimacy of the blue economy.

Definitions

This section defines some of the key terms employed in the chapter.

Values

Broadly, values are goals, outcomes or actions that are seen as desirable or worthwhile. The focus of this chapter is specifically on moral values (or ethical values – the terms shall be used interchangeably). Moral values are goals, outcomes or actions that should be undertaken or pursued. These include notions like human rights, honesty, animal welfare and environmental stewardship. Moral values are prescriptive in the sense that they describe what ought to be done: they attach to ideas about right and wrong, good and bad. Moral philosophical theories are used to explore, defend and critique claims about moral values. These include consequentialist theories that focus on creating good outcomes (Bentham 1789/1948; Mill 1861/2001), deontological theories that focus on principles of action (Kant 1785/2008), and political theories that explore rights, legitimacy and distributive justice (Locke 1690/1947; Rawls 1971).

Moral values also have a descriptive sense, insofar as they are psychological states held by human beings that play a role in determining their actions. Psychologically, values are enduring prescriptive beliefs about the personal or social desirability of an act or goal. They serve as imperatives for action as well as standards for judging actions. They are always centrally connected to the subject's cognitive system, interlocking with many other beliefs and attitudes (Rokeach 1976; Breakey 2018b).

Values may be held by an individual in their personal capacity, that they bring to their workplace (e.g., 'I have a strong commitment to environmental sustainability, that guides everything I do.'). As will be later explored, values may also be ascribed to an institution (e.g., 'In this organisation, safety always comes first.').

Risk

Every claim about risk includes an implicit assumption about value. If there is not a desired goal at stake, there is no risk. In many forms of risk, the values at stake are not moral values (e.g., supply chain vulnerabilities that create risks to production). Sometimes, however, an organisation will need to explicitly consider ethical risks. These come in two forms. First, since ethical obligations are intrinsically important, an organisation can work to reduce its risks of being involved in ethical wrongdoing as an end in itself. (That is, for no other reason than to do the right thing, for example, in the context of sustainable development, see Payne (2001)). Second, when ethical risks materialise, they can have an array of knock-on negative impacts, including to the organisation's brand and reputation, its employees (and capacity to retain and attract employees), the attention paid to it by regulatory and other public bodies and more. Naturally, these types of operational risk can translate into financial risk. For these reasons, organisations have both intrinsic and instrumental reasons to guard against ethical risks.

The blue economy

The concept of the blue economy first arose in official forums in 2012 at the United Nations Conference on Sustainable Development in Rio de Janeiro (UN 2012). It can be defined in several different ways.

In their influential work, Voyer and colleagues examine authoritative definitions of the blue economy. While noting important variations, they conclude: 'Most definitions include a focus on "triple bottom line objectives of environmental sustainability, economic growth and social equity, driven by an integrated oceans governance approach and technological innovation' (Voyer et al. 2018: 598). On this footing, normative (ethical) elements reside within the very concept of the blue economy, with the definitions including sociopolitical ethical principles (food and resource security; poverty alleviation; employment) and environmental precepts (sustainability; natural capital) as they apply to ocean-based industries.

These elements can be seen in the different lenses that may be used to frame the blue economy. Silver (2015) distilled four distinct lenses through which different actors perceived the blue economy:
1. Natural capital (by conservationists)

2. Livelihood (Small Island Developing States/fishers)
3. Good business (multinational corporations)
4. Drivers of innovation (tech industries)

Similar features of economic activity, environmental sustainability and social justice are captured in Smith-Godfrey's closely justified definition of the term as: 'the sustainable industrialisation of the oceans to the benefit of all' (Smith-Godfrey 2016: 60).

Following these authors, this chapter will understand the blue economy as economic activity on or with the marine environment, that sustains or restores that environment, and that pays heed to social and cultural priorities.

The benefits of having these normative standards within the definition help ensure that blue economy industries and activities achieve these worthy goals and, therefore, that the blue economy is intrinsically worthy of social and political support. On this footing, it would be incorrect for an unsustainable industry to brand itself as a part of the blue economy.

However, it should be noted that capturing normative standards into a descriptive concept can create difficulties. (An analogy can be drawn to the positivist philosophy in law, that sought to remove moral approval from the concept of law, to create space for a critique of law. Rather than debating 'Is this a law?,' the positivists argued the better question was, 'Is this a good law?') Several potential concerns arise in this respect.

First, the blue economy definition can stymie the capacity to morally critique an entity in the blue economy, precisely because once it is admitted as being part of the blue economy, it is necessarily perceived as socially and environmentally sustainable. The problem can arise that debate begins to centre on whether this industry is rightfully understood as a member of the blue economy rather than the questions that actually matter: Is this industry ethically, socially and environmentally justified? Can it raise its standards?

Second, the definition can create counterintuitive cases where entities (industries, corporations, operations) slip into and out of the category. For example, a new (or newly discovered) environmental impact might suddenly mean that an operation is no longer sustainable in its current form. If blue economy entities are sustainable by definition, then the operation is no longer a blue economy entity – until it improves its performance on this impact. This movement into and out of the category might cause confusion.

Third, when practically managing, governing and making policy in the blue economy, it will be necessary to engage both with industries whose status as sustainable might be questionable (e.g., cargo shipping) and entities that could be sustainable but currently are not (e.g., a poorly managed aquaculture operation). Often, when making decisions about the blue economy, it will be critical to include these operators as both key stakeholders and agents in the marine economy. Rather than excluding them as categorically outside the blue economy, the aim should be instead to pull them up to meet sustainability standards. This might be simpler if they are brought inside the conceptual ambit of the blue economy.

For this reason, the chapter will also allow a wide definition of the blue economy, covering more broadly any economic activity on or with the marine environment.

Key ethical issues and challenges

The section sketches the main ethical challenges (problem areas and risks) arising in the blue economy.

Unsurprisingly, several of the key ethical issues faced in the blue economy are sustainability challenges. Environmental sustainability is a critical issue for all blue economy activities, and ranges over several areas, including concerns with biodiversity, impacts from pollutants and industrial activity (e.g., aquaculture feed) on existing ecosystems, overfishing, the environmental impacts of accidents, energy use and more. Climate change adds a further dimension – and urgency – to blue economy environmental sustainability, as blue economy activities can contribute to climate risks (through energy use, especially diesel), work to ameliorate climate risks (through clean energy generation), and also be operationally challenged by the warming climate (e.g., aquaculture sites requiring cold water).

Social and cultural sustainability challenges also arise for blue economy activities, given their potential intrusion on, disruption of, or impact upon the resources required by local actors, including impacts on established or emerging local business (e.g., tourism operations, that can often be in tension with blue economy activities like aquaculture), recreation (fishing), residential life (faced with industrial levels of diesel engine noise) and cultural practices (especially those of local Indigenous peoples). Ethically, many of these impacts might be harmful and wrongful in themselves, though phrasing them as social and cultural sustainability concerns further implies that there will ultimately be operational (e.g., legal and regulatory) problems for the organisation. That is, its existence is not sustainable because of its social and cultural impacts.

Economic sustainability, understood as the financial viability of an operation, corporation or industry as a whole, can also be challenged in ways that implicate ethical issues. Productive industries create important social goods, including food security, energy security (including renewable energy through wind and wave power), employment (especially in regional areas with limited local industry) and more. For these reasons, economic sustainability can be an ethical issue. Unfortunately, economic sustainability can be in tension with environmental and social sustainability, as economic stressors on a commercial operation can exert pressures to cut corners or can narrow down the resources and attention available for fixing and responding to ethical risks. As such, economically unsustainable operations often have poor ethical and environmental outcomes.

Sustainability challenges are important, but they do not exhaust the issues facing the blue economy. These remaining challenges include issues of animal welfare (of both farmed salmon, but also wildlife like seals and animals like whales highly sensitive to noise pollution), supply chain injustices, concerns with governance, and corruption of the interface between commercial entities and government (Flanagan 2021).

There are contextual factors particular to the blue economy that make these challenges more pointed. These include the fact that technology and industrial processes for many blue economy industries are still evolving, potentially auguring in new ethical challenges or solutions. Relatedly, the newness of many blue economy activities means that some impacts, especially environmental impacts, are still unknown – as compared with established industries that have been around for decades, and whose impacts are predictable from past experience. The newness also carries the consequence that regulatory agencies and activities may be inchoate, meaning there can be a regulatory vacuum for some new industries, or more broadly that regulatory law or the activities of regulators are not fit-for-purpose. This issue can apply also to certification regimes, with uneven costs, authority, coverage, legitimacy and clarity across independent certifiers. As well, the vast, inaccessible, and largely unpopulated (by humans) waterscape that houses blue economy activities complicates regulation and governance efforts. Many blue economy activities occur out at sea, and even undersea, in remote and dynamic (even dangerous) environments, sometimes under cover of darkness and with unclear borders. All these features make it easy for actors to slip under the radar in their actions and reporting, away from the prying eyes of neighbours and journalistic media, and beyond the normal ambit of regulatory actors. Finally, the use of property/exclusionary rules on land is already challenged by the capacity of livestock, wildlife, water, sound and pollution to flow across legal boundaries, this issue is exacerbated in a liquid environment.

One final challenge with ethical implications is one that has impacted on almost all industries and activities from early 2020 to the time of writing, namely, the COVID-19 pandemic.

Stakeholder roles and social licence in the blue economy

Due to an array of factors, state and non-state agents can have a key role in shaping the blue economy and impacting on its ethical status. These factors include the role of quick-moving industry, with operations often on public resources shared with other users, with technology and production often outpacing regulation. In an industry with these features, there are few established expectations, the technology is still developing, and environmental impacts are unclear. This gives rise to a situation where social and legal controls can fail to keep pace with industrial activity.

One way this lack of fit between social expectations and industrial activity can manifest is through what has been called the social licence to operate (SLO), which stands as a potentially important factor in shaping blue economy ethical discourse. This section discusses the relationship between the SLO and the ethical challenges noted above.

Definitions of the SLO abound in the literature, with most centring around the notion of community or stakeholder acceptance of an activity (Newton, Farrelly, and Sinner 2020). (For ease, an activity will be referred to, but the SLO can apply to a law or regulation, a particular organisation or type of organisation, an overall industry or a general type of practice, as well as a specific activity.) Occasionally there will be a clause in these definitions noting that the activities in question are contested or that stakeholders include those who can impact on the activity (Baines and Edwards 2018; Melé and Armengou 2016). Some industries and/or countries will not use the term at all but merely refer to social acceptance. Indeed, this was the early terminology applied to aquaculture before SLO gained traction (Mather and Fanning 2019).

It is widely observed that acceptance can differ across stakeholders, suggesting that there is a plurality of SLOs, rather than a single SLO. This reflects the fact that the industry or corporation may have to justify itself to a number of communities on the basis that they deliver on values important to those communities. As well, the level of acceptance ranges across a continuum, from active resistance, vocal rejection, ignorance and apathy, grudging acquiescence, toleration, acceptance and support – all the way to feelings of ownership and identification with the industry (Boutilier and Thomson 2011). There are thus multiple areas of ambiguity within the SLO, including how many SLOs are relevant, how an overall SLO can be distilled from a diversity of stakeholder views, what stakeholders are involved and whether some of them count more than others (e.g., because they are more directly affected), and similar points of contention. These ambiguities weaken the usefulness of SLO as a normative principle, though there are no doubt some bright-line cases where all stakeholders and commentators would agree that social licence has been lost.

From an ethical point of view, the SLO can have both positive and negative qualities.

In terms of the positives, the SLO can be invoked when an affected community takes back control over an industry behaving in harmful ways (this aligns with the early invocations of SLO in the extractive industries in developing countries (Boutilier and Thomson 2011)). While law and regulation may have allowed the industry a legal licence to operate (perhaps through the industry succeeding in regulatory capture), the SLO occurs when a community asserts its rights as stakeholders to have a role in determining the nature and scope of industrial activity that directly impacts upon that community. Alternatively, the SLO might be invoked pre-emptively by an industry recognising its obligations to a community and proactively working to meet community expectations by raising its standards. This is arguably the situation in the first recorded invocation of SLO, which occurred in the US paper industry (Moore 1996). Both these good qualities could conceivably appear in the SLO being applied to the blue economy (Flanagan 2021). Because of the aforenoted dynamism in industrial activity and technological processes, industry may move ahead of law and regulation. This necessitates the more active involvement of stakeholders that SLO involves. As such, the SLO could constitute a valuable part of how ethics is understood, communicated and implemented in the blue economy.

However, the SLO also possesses ethically worrisome qualities. From the perspective of industry, SLO's ambiguity and amorphous nature can be a concern. Industry must be able to plan (within certain parameters) in order to make large-scale investment and operational decisions. Law creates a stable environment of expectations through which such decisions can be made (Bentham 1978/1802). But the SLO operates outside the law, and is subject to sudden change, creating a wide scope for unpredictable outcomes that may impact on operations. From an ethical perspective, this may be unfair and counterproductive (Ghori 2019). A second worry is that community sentiment may be misguided or misinformed, or improperly influenced by noisy, politically powerful or financially well-resourced actors, meaning that operations may be resisted on erroneous or emotional grounds, where a more rigorous process would have been better informed by scientific expertise (e.g., Murphy–Gregory 2018; Mather and Fanning 2019).

From the perspective of stakeholders, and broader ethical worries about environmental impacts, the ambiguity and lack of specificity may allow the SLO to be invoked as part of a greenwashing or ethics-washing campaign, with facile claims that it is held, or is an important priority for industry. In this way industry might exploit SLO rhetoric to avoid genuine engagement and appropriate ethical standards. An alternative concern is that all ethical and legitimacy related issues are seen by industry purely through an SLO lens – such issues only count insofar as, and only to the degree that, they constitute a threat to ongoing operations (Mather and Fanning 2019). This concern emerges in the early literature on SLO, which often focussed on a purely instrumental approach to discerning what the industry needs to do to achieve the SLO, rather than genuinely responding to serious ethical concerns (Santiago et al. 2021).

Worse again, the informality and unofficial nature of the SLO may arise because there are no official or quasi-official practices actively incorporating stakeholder views in a rigorous, systematic and legitimate process (e.g., see Cadman 2011). Reliance on the SLO as an effective check on industry wrongdoing, or as an appropriate manner by which stakeholder voices may be heard, may seem to obviate the development and rollout of improved (and perhaps legally enshrined) governance regimes.

On this footing, the prevalence and significance of the SLO is a self-reinforcing symptom of the lack of more legitimate and demanding ethical and governance practices.

Governing values for blue economy operations and institutions

Governing values refer to outcomes, actions and qualities that are ethical priorities in the blue economy (Breakey, Cadman, and Sampford 2017). They are answers to the question: What does humanity want the blue economy to do or to achieve? Governing values often have synergistic interactions, such that improving one value will overlap or assist with improving others. But they can also be in conflict, where prioritisation of one value will come at the direct or indirect sacrifice of another.

Governing values direct attention to specific areas of ethical concern. There are good reasons for wanting to be pluralist about governing values, and not taking a single type of value, or theory regarding that value, to be the exclusive focus (Breakey 2012). This is because most governing values communicate insights about an area of intrinsic ethical concern (Sampford 1994). It may be difficult within the confines of a theory or concept about one governing value to fully capture the richness and significance of an ethical concern at some distance from that theory.

For example, consider sustainable development – the first and arguably most important governing value for the blue economy discussed below. Sustainable development, if it is understood to include environmental, social and cultural sustainability, can seem to provide a comprehensive account of the ethical issues at stake in blue economy. As such, concerns about (say) animal welfare or unfair impacts on communities can appear to be addressed by the value of sustainable development, because these would impact upon long-term environmental and social sustainability. It is questionable whether this is true, however. Many regimes that treated various stakeholders unfairly, or engaged in animal cruelty, have historically been sustainable for generations on end. Yet even if sustainable development can capture these concerns, it appears to do so for the wrong reason. Animal cruelty or unfairness are not wrong because they are unsustainable. They are wrong immediately and intrinsically, irrespective of longer-term sustainability impacts. For this reason, this section will consider an array of distinct governing values, without attempting to reduce them all into the terms of an overarching master value.

Sustainable development

On many authoritative definitions, the value of sustainability is wedded intrinsically into the very concept of the blue economy. Arguably, commercial and productive marine activity can only be included within the blue economy if they include efforts at sustainability on social, cultural and especially environmental dimensions. There is thus a natural fit between the concepts of the blue economy and sustainable development, insofar as both are oriented around and prioritise productive and commercial activities (blue economy, sustainable development) while at the same time insisting that such activities are done within ethical and environmental bounds.

Definitions

There are several different definitions of sustainable development. In its first official rendering, sustainable development was defined as 'development that meets the needs of the present without compromising the ability of future generations to meet their own needs' (World Commission on Environment and Development 1987: 41). Later definitions included explicit concerns with social justice and equity alongside the pre-existing concern with ecological sustainability (Payne and Raiborn 2001), thus giving rise to the intersection of economic, social and environmental sustainability concerns – familiar from triple bottom line approaches to corporate social responsibility.

Each of these terms of economic, environmental and social sustainability can house deeper ambiguities. As Payne and Raiborn observe, even economic sustainability (or viability) could mean different things to different operations in different contexts (Payne and Raiborn 2001). Alexander and colleagues (2020) view economic, environmental and social sustainability as the three pillars of sustainable development, noting that social sustainability is the vaguest. In this way, various dimensions of justice can be included in social sustainability – since failures in justice will imperil ongoing community support for the activity (Saunders et al. 2020; see similarly, Farmery et al. 2019).

Ethical bases for sustainable development

From an ethical perspective, sustainable development can be justified in several different ways. The utilitarian ethical approach judges acts from their consequences – in particular, their overall consequences for sum total human and animal happiness (Singer 1993). The more an activity creates good results, and reduces or avoids inflicting harm and suffering, the more justifiable it is from a utilitarian standpoint. From a utilitarian perspective, sustainable development clearly has much to say for it. Development delivers many utilitarian goods, including prosperity, food security, employment and more. However, since utilitarianism takes a panoptic view, factoring in the near and long-term consequences of the act, not only for current humans and animals, but also for future ones, sustainability is critical.

Utilitarianism will not countenance the goods of current development if they come at the cost of a severely depleted and toxic future environment. As Payne and Raiborn (2001: 160) argue, 'no matter how high the costs of sustainable development are, the benefits of current and continued existence by the Earth's species *must* exceed that cost.' That said, Novaglio and colleagues (2022: 16) rightly observe that the pursuit of a more sustainable future is not itself without risk – in a utilitarian spirit, it must always be considered whether the expected social and environmental benefits of reforms outweigh the estimated costs.

Rather than focussing purely on consequences, another ethical approach (deontological ethics) focusses on fairness, rights and justice. Sustainability often intersects with claims of justice (Bogadóttir 2019; Lam 2016) because the presence of sustainability can mean that local community resources are not being destroyed in a way that would be unfair to the community. Sustainability can therefore drive a type of social contract where users gain access to resources only when they shoulder sustainability responsibilities (Lam and Pauly 2010). Equally, and on the basis of intergenerational justice, it can be unfair to future generations for the present population to enjoy greater material wealth while bequeathing a depleted world to future peoples. That said, Spahn (2018) argues that rights-based theories typically invoke a type of contractualism that aims to structure agreement between parties in collectively rational ways. While ethically desirable in many contexts, this process necessarily fails to incorporate the interests of future generations (who cannot possibly be included in present day decision-making procedures), meaning that an appeal to ecocentric ethics (see below) ultimately may be necessary to deliver sustainable development (Spahn 2018: 1862).

Both utilitarian and deontological thinking can justify the idea of stewardship – a value that prioritises sustainability in managing of natural resources, including fisheries (Klain et al., 2014). The global rush to develop the blue economy risks harming the marine environment and human wellbeing, and stewardship provides an approach that allows development within the constraints of sustainability and restoration.

The Sustainable Development Goals (SDGs)

Governing values may be supplied by ethical principle and theory. However, they can also be given a concrete form in official instruments – of which the UN SDGs are a prime example (United Nations General Assembly 2015). The UN's 17 SDGs, adopted by all UN Member States in 2015, aim to provide a shared blueprint for ongoing peace and prosperity for people and the planet. The SDGs:

recognize that ending poverty and other deprivations must go hand-in-hand with strategies that improve health and education, reduce inequality, and spur economic growth – all while tackling climate change and working to preserve our oceans and forests. (United Nations 2015)

Building on prior initiatives, including Agenda 21 (United Nations Conference on Environment and Development 1992) and the Millennium Development Goals (United Nations Millennium Summit 2000), the 17 SDGs may be understood as applications of the larger principle of sustainable development. Putting broad governing values (such as sustainable development) into a specified, authoritative form (such as the 17 SDGs) can be ethically important for two reasons. First, it gives more guidance to decision-makers regarding what the governing value requires, and how it might be applied in specific cases. Second, it provides additional forms of legitimacy and justifiability for the resulting principles and goals (Breakey 2021, 2018a). The processes of collective and inclusive decision-making, and formal endorsement through UN Member States, provide additional reasons for ethical respect and compliance with the SDGs.

The SDGs can ground ethical standards for the blue economy as they explicitly include many activities and products of the blue economy – such as economic benefits (SDG 1: No poverty; SDG 8: Decent work and economic growth) and food security (SDG 2: No hunger; SDG 3: Health and Wellbeing;) (United Nations General Assembly 2015). At the same time as highlighting many of the goods produced by blue economy industries, the SDGs prioritise environmental responsibilities. This occurs expressly in SDG 14 Life Below Water: 'Conserve and sustainably use the oceans, seas and marine resources for sustainable development (United Nations General Assembly 2015).' SDG 14b pertains directly to small-scale fisheries, calling for secure access to resources and markets for this sector (Said and Chuenpagdee 2019). The close relationship between the SDGs and blue economy activities allow them to be used as a basis for fairness in marine spatial planning (Ntona and Morgera 2018).

Critique

While sustainable development and the SDGs provide important guidance and justification for sustainable and equitable blue economy activities, this does not mean that these concepts are above critique. The notion of sustainability can be politicised to contest or lay territorial or other claims to sea and waterways (Silver et al. 2015; Stewart 2016; Fry and Tarte 2015). So too, the concept can paper over a serious tension between sustainable activities and the commercial activities undertaken by what are – after all – profit-seeking enterprises operating competitively in an environment where consumers may not attend to ethical issues in their purchasing decisions, and shareholders may focus on short-term horizons (Payne and Raiborn 2001: 160–1, 65).

Finally, SDGs are essentially anthropocentric (focussed on what humans value) rather than broader biocentric values (discussed below – focussed on what is good for life on the planet).

Sustainable development and the SDGs as governing values: Summary

Summing up, sustainable development – comprising economically, socially and environmentally sustainable economic activity – provides an important ethical basis for justifying blue economy activities, at the same time as it provides resources for guiding how those activities should occur and critiquing or even resisting them when they fail to live up to the demands of sustainability. The SDGs provide more specific detail on distinct sustainability goals, as well as providing those goals with additional institutional legitimacy.

Humanist ethics

Humanist ethical approaches are ones that invoke universal human values, including intergenerational equity, human rights, fairness, equity and justice. Above, humanist ethics approaches, including utilitarianism and deontology, were considered as bases for justifying sustainable development. However, such ethical approaches can also be directly employed to explore blue economy ethical issues.

Human rights

Human rights thinking provides an ethical approach that considers obligations that are owed to all human beings, purely on the basis of their status as human beings. Stemming from earlier ethical theorising about natural rights, human rights describe the entitlements that are required for people to flourish and live with dignity. They include concerns for freedoms of religion and speech, protections of due process and law, prohibitions on discrimination and entitlements for basic healthcare and social security. They also cover just and favourable conditions of work, and remuneration for work – which can apply to employment on fishing boats and other blue economy activities where worker exploitation is possible, and threats can arise of slavery, human trafficking, and forced or bonded labour (United Nations Environment Programme Finance Initiative 2021: 36). Like the SDGs, human rights find concrete form in major ethical instruments – such as the *Universal Declaration of Human Rights* (United Nations

General Assembly 1948) – developed by an international organisation through a process that garnered widespread legitimacy (Breakey 2018a; Glendon 2001).

With their shared humanist underpinnings, human rights and the SDGs are complementary approaches. Indeed, human rights stand as the only larger moral framework explicitly invoked by the SDGs (Spahn 2018: 1854). As might therefore be expected, some ethics commentators employ both human rights and the SDGs. For example, the human right to science is linked with SDG14 (United Nations General Assembly 2015) in the context of equity between industrial fisheries and small-scale farming on the matter of marine technology (Morgera and Ntona 2018).

Unlike the SDGs, human rights do not place an explicit value on environment or sustainability (Spahn 2018). However, it can be argued that there is a human right to have access to a liveable environment (Blackstone 1973), or that the right to health implies a right to a healthy environment (see, Spahn 2018: 1857).

In any case, human rights directly support many blue economy goals (contributing to human work, health, and food) and describe the ethical constraints (e.g., avoiding impact on local community stakeholders) that blue economy activities must observe. For example, the United Nations General Assembly's (2007) *Declaration on the Rights of Indigenous Peoples* recognises rights of Indigenous peoples to their distinct political, legal, economic, social and cultural institutions. This can include fishing and other activities within the blue economy which are supported by and contribute to all those institutions (Article 5). Other articles prohibit dispossession of Indigenous resources and grant Indigenous peoples rights to the conservation and protection of the environment and the productive capacity of their lands.

Some commentators employ human rights approaches to argue that communal fishing rights should be prioritised over individual rights, as the former can better assure the 'basic dignity of all members by distributing fishing rights in a manner consistent with human rights principles' (Song and Soliman 2019: 102). Similarly, others argue that the right to fish should be upheld as essential to local people in state legal frameworks.

However, rights are not always the apt method for determining ethical standards. Arguably, the individualisation of rights and decision-making has led to governance and regulatory regimes negatively impacting small-scale fisheries (Davis and Ruddle 2012).

Equity and justice

The fair distribution of resources, responsibilities, access and entitlements to individuals and communities is guided by ethical theories of distributive justice and understandings of equity (see, e.g., Rawls 1971). Applied to the challenge of an environmentally sustainable and socially equitable blue economy, these values interrogate the social impacts of environmental change, ecological degradation and pollution for different groups. Marine conservation, management, and development activities will all have different winners and losers (Bennett 2019). Distributive justice is critical in evaluating the fairness of these outcomes. For example, should local communities, towns or the state enjoy more of the profits from blue economy commercial activities? Should efforts be made to redirect more of the value of the international seafood trade to the fishing communities and small island countries where that value originated (World Bank Group 2016: 3)? And turning from fair shares of profits to fair burdens and impacts, principles of equity can be used to evaluate the potential injustices of reaping profits from imposing externalities on others – harmful impacts that are released as collective resources are appropriated and exploited.

Science values and knowledge

Humanist ethics can highlight the importance of improved knowledge and technological advances, where these work to fulfil ethical goals, such as reducing environmental impacts, or yielding greater knowledge about the functioning of ecological systems. The importance of these goods drives not only practices of knowledge development, but also data and information sharing, such as based on the FAIR (Findable, Accessible, Interoperable, Reusable) data principles (Novaglio et al. 2021: 8–10).

Communitarian ethics

Communitarian ethics focuses on the practices and traditions developed by particular cultures, and the standards of excellence, virtues and narratives that frame and draw upon these practices (MacIntyre 1981). This approach to blue economy ethics would highlight the tight relationships between cultural mores and practices, and the environments in which they have developed. Indeed, the word ethics stems from the ancient Greek words for both habit and habitat – stressing the interaction between local ecology and ethics (Rozzi 2019). Communitarian approaches to the blue economy would highlight the importance of local fishing rights and traditional interactions with the sea, especially by First peoples, but also by any longstanding local communities. Respecting such longstanding relationships with the marine environment could involve industry acknowledging the importance of a cultural licence to operate.

Ecocentric ethics

Many mainstream ethical theories are anthropocentric – that is, they take the freedom, wellbeing and flourishing of human beings as central (though some ethical theories, like utilitarianism, will include consideration of animal suffering and harm (Singer 2001)). Ecocentric ethics, in contrast, hold that there is intrinsic value in flora, fauna and ecosystems themselves (Sylvan 1973). These goods are not merely to be prized, protected and restored out of their instrumental benefits to current and future humans, but because they are owed ethical consideration in their own right. An influential example is Aldo Leopold's 'land ethic' (1968), which posits that the role of human beings should be reconceived from a conqueror of the land-community to a plain member of it.

Ecocentric ethics gives a stronger priority to non-human elements of world impacted by the blue economy – the rights of animals, the respect owed to local ecosystems, the importance of threatened species, the world-shaping concerns raised by climate change, and the need for not just respect but restoration of many habitats. This prioritisation can distinguish ecocentric ethics from other ethical approaches. For example, while sustainable development might consider development a given, ecocentric ethics would caution that development inherently favours human wellbeing and prosperity, which should not be privileged in ethical decision-making. From an ecocentric perspective, development is inherently suspect, given its tendency to use animals and ecosystems instrumentally as resources, rather than respectfully as valued members of a shared ethical community. That said, there can be considerable overlap between the practical demands of an ecocentric ethics and those humanist ethics approaches that take a long-term perspective (e.g., by including concerns for the rights and wellbeing of future generations), as the continued wellbeing of people is tied so closely, over the longer-term, to the flourishing of the planet.

Biodiversity

Biodiversity is often invoked as a critical goal of blue economy environmental sustainability or restoration. It is a value that calls for the integration of traditional knowledges with evidence-based science, as well as responsibility, reciprocity and trust – given that ecological systems often involve multiple national jurisdictions (Johnson et al. 2019). The idea of biodiversity can also be employed to create a broader ethical vision relevant to the blue economy that sees the biocultural homogenisation of monocultural mega-projects as socioenvironmental injustice (Rozzi and Rozzi, 2019). On this footing, biocultural diversity (of different cultures and geographies) is prized alongside biodiversity.

Ethics and finance

All the ethical approaches described above can attach directly to questions of finance. Just as the utilitarian ethical focus on the consequences for human and animal wellbeing can be used to evaluate blue economy activities, so too it can provide answers to what projects should be financed, and how this should be done. Equally, deontological ethical focus on rights and fairness can be used to interrogate whether finance can be used in inappropriate, unfair or dominating ways. For both these ethical approaches, there is nothing intrinsically desirable about economic growth – what matters for each will be the impact on human life and the environment. For example, at the most basic level of economic development, the key human goods that would be lionised by ethical theories of all types are the provision of sustenance, the sense of self-respect, and the release from servitude that economic development can deliver (these goods are noted in the context of seaweed farming in Indonesia by Muthalib et al. 2019). Development is not good in itself – but it can deliver critical ethical goods.

Finance and capital: Ethical issues

A key area of ethical concern, that can be supported through both human rights and distributive justice approaches, concerns access to capital, especially in cases where such access would create or improve basic livelihoods. Muthalib and colleagues (2019: 2255) found major problems with respect to capital access for poor seaweed farmers in Indonesia, including that farmers owned few assets, had little access to the banking world, and had no bankable collateral. These problems were exacerbated by pollution from mining companies, that often interfered with farmers capacities to produce and so to service their loans (Muthalib et al. 2019: 2779). As well as capital support from both public and private organisations, business management and entrepreneurship training for the farmers was seen as critical to fostering their empowerment through increased income. In the context of the COVID-19 pandemic (see below) and the ensuing clampdowns on aquaculture activities and drops in demand and price, these factors have made the situation of those with little access to institutional credit especially dire, as many need credit to tide their operations over until normalcy returns. (Hasan et al. 2021: 130)

From the reverse direction, there are ethical issues relating to how investment occurs, and how it could be done better. The World Bank Group (2016: 2) notes that some blue economy sectors will need little encouragement to develop, while others will require improved governance and planning to grow in a sustainable way. The transition to sustainable fisheries has hitherto largely been funded by non-private sources of capital (development agencies and philanthropic sources). In the World Bank view, good governance (including robust monitoring and enforcement) is necessary to ensure the sustainability and security of tenure that can encourage investment. Building market demand for sustainable seafood is a further important step in the process of developing sustainability, as well as reducing risk for investors (World Bank Group 2016: 6).

The Sustainable Blue Economy Finance Principles (United Nations Environment Programme 2018) aim to provide a guiding framework for banks, insurers and investors to finance a sustainable blue economy. The principles include environmental protection, framework compliance, risk-awareness, inclusivity and transparency – aiming to be solution-driven and science-led. As the UNEP (2018) observes, financial institutions provide the capital and insurance that drives marine industries, so financial decisions impact on future generations' lives and livelihoods. Its *Turning the Tide* guidance (2021) aims to respond to this by pointing out best practice activities to seek out for investment, as well as activities to challenge or even to avoid entirely.

In general, improvements in finance ethics and governance are one part of the way the overall ethical standards of the blue economy can be raised, and its promises secured. Novaglio and colleagues (2022: 10–16) see financial changes as a necessary part of the sustainable future they map out, where investor decision-making, shareholder dividends, and auditing practices account for environmental externalities and human wellbeing, and innovative financing mechanisms are designed to capture net social benefit in a progressive way, supporting activities with environmental and social benefits, and with greater demands made of high return and high-impact sectors.

Finally, there is arguably a need to better gauge and prioritise blue economy resources and opportunities. The World Bank Group (2016: 5) note that marine living resources are often not valued properly, leading some governments to mistakenly overvalue alternative and non-renewable (e.g., extractive) industries. So too, the UN Environment Programme (2021) observes that in 2017 SDG 14 Life Below Water (United Nations General Assembly 2015) received the least public funding of all the SDGs.

Profit-seeking and ethical action

A key question that arises at the intersection of finance and ethics is how the relationship between profit-seeking business and ethical prescriptions can be managed. How far can the pursuit of ethics and sustainable development align with industries' pursuit of profit, or more minimally of economic sustainability? Acknowledging that business cannot pursue 'totally altruistic environmental goals without any concern for profitability or longevity,' Payne and Raiborn (2001: 162) highlight the importance of focussing on the long-term over the short-term – as this horizon gives space for sustainability and reputation risks to be appropriately factored in. The authors warn though, that the fate of business is determined ultimately by consumers, and without their attention to ethical and environmental issues, economic drivers will continue to push in a different direction to ethical standards.

The intersection of ethical and sustainability concerns with financial and operational risks in the blue economy is described, sector-by-sector, in the UNEP's *Turning the Tide* report (United Nations Environment Programme Finance Initiative 2021), highlighting from an investment perspective the prudential rationale for avoiding ethically and environmentally unsustainable practices.

Grace and Cohen (2013: 33–35) explore this complex relationship between ethics and profit, noting that good ethics can be good for business in cases where: i) the two naturally coincide (e.g., when candour about industry impacts creates trust from local communities), ii) the two are engineered to coincide by external forces (e.g., where the business regulates itself to avoid the threat of intrusive external regulation), and iii) where additional action by the business along with good ethical behaviour can make ethics profitable (e.g., clever marketing displaying, or practices verifying, the business's genuinely high ethical standards). However, they note frankly that (just as with individuals acting ethically) there is no guaranteed correlation between ethics and self-interest. Two straightforward reasons the two can come apart are that a) ethical wrongdoing that is unlikely to be discovered can allow the business to attain an immediate material good, while avoiding any social or financial sanction, and b) business reputation can be burnished by a myriad of ethics-washing and greenwashing devices, and slick marketing campaigns, even absent any real ethical performance. For these reasons, ethics cannot be reduced to farsighted self-interest, and requires an intrinsic focus for industries, just as it does for ordinary individuals.

Blue growth

Specific ethical concepts applying to finance – and finance in the blue economy in particular – have been developed. Blue growth comes from the application of the concept of green growth (ensuring sustainable development) to the marine environment (Eikeset et al. 2018). Blue growth can be understood as a value that allows economic development to be pursued alongside goals of environmental sustainability and biodiversity. (However, just as with the blue economy, different actors define blue growth differently. For some actors, blue growth is simply any economic development in the marine environment, even if there is no concern with sustainability (Ertör and Hadjimichael 2020: 2).)

Against the idea of blue growth, some commentators raise concerns that such concepts inevitably invoke 'fairy tales of eternal economic growth' (Ertör and Hadjimichael 2020: 1). While sustainable economic activity is no doubt possible, it is another thing to claim that economic growth – in a finite and ecologically stressed world – can be done sustainably, especially as the time frame stretches further into the future. Consequently, non-growth notions such as de-growth are increasingly invoked (Childs 2020). Aiming to do more with less, blue de-growth pushes back against the economic and technological blue economy lens that sees oceans as vistas of untapped economic potential, ripe for exploitation.

Governing values and the COVID-19 pandemic

While shock events are unfortunately a common feature of seafood operations (White et al. 2021: 233), the COVID-19 pandemic created many serious impacts on the fish industry, including decreased (domestic but especially international) demand and selling price for fish, COVID-19 regulations impacting on fishing, processing or market (including restaurant) activities and seafood workers contracting the virus (White et al. 2021). The impact of these factors varied across sectors, states and countries.

Aquaculture was formally defined as an essential service in the US. However, the disruption of traditional marketing channels was critical – meaning not only loss of sales but having to hold market-ready product on farms (Senten, Engle, and Smith 2021). Knock-on effects included risks to the viability of (often small) business, the loss of live fish products of cultural importance to ethnic groups, the loss of labour to industries – and therefore of employment for many workers, animal welfare risks, and wellbeing concerns for employees (Senten, Engle, and Smith 2021: 359–65).

Similar issues arose in aquaculture in developing countries like Bangladesh, but in this case the crisis created new inequalities in supply chains, and changes to fish consumption driven by COVID-19 economic impacts elsewhere in the economy (e.g., jobs lost when textile industries closed down during self-isolation periods) (Hasan et al. 2021). Moreover, imposts such as the loss of viable small businesses, working-class jobs and food security, all imposed on a developing economy with existing concerns with child labour and extreme poverty, pose grave humanitarian risks.

In comparison, small-scale fisheries are already marginalised and often not prioritised by policymakers. The COVID-19 crisis has seen a massive impact through driving down demand and price, and at the same time social distancing and other restrictions can prevent boat fishing, fish market and fish processing activities (Bennett et al. 2020).

In these cases, it is the good that blue economy activities do (including food security, basic employment, support of livelihoods – especially of marginalised communities – see, e.g., World Bank Group (2016: 2)) that comes into sharp relief, as business-as-usual activities become under threat, and their ethical contributions become starkly visible.

Finally, it is worth observing that crises can create opportunities, and some have seen the disruption caused by the pandemic as furnishing an opportunity to be released from suboptimal path dependencies, and to discuss what a new, sustainable, and ethical blue economy might look like (e.g., Novaglio et al. 2021: 17).

Section summary

Many governing values are applicable to the blue economy, including sustainable development, humanist ethics such as human rights, ecocentric ethics and more. Some of these operate at the level of broad principle, and others have been specified in a way that makes clearer their application to blue economy activities. However, full specification through codes of ethical standards of corporate social responsibility (or other mechanisms of ethical standard-setting) has not yet occurred in a thoroughgoing way. As a result, it can be a challenge for blue economy actors to move from broad principles to their application in specific operations. It is one thing to have a commitment to sustainable development, but another to know what that commitment requires in a given situation.

Governance values for blue economy operations and institutions

Governance refers to: 'the structures and processes used to steer and coordinate interactions within an institution or institutional complex' (Breakey, Cadman, and Sampford 2017: 19). It draws attention to how things are done, rather than the why or the what. Governance values refer to the qualities of actions or regimes that allow them to reliably and visibly pursue the primary (governing) values. For example, the purpose of the blue economy is not inclusivity, transparency or accountability, but these values are nevertheless pivotal to ensure the blue economy can be trusted to deliver its promised values (e.g., of environmental and social sustainability).

Governance values can be employed to support the achievement of governing values (such as improving sustainability or promoting human rights). However, they also contribute to legitimacy in their own right (Breakey 2019; Cadman 2011). Equally though, there are some governing values that governance values can struggle to realise. Sustainability may be one of these. Spahn (2018: 1861) argues that normal processes of democratic and fair collective decision-making (procedural governance) cannot give fair consideration to future generations who cannot play any part in those processes.

Governance values can be presented on a schema running from 'thin' to 'thick' (Breakey, Cadman, and Sampford 2017). Thin governance values only cover minimum conditions for basic oversight. These include transparency, accountability and compliance activities. More legitimacy arises when thicker governance values are incorporated. Thickish governance values also include qualities regarding how the institution goes about making its decisions and who it includes in doing so. Finally, at the thick end of the continuum, stronger mechanisms of democracy and deliberation are included, as well as whether the organisation functions effectively.

Governing values can apply to two different areas: 1) the (collective and institutional) decision-making processes about what activities to perform, and 2) the activities in the blue economy themselves – such as fishing, aquaculture, energy generation and so on.

Governance values for decision-making processes

Decision-making processes refer to ethical ways that decision-makers and stakeholders can interact to develop alternatives and come to agreements. Processes can be defended in terms of their results (e.g., This type of process ensures strong protections for the environment.), and in terms of the legitimacy created by the process itself (e.g., All stakeholders were able to meaningfully contribute to the decision, and so should respect it.). As Cadman (2011) argues, governance structures and processes in combination deliver legitimate outcomes, and it is the interactions between stakeholders within those structures and processes that deliver legitimate outcomes, so long as those interactions are collaborative.

Several authors highlight mechanisms of participatory and procedural justice to resolve problems created by conflicting values. On this footing, an inclusive process of collaborative decision-making by informed stakeholders can respect the views of each, and develop solutions that warrant respect (e.g., Foley and McCay 2014). For example, one account of procedural justice requires that the dialogue outcome: treats people consistently; is neutral and unbiased; is based on accurate information; is correctable if decisions are found to be inaccurate; is based on ethical standards; and is representative of all stakeholders' voices in decision-making (Kim and Siddiki 2018). Interestingly, these findings suggest that relatively moderate levels of diversity in collaborative membership tends to be more beneficial for promoting perceptions of procedural justice than either low or high diversity or both. This type of justice is often employed to resolve or highlight cultural concerns: literature on Indigenous participation emphasises the importance of inclusion and participatory justice (Capistrano and Charles 2012; Norman 2017).

Governance values for blue economy activities

The governance challenges created by the blue economy create the need for innovative governance solutions and practices. Critically, many blue economy activities occur out at sea, in remote and dynamic environments, sometimes under cover of darkness and with unclear jurisdictional borders. Furthermore, often the activities, or their impacts, are undersea, reducing their visibility to media and stakeholder communities, and allowing the natural flow of water to carry away pollutants that, in other environments, could be traced to the offending industry (Flanagan 2021). All these features make it easy for actors to slip under the radar in their actions and reporting – even before the COVID-19 pandemic decreased human observers, and accountability monitoring (Bennett et al. 2020: 339).

Third-party certification plays an important role in ensuring sustainability in aquaculture – including social sustainability (Alexander, Amundsen, and Osmundsen 2020). Certification can allow for ethical and environmental standards higher than minimal or poorly enforced regulation to be entrenched and made accountable. To do so however, certification regimes must themselves have high governance standards – they must be independent and impartial and have mechanisms that address potential conflicts of interest (centrally, that certifiers can be well paid by allowing their brand to be used by industry for ethics-washing and greenwashing purposes). There must also be high standards of scientific expertise, testing and invigilation.

Even with high standards certification, problems can remain. Such certification can be costly, especially when scientific testing is specialised, leading to challenges for – as an example – aquaculture industries in New Zealand obtaining the services of European specialists. Such challenges have only increased with the impact of the COVID-19 pandemic, and the closing of national borders. In addition, there is a problem of complexity. Certification is rarely ethically or even environmentally comprehensive. That is, many certification regimes focus on specific issues and types of harms, rather than ensuring the overall health of ecosystems. A common response to this concern is to adopt multiple forms of certification, but this introduces significant complexity for food consumers and distributors to navigate.

A point just touched on in the above paragraph, which deserves particular attention, is the impact of the COVID-19 pandemic on governance standards. In these testing times, arguably a key governance value becomes resilience – the capacity to survive and adapt flexibly in altered contexts. (Cadman (2011: 42–43) notes durability in his governance framework.) However, such flexibility must itself be ethically informed. Financially and operationally stressed organisations can feel the need to cut corners or develop new workarounds, and these can come at an ethical cost.

Finally, governance values also apply to regulators, who must themselves continually monitor their independence, transparency, scientific expertise and methods of enforcement and invigilation of regulatory requirements. Indeed, even scientists themselves must heed governance values if they are to warrant trust by communities (Kelly, Fleming, and Pecl 2018).

Institutional integrity

Institutional integrity refers to whether the institution lives up to its publicly asserted values (Breakey, Cadman, and Sampford 2015). Many of the governing values listed above, as well as stakeholder and social licence demands, are externally mandated, in the sense that they originate in a source external to the duty-bearer. Integrity approaches work differently. Applied to individuals, they begin by asking a person what their values are: What do you stand for, what do you want to contribute, what will you publicly undertake to live up to (Breakey 2016)? Institutional integrity applies this same concept of integrity to institutions. The first vital questions that must be asked of any institution or organisation are: What is it for? Why should it exist? What justifies the organisation to the community in which it operates, given that the community generally provides privileges? Asking those questions involves an institutional and collective effort under an organisation's own formal and informal constitutional processes. An organisation that comes to a determination of its values, publicly proclaims them and reforms its operations so as to reliably realise those values, has institutional integrity (Preston and Sampford 2002). (Alternatively, an institution that engages in ethics-washing and puts forwards values it does not aim to live by is hypocritical.) The values it chooses serve as its public institutional justification – they express to the community why the institution is justified and deserves to be allowed to continue its activities (Breakey, Cadman, and Sampford 2015). They can come in the form of mission statements or statements of values.

Institutional integrity involves coherence integrity, which ensures that the values are operationalised throughout the organisation's structure and practices (Breakey, Cadman, and Sampford 2015). The organisation needs to develop internal processes and practices that ensure it will reliably achieve its public institutional justification. This will often involve the application of the thick governance values noted above.

Institutional integrity also includes context integrity, which refers to the environment in which the organisation exists, and whether the system around it – including actors like media, NGOs, regulators and government – has features that encourage its pursuit of its values or impede it doing so. Crucially, context integrity includes the relationships that the organisation pursues with these external bodies, and its power to curate and nurture those relationships in such a way as to encourage its pursuit of its publicly stated values (Breakey, Cadman, and Sampford 2015).

Especially important is the institution's interaction with regulatory and licensing bodies, and with government. If a blue economy organisation develops a siege mentality, resisting regulatory involvement and oversight so far as possible, then this can weaken the power of external compliance regimes to ensure the organisation works within acceptable bounds. After all, even if some aspects of regulatory action are intrusive or overly restrictive, many other aspects are bound to be legitimate and make important contributions to keeping the organisation ethical and sustainable.

On the other hand, the alternative challenge to context integrity occurs when the organisation manages to get too close to regulatory or government bodies and regulatory capture occurs (an allegation levelled at salmon farming in Tasmania by Flanagan (2021: 7)). At first, this arrangement can seem desirable for the organisation, because it allows it to proceed unencumbered by restrictions and external oversight. But regulatory capture can set the scene for severe ethical and operational risk. So long as the regulator is independent, impartial and effective and the regulation conforms acceptably to democratic sentiment, then an institution operating within its bounds gains a level of moral legitimacy: it is entitled to operate, because its actions occur within the parameters that a legitimate system of government has laid down. But once regulatory capture occurs, legal licence no longer confers legitimacy. Indeed, some commentators see SLO as a response to the lack of legitimacy of existing formal licences and political decisions (Newton et al., 2020, Bennett et al., 2020). Having subverted the agencies representing democracy and the rule of law, and which should be ensuring sustainable development – the organisation can no longer enjoy the legitimising support that comes from working within legal confines (Flanagan 2021: 7). Community support is likely to plummet in such cases, and social licence replaces legal licence as a legitimising factor. Unfortunately, if the community thinks government regulation cannot ensure ethical standards and sustainability, then they are more likely to opt for more drastic, all-or-nothing alternatives, such as complete bans.

A related context integrity issue for blue economy industries involves industry relationship with independent bodies and scientists, and the level of transparency that must be accorded these. Use of non-disclosure agreements and commercial-in-confidence arrangements are necessary and appropriate in many cases. However, care must be taken, lest such mechanisms start to blanket evidence of negative impacts that should be available to expert, political and community decision-making. While an industry might think it makes sense to keep control over any information that could be damaging to it, once it becomes apparent to a community that they are only able to access one side of the story, it can become almost impossible to recapture trust.

Understanding context integrity requires understanding an integrity system. The concept of an integrity system was inspired by the Fitzgerald reform process in Queensland in which good governance was promoted and corruption attacked by a combination of state institutions and agencies (courts, parliament, prosecutors), state watchdog agencies (ombudsman, auditor general, parliamentary committees), NGOs, laws, norms and incentive mechanisms (Sampford and Wood 1992; Sampford, Smith, and Brown 2005).

Integrity systems are constituted by the laws, norms, economic incentives, and institutional arrangements that deliver (or fail to deliver) publicly professed goals and values. The effectiveness of an integrity system depends on institutions and their relationships. An integrity system comprises the range of mechanisms, including laws, regulations and institutions, as well as the accepted practices, that support integrity in the exercise of power. It is important to recognise that an integrity system is not designed to merely prevent corruption or other governance failures but to increase the likelihood that institutions live up to the values they profess.

This is important for governments, industries and NGOs in developing their context integrity. Context integrity requires ensuring that other parts of the integrity system are supported, insofar as they keep the organisation playing its role – that is, delivering the values and goods that justify its existence.

Putting the pieces together: Legitimacy

This section draws together the SLO, governing values, governance values and institutional integrity to explore institutional and operational legitimacy in the blue economy.

This chapter has shown that blue economy ethics is complex. This group of industries raise a multitude of ethical concerns – each of which can implicate governing values, governance values, social licence issues and institutional integrity.

One way of responding to this complexity is through the idea of legitimacy. Social legitimacy refers to the actual support of an industry or its operations by a group (the term parallels the idea of the SLO). The focus here is on moral legitimacy, which refers to ethical reasons to tolerate or support an industry or organisation. If an institution possesses moral legitimacy, then this gives stakeholders good reason to accept it – ushering in social legitimacy.

Moral legitimacy is multidimensional in nature – meaning that there are many different and distinct features that ethical decision-makers can work through (Breakey 2021). For example, for any given activity, the following questions may be asked:

1. Is it ethical? This dimension tracks whether the activity itself is harmful or morally principles.
2. Is it fair? This dimension considers whether the costs, opportunities, externalities, benefits and risks are fairly distributed across relevant stakeholders. (These first two dimensions foreground the issues discussed in the governing values section above.)
3. Is it effective? This dimension considers whether the operation delivers its promised outcomes reliably and efficiently (perhaps compared to other operations, see, Buchanan and Keohane 2006).

4. Is it trustworthy? This dimension tracks whether the institution is honest, accountable and delivers on its claims and commitments. (It will focus on issues discussed in the institutional integrity section above.)
5. Does it make decisions appropriately? This dimension focuses on whether decisions are made impartially, based on relevant evidence and/or including input from stakeholders. (It will focus on the issues discussed in the governance values section above.)
6. Does it respect local ways and practices? This dimension stresses the importance of community, and the practices and traditions it creates. (It will focus on issues relevant to stakeholder roles and the SLO, noted above.)

Asking these questions (for further dimensions, see Breakey 2021) allows an industry to anticipate and respond comprehensively to ethical challenges, and to develop an ethical vision justifying and even celebrating its operations. These questions allow multidimensional legitimacy to be tracked for any institution or operation. However, for decisions that have specific environmental or local community issues, more focussed legitimacy frameworks can be optimal. For example, Cadman's (2011: 43–44) governance framework employs two principles distilled into four criteria and ten indicators. The indicators provide detailed specifications of key moral legitimacy dimensions, including inclusiveness, equality (in decision-making), resources (for participants), accountability, transparency, democracy, agreement and dispute settlement, behavioural change, problem-solving and durability. Such multidimensional legitimacy models and frameworks empower organisations to deal with the multitude of ethical issues in play in areas like the blue economy.

Conclusion

As a new and expanding type of industry, blue economy activities implicate an array of serious ethical issues – economic, social and environmental. At the same time, government regulation struggles to keep pace with development, scientific knowledge about impacts can be unclear, and much activity occurs in environments – both above and under the water – that challenge normal accountability and monitoring practices. Together, this gives rise to a perfect moral storm, where the legitimacy of operations, corporations and even entire industries can be called into question. Only by a robust and comprehensive engagement with the full suite of ethical issues in play can legitimacy be assured, and the host of positive ethical values that the blue economy can deliver be realised.

References

Alexander, Karen A., Vilde S. Amundsen, and Tonje C. Osmundsen. 2020. "Social Stuff' and All That Jazz: Understanding the Residual Category of Social Sustainability', *Environmental Science and Policy*, 112, 61–68.

Baines, James, and Peter Edwards. 2018. 'The Role of Relationships in Achieving and Maintaining a Social Licence in the New Zealand Aquaculture Sector', *Aquaculture* 485, 140–46.

Bennett, Nathan J. 2019. 'In Political Seas: Engaging with Political Ecology in the Ocean and Coastal Environment', *Coastal Management*, 47 (1), 67–87.

Bennett, Nathan J., Elena M. Finkbeiner, Natalie C. Ban, Dyhia Belhabib, Stacy D. Jupiter, John N. Kittinger, Sangeeta Mangubhai, Joeri Scholtens, David Gill, and Patrick Christie. 2020. 'The Covid-19 Pandemic, Small-Scale Fisheries and Coastal Fishing Communities', *Coastal Management*, 48 (4), 336–47.

Bentham, Jeremy. 1789/1948. *An Introduction to the Principles of Morals and Legislation* (New York: Hafner).

——. 1978/1802. 'Principles of the Civil Code.' in C.B. Macpherson (ed.), *Property: Mainstream and Critical Positions* (Toronto: University of Toronto), pp. 39–58.

Blackstone, William T. 1973. 'Ethics and Ecology', *The Southern Journal of Philosophy*, 11 (1-2), 55–71.

Bogadóttir, Ragnheiður. 2019. 'Blue Growth and Its Discontents in the Faroe Islands: An Island Perspective on Blue (De)Growth, Sustainability, and Environmental Justice', *Sustainability Science*, 15 (1), 103–15.

Boutilier, Robert G., and Ian Thomson. 2011. 'Modelling and Measuring the Social License to Operate: Fruits of a Dialogue between Theory and Practice', *Social License, 1, 1–10*.

Breakey, Hugh. 2012. 'Moral Pluralist Theories.' in Peter Bowden (ed.), *Applied Ethics: Strengthening Ethical Practices* (Prahran, Australia: Tilde University Press), pp. 17–29.

——. 2016. 'Compromise Despite Conviction: Curbing Integrity's Moral Dangers', *Journal of Value Inquiry*, 50 (3), 613–29.

——. 2018a. 'It's Right, It Fits, We Debated, We Decided, I Agree, It's Ours, and It Works: The Gathering Confluence of Human Rights Legitimacy', *Law and Philosophy*, 37 (1), 1–28.

——. 2018b. 'Same Duties, Different Motives: Ethical Theory and the Phenomenon of Moral Motive Pluralism', *Philosophical Studies*, 175 (2), 531–52.

——. 2019. 'Harnessing Multi-Dimensional Legitimacy for Codes of Ethics: A Staged Approach', *Journal of Business Ethics*, 70 (2), 359–73.

——. 2021. 'The Comprehensive Multidimensional Legitimacy Model: A Methodology for Applied Ethics Evaluation, Institutional Diagnosis and Practical Reform Initiatives', *Research in Ethical Issues in Organisations*, In Press.

Breakey, Hugh, Tim Cadman, and Charles Sampford. 2017. 'Governance Values and Institutional Integrity.' in Tim Cadman, Rowena Maguire and Charles Sampford (eds.), *Governing the Climate Change Regime: Institutional Integrity and Integrity Systems* (Surrey, UK: Routledge), pp. 16–44.

Breakey, Hugh, Timothy Cadman, and Charles Sampford. 2015. 'Conceptualizing Personal and Institutional Integrity: The Comprehensive Integrity Framework', *Research in Ethical Issues in Organizations*, 14, 1–40.

Buchanan, Allen, and Robert O. Keohane. 2006. 'The Legitimacy of Global Governance Institutions', *Ethics and International Affairs*, 20 (4), 405–37.

Cadman, Timothy. 2011. *Quality and Legitimacy of Global Governance* (London: Palgrave Macmillan).

Capistrano, Robert Charles G., and Anthony T. Charles. 2012. 'Indigenous Rights and Coastal Fisheries: A Framework of Livelihoods, Rights and Equity', *Ocean and Coastal Management*, 69, 200–09.

Childs, John. 2020. 'Performing 'Blue Degrowth': Critiquing Seabed Mining in Papua New Guinea through Creative Practice', *Sustainability Science*, 15 (1), 117–29.

Davis, Anthony, and Kenneth Ruddle. 2012. 'Massaging the Misery: Recent Approaches to Fisheries Governance and the Betrayal of Small-Scale Fisheries', *Human Organization*, 71 (3), 244–54.

Eikeset, Anne Maria, Anna B. Mazzarella, Brynhildur Davíðsdóttir, Dane H. Klinger, Simon A. Levin, Elena Rovenskaya, and Nils Chr Stenseth. 2018. 'What Is Blue Growth? The Semantics of "Sustainable Development of Marine Environments', *Marine Policy*, 87, 177–79.

Ertör, I., and M. Hadjimichael. 2020. 'Editorial: Blue Degrowth and the Politics of the Sea: Rethinking the Blue Economy', *Sustainability Science*, 15, 1–10.

Farmery, Anna K., Emily Ogier, Caleb Gardner, and Julia Jabour. "Incorporating ecologically sustainable development policy goals within fisheries management: An assessment of integration and coherence in an Australian context." *Journal of environmental management* 249 (2019): 109230.

Flanagan, Richard. 2021. *Toxic: The Rotting Underbelly of the Tasmanian Salmon Industry* (Melbourne: Penguin).

Foley, Paul, and Bonnie McCay. 2014. 'Certifying the Commons: Eco-Certification, Privatization, and Collective Action', *Ecology and Society*, 19 (2), 28.

Fry, Greg, and Sandra Tarte. 2015. *New Pacific Diplomacy* (Canberra: ANU Press).

Ghori, Umair. 2019. 'Encroachment of Social Licence in Australia's Trade and Investment', *University of Western Australia Law Review*, 46 (1), 55–89.

Glendon, Mary Ann. 2001. *A World Made New: Eleanor Roosevelt and the Universal Declaration of Human Rights* (New York: Random House).

Grace, Damian, and Stephen Cohen. 2013. *Business Ethics* (South Melbourne, Australia: Oxford University Press).

Hasan, Neaz A., Richard D. Heal, Abul Bashar, Alif Layla Bablee, and Mohammad Mahfujul Haque. 2021. 'Impacts of Covid-19 on the Finfish Aquaculture Industry of Bangladesh: A Case Study', *Marine Policy*, 130, 104577.

Johnson, David, Christopher Barrio Froján, Nicholas Bax, Piers Dunstan, Skipton Woolley, Pat Halpin, Daniel Dunn, Carolina Hazin, Maria Dias, Tammy Davies, Jorge Jiménez, Erick Ross, Cindy Van Dover, Giuseppe Notarbartolo Di Sciara, Erich Hoyt, Michael J. Tetley, Vikki Gunn, and Henning Von Nordheim. 2019. 'The Global Ocean Biodiversity Initiative: Promoting Scientific Support for Global Ocean Governance', *Aquatic Conservation*, 29 (S2), 162–69.

Kant, Immanuel. 1785/2008. *The Moral Law: Groundwork of the Metaphysic of Morals* (New York: Hutchinson's University Library).

Kelly, Rachel, Aysha Fleming, and Gretta T. Pecl. 2018. 'Social Licence for Marine Conservation Science', *Frontiers in Marine Science*, 5 (414), 1–6.

Kim, Jangmin, and Saba Siddiki. 2018. 'Linking Diversity of Collaborative Policymaking Venues with Procedural Justice Perceptions: A Study of US Marine Aquaculture Partnerships', *The American Review of Public Administration*, 48 (2), 159–74.

Klain, Sarah C., Rachelle Beveridge, and Nathan J. Bennett. (2014). "Ecologically sustainable but unjust? Negotiating equity and authority in common-pool marine resource management." *Ecology and Society* 19.4: 52. http://dx.doi.org/10.5751/ES-07123-190452

Lam, Mimi E. 2016. 'The Ethics and Sustainability of Capture Fisheries and Aquaculture', *Journal of Agricultural and Environmental Ethics*, 29 (1), 35–65.

Lam, Mimi E., and Daniel Pauly. 2010. 'Who Is Right to Fish? Evolving a Social Contract for Ethical Fisheries', *Ecology and Society*, 15 (3), 16.

Leopold, Aldo. 1968. *A Sand County Almanac: With Other Essays on Conservation from Round River* (New York: Oxford University Press).

Locke, John. 1690/1947. *Two Treatises of Government* (New York: Hafner).

MacIntyre, Alasdair. 1981. *After Virtue: A Study in Moral Theory* (London: Duckworth).

Mather, Charles, and Lucia Fanning. 2019. 'Social Licence and Aquaculture: Towards a Research Agenda', *Marine Policy*, 99 (January), 275–82.

Melé, Domènec, and Jaume Armengou. 2016. 'Moral Legitimacy in Controversial Projects and Its Relationship with Social License to Operate: A Case Study', *Journal of Business Ethics*, 136, 729–42.

Mill, John Stuart. 1861/2001. *Utilitarianism* (Cambridge: Hackett).

Moore, W.H. 1996. 'The Social License to Operate', *The Paper Industry Magazine*, 78 (10), 22–23.

Morgera, Elisa, and Mara Ntona. 2018. 'Linking Small-Scale Fisheries to International Obligations on Marine Technology Transfer', *Marine Policy*, 93, 295–306.

Murphy-Gregory, Hannah. 2018. 'Governance Via Persuasion: Environmental NGOs and the Social Licence to Operate', *Environmental Politics*, 27 (2), 320–40.

Muthalib, Abd A., Asrip Putera, Wali A. Rumbia, Pasrun Adam, Ahmad, M. Nuryadi, Andi B. Wawo, and Muh Nur. 2019. 'An Empowerment Model of Seaweed Farmers in Coastal Area of Southeast Sulawesi, Indonesia', *Aquaculture, Aquarium, Conservation and Legislation Bioflux*, 12 (6), 2252–60.

Newton, Mark J., Trisia A. Farrelly, and Jim Sinner. 2020. 'Discourse, Agency, and Social License to Operate in New Zealand's Marine Economy', *Ecology and Society*, 25 (1), 1–13.

Norman, Emma S. 2017. 'Standing up for Inherent Rights: The Role of Indigenous-Led Activism in Protecting Sacred Waters and Ways of Life', *Society and Natural Resources*, 30 (4), 537–53.

Novaglio, Camilla, Narissa Bax, Fabio Boschetti, Gholam Reza Emad, Stewart Frusher, Liam Fullbrook, Mark Hemer, Sarah Jennings., Ingrid van Putten, Lucy M. Robinson, Erica Spain, Joanna Vince, Michelle Voyer, Graham Wood, and Elizabeth A. Fulton. 2022. 'Deep Aspirations: Towards a Sustainable Offshore Blue Economy', *Reviews in Fish Biology and Fisheries*, 32, no. 1 (2022): 209–230.

Ntona, Mara, and Elisa Morgera. 2018. 'Connecting SDG 14 with the Other Sustainable Development Goals through Marine Spatial Planning', *Marine Policy*, 93, 214–22.

Payne, Dinah M., and Cecily A. Raiborn. 2001. 'Sustainable Development: The Ethics Support the Economics', *Journal of Business Ethics*, 32 (2), 157–68.

Preston, Noel, and Charles Sampford. 2002. 'Institutionalising Ethics.' in Charles Sampford, Noel Preston and Carmel Connors (eds.), *Encouraging Ethics and Challenging Corruption* (Annandale, Australia: Federation Press), pp. 32–68.

Rawls, John. 1971. *A Theory of Justice* (Cambridge, MA: Harvard University Press).

Rokeach, Milton. 1976. *Beliefs, Attitudes and Values: A Theory of Organization and Change* (London: Jossey-Bass Publishers).

Rozzi, Ricardo. 2019. 'Taxonomic Chauvinism, No More! Antidotes from Hume, Darwin, and Biocultural Ethics', *Environmental Ethics*, 41 (Fall), 249–82.

Said, Alicia, and Ratana Chuenpagdee. 2019. 'Aligning the Sustainable Development Goals to the Small-Scale Fisheries Guidelines: A Case for EU Fisheries Governance', *Marine Policy*, 107, 103599.

Sampford, Charles. 1994. 'Law, Ethics and Institutional Reform: Finding Philosophy, Displacing Ideology', *Griffith Law Review*, 1 (1), 1–38.

Sampford, Charles, Rodney Smith, and A. J. Brown. 2005. 'From Greek Temple to Bird's Nest: Towards a Theory of Coherence and Mutual Accountability for National Integrity Systems', *Australian Journal of Public Administration*, 64 (2), 96–108.

Sampford, Charles, and David Wood. 1992. 'The Future of Business Ethics: Legal Regulation, Ethical Standard Setting and Institutional Design', *Griffith Law Review*, 1 (1), 56–72.

Santiago, Ana Lúcia, Jacques Demajorovic, Dennys Eduardo Rossetto, and Hanabeth Luke. 2021. 'Understanding the Fundamentals of the Social Licence to Operate: Its Evolution, Current State of Development and Future Avenues for Research', *Resources Policy*, 70, 101941.

Saunders, Fred, Michael Gilek, Anda Ikauniece, Ralph Tafon, Kira Gee, and Jacek Zaucha. 2020. 'Theorizing Social Sustainability and Justice in Marine Spatial Planning: Democracy, Diversity, and Equity', *Sustainability*, 12 (6), 2560.

Senten, Jonathan, Carole R. Engle, and Matthew A. Smith. 2021. 'Effects of Covid -19 on U.S. Aquaculture Farms', *Applied Economic Perspectives and Policy*, 43 (1), 355–67.

Silver, Jennifer J., Noella J. Gray, Lisa M. Campbell, Luke W. Fairbanks, and Rebecca L. Grub. 2015. 'Blue Economy and Competing Discourses in International Oceans Governance', *Journal of Environment and Development*, 24 (2), 135–60.

Singer, Peter. 1993. *Practical Ethics* (Cambridge, UK: Cambridge University Press).

——. 2001. 'All Animals Are Equal . . . ' in Peter Singer (ed.), *Writings on an Ethical Life* (London: Fourth Estate), pp. 28–47.

Smith-Godfrey, S. 2016. 'Defining the Blue Economy', *Maritime Affairs (New Delhi, India)* 12 (1), 58–64.

Song, Andrew M., and Adam Soliman. 2019. 'Situating Human Rights in the Context of Fishing Rights – Contributions and Contradictions', *Marine Policy*, 103, 19–26.

Spahn, Andreas. 2018. '"The First Generation to End Poverty and the Last to Save the Planet?— Western Individualism, Human Rights and the Value of Nature in the Ethics of Global Sustainable Development', *Sustainability*, 10 (6), 1853.

Stewart, Alex. 2016. 'Fiji's Evolving Foreign Policy and Pacific Multilateral Order: Pre- and Post-Election.' in Steven Ratuva and Stephanie Lawson (eds.), *The People Have Spoken* (Canberra: ANU Press), pp. 229–48.

Sylvan, Richard. 1973. 'Is There a Need for a New, an Environmental Ethic?', *Proceedings of the XVth World Congress of Philosophy* 1, 205–10.

United Nations 2012 *Blue Economy Concept Paper* (Rio de Janeiro: United Nations Conference on Sustainable Development (Rio +20)) <https://sustainabledevelopment.un.org/content/documents/2978BEconcept.pdf> [Accessed 12 November 2021].

——. 2015. *The 17 Goals*, <https://sdgs.un.org/goals > [Accessed 12 November 2021].

United Nations Conference on Environment and Development 1992 *Agenda 21, Rio Declaration, Forest Principles* (Rio de Janiero: United Nations) <https://sustainabledevelopment.un.org/content/documents/Agenda21.pdf> [Accessed 31 January 2022].

United Nations Environment Programme. 2018. *The Sustainable Blue Economy Finance Principles*, <https://www.unepfi.org/blue–finance/> [Accessed 4 Nov 2020].

United Nations Environment Programme Finance Initiative.·2021. *Turning the Tide: How to Finance a Sustainable Ocean Recovery—a Practical Guide for Financial Institutions*, (Geneva: United Nations Environment Programme Finance Initiative), <https://www.unepfi.org/publications/turning-the-tide/ >[Accessed 12 November 2021].

United Nations General Assembly. 1948. *Universal Declaration of Human Rights*, Resolution 217 A (III) (New York) <https://www.un.org/en/about-us/universal-declaration-of-human-rights> [Accessed 12 November 2021].

——. 2007. *United Nations Declaration on the Rights of Indigenous Peoples*, A/RES/61/295 <https://www.un.org/development/desa/indigenouspeoples/declaration-on-the-rights-of-indigenous-peoples.html> [Accessed 12 November 2021].

——.·2015. *Transforming Our World: The 2030 Agenda for Sustainable Development*, (New York: United Nations), <https://sdgs.un.org/2030agenda> [Accessed 12 November 2021].

United Nations Millennium Summit 2000 United Nations Millennium Declaration (New York: United Nations, Deptartment of Public Information) <https://www.un.org/en/development/desa/pop ulation/migration/generalassembly/docs/globalcompact/A_RES_55_2.pdf> [Accessed 31 January 2022].

Voyer, M., G. Quirk, A. McIlgorm, and K. Azmi. 2018. 'Shades of Blue: What Do Competing Interpretations of the Blue Economy Mean for Oceans Governance?', *Journal of Environmental Policy and Planning*, 20 (5), 595–616.

White, Easton R., Halley E. Froehlich, Jessica A. Gephart, Richard S. Cottrell, Trevor A. Branch, Rahul Agrawal Bejarano, and Julia K. Baum. 2021. 'Early Effects of Covid-19 on US Fisheries and Seafood Consumption', *Fish and Fisheries*, 22 (1), 232–39.

World Bank Group.·2016. *Blue Economy Development Framework: Growing the Blue Economy to Combat Poverty and Accelerate Prosperity*, Oceans 2030: Financing the Blue Economy for Sustainable Development, <http://pubdocs.worldbank.org/en/446441473349079068/AM COECC-Blue-Economy-Development-Framework.pdf> [Accessed 4 November 2021].

World Commission on Environment and Development.·1987. *Our Common Future* (Oxford: Oxford University Press), <https://sustainabledevelopment.un.org/content/documents/5987our-common-future.pdf> [Accessed 13 October 2021].

Md. Wasiul Islam and Tapan Sarker

Chapter 24
Financing sustainable coastal and maritime tourism in the blue economy of the Asia-Pacific

Abstract: The coastal and marine environment is increasingly facing various challenges in the Asia-Pacific region due to multifaceted anthropogenic and natural reasons. This chapter explores the opportunities and challenges in promoting blue finance in enhancing a sustainable blue economy through the adoption of coastal and maritime tourism (CMT) in the Asia-Pacific region. Extant literature indicates various challenges in developing CMT in developing countries, including insufficient financing in this sector. Hence, this chapter aims to investigate how blue finance can promote sustainable development in developing countries. A conceptual framework is proposed, linking blue finance and sustainable development through strengthening the emerging blue economy, particularly by promoting sustainable CMT which can facilitate the conservation of the coastal and marine environment by transforming coastal communities into resilient communities. This chapter aims to draw some policy guidelines which might be useful for policymakers to focus on sustainable CMT as a means to stimulate the green economy through green finance and foster sustainable development.

Keywords: coastal and maritime tourism, blue economy, green finance, sustainable development, conservation, resilient communities, COVID-19

Introduction

The blue economy has been created as a separate economy to focus the resources of oceans. The blue economy encompasses a sustainable ocean economy to utilise ocean resources for continuing economic development and social prosperity ensuring the long-term protection of the environment. The blue economy contributes significantly to many developing economies of Asia and the Pacific (Wees 2020; Juneja et al. 2021; Walsh, Robertson, and Mehta 2020). The coastal and marine environment is often considered a popular tourist destination that has developed the coastal and maritime tourism (CMT) subsector and is significantly contributing to the blue economy, particularly the Asia-Pacific region. According to an Organisation for Economic Co-operation and Development (OECD) (2016) study, it is predicted that CMT will

https://doi.org/10.1515/9783110733488-024

replace the offshore oil and gas industry as the top ocean-based industry in terms of gross value added by 2030.

The coastal and marine environment is increasingly facing various challenges in the Asia-Pacific region due to multifaceted anthropogenic and natural reasons. Therefore, despite the immense contributions as well as huge potentials of CMT, this subsector is not free from challenges (United Nations Conference on Sustainable Development 2012; United Nations Conference on Trade and Development 2021b). Considering these challenges, massive financing or investment is essential in CMT to ensure the conservation of blue ecosystems. Presently, a new thread of blue finance has been popular to combat these challenges and to flourish the blue economy through CMT in a green and smarter or sustainable way (Edwards 2020; Walsh, Robertson, and Mehta 2020).

Against this backdrop, this chapter has taken initiative to investigate how blue finance can promote sustainable CMT in the blue economy of the Asia-Pacific region, based on an extant secondary literature review from various sources. This chapter will draw some policy guidelines which might be useful for policymakers to focus on sustainable CMT as one of the examples to stimulate the green economy through green finance and foster the sustainable development of the blue economy.

In this chapter, the blue economy and CMT in the Asia-Pacific are introduced. Aspects of the importance of blue financing, including its potential and its challenges are then discussed. Next, the impacts of COVID-19 on blue finance are examined. Then a conceptual framework is presented linking blue finance and sustainable development. Finally, some possible policy directions and conclusions are raised.

Background

Oceans constitute 72% of the world's surface and occupy more than 95% of the biosphere which support all forms of life and regulate global climate by producing oxygen, sequestering carbon dioxide, and recycling nutrients (UNCSD 2012). The ocean is Earth's largest ecosystem and the largest producer (at least 50%) of Earth's oxygen. It is the abode of most of the biodiversity on Earth. The impact of the oceans in the global economy is increasing by generating major economic opportunities for people with rapid growth in economic activities, innovation and business opportunities. Various industries have been developed based on the ocean biotic and abiotic resources which contribute significantly to the overall global economy. These also play crucial roles in sequestering the blue carbon and mitigating various climate change impacts.

The blue economy concept has been advanced via the advancement of the green economy which was emphasised at the Rio +20 United Nations Conference on Sustainable Development in Rio de Janeiro in 2012 . Following Rio +20, the concept of the blue economy was further matured through the development of the various institutional frameworks for sustainable development which was reflected in the Sustainable Development Goals (SDG 14). The blue economy is particularly targeted to coastal countries and is directly connected to reducing poverty and promoting environmental development.

This blue economy is dependent on ecosystem principles which consider oceans as development spaces where natural resources are explored with the consideration of conservation of those resources along with their ecosystems (United Nations Development Programme 2018). Moreover, the blue economy deals with exploring opportunities for income and growth with new jobs creation while maintaining ocean health. Consequently, the blue economy is considered as a framework for sustainable development particularly for developing countries where economies are more focussed on environmental resources exploitation to foster equity for benefit sharing and human resource development.

The Asia-Pacific region is bestowed with an impressive combination of natural and cultural resources. This region comprises excellent air transport infrastructure along with massive investment in the ground, ports and tourist service infrastructure (World Travel and Tourism Council 2020b). As a result, this region stands at the second position in the world in 2019 as the competitive region in terms of travel and tourism (World Travel and Tourism Council 2020a). Moreover, the Asia-Pacific region is known as the harbour of rich coastal and marine resources which attracts a considerable number of domestic and international tourists. The Sundarbans of Bangladesh and India is the world's single largest continuous stretch of mangrove forests. The Great Barrier Reef of Australia is also a famous tourist destination which is also a key ecologically vulnerable site in the region. East Asia-Pacific countries account for more than 50% of the Asia-Pacific's international tourist arrivals and profits. Moreover, the Gross Domestic Product (GDP) of southeast Asian countries has a high reliance on the tourism sector due to the high influx of international tourists.

Blue finance is known as a type of green investment which supports the green development of coastal and marine environments in local communities by transforming them into a strong and climate-resilient communities. Such finance takes initiatives to improve these blue ecosystems by funding different sustainable businesses which can minimise the negative impacts of various challenges like poverty, pollution and climate change (Edwards 2020; Walsh, Robertson, and Mehta 2020). Moreover, blue finance explores the risks and barriers to sustainable investment in the ocean. It also addresses ways of scaling-up such financing and the opportunities of investing in the ocean (Economist Impact: World Ocean Initiative 2018a). Some of the examples of such businesses are local wastewater treatment plants, ecotourism, better fisheries and forest management, capacity building, coral reefs and mangrove resilience, and so on. However, there is an acute shortage of blue financing in the world in ensuring marine resource conservation.

This chapter proposes conceptual framework linking blue finance and sustainable development through strengthening the emerging blue economy particularly by promoting sustainable CMT which can facilitate the conservation of the coastal and marine environment and transforming coastal communities into resilient communities. Moreover, the chapter explores how sustainable CMT can help develop a blue economy where blue finance (conservation finance) makes significant contributions. Furthermore, the access and types of such finance and their influences on low-carbon investments are discussed here. Such low-carbon investments and their implications in promoting green energy, developing ecotourism and other capacity building initiatives to reduce poverty, manage CMT, conserve the coastal and marine environment, manage waste disposal systems and develop sustainable food supply are discussed in this chapter.

Importance of the blue economy and CMT

The importance of the blue economy is well recognised and accepted. The United Nations and other major global institutions are now committed to the importance of protecting the ocean and its ecosystems. It is considered as a vital economy not only to boost up national or regional economies but also to ensure a balanced ecosystem, society and cultural harmony to promote its sustainable development. Though the blue economy significantly contributes to the global economy but the accurate value of the global blue economy is still undefined (UNCTAD 2021b). However, according to some sources, the global blue economy is worth around US 36 trillion per year which supports 80% of global trade by volume (UNCTAD 2012; Commonwealth Secretariat 2021; UNCTADUnited Nations Conference on Trade and Development 2016). The blue economy provides more than 3 billion people their livelihoods, mostly on islands and coastal areas of developing countries. In particular, more than 350 million jobs are solely connected to the fisheries sector serving food security (Turkas 2021; Commonwealth Secretariat 2021). However, according to the Organisation for Economic Cooperation and Development (OECD) (2016), the worth of the blue economy is assessed at USD 2.5 trillion annually making it equivalent to the world's seventh-largest economy, which is expected to double, generating around 40 million jobs by 2030 compared with its contributions of 2010 as the OECD (2016) has projected.

The blue economy plays a crucial role in many countries however, it is more crucial particularly for developing countries to safeguard the responsible use of oceans, seas and coastal areas for economic growth and at the same time to conserve the ecosystem through diminishing environmental risks and hazards. Moreover, it is vital for creating employment opportunities, improving human wellbeing and social equity, reducing poverty through lives and livelihoods, enhancing food and energy security, and so on (Commonwealth Secretariat 2021; Schmid 2020)

The share of the blue economy in the GDP of Asia-Pacific countries is very diverse. It varies from as low as 1% to as high as 87% in some of the island nations. This region is a significant provider of global food security, particularly through the fisheries sector. It shows that around 85% of the total population employed in the fisheries sector globally is from the Asia-Pacific region. This region is known as the backbone of global maritime trade with major sea lanes of communication within its region. Deep-sea mining is another promising sector in this region. China, India, Korea and Japan are contributing the most to this industry in Asia. This region also leads the global ship manufacturing industry (90% of global shipbuilding) mainly by the Asian countries – the Republic of Korea, China and Japan. Bangladesh (47.2%), India (25.6%) and Pakistan (21.5%) lead the ship-breaking industry in the world and maintain the maritime supply chain. The share of the blue economy in the GDP of Bangladesh in 2015 was 3.2%.

The World Bank introduced the first ever green bond in 2008, which created a market of almost USD 850 billion of issuances. Moreover, the World Bank started to work on the first ever blue bond of USD 15 million with the Seychelles in 2018 to champion sustainable marine and fisheries projects. So far, the Bank has managed around USD 5 billion that focusses on various challenges (like marine plastic pollution, access to clean water and good sanitation system) in and around the marine protected areas. Then, the Nordic Sea Blue Bond was launched in January 2019 by the Nordic Investment Bank.

Recreation and tourism, and more specifically CMT, are considered as one of the important services of the blue economy. Globally, CMT constitutes 5% of world GDP which contributes to 67% of total employment. This subsector is considered as one of five top export earners in 150 countries while it is at the top in 60 countries (Bangladesh General Economics Division 2021). CMT plays key importance in many developing countries of the world (UNCSD 2012). Up to 60% of the GDP of Small Island Developing States (SIDS) of this region are dependent on ocean-based tourism.

Globally sustainable CMT has great potential, this is especially so for the Asia-Pacific region where it can support ecotourism as well as conservation initiatives to restore fragile coastal and marine ecosystems (Economist Impact: World Ocean Initiative 2021a). CMT, especially ecotourism, and blue finance is identified as one of the new areas of opportunity in the blue economy sector.

Importance of blue financing

Blue finance is a type of green finance that promotes the sustainable development of coastal and marine ecosystems where the local coastal community has an important part to take in their overall development in terms of climate change, governance and other issues (Edwards 2020; Walsh, Robertson, and Mehta 2020). Some of the examples such green financing are initiatives that aim to strengthen the case for the ocean and coastal resilience with a view to conserve oceans and seas (SDG14).

Coastal communities, particularly of developing economies, play an important role in conserving the natural resources of the ocean. To do so they require global support by which they can contribute towards a blue economy as well as benefit both their communities and humanity. Moreover, it needs more individual and collective actions to ensure a blue economy to maximise prosperity for all (Economist Impact: World Ocean Initiative 2021a). Examples of such innovative financial instruments for the blue economy include blue bonds, results-based lending, ocean risk insurance, and payments for ecosystem services (Walsh, Robertson, and Mehta 2020). Several Asia-Pacific countries are taking several initiatives to strengthen their blue economy. As an example, the Maldives has planned to complete phase out their single-use plastic usage by 2023. Very recently they have banned the import of eight types of single-use plastics (Maldives Ministry of Environment Climate Change and Technology 2021). The following are some of the criteria for blue financing or eco-investing in the blue economy including sustainable CMT.

Sustainability

All the service providers in the blue economy, including CMT, need to consider the issues of sustainability in all their decision-making processes to achieve development. The investment needs to ensure a better environmental outcome by providing various environmental services and products to arrest environmental damages (i.e., environmental negative externalities). Blue financing should invest in preparing green policies to guide sustainable CMT operations. For example, hoteliers should consider the dimensions of sustainability in deciding whether they will go for investing in hotel construction and so on. Calculation of potential footprints may assist to choose more responsible CMT interventions.

Multi-stakeholders need to share their common understanding regarding the necessities of investments in the blue economy. In this regard, various evidence-based approaches and solutions to the issues and challenges of the blue economy will motivate them to invest to expedite ecosystem restoration and biodiversity conservation, that is, sustainable development. Moreover, it requires finance for more critical research that explores the effects of blue economy growth from a political economy perspective to mitigate various competing interests and conflicts among the stakeholders (Schmid 2020; Barbesgaard 2018).

Ecosystem revitalisation

This is a crucial part of financing in the blue economy including sustainable CMT (Economist Impact: World Ocean Initiative 2021b). The ecosystem plays a vital role in sustainable CMT where it is considered the most important tourist attraction *per se*. Blue finance should be allocated particularly where there is a necessity to revitalise the affected/damaged ecosystem. If there is enough evidence for sustainable CMT which can contribute to such ecosystem revitalisation, then there should have such financing so that the wellbeing of an ecosystem as well as the local community are ensured. In this case, tourists can assist in generating revenues to regenerate mangroves, coral reefs, wetlands and other habitats. Moreover, can be a catalyst towards sustainable CMT practice and generating new jobs for the locals. This will ultimately ensure a return on investment for investors whether it is government/private/PPP and national/international.

Tourists can facilitate the monitoring process of an ecosystem. For example, an amateur diver can collect photos and videos of a coral reef that can indicate the health status of this ecosystem. Moreover, the flow of tourists can often promote the protection of a protected area. Their feedback is used to make various decisions for the ecosystems. The example of Indonesia's Coral Triangle may be a good example to mention here. This habitat is known as one of the hotspots of marine biodiversity on the planet. However, the habitat was degraded in the recent past due to destructive fishing practices and poaching of many threatened species. Private investment promoted ecotourism in those islands, which provided the local people capacity building facilities and jobs to revitalise the vulnerable ecosystem through ensuring local protection and taking various conservation measures (Economist Impact: Wold Ocean Initiative 2018).

Incentives for the investors

The above-mentioned returns on investment and ecosystem revitalisation are some of the examples of incentives and motivations for investing in the blue economy, including CMT. Positive incentives such as bio-trade and eco-certification may be important facilitators to foster marine biodiversity conservation. Blue bonds need to be attractive enough for investors, especially the private sector, so that they are motivated to invest their resources in the bond or capital markets.

The innovative and creative financial solutions should focus on win-win-win outcomes, connecting the aspirations of coastal communities, the environment and the investors all at once. It may also focus on selling nature to save it reasoning and promoting market-based mechanisms to promote its conservation (Barbesgaard 2018).

Capacity building of community enterprises

There is also a need for awareness and capacity building of the concerned people to flourish the potential of the blue economy (Bangladesh General Economics Division 2021). The conservation of such sensitive ecosystems is largely dependent on the level of awareness of the local community and concerned official stakeholders, particularly those who are directly and indirectly involved with the management and governing of these ecosystems. The management, conservation and financing in these efforts are mostly technical and sophisticated, which warrant intensive capacity building initiatives at various levels and scales.

It has been found that over tourism is deteriorating the natural and cultural environments of CMT hotspots like Cox's Bazar, St. Martin Islands in Bangladesh as well as beaches of Bali, India and among others. Moreover, there is no management plan for most of the CMT destinations which require competent expertise and political willingness to have such technical and strategic documents through the interventions of concerned government departments. There should have significant awareness building and knowledge generation initiatives around various CMT destinations at all levels and scales *viz.*, consumers/tourists, tour operators, private businesses/entrepreneurs and local communities.

Partnerships

Blue finance needs to promote multi-stakeholder partnerships to include major actors like public, private, business entrepreneurship, not-for-profit organisations in financial markets, banks, investors, micro-credit entities, insurance companies, and so on (United Nations Environment Programme 2021). Resource mobilisation from different sources is warranted in this regard. Such sources of financing should cover both domestic and international institutions.

Governance

Such financing requires contributions in ensuring good governance of the coastal and ocean habitats through the delivery of long-term value to these ecosystems as well as shrink carbon and other greenhouse gas (GHG) emissions. Moreover, it needs to strengthen the resilient livelihoods of people who are dependent on these ecosystem resources considering ongoing climate change issues (Bangladesh General Economics Division 2021). Increased transparency, accountability, multi-stakeholder participation, rules of law, equity and balancing power among the stakeholders in the investment site can encourage investors to invest in the blue economy through capital markets. Moreover, the inclusion of climate change, environmental, social and governance factors in risk assessments is essential. The concerned stakeholders like investors, asset managers, insurers and banks are building their capacity to assess, value and price these risks.

Challenges of blue financing in the blue economy

The challenges of financing in the blue economy including CMT has been well discussed in the literature. A brief description is provided below on these major challenges.

Lack of universal standards and metrics

Currently, there is a lack of rigorous and universal standards and metrics to reveal that blue financing is advancing ocean health and the blue economy (Dahl 2010). There are several relevant frameworks of green financing like the Climate Bonds Initiative (Fatin and Whiley 2021), European Commission Sustainable Finance Taxonomy (Schütze and Stede 2021) and Green Bond Principles (Ehlers and Packer 2017). However, these initiatives and frameworks are considered not enough guidance for blue financing.

Underfunding of ocean investments

In general, there is an acute shortage of finance to achieve the SDGs. The United Nations estimates a global gap of 2.5 trillion annually to achieve these SDGs. However, the global funding gap for the blue economy is still to be reckoned accurately. Moreover, several pieces of research indicate that there is also a huge funding gap in attaining the targets related to the blue economy (SDG 14: life below water).

Evidence shows that at present, less than 1% of the total worth of the blue economy is financed by sustainable projects. It was committed only about USD 25.5 billion at the UN Ocean Conference in 2017 which was only about 17% of what was demanded achieving the SDG 14 by 2030 (Wees 2020). Another example shows, the shortage of finance is currently about seven times below of what is required to save the reefs.

The poverty of the local community

Poverty is considered the greatest global challenge to achieve the SDGs (United Nations 2012). The investment for the protection of marine resources is always challenging, particularly due to the poverty of local communities of many developing countries of the Asia-Pacific region. These people are dependent on fishing for their livelihoods. Therefore, merely outright banning resource harvest, even for a specific period, often does not work effectively to promote conservation initiatives of these marine resources (Turkas 2021).

Insufficient financial instruments for investments

Different types of government tax, subsidies and other incentives can influence financing in the blue economy and CMT both positively and negatively. However, the connections between these financial instruments and the blue economy are not available in many countries of the Asia-Pacific region, which hinders the financing in the blue economy (Walsh, Robertson, and Mehta 2020).

Insufficient scientific data and competent expertise

There are insufficient blue economy specialists to generate scientific and reliable data to plan for investment in the blue economy. Various sectors in the blue economy needs to be studied to assess the requirements of such investments for ensuring their sustainable development addressing the challenges faced, finding an innovative and attractive ways to invest, infrastructural design, monitoring and evaluation plans and so on.

Excess resource harvesting, unfair trade and ad hoc development

Resource regulation is one of the major challenges for facilitating sustainable development in the oceans (Singh 2021). Overfishing, excess harvesting of other biotic resources and unsustainable resource extraction from deep-sea mines threaten the environment of blue financing. Both legal and illegal resource extractions are causing such problems. For example, Cambodia, the Philippines, India, Indonesia are among the most heavily affected by such unregulated resource extractions, mainly fisheries resources. Moreover, an unhealthy working environment for the labourers, low payments and unfair trade is also deteriorating the natural resources of the ocean and creating big challenges for further investment (World Bank Group 2016).

Unplanned, unregulated and uncoordinated sectoral development in the land-coastal interface, as well as near-shore areas, are contributing to considerable environmental externalities that jeopardise the sustainable development growth of CMT (World Bank Group 2016). Moreover, coastal development for tourism can cause habitat destruction in areas like mangroves and coral reefs. Tourists produce various pollutants like soil, noise, water and air pollution. Cruise ships are responsible for emitting greenhouse gases and polluting water.

Marine pollution

Anthropogenic pressures are causing marine pollution is known as a massive challenge that affects the sensitive ecosystem (like mangroves, coral reefs, caves, and so on) of Asia-Pacific oceans. Unregulated shipping and their environmentally unfriendly operations, plastic pollution, effects of COVID-19 medical waste (particularly face masks and hand gloves) are aggravating marine pollution (Singh 2021) and putting pressure on investors to finance and solve these challenges. Scientists have projected there being more plastic than fish in the ocean by 2050 unless effective action is taken which would jeopardise the ocean environment (Turkas 2021; United Nations Environment Programme 2020). Of these, only 1418% of global plastic waste is recycled (Economist Impact: World Ocean Initiative 2018b). However, Morgan Stanley, which is working with the World Bank, sold USD 10 million worth of blue bonds in 2019 aiming to solve the challenge of plastic waste pollution in oceans.

Climate change

Though Pacific countries contribute very little (only 0.03%) to global carbon emissions, these countries, particularly the island nations, are often affected the most by climate change effects like sea level rise (nearly four times than the global average) along with various natural disasters such as cyclones, floods and so on. However, some of these island nations (Fiji, the Marshall Islands, Samoa, the Solomon Islands, Tuvalu, and Vanuatu) under the Pacific Blue Shipping Partnership have formed an agreement to lessen carbon emissions by 40% in 2030 and committed to achieving full decarbonisation by 2050 through technological advancement, particularly in the transportation industry (Martin 2019). The Asian Development Bank has suggested investing US 1.7 trillion per year between 2016 and 2030 in different climate-adjusted infrastructure of developing Asia, including transport, power, telecommunications, water supply and sanitation and other urban infrastructure.

Tourism is one of the sectors most affected by climate change. Adverse effects of climate change harm CMT by causing habitat destruction of beaches, mangroves and coral reefs. Tourism stakeholders are aware of these adverse effects and take a variety of corporate responsibility initiatives to tackle these effects (Economist Impact: World Ocean Initiative 2020).

Ocean governance

Ocean governance is a crucial issue for maintaining the health system of oceans as well as the blue economy. Poor governance of the ocean can deteriorate its ecosystem balance. South Asia has been struggling with ocean regulations as well as ocean finance (Singh 2021). There are many factors that hamper the governance of coastal areas and oceans which ultimately affect the environment of financing in the blue economy. These include poor enforcement of rules of law, absence of functional regulatory measures, lack of equity, transparency in issuing licences and permits, poor accountability of the concerned regulatory organisations and poor intersectoral/ministerial coordination. Other issues are stakeholder conflicts, poor participation of local stakeholders in monitoring ocean health and other community development interventions, lack of political commitments, mishandling of finance and integrity issues of the governing authorities.

There is a promising opportunity for blue financing to mitigate blue economy challenges if the following three conditions are met successfully. Firstly that, there is a standardised approach to valuing the natural resources of the blue economy. Secondly, state governments govern these resources effectively. Thirdly, private sector capital and initiatives are attracted and inspired to invest in the blue economy (Wees 2020).

Impacts of COVID-19: Financing for CMT and way forward

Several infectious diseases (e.g., COVID-19, influenza, Ebola, Zika, SARS, MERS-CoV, antibiotic-resistant bacteria, etc.) outbreaks have increased in the world significantly over the last 30 years and has affected the tourism industry considerably (World Travel and Tourism Council 2020a). The impact of ongoing COVID-19 on this industry is considered the most devastating in world history, which affects a significant toll on communities across the world. (Behsudi 2020; World Travel and Tourism Council 2021). According to a recent study, the COVID-19 pandemic has had an acute impact on the blue economy where the tourism sector has been affected most (71%), particularly in the Asia-Pacific region (Economist Impact: World Ocean Initiative 2020).

Economic impacts

According to the World Travel and Tourism Council, the global tourism sector was growing significantly before the ongoing COVID-19 pandemic in 2019, at more than

3.5% growth against the global economic growth of 2.5%. The Asia-Pacific performed the best among all regions in 2019 with a 5.5% growth in travel and tourism GDP which contributed 55% of all sector jobs in the global economy (see Table 24.1). The region has been dominating the world in creating jobs over the last six years in this sector. All the top five countries (and seven of the top ten countries) globally in terms of travel and tourism job creation over the last five years were in the Asia-Pacific region. India ranked the highest growth in the number of jobs created (6.36 million) followed by China (5.47 million) and the Philippines (2.53 million). However, according to the latest travel and tourism economic impact report (2021), the COVID-19 pandemic caused a reduction in GDP growth of 49.1% in 2020 with 62 million (34.1 million in the Asia-Pacific region) job losses. Domestic visitor spending decreased by 45%, while international visitor spending fell by an unprecedented 69.4% (World Travel and Tourism Council 2021). It is forecasted that global tourism receipts will not reach the levels of 2019 until 2023 (Behsudi 2020).

Table 24.1: Contributions of travel and tourism in the [global] economy.

Year	World GDP growth (%)	Asia-Pacific GDP growth (%)	Contribution to world GDP (%) (Asia-Pacific % of the world)	Contribution to job (million jobs) (Asia-Pacific = % of the world)
2018	3.9	6.4	10.4 (dm)	319 (dm)
2019	3.5	7.4	10.4 (34)	334 (185.1= 55.42%)
2020	−3.7	−53.7	5.5 (−49.1)	272 (151= 55.51%)

Source: World Travel and Tourism Council (2019, 2020b, 2021).
Source: dm = data missing.

Ecological impacts

Oceans are a poorly policed frontier, particularly during the ongoing COVID-19 pandemic. The reduced number of tourists due to the pandemic also reduced the revenues to spend for the conservation of these sensitive ecosystems (Juneja et al. 2021). Many additional impacts are still difficult to quantify, such as threats to the conservation of species and biodiversity, all directly linked to tourism. Many developing countries reported that illegal activities increased which were depleting the natural resources and biodiversity in and around the coastal and ocean areas due to the loss of jobs as a result of the COVID-19 pandemic. Many tourism-dependent people were forced to do that because of the unavailability of other legal alternative income generation opportunities for their livelihoods. The reduced number of tourists, or in fact no tourists, added to the conditions that led to illegal activity as the active presence and movements of tourists naturally acted to monitor those destinations which restricted illegal activities at those destinations.

Social impacts

Coastal communities were hardest hit, with an estimated USD 7.4 billion fall in GDP across SIDS due to the decline in tourism (Northrop et al. 2020). Seychelles and many other tourism-dependent nations have faced a virtual standstill by the pandemic. Pacific island nations such as Fiji was forecasted to reduce their GDP by 21% in 2020 (Behsudi 2020)These conditions have also created enormous social impacts at these CMT destinations such as loss of social harmony and equity, law breaking and various antisocial activities. There were also increases in severe crimes such as rape, human trafficking, hijacking, robbery, child abuse, infringement, sabotage, vandalism, chaos, social indiscipline and unrest, breaking the social chain of norms and command, and so on.

It has been observed that the COVID-19 pandemic has drastically changed the tourists' behaviour. Nowadays, tourists prefer safety and less-crowded outdoor activities to reduce the chance of being affected by the coronavirus. Consequently, a shift has been observed from mass tourism to dedicated nature-based tourism where CMT plays a major role. It is assumed that the demand for such nature-based tourism will be increased considerably in the post-pandemic era where domestic tourists will move around (Economist Impact: World Ocean Initiative 2021b)which will require increased finance to meet the increased demand.

Financing for CMT and way forward

The current situation strongly demands an increased and sufficient amount of liquidity support as blue finance over the next decade to recover CMT from the current financial crisis due to the COVID-19 pandemic (Economist Impact: World Ocean Initiative 2020; United Nations World Tourism Organization 2021). To fight back, most of the tourism-dependent economies of the world are currently trying hard to finance a broad range of policy measures to reduce the massive impacts of plunging tourism revenues on local communities and businesses. Consequently, cash transfers, grants, tax and debt relief, payroll support, loan guarantees (with and without interest) have been arranged by different countries (Behsudi 2020) to pat the wages and allowance of employees, rents, utility bills, VAT, taxes, loan interests, mortgage subsidy, infrastructure maintenance, employees' medical costs, insurance payments, capacity building, lockdown support to the tourism value chain of suppliers and intermediaries, including airlines. Moreover, it is recommended to harmonise travel and health protocols to address such crises in future. Therefore, many governments have had to finance in preparing and implementing standard operating procedures following health safety protocols for recovering their affected tourism sector, including CMT.

Many banks have ceased loan repayments in some instances for small to medium enterprises and large enterprises. A study shows that stimulus packages of USD 100 billion were provided across 24 economies as direct aid to the tourism industry and USD 300 billion as aid across other sectors that have considerable connection to the tourism sector. Some countries have taken provisions for providing support to the informal and casual workers of this sector. However, some new financing mechanisms (like revenue-sharing mechanisms among tourism service providers, government backed equity funds, etc.) are required to increase the financial support to the tourism-dependent communities to recover the tourism losses where a partnership between governments and the tourism industry has been sought. Additionally, innovative structural policies have been aimed for (Behsudi 2020) to interlink blue economy initiatives within the Asia-Pacific region through cooperation at the country-level and regional level along with their implementation at the national and subnational levels. All these initiatives in this region warrant special attention from various perspectives, including financing to protect the ocean ecosystems.

Sustainability is a crucial issue to deal with for addressing tourism practice in the post-COVID-19 pandemic era. Investment in sustainable tourism facilitates building resilience to withstand a crisis like the COVID-19. Such investment is well-known for the greater interest of the tourism sector. Some countries (like Costa Rica, the Seychelles, Malaysia and Thailand) have progressed considerably in investing in sustainable tourism and are currently enjoying the benefits amid the COVID-19 pandemic, a trend that is expected to continue post-pandemic. Such investments help the local communities to maintain their economic chain through other sources of income for sustaining their livelihoods. As an example, people from the Seychelles have increased their benefits through tuna exports during the pandemic to recover their tourism loss but it was a very small amount in comparison to tourism receipts (Behsudi 2020).

These investments also promote sequestering more carbon and biodiversity conservation of their surroundings as well as preserving their sociocultural values which ultimately advance the application of sustainability. However, most of the smaller tourism-dependent island nations have very few alternative sectors to switch over their resources. In some Marine Protected Areas (MPAs) in Costa Rica the issues of local communities are prioritised to enable them to make the necessary transition. In this regard, preparing business plans for local communities is considered crucial for declaring any area as a protected area/reserve. Moreover, many researchers suggest including the local communities in discussions around ocean protection to use their local knowledge as well as to ensure their overall wellbeing. Furthermore, they should be considered as a part of the governance of the areas.

A conceptual framework

The blue economic approach can be implemented following the guidance of SDGs of the United Nations. The UNCTAD (2021b) has recognised a framework which consists of five ocean economy pillars (see Table 24.2) of such an approach in line with SDG14 *viz.*, economic, environmental, social, scientific and technology and governance to pursue sustainable and inclusive development, technological capacity, innovation, policy and regulatory coherence in areas within and beyond national jurisdiction.

Table 24.2: Pillars of sustainable ocean development of the United Nations Conference on Trade and Development (UNCTAD).

Sustainable pillars	Characteristics
Economic	– Promotes sustainable economic growth of key ocean-based sectors. – Advances sustainable trade and improves market access for ocean-based goods and services. – Strengthens connectivity between people and markets and increases value addition.
Environmental	– Encompasses policies and actions for sustainable access to living marine resources. – Controls biodiversity depletion, advocates and enforces precautionary and ecosystem approaches. – Focuses on the impact of climate change and marine pollution and implements well-tailored mitigation and adaptation strategies.
Social	– Deals with inclusive human development. – Fosters livelihoods development of coastal populations, decent working conditions, empowerment through access to education and economic resources. – Specially focusses on marginalised and vulnerable people.
Scientific and technology	– Concentrates to increase scientific knowledge, technological access and collaboration in the area of ocean-based economies. – Encompasses low-carbon activities and renewable energy technologies for the use, maintenance and management of coasts and oceans. – Facilitates marine-related investments in applied research and development, technology and knowledge-sharing. – Boosts capacity building and cooperative frameworks within scientific and academic communities for the development of new and innovative ocean-based goods and services.
Governance	– Integrates relevant national and international regulatory and policy obligations to improve the blue economy of a country. – Includes policies to ensure compliance and enforcement of these institutional instruments and governance frameworks. – Strengthens the necessary interagency and intergovernmental cooperation.

Source: UNCTAD (2021b); UNCTAD (2021a).

This chapter has presented a conceptual framework (see Figure 24.1) based on the above discussions on blue economy and CMT to link between blue financing and sustainable CMT under the blue economy sector. This framework has seven parts. A short description of this framework is given below.

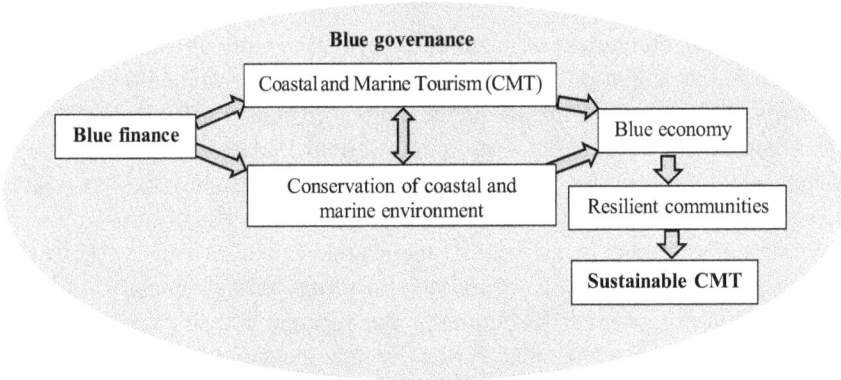

Figure 24.1: A conceptual framework on sustainable CMT through blue financing.

Conservation of coastal and maritime environment and CMT

All coastal countries must prioritise ocean, marine and coastal resources and their ecosystems in their all types of strategies and actions like trade, environment, climate change, and sustainable development. Moreover, all the pillars of sustainable ocean development of UNCTAD (see Table 24.2) need to be followed during any development activities carried out that impacts the coastal and marine environment. Coastal and marine pollution challenge the growth and developments of CMT as has already been discussed above. All types of environmental pollutions (including pollutions through CMT) and challenges are to be regulated through both binding and non-binding institutional instruments and governance arrangements to facilitate the conservation of coastal and maritime ecosystems. This will ultimately reduce the pressures on CMT and attract many investors to finance CMT development.

Blue financing in CMT and sustainable development

Governments should take proactive initiatives to help the CMT subsector through blue financing so that it can contribute towards sustainable development. They should incentivise the relevant stakeholders so that they can be motivated to facilitate sustainability in CMT. In this regard, governments may set minimum required standards for companies. Consequently, some certification systems may be developed by the government to promote CMT. Blue finance should encompass public and commercial finance, philanthropic capital and private equity to invest cooperatively in some innovative projects to create new local jobs to grow the local economies as well as to empower the local communities through ensuring positive social impacts to build upon the sustainable growth of the CMT subsector of the blue economy (World Bank Group 2016).

There are many challenges of sustainable blue financing as most of such finance is received as either grants or government money for a limited time (mostly for two years) which requires further applications to request further funds. To ensure blue finance is attractive and sustainable, various initiatives have been taken in different parts of the world. The Global Fund for Coral Reefs is one of the examples of such initiatives where a blended financing approach has been used which has combined grant money, concessional loans and private investment (Edwards 2020). This blue finance initiative has also been supported by a social enterprise which forms an organisation to facilitate the management and sustainability of finance for the marine protected areas. Further initiatives include, selling blue carbon credits through mangrove and seagrass conservation and restoration, ecotourism through charging entry and other fees for marine destinations, sustainable fisheries and among others. Such an approach is being implemented in the Dominican Republic and the Philippines as two pilot projects and are also planned for Belize, Cambodia and Cape Verde. It is expected to extend this approach in 20 marine protected areas by 2030 (Edwards 2020).

The blue economy and resilient communities

CMT under the blue economy should build a resilient community which is capable of reducing their vulnerability from the effects of a hazard or extreme events and responds creatively in a timely and effective manner. It grows the power of the community against various types of challenges to increase their long-term sustainability. CMT interventions should empower individual community members as well as the whole community to tackle these uncertainties and hardships. The community needs to integrate various plans concerning adaptation, risk reduction, ecosystem management, conflict risk reduction, alternative livelihoods and so on.

Good governance is considered as a crucial precondition to promote sustainable natural resource (like aquatic/marine/ocean resources) management and foster biodiversity conservation to build ecosystem as well as community resilience against various shocks and vulnerabilities including COVID-19 or climate change effects. Moreover, such governance arrangements will form an environment for the responsible private sector for their investments in the CMT value chain which will also foster local community empowerment. In this regard, different stakeholders (both public and private, knowledge centres, universities) should come forward to provide support to each other to foster research and development on the blue economy and resilient communities.

Governance and CMT

Governance is treated as the key focus to safeguard marine resources extractions and their trade. It demands a transparent, traceable, certified, safe and sustainable framework to meet the growing demand of consumers for the products and services which are produced in a sustainable way. The World Bank Group (2016) has suggested some governance proposals to improve the sustainable blue economy which is also applicable to sustainable CMT. These include reform to sectoral policies to reflect blue economy which also focusses on poverty alleviation, climate change and food security; builds public sectoral capacity and technical expertise to implement those policies; aligns economic interests considering long-term sustainability; promotes a healthy environment to foster CMT growth; strategic partnerships with donors; and utilisation of an inclusive multi-stakeholder approach and (public-private) dialogues.

International institutional instruments and governance arrangements should be followed by sustainable biodiversity-based value chains in CMT and other ocean-based sectors so that those can comply with the criteria of sustainability like the blue BioTrade principles (Kituyi and Bertarelli 2020). Considering the fragmented nature of the CMT and the interconnectedness of CMT challenges, there is an acute need for a common platform guided by an organisation outside of the CMT industry to bring together and organise the appropriate stakeholders for the betterment of this subsector (Economist Impact: World Ocean Initiative 2020).

Discussions and concluding remarks

Balanced and sustainable development is essential for both terrestrial and blue economies to foster the overall development of a country. There are a number of islands in the Asia-Pacific region where practising sustainable tourism by involving the local communities with the assistance of blue financing combining responsible private investments has progressed significantly which contributes to marine conservation by benefitting local communities. However, still many islands in this region are not performing as per the expectations. Currently, 57 countries in the world have established ocean-related policies, laws or regulations. The governments of Indonesia and Bangladesh have already integrated the coordination of ocean-related initiatives and issues. Nonetheless, there is a long way to move towards a sustainable ocean ecosystem. To date, only 7% of the ocean is protected through marine protected areas (MPAs), a long way from the target of 30%by 2030

(World Travel and Tourism Council 2020a). In addition only less than 2% of the ocean is protected as a no-take reserve (National Geographic 2021).

The CMT subsector is required to perform actively in protecting coastal and marine environments to achieve a healthy blue economy. In this regard, ecotourism has been suggested as an ideal approach for CMT operations. It is suggested that ecotourism practices at small-scale local level activities to support local communities by promoting procurement from local sources that provides a way to conserve their natural and cultural environment. It relegates adverse environmental impacts by creating environmental education and awareness. By generating revenues from the entry fees to the marine parks/MPAs/on-site local accommodation it fosters the protection of these marine habitats and benefits local communities. Moreover, such ecotourism practice facilitates reducing GHG emissions, maximises energy efficiency and the use sustainable materials for constructing infrastructure. Ecotourism may be even more important in a COVID-19 post-pandemic world as domestic tourists may start travelling first to these local destinations and small-scale resorts for their leisure and recreation. It is predicted that once governments withdraw the on-going lockdown measures the recovery process may be a great opportunity to explore ecotourism products and services. However, it is often noticed that there is insufficient capacity in the tourism industry to design a common roadmap towards its sustainability (Economist Impact: World Ocean Initiative 2020).

Ocean sustainability currently does not entice the required investment compared to other areas of sustainable development in the Asia-Pacific region. Conversely, research shows that 90% of institutional investors are interested in financing the sustainable blue economy (Economist Impact: World Ocean Initiative 2020). More investment is sought for research and development to strengthen technological advancements for monitoring the tourists' activities, reducing environmental adverse impacts by creative and innovative environment-friendly renewable energy, cruise shipping, food security, waste disposal and management. This includes plastic pollution along with other types of environmental pollution, decarbonisation, sustainable accommodation and other infrastructure facilities, and proving tourism products and services. Consequently, policymakers, business leaders, NGOs and the public should become increasingly aware of the urgent issues of ocean crises and take collaborative initiatives to raise awareness to solve these crises. Therefore, coordination among the investors including public funding agencies and philanthropic donors is sought to build greater risk tolerance in the sustainable CMT subsector of the blue economy.

Governance has been found to be an overarching issue to promote CMT through blue financing to boost up the overall blue economy. Good governance to ensure sustainable level ocean resource, blue finance management, secured tenure for the local communities, shared monitoring and evaluation of various institutional instruments and governance mechanisms are required to facilitate sustainable CMT development and encourage further blue financing in CMT.

This study has investigated how blue finance can promote sustainable CMT in the blue economy of the Asia-Pacific region. The study shows that despite the immense the potential of CMT in the developing countries in the Asia-Pacific region, there are very few sources of financing in CMT development and promotion. The market of green bonds has just started in in some countries in the region such as in Bangladesh through very few corporate entities. It will take time to grow the market, particularly in the coastal zones. Currently, the market of blue bonds is in the planning phase and will take some time to be executed. Considering the prospects of these sustainable or conservation bonds, scaling-up the issuance of these bonds for the coastal zones are required to ensure sustainable investments for CMT development along with other new and old sectors development.

Sustainable CMT may be implemented through practising nature-based tourism, more specifically ecotourism or community-based ecotourism, to foster poverty reduction, food security, women's empowerment, security of the coastal and marine zones, sociocultural support and so on. Considering these perspectives, it is also necessary to think about the importance of blue insurance in the region. Beyond the capital market, the government should take some other steps to ensure sustainable financing in these areas. However, the risks and challenges of issuing these bonds, insurance and implementing sustainable CMT should be studied to make such initiatives effective and efficient to fulfil the desired objectives.

Developing countries in the region should take lessons and learnings from some successful countries in conducting blue economy like the Seychelles or Indonesia in the fields of defining the blue economy, valuing the potential, addressing the challenges, and determining the institutional instruments and governance arrangements for promoting the blue economy (Alam 2021). There is a need for a management plan to preserve the health of the local marine environment and support ecosystem services.

If the blue economy is explored properly through maximising the sustainable use of coastal and marine ecosystem resources, they will be a valuable asset for national economies to enhance food security, generating new employment, alleviating poverty and reducing vulnerability and inequality. Consequently, it warrants planned massive investment to promote the sustainable blue economy where CMT plays a crucial role. Therefore, countries in the Asia-Pacific region require the adoption of an integrated approach to mobilise funds including foreign investment through developing fixed-income securities such as green and blue bonds.

References

Alam, Shamsul. 2021. 'Blue Bond – an Inventive Financing Solution for Blue Economy', *The Financial Express*, 4 June. <https://thefinancialexpress.com.bd/views/blue-bond-an-inventive-financing-solution-for-blue-economy-1622815987> [Accessed 9 January 2022].

Bangladesh General Economics Division.·2021. *Economy in Bangladesh through Sustainable Blue Bond: Assessing the Feasibility of Instituting Blue Bond in Bangladesh*, (General Economics Division, Planning Commision, Government of Bangladesh), <https://www.bd.undp.org/con tent/bangladesh/en/home/library/democratic_governance/promoting-sustainable-blue-economy-in-bangladesh-through-sustain.html> [Accessed 31 January 2022].

Barbesgaard, Mads. 2018. 'Blue Growth: Savior or Ocean Grabbing?', *The Journal of Peasant Studies*, 45 (1), 130–49.

Behsudi, Adam.·2020. *Wish You Were Here*, (IMF) <https://www.imf.org/external/pubs/ft/fandd/2020/12/impact-of-the-pandemic-on-tourism-behsudi.htm> [Accessed 22 August 2021].

Commonwealth Secretariat. 2021. *The Commonwealth Blue Charter*, <https://bluecharter.thecom monwealth.org/> [Accessed 31 January 2022].

Dahl, Richard. 2010. 'Green Washing: Do You Know What You're Buying?', *Environmental Health Perspectives*, 118, a246-a52.

Economist Impact: Wold Ocean Initiative. 2018. *Can Tourism Help Save the Ocean?*, <https://ocean.economist.com/protectors/articles/can-tourism-help-save-the-ocean> [Accessed 2 August 2021].

Economist Impact: World Ocean Initiative. 2018a. *Blue Finance*, <https://ocean.economist.com/blue-finance> [Accessed 5 August 2021].

——. 2018b. *Breathing Life into Plastic Waste* <https://ocean.economist.com/rethinking–plastics/breathing-life-into-plastic-waste/?utm_source=WOI&utm_medium=Banner> [Accessed 5 August 2021].

——. 2020. *A Sustainable Ocean Economy in 2030: Opportunities and Challenges*, <https://cdn.vev.design/private/Y00jvgKIBvZ1anyDSJNPOAQcI082/_jLT9hiqu_A_sustainable_ocean_econ omy_in_2030_%20copy.pdf.pdf> [Accessed 5 August 2021].

——. 2021a. *Life and Livelihoods: UN to Host Virtual World Ocean Day*, <https://ocean.economist.com/governance/articles/life-and-livelihoods-un-to-host-virtual-world-ocean-day> [Accessed 5 August 2021].

——. 2021b. *Will Tourism Recover from the Covid-19 Crisis Sustainably?*, <https://ocean.econo mist.com/governance/articles/will-tourism-recover-from-the-covid-19-crisis-sustainably> [Accessed 7 August 2021].

Edwards, Ben. 2020. 'What's the Future for "Blue Finance?', *Raconteur Media*, 22 July 2021. <https://www.raconteur.net/finance/investing/blue-finance/> [Accessed 31 January 2022].

Ehlers, Torsten, and Frank Packer. 2017. 'Green Bond Finance and Certification', *BIS Quarterly Review September*.

Fatin, Leena, and Andrew Whiley. 2021. 'Climate Bonds Initiative.' in Jan W. Dash (ed.), *World Scientific Encyclopedia of Climate Change: Case Studies of Climate Risk, Action, and Opportunity Volume 1* (London: World Scientific), pp. 57–61.

Juneja, Mani, Christina De Souza, Asha L. Giriyan, and Swati Ganeshan.·2021. *Contextualising Blue Economy in Asia-Pacific Region* (The Energy and Resources Institute), <https://www.teriin.org/policy-brief/contextualising-blue-economy-asia-pacific-region> [Accessed 31 January 2022].

Kituyi, Mukhisa, and Dona Bertarelli. 2020. *Why a Sustainable Blue Recovery Is Needed?*, <https://unctad.org/news/why-sustainable-blue-recovery-needed> [Accessed 5 August 2021].

Maldives Ministry of Environment Climate Change and Technology. 2021. *The Maldives Bans Single-Use Plastics Effective from Today* (Republic of Maldives), <https://www.environment. gov.mv/v2/en/news/11820> [Accessed 9 January 2022].

Martin, H.B. 2019 'Financing the "Blue Economy' *Wärtsilä* <https://www.wartsila.com/insights/arti cle/financing-the-blue-economy> [Accessed 16 December 2021]

National Geographic. 2021. *Protect the Blue: Marine Protected Areas*, <https://www.nationalgeo graphic.org/activity/protect-blue-mpas/> [Accessed 31 January 2022].

Nordic Investment Bank. 2019. *NIB Issues First Nordic–Baltic Blue Bond*, <https://www.nib.int/re leases/nib-issues-first-nordic-baltic-blue-bond> [Accessed 5 January 2022].

Northrop, E., M. Konar, N. Frost, and L. Hollaway. 2020. *Using the Ocean as a Tool for Global Economic Recovery*, <https://www.wri.org/blog/2020/coronavirus-ocean-blue-recovery> [Accessed 31 January 2022].

Organisation for Economic Cooperation and Development.·2016. *The Ocean Economy in 2030*, (Paris: OECD Publishing), <https://www.oecd.org/environment/the-ocean-economy-in-2030-9789264251724-en.htm> [Accessed 31 January 2022].

Schmid, Chris. 2020. *Dona Bertarelli Named UNCTAD Special Adviser for the Blue Economy* (United Nations Conference on Trade and Development), <https://unctad.org/news/dona-bertarelli-named-unctad-special-adviser-blue-economy> [Accessed 31 January 2022].

Schütze, Franziska, and Jan Stede. 2021. 'The EU Sustainable Finance Taxonomy and Its Contribution to Climate Neutrality', *Journal of Sustainable Finance and Investment*, December, 1–33.

Singh, Abhijit.·2021. *Blue Economy in the Indo-Pacific: Navigating between Growth and Conservation* (Observer Research Foundation), <https://www.orfonline.org/research/blue-economy-in-the-indo-pacific/> [Accessed 31 January 2022].

Turkas, Simon. 2021. *What Is the Blue Economy and How Can It Help My Island?*, <https://islandinnovation.co/what-is-the-blue-economy-and-how-can-it-help-my-island/> [Accessed 31 January 2022].

United Nations.·2012. *The Future We Want*, Outcome document of the United Nations Conference on Sustainable Development, Rio de Janeiro, Brazil, 20–22 June 2012), <https://sustainabledevelopment.un.org/content/documents/733FutureWeWant.pdf> [Accessed 31 January 2022].

United Nations Conference on Sustainable Development 2012 *Blue Economy Concept Paper* (Rio de Janeiro: United Nations Conference on Sustainable Development) <https://sustainabledevelopment.un.org/content/documents/2978BEconcept.pdf> [Accessed 31 January 2022].

United Nations Conference on Trade and Development.·2012. *Review of Maritime Transport 2012*, <https://unctad.org/system/files/official-document/rmt2012_en.pdf> [Accessed 20 April 2021].

——. 2016. *Oceans Economy and Ecosystem Services: Sustainable Fisheries and Coastal Tourism*, <https://unctad.org/meeting/oceans-economy-and-ecosystem-services-sustainable-fisheries-and-coastal-tourism-side-event> [Accessed 5 August 2021].

——. 2021a. *Oceans Economy and Fisheries*, <https://unctad.org/topic/trade-and-environment/ oceans-economy> [Accessed 5 August 2021].

——.·2021b. *Towards a Harmonized International Trade Classification for the Development of Sustainable Ocean-Based Economies*, <https://unctad.org/system/files/official-document/ ditcted2020d4_en.pdf> [Accessed 31 January 2022].

United Nations Development Programme.·2018. *Policy Brief on Leveraging the Blue Economy for Inclusive and Sustainable Growth*, <https://www.ke.undp.org/content/kenya/en/home/li

brary/strategic-policy-advisory-unit-/policy-brief–blue-economy-.html> [Accessed 31 January 2022].

United Nations Environment Programme. 2020. *Our Planet Is Drowning in Plastic* Pollution – *It's Time for Change!*, <https://www.unep.org/interactive/beat-plastic-pollution/> [Accessed 8 August 2021].

——. 2021. *Green Financing*, <https://www.unep.org/regions/asia-and-pacific/regional-initiatives/ supporting-resource-efficiency/green-financing> [Accessed 16 December 2021].

United Nations World Tourism Organization. 2021. *Advancing Harmonized Travel Protocols and Financing Tourism's Survival*, <https://www.unwto.org/news/advancing-harmonized-travel-protocols-and-financing-tourism-s-survival> [Accessed 16 December 2021].

Walsh, Melissa, Deborah Robertson, and Anouj Mehta.·2020. *The Role of Ocean Finance in Transitioning to a Blue Economy in Asia and the Pacific*, (Development Asia), <https://development.asia/explainer/role-ocean-finance-transitioning-blue-economy-asia-and-pacific> [Accessed 31 January 2022].

Wees, Ingrid van.·2020. *Building Blue Economy Ecosystems in Asia and the Pacific*, (Geneva: World Business Council for Sustainable Development), <https://www.wbcsd.org/Overview/Pano rama/Articles/Building-blue-economy-ecosystems-in-Asia-and-the-Pacific> [Accessed 31 January 2022].

World Bank Group.·2016. *Blue Economy Development Framework: Growing the Blue Economy to Combat Poverty and Accelerate Prosperity*, <https://thedocs.worldbank.org/en/doc/ 446441473349079068–0010022016/original/AMCOECCBlueEconomyDevelopmentFrame work.pdf> [Accessed 6 January 2022].

World Travel and Tourism Council.·2019. *Travel and Tourism Economic Impact 2019*, <https://wttc. org/Research/Economic-Impact> [Accessed 17 July 2020].

——.·2020a. *The Travel and Tourism Competitiveness Report 2019: Travel and Tourism at a Tipping Point*, <https://wttc.org/Research/Economic-Impact> [Accessed 17 July 2020].

——.·2020b. *Travel and Tourism: Global Economic Impact and Trends 2020*, <https://wttc.org/Re search/Economic-Impact> [Accessed 17 July 2020].

——.·2021. *Travel and Tourism Economic Impact 2021: Global Economic Impact and Trends*, <https://wttc.org/Portals/0/Documents/Reports/2021/Global%20Economic%20Impact% 20and%20Trends%202021.pdf?ver=2021-07-01-114957-177> [Accessed 31 January 2022].

Tek Maraseni, Sikha Karki, Upama Koju, Anita Shresta
and Timothy Cadman

Chapter 25
Evaluating the governance of sustainable development: The quality and legitimacy of the blue economy

Abstract: This chapter analyses multi-stakeholder perspectives on the governance and sustainability of different blue economy initiatives from both developed and developing countries. The study was conducted in 2020 using an anonymous online survey following an analytical method based on principles, criteria and indicators. Respondents rated the quality of these initiatives on a Likert scale (1-5) based on 11 indicators. The results show that the Sustainable Ocean Initiative received the highest score, while Marine permaculture scored the lowest. blue economy initiatives were considered inclusive by respondents; however, resources and capacity were deemed insufficient. Respondents from the Global South (developing countries) rated the initiatives higher than those from the Global North (developed countries) perhaps because developing countries are the prime beneficiaries of these programmes and receive more funding and assistance. These findings support policy and decision-makers formulating policies based on stakeholders' opinions and focussing on low-scoring initiatives. The blue economy is a growing sector with high potential for sustainable development; however, various factors, notably the COVID-19 pandemic, are obstructing its advancement. Therefore, effective communication, collaborative efforts and substantial and sustainable finance are vital for ensuring the sustainability of the blue economy in both the Global North and the Global South.

Keywords: blue economy, sustainability, governance, stakeholders, global north, global south, COVID-19

Introduction

The blue economy aims to close the gap between the ocean's economic potential and the urgent need for enhanced environmental stewardship, preservation and restoration (Voyer et al. 2018). To maintain the long-term viability of seas, coastal habitats and coastal inhabitants, international collaboration is necessary. This is especially true when it comes to monitoring and reporting on ocean ecosystems that are not under national jurisdiction (Smale et al., 2019). The Global Ocean Biodiversity Initiative (GOBI) has taken steps to build on the Census of Marine Life's

https://doi.org/10.1515/9783110733488-025

findings and guarantee that the best available marine biodiversity data is taken into account by governments and intergovernmental organisations (Johnson et al. 2019). The United Nations Decade of Ocean Science for Sustainable Development (2021–2030) (United Nations) will benefit from GOBI's support for ocean governance, which includes data development and expert consultation (Johnson et al. 2019). Proposed actions in the short and long-term include sharing expertise on water payment schemes, sustainably developing the water resources, linking tourism to development planning in coastal nations, investing in raising public awareness of biodiversity values, conventions to build institutional capacity, enhanced regulation and enforcement of environmental laws and policies and promoting multi-sectoral coordination. This will support the gathering of appropriate data to measure progress towards the Aichi Biodiversity Targets (Convention on Biological Diversity Secretariat n.d.-a) in specific regions using datasets (United Nations Environment Programme 2010).

It has been noted that to promote healthy and prosperous interaction between humans and the ocean, ocean governance should be reorganised (Rudolph et al., 2020) It is therefore important to understand stakeholders' perception of the blue economy and find an effective communication tool among stakeholders and clarity on the way, scope and scale of how the blue economy is defined. It is then necessary to find a way to match the scope and scale of the blue economy in terms of SDGs with stakeholders' expectations and delineate a realistic timeline to operationalise the UN's SDGs in the blue economy context (Lee, Noh, and Khim 2020).

If the blue economy model is to improve human wellbeing and social equity, while significantly reducing environmental risks and ecological scarcities, productive deliberation and meaningful participation of a diverse range of stakeholders to achieve effective and efficient outcomes will be essential. Assessing legitimacy of different global, regional, national and local initiatives from key stakeholders such as the academy, environment, government and others is necessary. Thus, this study aims to examine the perception of a variety of stakeholders on the governance and sustainability of the blue economy, particularly with respect to seven key initiatives under investigation. These are the blue economy generally, the Sustainable Ocean Initiative of the Convention on Biological Diversity (CBD), the Sustainable Blue Economy Finance Initiative (United Nations Environment Programme Finance Initiative n.d.), the Blue Carbon Initiative (Conservation International 2019) the Marine Stewardship Council (2002), marine permaculture and other global, regional, national or local activities. Furthermore, this study compares the views of stakeholders from both developed and developing countries towards these blue economy initiatives. This chapter commences with a delineation of the initiatives, continues with an explanation of the methods used to evaluate them, presents the findings of the investigation and concludes with a range of observations regarding the future of blue economy and its stakeholders going forward.

Key initiatives under the blue economy

Blue economy in general

The blue economy in general, has been an important topic of discussion when it comes to the future use of the world's oceans, including progress towards the UN SDGs. However, evidence of uniformity over-usage of common language or uniformity in sufficient understanding of the implications of the various ways of usages and enactment of the term remains unclear (Voyer et al. 2018). There are a number of challenges to be faced in the blue economy. These include the lack of common and agreed upon goals, the need to identify knowledge gaps, develop interdisciplinary approaches and learn how to communicate in a common language (in close collaboration with stakeholders). It is further necessary to find resolutions to conflicts of interests in trade-offs between uses of the ocean space and address frequent concern over who decides what should be open for public debate (Eikeset et al. 2018). Conversations about definitions, implementation techniques and covered sectors mustn't overlook critical ocean-based development priorities (Cisneros-Montemayor 2019).

The sustainable ocean initiative of the convention on biological diversity

The CBD developed seven criteria in 2008 to define ecologically or biologically significant areas (EBSAs) in open ocean waters and deep-sea habitats that ought to be protected (Dunn et al. 2014). The CBD method for describing EBSAs chooses areas of the ocean that are of great value because they provide important habitats and food sources for specific species (Johnson et al. 2019). According to *Living in Harmony with Nature by 2050* (International Union for the Conservation of Nature 2018), biodiversity is cherished, preserved, restored and sensibly exploited, maintaining ecosystem services, ensuring a healthy world and delivering benefits for all people (Sustainable Ocean Initiative 2014). The notion of other effective area-based conservation measures (OECMs) is explored in the context of the UN CBD Aichi Biodiversity Target 11 on marine protected areas and OECMs and their connections to the SDGs. The inclusion of the Aichi Biodiversity Targets in the SDGs may help to achieve a more systemic and complete implementation of SDG 14.5 on the conservation of at least 10% of marine and coastal regions. It states that OECMs contribute to biologically representative and well-managed marine protected area systems that are incorporated into larger governance systems like marine spatial planning. An analysis of policy coherence and coordination, for example, revealed both challenges and opportunities in the development of a blue economy agenda for Timor Leste. It has been stressed that existing methods may be sufficient to achieve blue economy goals without the need for additional legislation or policy (Voyer et al., 2018).

The 2014 Sustainable Ocean Initiative High level Meeting Pyeongchang Statement, (Johnson et al. 2019) outlined the Sustainable Ocean Initiative's approach. This approach focusses on achieving a balance between sustainable use and conservation, as well as the promotion of flexible and diverse approaches, identifying best practices, facilitating information sharing, learning from experiences and forming partnerships that can provide targeted capacity building, training and technical assistance.

The sustainable blue economy finance initiative

The UN Environment Programme Finance Initiative (UNEP-FI) defines finance for sustainable blue economy as those finance-related activities that promote sustainable blue economy by using the Sustainable Blue Economy Finance Principles (UNEPFI, 2018) when making financial decisions. This covers funding for long-term blue initiatives as well as funding for ocean-related industries in general (Sumaila et al. 2021). Over the last few decades, bilateral and multilateral development financing has poured into ocean-related activities such as fisheries and marine ecosystem protection, but financial efforts dubbed ocean or blue have just recently appeared. The Sustainable Blue Economy Finance Principles were revealed at the Economist World Ocean Summit 2018, marking a watershed moment in the history of the blue economy. The European Committee worked with the World Wide Fund for Nature (WWF), the European Investment Bank and the International Sustainability Unit to create this idea (Shiiba et al., 2022).

To fully address concerns as to the ocean's long-term viability, coastal towns and regions should adopt their policies, either as distinct documents or as different components of their development plans. Such documents should include a comprehensive list of tangible steps to secure their long-term viability and eventual transition to a sustainable blue economy. This would be consistent with Russia's most recent Arctic doctrine in 2020, in Moscow's Northern strategy is based on the principles of sustainability and climate change action (Tianming et al., 2021). Blue financing practices and identifying opportunities and challenges is a full-sized undertaking to improve connections between all stakeholders to illustrate attainable incentives for growing personal investment and public donations. As such, they would advocate a regulatory-driven financing mechanism incorporating the core ideas of blue finance in the context of marine governance, both at the worldwide and local levels. The proposed method would increase blue financing by looking for stability between economic growth and ocean sustainability (Shiiba et al., 2022).

Key policies actions are recommended: a) national and regional initiatives aimed at creating an enabling environment for the blue economy be encouraged; b) the blue economy's domestic resource mobilisation be considered; c) the sharing of knowledge and absorbing regional and other tools and lessons of good practice; d) a new strategy to gather and exchange information on the sources, instruments and uses of blue finance in and for small states, led by small states and supported by international development partners and e) an increase in small-state partnerships and new sources of blue financing be investigated (Rustomjee, 2016).

For example, tourism sector investment has scope for providing a long-term advantage for the benefit of capital for this area and sustainable management of the blue economy and could contribute to global GDP double what it is at present (White and Rahill 2021).

Marine stewardship council

The Marine Stewardship Council (MSC) (2002) has one of the most dominant and fastest growing certification initiatives with a global adoption rate of 12% of the seafood caught in 2017 (Wijen and Chiroleu-Assouline 2019). It was founded in 1996 as a conservation tool by Unilever and the World Wildlife Fund (WWF) as a voluntary standard aimed at preserving the world's threatened wild marine species (Wijen and Chiroleu-Assouline 2019; Foley 2013; Christian et al. 2013; Bush et al. 2013). It is based on the *Principles and Criteria for Sustainable Fishing* (MSC 2002), which is guided by the Food and Agriculture Organization (FAO) *Code of Conduct for Responsible Fisheries* (FAO 2021) and includes three key sustainability assessment principles: (1) fish stock health, (2) fishing impacts on marine ecosystems, and (3) the efficacy of the present fisheries management system (Foley 2013; Wijen and Chiroleu-Assouline 2019; Sutton 1996). *The MSC Chain of Custody Standard* (2019) covers the entire supply chain, from fisheries to processors to retailers (or from ocean to plate). This traceability of the standard verifies that a given product was captured and processed in line with MSC criteria by supply chain actors audited by third-party organisations (Gale and Haward 2004).

The MSC adoption rate was modest following the initial certification in 2001, but it picked up speed once it adopted the FAO's updated guidelines in 2005, which boosted the label's legitimacy and mollified its detractors (Gulbrandsen 2014, 2010; Woodcock et al. 2016; Tamm and Boström 2010).

The MSC's market supremacy is due in part to its scientific foundation, which is backed up by the use of legitimate market-based forms of environmental governance such as transparency, consistency, inclusion and impartiality (Bush et al. 2013; Boström 2006). In addition to the wider, longstanding campaigns conducted by various NGOs to raise awareness of the problem of sustainable fishing, MSC routinely conducts large-scale awareness campaigns in collaboration with NGOs (particularly WWF) and often with food stores (Wijen and Chiroleu-Assouline 2019; Jacquet and Pauly 2007; Ward 2008).

As the number of MSC certified fisheries has increased over the recent years, so has the criticism of the MSC process and its effectiveness (Christian et al. 2013;

Jacquet and Pauly 2007; Ward 2008; Gulbrandsen and Auld 2016; Jacquet, Hocevar, et al. 2010; Jacquet, Pauly, et al. 2010). Some authors have argued that the MSC guidelines lack social requirements such as good working conditions, minimum pricing and the inclusion of disadvantaged groups since they are focussed on the governance of the marine commons rather than sustainable development in general (Gulbrandsen 2010; Tamm and Boström 2010). The MSC approach also favours large-scale industrial fisheries over smaller-scale, more sustainable (Jacquet and Pauly 2008; Gulbrandsen 2009; Ponte 2012) ones and its Board of Directors is devoid of leadership from developing countries (Jacquet, Pauly, et al. 2010). MSC majority adopters are located in North America and North-western Europe and have largely excluded small fisheries in the developing world fisheries in South, whose capacity to apply for certification is lower (Wijen and Chiroleu-Assouline 2019; Bush et al. 2013; Foley 2013; Ponte 2012)

The blue carbon initiative

The Blue Carbon Initiative (Conservation International 2019) was launched in 2015 to promote climate change mitigation through restoration and sustainable use of coastal and marine ecosystems by Conservation International (CI), the Intergovernmental Oceanographic Commission of the United Nations Educational, Scientific, and Cultural Organization (IOC-UNESCO), and the International Union for Conservation of Nature (Thomas 2014). To achieve its goals, the Blue Carbon Initiative formed science and policy working groups (Thomas 2014; Howard et al. 2017). Blue carbon habitats, such as salt marshes, oceanic and estuarine mangroves and seagrasses constitute significant carbon stores and are extremely productive engines for sequestration of atmospheric carbon dioxide when compared to terrestrial ecosystems (Wylie, Sutton-Grier, and Moore 2016; Mcleod et al. 2011; Sifleet, Pendleton, and Murray 2011). In the previous half-century, up to 50% of blue carbon habitats have been destroyed and further deterioration and loss of these might account for up to 19% of worldwide deforestation emissions (Hopkinson, Cai, and Hu 2012; Macreadie et al. 2012; Donato et al. 2011; Pendleton et al. 2012). As the coastal ecosystems such as seagrasses, salt marshes and mangroves are cost-effective means to achieve positive climate change mitigation and adaptation outcomes, the Blue Carbon Initiative is currently focussed on them (Wylie, Sutton-Grier, and Moore 2016; Thomas 2014; Donato et al. 2011; Chmura et al. 2003).

Many nations with blue carbon resources are beginning to implement blue carbon restoration initiatives utilising carbon financing mechanisms, owing to the notable carbon sequestration and storage in coastal ecosystems (Herr et al. 2017; Wylie, Sutton-Grier, and Moore 2016). The compliance market is projected to increase as more nations and organisations strive to respond and adapt to climate change consequences by decreasing their carbon footprint and more blue carbon projects will ideally be included in this market (Wylie, Sutton-Grier, and Moore 2016).

While the blue carbon rationale is gaining traction, genuine interventions and fully completed initiatives, as well as new legislative measures are still uncommon and are frequently limited to modest mangrove restoration projects (McKinley et al. 2018). It faces challenges such as a lack of enforcement, human and financial limits and ambiguous or misguided government mandates (Herr et al. 2017).

The key three major knowledge gaps identified in the current Blue Carbon Initiative mechanism are (1) the effects of initiatives in degraded ecosystems (e.g. on biodiversity conservation) (Howard et al. 2017; Kauffman and Donato 2012); (2)); the absence of site-specific carbon sequestration data (Chmura 2013; Howard et al. 2017); and (3) the social-ecological effect of blue carbon projects at regional – rather than local – scales (Howard et al. 2017). Thomas (2016) and Vierros (2017) have identified an additional gap unfolding in the application and incorporation of local knowledge and values in blue carbon mechanisms.

Sea level rise and other consequences of climate change are crucial issues for blue carbon projects' long-term effectiveness (Rustomjee 2016). Blue carbon project managers must account for future climate change implications by potentially considering impacts for the next 100 years rather than just 20 or 50 (Wylie, Sutton-Grier, and Moore 2016; Contreras and Thomas 2019).

Marine permaculture

Permaculture has emerged alongside other sustainability-focussed movements and disciplines (Ferguson and Lovell 2014). Permaculture is 'an integrated, evolving system of perennial or self-perpetuating plant and animal species useful to man' (Holmgren 2020: 1). The recent definition broadened the concept as 'consciously designed landscapes which mimic the patterns and relationships found in nature while yielding an abundance of food, fibre, and energy for provision of local needs' (Holmgren 2020: 1).

Marine permaculture is a regenerative approach in which seaweed is produced beneath the ocean's surface (Gameau 2019). The Climate Foundation (2021) has stated that marine permaculture has the potential to restore natural ocean circulation and life while reducing climate change and providing food and economic security to millions of people who rely on the sea for their livelihoods. Seaweed, on the one hand, is gathered regularly and used for various purposes, including food, fertiliser and biofuel. On the other hand, it absorbs carbon from the atmosphere and restores alkalinity and ocean health, allowing shellfish and other sea creatures to flourish. 2040 Outreach (2021), has indicated that there is no need for fresh water, deforestation or fertiliser in marine permaculture. Seaweed farming processes can be modified to maximise climate advantages, which could boost seaweed farmers' income if they are well compensated (Duarte et al. 2017).

Seaweed farming has been practiced and its potential has been recognised worldwide (Araújo et al. 2021; Alemañ, Robledo, and Hayashi 2019; Campbell et al. 2019; Holdt and Kraan 2011; Rebours et al. 2014). However, some factors are impeding the development of this initiative. The availability of acceptable sites and competition for suitable places with other purposes, engineering systems capable of coping with difficult conditions offshore and rising market demand for seaweed products are some of the factors that limit the possibilities for expanding seaweed aquaculture and alteration in the local environment (Duarte et al. 2017; Campbell et al. 2019). Seaweed farming might not be able to replace world agriculture on a much wider scale, owing to production growth and cost limits, however, at a regional level, offsetting agriculture has potential, particularly in areas with strong climate policies (Froehlich et al. 2019).

Despite rising evidence of the importance of externally obtained organic matter for natural carbon sequestration, carbon credit systems currently exclude allochthonous carbon from their evaluations (Smale et al. 2018). Macroalgae should be included in blue economy accounting and activities (Krause-Jensen et al. 2018). Although seaweed offsetting is not a panacea for climate change, it is an important new tool for a more sustainable future (Froehlich et al. 2019).

Algae production, if incorporated into the agricultural system, might reduce nutrient losses and greenhouse gas emissions while also providing green energy (Ullmann and Grimm 2021). However, there is still a lack of understanding of seaweed farming and the uses of seaweeds (Radulovich et al. 2015). The expansion of seaweed farming and its usage as a feasible solution to food production and freshwater constraints must be communicated to decision-makers (Radulovich et al. 2015).

Other global, regional, national or local activities

These include other global, regional, national or local initiatives around the sustainable development of oceans in which stakeholders are involved or have been involved or have experienced. Some of these initiatives include but are not limited to the Channel Islands National Marine Sanctuary (local initiative), IPBES (global initiative), the UN Decade of Science National Plan of Action for Sharks and Rays, the Large Marine Ecosystems initiative, the Intergovernmental Oceanographic Commission (IOC), Ocean Decade, FAO programmes, the Convention on International Trade in Endangered Species of Wild Fauna and Flora (CITES activities), regional initiatives organised by OPOC (Office of the Pacific Ocean Commissioner, Pacific Islands Forum), the Pacific Islands Forum and the Secretariat of the Pacific Regional Environment Programme.

Aim of the study

There is a diverse range of states, nations, people, formal and informal institutions governing oceans for various uses and services. The effectiveness of ocean governance has been impacted by inconsistencies in sectoral approaches, conflicts between actors, jurisdictions with overlapping responsibilities and inadequate communication among governance organisations, all which must be addressed to develop effective governance for the sustainability of marine ecosystems (Balgos, Cicin-Sain, and Vander-Zwaag 2015; Stephenson et al. 2019; Alexander and Haward 2019). To create a sustainable blue economy, it is important to ensure that all associated stakeholders, including the corporate community, government, academia and civil society are involved (Heidkamp, Garland, and Krak 2021). This study therefore evaluates stakeholders' perceptions of their involvement in blue economy.

Methods

The framework of assessment of the quality of governance

The study investigates stakeholders' perceptions of the governance of seven different initiatives currently active in the blue economy space: the blue economy generally, the Sustainable Ocean Initiative of the CBD, the Sustainable Blue Economy Finance Initiative (UNEP), the Blue Carbon Initiative (Conservation International), the Marine Stewardship Council, Marine permaculture and other global, regional, national or local activities were examined using a hierarchical framework of principles, criteria and indicators. In this particular study the focus has been on determining governance quality, rather than ocean management or specific operational activities under the initiatives in question (Maraseni and Cadman 2015; Lammerts van Beuren and Blom 1997; Nhem and Lee 2020; Cadman et al. 2017). The analytical framework consists of two principles: meaningful participation and productive deliberation. Each of these principles is divided into two criteria each (i.e., four criteria in total). These four criteria are categorised into 11 indicators (see Table 25.1). The principle of meaningful participation is divided into interest representation which is further divided into three indicators: inclusiveness, equality, and resources. The criterion organisational responsibility is divided into two indicators: accountability and transparency. The two criteria under the principle of productive deliberation are decision-making and implementation criteria. The three indicators: democracy, agreement and dispute settlement come under decision-making. The last criterion, implementation, consists of another set of three indicators: behaviour change, problem-solving and durability. The ratings are analysed at the indicator level to measure the quality of governance. The detail of the framework is presented in Table 25.1:

Table 25.1: The framework of principles, criteria and indicators for evaluating governance quality.

Principle	Criterion	Indicator
Meaningful participation	Interest representation	Inclusiveness Equality Resources
	Organisational responsibility	Accountability Transparency
Productive deliberation	Decision-making	Democracy Agreement Dispute settlement
	Implementation	Behavioural change Problem-solving Durability

Source: Cadman (2011). Reproduced courtesy of Palgrave Macmillan.

Sample and design

Mixed-methods research approaches combine both qualitative and quantitative research methodology (Tashakkori and Teddlie 1998). Accordingly, the research method employed here comprised of a literature review; a quantitative method for rankings and statistical analysis of the stakeholders' perception using MS-excel and content analysis for analysing qualitative data from stakeholder's survey.

A survey was conducted online among individuals and representatives of institutions related to the blue economy using Survey Monkey (Momentive Inc n.d.) in October 2020. An email invitation link to a predesigned anonymous questionnaire was sent to stakeholders in global sustainable blue economy development initiatives. The email address of participants was obtained from websites, publicly available participants' lists from training workshops and information sessions advertised online.

The participants were asked to categorise themselves as belonging to one of the following sectors: environmental, social, economic, government, secretariat or other institutional component associated with the initiative(s), academic and other. Most importantly, participants were asked to categorise themselves as belonging to one of these two regions: Global North or Global South. The participants were asked to rank the quality of governance of the seven initiatives under investigation, on a Likert scale of one (very high) to five (very low) (Cadman 2009). The outcomes of the level of the indicator were combined to the criterion level, to determine the overall principle score. The two principle-level scores were combined to generate a total score (out of 55). Apart from the quantitative survey, participants in the survey were also given the option of writing their views/comments on each indicator. These comments are presented in the result section of this book chapter. Statistical tests, an Analysis of Variance (ANOVA), which compares differences between three or more groups (Field 2013) was conducted to determine whether there were significant differences in perceptions between these seven initiatives categories on the 11 indicators. The t-test, which is the statistical method of comparing means and testing for significant differences between two groups (Ross and Willson 2017; Grimm and Nesselroade 2019) was performed to find the difference in perceptions of Global North and Global South respondents for all 11 indicators of these initiatives. A twelfth question was asked, requesting respondents to rate their perceptions of the overall sustainability of the initiatives as well.

Study area and composition of stakeholder

Overall, there were 96 respondents. A majority of respondents were from the US (10), followed by Australia (6) and India (6), Mexico (5) and Nigeria (4). The respondents predominantly represented Global South (64%), that is, developing countries and the remaining (36%) of respondents were from Global North, that is, developed countries (see Figure 25.1).

Results and discussion

This section presents qualitative and quantitative analysis of multi-stakeholders' perspectives on the governance, management and sustainability of various blue economy initiatives.

Overall and initiatives wise consensus legitimacy ratings

The information regarding the mean initiative wise and overall consensus legitimacy rating on the 11 indicators of governance and sustainability is presented in Table 25.2. The Sustainable Ocean Initiative received the highest overall score (36.1 out of 55) while Marine permaculture received the lowest score (32.3). The Sustainable Ocean Initiative was supported by various stakeholders including local practitioners, government agencies, scientists, environmentalists and consumers (Hanekom 2020; Takeuchi 2010; Johnson et al. 2019).

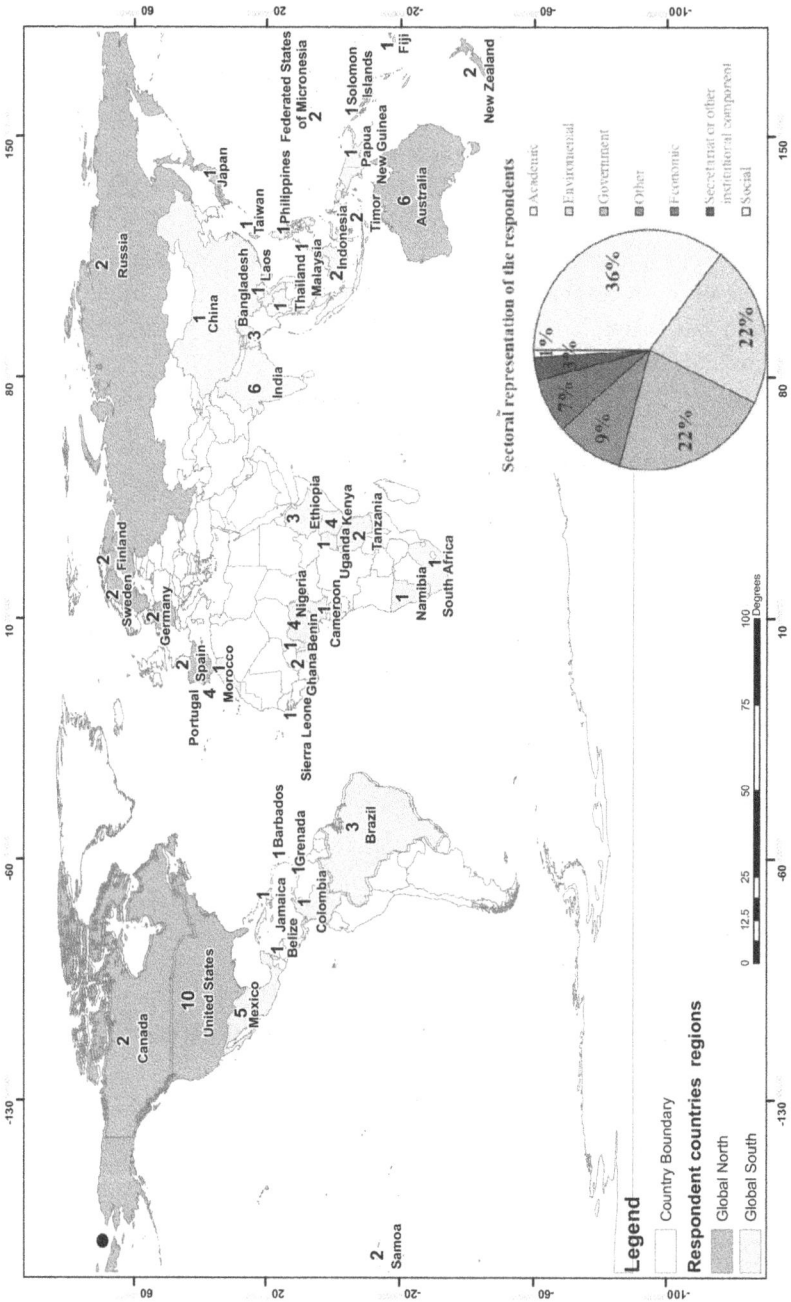

Figure 25.1: Study area map with the information on the number of participants and sectoral coverage chart.

Table 25.2: Summary of the consensus legitimacy rating of the initiatives over the indicators.

INITIATIVES	INDICATORS												
	Inclusiveness	Equality	Resources	Accountability	Transparency	Democracy	Agreement	Dispute Settlement	Behaviour change	Problem-Solving	Durability	Total (out of 55)	Sustainability score
Blue economy generally	**3.9**	3.3	2.2	3.1	3.2	3.1	3.1	2.9	3.4	3.4	3.4	35.1	3.7
Sustainable Ocean Initiatives	**3.9**	3.4	2.1	3.3	3.5	3.2	3.3	3.0	3.5	3.5	3.5	**36.1**	**3.8**
Sustainable Blue Economy Finance Initiatives	3.7	3.2	2.0	3.2	3.2	3.3	3.2	3.0	3.5	3.4	3.4	35.0	3.7
Blue Carbon Initiative	3.6	3.3	2.1	3.2	3.2	3.2	3.2	2.9	3.5	3.3	3.3	34.8	3.7
Marine Stewardship Council	3.3	3.1	**1.9**	3.1	3.1	3.1	3.2	2.9	3.3	3.2	3.3	33.7	3.6
Marine permaculture	3.1	3.0	**1.9**	2.9	3.0	3.0	3.0	2.9	3.2	3.2	3.1	**32.3**	**3.5**
Other (global, regional, national or local)	3.6	3.2	2.3	3.0	3.2	3.0	3.2	2.8	3.3	3.3	3.1	34.1	3.6
Weighted average**	**3.6**	3.2	**2.1**	3.1	3.2	3.1	3.2	2.9	3.4	3.3	3.3	34.4	3.7

Note: Weighted Average**: all sectors equally weighted.
Darker grey shading in the cells: highest score among each row of indictors for each initiative.
Lighter grey shading in the cells: lowest score among each row of indictors for each initiative.
Bold numbers: highest and lowest score among all.

Due to these benefits, a respondent from the Global South of the environmental sector explained, 'More youth should be engaged in the Sustainable Ocean Initiative.' The low ranking for marine permaculture could be because of a lack of knowledge among stakeholders with regards to this initiative and its application as it is rarely discussed at bigger events or in food production expansion, gap closure publications or aquaculture related discussion (Radulovich et al. 2015).

Inclusiveness received the highest scores among all the indicators for all the initiatives except in marine permaculture in which the indicators behaviour change and problem-solving received the highest scores. Likewise, in the case of the Marine Stewardship Council, behaviour change and durability received highest scores along with inclusiveness. Among all the initiatives, the blue economy generally and the Sustainable Ocean Initiative (CBD) received the highest score in the inclusiveness category, 3.9 out of 5.

Among all of these initiatives, the lowest scoring indicators were the resources. The Marine Stewardship Council and marine permaculture received the lowest score out of all the initiatives in the resources category, 1.9 out of five. As a result, there was a 40% difference in scores between the highest and lowest scores.

This suggests that the respondents are satisfied or optimistic about inclusion in almost all of the blue economy initiatives, whereas they believe that resources are the key limiting factor preventing these initiatives from achieving their objectives. This finding is consistent with those from other studies (Cadman et al. 2018; Cadman 2013).

There was a significant difference in perception of respondents over initiatives and indicators (see Table 25.2) with F-statistic much greater than the F-critical value and p-value<0.05 in an ANOVA test.

Despite the high overall rating for inclusiveness, opinions were diverse: a respondent said, 'The Working Group of Indigenous Minorities of Southern Africa is inclusive.' Another respondent said, 'The UNEP programme does not adequately cover the coastal region and seems to work with traditional organizations and exclude others.' Likewise, one respondent recommended, 'the Blue Carbon Initiative could be improved if it targets the local community who lives and interacts with the system.' The higher rating of inclusiveness is praiseworthy as the inclusion of stakeholders is an important component of global interest representation that varies significantly depending on the institutional framework (Koenig-Archibugi 2006: 13). An inclusive engagement, a detailed discussion and cooperation between actors such as policymakers, local communities, including Indigenous peoples and other underrepresented groups, civil society, academics and the private/business sector can all play a role in tackling global environmental concerns (Coscieme et al. 2020).

For the indicator resources, all the initiatives scored less than 50% (less than 2.5), showing that adequate resource management should be a serious priority for these initiatives. This finding is consistent with the perception of global stakeholders reported by Maraseni and Cadman (2015) where respondents both from the

Global South and Global North reported a lack of resources impeding their participation in global governance. The lowest ranking for the resources indicator corresponds to the results of a related governance study (Cadman et al. 2017; Cadman et al. 2018). Resources received the lowest score, which is concerning because a lack of resources limits an organisation's ability to participate effectively in decision-making and implementation (Cadman et al. 2016). blue economy activities and achievement of a sustainable future are hindered by a lack of technological and human capacity, lack of infrastructure as well as restricted financial resources (Lee et al. 2021; Novaglio et al. 2021). A respondent said, 'Sustainable development can be achieved when all goals are put under consideration but more so when the natural ecosystem like the marine ecosystem and biodiversity is put on top agenda for resource allocation and governance.' Similarly, another respondent from Global South said, 'Once the resources allocated to a certain sector is low, you cannot expect to have good governance, administration, therefore transparency become minimal.' Thus, adequate human, technical, and financial resources are required for efficient governance in the blue economy as well as for establishing a more sustainable future.

Interestingly, it is worth noting that respondents' perceptions regarding the sustainability of the initiatives investigated generally matched their perceptions regarding quality of governance. While there is a certain potential bias in these results, that is, that the blue economy is generally framed at the intergovernmental level as a concept imbued with the principle of sustainable development (recognising this is not the case in all regions, or policy forums), it is still surprising how consistently perceptions of quality of governance and sustainability tracked together in these results. Also of note is the fact that respondents scored both the governance quality and the sustainability of these initiatives so highly. The size of the respondent cohort may not be large enough to draw any definitive conclusions, but from this study at least, stakeholders within the blue economy seemed disposed favourably towards it. This is also partly because those who answered the survey might be deemed to be both insiders and potential beneficiaries from the activities investigated. A different set of results altogether might have ensued had the research deliberately targeted marginalised voices in the blue economy.

Respondents from the environment sector provided the highest scores for all indicators for all initiatives. These respondents rated inclusiveness of the blue economy generally and the Sustainable Ocean Initiative with a score of 4.1 out of 5, the highest of all sectors for this category. The government sector gave comparatively low ratings in most of the initiatives and indicators. The academic sector gave the lowest ranking for resources, with the Marine Stewardship Council receiving 1.6 out of 5 scores. An academic who provided low scores on resources said: 'More funding should be made available for research to support these initiatives and the eventual implementation of these initiatives.' The ANOVA test showed that the sector-wise results per initiative and indicator (see Table 25.3) was statistically significant

Table 25.3: Sector-wise consensus legitimacy rating of the initiatives over the indicators.

Initiatives	Sectors	Inclusiveness	Equality	Resources	Accountability	Transparency	Democracy	Agreement	Dispute settlement	Behaviour change	Problemsolving	Durability	Total (out of 55)	Sustainability score
Blue economy generally	Academic	3.9	3.3	1.8	2.9	3.2	2.9	3.1	2.7	3.3	3.3	3.3	33.7	3.6
	Environment	4.1	3.4	2.4	3.1	3.4	3.4	3.7	3.5	3.7	3.6	3.5	37.8	4
	Government	3.7	3.3	2.2	3.4	3.1	3.1	3.1	3	3.2	3.2	3.4	34.7	3.8
	Others	3.9	3.4	2.5	3.1	3.1	3.1	2.7	2.7	3.4	3.5	3.6	35	3.6
Sustainable Ocean Initiatives	Academic	4	3.5	1.9	3	3.4	3.1	3.3	2.8	3.5	3.4	3.4	35.3	3.9
	Environment	4.1	3.3	2.2	3.6	3.8	3.4	3.6	3.6	3.8	3.9	3.6	38.9	4.1
	Government	3.6	3.2	1.9	3.4	3.2	3.2	3.2	3.1	3.2	3.3	3.4	34.7	3.7
	Others	3.8	3.5	2.4	3.4	3.5	3.3	2.9	2.7	3.4	3.5	3.5	35.9	3.6
Sustainable Blue Economy Finance Initiatives	Academic	3.5	3.3	1.8	2.9	3.3	3	3.2	2.8	3.4	3.2	3.2	33.6	3.6
	Environment	3.9	3.3	2.1	3.2	3.1	3.3	3.6	3.6	3.6	3.7	3.7	37.1	3.9
	Government	3.6	3.1	2	3.4	3	3.4	3.1	3	3.4	3.3	3.2	34.5	3.8
	Others	4	3.1	2.3	3.2	3.4	3.4	2.9	2.9	3.5	3.3	3.4	35.4	3.6
Blue Carbon Initiative	Academic	3.7	3.2	1.9	3.1	3.3	3.1	3.2	2.8	3.5	3.3	3.2	34.3	3.6
	Environment	3.8	3.4	2.2	3.4	3.4	3.3	3.8	3.4	3.8	3.5	3.6	37.6	4.2
	Government	3.1	3.1	2	3.3	3	3.2	3.1	2.9	3.3	3.2	3.1	33.3	3.3
	Others	3.7	3.5	2.4	3.1	3.1	3.4	2.6	2.8	3.5	3.3	3.4	34.8	3.7

Marine Stewardship Council	Academic	3.3	3.1	**1.6**	2.8	3.1	2.9	3.2	2.7	3.2	3	3.1	32	3.5
	Environment	3.8	3.1	2.2	3.4	3.2	3.4	3.6	3.3	3.4	3.5	3.4	36.3	3.9
	Government	3.1	3	2	3.3	3.2	3.3	3.1	3	3.4	3.2	3.1	33.7	3.4
	Others	3.1	3.4	2.2	3.3	3.1	2.9	3	2.8	3.4	3.4	3.6	34.2	3.6
Marine permaculture	Academic	3.2	3.1	1.7	2.8	3.1	3	3.1	2.9	3.3	3.2	3.1	32.5	3.7
	Environment	3.4	3	2.1	2.7	3.1	3.1	3.1	3	3.3	3.2	3.1	33	3.7
	Government	2.8	2.7	1.9	3.2	2.8	3.1	3.1	2.8	2.9	3.1	2.7	31.1	3.2
	Others	3.1	3.4	2.3	3	2.8	2.9	2.7	2.8	3.3	3.4	3.4	33.1	3.4
Other global, regional, national, local initiatives	Academic	3.7	3	2.4	3.1	3.5	3.1	3.4	2.8	3.6	3.4	3.5	35.5	3.9
	Environment	3.6	3.1	2.1	2.7	3.1	2.9	3.4	3.4	3.4	3.4	3.1	34.2	3.8
	Government	3.5	3.2	2.1	3.3	3.2	3.1	3.1	2.7	3.1	3.3	3.1	33.7	3.3
	Others	3.4	3.6	2.4	2.8	2.8	2.9	2.9	2.4	3.2	3.1	3	32.5	3.4
Average of all sectors**	Academic	3.6	3.2	1.9	2.9	3.3	3.0	3.2	2.8	3.4	3.3	3.3	33.8	3.7
	Environment	3.8	3.2	2.2	3.2	3.3	3.3	3.5	3.4	3.6	3.5	3.4	36.4	3.9
	Government	3.3	3.1	2.0	3.3	3.1	3.2	3.1	2.9	3.2	3.2	3.1	33.7	3.5
	Others	3.6	3.4	2.4	3.1	3.1	3.1	2.8	2.7	3.4	3.4	3.4	34.4	3.6

Note: 1) Average of all sectors, **all sectors equally weighted; 2) Numbers darker grey highlighted: highest score among the indicators between different sectors within initiative; 3) Numbers lighter grey highlighted: lowest score among the indicators between different sectors within initiative; 4) Darker grey shading in the cells: highest scoring among each row of the sector-wise scores for the indictors for each initiative; 5) lighter grey shading in the cells: lowest scoring among each row of the sector-wise scores for the indictors for each initiative; 6) Bold numbers: highest and lowest score among all.

with an F-statistic much greater than F-critical value and p-value less than 0.05 at 95% CI.

The blue carbon community is dominated by biological scientists, environmental sectors and non-government policy experts (Nunes, Svensson, and Markandya 2017; Thomas 2014). The majority of the blue economy initiatives undertaken for the study were begun by non-government (mostly environmental) actors (Thomas 2014; Grip 2017; Gulbrandsen 2009), which could be one of the key reasons why government respondents gave the lowest scores and environmental sector respondents gave the highest scores. For example, despite the MSC's ties to the FAO code of conduct and other international fisheries agreements and given the long history of international fisheries governance, some European governments have expressed reservations about the scheme, questioning the right of non-state bodies to govern common pool resources like fish stocks (Gulbrandsen 2006, 2009). These states have contended that non-state players lack the essential experience and mandate to administer fisheries and that the MSC was an attempt to construct a private transnational management regime outside of national sovereignty (Gulbrandsen 2009). Unlike other standards agencies, the MSC does not give governments a special status. Instead, they are treated equally to all other stakeholders, such as NGOs, fishers, producers and retailers. These factors may impact government agencies' assessment that the MSC lacks legitimacy in the fishing industry and among governments (Stokke 2004; Gulbrandsen 2009; Bush et al. 2013; Christian et al. 2013)

Some of the respondents from the government sector mentioned that these initiatives need to develop a framework of engagement and should spend more time communicating with the public. A respondent from the government sector added that these initiatives must be embedded into government policies and priorities before they can be sustainable and provide the resources, capacity and legislative frameworks that are required for implementation.

Another reason is inadequacy in the knowledge of the issues, as well as practical guidance, tools and ways to assist government decision-makers in effectively taking these initiatives' considerations into account (Bennett 2018). Also, there is a growing gap between international goals for the blue economy and the practical realities and injustices that accompany their execution (Barbesgaard 2018; Bennett, Govan, and Satterfield 2015). One of the respondents from the government sector in the survey mentioned that 'Most blue economy investment is still relatively unsophisticated with inadequate market history and all the challenges of sustaining new initiatives and many proposals also lack adequate stability for private investors.' While another respondent from the government sector said that 'sometimes it gets overwhelming to see so many initiatives by so many international and regional organisations when all are talking about the same thing.'

When it comes to the use and management of blue economy related activities, there is insufficient integration between the many approaches pushed by governments in their collaborations with development partners on the one hand and environmental authorities and organisations on the other. More international and regional collaboration is needed, emphasising coherence in development aid and fisheries development (Ababouch and Carolu 2015).

However, gradually more and more actors are becoming interested in fundamental problems about how to manage ocean resources, such as who should control them, who should have access to them, on what conditions and for what purpose. A question is: what function do coastal and maritime resources play in society? These issues are increasingly being debated under the banner of blue growth, with international environmental non-governmental organisations such as the World Wide Fund for Nature (WWF) and Conservation International, the financial sector such as Credit Suisse and Goldman Sachs, and even military companies such as Lockheed Martin driving the debate (Barbesgaard 2018). Studies of certification and labelling initiatives created and administered by the environmental sector have begun to investigate the relationship between governments and private transnational governance systems. Scholars are integrating the state into the study of ostensibly private social and environmental certification and labelling systems, commonly referred to as non-state market-driven governance (NSMD) (Cashore 2002; Gulbrandsen 2010). Clapp, Newell, and Brent (2018) have stated that 'large environmental non-governmental organisations (NGOs) have successfully leveraged the blue economy framework as a new vehicle for enabling finance capital to penetrate marine areas.' Bond (2019) has also mentioned in his study the huge role of the environmental leaders in activity, products or services in adding value to the image of their regions and the Atlantic Area regarding the blue economy.

Region wise consensus legitimacy rating of all initiatives

Overall, the respondents from the Global South (developing countries) consistently provided higher ratings than those from the Global North (developed countries) on all indicators and initiatives, except for democracy and equality. Global South respondents gave the Sustainable Ocean Initiative the highest out of all the initiatives in the inclusiveness category, with a score of 4.1 out of 5. Similarly, the lowest scoring indicators for all initiatives in both regions were resources. The Sustainable Ocean Initiative and the Marine Stewardship Council, both from the Global North region, scored the lowest out of all the initiatives in the resources indicator, with 1.6 out of 5 scores (see Table 25.4).

The t-test revealed a statistically significant difference (p-value < 0.05 and p-value <0.01) in ratings between the Global North and Global South respondents for all initiatives excluding the Sustainable Blue Economy Finance Initiatives. The score from the Global South is almost always greater than the score from the Global North. This may be because countries in the Global South are typically the primary beneficiaries of these programmes and receive more funds for projects and assistance

Table 25.4: Sector-wise consensus legitimacy rating of the initiatives over the indicators.

Initiatives		Inclusi-veness	Equality	Reso-urces	Accounta-bility	Trans-parency	Dem-ocracy	Agree-ment	Dispute settlement	Behavioural change	Problem-solving	Durability	Total (out of 55)	Sustaina-bility score
Blue economy generally	Global North (35)	3.6	3.2	1.9	2.8	3.0	3.0	2.9	2.6	3.1	3.1	3.2	32.4	3.3
	Global South (61)	3.9	3.2	2.4	3.3	3.4	3.2	3.4	3.3	3.5	3.5	3.5	**36.6**	3.9
Sustainable Ocean Initiatives	Global North (35)	3.6	3.3	**1.6**	3.1	3.3	3.3	3.0	2.5	3.1	3.1	3.3	33.2	3.5
	Global South (61)	**4.1**	3.5	2.3	3.4	3.5	3.2	3.4	3.2	3.6	3.7	3.5	**37.4**	4.0
Sustainable Blue Economy Finance Initiatives	Global North (35)	3.5	3.1	1.7	3.1	3.3	**3.4**	3.0	2.7	3.2	3.1	3.3	33.4	3.4
	Global South (61)	3.8	3.3	2.1	3.2	3.2	3.2	3.3	3.2	3.6	3.5	3.4	**35.8**	3.9

Blue Carbon Initiative	Global North (35)	3.4	3.2	1.8	3.0	3.0	3.3	2.9	2.6	3.2	3.0	3.1	32.5	3.3
	Global South (61)	3.7	3.3	2.2	3.3	3.3	3.1	3.3	3.1	3.6	3.5	3.5	35.9	3.9
Marine Stewardship Council	Global North (35)	3.0	3.2	1.6	3.0	3.1	3.0	3.1	2.6	3.0	2.9	3.3	31.8	3.2
	Global South (61)	3.5	3.1	2.1	3.2	3.2	3.1	3.3	3.1	3.5	3.4	3.3	34.8	3.8
Marine permaculture	Global North (35)	2.9	3.1	1.7	2.7	2.9	3.0	2.8	2.6	3.0	2.9	3.0	30.6	3.1
	Global South (61)	3.2	3.0	2.1	3.0	3.0	3.0	3.1	3.0	3.3	3.4	3.1	33.2	3.7
Other (global, regional, national or local)	Global North (35)	3.1	3.4	1.9	2.7	3.0	3.0	3.1	2.4	3.1	2.8	3.0	31.5	3.2
	Global South (61)	3.8	3.1	2.4	3.1	3.2	3.0	3.3	3.0	3.4	3.5	3.3	35.1	3.7

(continued)

Table 25.4 (continued)

Initiatives		Inclusiveness	Equality	Resources	Accountability	Transparency	Democracy	Agreement	Dispute settlement	Behavioural change	Problem-solving	Durability	Total (out of 55)	Sustainability score
Average of all sectors**	Global North	3.3	3.2	1.7	2.9	3.1	3.1	3.0	2.6	3.1	3.0	3.2	32.2	3.3
	Global South	**3.7**	3.2	2.2	3.2	3.3	3.1	3.3	3.1	3.5	3.5	3.4	**35.5**	3.8

Note: Average of all sectors**: all sectors equally weighted.
Darker grey shading in the cells: highest score among each row of the region wise scores for the indictors for each initiative.
Lighter grey shading in the cells: lowest scoring among each row of the region wise score for the indictors for each initiative.
Bold numbers: highest and lowest score among all.

(Cadman and Maraseni 2012, 2011). One of the respondents from the Global South said, 'The blue economy can be a cornerstone for development, particularly in developing countries.' Another respondent from the Global South said 'We see the vital link between the ocean and climate change mitigation as well as the competing interests between conservation and sustainable management of ocean resources. It is always an interesting balancing act in international forums and in particular with respect to the various blue economy dialogues.' A respondent from the Global North lamented: 'I have rarely been helped with resources, which is a barrier for a small non-profit firm of limited means.' Also, the Global South region had more participants from the environmental sector (see Figure 25.2), who gave higher scores to the indicators, which could be one of reasons for the respondents from the Global North providing lower ratings overall.

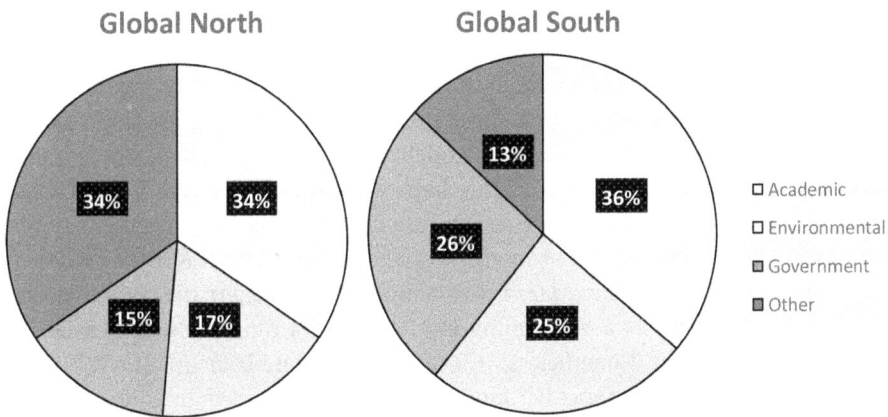

Figure 25.2: Sectoral representation of the participants in the Global North and the Global South region.

Conclusion

Analysing stakeholder perceptions of the governance and sustainability of blue economy initiatives and activities provides a comprehensive view of attitudes toward ocean initiatives that may have an impact on the sustainability of the ocean. This study revealed a considerable divide in perceptions of respondents on blue economy initiatives. The perception varied with respect to indicators, initiatives as well as sectors and location of respondents.

Based on the indicator-wise results, all the respondents believed that these blue economy initiatives lacked adequate resources. Taking this into account, if these initiatives stress delivering appropriate and timely technical, economic and other resources to the relevant stakeholders, the initiatives will function smoothly and have positive impact on the blue economy's long-term viability.

The Sustainable Ocean Initiative received the highest score out of all the initiatives, while on the other hand, marine permaculture scored the lowest. These rankings suggest that the Sustainable Ocean Initiative is doing its job better in comparison to the other initiatives under consideration.

The government sector is a nation's primary body responsible for sustainability. So, for any of these voluntary blue economy efforts to succeed, it must collaborate with the concerned government body working on the blue economy. Findings shows that these initiatives might not have placed high priority on government sector stakeholders and thus, they may need to set priorities and develop plans and policies in a way to create a conducive environment for greater involvement of government stakeholders.

In comparison to the Global North (developed countries), the Global South (developing countries) gave higher ratings to nearly all the indicators and all the initiatives suggesting that the Global North are less satisfied with these activities than those from the Global South. Based on the literature as well as the comments of the respondents, this is mostly because these programmes have a strong emphasis on the Global South and provide a variety of deliverables and resources. These initiatives should not only focus on providing large amounts of resources to the Global South, assuming that they are the ones who are most in need, but also work on providing sufficient technical and economic resources to the Global North as well, either by increasing the initiative's resources or by finding an alternative way to do so.

The blue economy is a burgeoning industry with a tremendous potential for long-term development. Nonetheless, it faces a number of obstacles. The COVID-19 pandemic has had an even greater impact on oceans and coasts that have already been affected by the increasing unsustainable exploitation of marine resources for economic purposes. It has shown the extent of human dependency on the ocean, as well as the relationship between human wellbeing, the economy and the sea. It has also emphasised the importance of collaborating to solve common problems and allocating resources to areas that demand urgent attention. The surprisingly high scores allocated by respondents to all initiatives, and notably regarding blue economy sustainability, are also noteworthy. More research is required to determine if this reflects a broader perspective, or if marginalised and excluded communities from the blue economy would feel the same way as those who took part in this study.

Nevertheless, the findings can help policy and decision-makers focus on initiatives with lower scores and formulate policies based on the perspectives of stakeholders with an interest in and influence over blue economy activities. Thus, better stakeholder understanding, collaborative efforts, effective communication about blue economy initiatives and, most importantly, substantial and sustainable finance are critical to achieving long-term development goals and ensuring the sustainability of the blue economy in both the Global North and the Global South, as well as recover from COVID-19's effects on the blue economy. For the blue economy to be sustainable moving forward, all voices and needs must be included in this emerging frontier, if it is not to repeat the mistakes of terrestrial development.

References

2040 Outreach. 2021. *2040 Marine Permaculture*, <https://whatsyour2040.com/marine-permacul ture/> [Accessed 20 January 2022].

Ababouch, Lahsen, and C. Carolu. 2015. 'Fisheries and Aquaculture in the Context of Blue Economy', *Feeding Africa*, 2 (21–23), 13.

Alemañ, Alejandro Espi, Daniel Robledo, and Leila Hayashi. 2019. 'Development of Seaweed Cultivation in Latin America: Current Trends and Future Prospects', *Phycologia*, 58 (5), 462–71.

Alexander, K.A., and M. Haward. 2019. 'The Human Side of Marine Ecosystem-Based Management (EBM): 'Sectoral Interplay' as a Challenge to Implementing EBM', *Marine Policy*, 101, 33–38.

Araújo, Rita, Fatima Vázquez Calderón, Javier Sánchez López, Isabel Costa Azevedo, Annette Bruhn, Silvia Fluch, Manuel Garcia Tasende et al. "Current status of the algae production industry in Europe: an emerging sector of the blue bioeconomy." *Frontiers in Marine Science* 7 (2021): 626389.

Balgos, Regions Miriam C., Biliana Cicin-Sain, and David L. VanderZwaag. 2015. 'A Comparative Analysis of Ocean Policies in Fifteen Nations and Four Regions.' in Regions Miriam C Balgos, Biliana Cicin-Sain and David L VanderZwaag (eds.), *Routledge Handbook of National and Regional Ocean Policies* (Routledge), pp. 45–90.

Barbesgaard, Mads. 2018. 'Blue Growth: Savior or Ocean Grabbing?', *The Journal of Peasant Studies*, 45 (1), 130–49.

Bennett, Nathan J. 2018. 'Navigating a Just and Inclusive Path Towards Sustainable Oceans', *Marine Policy*, 97, 139–46.

Bennett, Nathan James, Hugh Govan, and Terre Satterfield. 2015. 'Ocean Grabbing', *Marine Policy*, 57, 61–68.

Bond, Patrick. 2019. 'Blue Economy Threats, Contradictions and Resistances Seen from South Africa', *Journal of Political Ecology*, 26 (1), 341–62.

Boström, Magnus. 2006. 'Establishing Credibility: Practising Standard-Setting Ideals in a Swedish Seafood-Labelling Case', *Journal of Environmental Policy and Planning*, 8 (2), 135–58.

Brodie Rudolph, Tanya, Mary Ruckelshaus, Mark Swilling, Edward H. Allison, Henrik Österblom, Stefan Gelcich, and Philile Mbatha. "A transition to sustainable ocean governance." *Nature communications* 11, no. 1 (2020): 1–14.

Bush, Simon R., Hilde Toonen, Peter Oosterveer, and Arthur P.J. Mol. 2013. 'The 'Devils Triangle' of MSC Certification: Balancing Credibility, Accessibility and Continuous Improvement', *Marine Policy*, 37, 288–93.

Cadman, Tim. 2009. *Quality, Legitimacy and Global Governance: A Comparative Analysis of Four Forest Institutions*, Doctoral thesis, University of Tasmania.

Cadman, Tim, and Tek Maraseni. 2011. 'The Governance of Climate Change: Evaluating the Governance Quality and Legitimacy of the United Nations' REDD-Plus Programme', *The International Journal of Climate Change: Impacts and Responses*, 2 (3), 103–24.

——. 2012. 'The Governance of REDD+: An Institutional Analysis in the Asia Pacific Region and Beyond', *Journal of Environmental Planning and Management*, 55 (5), 617–35.

Cadman, Timothy. 2011. *Quality and Legitimacy of Global Governance: Case Lessons from Forestry* (London, UK: Palgrave Macmillan).

———. 2013. 'Applying an Empirical Evaluation to the Governance Legitimacy of Carbon Offset Mechanisms on the Basis of Stakeholder Perceptions.' in Timothy Cadman (ed.), *Climate Change and Global Policy Regimes: Towards Institutional Legitimacy* (London: Palgrave Macmillan UK), pp. 79–95.

Cadman, Timothy, Tek Maraseni, Hugh Breakey, and Hwan-ok Ma. 2018. 'Representing Whose Access and Allocation Interests? Stakeholder Perceptions and Interests Representation in Climate Governance.' in Beth Edmondson and Stuart Levy (eds.), *Transformative Climates and Accountable Governance* (Cham, Switzerland: Springer International Publishing), pp. 223–49.

Cadman, Timothy, Tek Maraseni, Breakey Hugh, López-Casero Federico, and Hwan Ok Ma. 2016. 'Governance Values in the Climate Change Regime: Stakeholder Perceptions of REDD+ Legitimacy at the National Level', *Forests*, 7 (10), 212.

Cadman, Timothy, Tek Maraseni, Hwan Ok Ma, and Federico Lopez-Casero. 2017. 'Five Years of REDD+ Governance: The Use of Market Mechanisms as a Response to Anthropogenic Climate Change', *Forest Policy and Economics*, 79, 8–16.

Campbell, Iona, Adrian Macleod, Christian Sahlmann, Luiza Neves, Jon Funderud, Margareth Øverland, Adam D. Hughes, and Michele Stanley. 2019. 'The Environmental Risks Associated with the Development of Seaweed Farming in Europe – Prioritizing Key Knowledge Gaps', *Frontiers in Marine Science*, 6 (2019): 107.

Cashore, Benjamin. 2002. 'Legitimacy and the Privatization of Environmental Governance: How Non–State Market–Driven (Nsmd) Governance Systems Gain Rule–Making Authority', *Governance*, 15 (4), 503–29.

Chmura, Gail L. 2013. 'What Do We Need to Assess the Sustainability of the Tidal Salt Marsh Carbon Sink?', *Ocean and Coastal Management*, 83, 25–31.

Chmura, Gail L., Shimon C. Anisfeld, Donald R. Cahoon, and James C. Lynch. 2003. 'Global Carbon Sequestration in Tidal, Saline Wetland Soils', *Global Biogeochemical Cycles*, 17 (4), 1111.

Christian, Claire, David Ainley, Megan Bailey, Paul Dayton, John Hocevar, Michael LeVine, Jordan Nikoloyuk, Claire Nouvian, Enriqueta Velarde, Rodolfo Werner, and Jennifer Jacquet. 2013. 'A Review of Formal Objections to Marine Stewardship Council Fisheries Certifications', *Biological Conservation*, 161, 10–17.

Cisneros-Montemayor, Andrés M. 2019. 'A Blue Economy: Equitable, Sustainable, and Viable Development in the World's Oceans.' in W. Cheung, Y. Ota and A. Cisneros-Montemayor (eds.), *Predicting Future Oceans: Sustainability of Ocean and Human Systems Amidst Global Environmental Change* (Amsterdam: Elsevier), pp. 395–404

Clapp, J., P. Newell, and Z.W. Brent. 2018. 'The Global Political Economy of Climate Change, Agriculture and Food Systems', *The Journal of Peasant Studies*, 45 (1), 80–88.

Conservation International. 2019. *The Blue Carbon Initiative*, <https://www.thebluecarboninitiative.org/> [Accessed 28 January 2022].

Contreras, Carolina, and Sebastian Thomas. 2019. 'The Role of Local Knowledge in the Governance of Blue Carbon', *Journal of the Indian Ocean Region*, 15 (2), 213–34.

Convention on Biological Diversity Secretariat. n.d.-a. *Aichi Biodiversity Targets*, <https://www.cbd.int/sp/targets/> [Accessed 28 January 2022].

———. n.d.-b. *Sustainable Ocean Initiative*, <https://www.cbd.int/soi/> [Accessed 28 January 2022].

Coscieme, Luca, Håkon da Silva Hyldmo, Álvaro Fernández-Llamazares, Ignacio Palomo, Tuyeni H. Mwampamba, Odirilwe Selomane, Nadia Sitas, Pedro Jaureguiberry, Yasuo Takahashi, Michelle Lim, Maria P. Barral, Juliana S. Farinaci, Julio Diaz-José, Sonali Ghosh, Joyce Ojino, Amani Alassaf, Bernard N. Baatuuwie, Lenke Balint, Zeenatul Basher, Fanny Boeraeve, Sugeng Budiharta, Ruishan Chen, Maylis Desrousseaux, Gregory Dowo, Catherine Febria, Houda Ghazi, Zuzana V. Harmáčková, Rodolfo Jaffe, Mphatso M. Kalemba, Cosmas K. Lambini, Felicia P.S. Lasmana, Assem A.A. Mohamed, Aidin Niamir, Patricio Pliscoff, Rahat Sabyrbekov, Uttam

B. Shrestha, Aibek Samakov, Anna A. Sidorovich, Laura Thompson, and Mireia Valle. 2020. 'Multiple Conceptualizations of Nature Are Key to Inclusivity and Legitimacy in Global Environmental Governance', *Environmental Science and Policy*, 104, 36–42.

Donato, Daniel C., J. Boone Kauffman, Daniel Murdiyarso, Sofyan Kurnianto, Melanie Stidham, and Markku Kanninen. 2011. 'Mangroves among the Most Carbon-Rich Forests in the Tropics', *Nature Geoscience*, 4 (5), 293–97.

Duarte, Carlos M., Jiaping Wu, Xi Xiao, Annette Bruhn, and Dorte Krause-Jensen. 2017. 'Can Seaweed Farming Play a Role in Climate Change Mitigation and Adaptation?', *Frontiers in Marine Science*, 4 (2017): 100.

Dunn, Daniel C., Jeff Ardron, Nicholas Bax, Patricio Bernal, Jesse Cleary, Ian Cresswell, Ben Donnelly, Piers Dunstan, Kristina Gjerde, and David Johnson. 2014. 'The Convention on Biological Diversity's Ecologically or Biologically Significant Areas: Origins, Development, and Current Status', *Marine Policy*, 49, 137–45.

Eikeset, Anne Maria, Anna B. Mazzarella, Brynhildur Davíðsdóttir, Dane H. Klinger, Simon A. Levin, Elena Rovenskaya, and Nils Chr Stenseth. 2018. 'What Is Blue Growth? The Semantics of "Sustainable Development of Marine Environments"', *Marine Policy*, 87, 177–79.

Ferguson, Rafter Sass, and Sarah Taylor Lovell. 2014. 'Permaculture for Agroecology: Design, Movement, Practice, and Worldview. A Review', *Agronomy for Sustainable Development*, 34 (2), 251–74.

Field, Andy. 2013. *Discovering Statistics Using IBM SPSS Statistics* (London: Sage Publications).

Foley, Paul. 2013. 'National Government Responses to Marine Stewardship Council (MSC) Fisheries Certification: Insights from Atlantic Canada', *New Political Economy*, 18 (2), 284–307.

Food and Agriculture Organization of the United Nations. 2021. *Code of Conduct for Responsible Fisheries*, (Rome: FAO), <https://www.fao.org/fishery/en/code> [Accessed 21 January 2022].

Froehlich, Halley E., Jamie C. Afflerbach, Melanie Frazier, and Benjamin S. Halpern. 2019. 'Blue Growth Potential to Mitigate Climate Change through Seaweed Offsetting', *Current Biology*, 29 (18), 3087–93. e3.

Gale, Fred, and Marcus Haward 2004 *Public Accountability in Private Regulation: Contrasting Models of the Forest Stewardship* Council *(FSC) and Marine Stewardship Council (MSC)* (Citeseer Australasian Political Studies Association Conference, University of Adelaide)

Gameau, Damon. 2019. *2040: A Handbook for the Regeneration* (Australia: Macmillan).

Global Ocean Biodiversity Initiative. *About Gobi*, <https://gobi.org/about/> [Accessed 28 January 2022].

Grimm, Laurence G., and K. Paul Nesselroade. 2019. *Statistical Applications for the Behavioral and Social Sciences*: (New York: John Wiley and Sons, Inc.).

Grip, Kjell. 2017. 'International Marine Environmental Governance: A Review', *Ambio*, 46 (4), 413–27.

Gulbrandsen, Lars H. 2006. 'Creating Markets for Eco-Labelling: Are Consumers Insignificant?', *International Journal of Consumer Studies*, 30 (5), 477–89.

——. 2009. 'The Emergence and Effectiveness of the Marine Stewardship Council', *Marine Policy*, 33 (4), 654–60.

——. 2010. *Transnational Environmental Governance: The Emergence and Effects of the Certification of Forest and Fisheries*: (Edward Elgar Publishing).

——. 2014. 'Dynamic Governance Interactions: Evolutionary Effects of State Responses to Non-State Certification Programs', *Regulation and Governance*, 8 (1), 74–92.

Gulbrandsen, Lars H., and Graeme Auld. 2016. 'Contested Accountability Logics in Evolving Nonstate Certification for Fisheries Sustainability', *Global Environmental Politics*, 16 (2), 42–60.

Hanekom, Anton. 2020. 'South African Initiative to End Plastic Pollution in the Environment', *South African Journal of Science*, 116, no. 5–6 (2020): 1–2.

Heidkamp., C Patrick, Michaela Garland, and Louie Krak. 2021. 'Enacting a Just and Sustainable Blue Economy through Transdisciplinary Action Research', *The Geographical Journal*, 0 (1), 1–13.

Herr, Dorothée, Moritz von Unger, Dan Laffoley, and Alexis McGivern. 2017. 'Pathways for Implementation of Blue Carbon Initiatives', *Aquatic Conservation: Marine and Freshwater Ecosystems*, 27, 116–29.

Holdt, Susan Løvstad, and Stefan Kraan. 2011. 'Bioactive Compounds in Seaweed: Functional Food Applications and Legislation', *Journal of Applied Phycology*, 23 (3), 543–97.

Holmgren, David 2020. *Essence of Permaculture* (Victoria: Melliodora Publishing).

Hopkinson, Charles S., Wei-Jun Cai, and Xinping Hu. 2012. 'Carbon Sequestration in Wetland Dominated Coastal Systems—a Global Sink of Rapidly Diminishing Magnitude', *Current Opinion in Environmental Sustainability*, 4 (2), 186–94.

Howard, Jennifer, Elizabeth McLeod, Sebastian Thomas, Erin Eastwood, Matthew Fox, Lauren Wenzel, and Emily Pidgeon. 2017. 'The Potential to Integrate Blue Carbon into MPA Design and Management', *Aquatic Conservation: Marine and Freshwater Ecosystems*, 27, 100–15.

International Union for the Conservation of Nature 2018 *Living in Harmony with Nature by 2050* (Sharm el-Sheikh, Egypt: 4th Science Forum) <https://www.iucn.org/commissions/commission-ecosystem-management/our-work/cems-thematic-groups/ecosystems-and-invasive-species/towards-living-harmony-nature-2050-cop14> [Accessed 28 January 2022].

Jacquet, Jennifer, John Hocevar, Sherman Lai, Patricia Majluf, Nathan Pelletier, Tony Pitcher, Enric Sala, Rashid Sumaila, and Daniel Pauly. 2010. 'Conserving Wild Fish in a Sea of Market-Based Efforts', *Oryx*, 44 (1), 45–56.

Jacquet, Jennifer L., and Daniel Pauly. 2007. 'The Rise of Seafood Awareness Campaigns in an Era of Collapsing Fisheries', *Marine Policy*, 31 (3), 308–13.

Jacquet, Jennifer, and Daniel Pauly. 2008. 'Funding Priorities: Big Barriers to Small-Scale Fisheries', Conservation Biology, 22 (4), 832–35.

Jacquet, Jennifer, Daniel Pauly, David Ainley, Sidney Holt, Paul Dayton, and Jeremy Jackson. 2010. 'Seafood Stewardship in Crisis', *Nature*, 467 (7311), 28–29.

Johnson, David, Christopher Barrio Froján, Nicholas Bax, Piers Dunstan, Skipton Woolley, Pat Halpin, Daniel Dunn, Carolina Hazin, Maria Dias, Tammy Davies, Jorge Jiménez, Erick Ross, Cindy Van Dover, Giuseppe Notarbartolo Di Sciara, Erich Hoyt, Michael J. Tetley, Vikki Gunn, and Henning Von Nordheim. 2019. 'The Global Ocean Biodiversity Initiative: Promoting Scientific Support for Global Ocean Governance', *Aquatic Conservation: Marine and Freshwater Ecosystems*, 29 (S2), 162–69.

Kauffman, J. Boone, and Daniel C. Donato. 2012. *Protocols for the Measurement, Monitoring and Reporting of Structure, Biomass and Carbon Stocks in Mangrove Forests* (Citeseer) <https://WP86CIFOR.pdf> [Accessed 26 February 2022].

Koenig-Archibugi, M. 2006. 'Introduction: Institutional Diversity in Global Governance.' in M. Koenig-Archibugi and M. Zurn (eds.), *New Modes of Governance in the Global System: Exploring Publicness, Delegation and Inclusiveness* (Basingstoke, UK: Palgrave Macmillan), pp. 13.

Krause-Jensen, Dorte, Paul Lavery, Oscar Serrano, Núria Marbà, Pere Masque, and Carlos M. Duarte. 2018. 'Sequestration of Macroalgal Carbon: The Elephant in the Blue Carbon Room', *Biology Letters*, 14 (6), 20180236.

Lammerts van Beuren, Erik M., and Esther M. Blom. 1997. *Hierarchical Framework for the Formulation of Sustainable Forest Management Standards* (Leiden, The Netherlands: The Tropenbos Foundation).

Lee, Ki-Hoon, Junsung Noh, and Jong Seong Khim. 2020. 'The Blue Economy and the United Nations' Sustainable Development Goals: Challenges and Opportunities', *Environment International*, 137, 105528.

Lee, Ki-Hoon, Junsung Noh, Jongmin Lee, and Jong Seong Khim. 2021. 'Blue Economy and the Total Environment: Mapping the Interface', *Environment International*, 157, 106796.

Macreadie, Peter I., Katie Allen, Brendan P. Kelaher, Peter J. Ralph, and Charles G. Skilbeck. 2012. 'Paleoreconstruction of Estuarine Sediments Reveal Human-Induced Weakening of Coastal Carbon Sinks', *Global Change Biology*, 18 (3), 891–901.

Maraseni, Tek Narayan, and Tim Cadman. 2015. 'A Comparative Analysis of Global Stakeholders' Perceptions of the Governance Quality of the Clean Development Mechanism (CDM) and Reducing Emissions from Deforestation and Forest Degradation (REDD+)', *International Journal of Environmental Studies*, 72 (2), 288–304.

Marine Stewardship Council. 2002. *MSC Principles and Criteria for Sustainable Fishing.* <https://www.msc.org/docs/default-source/default-document-library/for-business/program-documents/chain-of-custody-program-documents/msc-chain-of-custody-standard_default-version-v5-0.pdf> [Accessed 21 January 2022]

——. 2019. *MSC Chain of Custody Standard: Default Version.* <https://www.msc.org/docs/default-source/default-document-library/for-business/program-documents/chain-of-custody-program-documents/msc-chain-of-custody-standard_default-version-v5-0.pdf> [Accessed 21 January 2022]

McKinley, Emma, Oscar Aller-Rojas, Caroline Hattam, Celine Germond-Duret, Inés Vicuña San Martín, Charlotte Rachael Hopkins, Héctor Aponte, and Tavis Potts. 2018. 'Charting the Course for a Blue Economy in Peru: A Research Agenda', *Environment, Development and Sustainability*, 21 (5), 2253–75.

Mcleod, Elizabeth, Gail L. Chmura, Steven Bouillon, Rodney Salm, Mats Björk, Carlos M. Duarte, Catherine E. Lovelock, William H. Schlesinger, and Brian R. Silliman. 2011. 'A Blueprint for Blue Carbon: Toward an Improved Understanding of the Role of Vegetated Coastal Habitats in Sequestering CO_2', *Frontiers in Ecology and the Environment*, 9 (10), 552–60.

Momentive Inc. n.d. *Survey Monkey.* <www.momentive.ai> [Accessed 31 January 2022]

Nhem, Sareth, and Young-jin Lee. 2020. 'Exploring Perspectives in Assessing the Quality of Governance of the Reducing Emissions from Deforestation and Forest Degradation (REDD+) Pilot Project in Cambodia: Use of Q Methodology', *Journal of Mountain Science*, 17 (1), 95–116.

Novaglio, Camilla, Narissa Bax, Fabio Boschetti, Gholam Reza Emad, Stewart Frusher, Liam Fullbrook, Mark Hemer, Sarah Jennings, Ingrid Van Putten, and Lucy M. Robinson. 2021. 'Deep Aspirations: Towards a Sustainable Offshore Blue Economy', *Reviews in Fish Biology and Fisheries*, 32, no. 1 (2022): 209–230.

Nunes, Paulo A.L.D., Lisa Emelia Svensson, and Anil Markandya. 2017. *Handbook on the Economics and Management of Sustainable Oceans* (Cheltenham: Edward Elgar Publishing).

Pendleton, Linwood, Daniel C. Donato, Brian C. Murray, Stephen Crooks, W. Aaron Jenkins, Samantha Sifleet, Christopher Craft, James W. Fourqurean, J. Boone Kauffman, and Núria Marbà. 2012. 'Estimating Global "Blue Carbon Emissions from Conversion and Degradation of Vegetated Coastal Ecosystems', *PLoS One*, 7 (9), e43542.

Ponte, Stefano. 2012. 'The Marine Stewardship Council (MSC) and the Making of a Market for 'Sustainable Fish", *Journal of Agrarian Change*, 12 (2-3), 300–15.

Radulovich, Ricardo, Amir Neori, Diego Valderrama, C.R.K. Reddy, Holly Cronin, and John Forster. 2015. 'Chapter 3 – Farming of Seaweeds.' in Brijesh K. Tiwari and Declan J. Troy (eds.), *Seaweed Sustainability* (San Diego: Academic Press), pp. 27–59.

Rebours, Céline, Eliane Marinho-Soriano, José A. Zertuche-González, Leila Hayashi, Julio A. Vásquez, Paul Kradolfer, Gonzalo Soriano, Raul Ugarte, Maria Helena Abreu, and Ingrid

Bay-Larsen. 2014. 'Seaweeds: An Opportunity for Wealth and Sustainable Livelihood for Coastal Communities', *Journal of Applied Phycology*, 26 (5), 1939–51.

Ross, Amanda, and Victor L. Willson. 2017. *Basic and Advanced Statistical Tests* (Rotterdam: Sense Publishers).

Rustomjee, Cyrus 2016 *Developing the Blue Economy in Caribbean and Other Small States* (Ontario: Centre for International Governance Innovation 2016)

Shiiba, Nagisa, Hsing Hao Wu, Michael C. Huang, and Hajime Tanaka. "How blue financing can sustain ocean conservation and development: A proposed conceptual framework for blue financing mechanism." *Marine Policy* 139 (2022): 104575.

Sifleet, Samantha, Linwood Pendleton, and B.C. Murray.·2011. *State of the Science on Coastal Blue Carbon: A Summary for Policy Makers*, (Nicholas Institute for Environmental Policy Solutions), <https://nicholasinstitute.duke.edu/sites/default/files/publications/state-of-science-coastal-blue-carbon-paper.pdf> [Accessed 20 January 2022].

Smale, Dan A., Pippa J. Moore, Ana M. Queirós, S. Higgs, and Michael T. Burrows. 2018. 'Appreciating Interconnectivity between Habitats Is Key to Blue Carbon Management', *Frontiers in Ecology and the Environment*, 16 (2), 71–73.

Stephenson, Robert L., Alistair J. Hobday, Christopher Cvitanovic, Karen A. Alexander, Gavin A. Begg, Rodrigo H. Bustamante, Piers K. Dunstan, Stewart Frusher, Maree Fudge, and Elizabeth A. Fulton. 2019. 'A Practical Framework for Implementing and Evaluating Integrated Management of Marine Activities', *Ocean and Coastal Management*, 177, 127–38.

Stokke, Olav Schram 2004 *Labelling, Legalisation and Sustainable Management of Forestry and Fisheries* (The Hague, Netherlands: Fifth Pan-European International Relations Conference)

Sumaila, U. Rashid, Melissa Walsh, Kelly Hoareau, Anthony Cox, Louise Teh, Patrízia Abdallah, Wisdom Akpalu, Zuzy Anna, Dominique Benzaken, and Beatrice Crona. 2021. 'Financing a Sustainable Ocean Economy', *Nature Communications*, 12 (1), 1–11.

Sustainable Ocean Initiative.·2014. *Action Plan for the Sustainable Ocean Initiative (2015-2020)*, (Seoul, Korea: Sustainable Ocean Initiative Global Partnership), <https://www.cbd.int/doc/meetings/mar/soiom-2014-02/official/soiom-2014-02-actionplan-en.pdf> [Accessed 19 January 2022].

Sutton, Michael. 1996. 'The Marine Stewardship Council: New Hope for Marine Fisheries', *Naga, the ICLARM Quarterly*, 19 (3), 10–12.

Takeuchi, Kazuhiko. 2010. 'Rebuilding the Relationship between People and Nature: The Satoyama Initiative', *Ecological Research*, 25 (5), 891–97.

Tamm, K., and M. Boström. 2010. *Transnational Multistakeholder Standardization. Organizing Fragile Non-State Authority* (Cheltenham, UK and Northampton, MA: Edward Elgar).

Tashakkori, Abbas, and Charles Teddlie. 1998. *Mixed Methodology: Combining Qualitative and Quantitative Approaches*: (Sage).

The Climate Foundation.·2021. *Marine Permaculture Offshore Executive Summary*, (The Climate Foundation), <https://www.climatefoundation.org/uploads/3/0/2/0/30209783/marine_permaculture_exec_summ_august_2019_two_pager.pdf> [Accessed 20 January 2022].

Thomas, Sebastian. 2014. 'Blue Carbon: Knowledge Gaps, Critical Issues, and Novel Approaches', *Ecological Economics*, 107, 22–38.

——. 2016. 'Between Tun Mustapha and the Deep Blue Sea: The Political Ecology of Blue Carbon in Sabah', *Environmental Science and Policy*, 55, 20–35.

Tianming, Gao, Vasilii Erokhin, Aleksandr Arskiy, and Mikail Khudzhatov. "Has the COVID-19 Pandemic Affected Maritime Connectivity? An Estimation for China and the Polar Silk Road Countries." *Sustainability*, 13, no. 6 (2021): 3521.

Ullmann, Jörg, and Daniel Grimm. 2021. 'Algae and Their Potential for a Future Bioeconomy, Landless Food Production, and the Socio-Economic Impact of an Algae Industry', *Organic Agriculture*, 11 (2), 261–67.

United Nations. *Decade of Ocean Science for Sustainable Development*, <https://www.oceande cade.org/> [Accessed 19 January 2022].

United Nations Environment Programme.·2010. *The State of Biodiversity in Latin America and Carribean,* <https://www.cbd.int/gbo/gbo3/doc/StateOfBiodiversity-LatinAmerica.pdf> [Accessed 20 January 2022].

United Nations Environment Programme Finance Initiative (UNEPFI). 2018. *The Sustainable Blue Economy Finance Principles,* <https://www.unepfi.org/blue-finance/the-principles/> [Accessed 28 January 2022].

——. n.d. *United Nations' Sustainable Blue Finance Initiative: Mobilising Capital for a Sustainable Ocean*, <https://www.unepfi.org/blue-finance/> [Accessed 28 January 2022].

Vierros, Marjo. 2017. 'Communities and Blue Carbon: The Role of Traditional Management Systems in Providing Benefits for Carbon Storage, Biodiversity Conservation and Livelihoods', *Climatic Change*, 140 (1), 89–100.

Voyer, Michelle, Genevieve Quirk, Alistair McIlgorm, and Kamal Azmi. 2018. 'Shades of Blue: What Do Competing Interpretations of the Blue Economy Mean for Oceans Governance?', *Journal of Environmental Policy and Planning*, 20 (5), 595–616.

Ward, Trevor J. 2008. 'Barriers to Biodiversity Conservation in Marine Fishery Certification', *Fish and Fisheries*, 9 (2), 169–77.

White, E.M., and B. Rahill.·2021. *Blue Natural Capital*, (Washington DC: International Finance Corporation), <https://openknowledge.worldbank.org/bitstream/handle/10986/35476/Blue-Natural-Capital-Enhancing-Business-Outcomes-and-Sustainability-of-Coastal-Tourism-Markets.pdf?sequence=1&isAllowed=y> [Accessed 21 January 2022].

Wijen, Frank, and Mireille Chiroleu-Assouline. 2019. 'Controversy over Voluntary Environmental Standards: A Socioeconomic Analysis of the Marine Stewardship Council', *Organization and Environment*, 32 (2), 98–124.

Woodcock, Ben A., Nicholas J.B. Isaac, James M. Bullock, David B. Roy, David G. Garthwaite, Andrew Crowe, and Richard F. Pywell. 2016. 'Impacts of Neonicotinoid Use on Long-Term Population Changes in Wild Bees in England', *Nature Communications*, 7 (1), 1–8.

Wylie, Lindsay, Ariana E. Sutton-Grier, and Amber Moore. 2016. 'Keys to Successful Blue Carbon Projects: Lessons Learned from Global Case Studies', *Marine Policy*, 65, 76–84.

Graham Wood

Chapter 26
How green is the blue economy?

Abstract: The chapter begins by comparing the 10,000 years of the (largely) terrestrial economy, with the (relatively) recently emerging blue economy. The history of the terrestrial economy has been one of trial and error in terms of how sustainable or green it may be characterised as being. What lessons can be applied now to avoid some of those errors in the blue economy?

Using this comparison as motivation, the chapter will involve a discussion of the concepts of planetary boundaries, ecosystem services and natural capital, the contrasts between domesticated and non-domesticated space; strong and weak sustainability; intrinsic and instrumental environmental values; shallow and deep environmental ethics; and biocentric and anthropocentric conceptual frameworks. The analysis will involve a critical examination of the concept sustainable development drawing on a number of approaches including those motivated by the Brundtland definition of sustainable development (World Commission on Environment and Development 1987). The analysis will also point to a number of examples to illustrate the concepts central to sustainability. Finally, a series of specific questions will be identified and examined in order to address the overarching question of this chapter: how green is the blue economy?

Keywords: environmental history, planetary boundaries, strong sustainability, weak sustainability, biocentric, anthropocentric, environmental justice, COVID-19

Introduction

The chapter will give the reader the conceptual resources needed to answer the question: how green is the blue economy. The chapter beings with some preliminary discussion of relevant distinctions. Next the history of humanity's modification of the environment is considered to provide some context and relevant insights. This is followed by the presentation of a series of conceptual frameworks.

https://doi.org/10.1515/9783110733488-026

Preliminaries

On the question: How green is the blue economy?

Rather than answer the question how green is the blue economy? this chapter will ask it. Here is why. Firstly, any answer will depend on what is meant by the word green and this will vary depending on the position of the person using the word. There are a number of issues that affect the meaning of the word green and what meaning is adopted, and that is because green (as it is used here) is an essentially contested concept (Gallie 1956). These issues will be examined in detail. Secondly, to answer the question, it is necessary to have a sufficient level of knowledge of the nature of the blue economy. The author of this chapter does not possess sufficient knowledge of the nature of the blue economy, so will not offer to answer the question. But readers of this chapter will be able to draw upon their own knowledge of the blue economy. So, what this chapter will do is provide a set of conceptual resources for the reader. When combined with a sufficient knowledge of the actual nature of the blue economy, readers will be able to answer the question for themselves.

The meanings of the words blue and green

The blue economy will be understood as referring to that part of the economy associated with the ocean. Importantly, there are a number of ways the term blue economy is used in the literature (Smith-Godfrey 2016). In some contexts, the term blue economy is used in an evaluative sense, where the use of the word blue is taken to be an endorsement. However, here blue economy will be used as a purely descriptive term, that is, to refer to the ocean economy.

However, the word green will be used as an evaluative term, as a default position its application will be taken to be an endorsement. However, different people have different positions on how green the blue economy should be. So, it is possible that, on one person's understanding the blue economy is too green and, on another person's, understanding it is not green enough. But either way the question: how green is the blue economy? will be understood as an essentially evaluative question.

Descriptions/predictions versus prescriptions

The distinction between description/prediction and prescription is important. Description is a characterisation of past or present objects, events or states of affairs that does not involve evaluative judgements of those objects, events or states of affairs. Some assume that it is impossible to describe in a value-free way. For discussion of this issue see McMullin (2001). Such people assume that values (be they personal, social, institutional, or political) are always involved in any purported value-free description. This is a denial of the fact/value distinction. However, in this chapter it will be assumed that it is possible to describe large parts of the world independently from values. This assumption is consistent with the existence of the is/ought gap (Hume 1984: 521).

Associated with description is prediction. Here it will be assumed that prediction is a characterisation of the state of future objects, events or states of affairs, and again these characterisations do not involve evaluative judgements. Humans use many methods for predicting the future. Sciences such as physics, chemistry and biology are the best method humans have yet devised for prediction. Science is not perfect at prediction, but within certain limits it is reasonably good. This chapter will assume that it is possible to describe and predict (however imperfectly) the nature of, and processes associated with, the blue economy.

Prescription is distinct from both description and prediction. Prescriptions are characterisations of what should, or ought, be the case. One person may take the view that the present state of certain objects, events or states of affair is the way they should be, and in such cases that person will not take action to change the status quo. Alternatively, another person may take the view that the present state of certain objects, events or states of affairs is not the way they should be, and so that person, assuming they have the power to do so, many take action to change the status quo.

Pragmatic and ethical prescriptions

Two forms of prescription are relevant here. Both can be understood with reference to how people should act but the should in each case is understood differently. The first use of should is pragmatic, the second is ethical.

Pragmatic should claims relate to situations in which a person A seeks a certain outcome Z and there are certain things X and Y that need to happen for Z to occur. Thus, A should act to bring about X and Y so that Z occurs. Person A may be motivated by a range of motivations, for example, personal preference, but for the purpose of this analysis it is assumed that ethical considerations are not the motivations. In this situation the should is a pragmatic prescription.

Ethical should claims relate to a situation in which a person B seeks a certain outcome W and there are certain things U and V that need to happen for that outcome to occur. Thus, B should act to bring about U and V so that W occurs. Person B may be motivated by a range of ethical motivations, and the nature of possible ethical motivations will be considered later in this chapter. In this situation the should is an ethical prescription.

In order to understand the distinction, consider one person who does not experience any ethical motivation at all in some situation. In other words, they are not motivated by ethics to do anything in this situation. So, if they think they should do anything it is not because they think ethical considerations prescribe action. Nonetheless they may well have a rich and complex set of assumptions about what they should do.

For the purposes of the distinction drawn here, it is assumed that the pragmatic sense of should and the ethical sense of should can be considered independently. However, it is often the case that pragmatic and ethical prescriptions are not considered independently simply because of the complex set of relations within which people exist.

It is possible to interpret the question how green is the blue economy? in a purely pragmatic sense. To illustrate this, consider a person that feels no ethical motivations. Even in the absence of any ethical motivations, this person may have an interest in how well the ocean ecosystem is functioning in the service of their own ends. Assuming that this person wishes to gain some benefit from the ocean, then there are certain actions that person should pursue (or endorse) and there are certain actions that that person should not pursue (or not endorse). This pragmatic analysis of the question how green is the blue economy? aligns with a use of the word green that could simply mean good housekeeping in a purely self-interested sense of that phrase.

In contrast to the purely pragmatic analysis of the question is the ethical analysis of the question. In this case in addition to pragmatic shoulds there are also ethical shoulds. Here it will be assumed that ethical shoulds arise because of ethical motivations. However, this is only one way to characterise the nature and origins of ethical shoulds. There is much debate in metaethics about the nature and origins of ethical shoulds, for example, see Copp (2006). But a full analysis is beyond the scope of this chapter. For present purposes it is enough to acknowledge that people are subject to a range of ethical motivations, that may be directed toward a range of entities, objects, events or states of affairs, including but not limited to themselves, other humans, other individual non-human organisms, other species, ecosystems and other features of the Earth, such as rivers and mountains.

In the normal course of psychological development humans come to experience ethical motivations and as such they are referred to as moral agents. Those humans may experience ethical motivations toward other moral agents (other humans who have undergone the normal course of psychological development), or other entities that are not moral agents themselves. Entities that are not themselves moral agents, but nonetheless are granted ethical standing are termed moral patients. Moral agents hold other moral agents morally accountable for their actions, but do not hold moral patients morally accountable.

Environmental history

Later in the chapter a range of conceptual resources will be introduced relevant to readers when answering the question how green is the blue economy? for themselves. But before that it will be valuable to review some environmental history.

What follows is a review of environmental history on land over approximately the last 10,000 years. The purpose of this review is two-fold. Firstly, it provides insights into how humanity has modified the land over that period, and secondly, drawing on those insights it gives the reader a chance to reflect on how the next 10,000 years might unfold in terms of how humanity modifies both land and sea. Thus, the reader is invited to imagine what the next 10,000 years will look like (and prediction) and what it should look like (a prescription) on both land and sea.

Homo sapiens (evolutionarily modern humans) emerged around 200,000 years ago and existed in hunter-gather groups up until around 10,000 years ago, when humans first began to domesticate crops and animals. Humans have always modified the biosphere to a greater or lesser extent. The nature and extent of this modification can be understood with reference to five periods of cultural ecology suggested by Thompson (1989) and used by Simmons (1993) whose analysis will be drawn upon here. The five periods are: hunter-gathering and early agriculture; riverine civilisations; agricultural empires; The Atlantic-industrial era; and The Pacific-global era.

Hunter-gathering and early agriculture

Hunter-gathering was the first period of cultural ecology, before the establishment of towns and cities, where human groups moved around over relatively large territory. While the impact of hunter-gathering on the environment was relatively small in comparison to more recent human activity, it still occurred. The significance of that impact varied.

Sometimes it was not obvious. For example, analysis of the composition of forests in Peru indicates that hunter-gather groups have lived in those forests for thousands of years without affecting the nature of that forest (Piperno et al. 2021).

Sometimes it was very obvious. Many assume that humans were responsible for the extinction of many mammals and birds in Australia (during the Pleistocene) in the Americas (at the end of the Pleistocene) and across the Pacific (in the Holocene) (Meltzer 2015). This extinction event is most marked in North America where two-thirds of the megafauna disappeared from the fossil record (Simmons 1993: 4).

And sometimes it was more nuanced. Hunter-gather groups used fire to clear the land and stimulate new growth of plants that in turn attracted animals that could then be hunted. For example, in Tasmania, Indigenous people used fire to convert forest to fern heath and tussock grassland attracting wallabies, bandicoots and possums that where then hunted (Simmons 1993: 5).

While there were impacts, hunter-gather societies managed their environmental impact using a range of beliefs and cultural practices, for example, rituals that lead to regular variation of hunting areas, or beliefs that protected some species from hunting (Simmons 1993: 7).

Riverine civilisations and agricultural empires

The next phase of cultural ecology is the period of riverine civilisations first emerging in Mesopotamia, Egypt and the Indus and Yellow River valleys. In this phase humans began controlling water on a large-scale using irrigation, mitigating against the limiting effect of seasonal variability of rain. This allowed for food to be produced in larger amounts that in turn allowed for the development of complex civilisations. However, along with the benefits of civilisation, there were environmental costs such as, salinity and siltation problems (Morozova 2005). For example, by 1700 BCE salinity and siltation were serious problems in Mesopotamia, and these environmental issues coincided with more than an estimated 50% decline in human population between 1900 BCE and 1600 BCE (Simmons 1993: 13).

Following the riverine civilisations, that were reasonably localised in geographical regions (e.g., the land surrounding the Nile), were the agricultural empires that extended over larger areas, such as Roman, Indian and Chinese civilisations. This form of cultural ecology existed in various manifestations up to the industrial revolution.

During this time human technological capacity for environmental modification continued to increase, leading to further food surpluses that in turn lead to increasing social complexity. As was the case previously, the management of the technological capacity for environmental modification was often incorporated into the beliefs and customs of the civilisations themselves, such as is illustrated by the water temples of Bali (Lansing 1987). But, in contrast to environmental management practices that were embedded within cultural beliefs and practices, sometimes what might be seen today as positive environmental outcomes were actually side-effects of the pursuit of other interests and purposes. For example, in medieval Europe kings and princes designated large areas as royal forest for the purpose of preserving habitat for the game they wished to hunt. This had the side-effect of preserving areas of forests as reasonably undisturbed ecosystems. And the Venetian republic maintained a forest for the explicit purpose of ensuring a supply of wood for use in shipbuilding within the Arsenal (Simmons 1993: 22–26). So, it is important to remember that environmental modification (that might be considered good, neutral or bad) can sometimes be explicitly pursued or can be the side-effect of other pursuits.

It is interesting to note that within all of the cultural ecologies up to this point there was a recognisable connection between environmental management and cultural beliefs and practices. After this point there is a less obvious connection between environmental management and cultural beliefs and practices (Wood 2019).

This may be a function of the speed of environmental modification that has occurred since the beginning of the industrial revolution. Perhaps the speed of the change meant that insights into appropriate environmental management practices did not have time to be embedded within the wider set of cultural beliefs and practices.

The Atlantic-industrial and Pacific-global eras

The industrial revolution began in Britain at the end of the eighteenth century. This involved large-scale use of energy derived from fossil fuels and fundamentally changed the relationship between humans and the non-human world. The significant transformation that the industrial revolution began continues to this day. There are many dimensions to the transformation that began with the industrial revolution. But one way of understanding the difference between the hunter-gather era and the present industrial era is in terms of energy consumption via the use of fossil fuels. The energy available to humans in the form of fossil fuels has resulted in a greatly increased capacity for environmental modification. Fossil fuel powered machines and motors on both land and sea have allow humans to act in ways that were not possible in the pre-fossil fuel era.

Lessons from environmental history

The purpose of reviewing environmental history is to highlight the fact that humans have come to dominate the terrestrial portions of the planet, and that domination has brought with it benefits to humans, but it has also brought with it costs to the environment. Through the last 10,000 years humans have learnt perhaps too slowly what is appropriate and what is not appropriate in terms of environmental modification on land. There is now the opportunity to apply these lessons to the next 10,000 years on the oceans (and the land).

Humans have always interacted with the oceans, but most of the human domination of the planet has involved modifications of terrestrial ecosystems. Humans are now beginning what might be considered the equivalent of both the agricultural and industrial revolutions in the oceans. Indeed, as Marra (2005: 175) observes: 'Following the cultivation of land for food, society must take the next step: large-scale domestication of the ocean.' However, not everyone agrees that large-scale domestication of the ocean must occur. But to the extent that domestication of the ocean will occur: how should that proceed? The question how (if at all) should the domestication of the ocean proceed? is one among several asked in this chapter that will help the reader answer the central question: how green is the blue economy?

Land degradation and ocean degradation

An important lesson learnt from the past 10,000 years of humanity's agricultural and relatively more recent industrial use of the terrestrial environment is that the environment can be degraded. This lesson can be applied to the marine environment as humanity attempts to avoid the equivalent mistakes. Obviously, the marine environment is different to the terrestrial environment, but there are still important parallels between the two, such that the lessons learnt on land can be applied in the oceans. One parallel will be examined here. The purpose of drawing this particular parallel is simply illustrative. It is intended to prompt in the mind of the reader further parallels.

Consider the parallel between widespread land degradation and widespread ocean degradation. There are a number of forms of land degradation, including soil erosion, salination and desertification. In a general sense, half of the land area of the planet has been disturbed by humans in some way, and when excluding land that is uninhabitable by humans (i.e., areas of rock, ice or barren land) three-quarters of all habitable land has been disturbed in some way (Hannah et al. 1994). But to focus on desertification, Eswaran, Lal, and Reich (2001: 30) report that 'Desertification is experienced on 33% of the global land surface and affects more than one billion people, half of whom live in Africa.'

An equivalent to desertification on land might be ocean acidification. As CO_2 is released with the burning of fossil fuels a portion of that CO_2 dissolves in the ocean. This changes the pH of the ocean making it more acidic over time. One consequence of this is that marine organisms that have shells are affected. The increased acidity of the ocean reduces the organism's capacity to maintain its shell because the increased acidity leads to increased rates of the shell being dissolved by the more acidic water. Thus, acidification has 'the potential for direct and profound impacts on our living marine ecosystems' (Feely, Doney, and Cooley 2009: 46). One of the many implications of both land degradation and ocean degradation, is biodiversity loss. The question: what is the appropriate attitude to biodiversity loss? is another question that will help the reader answer the central question: how green is the blue economy?

Some distinctions

When considering the question: what is the appropriate attitude to biodiversity loss?, a number of distinctions are relevant. Firstly, the distinction between facts and values, secondly, the distinction between description and prescription, and thirdly, the distinction between pragmatic and ethical prescriptions.

The previous section introduced the concept of biodiversity loss. For the purposes of this chapter, it will be assumed that humans are causing biodiversity loss.

But is biodiversity loss a bad thing? Biodiversity loss may not be a bad thing. If a person has no interest in maintaining the current set of species that exist on the planet, it may not be a bad thing. As the geological record shows, biodiversity recovered after the five mass extinction events of the past, so the fact that biodiversity is being lost now is not, in and of itself, enough to conclude that it is a bad thing. It is only a bad thing if a particular value judgement is made about these facts. Namely, the judgement that they are bad. For members of species that would replace the current set of species (after the biosphere recovers on the other side of the next mass extinction), presumably it would be a good thing. However, if a person makes the judgement that they are bad then, for that person at least, they are bad. But in what sense are they bad? Two possibilities are relevant here. Biodiversity loss may be bad pragmatically, or it may be bad ethically.

If entities that have ethical standing are impacted sufficiently negatively by biodiversity loss, then these events are bad ethically, and thus ethical prescriptions, that these events should not happen, may be relevant. If no entities that have ethical standing are impacted sufficiently negatively by biodiversity loss, then these events are not bad ethically. However, they may be bad pragmatically.

The previous section also introduced the concept of degradation. Is land and ocean degradation a bad thing? Before addressing this question, it should be acknowledged that the word degradation is usually understood as essentially carrying a negative connotation, in that all degradation is bad. So, to avoid begging the question here, the negative connotation will be set aside. In other words, the question being addressed here is this: is the value-free $^{(vf)}$ physical process that is usually identified by the word degradation a bad thing? Call this land or ocean degradation.^{vf}

And, as was the case with the concept of biodiversity loss, land or ocean degradation^{vf} may not be a bad thing. If a person has no interest in maintaining a certain capacity of land or ocean (that is lost when the land or ocean undergoes degradation^{vf}) then it is not a bad thing. It is only a bad thing if a particular value judgement is made about these facts. Namely, the judgement that they are bad. If a person makes the judgement that they are bad then, for that person at least, they are bad. But in what sense are they bad? Two possibilities are relevant here. Land or ocean degradation^{vf} may be bad pragmatically, or they may be bad ethically.

If entities that have ethical standing are impacted sufficiently negatively by land or ocean degradation,^{vf} then these events are bad ethically and thus ethical prescriptions that these events should not happen may be relevant. If no entities that have ethical standing are impacted sufficiently negatively by land or ocean degradation,^{vf} then these events are not bad ethically. However, they may be bad pragmatically.

Of course, many humans do have an interest in both maintaining biodiversity and avoiding land and ocean degradation.^{vf} If one assumes that all humans have ethical standing and that at least some humans will be impacted sufficiently negatively by biodiversity loss and land/ocean degradation^{vf} then both are ethically bad. The threshold at which some impact is sufficiently negative will vary on a number of factors and a full analysis of those factors will again take us beyond the scope of this chapter. But each person will have their own position on what that threshold is, and society more broadly will come to a socially mediated position on that threshold through a range of social processes.

Conceptual frameworks

Anthropocentrism versus non-anthropocentrism

The previous section was focussed on the impact of biodiversity loss and biosphere degradation on humans but that is not the only possibility. For example, if one assumes that non-human organisms have ethical standing and that at least some non-human organisms will be impacted sufficiently negatively by biodiversity loss and land/ocean degradation,[vf] then both are ethically bad.

A way to understand concerns beyond the human sphere is to use the concept of circles of concern. Imagine a set of concentric circles that represent a hierarchy of concerns that one individual may have. Contained within the central circle are the things of greatest concern to the individual. And contained within each of the other circles of the set are other things of less concern, such that the distance from the centre of the set of concentric circles represents the level and nature of concern the individual has for the thing.

For example, perhaps for one person only the interests of themselves and their close friends and family and pets are of primary concern, so it is only these interests that are represented in the central circle of the set. The next group of concerns for this person might be the social, economic and environmental circumstances that serve the interests of the entities in the central circle. Perhaps the next group of concerns for this person might be the interests of other humans that are not in their inner circle. Perhaps the next group of concerns for this person might be the social, economic and environmental circumstances that serve the interests of these other humans.

But this is not the only possibility. For another person perhaps all the interests of all humans are of primary concern, so it is these interests that are represented in the central circle of the set. The next group of concerns for this person might be the social, economic and environmental circumstances that serve the interests of all humans.

Both these examples assume that concerns associated with humans, either particular humans, or all humans, are located within the central circle. Broadly speaking this is anthropocentrism. But anthropocentrism is not the only possibility.

It may be that for another person the central circle contains the interests of all animals with a certain level of sentience (such that they are able to experience pleasure and pain). Broadly speaking this is sentiocentrism, and includes the position advocated by Singer (1993). Other concerns located in circles further from the centre related to aspects of the environment that serve the interests of all sentient organisms.

Or it may be that for another person the central circle contains the interests relevant to the maintenance of the integrity of the biosphere as a whole. Broadly speaking this is biocentrism and includes positions such as deep ecology (Sessions 1995) and the land ethic (Callicott 2001). Other concerns located in circles further from the centre related to the non-living aspects of the environment (e.g., the chemical composition of the ocean) that serve the interests of the biosphere as a whole.

To repeat, these different hierarchies of concern are generally labelled anthropocentrism (when humans dominate the concerns within the central circles), sentiocentrism (when sentient organisms dominate the concerns within the central circles, and humans are not considered more important than other sentient species) and biocentrism (when the interests of the biosphere dominate the concerns within the central circles and sentient organism are not considered more important than other non-sentient organisms).

Different people may locate their concerns for different entities, objects, events and states of affairs within different circles in the set of concentric circles. The choices they make may be motivated by individual preference, or practical or ethical considerations. One way to understand the hierarchy of concerns is by classifying entities, objects, events or states of affairs as either instrumentally valuable or intrinsically valuable and locating the things of intrinsic value closer to the centre of the set of concentric circles and things of instrumental value further from the centre of the set of concentric circles.

Instrumental versus intrinsic value

Now consider the distinction between instrumental value and intrinsic value. An entity, object, event, or state of affairs has instrumental value when it is serves some purpose to achieve some other thing. Perhaps this other thing is only instrumentally valuable as well. It may serve yet some other purpose. Indeed, there may be long strings of instrumental relationships between a series of entities, objects, events or states of affairs. But if all the assumed value in any set of instrumental relationships is only of this instrumental sort, then in effect there is no value at all. There must be some value that is not instrumental. It is this non-instrumental value that affects all the instrumental things in the set and imbues them all with their instrumental value. Call this value intrinsic value.

O'Neill (2001: 164–65) offers a number of characterisations of intrinsic value, three of which will be considered here. One sense of intrinsic value is value experienced by a valuer for its own sake. The valuable entity, object, event or state of affairs is not used to attain anything else, rather it is valuable for its own sake. For example a person may not benefit in any practical sense from studying birds, but nonetheless may value studying birds for its own sake (O'Neill 2001: 164).

Another sense of intrinsic value is related to the granting of ethical standing to an entity, object, event or state of affairs. This granting of ethical standing is often associated with the assumption that the entity, object, event or state of affairs is an end in itself. This is the central idea of the humanity version of Kant's categorical imperative: 'Act in such a way that you always treat humanity, whether in your own person or in the person of any other, never simply as a means, but always at the same time as an end' (Kant 1964: 429).

Humans are usually taken to be ends in themselves, but other entities, objects, events or states of affairs may also be taken to be ends in themselves. The guiding idea here is that because a thing is an end in itself, it is worthy of ethical standing. Thus, non-human entities could be granted the same status if one adopts a modified biocentric version of the categorical imperative as follows: Act in such a way that you always treat life, whether in your own species or in any other, never simply as a means, but always at the same time as an end.

The final sense of intrinsic value is to be considered here is based on the assumed existence of objective value. Objective value is an important concept in environmental philosophy, as it is in all of ethics, simply because moral judgements are taken by most people to be objectively prescriptive (Mackie 1977: 35).

Shallow and deep environmental ethics

The distinction between instrumental and intrinsic values is helpful in understanding the distinction between shallow and deep environmental ethics.

Shallow environmental ethics aligns with the assumption that all intrinsic values are closely associated with humans. Any values in the non-human world are instrumental values. To illustrate this, take the case above of a person studying the behaviour of birds for their own sake. A person endorsing a shallow environmental ethic may seek to protect the habitat of the birds and seek to ensure that birds persist in their habitat, but all of this is pursued instrumentally. The relevant intrinsic value is related to the actual study of the birds. The study itself is taken, by the studier of birds, to be intrinsically valuable and because the studier of birds is a person, that person is granted ethical standing so the interests of that person (in this case the interest in studying birds for its own sake) are to be respected. Or as O'Neill puts it, because 'y is of value to x, and x has ethical standing, then there is a prima facie ethical duty for ethical agents not to deprive x of y' (2001: 165).

Of course, there are much more serious far-reaching interests (other than studying birds) that are respected in shallow environmental ethics, such as the maintenance of complex social, economic and political structures that further individual and collective human interests. But they are all ultimately based on intrinsic values located within the human realm (and closely related to the ethical standing of humans).

In contrast, deep environmental ethics aligns with the assumption that there are intrinsic values associated with the non-human world, and these intrinsic values are taken to imply ethical standing.

Thus, again taking the example above, it is not that a person happens to find intrinsic value in studying birds in their habitat. Rather, it is taken to be the case that birds, or indeed the environment that offers birds a habitat, are intrinsically valuable in and of themselves, and that may also imply ethical standing. And perhaps this value is taken to be objective value.

Weak versus strong sustainability

Another distinction of relevance to this analysis is the distinction between weak and strong sustainability. See Davies (2013) for review. Weak and strong sustainability can be understood with reference to different assumptions about the preservation of different forms of capital. Capital is the stock of resources that can be used to serve the interests of humans. Capital exists in a number of forms. Natural capital potentially includes all the physical matter on Earth (excluding humans, and the matter already modified by humans) and the incoming energy from the sun that could be appropriated for human use. In a biocentric sense all living organisms benefit to some extent from this natural capital. But of course, in a narrower anthropocentric sense, many plants and non-human animals are understood as the natural capital itself. As well as natural capital there are a number of other forms of capital, including such things as financial wealth, manufactured goods and the social institutions and industrial infrastructure that create and constitute much of human culture.

Natural capital, say in the form of forests, can be converted into timber, that can in turn be converted into houses (timber and houses both being forms of manufactured capital) that can in turn contribute to the provision of protection from the elements and associated security that constitutes what might be identified as the social capital that is a home (and that becomes very obviously absent when a person is homeless).Weak sustainability is the position that assumes that any form of capital can be converted into any other form of capital in the pursuit of maintaining or increasing the total amount of capital available to serve the interests and purposes of humans. In other words, no form of capital must be maintained independently from the overall goal of maintaining or increasing the total amount of capital. Strong sustainability is the position that some natural capital must be maintained. There are two reasons for the assertion that some natural capital must be maintained. One reason is a purely anthropocentric reason, based on the assumption that if a certain amount of natural capital is not maintained then eventually the total amount of capital will not be maintained. Maintaining a certain level of biodiversity to maintain the stability of ecosystems upon which humans depend can be characterised in this way. The other reason is a biocentric reason, based on the assumption that that which is characterised as natural capital is also to be understood as having ethical standing in its own right. Because these features of the biosphere (characterised by some as natural capital) have ethical standing in their own right they must be maintained, even if the so-called natural capital could be converted into other forms of capital that would be more valuable in terms of the interests of humans.

Environmental justice

Up to this point, the themes of the chapter have tended to involve a contrast between the human and the non-human world. Indeed, it might be assumed that the word green is a word that presumes that the non-human world is to be afforded a higher (possibly ethical) significance. This is true. But it is not the only way the word green is used. Some, when using the word green, take it to have a wider meaning, and this wider meaning often includes what has become known as environmental justice.

Environmental ethics can be contrasted with environmental justice as follows. While environmental ethics addresses the ethical dimensions of the relationship between the human and the non-human, environmental justice addresses issues of justice among different individual humans or groups of humans when the issues of justice relate directly to environmental costs and benefits, and particularly when the environmental costs and benefits are distributed in unjust ways (Figueroa and Mills 2001: 426–27). Two important dimensions of environmental justice are: (1) distributive justice, involving how environmental benefits and burdens are distributed, and (2) participatory justice, how distributive decisions are made (Figueroa and Mills 2001: 427).

If it is assumed that the concept green includes respect for environmental justice, then when addressing the question how green is the blue economy? it is necessary to consider a wide range of issues of environmental justice. For example, when decisions are made among a group of nation-states about access to fisheries, are just processes followed and are the outcomes of these processes themselves just? And are the benefits and costs associated with the blue economy distributed fairly between nation-states and among the individuals within any one nation-state?

One example where environmental justice is particularly relevant is the place of Small Island Developing States in the blue economy. One issue that is already an existential challenge for such states is the effects of climate change, such as sea level rise, and more extreme weather events, and thus, the instantiation of environmental justice is of the utmost importance now for these states. And COVID-19 presents another challenge for these states. Both climate change in the long-term and COVID-19 in the short-term present themselves as direct challenges to the resilience (and more generally the sustainability) of these states, which leads on to the theme of sustainable development.

Sustainable development

While environmental justice might be principally understood to relate to ethical considerations among the current generation of humans, sustainable development can principally be understood to relate to ethical considerations between the current generation of humans and future generations of humans. The Brundtland definition of sustainable development is development that 'meets the needs of the present without compromising the ability of future generations to meet their own needs' (World Commission on Environment and Development 1987: 8). Sustainable development can be understood as functioning as a criterion of 'acceptable environmental modification' (Holland 2001: 400). Or putting it in more explicitly economic terms, sustainable development requires 'holding the scale of the human economic subsystem [. . .] to within the biophysical limits of the overall ecosystem on which it depends' (Goodland 2002: 2).

The idea of acceptable environmental modification (Holland 2001) and the idea of holding the human economic subsystem to with the limits of the biophysical environment (Goodland 2002), are two ways of thinking about other ideas, such as acknowledging the importance of ecosystem services (see Buckwell and Morgan chapter in this volume, the capacity for resilience to shock, for example, in the context of COVID-19 see Béné (2020), and the concept of planetary boundaries (Steffen et al. 2015).

Sustainable development is often understood to be essentially anthropocentric. But an anthropocentric position is not the only position available. A biocentric position is also possible. Building on Holland's observation that sustainable development is effectively functioning as a criterion for 'acceptable environmental modification' (Holland 2001: 400), it is possible to create a biocentric version of the Brundtland definition of sustainable development (World Commission on Environment and Development 1987). A biocentric version of the Bruntland definition (one that presupposes strong sustainability) might be: sustainable environmental modification is modification that meets the needs of the present set of species without compromising the ability of future sets of species to meet their own needs.

An invitation to reflect on some questions and a case study

The next section of the chapter invites the reader to reflect upon questions and a case study in the light of the conceptual frameworks examined above to help them address the question how green is the blue economy? for themselves.

What is of intrinsic value?

Different people will consider different things to be of intrinsic value. For current purposes it will be assumed that some aspects of human existence are of intrinsic value. Perhaps some people will think human life itself is intrinsically valuable. Others may think that it is not human life (in and of itself) that is intrinsically valuable. But rather it is certain aspects of a human life that are intrinsically valuable (e.g., it is the flourishing of a human life that is intrinsically valuable rather than the mere existence of a life).

Some people may consider many aspects of the non-human world to be of intrinsic value. And these people may draw the same distinction between the intrinsic value of non-human life itself versus the intrinsic value of aspects of non-human life (e.g., flourishing versus mere existence). Other people may consider no aspects of the non-human world to be of intrinsic value. Why a person may consider any of the above entities to have intrinsic value is a big question and addressing it is beyond the scope of this chapter. But nonetheless readers can reflect upon what they consider to be intrinsically valuable.

What has ethical standing?

Different people will consider different things to have ethical standing. This may or may not be related to their position on what is intrinsically valuable. Some people may consider that only humans have ethical standing. Some people may consider that some or all sentient organisms have ethical standing. Some people may consider that all living organisms have ethical standing. Some people may consider that ecosystems or features of a landscape such as rivers and mountains have ethical standing. And again, why a person may consider any of the above entities to have ethical standing is a big question and addressing it is beyond the scope of this chapter. But, again, readers can reflect upon what entities they themselves consider to have ethical standing.

What is the relationship between intrinsic value and ethical standing?

The answers to the previous two questions will be related to different worldviews. And people holding different worldviews will answer these two questions differently. While there are many different worldviews that are relevant here, including a broad range of religious and non-religious worldviews, two pairs of concepts are particularly relevant. These are the pair anthropocentrism/biocentrism and the pair shallow environmental ethics/deep environmental ethics.

One way to understand the first pair is with reference to intrinsic values. People who hold an anthropocentric worldview may recognise intrinsic value only in the human world, or perhaps prioritise the intrinsic values of the human world over any intrinsic values that they recognise in the non-human world. People who hold a biocentric worldview may recognise equal intrinsic value in all of life (or if not all of life, then a significant portion of non-human life).

One way to understand the second pair is with reference to ethical standing. People who endorse a shallow environmental ethic recognise the ethical standing of humans and acknowledge that humans depend upon the non-human world. Because of that dependence relation humans have an ethical responsibility to manage the non-human world for the sake of the humans, but not for the sake of the non-human world itself. People who endorse a deep environmental ethic recognise the ethical standing of all of life (or if not all of life, then a significant portion of non-human life) and because of that ethical standing, humans have a responsibility to interact with that portion of the non-human world ethically.

Different people hold different worldviews, and these different worldviews will inform each person's answer to the next question: what percentage of the biosphere should be appropriated for human use?

What percentage of the biosphere should be appropriated for human use?

Consider the question: what percentage of the biosphere should be appropriated for human use? The motivation for asking this question is simply to prompt reflection in the mind of the reader. Here two possible answers will be considered: (option 1) as close to 100% as possible, or (option 2) some percentage considerably less than 100%. The characterisation of option 1 simply acknowledges the fact that no human system of appropriation is totally efficient. So even if the aim was to appropriate 100% of the biosphere for human use that would not in fact be possible.

Why might a person choose option 1? One reason might be that a person assumes that humans are the only organisms that are of significance, and the presence of all other organisms only serves the interests and purposes of humans. It is important to note that the point of option 1 is not that 100% of all biomass is constituted by human beings, for context see Bar-on, Phillips and Milo (2018). But rather that all of the biosphere serves the interests and purposes of humans. There may be many plants and animals, but they are to be understood as only of instrumental value, and their instrumental value ultimately serves the interests of humans. Adopting option 1 could be taken to imply that a person acknowledges no intrinsic values other than those directly relating to human interests and purposes.

Now consider option 2: why might a person hold that humans should appropriate the biosphere at some percentage considerably below 100%? The answer might be that humans recognise significance in the non-human world, for example, intrinsic value or ethical standing. And this might imply to some humans that humanity, as a whole, should limit itself to some percentage of appropriation of the biosphere significantly less than 100%.

The appropriation question currently being considered refers to the biosphere as a whole. But that is not the only option. Two more specific questions can be asked: what percentage of the terrestrial biosphere should be appropriated for human use? and what percentage of the marine biosphere should be appropriated for human use? These two more specific questions are worth reflecting upon. Furthermore, are the answers to these questions the same or different? And if different, why are the different?

Perhaps a person considers the fact that humans are terrestrial animals relevant. Perhaps a person considers that appropriation of the terrestrial biosphere by humans can be justified in ways that the equivalent appropriation of the marine biosphere cannot be justified. This may relate to the concept of autonomy of some non-human realms. Some people may assume that some of the biosphere is not ours.

The answer to the question what percentage of the marine biosphere should be appropriated for human use? informs the answer to the question how green is the blue economy?

Thus, one dimension of the question how green is the blue economy? is how much of the marine biosphere should be left to be an end in itself. And importantly this issue is relevant even if some percentage of the marine biosphere is appropriated for human use because it relates to the overall scale of the blue economy. The other dimension of the question relates to the internal nature of the blue economy. Of the blue economy itself (i.e., that portion of the marine biosphere that has not been left to be an end in itself and perhaps has been domesticated) the question asks: how green is the internal nature of the blue economy?

To consider these two questions from a slightly different perspective, imagine a blue economy that is considered suitably green when considered from within, but then when the overall scale of the blue economy is considered, it is discovered that there is no part of the ocean that is not appropriated for human use, so effectively the blue economy has not left any of the ocean to be an end in itself or undomesticated. And this could be judged not to be sufficiently green because some of ocean should have been left outside of the blue economy, left undomesticated or undisturbed. A related issue is the identification of some parts of the ocean as wilderness (Barr and Kliskey 2014).

Case study: Seals and a fish farm

This case study is offered to provide concrete examples to further help the reader understand their own positions on the question: how green is the blue economy? The same case study can be used to reflect upon the question: what percentage of the ocean should be domesticated? And when considering this question, a spectrum can be considered. At one end of the spectrum is the position that 100% of the ocean should be domesticated, and at the other end is the position that 0% of the ocean should be domesticated. Both extreme ends of the spectrum are unrealistic for a number of reasons. But nonetheless this domestication spectrum serves a valuable purpose as a prompt for the reader's own reflection.

One issue that will continually need to be addressed in the blue economy is the interactions between human activity and the activity of wild animals. Consider the example of a fish farm that is located within the habitat of seals. Fish are a food source for seals and seals will engage in activity associated with seeking out and eating the fish.

The Tasmanian Government Seal Management Framework (2018: 2) notes that farming of Atlantic salmon and ocean trout began in Tasmania in the mid-1980s and is now the largest primary industry in the state. It also lists a number of issues that the framework is designed to manage including seals entering and interfering with fish containment pens, seals being trapped or entangled in marine farm infrastructure and risks to the wellbeing of both seals and marine farm staff as a result of the presence of seals in and around fish farms. All of this may result in reduced production of fish, injury to humans working on the farms, and injury to seals (either through their own actions, or as a result of actions taken by humans to deter the seals). So effective management of the interaction between human activity and the activity of seals is essential.

Any specific strategy to manage the interactions of seals with fish farming activity can be located on a spectrum of management strategies. Call this the management strategies spectrum to distinguish it from the domestication spectrum introduced above. At one end of the management strategies spectrum is a point at which only human interests are considered. At this end of the spectrum there would be no consideration given to animal welfare and so there would be no legal requirements to limit any action taken to control the activity of the seals. At this point of the spectrum there will be legal requirements, but these will be motivated by something other than animal welfare, such as human safety. Moving away from this end of the spectrum the welfare of animals will become relevant. At the point on the spectrum at which animal welfare becomes relevant animals are taken to be moral patients. As noted previously, moral patients are not expected to act morally, but moral agents, for example normal human adults, are expected to act morally toward them. Due to the seals status as moral patients (where their welfare must be taken into account for moral reasons), legislation may be put in place to ensure the welfare of the animals. Somewhere near this point on the spectrum is where the current management strategy is located.

But it is not the end of the spectrum. Positions further away still from the purely human priorities end of the management strategies spectrum are conceivable. These might consider not only the welfare of seals, where that welfare is taken to mean minimisation of harms related to the seals interactions with the farming infrastructure but might consider the rights of seals. Some may hold that not only do humans have a moral responsibility to attend to the welfare of animals, but humans also have a moral responsibility to attend to the rights of animals. What rights might seals have in relation to fish farms?

This issue can be understood in general terms by considering the example of sharks killing humans who swim in the ocean. When a shark is killing humans close to a popular swimming beach there are often two responses among humans. The first is to assume that the shark should be killed. However, the second is to assume that the shark should not be killed, because the shark has a right to be doing what it is doing. Hammerton and Ford (2018) use the comparison between the human right to leisure (included in Article 24 of the Universal Declaration of Human Rights (United Nations 1948)) and a species right to essential habitat. The specific details of the comparison are not of central importance here, rather the point is this: do humans have the right to stop other animals doing what those other animals naturally do when it is humans that are the ones entering the other animal's essential habitat?

This same issue can be recognised in the case of seals seeking to eat fish from fish farms. The equivalent question is: do seals have a right to seek to eat fish that are in the ocean? And if they do, what rights do humans farming fish in the ocean have to stop them? This may seem like a radical position, but this represents another position on the spectrum of management strategies. And perhaps the other end of the spectrum, not examined in detail here, is the position that humans are land animals and therefore should not be domesticating the ocean at all. Here it should be obvious that there are important parallels between the management strategy spectrum and the domestication of the ocean spectrum.

Consideration of both the management strategy spectrum and the domestication of the ocean spectrum is useful because it allows reflection on what locations on these spectra are green and highlights the fact that different people will have different assumptions about (1) what is green and (2) what is the appropriate position on these spectra for humans and human activity. And, as noted previously, even if the extreme ends of the spectra are not attractive to many, the description of those extreme ends is valuable as it serves to illustrate all possible positions.

Conclusion

In this chapter a number of conceptual resources have been presented and a range of questions have been asked, all in the service of addressing the central question: how green is the blue economy? The reader who has some knowledge of the nature of the blue economy will be able to use that knowledge in combination with the conceptual resources presented here to answer this central and important question.

References

Bar-on, Yinom M., Rob Phillips, and Ron Milo. 2018. 'The Biomass Distribution on Earth', *Proceedings of the National Academy of Sciences*, 115 (25), 6506–11.

Barr, Bradley W., and Andrew D. Kliskey. 2014. 'Perceptions of Wilderness and Their Application to Ocean and Coastal Waters', *Ocean and Coastal Management*, 96, 1–11.

Béné, Christophe. 2020. 'Resilience of Local Food Systems and Links to Food Security – a Review of Some Important Concepts in the Context of Covid-19 and Other Shocks', *Food Security*, 12, 805–22.

Callicott, J.B. 2001. 'The Land Ethic.' in Dale Jamieson (ed.), *A Companion to Environmental Philosophy* (Oxford: Blackwell), pp. 204–17.

Copp, David (eds.) 2006. *The Oxford Handbook of Ethical Theory*, (Oxford: Oxford University Press).

Davies, George Randal. 2013. 'Appraising Weak and Strong Sustainability: Searching for a Middle Ground', *Consilience: The Journal of Sustainable Development*, 10, 111–24.

Eswaran, H., R. Lal, and P.F. Reich. 2001. 'Land Degradation: An Overview.' In E. M. Bridges, I. D. Hannam, L. R. Oldeman, F. W.T. Penning de Vries, S. J. Scherr, S. Sombatpanit, R. N. Leslie, T. Compo and A. Prueksapong (eds.), *Response to Land Degradation* (Boca Raton, FL: CRC Press), pp. 20–35.

Feely, Richard A., Scott C. Doney, and Sarah R. Cooley. 2009. 'Ocean Acidification: Present Conditions and Future Changes in a High-Co$_2$ World', *Oceanography*, 22 (4), 37–47.

Figueroa, Robert, and Claudia Mills. 2001. 'Environmental Justice.' In Dale Jamieson (ed.), *A Companion to Environmental Philosophy* (Oxford: Blackwell), pp. 426–38.

Gallie, W.B. 1956. 'Essentially Contested Concepts', *Proceedings of the Aristotelian Society*, 56, 167–98.

Goodland, R. 2002. 'Sustainability: Human, Social, Economic and Environmental.' In T. Munn (ed.), *The Encyclopedia of Global Environmental Change* (New York: John Wiley and Son), pp. 174–96.

Hammerton, Zan, and Akkadia Ford. 2018. 'Decolonising the Waters: Interspecies Encounters between Sharks and Humans', *Animal Stuides Journal*, 7 (1), 270–303.

Hannah, Lee, David Lohse, Charles Hutchinson, John L. Carr, and Ali Lankerani. 1994. 'A Preliminary Inventory of Human Disturbance of World Ecosystems', *Ambio*, 23 (4/5), 246–50.

Holland, Alan. 2001. 'Sustainability.' in Dale Jamieson (ed.), *A Companion to Environmental Philosophy* (Oxford: Blackwell), pp. 399–401 27.

Hume, David. 1984. *A Treatise of Human Nature* (London: Penguin Books).

Lansing, J. Stephen. "Balinese "water temples" and the management of irrigation." *American anthropologist*, 89, no. 2 (1987): 326–341.

Kant, Immanuel. 1964. *Groundwork of the Metaphysics of Morals* (New York: Harper and Row).

Mackie, J.L. 1977. *Ethics: Inventing Right and Wrong* (London: Penguin).

Marra, John. 2005. 'When Will We Tame the Oceans', *Nature*, 436 (14 July), 175–76.

McMullin, Ernan. 2001. 'Values in Science.' in William H. Newton-Smith (ed.), *A Companion to the Philosophy of Science* (Oxford: Blackwell), pp. 550–60.

Meltzer, D. 2015. 'Pleistocene Overkill and North American Mammalian Extinctions', *Annual Review of Anthropology*, 44, 33–53.

Morozova, Galina S. 2005. 'A Review of Holocene Avulsions of the Tigris and Euphrates Rivers and Possible Effects on the Evolution of Civilisations in Lower Mesopotamia', *Geoarchaeology: An International Journal*, 20 (4), 401–23.

O'Neill, John. 2001. 'Meta-Ethics.' in Dale Jamieson (ed.), *A Companion to Environmental Philosophy* (Oxford: Blackwell), pp. 163–76 11.

Piperno, Dolores R., Crystal H. McMichael, Nigel C.A. Pitman, Juan Ernesto Guevara Andino, Marcos Ríos Paredes, Britte M. Heijink, and Luis A. Torres-Montenegro. 2021. 'A 5,000-Year Vegetation and Fire History for Tierra Firme Forests in the Medio Putumayo-Algodón Watersheds, Northeastern Peru', *Proceedings of the National Academy of Sciences*, 118, no. 40 (2021): 2022213118.

Sessions, George (eds.) 1995. *Deep Ecology for the Twenty-First Century*, (Boston: Shambhala).

Simmons, I.G. 1993. *Environmental History: A Concise Introduction* (Oxford: Blackwell).

Singer, Peter. 1993. *Practical Ethics* (Cambridge, UK: Cambridge University Press).

Smith-Godfrey, S. 2016. 'Defining the Blue Economy', *Maritime Affairs: Journal of the National Maritime Foundation of India*, 12 (1), 58–64.

Steffen, Will, Katherine Richardson, Johan Rockström, Sarah E. Cornell, Ingo Fetzer, Elena M. Bennett, Reinette Biggs, Stephen R. Carpenter, Wim de Vries, Cynthia A. de Wit, Carl Folke, Dieter Gerten, Jens Heinke, Georgina M. Mace, Linn M. Persson, Veerabhadran Ramanathan, Belinda Reyers, and Sverker Sörlin. 2015. 'Planetary Boundaries: Guiding Human Development on a Changing Planet', *Science*, 347, no. 6223 (2015): 1259855.

Tasmanian Government.·2018. *Seal Management Framework 2018: For the Mitigation of Seal Interactions with Aquaculture Staff and Infrastructure in Tasmania*, Parks Department of Primary Industries, Water and Environment (Hobart: Tasmanian Government), <https://dpipwe.tas.gov.au/Documents/Seal%20Management%20Framework.pdf> [Accessed 21 November 2021].

Thompson, W.I. 1989. *Imaginary Landscape. Making Worlds of Myth and Science* (New York: St Martin's Press).

United Nations. 1948. *Universal Declaration of Human Rights*, <https://www.un.org/sites/un2.un.org/files/udhr.pdf> [Accessed 4 November 2021].

Wood, Graham. 2019. 'Understanding Historical and Contemporary Ethics and Earth Ethics.' in Julia Grieves, Brian Adams and Emma Brindal (eds.), *Earth Ethics Australia* (Banyo, Australia: Australian Earth Laws Alliance), pp. 7–11.

World Commission on Environment and Development. 1987. *Our Common Future* (Oxford: Oxford University Press).

Sam Zak, Bailey Chappel, Connor Pilger, Bart Oor,
Theresa Theuretzbacher, Rebecca Truman and Brian von Herzen

Chapter 27
Finance approaches supporting social enterprise, non-profits and for-purpose organisations: A marine permaculture case study

Abstract: The Green Climate Fund has yet to raise even 15% of its funding target to meet initial objectives of the United Nations Sustainable Development Goals (SDGs). Funding solutions in carbon markets and public goods often requires non-traditional finance approaches. The Climate Foundation has leveraged non-profit finance over the past decade to support development and validation of marine permaculture design principles, a bold and visionary emerging field that can transform humanity's marine relationships from extraction to regeneration and help address climate change, the regenerative blue economy and sustainable development.

This chapter discusses a spectrum of opportunities to leverage capital for marine permaculture development. The three broad areas of funding opportunities discussed comprise philanthropy, emerging forms of decentralised finance, and more conventional forms of commercial fundraising. Also outlined are the advantages and disadvantages of each approach to commercialising sustainable solutions while ensuring that governance principles and the core mission remain. This narrative is based largely on the Climate Foundation's experience, including tech funding work from Silicon Valley advancing the development of marine permaculture. The chapter concludes with a summary of funding, noting the different forms of fundraising that are appropriate for different phases of innovation development.

Keywords: marine permaculture, regenerative finance, fintech, decentralised finance, blended finance, COVID-19

Introduction

Achieving the objectives outlined in the UN Sustainable Development Goals (SDGs) is a monumental challenge that requires engagement from economic and social sectors across the Global North and South. Crucially, investment is needed in potentially game-changing regenerative solutions that produce positive outcomes for nature and society, ensuring that both people and the planet can thrive. Given the challenges that incumbent companies face in changing their core business models

https://doi.org/10.1515/9783110733488-027

(Christensen 2013), delivering such solutions will likely be contingent upon new, smaller enterprises able to bring disruptive solutions to commercial scale. Unfortunately, such solutions are chronically underfunded by both government and private equity due to limited capacity to accept risk and, in part, because investors typically cannot capitalise on public goods and spill overs. Furthermore, funding to commercialise such innovations often comes at the cost of ceding control of the innovation itself, potentially compromising governance principles and possibly undermining the contribution to sustainable development.

The Climate Foundation is a non-profit 501c3 NGO formed in 2007 to research and develop economically sustainable models and market-transformative solutions that can contribute to sustainable development and are aligned with three core missions: 1) providing food security, 2) regenerating ecosystems, and 3) helping balance carbon. This chapter draws upon Dr Brian von Herzen's four decades of experience developing technological solutions in Silicon Valley and at the Climate Foundation developing ground-breaking sustainable solutions with a focus on marine permaculture.

Developing solutions such as marine permaculture is capital intensive and requires multi-million-dollar investments to achieve full potential. This chapter outlines best practices and identifies key opportunities for leveraging decentralised finance to advance innovations. These different forms of capital-raising range from small five-figure grants to investments of over one hundred million dollars.

The first section outlines marine permaculture trials to date, the long-term vision for this solution, and its potential contributions to sustainable development in reference to the SDGs.

The second section discusses philanthropic capital-raising from private foundations, big international NGOs, government grants and philanthropic crowdfunding, along with advantages and disadvantages of each approach, as well as the impact of COVID-19.

The third section identifies and explores emerging areas of decentralised finance identified alongside collaborators at 180 Degrees Consulting. Options related to raising capital from the crowd are explored, including philanthropic crowdfunding and reward-based crowdfunding, both of which are being considered to support the development of marine permaculture. Similarly, the potential of leveraging equity-based crowdfunding is compared with that of successful business ventures.

Finally, the fourth section reflects on conventional forms of funding and best practices for innovative companies seeking to contribute to sustainable development. Areas discussed include beneficent impact funding, angel investing, concessionary capital and catalytic capital combined with market rate capital. Also explored are licensing terms to ensure that governance principles remain intact even after substantial dilution by private investment, along with the promise of leveraging large amounts of capital, including public non-dilutive funding, through catalytic capital, project finance and social impact bonds.

Figure 27.1 displays a heatmap of different funding approaches for the development of marine permaculture relative to key criteria.

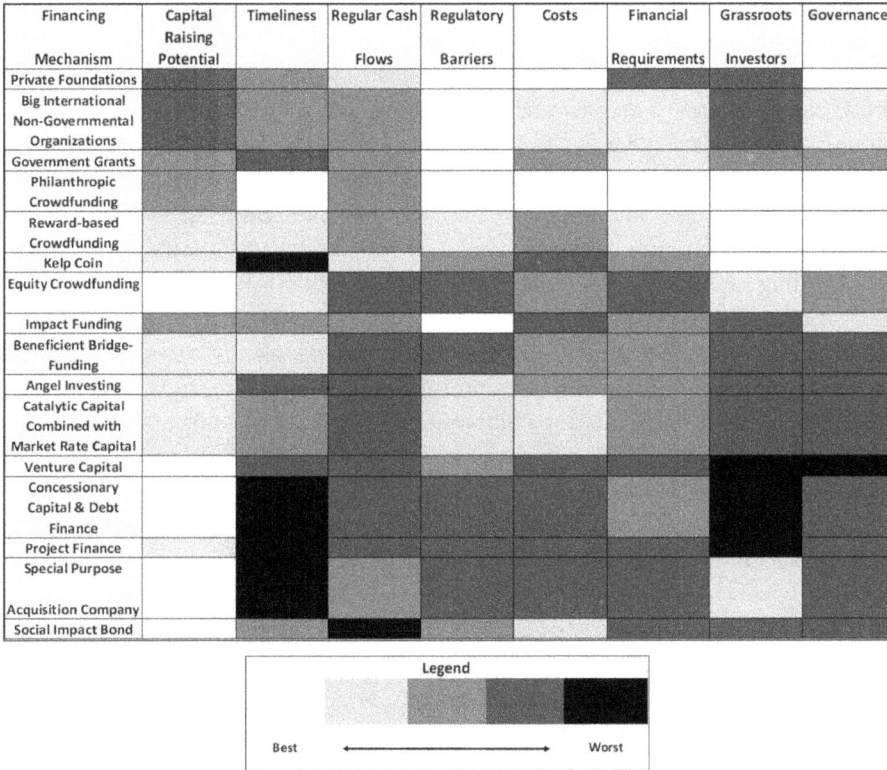

Financing Mechanism	Capital Raising Potential	Timeliness	Regular Cash Flows	Regulatory Barriers	Costs	Financial Requirements	Grassroots Investors	Governance
Private Foundations								
Big International Non-Governmental Organizations								
Government Grants								
Philanthropic Crowdfunding								
Reward-based Crowdfunding								
Kelp Coin								
Equity Crowdfunding								
Impact Funding								
Beneficient Bridge-Funding								
Angel Investing								
Catalytic Capital Combined with Market Rate Capital								
Venture Capital								
Concessionary Capital & Debt Finance								
Project Finance								
Special Purpose Acquisition Company								
Social Impact Bond								

Legend

Best ⟵——————⟶ Worst

Figure 27.1: Heatmap of fundraising approaches relative to key criteria.

The chapter concludes by summarising findings. This spectrum of fundraising options discussed may be useful for advancing other ground-breaking solutions for sustainable development.

Marine permaculture vision and contributions to sustainable development

Marine permaculture vision

Marine permaculture is a type of mariculture using the principles of permaculture to regenerate seaweed forests and other ecosystems offshore. By doing so, marine permaculture can contribute to sustainable development when implemented at scale. On a marine permaculture platform, renewable power enables irrigation of seaweed forests with cooler, nutrient-rich waters from between 100 and 500-metres depth. This irrigation mitigates marine heatwaves that have led to ocean stratification and decimated natural macroalgae ecosystems in many regions of the world (Thomsen et al. 2019; Straub et al. 2019; Wernberg et al. 2016). A submersible marine permaculture platform provides the substrate that seaweeds need to grow. Regenerating natural upwelling reduces mixed layer temperatures to levels closer to those measured pre-industrially. It thus comprises a form of deep-water irrigation, analogous to terrestrial irrigation but with water that is cooler and has higher nutrients than the surface mixed layer.

Marine permaculture platforms can also contribute to sustainable development by providing multiple ecosystem services and economic benefits through sustainable, marketable yields of fish and seaweeds. The technology is being designed for application in biomes ranging from tropical waters to temperate zones. The Climate Foundation has conducted trials around the world, including Hawaii, the US East Coast, Puerto Rico, Australia, the Philippines and Indonesia. Trials are being prioritised starting in regions with regulatory frameworks that facilitate seaweed cultivation and with low operational costs.

The long-term vision for marine permaculture is to establish a distributed network of community-owned platforms generating value and benefits throughout the population they serve, especially, but not exclusively, in developing regions. Hardware and intellectual property rights to build, operate and maintain marine permaculture platforms could be leased on reasonable terms to collaborating partners through a franchise model, for example, as has been done for numerous businesses around the world. Lease-to-own models could also be used. Each 100 hectares of marine permaculture would provide a regular harvest of seaweed and fish that would support more than a dozen families. Cooperatives could also own processing infrastructure such as biorefineries, to generate seaweed-based products and ensure that much of the revenue produced stays within the community.

Such a lease-to-own community-owned franchise model would depend upon a two-step strategy that would enable community projects to access marine permaculture development and improvements as needed. The first step is developing vertically integrated value chains to demonstrate and perfect the technology. Next is extending projects to other regions of the world through such models to enable marine permaculture to scale rapidly with many benefits distributed to the community. This model embodies some core principles championed by ecological economists, notably developing regenerative economic activity that aligns with natural systems and distributes returns across the value chain (Raworth 2017). Sustaining these core principles is key to achieving the equitable governance objectives for marine permaculture.

The first marine permaculture projects are likely to be deployed in Pacific coastal and Small Island Developing States. However, the technology is applicable to both industrialised and non-industrialised countries, both of which share a critical need for sustainable development and ecosystem regeneration. Indeed, sustainable development represents a goal all nations should strive for. New development frameworks, such as Kate Raworth's (2017) doughnut economics, combines the Stockholm Resilience Centre's planetary boundaries framework (Steffen et al. 2015) with a social foundation for what people need to lead to live a good life. As research from the University of Leeds has demonstrated (O'Neill et al. 2018), no country in the world has yet managed to achieve a balance of living within environmental limits while sustaining its population's wellbeing. Although the exact nature of countries' development needs differ, such findings reinforce Raworth's assertion that all are developing countries now (Horner 2019). Striving for balance also lies at the heart of the SDGs, which concern all countries of the world, all sectors of government, the private sector and civil society alike.

Contribution to sustainable development

If deployed at scale, the marine permaculture model developed by the Climate Foundation can make a meaningful contribution to most of the 17 SDGs (sustainabledevelopmentUN.org n.d.) and targets outlined by the United Nations in 2015. These contributions are summarised below.

SDG 2 Zero hunger

To meet the demands of a growing population, the Food and Agriculture Organisation of the United Nations (2017) estimates that by 2050, food production will need to increase 50% over 2012 baselines. Increased land use demands coupled with the need to protect land-based carbon sinks underscore the importance of marine productivity to achieving universal food security in this century. Indeed, the World Bank has endorsed macroalgae cultivation as a viable means of providing food security in tropical developing countries (Bjerregaard et al. 2016). Moreover, aquaculture is one of the fastest growing food sectors on the planet (Duarte et al. 2017), with macroalgae cultivation demonstrating significant growth rates of 8% per year (United Nations Food and Agriculture Organisation 2018). Marine permaculture can support this continued expansion, particularly in tropical climates by:
1. Expanding the production season with deep-water irrigation and bringing cultivation to offshore environments
2. Helping build climate resilience into conventional seaweed aquaculture by mitigating the impacts of marine heat waves that have decimated crops
3. Regenerating marine life and fish stocks, especially if marine permaculture arrays are strategically located near or within marine protected areas, for example, as demonstrated by seaweed projects by Coast 4C in the Philippines

4. Providing sustainable fodder for animal feed and fish meal; harvesting sea-weeds can free up land for human food production that would otherwise be devoted to livestock feed
5. Diversifying the food system, thereby building resilience to climate-related shocks (e.g., drought, flood, wildfire, disease, pest infestation)

SDG 3 Good health and wellbeing

As nutrient-rich superfoods, edible seaweeds provide multiple health benefits. Their widespread dietary uptake could contribute to global health and wellbeing. Several studies demonstrate that including small amounts of seaweed in diets may help improve cardiovascular health and reduce blood pressure (Hata et al. 2001; Wada et al. 2011; Houston 2014). Seaweed's high omega-3 polyunsaturated fatty acids DHA and EPA have also been found to benefit cognitive function (Stark et al. 2016) and improve symptoms of depression (Hallahan et al. 2016). Studies have also shown that adding seaweed supplements to animal feed can help improve animal health, reducing the need for antibiotics (Morais et al. 2020).

SDG 8 Decent work and economic growth, SDG 9 Industry, innovation and infrastructure and SDG 10 reduced inequalities

The High Level Panel for a Sustainable Ocean Economy has highlighted the seaweed revolution as a regenerative economic input and new industry with enormous growth opportunities for the blue economy (Stuchtey et al. 2020). This growth potential is reflected by the multiple end-uses for seaweeds, including food, animal feed, fertil-isers, hydrocolloids, nutraceuticals and cosmetics. Other emerging and potential products include bioplastics, fabrics and biofuels. Such alternatives embody princi-ples of responsible production and consumption that are critical to the sustainable economy. For example, using seaweed in bio stimulants and bio-fertilisers can also support the sustainable intensification of agriculture while closing the nitrogen cycle. This intervention, in turn, can help reduce and remediate oceanic dead-zones caused by fertiliser runoff (Neveux et al. 2018). Similarly, short-lived biodegradable bioplastics offer a sustainable replacement for single-use plastics.

Marine permaculture codesign and optimisation with coastal communities will accelerate innovation while enabling the communities to retain more of the rewards of their efforts. Marine permaculture can help promote economic diversification, in-troduce new opportunities and, with integrated government planning, establish a new industrial base. These economic opportunities can help reduce intra-country inequalities commonly found between cities and rural and coastal areas in develop-ing and developed countries.

SDG 13 climate action

As noted above, many seaweed derived products can mitigate climate change by displacing high-carbon-intensity products with lower intensity seaweed alternatives. Marine permaculture not only fixes carbon, but also sequesters it. Seaweeds shed biomass as they grow, much of it sequestered permanently in sediment or within the deep ocean throughout welling of carbon export (Krause-Jensen and Duarte 2016; Santos et al. 2021; Ortega, Geraldi, and Duarte 2020). Furthermore, residual seaweed from creating seaweed-based products can be sunk into the middle and deep ocean as a blue carbon sink. Attributing the sequestered carbon to the products and services generated by the seaweed could enable creation of carbon negative, climate-positive products and services.

Once at scale, marine permaculture contributes to climate adaptation by mitigating ocean warming, marine heatwaves and their associated detrimental impacts on seaweed production and seaweed ecosystems. On some islands in Indonesia, seaweed production decreased by 60% between 2016 and 2017 due to ice-ice syndrome associated with marine heat waves caused by climate warming (Hunt 2021). Introducing deep-water irrigation could mitigate such extreme events while boosting productivity and enabling year-round cultivation. To date, the Climate Foundation's trials cultivating the red seaweed *Kappaphycus spp.* have demonstrated dramatically increased growth in comparison to control trials, as shown in Figure 27.2.

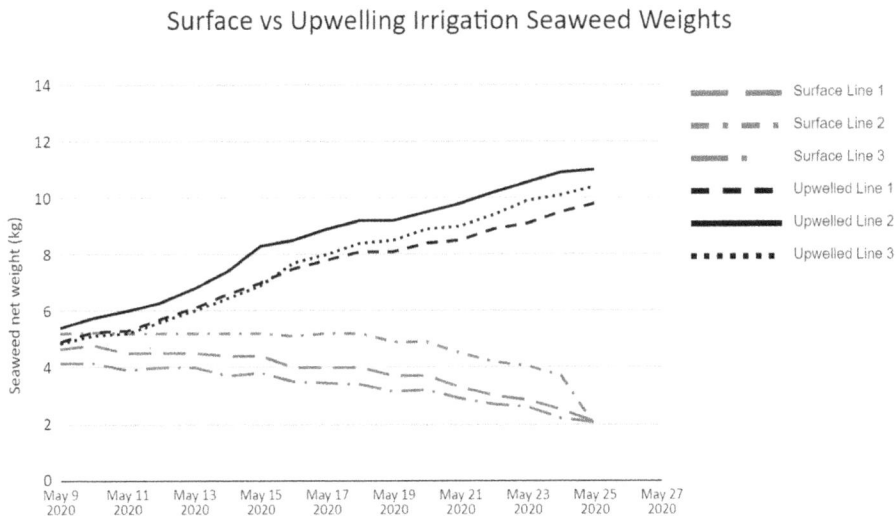

Figure 27.2: *Kappaphycus spp.* net weights with irrigation from surface water between May 9th and May 27th, 2020. From Climate Foundation trials in the Philippines.

SDG 14 Life Below water

Marine permaculture ecosystem services improve life below water. The benefits to local marine life of replicating natural seaweed forests offshore include locally reduced ocean acidification and eutrophication through photosynthesis (Buschmann et al. 2017; Krause-Jensen et al. 2018; Duarte et al. 2017). Moreover, marine permaculture arrays can provide habitat and nurseries for juvenile fish, supporting the regeneration of marine life (Buschmann et al. 2017; Vásquez et al. 2013; Campbell et al. 2019). Strategic staffed presence of marine permaculture alongside Marine Protected Areas can further ensure the protection of these areas and maximise their benefits through spill overs.

Philanthropic capital

Philanthropic capital can be raised from high-net-worth individuals and associated private foundations, big international non-governmental organisations (BINGOs), public grants and social-media-enabled crowdfunding. Securing capital from any of these sources poses some challenges. Nonetheless, these streams can be invaluable to drive research and development and can even enable commercialisation.

Private foundations

Private foundations can provide early, non-dilutive research and development capital to advance innovation. Smaller foundations in particular, are often more open to investing in yet-to-be-proven approaches or those that carry a higher level of risk. Furthermore, obtaining philanthropic funding can be less bureaucratic and more expeditious than government funding processes. A less resource-intensive process works well for typically lean innovation organisations.

Effective working relationships between the funding source and recipient can result in a relatively stable, low-cost funding stream with less constraint on the use of funds for the innovation. Moreover, should sufficient capital be provided, philanthropic funding can enable the social enterprise to achieve commercialisation and economic self-sufficiency without having to access conventional equity markets. Thus supported, the social enterprise remains wholly owned by collaborating partners, retaining its governance principles and ensuring maximum impact on sustainable development.

In contrast, it is also not unusual for private foundation funding to be intermittent, requiring supplemental capital resources. The intermittency can be exacerbated by external shocks that limit funding capacity or redirect priorities to more pressing issues. This has been the case for many NGOs as a result of the COVID-19 pandemic and the global financial crisis that began in 2008. Maintaining intermittent funding may require more give-and-take on project priority and direction between the source and recipient.

Big international non-governmental organisations (BINGOs)

Grants provided by BINGOs, particularly those with a focus on sustainable development and conservation, can give projects a substantial boost. These funding organisations often have access to significant capital resources. Winning grants from BINGOs with high name recognition can attract positive publicity and serve as validation of the innovation. Being connected with a BINGO can also enhance networking with both private funders and government project managers controlling significant capital or administering exclusive programmes. BINGOs can also serve as powerful convening bodies able to assemble groups of relevant stakeholders to tackle key issues around a specific area, which can further boost the organisation's profile and the innovation being developed.

Though they have advantages, BINGOs often have been slow to support unproven technologies or approaches even if they have transformational potential, particularly if the outcome is uncertain or possibly comes with unintended consequences. For instance, multiple proposals aiming to protect coral reefs from thermally induced photobleaching – an existential threat given that two degrees of warming will essentially eliminate coral reefs (Hoegh-Guldberg et al. 2018) have not raised funding from large international conservation organisations due to the headline risk of adverse side-effects. Consequently, other projects are often selected due to lower risk and higher likelihood of success. As a result, financing ambitious projects is challenging due to risk profiles and the absence of innovation financing.

Specific mandates to select BINGO projects for funding can also be a challenge as funding categories often focus on specific issues, leading to siloed programme objectives and single-purpose projects. Projects such as marine permaculture, with moderate-to-high impact across multiple SDGs, can fail to receive high scores when they are not credited for benefits spread across several programme areas. This silo effect makes it difficult to secure funding for integrated, multi-disciplinary and transformational solutions. The same reductionist limitations can also occur within larger private foundations with entrenched bureaucracies. Furthermore, winning BINGO grants requires substantial time and effort upfront to establish connections and prepare detailed applications, and thereafter, to maintain relationships and submit regular data and reports on progress and outcomes.

Government grants

Compared to the philanthropic funding mechanisms discussed above, government grants can offer larger blocks of funding. However, they also tend to have the most competitive and complex application and selection processes. Moreover, governments need to justify spending public money. Application processes often require matching private funds and/or partnerships with academic research institutions. Regular and detailed progress reports are typically required and impose a significant administrative burden. Calls for proposals for relevant programmes can be intermittent, making it necessary to monitor and pursue multiple funding streams for a single project.

Smaller government grant programmes tend to be risk averse, while some larger innovation grants can be forward-looking and aim to implement transformative change. Indeed, the Climate Foundation has received substantial grants from a number of bodies including AgriFutures Australia, US Fish and Wildlife Service, and the Australian government's Department of Foreign Affairs and Trade's Blue Economy Challenge. These transformation-oriented grants can drive innovation in areas that the private sector would not fund. For instance, the US' Advanced Research Projects Agency – Energy was set up to research promising new ideas for bolstering US energy security, which includes the MARINER programme devoted to exploring all aspects of growing macroalgae for biofuels, including cultivating seaweed at scale offshore. The size of the grants is a major advantage of the programme. Amounts generally range from half a million to five million dollars. Such funding is released in multiple stages to support early technology readiness level innovations that private sector funders typically consider too high-risk. Public grants can also serve to de-risk investment, thereby helping crowd-in investment from private sector sources both during the innovation stage and later once the innovation has been validated (Mazzucato 2021). Government funding can, therefore, help deliver the ground-breaking innovation sustainable development requires to scale as discussed below.

Philanthropic crowdfunding

Philanthropic crowdfunding is a relatively new form of capital-raising, enabling organisations to raise thousands of small donations from a diverse range of supporters. Capital can be raised through one-off campaigns or from repeat donors who support the work of the organisation on a subscription basis. The Climate Foundation has run two successful crowdfunding campaigns to support marine permaculture. Together they raised over AU\$1 million, greatly exceeding initial goals.

A number of core factors contributed to the success of these campaigns. First, campaign partners are critically important. In the Australian crowdfunding effort conducted from April to November 2019, the Climate Foundation, its partners, and the impact production team from the Australian documentary *2040* (2019) each played a key role providing the campaign credibility, visibility and support. Corporate matching was key to the campaign. The prospect of a dollar-for-dollar match for their contribution was a major incentive for donors. The University of Tasmania also provided academic support for the project, indicating that it was in the public interest. Finally, the *2040* documentary film, which featured marine permaculture as one of five key solutions, was a core marketing and publicity element of the campaign. The film's striking video materials, empowering narrative, and call to action conveyed marine permaculture's potential when implemented at scale and inspired thousands of viewers to contribute. Short video excerpts created by the production team proved to be particularly effective on social media, especially on platforms like Twitter and Facebook. Moreover, anchoring the campaign in a specific location and pledging to solve a specific problem, the disappearance of seaweed forests in Australia, helped the campaign resonate with people throughout the country. Support in social media from respected figures such as environmental entrepreneur Paul Hawken and environmental activist Bill McKibben expanded the campaign's reach and increased its impact. Overall, the Climate Foundation found that combining a bold climate solution with key supporters and impactful media and publicity can produce inspirational and successful philanthropic crowdfunding campaigns.

The Climate Foundation's philanthropic crowdfunding experience has resulted in positive outcomes. However, developing a campaign that generates widespread interest from thousands of supporters requires substantial investment in public relations. The proliferation of online crowdfunding campaigns has brought scaling, with some platforms offering to host and run campaigns. Engaging with such services can be risky, as the crowdfunding campaign might fail to meet its goals but could involve substantial cost and time investment to conduct. Furthermore, given the public exposure and active engagement with donors, philanthropic crowdfunding campaigns pose some reputational risk if the project fails to meet its objectives.

Online subscription platforms that generate regular payments to digital content creators are another form of philanthropic crowdfunding with potential to help NGOs leveraging technology for sustainable development. The platforms were originally developed to help creative content providers with extra income that may complement other revenue. A notable example is Patreon, which launched in 2013. Patreon clients, called patrons, set membership tiers with different, but moderately priced levels to which content followers subscribe. The platform is widely used by musicians, artists, writers, journalists and video content creators and has enjoyed rapid growth in popularity and revenue generation, which has increased exponentially since 2017, almost doubling for four consecutive years (Conte 2020).

While the majority of revenues on such platforms are generated by creative artists (Dean 2021), a number of NGOs are registered on Patreon. The platform enables donors to make regular small contributions to these organisations. The key to successfully using this platform is for NGOs to provide regular, engaging content for each tier of supporters. Such content should include progress updates, new developments, milestones met, media coverage and messaging that gives subscribers the sense that their donations are helping the NGO meet its objectives. However, a challenge is to design and support tiered levels of content that are satisfying to contributors at each level. Furthermore, similar to the philanthropic crowdfunding discussed previously, the subscription model requires activities different from and in addition to those devoted to the NGO's core mission, in contrast to content creators receiving payments for their core work.

Distributed finance

This section draws upon the Climate Foundation's collaboration with partners from 180-Degrees Consulting Australia and others who have helped identify distributed near to medium-term funding opportunities for marine permaculture. Emerging financial technology development, also known as fintech, aims to transform many traditional methods of delivering financial services. The possibilities of fintech innovation are vast and complex in their suitability across industries. As shown in Table 27.1, the multiple forms of crowdfunding outlined provide particularly effective and simple opportunities to raise capital over time.

Table 27.1: Potential crowdfunding rewards to incentivise donations.

Potential rewards	Description
Early Updates and previews	Regular, multi-media reports providing the latest news, updates and next steps will generate a sense of involvement with the project.
Seaweed products	Providing supporters with seaweed products.
Ecotourism trips to the platform	Allowing supporters to visit a marine permaculture array and potentially dive on the site.
Kelp Coin (outlined in detail below)	Providing supporters above a threshold with Kelp Coin as an incentive represents a reward that can mature in value over time.
Discounts	Giving supporters a small, one-time family and friends discount to any products produced in the future. Furthermore, involving family and friends, will introduce more people to the cause.

Reward-based crowdfunding

Reward-based crowdfunding solicits donors to fund individuals, projects or organisations in exchange for non-monetary rewards such as products or services. It is increasingly being used to finance innovative technology programmes. A prominent example of successfully using reward-based crowdfunding is the seaweed-based food company Akua (Republic.co 2021). This enterprise raised over US 1 million through a crowdfund campaign to create a kelp-burger, by promising to send backers seaweed burgers once the company was commercially established. This crowdfunding option can run parallel with or replace equity crowdfunding or other fundraising strategies, while simultaneously supporting marketing efforts overall.

As with philanthropic crowdfunding, the success of such campaigns is dependent on developing an effective implementation strategy that encompasses effective marketing, engaging digital content, good timing and the support of influential backers.

Decentralised finance and blockchain security

Blockchain technology has significant potential for use by NGOs to support their social missions (Novak 2018). The distributed, peer-to-peer nature of transactions can improve organisational transparency, reduce intermediation costs and liabilities, and ultimately raise significant capital. Such technology can also help NGOs access a network of like-minded people who are keen to support the development of regenerative innovations and ideas. For example, several cryptocurrencies, such as SEEDS, Athana, Zilliqa, and others, are designed to provide returns to community projects and projects supporting organisations implementing regenerative solutions. Blockchain tokens can be designed to be ecologically sustainable by reducing energy input costs by orders of magnitude relative to first generation blockchains. By participating in an established blockchain network, NGOs can access a wider audience and increased potential for investment in their projects.

Using blockchain to issue digital tokens is a potentially fruitful project development approach for marine permaculture. One concept being explored by the Climate Foundation is Kelp Coin®. Kelp Coin tokens represent forward contracts on a tonne of living kelp forest growing on a marine permaculture platform. Each tonne represents a fixed quantity of carbon, which is the asset to which the token value is pegged. Early vintage Kelp Coins were launched at an initial valuation of USD 100, with pricing updates over time to reflect market trends.

Kelp Coins differ from traditional cryptocurrencies that have no inherent value and are not tied to any assets. Additionally, the owner of the Kelp Coin retains a certain control over the one tonne of kelp to which it is linked. For example, the owner may choose to sink the seaweed, at which point the seaweed would become retired and converted into a recognised carbon offset, once suitable methodologies are in place. The Climate Foundation intends for mature tokens to be traded on networks to connect purchasers of carbon offset or ecosystem service credits with suppliers, such as Nori or Regen Networks. Alternatively, the coin could mature and act as an investment vehicle once the seaweed has been purchased by a buyer or traded on the blockchain. Hence, there is significant optionality for the investor, who can choose to pursue capital gains, promote environmental sustainability and purchase seaweed, all from a singular token. The Kelp Coin forward-contract model can also enable direct financing of marine permaculture projects. With an anticipated Kelp Coin maturity of 48 months, new projects can be financed and launched in advance of third-party validation of the kelp forest biomass growing on the platforms.

The development of the Kelp Coin poses both benefits and challenges. Maintaining and managing blockchain ledgers represents an ongoing commitment. Multiple economic, financial and technological risks need to be acknowledged, with cybersecurity a key distinguishing feature of well-designed blockchains (Gurdgiev and Fleming In press). There are also considerable regulatory and legal confines that must be considered (Nguyen et al. 2021).

Kelp Coin offers substantial benefits beyond the ability to raise capital. Kelp Coin would likely attract strong marketing attention to Climate Foundation projects, and to marine permaculture technology overall. Introducing a new, participatory way of funding natural capital could gain the attention of grassroot supporters, especially given the recent surge in popularity of cryptocurrencies. The reasonable buy-in price of Kelp Coin would also enable community-level participation. Indeed, a small-scale trial undertaken with little, if any publicity, has so far resulted in the issuance of numerous Kelp Coins validating the initial grassroots interest.

Kelp Coin could also serve as a token of gratitude issued to voluntary collaborators helping to develop marine permaculture, comparable to how music festivals provide festival season passes in gratitude to voluntary collaborators that help organise, assemble, operate and dismantle an entire ecovillage for tens of thousands of participants each year. For example, the Woodford Folk Festival (2020) recruits thousands of volunteers every year to help build, run and dismantle their village.

There is great potential for a whole ecosystem of products to be generated from marine permaculture arrays operating at scale. Such high-value, seaweed derived products include, cosmetics, bio-fertilisers and seafoods that could be offered for purchase at a discount when Kelp Coin is used in the transaction. Supporters might also be engaged in a loyalty programme that rewards the purchase and use of Kelp Coin.

Finally, there is growing interest in seaweed for economic uses among large organisations. Such uses require large and reliable supplies of biomass, and the Kelp Coin could be used to help meet that demand through a forward-contract supply offering. The Climate Foundation could seek investment in marine permaculture technology via the Kelp Coin blockchain, and in return offer a consistent, large and discounted future seaweed supply.

Equity crowdfunding

Once an innovation approaches commercialisation, equity crowdfunding can be used to launch a for-profit enterprise. Equity-based crowdfunding emerged in the early 2000s and is expanding today in several countries. Equity crowdfunding enables ventures to leverage investment from the crowd comprising hundreds to thousands of non-accredited investors. These investors are motivated to support budding initiatives but do not meet the standard income threshold for traditional offerings. Typically, they are more interested in funding innovations they believe in, rather than generating a significant return on their investment.

An equity crowdfunding offering can promise future equity to investors should the company do well in the future. For example, a simple agreement for future equity (SAFE) note gives investors a right to future equity without setting the price per share at the time of the initial investment. Numerous online equity crowdfunding platforms are available for equity crowdfunding, which generally charge a flat fee to launch a crowd-funder and a commission on the capital raised. Such platforms have varying degrees of reach in terms of the network benefit of the online platform. See Table 27.2 for a comparison of two main crowdfunding platforms used in Australia. Many platforms have similar offerings, including developing and supporting marketing campaigns.

To date, a number of environmentally driven companies seeking to contribute to sustainable development have successfully leveraged equity crowdfunding platforms to support their development. The company Oddbox (Seedrs 2018), which aims to reduce food waste in the UK, raised over GBP 500,000 in 2018. Similarly, C-Combinator (WeFunder 2021), a seaweed company aiming to turn sargassum into high-value products, raised over USD 300,000 through equity crowdfunding in the US. Such platforms enable startups to raise large amounts of capital relatively quickly without conceding too much control of the venture to investors. For instance, at the time of this writing Australian regulations cap equity crowdfunding at AUD 5 million although it is only open to companies with gross assets of no more than AUD 25 million. As with other types of crowdfunding, success is dependent on marketing campaigns to generate excitement and support. Effective strategies may include elements of reward-based

Table 27.2: Comparing Australia's two most widely used equity-based crowdfunding platforms: Equitise and OnMarket.

EC platform	Background (size, experience, etc.)	Application process/ eligibility	Fees	Support (e.g., advertising, legal, etc.)
Equitise	*(Aus and NZ)* Database of 50,000 investors, 86% success rate, average raise of $500k, 6 years exp	5-minute expression of interest before contact to create a plan. Send in a business plan and website link and they research	$2,500$10k upfront for marketing & launch, 6% commission on capital	Boost campaign, support after capital goal with market leading share registry and secondary market services
OnMarket	Currently the most successful campaign in Aus ($2.1mill for DC Power) Same strategy as Equitise	1) Register interest 2) OnMarket performs Due Diligence process 3) Building campaign 4) Going out to crowd	$10k establishment fee for marketing & launch, 7.5% commission on capital	Support in developing campaign, mapping out marketing and promotion plans and management of shareholders

crowdfunding by offering perks to investors, such as promises to receive future products, as was done by Akua and C-Combinator.

The downside of using equity crowdfunding platforms is inherent uncertainty. Given crowdfunding's public nature, the potential for raising future money from a platform's crowd may be exhausted should an initial campaign be unsuccessful. Conversely, successful campaigns can lead to multiple raises over many years, allowing companies to bypass other funding approaches. Even established companies might incorporate equity crowdfunding in their overall funding strategy not only to raise capital, but also to engage with customers and build the company's brand. The craft brewery Brewdog has run over eight equity raises (Stoller 2020). A recent campaign raised over GBP 30 million with the objective of helping the company improve its environmental performance and become carbon negative. As well as selling equity in the company, Brewdog aims to build a sense of community among its over 120,000 small-time investors and to turn them into brand ambassadors (Stoller 2020), by offering discounts on products and through invitations to annual general meetings (Brewdog 2021). While such approaches remain relatively new, they nonetheless reflect the possibility of using alternative platforms to raise significant amounts of capital, while building a community of supporters around social enterprises for sustainable development.

Conventional and hybrid forms of funding focussing on sustainable development

The following section outlines more conventional forms of funding and hybrids available to startups with reflections on best practices to ensure that core governance and missions of startups focussed on long-term sustainable impact remain in place through the commercialisation process.

Impact funding

Impact funding is a form of financing that foundations and investors provide to startups under the condition that the funding amounts be reimbursed. Typically, this is in the form of a recoverable grant whereby the money invested is expected to be paid back at a later date once the innovation has been licensed and is generating revenues. In some contexts, this kind of financing is considered philanthropic and is tax deductible. Although the expectation that the grant will have to be repaid is a disadvantage, such funding provides a benefit in that there are few constraints placed into the contract so that the governance principles are not compromised.

Beneficent bridge funding

Beneficent bridge funding is a fintech innovation created by the Climate Foundation. Under this model, funders would provide a grant to a non-profit organisation developing solutions for sustainable development. The funding would support the research and development of innovations that could prove to be economically sustainable and licensable. Given that the contribution is provided to a non-profit research institute, the grant would be tax deductible in year zero of the investment. Later, should the research be successful, the technology could be licensed to a startup enterprise able to accept equity investment. At that point, impact funders could be invited to a seed round of equity investment in a company commercialising the technology. As conceived, Beneficent bridge™ funding provides impact funders with an immediate tax deduction for research with public impact, depending on their specific jurisdiction, and potential for future investment in an industry commercialising an innovation that contributes to achieving SDGs.

Angel investing

Angel investment is typically sought in the innovation's startup phase when risks of failure are high and prospects for returns are low. The prospect of future fundraising rounds diluting equity shares makes commercial investors unwilling to provide startup support. Angel investing has been growing in popularity in recent years and is commonplace in Silicon Valley, where a number high-net worth individuals opt to invest their own money in innovative companies they believe in. It is not uncommon for startups to engage in a mentorship with angel investors, who are often retired entrepreneurs. Investment amounts depend on the angel investor. Angels at times are willing to take early stage risks on investments that are still being qualified by venture capitalists.

The downsides of angel investing are similar to those of philanthropic funding from foundations. Relationships can be difficult to manage, and it is not easy for transformative solutions to fit into the various investment silos in which angels are seeking to invest. Investment capital was less available during the pandemic, however, the pandemic shift towards meeting and interacting digitally has resulted in investors increasingly backing startups without having met the founders in person. This trend has created greater opportunities for internationally based teams. As with working remotely, this trend is likely to continue in the years ahead.

Catalytic capital combined with market rate capital

Catalytic capital combined with market rate capital, as is being pioneered by the Azolla Fund (Prime Coalition n.d.), for example, also holds promise to help fund innovative ideas for sustainable development. The fund is named after the Azolla event, the period in geological history 49 million years ago when an aquatic fern is believed to have sequestered over a thousand gigatons of carbon dioxide from the atmosphere in about 800,000 years (Brinkhuis et al. 2006). It aims to finance and scale mission-oriented startups for sustainable development that could have a leading impact on climate change and transition to the low-carbon economy (Prime Coalition n.d.).

There are two phases to Azolla Fund financing. The first involves catalytic capital, that is, capital provided at higher risk than would be normally acceptable to venture capital (VC) funds. The catalytic capital is leveraged from philanthropic funders and is only provided to high-risk investments with potential for ground-breaking impacts. Depending on the startup, this might also involve a concessionary rate of return to investors. Once these startups have reached sufficient maturity, the fund then provides market rate capital, that is, capital provided with market rate expectation of risk and returns to enable companies in the catalytic stage to become venture-fundable through a Series A funding round. The Azolla Fund was prototyped by the Prime

Impact Fund with over a dozen investments. Such funds could represent improvement over traditional approaches to VC scaling of startups for sustainable development.

Venture capital

VC is usually one of the early outside sources of equity for startups striving to reach commercialisation (La Rocca, La Rocca, and Cariola 2011). Especially in the early stages, venture capitalists advise the company, providing financial and business guidance (Fluck 2000). A startup's long-term goals should be well aligned with the objectives of the venture capitalists to assure that mission and governance objectives and principles underpinning transformative innovations can be maintained. This section outlines what these risks are and what measures might be taken to avoid them, to ensure that the governance principles remain in place.

Late-stage investors abound in the VC world today. There may be a dozen late-stage investment groups for every early stage lead investor or seed firm. Many ground-breaking innovations for sustainable development find it difficult to obtain funding from VC funds that perceive the startup as too high-risk or that they would be unable to capitalise on spill overs and public goods produced. As a result, potentially transformative or disruptive solution startups must seek out early stage VC firms willing to lead a round. Many impact investors simply check the box on impact, while expecting a market rate of return on investment. At the same time, high-impact innovations with a deep technology stack, such as marine permaculture, are more difficult for due diligence teams to assess for risk without deep in-house technical expertise. These challenges increase a perception of high-risk. Should the innovation reach a point at which it is ready to be funded by VC, maintaining the original governance principles and core objectives of the at purpose enterprise can be a challenge. Investors increase their ownership role in the enterprise during commercialisation and expansion funding that may occur over several rounds. A possible result is that investors gain increasing authority over startup governance (Goldstein 2018), a result that can lead to dilution of governance principles.

Dilution of startup governance control is a real issue; however, it is still possible to protect the fundamental principles to ensure that transformative impact objectives for sustainable development remain in place. For example, establishing a public benefit corporation with triple bottom line principles directly in its constitution offers a legal mechanism to protect the principles throughout capital raises and changes in leadership (benefitcorp.net n.d.). The public benefit or B-Corp approach provides directors and officers authority to consider the interest of all stakeholders, including employees and customers and the environment. This authority is perhaps one of the least controversial ways of ensuring the triple bottom line of people, planet and profit is addressed. This approach is relatively straightforward for newly established organisations, but could require existing organisations to amend their constitutional documents (Marquis 2020).

Another approach to protect governance principles is to create a golden share or even two classes of shares; voting and non-voting or shares that have very different levels of voting rights. This was done by the company Alphabet as a means of ensuring that insiders maintained governance even with a minority interest (Duggan 2021). Similarly, Berkshire Hathaway created two classes of shares in 1996, with class B shares having 1/10,000th of the voting rights of class A shares. This ensured that like-minded shareholders with the long-term interest of the company at heart maintained a commanding position. Adopting such an approach could help ensure that investors whose interests are aligned with the founding principles of the company have a commanding control over the company's direction.

Concessionary capital and government debt finance

Concessionary capital is a form of investment typically associated with growing, revenue-producing enterprises that are more mature and have a lower level of risk. The investors are willing to accept a below-market rate of return and/or a smaller share of equity for a capital project that has clear social or ecological benefits. With lower expectations for return, investors are more patient and have longer payback horizons. In some cases, concessionary capital can be provided by impact angel investors with regenerative objectives, however, it is often provided by government agencies who recognise the social benefits of investments.

Government or national bank backed loan guarantees can be a source of concessionary interest rate debt finance for large projects. Often, when untested innovations that are high-risk but could provide significant public benefits enter the market, government loan guarantees can mitigate the private sector's hesitancy to back such projects. Typically, these projects require high levels of capital, in the hundreds of millions. Often, a condition for obtaining government loan guarantees is that companies or projects contribute to meeting national objectives through their value propositions. The US Department of Energy's loan guarantee programme, which has provided over USD 40 billion in loans and loan guarantees (US Department of Energy n.d.-a), supports projects directed toward improving national energy security and sovereignty.

Many governments provide loan guarantees to projects that help meet core SDGs. In Europe, for example, it is common for governments to provide loan guarantees to banks, who will then loan funds for social purpose and outcomes projects. Often, receiving such a government backed loan guarantee requires external validation such as having first obtained another subsidy or grant previously. The federal government serving as guarantor in the event of failure has the effect of unlocking private capital to finance key projects needed to achieve societal goals. With assurances from central government agencies that losses will be underwritten if the company files for bankruptcy, private sector lenders, such as large banks, are more likely to issue loans to potentially risky projects. These programmes enable projects to secure potentially large amounts of debt capital at a concessionary rate and protect the core mission of the innovation.

Government programmes also exist that provide direct loans as opposed to loan guarantees. A notable example is the automotive company Tesla, which received a loan of USD 465 million from the US Department of Energy (US Department of Energy n.d.-b) during the early years when it was struggling to attract capital from private funders (Mazzucato 2021). Academics such as Mariana Mazzucato argue that the public sector can at times be surprisingly entrepreneurial given its key role in financing and driving many ground-breaking innovations, including the technology behind the worldwide web and the iPhone (Mazzucato 2011). They further argue that the public sector should behave more like venture capitalists and be far more muscular in directing and funding innovation to resolve tough societal challenges for which innovation is chronically underfunded. A variety of public funding programmes are available for transformational innovations, such as Horizon Europe and the European Innovation Council. These programmes aim to invest in high-risk areas that could transform the European economy. Programmes such as these are often very well-funded and have objectives that are in line with sustainable development. The downside is that competition for funding is fierce and there is often a need to build a broad coalition of different institutions, such as universities from multiple countries, in order to qualify. This complicates the application process and may contribute to mission creep or changing the project scope to align with coalition partner priorities.

Project finance

Project finance provides a means to leverage greater funding by attaching research and development for innovations to larger, technology implementation projects already established and funded by banks and private equity. For example, a multibillion-dollar investment to implement a one-gigawatt solar energy project might have 1020% set aside for pilot scale demonstration of more advanced technology, such as aquatic solar. The payback on the project is secured through the established technology, however, the set aside funded project provides further technical incentive and potential for future positive returns. The research and development aspect of the commercial project justifies marketing it as having new and innovative characteristics. Put colloquially, it can be the sizzle that sells the steak. Furthermore, once the new technology is validated at pilot scale, it can be more readily financed for larger scale development.

Marine permaculture development could benefit from a different coupling of project finance objectives, for example, combining offshore mariculture projects with the decommissioning of oil rigs. Depending on location, the cost of decommissioning an oil rig, which involves capping wells and partially or completely removing the structure, ranges from the millions to billions of dollars. A re-envisioned decommissioning project could incorporate offshore mariculture trials, renewable energy systems and finfish aquaculture. Repurposing the oil rig could save money on decommissioning and give new life to materials destined for scrap while also creating economic opportunity and potentially retaining jobs. Operations could be taken up by cooperatives with key research and development assets to advance innovation in sustainable development. A successful model could then be scaled to decommissioning projects around the world.

Special purpose acquisition company

Special purpose acquisition companies (SPAC) are publicly held investment vehicles created to merge with a company, and thereby bring it public. SPACs have raised significant investment for startups in recent years, effectively taking even pre-revenue new enterprises public. Also known as a blank cheque company, a SPAC is listed on a stock exchange with the intention of acquiring one or more private companies through merger at a future date. It is usual, upon creation of a SPAC, to create a trust with liquid assets. The SPAC has two years to acquire target companies, which are typically privately held. Should it fail to do so within that time frame, funds held in the trust are returned to investors. Customarily, the purposes and intent of the SPAC are set out in advance of the offering. Further details of the investment are finalised later in negotiation as part of the merger process.

The advantage of SPACs for startups is that they provide a means to raise capital from public markets without the uncertainties and stock volatility of a traditional initial public offering. Moreover, a startup can hold shares to ensure that the governance principles of the company are maintained. Fees involved in mergers may reduce near-term returns on investment. However, proponents argue that SPACs are part of the democratisation of early-stage investing, enabling the public to invest in pre-revenue companies that could later experience dynamic growth. Another key advantage of SPACs is their popularity and the amount of money flowing into them. In 2020, US 76 billion was invested into SPACs, up from 13 billion in 2019, validating this as an approach with high growth of investment (Kostin and Conners 2021). As such, SPACs could serve as an effective means for unproven ventures that have yet to be commercialised to obtain significant funding, as with the case of Virgin Galactic, which used a SPAC to go public in 2019 (Fernholz 2021). SPACs might be leveraged to help develop marine permaculture products and services, for example. A SPAC could be created potentially for a collection of seaweed companies, thereby tapping into growing interest and excitement around seaweed.

As part of the SPAC, multiple companies with complementary roles within an industry in startup phases or already with revenue could be funded and scaled.

Social impact bond

A social impact bond (SIB) is a performance-based contract between the government and a provider to achieve socially beneficial outcomes. The agreement between the parties details the project objectives, performance metrics and amount to be paid to the provider upon achieving specified outcomes. Investors provide upfront funding for the project. Within this framework, the investor and the provider bear the risk of project failure. Buoyed by trends towards social impact investing, the popularity of SIBs has grown substantially over recent years. They have most commonly been used to increase efficiency and effectiveness in delivering social services, such as healthcare to disadvantaged communities. It is based on anticipated savings in public programmes that the government pays providers when they meet the performance criteria. SIBs' potential to reduce public costs while contributing to public wellbeing and attracting financing from diverse sources, makes them worthy of consideration for NGOs pursuing innovations in sustainable development. Even so, transaction costs, execution risk, and difficulties measuring tangible social impact can impede interested parties (Mulgan et al. 2011).

However, despite these conditions, the company can receive private capital upfront regardless of whether or not the criteria set out are met. Additionally, there are examples of large amounts of capital being raised through SIBs. The first SIB agreement in Australia raised over AUD 7 million and generated a 10% return for investors per year. Another SIB in 2018 raised over 9 million and is still yet to be completely fulfilled. SIBs are therefore a significant fundraising avenue for ambitious ventures; where potential impact is large, but the likelihood of success is less clear. The Young Foundation (Mulgan et al. 2011) suggests that there are seven critical success factors for SIBs, with clear evidence of efficacy, measurable impact and government receptiveness being key for businesses seeking successful social investment. The Foundation also sets out a set of tests organisations can apply to determine if SIBs are appropriate for them to pursue (Mulgan et al. 2011).

Unfortunately, some countries have been slow to adopt SIBs. Indeed, in some countries where SIBs are used, many have struggled in the market due to overly complex documentation and set up requirements, lack of application and their low capitalisation magnitude, which is mostly well under AUD 7 million.

As an example, for the Climate Foundation to leverage a SIB would require a government to understand the positive impacts of marine permaculture on ocean regeneration and potential for ecosystem services and carbon export measurement and sequestration. There has currently been little to no focus on environmental pursuits in Australian SIBs. National governments including the Philippines or Indonesia might recognise the social and economic benefits of entering into a SIB and be willing to consider doing so. Government assurance of payment would be a key element of such a SIB. However, it could represent a potential funding stream in the future, should the need for carbon sequestration and improved ocean regeneration move up the government's agenda.

Conclusion

Addressing climate change by regenerating healthy climate conditions is likely to be one of the greatest challenges humankind has ever undertaken. To date, governments and markets have failed to fund climate solutions required to respond effectively to the magnitude of the existential threat facing civilisation today. Given the sheer number of market failures that surround the provision of public environmental goods and the climate crisis, transformative leadership and governance is undoubtedly required to leverage public and private capital needed to build and scale integrated solutions and set necessary boundary conditions for solutions to scale, such as significant, predictable and reliable carbon pricing. Social enterprises and NGOs seeking to leverage funding for ground-breaking but possibly risky projects thus need to explore creative ways to leverage funding while preserving innovation and governance objectives.

This chapter has covered a spectrum of fundraising approaches ranging from small-scale grants to hundred-million-dollar investments that can leverage capital-raising for potentially ground-breaking innovations that could advance sustainable development and assist in achieving UN SDGs. Though surely incomplete, this list is intended to provide an indicative spectrum of funding approaches.

Table 27.3 and Figure 27.3 illustrate at which stages, as defined by timeframe, funding goal and maturity, different funding approaches might be used to support marine permaculture development and commercialisation. While some of these funding opportunities could not be fully explored in the chapter due to space limitations, a spectrum of alternative funding outlined provides a promising view of the fintech transformations to come, even in this decade.

From the Climate Foundation's experience, cultivating private philanthropic relationships has been key, especially at the earlier stages of innovations, to adroitly enable progress through the technology readiness levels. Cultivating partner relationships and allocating adequate resources to maintain them are key to successful programme development. Decentralised finance, which can encompass philanthropy, reward-based crowdfunding and equity crowdfunding, is a growing trend

Table 27.3: Breakdown of different funding timelines with their respective objectives and funding streams.

	Horizon 1: Early R&D Funding	Horizon 2: Demonstration of sustainable economic models	Horizon 3: Scaling revenue base and building hectare-scale projects	Horizon 4: Large Projects: building arrays over KM^2 scale
Time	0–1 years	1–3 years	3+ years	10+ years
Goal	$750k	$3.5M	$10M	>$30M
Maturity	Early market engagement and Revenues	Demonstration of sustainable revenues	Cash flow positive	High return on investment
Funding Streams	– Philanthropic Capital – Reward Crowdfunding – Philanthropic Crowdfunding – Impact Funding	– Scaled Philanthropic Capital – Kelp Coin – Partnerships with Buyers – Equity Crowdfunding – VC – Catalytic Capital – Angel Investing – Beneficent Bridge Funding – SPAC – Impact Funding	– Project Finance – Private equity/ Projects – Social Impact Bonds – Concessionary Debt Finance – Franchising – Impact Funding – Green Banks	– Private equity/ Projects – Market rate investment – Debt finance – Franchising – Green Banks

with the potential to provide a variety of opportunities that can be leveraged by for-purpose organisations. By creatively and continuously engaging funders, be they organisations or individuals, to build excitement, enthusiasm and a sense of community around key innovations, a decentralised finance campaign can generate funding that carries all the way through to economic sustainability while achieving long-term SDG objectives.

Finally, conventional funding such as venture capital for commercialising start-ups have been contrasted to public and private philanthropic funding. It should be noted that transitioning a project from philanthropic support to commercialisation requires careful planning and timing. Moreover, potential pitfalls and merits of equity finance for-purpose-driven organisations have been described. Ensuring governance continuity supportive of the innovation is crucial for scaling through the years to achieve SDG objectives globally in the long-term. The chapter has also explored the potential of innovations in blended finance that can raise significant amounts of capital from public-private sources to enable large projects in multiple stages with concurrent technology validation.

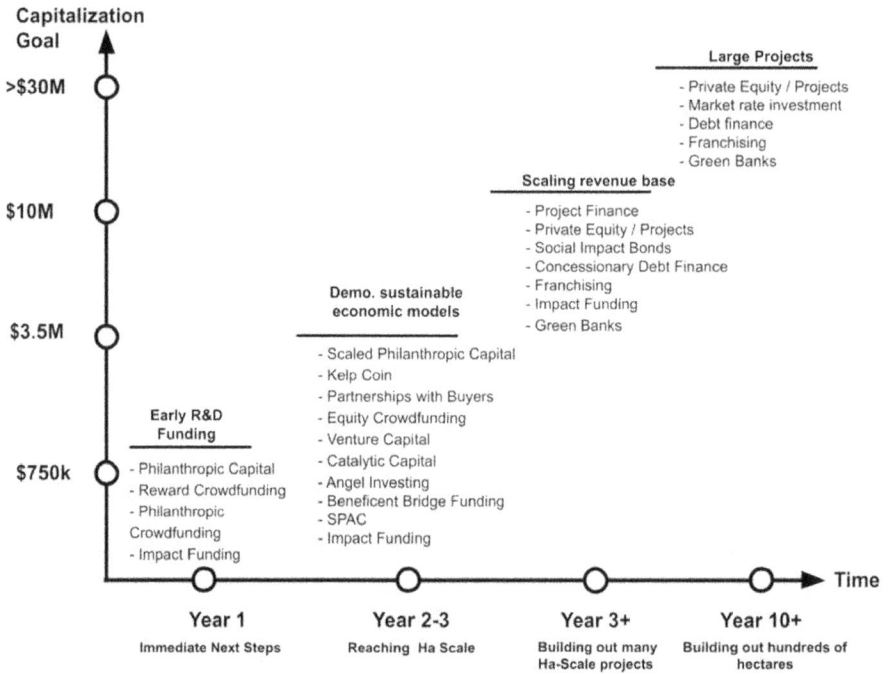

Figure 27.3: Breakdown of different funding timelines with their respective objectives and funding streams.

Taken together, these approaches indicate the types of fundraising that can help social enterprise, non-profits and startups alike raise impact capital and scale to implement solutions needed this century.

References

benefitcorp.net. n.d. *What Is a Benefit Corporation?*, <https://benefitcorp.net/> [Accessed 12 November 2021].

Bjerregaard, Rasmus, Diego Valderrama, Ricardo Radulovich, James Diana, Mark Capron, Cedric Amir Mckinnie, Michael Cedric, Kevin Hopkins, Charles Yarish, and Clifford Goudey.·2016. *Seaweed Aquaculture for Food Security, Income Generation and Environmental Health in Tropical Developing Countries*, (Washington DC: The World Bank), <https://documents1.world bank.org/curated/en/947831469090666344/pdf/107147-WP-REVISED-Seaweed-Aquaculture-Web.pdf> [Accessed 31 January 2022].

Brewdog. 2021. *Equity for Punks Tomorrow, Tomorrow Starts Today: Share Offer Information Securities Note*, <https://downloads.ctfassets.net/b0qgo9rl751g/2KHoBJQYw21fcXvQBVHiCp/55c588839f9c3645aa62025ab1e4c40d/EFP_T_prospectus.pdf> [Accessed 12 November 2021].

Brinkhuis, Henk, Stefan Schouten, Margaret E. Collinson, Appy Sluijs, Jaap S. Sinninghe Damsté, Gerald R. Dickens, Matthew Huber, Thomas M. Cronin, Jonaotaro Onodera, and Kozo

Takahashi. 2006. 'Episodic Fresh Surface Waters in the Eocene Arctic Ocean', *Nature*, 441 (7093), 606–09.

Buschmann, Alejandro H., Carolina Camus, Javier Infante, Amir Neori, Álvaro Israel, María C. Hernández-González, Sandra V. Pereda, Juan Luis Gomez-Pinchetti, Alexander Golberg, Niva Tadmor-Shalev, and Alan T. Critchley. 2017. 'Seaweed Production: Overview of the Global State of Exploitation, Farming and Emerging Research Activity', *European Journal of Phycology*, 52 (4), 391–406.

Campbell, Iona, Adrian Macleod, Christian Sahlmann, Luiza Neves, Jon Funderud, Margareth Øverland, Adam D. Hughes, and Michele Stanley. 2019. 'The Environmental Risks Associated with the Development of Seaweed Farming in Europe – Prioritizing Key Knowledge Gaps', *Frontiers in Marine Science*, 6 (2019): 107.

Christensen, Clayton M. 2013. *The Innovator's Dilemma: When New Technologies Cause Great Firms to Fail* (Cambridge, MA: Harvard Business Review Press).

Conte, Jack 2020 'Create on Your Terms with Your Community' *Patreon Blog* <https://blog.patreon.com/patreon-series-e-announcement> [Accessed 12 November 2021]

Dean, Brian.·2021. *Patreon: Subscriber and Creator Statistics for 2021*, (Backlinko), <https://backlinko.com/patreon-users> [Accessed 12 November 2021].

Duarte, Carlos M., Jiaping Wu, Xi Xiao, Annette Bruhn, and Dorte Krause-Jensen. 2017. 'Can Seaweed Farming Play a Role in Climate Change Mitigation and Adaptation?', *Frontiers in Marine Science*, 4, 100.

Duggan, Wayne. 2021. 'Goog Vs. Googl: Why 2 Classes of Alphabet Stock?', *money.usnews.com*. <https://money.usnews.com/investing/articles/goog-vs-googl-stock-difference> [Accessed 12 November 2021].

Fernholz, Tim. 2021. 'How the Rocket Business Launched a Wave of Blank Check Acquisitions', *Quartz*. <https://qz.com/1979846/virgin-galactic-launched-a-wave-of-space-spacs/> [Accessed 12 November 2021].

Fluck, Zsuzsanna.·2000. *Capital Structure Decisions in Small and Large Firms: A Life-Cycle Theory of Financing*, (New York: New York University), <https://w4.stern.nyu.edu/finance/docs/WP/1999/pdf/wpa99069.pdf> [Accessed 12 November 2021].

Goldstein, Jesse. 2018. *Planetary Improvement: Cleantech Entrepreneurship and the Contradictions of Green Capitalism* (Cambridge, MA: MIT Press).

Gurdgiev, Constantin, and Adam Fleming. In press. 'Informational Efficiency and Cybersecurity Threats: A Social Impact Finance Perspective of the Systemic Threats to Blockchain Applications.' in Thomas Walker, Jane McGaughey, Sherif Goubran and Nadra Wagdy (eds.), *Innovations in Social Finance: Transitioning Beyond Economic Value* (London: Palgrave Macmillan), pp. 347–72 Chapter 12.

Hallahan, Brian, Timothy Ryan, Joseph R. Hibbeln, Ivan T. Murray, Shauna Glynn, Christopher E. Ramsden, John Paul SanGiovanni, and John M. Davis. 2016. 'Efficacy of Omega-3 Highly Unsaturated Fatty Acids in the Treatment of Depression', *British Journal of Psychiatry*, 209 (3), 192–201.

Hata, Yoshiya, Kumiko Nakajima, Jun-ichi Uchida, Hidemasa Hidaka, and Takahisa Nakano. 2001. 'Clinical Effects of Brown Seaweed, Undaria Pinnatifida (Wakame), on Blood Pressure in Hypertensive Subjects', *Journal of Clinical Biochemistry and Nutrition*, 30, 43–53.

Hoegh-Guldberg, O., D. Jacob, M. Taylor, M. Bindi, S. Brown, I. Camilloni, A. Diedhiou, R. Djalante, K. Ebi, F. Engelbrecht, J. Guiot, Y. Hijioka, S. Mehrotra, A. Payne, S.I. Seneviratne, A. Thomas, R. Warren, and G. Zhou. 2018. 'Impacts of 1.5ºc Global Warming on Natural and Human Systems.' in V. Masson-Delmotte, P. Zhai, H. O. Pörtner, D. Roberts, J. Skea, P.R. Shukla, A. Pirani, W. Moufouma-Okia, C. Péan, R. Pidcock, S. Connors, J. B.R. Matthews, Y. Chen, X. Zhou, M. I. Gomis, E. Lonnoy, T. Maycock, M. Tignor and T. Waterfield (eds.), *Global*

Warming of 1.5°C. An IPCC Special Report on the Impacts of Global Warming of 1.5°C above Pre-Industrial Levels and Related Global Greenhouse Gas Emission Pathways, in the Context of Strengthening the Global Response to the Threat of Climate Change, Sustainable Development, and Efforts to Eradicate Poverty (Intergovernmental Panel On Climate Change), Chapter 3.

Horner, Rory 2019 'Are We All Developing Countries Now?' *Debating Development Research* <http://www.developmentresearch.eu/?p=400> [Accessed 12 November 2021]

Houston, Mark. 2014. 'The Role of Nutrition and Nutraceutical Supplements in the Treatment of Hypertension', *World Journal of Cardiology*, 6 (2), 38.

Hunt, Pascale 2021. '"Great Reboot or Short-Term Saviour? Bali's Seaweed Farming Revival', *The Fish Site*. <https://thefishsite.com/articles/great-reboot-or-short-term-saviour-balis-seaweed-farming-revival> [Accessed 12 November 2021].

Kostin, David, and Cormac Conners. 2021. '2020: The Year of the SPAC', *Goldman Sachs: Global Macro Research*, pp. 12–13. <https://www.goldmansachs.com/insights/pages/top-of-mind/the-ipo-spac-tacle/report.pdf> [Accessed 12 November 2021].

Krause-Jensen, Dorte, Paul Lavery, Oscar Serrano, Núria Marbà, Pere Masque, and Carlos M. Duarte. 2018. 'Sequestration of Macroalgal Carbon: The Elephant in the Blue Carbon Room', *Biology Letters*, 14 (6), 20180236.

Krause-Jensen, Dorte, and Carlos M. Duarte. 2016. 'Substantial Role of Macroalgae in Marine Carbon Sequestration', *Nature Geoscience*, 9 (10), 737–42.

La Rocca, Maurizio, Tiziana La Rocca, and Alfio Cariola. 2011. 'Capital Structure Decisions During a Firm's Life Cycle', *Small Business Economics*, 37 (1), 107–30.

Marquis, Christopher. 2020. 'The B Corp Movement Goes Big', *Stanford Social Innovation Review*, 18 (4), 22–29.

Mazzucato, Mariana. 2011. 'The Entrepreneurial State', *Soundings*, 49 (49), 131–42.

——. 2021. *Mission Economy: A Moonshot Guide to Changing Capitalism* (London: Penguin UK).

Morais, Tiago, Ana Inácio, Tiago Coutinho, Mariana Ministro, João Cotas, Leonel Pereira, and Kiril Bahcevandziev. 2020. 'Seaweed Potential in the Animal Feed: A Review', *Journal of Marine Science and Engineering*, 8 (8), 559.

Mulgan, Geoff, Neil Reeder, Mhairi Aylott, and Luke Bo'sher.·2011. *Social Impact Investment: The Challenge and Opportunity of Social Impact Bonds*, (London: The Young Foundation), <https://youngfoundation.org/wp-content/uploads/2012/10/Social-Impact-Investment-The-opportunity-and-challenge-of-Social-Impact-Bonds-March-2011.pdf> [Accessed 31 January 2022].

Neveux, Nicolas, John J. Bolton, Annette Bruhn, David A. Roberts, and Monique Ras. 2018. 'The Bioremediation Potential of Seaweeds: Recycling Nitrogen, Phosphorus, and Other Waste Products.' in Stephane La Barre and Stephen S. Bates (eds.), *Blue Biotechnology: Production and Use of Marine Molecules* (Weinheim, Germany: Wiley-VCH GmbH), pp. 217–39.

Nguyen, Loan T.Q., Thinh G. Hoang, Linh H. Do, Xuan T. Ngo, Phuong H.T. Nguyen, Giang D.L. Nguyen, and Giang N.T. Nguyen. 2021. 'The Role of Blockchain Technology-Based Social Crowdfunding in Advancing Social Value Creation', *Technological Forecasting and Social Change*, 170, 120898.

Novak, Mikayla. 2018. 'Crypto-Altruism: Some Institutional Economic Considerations', *Available at SSRN 3230541*.

O'Neill, Daniel W., Andrew L. Fanning, William F. Lamb, and Julia K. Steinberger. 2018. 'A Good Life for All within Planetary Boundaries', *Nature Sustainability*, 1 (2), 88–95.

Ortega, Alejandra, Nathan R. Geraldi, and Carlos M. Duarte. 2020. 'Environmental DNA Identifies Marine Macrophyte Contributions to Blue Carbon Sediments', *Limnology and Oceanography*, 65 (12), 3139–49.

Prime Coalition. n.d. *What Is Prime*, <https://primecoalition.org/what-is-prime/> [Accessed 12 November 2021].

Raworth, Kate. 2017. *Doughnut Economics: Seven Ways to Think Like a 21st-Century Economist* (White River Junction, VT: Chelsea Green Publishing).

Republic.co. 2021. *AKUA: Meat-Alt Company Making Plant-Based Foods from Regenerative Aquaculture*, <https://republic.co/akua> [Accessed 12 November 2021].

Santos, Isaac R., David J. Burdige, Tim C. Jennerjahn, Steven Bouillon, Alex Cabral, Oscar Serrano, Thomas Wernberg, Karen Filbee-Dexter, Julia A. Guimond, and Joseph J. Tamborski. 2021. 'The Renaissance of Odum's Outwelling Hypothesis In'blue Carbon' Science', *Estuarine, Coastal and Shelf Science*, 255, 107361.

Seedrs. 2018. *Oddbox: Oddbox Fights Food Waste on Farms and Delivers Delicious Wonky Produce for Cheaper*, <https://www.seedrs.com/oddbox> [Accessed 12 November 2021].

Stark, K.D., M.E. Van Elswyk, M.R. Higgins, C.A. Weatherford, and N. Salem, Jr. 2016. 'Global Survey of the Omega-3 Fatty Acids, Docosahexaenoic Acid and Eicosapentaenoic Acid in the Blood Stream of Healthy Adults', *Progress in Lipid Research*, 63, 132–52.

Steffen, Will, Katherine Richardson, Johan Rockström, Sarah E. Cornell, Ingo Fetzer, Elena M. Bennett, Reinette Biggs, Stephen R. Carpenter, Wim De Vries, and Cynthia A. De Wit. 2015. 'Planetary Boundaries: Guiding Human Development on a Changing Planet', *Science*, 348, no. 6240 (2015): 1217.

Stoller, Kristin 2020. 'The New Beer Barons: How Two Scottish Kids Turned Wild Flavors, Crowdfunding and Plenty of Attitude into a $2 Billion Business', *Forbes* <https://www.forbes.com/sites/kristin stoller/2020/01/14/the-new-beer-barons-how-two-scottish-kids-turned-wild-flavors-crowdfunding-and-plenty-of-attitude-into-a-2-billion-business/?sh=26fbf1b029c4> [Accessed 12 November 2021].

Straub, Sandra C., Thomas Wernberg, Mads S. Thomsen, Pippa J. Moore, Michael T. Burrows, Ben P. Harvey, and Dan A. Smale. 2019. 'Resistance, Extinction, and Everything in between—the Diverse Responses of Seaweeds to Marine Heatwaves', *Frontiers in Marine Science*, 6, 763.

Stuchtey, M., Adrien Vincent, Andreas Merkl, Maximilian Bucher, Peter M. Haugan, Jane Lubchenco, and Mari Elka Pangestu.·2020. *Ocean Solutions That Benefit People, Nature, and the Economy*, (Washington DC: World Resource Institute), <https://www.oceanpanel.org/ocean-action/people-nature-economy-report.html> [Accessed 12 November 2021].

sustainabledevelopmentUN.org. n.d. *Final List of Proposed Sustainable Development Goal Indicators*, <https://sustainabledevelopment.un.org/content/documents/11803Official-List-of-Proposed-SDG-Indicators.pdf> [Accessed 12 November 2021].

Thomsen, Mads S., Luca Mondardini, Tommaso Alestra, Shawn Gerrity, Leigh Tait, Paul M. South, Stacie A. Lilley, and David R. Schiel. 2019. 'Local Extinction of Bull Kelp (Durvillaea Spp.) Due to a Marine Heatwave', *Frontiers in Marine Science*, 6, 84.

United Nations Food and Agriculture Organisation.·2017. *Annual Report: The Future of Food and Agriculture—Trends and Challenges*, (Rome: FAO), <https://www.fao.org/3/i6583e/i6583e.pdf> [Accessed 12 November 2021].

——.·2018. *The State of World Fisheries and Aquaculture 2018 – Meeting the Sustainable Development Goals*, The State of the World, (Rome: FAO), <http://www.fao.org/3/i9540en/I9540EN.pdf> [Accessed 12 November 2021].

US Department of Energy. n.d.-a. *Loan Programs Office*, <https://www.energy.gov/lpo/loan-programs-office> [Accessed 12 November 2021].

——. n.d.-b. *Loans Program Office: Tesla*, <https://www.energy.gov/lpo/tesla> [Accessed 12 November 2021].

Vásquez, Julio A., Sergio Zúñiga, Fadia Tala, Nicole Piaget, Dení Rodríguez, and J.M. Alonso Vega. 2013. 'Economic Valuation of Kelp Forests in Northern Chile: Values of Goods and Services of the Ecosystem', *Journal of Applied Phycology*, 26 (2), 1081–88.

Wada, Keiko, Kozue Nakamura, Yuya Tamai, Michiko Tsuji, Yukari Sahashi, Kaori Watanabe, Sakiko Ohtsuchi, Keiko Yamamoto, Kyoko Ando, and Chisato Nagata. 2011. 'Seaweed Intake and Blood Pressure Levels in Healthy Pre-School Japanese Children', *Nutrition Journal*, 10 (1), 1–7.

WeFunder. 2021. *Invest in C-Combinator*, <https://wefunder.com/ccombinator/buzz> [Accessed 12 November 2021].

Wernberg, Thomas, Scott Bennett, Russell C. Babcock, Thibaut De Bettignies, Katherine Cure, Martial Depczynski, Francois Dufois, Jane Fromont, Christopher J. Fulton, and Renae K. Hovey. 2016. 'Climate-Driven Regime Shift of a Temperate Marine Ecosystem', *Science*, 353 (6295), 169–72.

Woodford Folk Festival. 2020. *Woodfordia Presents: Woodford Folk Festival*, <https://woodfordfolkfestival.com/about/> [Accessed 12 November 2021].

Conclusion

All authors

Chapter 28
Sustainable development and finance post-pandemic – future directions and challenges

Abstract: Sustainable development, finance and related global policies and mechanisms have evolved over the decades. Today, regional initiatives for classifying sustainable activities exist, and several decades' research and development of ecosystem services and natural capital have identified and tested alternative economic models. The World Bank has the potential to finance them and sustainability at the landscape scale is achievable. But economic and environmental values can come into conflict. In developing countries, sustainable alternatives exist in business activities such as coastal and marine tourism. Financing small businesses through sound digital infrastructure is critical, as is the use of public fiscal instruments for the sustainable use of natural resources. Despite its developed status, renewable energy policies in the EU are leading to forest destruction. Financial vehicles such as green bonds have a similar potential. To avoid greenwashing, more focus needs to be on meeting the needs of those at the base of the economic pyramid, resourcing them with smart technologies and valuing civic engagement. Climate finance must be ethical and its allocation have integrity; this will foster community resilience. To avoid repeating the mistakes of terrestrial development, the world's oceans need to be protected and new business models adopted in this expanding frontier. Now is the time for all sectors to create a sustainable future for the planet and its inhabitants in the post-COVID, post-carbon era to come.

Keywords: blue economy, climate finance, private finance, public finance, sustainable development and finance, COVID-19

Part 1: Origins and evolution of sustainable development and finance

Sustainable development and finance have been on the international policy agenda for several decades now and in the wake of various global shocks have undergone some transformation, most obviously in the pivot towards green growth in the wake of the 2008 Global Financial Crisis (Mundaca et al. 2016). The mainstream approaches to sustainability fail to recognise the political nature of sustainability,

https://doi.org/10.1515/9783110733488-028

that is the socioeconomic processes that result in environmental degradation poverty and injustice (Castro 2004).

Economic growth today is diametrically opposed to the sustainability of the Earth Higgins (2013). A balanced economic and political environment should mean private sector investment in green initiatives and climate action is already occurring (Clark, Reed, and Sunderland 2018). Yet the reality is that conventional markets completely dominate the finance space and sustainable development is a tiny tranche of those activities. A profound paradigm shift is necessary if there is to be long-term political and private sector support for sustainable financial markets, over and against the destruction and degradation of nature, which other sources of capital aspire to, rather than its restoration and maintenance (Parker and Cranford 2010).

In Part 1 of this Handbook, the authors interrogated some of the most symbolic institutions, discourses and mechanisms underpinning sustainable development and finance. In Chapter Two, Ahlström and Sjåfjell analysed and critiqued the EU Taxonomy Regulation by means of a helpful framework for understanding the complexity and uncertainty surrounding legal and sustainable approaches to development and finance. But policy tensions with post-COVID-19 recovery plans mean that national plans will be assessed against unambitious targets of expenditure for sustainability-related investments. Integrating established policy principles into the finance field may create more effective responses to steer through the fog of uncertainty.

In Chapter Three, Andrew Buckwell and Edward A. Morgan discussed ecosystem services and natural capital and their application in the field of sustainable finance. They concluded that the means of valuing nature cannot be relied on for every aspect of decision-making around sustainable finance. Ecosystem services provision is often in a non-linear, has a long-term timeframe and is complex. Social biases can also influence models of valuation. The drive to speak the language acceptable to policymakers has been to emphasise the monetary value of nature, which has been pitted against the idea that nature can have intrinsic values, regardless of human systems of valuation. Understanding the nuances of these values can enable better uptake of these concepts into sustainable finance going forward and in recognition of COVID-19.

In Chapter Four, Susan Park reflected that over the past decade, the World Bank Group has pivoted strongly towards the private sector and public private partnerships drive much of the sustainable development agenda, for example, in biodiversity, away from the previously stated aim of promoting public goods, such as the environment. This cuts to the core weakness of the institution, the author concluded, as promising to end upstream lending for oil and gas while also creating economically viable energy solutions for developing countries. These contending issues feed into how and what sustainability-related development solutions are offered, how borrower ownership is to be preserved and how private sector processes are offset, while public goods such as health are maintained. How the World Bank will provide post-COVID-19 financing for reducing carbon intensive development in ways that provide the payoffs intended for the environment will be interesting to see.

In Chapter Five, in their second joint offering, Edward A. Morgan and Andrew Buckwell explored landscape planning and economics for sustainable finance. The conclusions were that land use planning and resource management in landscapes often undervalues the multiple ecosystem services provided by the habitats in a landscape. Trying to value the landscape economically tends to focus on one direct use value at a time (e.g., timber) and fails to integrate management planning (e.g., for watersheds) across the landscape. The total economic value of a landscape needs to be taken into consideration to help stakeholders identify and weigh up the values contained in the landscape. Knowing the value of ecosystem services can inform deliberations at the landscape level and ensure the good use and fair trade of a landscape's interconnected values.

In Chapter Six, Chris Taylor looked at the extent to which neoliberalism and liberal environmentalism have outsourced the sustainability of forest management to the market through independent, third-party certification. On the one hand, this has removed state control, creating a form of governing by distance, while on the other creating opportunities for more direct involvement of civil society and other stakeholders in the evaluation of management activities. This poses its own risks, notably through the handing of responsibility for oversight to auditors conducting assessment, who may or may not take the knowledge and information provided by stakeholders into consideration.

Part 2: Public finance for sustainable development

Development is a complex process and cannot be programmed through linear interventions and government decisions can determine the future of an entire generation. Achieving the goal of a society based on knowledge and innovation for future generations and creating a favourable environment for sustainable development, requires collaboration between government, civil society and business (Arnăut 2014). In this regard, more flexible approaches to the use of public finance and thoughtful tax measures could aid recovery in the post-COVID era and strengthen sustainable development.

The strategic directions of sustainable development are set by each country and governed by policies, tools and scenarios that have real life consequences. These can be positive or negative towards supporting human development. Public financing is essential in reaching SDG goals and targets. The size and structure of public expenditures, including budgetary expenditure, are essential to assume the tasks taken on by the state as responsibilities. At the same time, the sensible and effective use of public funds in strategic areas of public services, such as health or social welfare (Piotrowska-Marczak and Kietlińska 2001) or state-accredited superannuation schemes is part of a successful sustainability outcome.

Sustainability-related spending can improve quality of life and increase competitiveness of the economy. However, an increase in sustainable development related spending alone will not improve the perspectives of sustainable development, but rather, how effectively those resource allocations are spent. Increasing expenditure on sustainable development that results in growing budgetary imbalances at the expense of other sectors is not a solution. A continuous increase in the amount spent on environmental protection, education, health, social security and culture may result in considerable increases in total public spending but it may also increase budget deficits and debts, putting sustainable development at risk. Shifting the burden of financing partly onto the private sector using the system of adequate stimuli and incentives is also an important measure (Marin et al. 2012; Lucian et al. 2011). However, it may be difficult for the private sector to fully replace public funding but at least the danger of impacting on other critical issue areas is mitigated (Kepui, Chamala, and Shadur 1996).

However, analyses of sustainable development have shown that the main financing sources for sustainable development continue to be located within the public sector. This is due largely to the absence of sustainability-oriented financial markets as existing financial instruments do not adequately address the SDGs (Gambetta et al. 2019). Regrettably, while national public funding in developing and low-income countries doubled between 2002 and 2011, it has now plateaued and is insufficient to meet sustainable development needs (United Nations Development Programme 2018). A similar analogy can be drawn with responses to COVID-19. After an initial flurry of measures to address the pandemic, commitment waned and infections spread. Combatting climate change, in the context of sustainable development and poverty alleviation, the overarching principles of the Paris Agreement, for example, cannot occur without an ongoing financial commitment and political will. In the absence of these, the scourge of poverty and unsustainable development – as well as climate change and other environmental emergencies – will continue to afflict society for the foreseeable future.

In Part 2 of this Handbook, the authors drew a range of conclusions in their chapters. Southern scholars looked to the future for sustainable development in emerging economies. In Chapter Eight, Zaman and Sarker provided a set of prescriptive suggestions for the future of public finance for sustainable development. SDG financing needs a viable and effective blend of financial and non-financial resources, addressing real-world problems. Governments have an essential role to play in the low-carbon transition of their countries. Carbon revenues may have a beneficial impact and lead to the funding of development plans in other sectors that facilitate social infrastructure and education. Climate public expenditure needs to be well-coordinated between government agencies. In addition, effective global, regional, bilateral and multilateral cooperation needs to be folded into national governments' efforts to finance SDGs. Dey and Basak argued in Chapter Nine, that a time will come when digital finance will be available to the masses in all countries. Governments and the private sector both face challenges to evolve and adapt to the new era of digital finance. Doing so could open up new opportunities for billions of people, ensuring the achievement of the SDGs. To get the full benefit of the SDGs, however, digital financial services need to be well-governed. In Chapter Ten, Nurfatriani, Salminah and Kurniasari. see in the COVID-19 pandemic a moment to seize that future. There are already many fiscal instruments at the government's disposal to encourage the shift from brown to green development and the private sector should be encouraged to invest in mass-labour green projects, based on the sustainable management of Indonesia's abundant natural resources.

In Chapter Eleven, Kun subverted this optimistic Southeast Asian perspective, for a darker, European reality. Here mechanisms for sustainable development, climate change management and renewable energy have become a toxic mix. In combatting climate change by reducing fossil fuel emissions, the EU has embraced the burning of biomass, mostly trees, as an alternative, with negative environmental consequences. The rhetoric of sustainability is there through such financial instruments as a green taxonomy. But unsustainable, forest-reliant business models, exploiting loopholes in existing international climate policy and EU regulations, prevent the effective implementation of genuinely sustainable activity. Not only do nation-states and policies have to be flexible and innovative in their use of public finance to support sustainable development and COVID recovery, they also have to avoid negative interactions with existing rules. In the case of the EU Taxonomy, it appears that a progressive measure aimed at encouraging the uptake of sustainability in private sector activity is in conflict with business-as-usual models of profit maximisation and cost-externalisation.

Part 3: Private finance for sustainable development

The business community has a vital role to play in contributing to the achievement of the SDGs, while government is in the primary position to overcome the barriers to the transition to a sustainable economy. Sustainable finance does not remake private economic behaviour. Hence, a pragmatic and proactive approach by policymakers is necessary to bring reform into conventional economic behaviour. Regulators should provide definitive guidance to the share of responsibilities on private entities concerning SDGs or planetary boundaries. Policies should drive sustainable environmental as well as economic practices and leverage private sector resources. Where possible, business costs associated with adopting clean energy should be internalised within genuinely sustainable markets, rather than via governmental (taxpayer) subsidies. Incentive measures that align the private sector with environmental outcomes and create green employment will lead to increased public support and business uptake (Hart 2013).

It continues to be difficult to connect the corporate internal system, structure and culture with public interest objectives. Different risks, such as legal and political risk, financial risk (default risk, liquidity risk, inflation risk, interest rate risk, investment risk, risks of pandemic outbreaks, etc.) need to be taken into consideration by the state when creating the right investment climate for the private sector. While the contribution of civil society and the public sector is vital in achieving the SDGs, the private sector's role is also critical as it can help mobilise much needed capital to finance the SDG agenda. Accountability to stakeholders does not mean just profit maximisation but reducing businesses' share of carbon emissions and not overstepping planetary boundaries. The patchy support for the SDGs is related to the business community's conception of sustainability, which generally emphasises continuity, efficiency and cost savings over environmental performance (Wynn and Jones 2020).

There is an emerging need for private investment in economically and environmentally sustainable development projects, which would deliver jobs and inclusive growth, improve relationships with customers and employees, and spur business growth and innovation. Unlocking private finance to fulfil sustainable development commitments can bridge the gap between the levels of finance required and the level currently invested (Clark, Reed, and Sunderland 2018) as public investment will be not sufficient to finance low-carbon projects. Collaboration amongst the actors can improve the understanding of the underlying benefits of ecosystem protection and planetary conservation. Here it is encouraging to see the collaboration between business, unions and private sector investors getting behind the Just Transition movement to ensure green jobs in the post-carbon economy, using such private governance standards as the Principles for Responsible Investment (PRI) (Robins, Brunsting, and Wood 2018). Examining other financial and non-financial benefits that are often overlooked could provide partnership opportunities, making sustainable development and finance more attractive.

In Part 3 of this Handbook, author contributions were diverse, reflecting the contradictions and diverse localities of sustainable finance. From their Southern perspective, in Chapter Thirteen, Ferrando et al. explored the framework of sustainable finance, where green bonds are increasing in popularity. Green bonds have expanded globally from different loci but have territorialised themselves and adapted to local contexts. How these tools play out on the ground have real, political, social, legal and financial consequences for what is defined as green, the social and environmental implications for climate change action and the role played by financial investors. The debtor-creditor relationship and use of debt historically have perpetuated an uneven distribution of power. Financing the green transition by bonds puts future generations in debt to a crisis that was not of their making and has favoured players who can afford to cash in on indebtedness. The flow of capital from the North to the South as climate-linked debt instead of grants and reparations, ignores historical obligations and puts creditors in charge of expanding the economy. Whether green bonds will prevent the climate catastrophe and whether this will also mean a social disaster, is not yet known.

Dembek and York noted in Chapter Fourteen that while the developed world struggled with isolation during COVID-19, many base of the pyramid (BoP) communities had no option but face-to-face interaction. With limited access to technology, micro-entrepreneurs and BoP customers pivoted to e-commerce. BoP business models have had to rapidly adapt, requiring flexible and responsive sources of finance. Here, there is a critical role to be played by robust digital payment infrastructures, micro-insurance and sources of working capital. The pandemic has shown how little resilience the very poor have when confronted by systemic disruption. Even with modest savings or remittance networks, BoP communities experienced widespread loss of income opportunities, particularly women, children, people with disabilities and other marginalised groups. BoP models should go beyond sources of income and incorporate safeguards, recognise human capital, natural capital and social capital, all of which underpin financial resilience. COVID-19 presents the international community with an opportunity to build better, stronger, more sustainable and more resilient systems in a green post-pandemic world. Developing sustainably relies on systems-level processes with leverage for change, alternative approaches and putting mechanisms in place to support solutions as they arise. In their pursuit of sustainable development and poverty alleviation business and capital should maximise their potential to respond quickly to the sustainable production and consumption patterns that have arisen during the pandemic.

In Chapter Fifteen, in an interesting perspective mirroring Dey and Basak (Chapter Nine), Arnab Bose and colleagues looked at the digital future for finance in India. COVID-19 was not a moment when Artificial Intelligence (AI) and blockchain technologies came to the fore. While the next pandemic will most likely have a role for AI, this is not to say that AI and blockchain were completely absent this time around. But the scale required to help combat the virus was not reached and still has to evolve. For that ecosystem to develop multiple approaches are required. The authors call on stakeholders to begin a dialogue with each other to enable technology makers to collaborate on working to achieve the SDGs. Many tools are required for managing risks when using AI or blockchain for sustainable development in a country like India.

In another alternative model for understanding the economy in Chapter Sixteen, Tony Bradley opened up the debate about what data, criteria and assumptions are made about the environment-related engagement of households in the economy. If some consistency and comparability can be arrived at on these, both in relation to localities, within a country such as the UK and between societies, that gives further opportunities for policy, philanthropy and impact investment decisions towards new core economic household environmental production. Consistent standards over methodology and assumptions in relation to civic engagement will enable such valuations. This applies equally to developed, mid-developing and less developed countries. Such approaches to valuation can assist policymakers in targeting their strategies more directly. Non-monetary financial transactions of citizens in the economy cannot be ignored. Doing so would mean missing one of the most significant aspects of mitigating the ecological crises of the twenty-first century. In this respect, a lot can be learnt from responses beyond the nation-state, and neoliberalism, such as the UK's community-driven COVID-19 Mutual Aid Groups.

Part 4: Climate finance for sustainable development

Of the original three mechanisms of the Kyoto Protocol (KP), Joint Implementation (JI), International Emissions Trading (IET), and the Clean Development Mechanism (CDM), only the CDM was genuinely global in nature. Technology and finance were directed to Southern countries from Northern countries to allow them to reduce greenhouse gas emissions through the offset of industrial emissions, thereby providing support for sustainable development. The number of registered CDM projects grew from 62 to over 7,000 when the commitment period ended, offsetting in excess of a billion tonnes of CO_2 emissions (Maraseni and Cadman 2015: 2–3). However, the CDM was presented in the analysis of the time as re-territorialising the South and the regulation over sinks spaces such as forest-based offsets represented an imperial model of global environmental governance, an 'empire of carbon management and control' (Paterson and Stripple 2007: 163). How carbon and sustainability markets emerge in the new Sustainable Development Mechanism (SDM) remains to be seen, particularly as CDM projected-derived credits are still in the mix, and the old compliance/voluntary approaches are still being rethought.

In Part 4 of the Handbook the authors looked at some of the existing institutions of climate finance, old and new, which are driving or funding investment. Roppongi explored the pressing challenges of climate finance sustainability in the light of the global crisis in Chapter Eighteen. The pandemic has impacted global and national economies, increased global debt, unleashed fiscal constraints in both developing and developed countries, which has impacted multilateral institutions. Frameworks to mobilise finances for the greater good require frameworks and methodologies but institutional constraints and conflicts of interest are hampering efforts to combat climate change. The financial system and business models have to have greater alignments in financial flows towards climate-oriented goals. This is essential for improving the system and expanding the financial pool of resources for implementing the Paris Agreement and SDGs. This is a once-in-generation opportunity to comprehensively change the financial system for a sustainable post-pandemic recovery.

Radunsky argued in Chapter Nineteen that institutions, such as the Adaptation Fund (AF) and other funds, are essential in managing climate risks. Adaptation activities are much more context specific than policy-initiatives such as decarbonisation and institutions specialising in adaptation such as the AF have a role to play now and in the future. But increasing adaptation finance to address climate change impacts now must not reduce mitigation finance or compromise on goals of carbon neutrality. Strengthening international cooperation is essential, on a par with countries' efforts to strengthen international cooperation post-COVID to prevent and combat further pandemics. Governments can learn from their risk management of the pandemic to improve risk management in disaster and risk reduction in the future. The need to address the adaptation gap has also been recognised by several countries and there is an urgent speed up the support for those vulnerable to the worsening outcomes of climate change. Adaptation is only adequate if loss and damage are negligible, requiring action to address both the adaptation gap and the mitigation gap. If not, more people will suffer. Everyone must contribute to closing those gaps.

Writing in Chapter Twenty on the ongoing developments in Article 6 of the Paris Agreement (PA), Rob Hales presented ten principles for responsible investment in climate mitigation activities, which are reproduced in full here:

- Principle 1: Nature-based offset solutions should only be used for abating 10% of an organisation's operational emissions. This is based on the new Science Based Targets Standard announced in 2021.
- Principle 2: For organisations that have fossil fuel emissions of greater than 10% of emissions that cannot be abated through present technology then rapid fossil fuel emissions reduction in existing, easy to abate emissions should be implemented.
- Principle 3: Nature-based offset solutions should not be used in the abatement of an organisation's fossil fuel emissions if an alternative abatement action presently exists. Rapid reductions in fossil fuel emissions are imperative.
- Principle 4: An offset must be used in real-time and future unproven offset abatement strategies such as carbon capture and storage should not be used in net-zero emission planning.
- Principle 5: Offsets should include measurable co-benefits to local communities if the offset occurs within the locality of the community. Literature on a just transition should inform best practice.
- Principle 6: Where Indigenous communities are involved in offsets, then the principle of Free Prior Informed Consent should govern the inclusion (or not) of Indigenous peoples in the offset project.
- Principle 7: Offsets should be reported with robust transparency and accountability processes at the organisation level.

- Principle 8: Carbon offsets used in once country by a country cannot be used in other countries – offsets need to be cancelled upon initial trade. The use of offsets should support high ambition Nationally Determined Contributions (NDCs).
- Principle 9: Nature-based solutions used as offsets need to have positive conservation and biodiversity benefits.
- Principle 10: Offsets should have adaptation benefits as well as mitigation benefits.

Hales concluded by recommending that such principles be used for the development of standards covering mitigation activities.

In Chapter Twenty-One, Andrea Young suggested systemic change is needed when complex challenges such as climate change and the pandemic arise, with all their economic, social and environmental impacts on the poor, social inequality and loss of biodiversity. Now is the time for governments and civil society to seize this moment to increase public understanding of the impacts of climate change, which will create lasting and future, impacts. But the mechanisms used to address crises such as COVID-19, an economic downturn, rising global poverty or even climate neutrality will require more funding, especially if increased climate action and sustainable industrial innovation are to come about. All actors should use this moment wisely and develop instruments for a transformative post-carbon economy.

Part 5: The blue economy and sustainable development

Some of the tensions inherent in the use of terrestrial resources are now potentially playing out the marine environment on the assumption the oceans' resources are to be exploited by humans, yet simultaneously protected for their inherent values, reflecting the greater problems with the concept of sustainable development itself. There are some deep philosophical and moral questions to be asked about the ethics and values of the blue economy and the role that blue finance can play in advancing sustainable development, particularly for communities dependent on the oceans for their livelihood.

In Part 5, the authors reflected on the complexities and contradictions in the use of the world's oceans by humans and the wake of COVID-19. In Chapter Twenty-Three, Hugh Breakey discussed the blue economy as a new and expanding area of growth for industry. Activities in the ocean involve a range of ethical challenges, whether economic, social or environmental. Government regulation appears unable to keep up with development and the science about the impacts is uncertain with economic activity being in environments above and below sea level that are difficult for normal accountability and monitoring practices to take place. This has the potential to create explosive stakeholder situations, where the legitimacy of the actors involved is called into question by the community. The full suite of ethical issues in play needs to be confronted head on by all parties in order that legitimacy is assured and all the positive ethical values of the blue economy realised.

In Chapter Twenty-Four, Islam and Sarker explored the potential of coastal and marine tourism in a Southeast Asian context. Nature-based tourism, ecotourism and community-based ecotourism all have the potential to contribute to poverty reduction, address food security, empower women, help ensure the security of the coastal and marine zones and make a positive sociocultural contribution, but they are in their infancy in the region. Developing economies in the region could learn from the Seychelles or Indonesia. But wherever development occurs, management plans to support ecosystem services and preserve the health of the marine environment need to be in place. For the blue economy to succeed sustainably in the Asia-Pacific, the region requires a more integrated approach for mobilising finance and investment.

In a surprising finding in Chapter Twenty-Five, Maraseni et al. presented the results of a global survey which found that international stakeholders, across most sectors, North and South, were generally satisfied with sustainable development in terms of how it was playing out through the various international state and non-state initiatives on the oceans. In comparison to the Global North (developed countries), the Global South (developing countries) almost consistently rated the governance quality of all the initiatives investigated higher, which begs the question as to why the Global North was less satisfied. The authors suggest this is because these programmes have a strong emphasis on the Global South and provide a variety of resources and programmes. These international, often intergovernmental, forums should provide resources to the Global South, but they should not forget the North has technical, economic and institutional capacity building needs of its own, most notably in strengthening civil society through democratic engagement.

Graham Wood asked readers in Chapter Twenty-Six to give consideration to both the management strategy and the domestication of the ocean perspectives, as it allows reflection on differing community assumptions about what is green and where people sit on the management/domestication side of the equation. Few opt for or are attracted by extremes but they are nevertheless valuable to serve as illustrations of all possible positions. In this helpful chapter, readers are encouraged to reflect on what development is for, who and what it affects, and who it benefits.

In Chapter Twenty-Seven, Zak and fellow collaborators delivered a message straight from those active on the ocean. New technology is in full operation, through digital, fiscal, financial, social and environmental projects and programmes. Mobilising capital is essential, but it is generated more from partnership models and sources of new sustainable finance, rather than relying on the old. Blended finance and other means of revenue-raising can generate significant amounts of capital from public-private sources to enable larger scale projects.

In conclusion, ensuring an innovative and resilient approach to sustainable development and finance will be essential in scaling-up to meet SDG goals and targets, and recovering from COVID-19. Reconciling the tensions between environmental and economic conceptions of development, exemplified in the concept of growth itself, and fundamental to living in a post-carbon society, may be more difficult.

References

Arnăut, Adriana 2014. *Role of Government and Civil Society in Sustainable Development, Institutional Repository of Moldova State University* (Moldova: Moldova State University).

Castro, Carlos J. 2004. 'Sustainable Development: Mainstream and Critical Perspectives', *Organization and Environment*, 17 (2), 195–225.

Clark, Robyn, James Reed, and Terry Sunderland. 2018. 'Bridging Funding Gaps for Climate and Sustainable Development: Pitfalls, Progress and Potential of Private Finance', *Land Use Policy*, 71, 335–46.

Gambetta, Nicolás, Paula Azadian, Victoria Hourcade, and María Elisa Reyes. 2019. 'The Financing Framework for Sustainable Development in Emerging Economies: The Case of Uruguay', *Sustainability*, 11 (4), 1059.

Hart, Craig. 2013. *Climate Change and the Private Sector: Scaling up Private Sector Response to Climate Change:* (London: Routledge).

Higgins, Karen L 2013 'Economic Growth and Sustainability–Are They Mutually Exclusive', *Elseiver Connect* <https://www.elsevier.com/connect/economic-growth-and-sustainability-are-they-mutually-exclusive> [Accessed 24 February 2022].

Kepui, Tim P, Shankariah Chamala, and Mark A Shadur. 1996. 'The Role of Culture in Development Management: Case Studies of a Public and a Private Sector Organization in Papua New Guinea', *Sustainable Development*, 4 (3), 111–20.

Lucian, Unița, Rahotă Daniela, Maghiar Teodor Traian, and Straciuc Oreste. 2011. 'The Role of the Preventive Medicine in Sustainable Development. A Study Case on the Private Medicine Sector in Oradea', *Annals of the University of Oradea, Economic Science Series. (20)*, 2, 116–23.

Maraseni, Tek Narayan, and Tim Cadman. 2015. 'A Comparative Analysis of Global Stakeholders' Perceptions of the Governance Quality of the Clean Development Mechanism (CDM) and Reducing Emissions from Deforestation and Forest Degradation (REDD+)', *International Journal of Environmental Studies*, 72 (2), 288–304.

Marin, Camelia, Roxana Dorobantu, Diana Codreanu, and Ruxandra Mihaela. 2012. 'The Fruit of Collaboration between Local Government and Private Partners in the Sustainable Development Community Case Study: County Valcea', *Economy Transdisciplinarity Cognition*, 15 (2), 93.

Mundaca, Luis, Lena Neij, Anil Markandya, Peter Hennicke, and Jinyue Yan. 2016. 'Towards a Green Energy Economy? Assessing Policy Choices, Strategies and Transitional Pathways', *Applied Energy*, 179, 1283–92.

Parker, Charlie, and Matthew Cranford. 2010. *The Little Biodiversity Finance Book: A Guide to Proactive Investment in Natural Capital (PINC)* (Oxford: Global Canopy Programme).

Paterson, Matthew, and Johannes Stripple. 2007. 'Singing Climate Change into Existence on the Territorialization of Climate Policymaking.' in Mary Pettenger (ed.), *The Social Construction of Climate Change: Power, Knowledge, Norms, Discourses* (London: Ashgate Publishing ltd), pp. 149–72

Piotrowska-Marczak, Krystyna, and Krystyna Kietlińska. 2001. 'Reforming Health and Social
    Services in Poland-an Overview', *Public Management Review*, 3 (2), 281–93.
Robins, Nick, Vonda Brunsting, and David Wood.·2018. *Climate Change and the Just Transition:
    A Guide for Investor Action*, (London: Grantham Research Institute on Climate Change and the
    Environment, London School of Economics), <https://www.lse.ac.uk/granthaminstitute/wp-
    content/uploads/2018/12/Climate-change-and-the-just-transition_Guide-for-investor-action.
    pdf> [Accessed 24 February 2022].
United Nations Development Programme.·2018. *Financing the 2030 Agenda – an Introductory
    Guidebook for UNDP Country Offices*, (New York: UNDP), <https://www.uncclearn.org/
    resources/library/financing-the-2030-agenda-an-introductory-guidebook-for-undp-country-
    offices/> [Accessed 24 February 2022].
Wynn, Martin, and Peter Jones. 2020. 'The Sustainable Development Goals, the ICT Industry and
    ICT4D Research.' in Tay Keong Tan, Milenko Gúdić and Patricia M. Flynn (eds.), *Struggles and
    Successes in the Pursuit of Sustainable Development* (London: Routledge), pp. 84–95.

List of abbreviations and acronyms

AAAA	Addis Ababa Action Agenda
ADB	Asian Development Bank
ADBI	Asian Development Bank Institute
AF	Adaptation Fund
AFB	Adaptation Fund Board
AfDB	African Development Bank
AFOLU	Agriculture, forestry and other land use
AI	Artificial intelligence
AIIB	Asian Infrastructure Investment Bank
ANOVA	An Analysis of Variance
APBN	Indonesia state budget
ASCI	Administrative Staff College of India
ASEAN	Association of Southeast Asian Nations
BA	Biennial Assessments
BAU	Business-as-usual
BAZNAS	National Zakat Agency Indonesia
BEIS	Business, Energy and Industrial Strategy
BETA	Bureau d'Économie Théorique et Appliquée
BEUC	The European Consumer Organisation
BIGM	Bangladesh Institute of Governance and Management
BINGO	Big international non-governmental organisations
BIS	Bank for International Settlements
BKPM	Indonesia Investment Coordinating Board
BoP	Base of the economic pyramid
BR	Biennial reports
BNDES	Brazilian Development Bank
BPDLH	Environmental Fund Management Agency Indonesia
CA	Competent Agencies
CAO	Compliance Advisor/Ombudsman
CBA	Cost benefit analysis
CBD	Convention on Biological Diversity
CBF	Capacity building framework
CBI	Climate Bonds Initiative
CBS	Climate Bond Standard and Certification Scheme
CBT	Climate budget tagging
CDM	Clean Development Mechanism
CE	Choice experiments
CEMADEN	Brazilian National Center of Monitoring and Early Warning of Environmental Disasters
CER	Certified emissions reductions
CGAP	Consultative Group to Assist the Poor
CHP	Coal-to-gas and cogeneration
CI	Conservation International
CICERO	Centre for International Climate and Environmental Research
CICES	Common International Classification of Ecosystem Services
CIF	Climate Investment Fund
CITES	Convention on International Trade in Endangered Species of Wild Fauna and Flora

https://doi.org/10.1515/9783110733488-029

CIV	Collective investment vehicles
CMT	Coastal and maritime tourism
COP	Conference of the Parties
CPI	Climate Policy Initiative
CSO	Civil society organisations
CSSE	Center for Systems Science and Engineering
CTCN	Climate Technology Centre and Network
CTF	Clean Technology Fund
CV	Contingent valuation
DA	Doha Amendment
DAC	Development Assistance Committee
DAK	Special Allocation Fund Indonesia
DFI	Development finance institutions
DFS	Digital financial services
DID	Regional Incentive Fund Indonesia
DTU	Technical University of Denmark
EASAC	European Academies Science Advisory Council
EBI	European Investment Bank
EBM	Ecosystem-Based Management
EBRD	European Bank of Reconstruction and Development
EBSA	Ecologically or biologically significant areas
EEA	European Environment Agency
EIT	Economies in transition
EMDE	Emerging markets and developing economies
EME	Emerging market economies
ENGO	Environmental non-governmental organisations
EP	European Parliament
EPA	United States Environment Protection Agency
ERU	Emission reduction units
ES	Ecosystem services
ESSD	Environmentally and Socially Sustainable Department
ETS	Emission Trading System
EUGBS	European Green Bond Standard
EUTR	EU Timber Regulation
EV	Electric Vehicle
FAIR	Findable, Accessible, Interoperable, Reusable
FAO	Food and Agriculture Organization of the United Nations
FATF	Financial Action Task Force
FiT	Feed-in Tariff
FMU	Forest Management Units
FSC	Forest Stewardship Council
GATT	General Agreement on Tariffs and Trade
GBP	Green Bond Principles
GCF	Green Climate Fund
GDP	Gross Domestic Product
GEEREF	Global Energy Efficiency and Renewable Energy Fund
GEF	Global Environment Facility
GESI	Gender and social inclusion
GFANZ	Glasgow Financial Alliance for Net-Zero

GFL	Green Finance for Latin America and the Caribbean Platform
GFR	Green Fiscal Reform
GGGI	Global Green Growth Indonesia
GHG	Greenhouse gas
GISP	Global Invasive Species Program
GLAN	Global Legal Action Network
GOBI	Global Ocean Biodiversity Initiative
GPI	Genuine Progress Indicator
GRIPS	Graduate Institute for Policy Studies
H&C	Heating and cooling
HDI	Human Development Index
HEV	Hybrid and electric vehicles
HHSA	Household satellite accounts
HLEG	High Level Expert Group
IA	Implementing agency or agencies
IADB	Inter-American Development Bank
IBRD	International Bank for Reconstruction and Development
ICAP	International Carbon Action Partnership
ICMA	International Capital Market Association
ICRISAT	International Crops Research Institute for Semi-Arid Tropics
ICT	Information and communications technology
IDA	International Development Association
IDB	International Development Bank
IDBG	Inter-American Development Bank Group
IDFC	International Development Finance Club
IDR	Indonesian Rupiah
IDRBT	Institute for Development and Research in Banking Technology
IET	International Emission Trading
IFC	International Finance Corporation
IGLP	Institute of Global Law and Policy
IMF	International Monetary Fund
ITMO	Internationally transferred mitigation outcome
IOC	Intergovernmental Oceanographic Commission
IoT	Internet of Things
IPBES	Intergovernmental Science-Policy Platform on Biodiversity and Ecosystem Services
IPCC	Intergovernmental Panel on Climate Change
IPPKH	Borrow-to-use area permits
IRM	Initial resource mobilisation
IsDB	Islamic Development Bank
ITTC	International Tropical Timber Council
ITTO	International Tropical Timber Organisation
JI	Joint Implementation
JRC	Joint Research Centre
KLHK	Ministry of Environment and Foresty Indonesia
KP	Kyoto Protocol
KRISNA	Planning and Budgeting System Collaboration Indonesia
KTH	Forest Farmers Group Indonesia
KUPS	Social Forestry Business Group Indonesia
KuU	Known, unknown, unknowable

KwH	Kilowatt-hour
LCDF	Least Developed Countries Fund
LDC	Least Developed Countries
LDCF	Least Developed Countries Fund
LEV	Low emissions vehicles
LIDC	Low-income developing countries
LTF	Long-term climate finance
LULUCF	Land use change and forestry
MC	Marginal cost
MDB	Multilateral Development Bank
MDG	Millennium Development Goals
MEA	Millennium Ecosystem Assessment
MEP	Members of the European Parliament
MFF	Multiannual Financial Framework
MFS	Mobile financial services
MIE	Multilateral Implementing Entities
MIGA	Multilateral Investment Guarantee Agency
MoEF	Ministry of Environment and Forestry Indonesia
MP	Marine permaculture
MPA	Marine Protected Areas
MPI	Multidimensional Poverty Index
MRF	Materials Recovery Facilities
MRV	Measurement, reporting and verification
MS	Member States
MSC	Marine Stewardship Council
MSME	Micro, small and medium enterprises
NAP	National Adaptation Plan
NAZCA	Global Climate Action Portal
NCA	National Competent Authorities
NCF	National Climate Fund
NCP	Natural Capital Protocol
NDB	New Development Bank
NDC	Nationally Determined Contribution
NDE	National Designated Entities
NEAP	National Environmental Action Plans
NECP	National Energy and Climate Plans
NEK	Carbon Economic Value Indonesia
NGEU	Next Generation EU Instrument
NGFS	Network for Greening the Financial System
NGO	Non-government organisations
NICE	National Institute for Health and Clinical Excellence UK
NIE	National Implementing Entities
NITI Aaygog	National Institution for Transforming India Policy Commission
NPV	Net present value
NRDC	Natural Resources Defence Council
NSMD	Non-state market-driven
NTFP	Non-Timber Forest Products
NTSR	Non-Tax State Revenue
NWP	Nairobi Work Programme

ODA	Official Development Assistance
OECD	Organisation for Economic Co-operation and Development
OECM	Other effective area-based conservation measures
OMGE	Overall mitigation in global emissions
ONS	Office for National Statistics UK
OPOC	Office of the Pacific Ocean Commissioner, Pacific Islands Forum
PA	Paris Agreement
PBoC	People's Bank of China
PCF	Prototype Carbon Fund
PDF	Project Development Facility
PEFC	Programme for the Endorsement of Forest Certification
PEN	National Economic Recovery Programmes Indonesia
PES	Payment for ecosystem services
PINC	Proactive Investment in Natural Capital
PJ	Peta joule
PLTMH	Power Plants Micro Hydro Power Indonesia
PMA	State equity participation Indonesia
PP	Priority working programmes
PRI	Program-Related Investments
PSF	Private Sector Facility
PV	Present value
QALY	Quality adjusted life years
RBI	Reserve Bank of India
RCT	Randomised control trials
RED	Renewable Energy Directive EU
REDD	Reducing Emissions from Deforestation and Forest Degradation
REDII	Revision of the Renewable Energy Directive EU
REKK	Regional Energy Research Centre Hungary
RES	Renewable Energy Sources
RIE	Regional Implementing Entities
ROI	Return on investment
RPJMN	National Medium Development Planning Indonesia
SAFE	Simple agreement for future equity
SBSTA	Subsidiary Body for Scientific and Technological Advice
SCCF	Special Climate Change Fund
SCF	Standing Committee on Finance
SDGs	Sustainable Development Goals
SDM	Sustainable development mechanism
SEBI	Securities and Exchange Board of India
SEEA	System of Environmental Economic Accounting
SFM	Sustainable forest management
SIB	Social impact bond
SIDS	Small Island Developing States
SLO	Social licence to operate
SMART	Sustainable Market Actors for Responsible Trade
SME	Small and medium-sized enterprises
SoEF	Status of Europe's Forest
SP	Safeguard policies
SPAC	Special purpose acquisition companies

SPO	Second party opinion
SPV	Special purpose vehicles
TAKE	Ecological-Based District Budget Transfer Indonesia
TAPE	Ecological-Based Provincial Budget Transfer Indonesia
TAR	Third Assessment Report
TEEB	The Economics of Ecosystems and Biodiversity
TEG	Technical Expert Group
TERI	The Energy and Resources Institute
TESV	Total ecosystem service value
TEV	Total economic value
TKDD	Transfers to Regional Governments and Villages Indonesia
TLFF	Tropical Landscapes Finance Facility
TM	Technology Mechanism
TOSSD	Total Official Support for Sustainable Development
UKRI	United Kingdom Research and Innovation
UNCBD	United Nations Convention on Biological Diversity
UNCCD	United Nations Convention to Combat Desertification
UNCED	UN Conference on Environment and Development
UNCHE	UN Conference on the Human Environment
UNCTAD	United Nations Conference on Trade and Development
UNDP	United Nations Development Programme
UNEP	United Nations Environment Programme
UNFCCC	United Nations Framework Convention on Climate Change
VC	Venture capital
VCMI	Voluntary Carbon Market Integrity
WEF	World Economic Forum
WRAP	Waste and Resources Action Programme
WRI	World Resources Institute
WTO	World Trade Organisation
WTP	Willingness-to-pay
WWF	World Wildlife Fund

List of figures

https://doi.org/10.1515/9783110733488-030

List of tables

https://doi.org/10.1515/9783110733488-031

Index

https://doi.org/10.1515/9783110733488-032

www.ingramcontent.com/pod-product-compliance
Lightning Source LLC
Chambersburg PA
CBHW081210220326
41598CB00037B/6730